Tom Christianson

Classic Interlinear Translations

COMMENTARIES OF

CÆSAR

ON THE

GALLIC WAR

The original text reduced to the natural English order

WITH A LITERAL

**Interlinear Translation of the
First Seven Books**

DAVID McKAY COMPANY, INC.
NEW YORK

Copyright 1952, by
David McKay Co., Inc.

Copyright, 1893, by
ARTHUR HINDS & CO.

Copyright, 1924, by
HANDY BOOK CORP.

Reprinted October 1964

Printed in the United States of America

PUBLISHER'S NOTE

The Interlinear Translations of the Greek and Latin Classics have been in print for many years. Caesar's Gallic Wars first appeared in 1893. Since then countless students and scholars have turned to this translation for assistance in elucidating a difficult passage. It has thus become, in its own way, a classic of which we, the publishers, feel justly proud.

The order of the Latin version follows the natural order of English, and those words that are understood in the original are supplied. This system has proved of great help in understanding Latin grammar and the construction of a Latin sentence. It is our hope that it will continue to be an aid in appreciating the beauty and greatness of one of the world's foremost authors.

PREFACE

In preparing the Classic Series of Interlinear Translations the publishers have insisted upon a faithful adherence to two obvious essentials: the reduction of the original text to the natural order, and, as far as possible, a strictly literal version.

In all cases, however, where the meaning as thus literally rendered is not sufficiently intelligible, explanatory words or phrases have been added.

It is hoped that the plan will be appreciated of inserting all explanatory words and phrases, by means of brackets, in immediate conjunction with the text, thus obviating the annoyance and the serious loss of time that attend frequent reference to notes by numbered paragraphs in an appendix.

The superiority is readily apparent of the interlinear over other translations, not only in the saving of time, but also for all purposes of careful study; making possible as well as convenient and easy, a correct solution of idioms, a quick insight into the sense, a facile and lucid rearrangement of the context in the English order, and a practical comparison of both the similarities and the contrasts of construction.

COMMENTARIES OF CAESAR
ON THE GALLIC WAR

PRIMUS LIBER
FIRST BOOK

COMMENTARIORUM
OF COMMENTARIES

CAII JULII CÆSARIS,
OF CAIUS JULIUS CÆSAR,

DE

ON

GALLICO BELLO.
GALLIC WAR.

Cæsar, in narrating the war which he carried on in Gaul, first describes Gaul, then recounts two battles against the Helvetians and one against the Germans.

1. Omnis Gallïa est divisa in tres partes: unam
All Gaul is divided into three parts: one
quarum Belgæ incŏlunt; aliam Aquitani; tertiam,
of which the Belgæ inhabit; another the Aquitani; the third,
qui linguâ ipsorum appellantur
(those) who in (the) language of themselves are called
Celtæ, nostrâ, Galli. Omnes hi diffĕrunt inter
Celtæ, in ours, Gauls. All these differ between
se linguâ, institutis, legĭbus. Flumen
themselves in language, institutions, (and) laws. The river

DE BELLO GALLICO

Garumna divĭdit Gallos ab Aquitanis,
Garonne divides the Gauls from the Aquitani,

Matrona et Sequăna à Belgis. Belgæ sunt
the Marne and Seine from the Belgæ. The Belgæ are

fortissĭmi omnĭum horum: proptereă quòd absunt
the bravest of all these: because that they are distant

longissĭmè à cultu atque humanitate
farthest from the cultivation and humanity (refinement)

Provincĭæ; que mercatores minĭmè sæpe
of the Province (Provence); and merchants least often

commëant ad ĕos, atque important ĕa,
resort to them, and import those (things),

quæ pertĭnent ad anĭmos effeminandos.
which appertain to minds to be effeminated (to effeminate

Sunt proxĭmi Germanis, qui
their minds). They are nearest to the Germani, who

incŏlunt trans Rhenum, cum quĭbus gĕrunt
inhabit beyond the Rhine, with whom they carry-on

bellum continenter: de quâ caussâ Helvetĭi
war continually: from which cause the Helvetii

quŏque præcedunt relĭquos Gallos virtute;
also go before (excel) remaining Gauls in valour;

quòd contendunt cum Germanis quotidianis prœlĭis
because they contend with the Germani in daily battles

fĕrè, quum aut prohĭbent ĕos suis
almost, when either they prohibit them from their own

finĭbus, aut ipsi gĕrunt bellum in
borders, or they (themselves) carry-on war in

finĭbus eorum. Una pars eorum, quam
the borders of them. One part of them, which

dictum-est Gallos obtinere, căpit initĭum à
it has been said the Gauls to hold, takes beginning from

flumĭne Rhodăno; continetur flumĭne Garumnâ,
river Rhone; it is bounded by river Garonne,

Oceăno, finĭbus Belgarum; etĭam attingit
by the ocean, by the borders of the Belgæ; also it touches

LIBER I. 3

flumen	Rhenum	à	Sequănis	et
(reaches to) the river	Rhine	from	the Sequani	and

Helvetiis;	vergit	ad	Septentriones.
the Helvetii;	it inclines	to	the seven-stars (the North).

Belgæ	oriuntur	ab	extremis	finĭbus	Galliā
The Belgians	rise	from	the farthest	borders	of Gaul:

pertĭnent	ad	inferiorem	partem	flumĭnis	Rheni;
they reach	to	the lower	part	of the river	Rhine;

spectant	in	Septentriones	et	orientem	solem.
they look	unto	the North	and	the rising	sun.

Aquitanĭa	pertĭnet	à	flumĭne	Garumnā	ad
Aquitania	reaches	from	the river	Garonne	to

Pyrenæos	montes,	et ĕam	partem	Oceăni,
the Pyrenean	mountains,	and that	part	of the ocean,

quæ	spectat	ad	Hispaniam,	inter	occasum
which	looks	to	Spain,	between	the going-down

Solis	et	Septentriones.
of the sun (West)	and	the North.

2. | Orgetŏrix | fŭit | longè | nobilissĭmus | et | ditissĭmus |
|---|---|---|---|---|---|
| Orgetorix | was | by far | the most noble | and | richest |

ăpud	Helvetĭos.	Is,	Marco	Messalā	et	Marco
among	the Helvetii.	He,	Marcus	Messala	and	Marcus

Pisone	consulĭbus,	inductus	cupiditate	regni,
Piso	(being) consuls,	induced	by desire	of the kingdom,

fecit	conjurationem	nobilitatis;	et	persuasit
made	a conspiracy	of the nobility;	and	persuaded

civitati,	ut	exirent	de	sŭis	finĭbus
to the state	that	they should go out	from	their-own	borders

cum	omnĭbus	copĭis:	esse	perfacĭle,	quum
with	all	forces:	to be	very-easy,	when

præstarent (imp. subj.)	omnĭbus	virtute,	potiri
they did excel	to all	in valour,	to gain

imperĭo	totius	Galliæ.	Persuasit	id	ĕis
the empire	of the whole	Gaul.	He persuaded	that	to them

hoc	facilius,	quòd	Helvetĭi	continentur
by this	more easily,	because	the Helvetii	are contained (hemmed

undĭque	natura	lŏci;	ex unâ parte,
in) on every side	by the nature	of the place;	out-of one part,
latissĭmo	atque	altissĭmo	flumĭne Rheno,
by the widest (very wide)	and	deepest	river Rhine,
qui divĭdit	Helvetĭum	agrum	à Germanis:
which divides	the Helvetian	land	from the Germani:
ex altĕrâ	parte,	altissĭmo	monte Jurâ,
out-of the other	part,	by the highest	mountain Jura,
qui est inter	Sequănos	et	Helvetĭos;
which is between	the Sequani	and	the Helvetii; (out of)
tertĭâ,	lăcu	Lemano,	et
third (part),	by lake	Lemanus (the lake of Geneva),	and
flumĭne Rhodăno,	qui	divĭdit nostram	provincĭam
by the river Rhone,	which	divides our	province
ab	Helvetĭis.	Fiebat	
(Provence) from	the Helvetii.	It was made (it happened)	

his rebus, ut et vagarentur (imp. sub) mĭnŭs
by these things, that both they did rove less

latè et possent (imp. sub.) mĭnŭs facĭlè inferre
widely and were able less easily to-bring-on

bellum finitĭmis. De quâ caussâ homĭnes
war to bordering (nations). From which cause men

cupĭdi bellandi afficiebantur magno dolore. Autem
desirous of warring were affected with great pain. But

arbitrabantur se habere angustos fines, pro
they did deem themselves to have narrow borders, for

multitudĭne homĭnum et pro glorĭâ belli atque
the multitude of men and for the glory of war and

fortitudĭnis; qui patebant ducenta et
of bravery; which did lie open (extend) two-hundred and

quadraginta millĭa passŭum in longitudĭnem, centum
forty thousands of paces into length, a hundred

et octoginta in latitudĭnem.
and eighty into width.

3. Adducti his rebus, et permoti auctoritate
Induced by these things, and excited by the authority

LIBER I.

Orgetorĭgis,	constituerunt	comparare	ĕa,
of Orgetorix	*they determined*	*to prepare*	*those (things)*

quæ	pertinerent (imp. sub.)	ad proficiscendum;	coëmĕre
which	*did pertain*	*to setting-out;*	*to buy up*

quàm	maxĭmum		numĕrum
as	*the greatest*	*(the greatest possible)*	*number*

jumentorum	et	carrorum;	facĕre	quàm
of beasts of burden	*and*	*of waggons;*	*to make*	*as*

maxĭmas	sementes,	ut	copĭa	frumenti	suppetĕret
the greatest	*sowings,*	*that*	*plenty*	*of corn*	*might supply*

in	itinĕre;	confirmare	pacem	et	amicitĭam	cum
in	*the journey;*	*to confirm*	*peace*	*and*	*friendship*	*with*

proxĭmis civitatĭbus.	Duxerunt	biennĭum
the nearest states.	*They led (thought)*	*the space-of-two-*

	esse	sătis	sĭbi	ad	ĕas	res
years	*to be*	*enough*	*for themselves*	*to*	*those*	*things*

conficiendas;	confirmant	lege	profectionem
to be accomplished;	*they confirm*	*by law*	*(their) departure*

in	tertĭum	annum.	Orgetŏrix	deligĭtur	ad
upon (for)	*the third*	*year.*	*Orgetorix*	*is chosen*	*to*

ĕas	res	conficiendas.	Is	suscepit	sĭbi
those	*things*	*to be accomplished.*	*He*	*undertook*	*to himself*

legationem	ad	civitates.	In	ĕo	itinĕre	persuadet
an embassy	*to*	*the states.*	*In*	*that*	*journey*	*he persuades*

Castĭco,	filĭo	Catamantaledis,	Sequāno,	pătcr
to Casticus,	*son*	*to Catamantales,*	*a Sequanian,*	*the father*

cujus	obtinuĕrat	regnum	in	Sequānis	multos
of whom	*had held*	*the kingdom*	*in*	*the Sequani*	*many*

annos,	et	appellatus-ĕrat	amicus	à	Senatu	que
years,	*and*	*had been called*	*friend*	*by*	*the Senate*	*and*

Romano	popŭlo,	ut	occuparet	regnum	in
Roman	*people,*	*that*	*he should occupy*	*the kingdom*	*in*

suâ	civitate,	quod	pătcr	antè	habuĕrat:	que
his-own	*state,*	*which*	*(his) father*	*before*	*had had:*	*and*

item	persuadet	Ædŭo	Dumnorĭgi,	fratri
likewise	*he persuades*	*to the Æduan*	*Dumnorix,*	*the brother*

DE BELLO GALLICO.

Divitiăci, qui ĕo tempŏre obtinebat principatum
of Divitiacus, who in that time did hold sovereignty

in sŭâ civitate, ac ĕrat maxĭmè acceptus,
in his state, and was chiefly acceptable

plebi, ut conaretur ĭdem;
to the common people, that he should attempt the same (thing);

que dat sŭam filiam in matrimonĭum ĕi.
and gives his daughter into marriage to him.

Prŏbat illis esse perfacĭle factu
He proves to them to be (that it was) very-easy to be done

perficĕre conata, proptereă quŏd ipse
to effect (the things) attempted, because that (he) himself

esset (imp. subj.) obtenturus imperĭum sŭæ
was about-to-hold (obtain) the empire of his

civitatis: esse non dubĭum quin
state: to be (that it was) not doubtful but-that

Helvetĭi possent (imp. subj.) plurĭmum totius
the Helvetians were able most of all

Gallĭæ: confirmat, se conciliaturum
Gaul: he confirms (affirms), himself about-to-procure

regna illis sŭis copĭis que sŭo exercĭtu.
the kingdoms for them with his stores and with his army.

Adducti hâc oratione, dant inter se
Induced by this speech, they give between themselves

fĭdem et jusjurandum; et regno
faith and oath; and the kingdom (rule)

occupato per tres potentissĭmos ac firmissĭmos
being occupied by three most powerful and most firm

popŭlos, sperant sese posse potiri totius
peoples, they hope themselves to be able to possess of all

Gallĭæ.
Gaul.

4. Ut ĕa res enuntiata-est Helvetĭis per
When that thing was declared to the Helvetii by

indicĭum, sŭis morĭbus coëgerunt Orgetorĭgem dicĕre
discovery, by their customs they forced Orgetorix to say

5] **LIBER I.** 7

    caussam ex vinculis. Oportebat
(plead) (*his*) *cause* *from* (in) *bonds.* *It did behove*

pœnam sequi damnatum, ut cremaretur
punishment *to follow* (*him*) *condemned,* *that he should be burnt*

igni. Die constitutâ dictionis caussæ,
with fire. *In the day* *appointed* *of saying* (pleading) *of cause,*

Orgetörix coëgit omnem suam familiam, ad decem
Orgetorix *collected* *all* *his* *household,* *to* *ten*

millia hominum, ad judicium ;   et
thousands *of men,* *to* *the judgment* (place of trial); *and*

conduxit eòdem omnes suos clientes que
he led-together *to same place* *all* *his* *clients* *and*

 obæratos, quorum habebat magnum numerum:
bond-men-for-debt, *of whom he did have* *a great* *number :*

per eos, eripuit se ne-diceret caussam.
by *them,* *he rescued* *himself that he might not say* *cause*

     Quum civitas, incitata ob
(from taking his trial). *When the state, excited on-account-of*

eam rem, conaretur (imp. subj.) exequi suum jus
that thing, *did endeavour* *to execute* *its* *right*

armis, que magistratus cogerent (imp. subj.)
by arms, *and* *the magistrates* *did collect*

multitudinem hominum ex agris, Orgetörix mortuus-est;
a multitude *of men out of the lands, Orgetorix* *died;*

neque suspicio abest,' ut Helvetii arbitrantur, quin
nor suspicion is absent, as the Helvetii *think,* *but-that*

ipse consciverit (perf. subj.) mortem sibi.
himself *committed*   *death* *to himself.*

5. Nihilominùs post mortem ejus Helvetii
 Nevertheless *after* *the death* *of him* *the Helvetii*

conantur facere id, quod constituerant, ut
endeavour *to do* *that,* *which* *they had determined,* *that*

 exeant è suis finibus. Ubi jam arbitrati-sunt
they may go-out from their borders. When now *they deemed*

 se paratos-esse ad eam rem, incendunt
(*themselves* *to have been prepared* *to* *that* *thing, they set-fire-to*

DE BELLO GALLICO. [6

omnĭa   sŭa   oppĭda,   ad   duodĕcim   numĕro,   vicos
all   their towns,   to   twelve   in number, streets

       ad   quadringentos,   relĭqua   privata ædificĭa;
(villages) to four-hundred, the remaining private buildings;

comburunt omne frumentum, præter   quod   ĕrant
they burnt-up all the corn, except (that) which they were

portaturi   cum   se; ‖   ut,   spe   reditionis
about-to-carry with themselves; that, the hope of a return

dŏmum   sublatâ,   essent   paratiores   ad
home   being taken-away, they might be more ready   to

omnĭa pericŭla   subeunda: ‖   jŭbent   quemque
all   dangers   to be undergone : they order   each

afferre   dŏmo   sĭbi   molĭta   cibarĭa   trĭum
to bring from home for himself ground provisions of (for) three

ŧnensĭum. ‖ Persuadent   Rauracis,   et   Tulingis,
months.   They persuade to the Rauraci, and to the Tulingi,

et   Latobrĭgis,   finitĭmis,   utì   usi
and to the Latobrigi, neighbouring (people), that having used

eodem   consilĭo,   sŭis   oppĭdis   qne   vicis
with the same counsel,   their   towns   and   villages

exustis,   proficiscantur   unà   cum   iis: ‖ que
being burnt up, they may depart together with   them: and

adsciscunt   socĭos   sĭbi,   Boïos,   qui   incoluĕrant
they take-to allies to themselves, the Boii, who had dwelt

trans   Rhenum,   et   transiĕrant   in   Norĭcum
beyond the Rhine, and   had passed over into the Norican

agrum,   que   oppugnârant   Norĭcam,   receptos   ad
land,   and had assaulted   Norica,   received   to

se.
themselves.

6. Erant   omnino   dŭo   itinĕra,   quĭbus
There were   in-all   two   journies (roads), by which

itinerĭbus   possent   exire   dŏmo;   unum
roads   they might be able to go forth from home; one

per   Sequănos   angustum et difficĭle,   inter   montem
through the Sequani   narrow and difficult· between mountain

LIBER I.

Juram	et	flumen	Rhodanum,	quo	singŭli
Jura	and	the river	Rhone,	by which	single

carri	vix	ducerentur;	autem	altissimus
waggons	scarcely	could be led;	but	the highest (a very

	mons	impendebat,	ut	perpauci	facĭlĕ,
high)	mountain	did hang-over,	that	very few	easily

possent	prohibere;	altĕrum	per nostram
would be able	to prohibit;	the other	through our

provinciam,	multò	facilĭus	atque	expeditĭus;
province,	by-much	more easy	and	more ready;

proptereă	quòd	inter	fines	Helvetiorum	et
because	that	between	the borders	of the Helvetii	and

Allobrŏgum,	qui	nuper	pacati-ĕrant,
of the Allobroges,	who	lately	had been reduced to peace,

Rhodănus	flŭit,	que	is	nonnullis	lŏcis	transitur
the Rhone	flows,	and	that	in some	places	is passed

vădo.	Geneva	est	extremum	oppĭdum	Allobrŏgum
by ford.	Geneva	is	the farthest	town	of the Allobroges

que	proxĭmum	finĭbus	Helvetiorum;	ex	ĕo
and	nearest	to the borders	of the Helvetii;	from	that

oppĭdo	pons	pertĭnet	ad	Helvetĭos.	Existimabant
town	a bridge	reaches	to	the Helvetii.	They did think

sese	vel	persuasuros	Allobrogĭbus,	quòd
themselves	either	about-to-persuade	to the Allobroges,	because

viderentur (imp. subj.)	nondum	bŏno	anĭmo	in
they did seem	not-yet	with good	mind	towards

Romanum	popŭlum;	vel	coacturos	vi,
the Roman	people;	or	about-to-force	by violence,

ut	paterentur	ĕos	ire	per	sŭos	fines.
that	they should suffer	them	to go	through	their	borders.

Omnĭbus rebus	comparatis	ad	profectionem,
All things	being prepared	to	(their) departure,

dicunt	dĭem,	quâ	dĭe	omnes	conveniant
they say (appoint)	a day	in which	day	all	may assemble

ad	ripam	Rhodăni.	Is	dĭes	ĕrat	ante	quintum
at	the bank	of the Rhone.	That	day	was	before	the fifth

10   DE BELLO GALLICO   [7

diem	kalendarum	Aprilis;	Lucio	Pisone,
day	of the Kalends	of April (27th March);	Lucius	Piso;

Aulo Gabinio   consulibus.
Aulus Gabinius (being) consuls.

7. Quum id nuntiatum-esset (pl. perf. subj.) Caesari,
When that had been told   to Cæsar,

eos   conari   facere   iter   per   nostram
them to endeavour to make a journey through our

provinciam, maturat proficisci ab urbe, et
province, he hastens to depart from the city, and

contendit   in ulteriorem Galliam itineribus quàm
strains (marches) into farther Gaul by journies as

maximis potest, et pervenit ad Genevam. Imperat
greatest he can, and arrives at Geneva. He orders

toti provinciae   quàm maximum
to the whole province (to furnish) as greatest (the greatest

numerum militum. Una legio erat omnino
possible) *number of soldiers. One legion was in-all*

in alteriore Gallia. Jubet pontem, qui erat
in farther Gaul. He orders the bridge, which was

ad Genevam, rescindi. Ubi Helvetii facti-sunt
at Geneva, to be cut down. When the Helvetii were made

certiores de adventu ejus, mittunt nobilissimos
more certain of the arrival of him, they send the noblest

civitatis legatos ad eum; cujus legationis
of the state (as) ambassadors to him; of which embassy

Numeius et Verodoctius obtinebant principem locum:
Numeius and Verodoctius did hold the chief place:

qui dicerent esse sibi in animo,
who should say to be to themselves in mind (that they

sine ullo maleficio facere iter per
intended), *without any mischief to make a journey through*

provinciam, proptereà quòd haberent (imp. subj.) nullum
the province, because that they did have no

aliud iter: rogare, ut liceat sibi
other journey (route): *to ask, that it may be-lawful to themselves*

| facĕre id voluntate ejus. | Cæsar, quòd tenebat |
| to do that by the will of him. | Cæsar, because he did hold |

| memoriâ, Lucium Cassium | consŭlem occisum, que |
| in memory, Lucius Cassius | the consul being slain, and |

| exercĭtum ejus pulsum | ab Helvetiis, et missum |
| the army of him driven (routed) | by the Helvetii, and sent |

| sub jŭgum, putabat | non concedendum; nĕque |
| under the yoke, did think (it) | not to be conceded; nor |

| existimabat homĭnes | inimico anĭmo, facultate |
| did he think men | with unfriendly mind, liberty |

| itinĕris faciundi | per provinciam dătâ, |
| of journey to be made | through the province being given, |

| temperaturos ab injuriâ et maleficio: | tămen ut |
| about to-refrain from injury and mischief: | however that |

| spatium posset intercedĕre, | dum milĭtes, |
| a space might be able to intervene, | whilst the soldiers, |

| quos imperavĕrat, convenirent, | respondit, se |
| whom he had ordered, might assemble, | he replied, himself |

| sumpturum diem ad | deliberandum; si |
| about-to-take a day (time) to | deliberate; if |

| vellent (imp. subj.) quid | reverterentur ad |
| they did will any-thing | they might return at |

idus Aprilis.
the ides of April.

8. Interĕa ĕâ legione, quam habebat
 Meanwhile with that legion, which he did have

| cum se que militĭbus | qui convenĕrant ex |
| with himself and with the soldiers | who had assembled from |

| provinciâ, perducit | murum in altitudĭnem |
| the province, he leads-along | a wall into height |

| sexdĕcim pĕdum, que fossam | à lăcu Lemano, |
| of sixteen feet, and a trench | from the lake Lemanus, |

| quem flumen Rhodănum influit, | ad montem Juram, |
| which the river Rhone flows-into, | to mountain Jura, |

| qui divĭdit fines | Sequanorum ab Helvetiis, |
| which divides the borders | of the Sequani from the Helvetii, |

děcem ·et nŏvem   millĭa   pasŭum.   Eo opĕre
ten and nine (nineteen) thousands of paces.   That work

  perfecto,   disponit   præsidĭa,   communit castella,
being completed, he disposes   garrisons,   he fortifies castles;

/quò   posset   prohibere   facilĭus,   si
that   he might be able   to prevent   more easily, if

conarentur   transire,   se   invito.
they should endeavour to pass over, himself   (being) unwilling.

Ubi   ĕa   dĭes venit,   quam   constituĕrat   cum
When   that   day   came,   which   he had appointed with

  legatis,   et   legati   reverterunt ad ĕum ;
the ambassadors, and the ambassadors   returned   to him;

nĕgat   se,   more   et   exemplo   Romani
he denies himself,   by the custom and example   of the Roman

popŭli,   posse   dăre   ĭter   per   provincĭam ulli;
people, to be able to give a journey through the province to any;

et ostendit   prohibiturum,   si   conentur (pres.
and shows (himself) about to prohibit, if   they attempt

subj.) facĕre   vim.   Helvetĭi   dejecti   ĕâ
  to make violence.   The Helvetii   cast down   from that

spe,   alĭi,   navĭbus   junctis,   que complurĭbus
hope, others (some), ships   being joined, · and a great-many

ratĭbus   factis,   alĭi   vădis   Rhodăni,   quà
rafts   being made,   others   by fords   of the Rhone,   where

minĭma altitudo flumĭnis   ĕrat, nonnunquam   interdĭu,
least   depth   of river   was,   sometimes   in day-time,

sæpĭùs   noctu,   conati   si   possent (imp.
more often by night,   having endeavoured if they were able

subj.)   perrumpĕre,   repulsi   munitione
     to break through,   repulsed   by the fortification

opĕris,   et   concursu   et   telis
of the work,   and   by the encounter   and   weapons

milĭtum,   destiterunt   hoc   conatu.
of the soldiers, they desisted from this   endeavour.

9. Una   vĭa   per   Sequănos   relinquebatur;
  One   way   through   the Sequani   was left;

LIBER I.

qua, Sequănis invitis, potĕrant non
by which, the Sequani (being) unwilling, they were able not

ire propter angustĭas. Quum possent (imp.
to go on-account-of the defiles. When they were able

subj.) non persuadere iis suâ sponte,
not to persuade to them by their-own accord,

mittunt legatos ad Dumnorĭgem Æduum,
they send ambassadors to Dumnorix the Æduan,

ut, ĕo deprecatore, impetrarent hoc à
that, he (being) intercessor, they might obtain this from

Sequănis. Dumnŏrix potĕrat plurĭmum
the Sequani. Dumnorix was able most (had very great in-

ăpud Sequănos gratĭâ et largitione, et
fluence) *with the Sequani by favour and by largess, and*

erat amicus Helvetĭis, quòd duxĕrat in
was friendly to the Helvetii, because he had led into

matrimonĭum filĭam Orgetorĭgis ex eâ civitate;
marriage the daughter of Orgetorix out-of that state;

et adductus cupiditate regni, studebat nŏvis
and induced by a desire of (for) power, he did study for new

rebus; et volebat habere quamplurĭmas
things (revolution); and did will to have very-many

civitates obstrictas suo beneficĭo sĭbi. Ităque
states bound by-his benefit to himself. Therefore

suscĭpit rem, et impĕtrat à Sequănis,
he undertakes the thing, and obtains from the Sequani,

ut patiantur Helvetĭos ire per suos
that they may suffer the Helvetii to go through their

fines, que perficit ŭti dent obsĭdes inter
borders, and effects that they may give hostages between

sese; Sequăni ne prohibĕant
themselves; the Sequani lest they may prohibit (that they

Helvetĭos itinĕre; Helvetĭi,
may not prohibit) *the Helvetii from the journey; the Helvetii,*

ut transĕant sĭne maleficĭo et injurĭâ.
that they may pass without mischief and injury.

DE BELLO GALLICO. [10

10. Nuntiatur Caesări, esse Helvetĭis in
It is announced to Cæsar, to be to the Helvetii in

anĭmo, facĕre ĭter per agrum
mind, to make the journey through the land

Sequanorum et Æduorum in fines
of the Sequani and of the Ædui into the borders

Santŏnum, qui absunt non longè à
of the Santones, who are distant not far from

finĭbus Tolosatĭum, quae civĭtas est in provincĭâ.
borders of the Tolosates, which state is in the province.

Si id fiĕret intelligebat futurum
If that should be done he did understand (it) about-to-be

cum magno pericŭlo provinciae, ut haberet
with great danger of the province, that it should have

bellicosos homŭnes, inimicòs Romani popŭli,
warlike men, enemies of the Roman people,

finitĭmos lŏcis patentĭbus et maxĭmè
bordering to places open and chiefly

frumentarĭis. Ob éas caussas praefecit
abounding-in-corn. On-account-of those causes he set-over

Titum Labienum legatum ĕi munitioni quam
Titus Labienus lieutenant to that fortification which

fecĕrat : ipse contendit in
he had made : he (himself) strained (hastened) into

Italĭam magnis itinerĭbus que ĭbi conscribit dŭas
Italy by great journies and. there he levies two

legiones ; et educit ex hibernis tres,
legions ; and he leads-out out-of winter-quarters three,

quae hiemabant circum Aquileïam ; et quâ
which did winter around Aquileia ; and by which

ĭter ĕrat proxĭmum in citeriorem Gallĭam
(way) the journey was nearest into hither Gaul

per Alpes, contendit ire cum his
through the Alps, he strains (hastens) to go with these

quinque legionĭbus. Ibi Centrones et Garocĕli,
five legions. There the Centrones and the Garocĕli,

11] LIBER I. 15

et	Caturīges,	superiorībus	lŏcis	occupatis,
and	the Caturiges,	the higher	places	being occupied,

conantur	prohibere	exercĭtum	itinĕre.	His
endeavour	to prohibit	the army	from the journey.	These

pulsis	complurĭbus	prœlĭis,	pervenit	ab
being routed	in several	battles,	he arrived	from

Ocĕlo,	quod est extremum	citerioris	provinciæ,
Ocelum,	which is the extreme (town)	of the hither	province,

in	fines	Vocontiorum	ulterioris	provinciæ
into	the borders	of the Vocontii	of the farther	province

septĭmo	dĭe;	inde in	fines	Allobrŏgum;
in the seventh	day;	thence into	the borders	of the Allobroges ;

ducit	exercĭtum	ab	Allobrogĭbus	in	Segusianos.
he leads	the army	from	the Allobroges	into	the Segusiani.

Hi sunt primi	extra	provinciăm	trans	Rhodănum.
These are the first	without	the province	beyond	the Rhone.

11. Helvetii jam transduxĕrant sŭas copĭas
The Helvetii already had led-over their forces

per	angustĭas	et	fines	Sequanorum	et
through	the defiles	and	borders	of the Sequani	and

pervenĕrant	in	fines	Æduorum,	que
had arrived	into	the borders	of the Ædui,	and

populabantur	agros	eorum.	Ædŭi,	quum
did lay waste	the lands	of them.	The Ædui	when

possent (imp. subj.)	non	defendĕre	se	que
they were able	not	to defend	themselves'	and

sŭa	ab	his,	mittunt	legatos	ad
their-own (effects)	from	these,	send	ambassadors	to

Cæsărem	rogatum	auxilĭum;	"se	omni	tempōre
Cæsar	to ask	aid ;	" themselves	in all	time

merĭtos-esse	ita	de	Romano	popŭlo,	ut,
to have deserved	so	of	the Roman	people,	that,

pene	conspectu	nostri	exercĭtûs,	ăgri
almost	in sight	of our	army,	(their) lands

debuĕrint (perf. subj.)	non	vastari,	libĕri
ought	not	to be laid-waste,	the children

16   DE BELLO GALLICO.   [12

eorum	abduci	in	servitutem,	oppĭda
of them	*to be led away*	*into*	*slavery,*	*the towns*

expugnari."	Eodem	tempŏre,	quo
o be taken-by-storm."	*In the same*	*time,*	*in which*

Ædŭi,	Ambarri	quŏque,	necessarĭi	et	consanguinĕi
the Ædui,	*the Ambarri*	*also,*	*friends*	*and*	*kinsmen*

Æduorum,	facĭunt	Cæsărem	certiorem,
of the Ædui,	*make*	*Cæsar*	*more certain* (inform Cæsar),

"sese,	agris	depopulatis,	non facĭlè prohibere
"themselves,	*the lands*	*being depopulated,*	*not easily to prohibit*

vim	hostĭum	ab	oppĭdis."	Item
the violence	*of the enemies*	*from*	*the towns."*	*Likewise*

Allobrŏges,	qui	habebant	vicos	que
the Allobroges,	*who*	*did have*	*streets* (villages)	*and*

possessiones	trans Rhodănum,	recipĭunt	se	fŭgâ
possessions	*beyond the Rhone,*	*betake*	*themselves*	*in flight*

ad Cæsărem;	et demonstrant,	nĭhil	relĭqui
to Cæsar;	*and show,*	*nothing*	*of remaining* (*property*)

esse	sĭbi	præter	sŏlum	agri.	Adductus
to be	*to themselves*	*beside*	*the soil*	*of the land.*	*Induced*

quĭbus	rebus,	Cæsar	statŭit	non	expectandum
by which	*things,*	*Cæsar*	*resolved*	*not*	*to be waited*

sĭbi,	dum,	omnĭbŭs
to (by) *himself* (that he ought not to wait),	*until,*	*all*

fortunis	sociorum	consumptis,	Helvetĭi
the fortunes	*of the allies,*	*being consumed,*	*the Helvetii*

pervenirent	in	Santŏnes.
should arrive	*into*	*the Santones.*

12. Arar	est flumen,	quod	inflŭit in
The Arar (the Saone)	*is a river,*	*which*	*flows into*

Rhodănum	incredibĭli	lenitate	per	fines
the Rhone	*with incredible*	*smoothness*	*through*	*the borders*

Æduorum	et	Sequanorum;	ita	ut	possit
of the Ædui	*and*	*of the Sequani;*	*so*	*that*	*it may be able*

non	judicari	ocŭlis	in	utram	partem
not	*to be judged*	*by the eyes*	*into*	*whether-of-the-two*	*part*

LIBER I.

fluat.	Helvetii	transibant	id,	ratibus	ac
it flows.	*The Helvetii*	*did pass-over*	*that,*	*rafts*	*and*

lintribus	junctis.	Ubi	Caesar	factus-est	certior
boats	*being joined.*	*When*	*Caesar*	*was made*	*more certain*

per	exploratores,	Helvetios	jam	transduxisse
by	*scouts,*	*the Helvetii*	*already*	*to have-led-over*

id	flumen	tres	partes	copiarum,	vero	quartam
that	*river*	*three*	*parts*	*of (their) forces,*	*but*	*the fourth*

partem	esse	reliquam	citra	flumen	Ararim;
part	*to be*	*remaining*	*on-this-side*	*the river*	*Arar (Saone);*

de	tertia	vigilia	profectus	e
from (at)	*the third*	*watch (midnight)*	*having set-out*	*from*

castris	cum	tribus	legionibus	pervenit	ad	eam
the camps	*with*	*three*	*legions*	*he arrives*	*to*	*that*

partem,	quae	nondum	transierat	flumen.
part,	*which*	*not-yet*	*had passed*	*the river.*

Aggressus	eos	impeditos	et	inopinantes
Having attacked	*them*	*encumbered*	*and*	*unaware*

concidit	magnam	partem	eorum;	reliqui
he cut-up (slew)	*a great*	*part*	*of them;*	*the rest*

mandarunt	sese	fugae	atque	abdiderunt	in
committed	*themselves*	*to flight*	*and*	*hid (themselves)*	*into*

proximas	silvas.	Is	pagus	appellabatur	Tigurinus:
the nearest	*woods.*	*That*	*district*	*was called*	*the Tigurine:*

nam	omnis	Helvetia	civitas	divisa-est	in
for	*all*	*the Helvetian*	*state*	*has been divided*	*into*

quatuor	pagos.	Hic	unus	pagus,	quum
four	*districts.*	*This*	*one*	*district,*	*when*

exisset (pl. perf. subj.)	domo,	memoria
it had gone-out	*from home,*	*in the memory*

nostrorum	patrum,	interfecerat	Lucium	Cassium
of our	*fathers,*	*had slain*	*Lucius*	*Cassius*

Consulem,	et	miserat	exercitum	ejus	sub
the Consul,	*and*	*had sent*	*the army*	*of him*	*under*

jugum.	Ita	sive	casu,	sive	consilio
the yoke.	*Thus*	*whether*	*by chance,*	*or*	*by the counsel*

immortalium   Deorum,   pars   Helvetiæ   civitatis,
of the immortal   Gods,   the part   of the Helvetian   state,

quæ   intulerat   insignem   calamitatem   Romano
which   had brought-on   a remarkable   calamity   to the Roman

populo,   ea   princeps   persolvit   pœnas.   In quâ
people,   that   chief (first)   paid   penalties.   In which

re   Cæsar   ultus-est   non   solùm   publicas   sed   etiam
thing   Cæsar   avenged   not   only   public   but   also

privatas   injurias ;   quòd   Tigurini   interfecerant
private   injuries ;   because   the Tigurini   had slain

Lucium   Pisonem   legatum,   avum   Lucii
Lucius   Piso   the lieutenant,   grandfather   of Lucius

Pisonis   soceri   ejus,   eodem   prœlio,
Piso   ather-in-law   of him (Cæsar),   in the same   battle,

quo   Cassium.
in which (they slew)   Cassius.

13. Hoc   prœlio   facto,   ut   posset
This   battle   being made,   that   he might be able

consequi   reliquas   copias   Helvetiorum,   curat
to reach the remaining forces   of the Helvetii, he takes-care

pontem   faciendum   in   Arare,   atque   ita   transducit
a bridge   to be made   in   the Arar,   and   so   leads-over

exercitum.   Helvetii   commoti   repentino   adventu
the army.   The Helvetii   moved   by the sudden   arrival

ejus,   quum   intelligerent (imp. subj.)   illum
of him,   when   they did understand   him

fecisse   uno   die   id,   quod   ipsi
to have done   in one   day   that,   which   themselves

confecerant   ægerrimè   viginti   diebus,   ut
had accomplished   most-hardly   in twenty   days,   that

transirent   flumen,   mittunt   legatos   ad
they might pass   the river,   send   ambassadors   to

eum ;   cujus   legationis   Divico   fuit   princeps,   qui
him :   of which   embassy   Divico   was   chief,   who

fuerat   dux   Helvetiorum   Cassiano   bello.
had been   leader   of the Helvetii   in the Cassian   war

LIBER 1.

Is	ita	egit	cum	Caesare;	"si	Romanus
He	thus	acted (treated)	with	Caesar;	"if	the Roman

populus	faceret	pacem cum	Helvetiis,	Helvetios
people	would make	peace with	the Helvetii,	the Helvetii

ituros	in eam partem,	atque	futuros
about-to-go (would go)	into that part,	and	about-to-b

ibi,	ubi	Caesar	constituisset	atque
there,	where	Caesar	might have appointed	and

voluisset	esse;	sin	perseveraret
might have willed (them)	to be;	but if	he should persevere

persequi	bello,	reminisceretur	veteris
to pursue	with war,	he should remember	of the old

incommodi	Romani	populi,	et
inconvenience (misfortune)	of the Roman	people,	and

pristinae	virtutis	Helvetiorum:	quod
of the ancient	valour	of the Helvetii:	because

adortus-esset (pl. perf. subj.)	improviso	unum	pagum,
he had assaulted	unexpectedly	one	district;

quum	ii,	qui	transissent (pl. perf. subj.)	flumen,
when	those,	who	had passed	the river,

possent (imp. subj.)	non ferre	auxilium	suis:
were able	not to bring	aid	to their (men);

tribueret	ne	aut	magnopere	suae	virtuti
he should assign	not	either	greatly	to his	valour

ob	eam	rem, aut	despiceret	ipsos.
on-account-of	that	thing or	should despise	themselves.

Se	ita	didicisse	à	suis	patribus
Themselves	so	to have learned	from	their	fathers

que	majoribus,	ut	contenderent	magis
and	ancestors,	that	they should contend	more

virtute	quàm	niterentur	dolo,	aut
by valour	than	they should strive	by deceit,	or

insidiis.	Quare	committeret	ne,	ut
with ambushes.	Wherefore	he should commit	not,	that

is	locus,	ubi	constitissent (pl. perf. subj.),
that	place,	where	they had stood

caperet   nomen   ex   calamitate   Romani
should take   *(its) name* *from* *the calamity* *of the Roman*

populi,   et   internecione   exercitus,   ac
people,   *and* *the destruction* *of the army,*   *and*

prodĕret   memoriam.
should deliver (hand down) *the memory (of it).*

14. Caesar   respondit ita   his;   " eò
    Cæsar *answered* *thus* *to these (words);* *"therefore*

minus   dubitationis dari   sibi,   quòd
less   *of doubt*   *to be given* *to himself,*   *because*

teneret (imp. subj.) eas   res   memoriâ,   quas
he did hold   *those* *things* *in memory,* *which*

Helvetii   legati   commemorâssent (pl. perf.
the Helvetian *ambassadors*   *had mentioned,*

subj.), atque ferre   eò   gravius,   quò
        and *to bear* *by that* *more heavily,*   *by which*

          accidissent (pl. perf. subj.) minùs   merito
(because) *they had befallen*   *less*   *by the merit*

Romani   populi,   qui   si   fuisset (pl. perf. subj.)
of the Roman *people,* *which* *if* *it had been*

conscius   sibi   alicujus   injuriæ,   fuisse   non
conscious *to itself* *of some*   *injury,*   *to have been* *not*

difficile   cavere;   sed   deceptum   eo,   quòd
difficult *to beware*   *but* *being deceived* *in this,* *because*

neque   intelligeret (imp. subj.)   commissum
neither *it did understand*   *(fault) committed*

à   se,   quare   timeret;   neque   putaret
by   *itself,* *wherefore*   *it should fear;* *nor*   *did it think*

(imp. subj.) timendum   sine   caussâ.   Quòd   si
              to be feared *without*   *cause.*   *But* *if*

vellet (imp. subj.) oblivisci   veteris   contumeliæ,
he did will   *to forget*   *of the ancient* *insult,*

num   etiam   posset   deponere   memoriam
whether *also*   *would he be able* *to lay-down* *the memory*

recentium   injuriarum, quòd,   eo   invito,
of fresh   *injuries,* *that,* *he* *(being) unwilling,*

tentâssent (pl. perf. subj.)　ĭter　　per　　Provincĭam
they had attempted　　　　　　*a journey through the Province*

peŕ　vim,　quòd　vexâssent (pl. perf. subj.)　Ædŭos,
by violence,　that　they had harassed　　　　*the Ædui,*

quòd　Ambarros,　quòd　　Allobrŏges?　　Quòd
that　the Ambarri,　that　the Allobroges?　　That

gloriarentur (imp. subj.) tam insolenter　sŭâ　victorĭâ;
they did boast　　　　*so　insolently　in their victory;*

que quòd　admirarentur　se　tulisse　injurĭas
and that　they did wonder　himself to have borne the injuries

impunè　tam dĭu,　pertinere　eòdem.
with-impunity　so long,　to pertain　to the same (point).

Enim　immortales　Dĕos　　consuêsse,
For　the immortal　Gods　to have been accustomed,

quò　homĭnes　dolĕant　gravĭùs　ex
in-order-that　men　may grieve · more heavily　from

commutatione rerum,　quos　vĕlint　ulcisci
the change　of things,　whom　they may wish　to punish

pro　scelĕre　eorum,　interdum　concedĕre
for　the wickedness　of them,　sometimes　to grant

secundĭores　res　his,　et　diuturniorem
more prosperous　things　to these,　and　more-lasting

impunitatem.　Cùm　ĕa　sint (pres. subj.)
impunity.　When (since) those (things) are

ĭta,　tămen si　obsĭdes　dentur　sĭbi　ab ĭis,
so,　yet　if hostages　may be given　to himself　by them,

ŭtì　intellĭgat　　facturos　ĕa
that　he may understand (them)　about-to-do　those (things)

quæ　polliceantur (pres. subj.);　et si　satisfacĭant
which　they promise;　　　　　and if　they may satisfy

Ædŭis　de　injurĭis,　quas
to the Ædui　concerning　the injuries,　which

intulĕrint (perf. subj.)　ipsis　que　socĭis
they have brought-on　to themselves　and　to the allies

eorum,　ĭtem　si Allobrogĭbus,　sese　esse
of them,　likewise　if to the Allobroges,　himself　to be

facturum	pacem	cum	iis."	Divico	respondit:
about-to-make	peace	with	them."	Divico	answered:

"Helvetios	institutos-esse	ita	à	majoribus,
"the Helvetii	to have been instructed	so	by	(their) ancestors,

uti	consueverint (perf. subj.)	accipere,	non	dare
that	they have been accustomed	to receive,	not	to give

obsides;	Romanum	populum	esse	testem	ejus	rei."
hostages;	the Roman	people	to be	witness	of that	thing."

Hoc	responso	dato,	discessit.
This	answer	being given,	he departed.

15.
Postero	die	movent	castra	ex	eo
On the following	day	they move	the camps	from	that

loco.	Caesar	facit	idem;	que	praemittit
place.	Caesar	does	the same;	and	sends-forward

omnem	equitatum	ad	numerum	quatuor	millium,
all	the cavalry	to	the number	of four	thousands,

quem	habebat	coactum	ex	omni	provinciâ,
which	he did have	collected	from	all	the province,

et	Æduis	atque	sociis	eorum;
and	from the Ædui	and	from the allies	of them;

qui	videant	in	quas	partes	hostes	faciant
who	may see	into	what	parts	the enemies	may make

iter:	qui,	insecuti	cupidiùs
(their) journey:	who,	having followed-up	more (too) eagerly

novissimum	agmen,	committunt	proelium
the last	troop (the rear),	join	battle

cum	equitatu	Helvetiorum	alieno
with	the cavalry	of the Helvetii	in strange (unfavourable)

loco,	et	pauci	de	nostris	cadunt.	Quo
place,	and	a few	of	our (men)	fall.	By which

proelio	Helvetii	sublati,	quòd	quingentis
battle	the Helvetii	being elated,	because	with five-hundred

equitibus	propulerant	tantam	multitudinem
horsemen	they had repulsed	so-great	a multitude

equitum,	coeperunt	subsistere	audaciùs;
of horsemen,	began	to withstand	more boldly,

nonnunquam	ex	novissĭmo	agmĭne	lacessĕre
sometimes	*out-of*	*the last*	*troop* (the rear)	*to challenge*

prœlĭo	nostros.	Cæsar	continebat	sŭos
with battle	*our (men).*	*Cæsar*	*did withhold*	*his (men)*

à	prœlĭo,	ac	habebat	sătis in
from	*battle,*	*and*	*did have* (thought it)	*enough in*

præsentĭâ,	prohibere	hostem
presentness (for the present),	*to prohibit*	*the enemy*

rapinis,	pabulationĭbus,	que	populationĭbus.
from rapines,	*from foragings,*	*and*	*from wastings.*

Ita	circĭter	quindĕcim	dĭes fecerunt	ĭter,
So	*about*	*fifteen*	*days they made*	*the journey,*

ŭtĭ	inter	novissĭmum	agmen	hostĭum et
that	*between*	*the last*	*troop*	*of the enemies and*

nostrum	primum,	non	amplĭùs	quinis aut
our	*first* (van),	*not*	*more*	(than) *five or*

senis	millĭbus	passŭum	interesset.
(than) *six*	*thousands*	*of paces*	*might intervene.*

16. Intĕrim	Cæsar	quotidĭe	flagi-
Meanwhile	*Cæsar*	(began) *daily*	*to demand-*

tare	Ædŭos	frumentum,	quod	pol-
earnestly from	*the Ædui*	*the corn,*	*which*	*they*

licĭti-essent (pl. perf. subj.)	publĭcè. Nam	propter
had promised	*publicly. For*	*on-account-of*

frigŏra	(quòd	Gallĭa	posĭta est sub
the colds	(*because*	*Gaul*	*is situated towards*

Septentrionĭbus (pl.),	ut	dictum-est	antè,)	non
the North,	*as*	*has been said*	*before,)*	*not*

mŏdò	frumenta	ĕrant	non	matura in	agris sed
only	*the corns*	*were*	*not*	*ripe in*	*the lands but*

ne	quĭdem	sătis	magna	copĭa, pabŭli
not	*indeed* (even)	*sufficiently*	*great*	*plenty, of forage*

suppetebat.	Autem	potĕrat	mĭnùs uti	ĕo
was supplied.	*But*	*he was able*	*less to use*	*with that*

frumento,	quod	subvexĕrat	navĭbus flumĭne
corn,	*which*	*he had-carried-up*	*in ships by the river*

DE BELLO GALLICO.

Arăre, proptereă quòd Helvetii averterant
Arar, because that the Helvetii had turned-away

iter ab Arăre, à quĭbus nolebat
the journey from the Arar, from which he was unwilling

discedĕre. Ædŭi ducĕre
to depart. The Ædui (began) to lead (to put off)

diem ex die, dicĕre conferri,
day from (after) day, to say (the corn) to be brought-together,

comportari, adesse. Ubi intellexit
to be conveyed, to be-present (at hand). When he understood

se duci diutiùs, et diem instare,
himself to be led (put-off) longer, and the day to urge-on

quo die oporteret metiri
(drew near), in which day it would behove to measure-out

frumentum militĭbus; principĭbus corum
corn to the soldiers; the chiefs of them

convocatis, quorum habebat magnum
being called together, of whom he did have a great

numĕrum in castris, in his Divitiaco
number in the camps, in (among) these Divitiacus

et Lisco, qui praeĕrat summo magistratŭi
and Liscus, who was-over the highest magistracy

(quem Ædŭi appellant Vergobretum, qui creatur
(whom the Ædui name Vergobretus, who is created

annŭus que habet potestatem vitæ que necis
annual and has the power of life and of death

in suos), accusat eos gravĭter,
over his-own (people)), he accuses them heavily,

quòd quum posset (imp. subj.) nĕque emi,
because when it was able neither to be bought,

nĕque sumi ex agris, tempore tam
nor to be taken from the lands, in a time so

necessario, hostĭbus tam propinquis,
necessary, the enemies (being) so near,

sublevetur (pres. subj.) non ab iis; praesertim quum,
he is succoured not by them; especially when,

ex	magnā	parte	adductus	precĭbus	eorum
from	*great*	*part*	*induced*	*by the prayers*	*of them*

	suscepĕrit (perf. subj.)	bellum:	querĭtur	etĭam
	he has undertaken	*the war:*	*he complains*	*also*

multò	gravĭùs	quòd	destitutus-sit (perf. subj.).
by much	*the more heavily*	*that*	*he has been left destitute (of corn).*

17.
Tum	demum	Liscus	adductus	oratione
Then	*at-last*	*Liscus*	*induced*	*by the speech*

Cæsăris,	proponit	quod antĕà	tacuĕrat:
of Cæsar,	*sets-forth*	*(that) which before*	*he had kept-silent:*

esse		nonnullos,	auctorĭtas	quorum
to be	*(that there are)*	*some,*	*the authority*	*of whom*

valĕat (pres. subj.)	plurĭmùm	ăpud	plebem,
avails	*most (very much)*	*with*	*common-people,*

qui	privati	possint (pres. subj.)	plus
who	*(being) private (persons)*	*can (do)*	*more*

quàm	magistratus	ipsi,	hos	seditiosâ
than	*the magistrates*	*themselves,*	*these*	*by seditious*

et	imprŏbâ	oratione	deterrere	multitudĭnem	ne
and	*wicked*	*speech*	*to deter*	*the multitude*	*lest*

confĕrant	frumentum;	quòd	dicant
they may bring-together	*the corn;*	*because*	*they say*

(pres. subj.) præstare,	si jam	possint
to excel (to be better),	*if now*	*they may be able*

non	obtinere	principatum	Gallĭæ,	perferre
not	*to obtain*	*the sovereignty*	*of Gaul,*	*to endure*

imperĭa	Gallorum	quàm	Romanorum;	nĕque
the commands	*of the Gauls*	*than*	*of the Romans;*	*nor*

debĕant (pres. subj.)	dubitare	quin,	si	Romani
ought they	*to doubt*	*but-that,*	*if*	*the Romans*

superavĕrint	Helvetĭos,	sint (pres. subj.)
shall have overcome	*the Helvetii,*	*they are*

erepturi	ibertatem.	Ædŭis	unà
about to snatch-away	*liberty*	*from the Ædui*	*together*

cum	relĭquâ	Gallĭâ:	ab	ïisdem	nostra
with	*remaining*	*Gaul:*	*by*	*the same (persons)*	*our*

consilĭa,	quæque	gerantur (pres. subj.)		in	castris,
counsels,	whatsoever	are carried-on		in	the camps,

enuntiari	hostĭbus	hos	posse	non
to be announced	to the enemies;	these	to be able (could)	not

coërceri	à	se:	quin-etĭam, quòd
to be restrained	by	himself:	moreover, because

enuntiârit (perf. subj.)	rem	necessariò	Cæsări,
he told	the thing	necessarily	to Cæsar,

sese	intelligĕre	cum	quanto periclŭo
himself	to understand	with	how-great danger

fecĕrit (perf. subj.)	id;	et	ob ĕam	caussam
he has done	it;	and	for that	cause

tacuisse	quamdĭu potuĕrit. (perf. subj.)
to have kept-silence	as-long-as he could.

18.
Cæsar	sentiebat	Dumnorĭgem	fratrem
Cæsar	did perceive	Dumnorix	the brother

Divitiăci	designari	hâc oratione	Lisci;
of Divitiacus	to be marked-out	by this speech	of Liscus;

sed, quòd	nolebat	ĕas	res	jactari
but, because	he did-not-will	those	things	to be tossed

(debated)	plurĭbus	præsentĭbus,	dimittit
	more	(being) present,	he dismisses

concilĭum,	retĭnet	Liscum: quærit	ex
the council,	he retains	Liscus: he seeks	from (him)

solo ĕa,	quæ	dixĕrat in	conventu.
alone those (things),	which	he had said in	the assembly.

Dicit	liberĭûs, atque	audaciûs. Rĕperit
He speaks	more-freely, and	more-boldly. He finds

eădem	esse	vera ab aliis	secretò.
the same (things)	to be	true from others	apart.

Dumnorĭgem	ipsum esse	summâ	audaciâ,
Dumnorix	himself to be	with (of) the highest	boldness,

magnâ gratĭâ	ăpud	plebem	propter
in great favour	with	the common-people	on-account-of

liberalitatem,	cupĭdum	novarum rerum;
(his) liberality,	desirous	of new things (revolution);

habere	portoria	que	omnia	reliqua
to have	the customs-duties	and	all	the remaining

vectigalia	Æduorum	complures	annos	redempta
taxes	of the Ædui	many	years	purchased

parvo	pretic;	proptereā	quòd, ille	licente, nemo
for a small	price;	because	that, he	bidding, no-one

audĕat (pres. subj.)	liceri contrà;	his	rebus
dares	to bid against (him);	by these	things

et	auxisse	sŭam	familiarem rem,	et
both	to have increased	his	family estate,	and

comparâsse	magnas	facultates	ad	largiendum
to have procured	great	means	to	bestow:

semper	alĕre	magnum	numĕrum	equitatûs
always	to maintain	a great	number	of cavalry

sŭo	sumptu,	et	habere	circum
at his-own	expense,	and	to have (them)	around

se:	nĕque	posse	largĭter	solùm
himself:	nor	to be able (to bestow)	largely	only

dŏmi,	sed etiam ăpud	finitĭmas	civitates;	atque
at home,	but also with	the bordering	states;	and

caussâ	hujus	potentĭæ,	collocâsse
by reason	of this	power,	to have placed (given in

	matrem in	Biturigĭbus,	homĭni illic
marriage)	(his) mother in	the Bituriges,	to a man there

nobilissĭmo et	potentissĭmo;	ipsum habere	uxorem
most-noble and	most-powerful;	himself to have	a wife

ex	Helvetiis	collocâsse	sororem ex
out-of	the Helvetii:	to have placed	a sister out-of

matre,	et sŭas propinquas	nuptum	in	alias
mother,	and his kinswomen	to be married	into	other

civitates:	favere et cupĕre		Helvetiis
states:	to favour and to desire (wish well)		to the Helvetii

propter	ĕam affinitatem:	etiam	odisse
on-account-of	that alliance:	also	to have hated

Cæsărem	et Romanos	sŭo	nomĭne,
Cæsar	and the Romans	from his-own	name (account).

quòd	potentĭa	ejus	diminuta-sit (perf. subj.)
because	the power	of him	has been diminished

adventu	eorum,	et	Divitĭăcus	frater	restitutus
by the arrival	of them,	and	Divitiacus	(his) brother	restored

in	antiquum	lŏcum	gratĭæ	atque	honoris:	si
into	the ancient	place	of favour	and	of honour:	if

quid	accĭdat	Romanis,	venire	in
any (thing)	may happen	to the Romans,	to come	into

summam	spem	regni	obtinendi	per
the highest	hope	of the kingdom	to be obtained	through

Helvetĭos;	imperĭo	Romani	popŭli,	non
the Helvetii;	(under) the empire	of the Roman	people,	not

mŏdò	desperare	de	regno,	sed	etĭam	de	ĕâ
only	to despair	of	the kingdom,	but	also	of	that

gratĭâ	quam	habĕat. (pres. subj.)	Cæsar	etĭam	reperiebat
favour	which	he has.	Cæsar	also	did find

inquirendo,	quòd	adversum	prœlĭum	equestre (adj.)
by inquiring,	that	the adverse	battle	of cavalry

factum-esset (plup. subj.)	paucis	diebus	antè,
had been made	in a few	days	before,

initĭum	ejus	fŭgæ	factum-esse	à	Dumnorĭge
the beginning	of that	flight	to have been made	by	Dumnorix

atque	equitĭbus	ejus,	(nam Dumnŏrix	præĕrat
and	by the horsemen	of him,	(for Dumnorix	was-over

	equitatŭi,	quem	Ædŭi	misĕrant
(commanded)	to the cavalry,	which	the Ædui	had sent

auxilĭo Cæsări;)	que	fŭgâ	eorum	relĭquum
for aid to Cæsar;)	and	by the flight	of them	the remaining

equitatum	perterrĭtum-esse.
cavalry	to have been dismayed.

19. Quĭbus	rebus	cognĭtis,	quum	certissĭmæ
Which	things	being known,	when	surest

res	accedĕrent (imp. subj.)	ad	has	suspiciones;
things	did accede (confirmed)	to	these	suspicions;

quòd	traduxisset (pl. perf. subj.)	Helvetĭos	per
because	he (Dumnorix) had led-over	the Helvetii	through

fines	Sequanorum;	quòd	curâsset
the borders	*of the Sequani;*	*because*	*he had taken-care*

(pl. perf. subj.) obsĭdes dandos inter eos: quòd
hostages to be given between them: because

fecisset (pl. perf. subj.) omnĭa ĕa non mŏdò
he had done all those (things) not only

injussu sŭo et civitatis, sed etĭam
without-order his (of him) and of the state, but also

ipsis inscientĭbus; quòd accusaretur (Imp. subj.)
themselves not-knowing; because he was accused

à magistratu Æduorum, arbitrabatur sătis
by the magistrate of the Ædui; he (Cæsar) did deem enough

caussæ esse quare, aut ipse animadvertĕret
of cause to be wherefore, either himself should animadvert

in ĕum, aut juberet civitatem animadvertĕre.
(punish) upon him, or should order the state to punish (him).

Unum repugnabat omnĭbus his, quòd cognovĕrat
One (thing) did oppose to all these, that he had known

summum studĭum fratris Divitiăci in
the highest zeal of (his) brother Divitiacus unto

Romanum popŭlum, summam voluntatem in se,
the Roman people, (his) highest good-will unto himself,

egregĭam fĭdem, justitĭam, temperantĭam. Nam
(his) prę-eminent faith, justice, temperance. For

verebatur, ne offendĕret anĭmum Divitiăci
he did fear, lest he should offend the mind of Divitiacus

supplicĭo ejus. Ităque prĭus quàm
by the punishment of him. Therefore sooner than

conaretur quidquam, jŭbet Divitiăcum
he should attempt anything, he orders Divitiacus

vocari ad se; et quotidianis
to be called to himself; and the daily (usual)

interpretĭbus remotis, colloquĭtur cum ĕo,
interpreters being removed, he converses with him,

per Caĭum Valerĭum Procillum, princĭpem
through Caius Valerius Procillus, chief

provinciæ Galliæ, suum familiarem, cui
of the province of Gaul, his intimate (friend), to whom

habebat summam fidem omnium rerum;
he did have the highest faith (confidence) *of all things;*

simul commonefăcit, quæ dicta-sint
at-the-same-time he reminds, what (things) *may have been said*

de Dumnorige in concilio Gallorum, ipso
of Dumnorix in the council of the Gauls, himself (Divitiacus)

præsente; et ostendit quæ quisque dixĕrit
(being) present; and shows what every-one has said

(perf. subj.) separatim de eo apud se: petit
separately of him to himself (Cæsar): *he asks*

atque hortatur ut, sine offensione animi ejus,
and exhorts that, without offence of the mind of him,

vel ipse statuat de eo, caussâ
either he himself (Cæsar) *may determine of him,* (his) *case*

cognită; vel jubĕat civitatem statuĕre.
being known; or may order the state to pass judgment.

20. Divitiăcus complexus Cæsărem cum multis
Divitiacus having embraced Cæsar with many

lacrymis cœpit obsecrare, "ne-statuĕret
tears began to beseech, " that he would not determine

quid gravius in fratrem; se
any-thing more heavy against (his) *brother; himself*

scire illa esse vera nec quenquam capĕre
to know those (things) *to be true; nor any-one to take*

plus doloris ex eo, quàm se; proptereă quòd
more of grief from that, than himself; because that

(quum ipse posset (imp. subj.) plurĭmum gratiă
(when himself was able (to do) most in influence

domi atque in reliquă Galliă, ille minĭmum
at home, and in the remaining Gaul, he (Dumnorix) *least*

propter adolescentĭam) crevisset (pl. perf. subj.)
on-account-of (his) *youth) had increased* (in power)

per se; quibus opibus ac nervis
through himself (Divitiacus); *which means and nerves* (strength)

LIBER I.

uteretur (imp. subj.)	non	solùm	ad	gratiam
he did use	*not*	*only*	*to*	*((Diviaticus') influence*

minuendam,	sed	penè	ad	sŭam	perniciem;
to be diminished,	*but*	*almost*	*to*	*his*	*destruction;*

sese	tămen	commoveri	et	fraterno	amore
himself	*however*	*to be moved*	*both*	*by fraternal*	*love*

et	existimatione	vulgi:	quòd	si
and	*by the esteem*	*of the common-people:*	*because*	*if*

quid	gravius	accidisset	ĕi
any (thing)	*more heavy*	*should have happened*	*to him*

à	Cæsăre,	cùm	ipse	teneret (imp. subj.)
from	*Cæsar,*	*when*	*he himself*	*did hold*

ĕum	lŏcum	amicitiæ	ăpud	ĕum,	nemĭnem
that	*place*	*of friendship*	*with*	*him,*	*no-one*

existimaturum	non	factum	sŭâ	voluntate;
about-to-think (the thing)	*not*	*done*	*with his*	*will;*

futurum	ex	quâ	re,	ŭtì	anĭmi
about-to-be	*from*	*which*	*thing,*	*that*	*the minds*

totius	Galliæ	averterentur	à	se."
of the whole	*Gaul*	*would be turned-away*	*from*	*himself."*

Quum	flens	petĕret (imp. subj.)	hæc
When	*weeping*	*he did seek*	*these (things)*

à	Cæsăre	pluribus	verbis,	Cæsar	prehendit
from	*Cæsar*	*in many*	*words,*	*Cæsar*	*takes*

dextram	ejus;	consolatus,	rŏgat (ut)
the right-hand	*of him;*	*having consoled,*	*he asks (that)*

faciat	finem	orandi:	ostendit	gratiam
he may make	*an end*	*of praying:*	*he shows*	*the favour*

ejus	esse	tanti	ăpud	se,	ŭtì
of him	*to be*	*of so-much (account)*	*with*	*himself,*	*that*

condonet	et	injuriam	Reipublĭcæ	et
he might forgive	*both*	*the injury*	*of the Republic*	*and*

sŭum	dolorem,	voluntati	ac	precĭbus
his-own	*grief,*	*to the will*	*and*	*to the prayers*

ejus.	Vŏcat	Dumnorĭgem	ad	se;	adhĭbet
of him.	*He calls*	*Dumnorix*	*to*	*himself;*	*he applies*

(sends for)	fratrem; brother;	ostendit he shows	quæ what	reprehendat (pres. he blames
subj.) in in	eo; him;	proponit he sets-forth	quæ ipse what himself	intelligat understands
(pres. subj.),	quæ what	civitas the state	queratur (pres. subj.); complains-of;	
monet, he warns,	ut that	vitet he may avoid	omnes suspiciones all suspicions	in into (for)
reliquum the remaining	tempus; time;	dicit he says	se himself	condonare to forgive
præterita past (things)	fratri to (his) brother		Divitiaco. Divitiacus.	Ponit He places
custodes keepers	Dumnorigi, to Dumnorix,	ut that	possit he may be able	scire to know
quæ what (things)		agat (pres. subj.) he does	cum with	quibus whom

loquatur (pres. subj.)
he speaks.

21. Eodem die factus certior ab
 In the same day being made more sure by

exploratoribus, hostes consedisse sub
scouts, the enemies to have sat-down under (at the

montem, octo millia passuum ab
foot of) *the mountain, eight thousands of paces from*

castris ipsius; misit qui cognoscerent,
the camps of himself; he sent (persons) who might know,

qualis esset natura montis, et
what-sort might be the nature of the mountain, and

qualis ascensus in circuitu: renuntiatum-est
what-sort the ascent in a circuit: it was announced

esse facilem. De tertia vigilia jubet
to be easy. From (at) *the third watch he orders*

Titum Labienum legatum pro Prætore
Titus Labienus lieutenant for Prætor (with prætorian powers)

cum duabus legionibus, et iisdem ducibus, qui
with two legions, and the same guides, who

cognovĕrant	ĭter,	ascendĕre	summum	jŭgum
had known	*the route,*	*to ascend*	*the highest*	*top*

montis;		ostendit	quid	sit	sŭi consilii,
of the mountain;		*he shows*	*what*	*may be*	*of his counsel*

	Ipse	de	quartâ	vigiliâ
(design).	He himself	from (at)	the fourth	watch

eodem	itinĕre,	quo	hostes	iĕrant,
by the same	*route,*	*by which*	*the enemies*	*had gone,*

contendit	ad	ĕos, que	mittit	antĕ	omnem equitatum.
hastens	*to*	*them, and*	*sends*	*before*	*all the cavalry.*

Publĭus	Considĭus,	qui	habebatur peritissĭmus
Publius	*Considius,*	*who*	*was deemed most-skilled*

militaris	rĕi, et	fuĕrat	in exercĭtu	Lucĭi
of military	*affair, and*	*had been*	*in the army*	*of Lucius*

Syllæ,	et	postĕa	in	Marci Crassi,
Sylla,	*and*	*afterwards*	*in (the army)*	*of Marcus Crassus,*

præmittĭtur	cum	exploratorĭbus.
is sent-forward	*with*	*the scouts.*

22.
Primâ	luce,	quum	summus	mons
In the first	*light,*	*when*	*the highest*	*mountain*

teneretur (imp. subj.)		à	Tito Labieno,	ipse
was held		*by*	*Titus Labienus,*	*he himself*

abesset (imp. subj.)	non	longĭus	mille et
was absent	*not*	*farther (than)*	*a thousand and*

quingentis	passĭbus	ab castris	hostĭum;
five-hundred	*paces*	*from the camps*	*of the enemies*

nĕque,	ut	compĕrit	postĕa	ex captivis,
nor,	*as*	*he found*	*afterwards*	*from the captives,*

aut	adventus	ipsius,	aut Labieni
either	*the arrival*	*of himself,*	*or of Labienus*

cognĭtus-esset (pl. perf. subj.);	Considĭus,	ĕquo
had been known;	*Considius,*	*(his) horse*

admisso,	accurrit	ad ĕum;	dicit.
being spurred-on,	*runs*	*to him;*	*he says,*

montem	quem	voluĕrit (perf. subj.)	occupari
the mountain	*which*	*he willed*	*to be occupied*

DE BELLO GALLICO. 22

à	Labieno,	teneri	ab	hostibus :	se
by	Labienus,	to be held	by	the enemies :	himself

cognovisse	id	à	Gallicis	armis	atque	insignibus.
to have known	that	from	Gallic	arms	and	ensigns.

Cæsar	subducit	suas	copias	in	proximum	collem,
Cæsar	leads-away	his	forces	into	the nearest	hill,

instruit	aciem.	Labienus,	ut	præceptum-erat
he arrays	the line.	Labienus,	as	had been directed

ei	à	Cæsare,	ne-committeret	prœlium,
to him	by	Cæsar,	that he should not engage	battle,

nisi	copiæ	ipsius	visæ-essent (pl. perf. subj.)
unless	the forces	of himself	had been seen

prope	castra	hostium,	ut	impetus	fieret
near	the camps	of the enemies,	that	the attack	might be made

in	hostes	undique	uno	tempore,
against	the enemies	on-every-side	in one	time,

monte	occupato,	expectabat	nostros,
the mountain	being occupied,	did await	our (men),

que	abstinebat	prœlio.	Denique,	multo	die
and	did abstain	from battle.	Finally,	in much	day

			Cæsar	cognovit	per
(when the day	was far advanced		Cæsar	knew	by

exploratores,	et	montem	teneri	à	suis,
scouts,	both	the mountain	to be held	by	his-own

	et	hostes	movisse	castra,	et
(men),	and	the enemies	to have moved	camps,	and

Considium	perterritum	timore	renuntiâsse	pro
Considius	dismayed	by fear	to have related	for

viso,	quod	vidisset (pl. perf. subj.)	non.
seen,	(that) which	he had seen	not.

Eo	die,	intervallo	quo	consuêrat,
In that day,	in the interval	with which	he had been accustomed,	

sequitur	hostes,	et	ponit	castra	tria	millia
he follows	the enemies,	and	places	camps	three	thousands

passuum	ab	castris	eorum.
of paces	from	the camps	of them.

23. Postridie ejus diei, quòd biduum
The day-after of that day, because space-of-two-days

| omnino | supererat, | quum | oporteret (imp. subj.) |
| altogether | did remain, | when | it did behove |

| metiri | frumentum | exercitu (exercitui); | et |
| to measure-out | corn | to the army; | and |

| quòd | aberat | à | Bibracte, | longè |
| because | he was distant | from | Bibracte, | far |

| maximo | ac | copiosissimo | oppido | Æduorum, |
| the greatest | and | most-wealthy | town | of the Ædui, |

| non | amplius | octodecim | millibus | passuum; |
| not | more (than) | eighteen | thousands | of paces; |

existimavit prospiciendum frumentariæ rei;
he deemed should be provided the corn thing (supply)

| et | avertit | iter | ab | Helvetiis | ac |
| and | he turns-away | the journey | from | the Helvetii | and |

| contendit | ire | Bibracte. | Ea | res | nuntiatur |
| hastens | to go | (to) Bibracte. | That | thing | is announced |

| hostibus | per | fugitivos | Lucii | Æmilii, |
| to the enemies | by | fugitives | of Lucius | Æmilius, |

| Decurionis | equitum | Gallorum. | Helvetii, |
| Captain | of horsemen | of Gauls. | The Helvetii, |

| seu | quòd | existimarent (imp. subj.) | Romani |
| either | because | they did deem | the Romans |

| discedere | perterritos | timore, | eo | magis | quòd |
| to depart | dismayed | with fear, | by that | more | because |

| pridie | superioribus | locis | occupatis, |
| the-day-before | the higher | places | being occupied, |

| commisissent (pl. perf. subj.) | non | prœlium, | sive |
| they had committed | not | battle, | or |

| quòd | confiderent (imp. subj.) | posse | inter- |
| because | they did trust | to be able | to be inter- |

| cludi | frumentariâ | re; | consilio |
| cepted | from corn | thing (provisions); | (their) counsel |

| commutato | atque | itinere | converso, | cœperunt |
| being altered | and | the route | being changed, | they began |

insĕqui	to follow-up
ac	and
lacessĕre	to provoke
nostros	our (men)
à	from
novissĭmo agmĭne.	the last troop.

24.
Postquam	After-that
Cæsar	Cæsar
animadvertit	observed
id,	that,
subducit sŭas copĭas	he leads-away his forces
in proxĭmum collem	into the nearest hill
que misit equitatum,	and sent cavalry,
qui sustineret	which might sustain
impĕtum hostĭum.	the attack of the enemies.
Ipse interim	Himself meanwhile
instruxit triplĭcem acĭem	arrayed a triple line
quatŭor veteranarum legionum	of four veteran legions
in medĭo colle;	in the middle hill;
ita ŭti collocaret	so that he might place
supra se,	above himself,
in summo jŭgo,	in the highest top,
dŭas legiones quas conscripsĕrat	two legions which he had levied
proxĭmè	very-lately
in citeriore Gallĭâ,	in hither Gaul,
et omnĭa auxilĭa,	and all the aids (auxiliaries),
et compleret	and might fill
totum montem hominĭbus.	the whole mountain with men.
Intereă jussit	In-the-mean-time he ordered
sarcĭnas conferri	the baggages to be brought-together
in unum lŏcum	into one place
et ĕum muniri	and it to be fortified
ab ĭis, qui constitĕrant	by those, who had stood
in superiore acĭe.	in the higher line.
Helvetĭi, secuti	The Helvetii, having followed
cum omnĭbus sŭis carris,	with all their waggons,
contulerunt impedimenta	brought-together the baggages
in unum lŏcum:	into one place:
Ipsi confertissĭmâ acĭe,	Themselves in thickest line,
nostro equitatu rejecto,	our cavalry being thrown-back,
phalange factâ,	a phalanx being made,
successerunt	came-up
sub nostram primam acĭem.	under our first line.

25. Cæsar, sŭo primùm, deinde ĕquis
Cæsar, his-own (horse) first, then the horses

omnĭum remotis è conspectu, ut perĭcŭlo
of all being removed from sight, that the danger

æquato, tollĕret spem fūgæ,
being made-equal, he might take-away the hope of flight,

cohortatus sŭos, commisit prœlĭum.
having encouraged his (men), engaged battle.

Milĭtes, pilis missis è superiore lŏco,
The soldiers, javelins being sent from the higher place,

facĭlè perfregerunt phalangem hostĭum : ĕâ
easily broke-through the phalanx of the enemies. it

disjectâ, fecerunt impĕtum in ĕos districtis
being dispersed, they made an attack upon them with drawn

gladĭis. Erat magno impedimento Gallis ad
swords. It was to great impediment to the Gauls to

pugnam, quòd plurĭbus scutis eorum transfixis
the fight, that many shields of them being pierced-through

et colligatis uno ictu pilorum, cùm
and bound-together by one stroke of javelins, when

ferrum inflexisset (pl. perf. subj.) se, potĕrant
the iron had bent-in itself, they were able

nĕque evellĕre, nĕque, sinistrâ impeditâ,
neither to pluck-out, nor, the left (hand) being entangled,

pugnare sătis commŏdè : ut multi, brachĭo
to fight sufficiently conveniently : that many, the arm

dĭu jactato, præoptarent (imp. subj.)
a long-time being tossed-about, wished-rather

emittĕre scutum mănu, et pugnare nudo
to send-forth shield from the hand, and to fight with naked

corpŏre. Tandem defessi vulnerĭbus cœperunt et
body. At length wearied with wounds they began both

referre pĕdem, et quòd mons
to carry-back foot (to retreat), and because the mountain

subĕrat circĭter mille passŭum,
was-under (was at hand) about a thousand of paces,

recipĕre	se	ĕŏ.	Monte	capto,
to betake	*themselves*	*thither.*	*The mountain*	*being taken,*

et	nostris	succedentĭbus,	Boïi	et	Tulingi,
and	*our (men)*	*going-up,*	*the Boii*	*and*	*Tulingi,*

qui	claudebant	agmen	hostĭum	circĭter
who	*did close*	*the troop*	*of the enemies*	*(with) about*

quindĕcim	millĭbus	homĭnum,	et ĕrant	præsidĭo
fifteen	*thousands*	*of men,*	*and were*	*for a guard*

novissĭmis,	agressi	nostros, ex
to the last (rear),	*having attacked*	*our (men) from (on)*

itinĕre	aperto latĕre,	circumvenire ;
(their) route	*in open side (flank),*	*(began) to surround ;*

et	Helvetïi	qui	recepĕrant	se in
and	*the Helvetii*	*who*	*had betaken*	*themselves unto*

montem,	conspicati	id,	cœperunt rursus
the mountain,	*having beheld*	*that,*	*began again*

instare	et	redintegrare	prœlĭum. Romani
to press-on	*and*	*to renew*	*the battle. The Romans*

intulerunt	signa	conversa	tripartitò ;
brought-on (advanced)	*the standards*	*turned*	*in-three-parts ;*

prima	ac	secunda acĭes,	ut resistĕret
the first	*and*	*second line,*	*that it might resist*

victis	et	submotis ;	tertĭa ut
to the conquered	*and*	*moved-away (repulsed) ;*	*the third that*

excipĕret	venientes.	Ita	pugnatum-est
it might receive	*(those) coming.*	*Thus*	*it was fought*

ancipĭti	prœlĭo	dĭu	atque acrĭter.
with doubtful	*battle*	*a long-time*	*and sharply.*

26.
Quum	possent (imp. subj.)	non	sustinere
When	*they were able*	*not*	*to sustain*

impĕtum	nostrorum	diutĭùs, altĕri	receperunt
the attack	*of our (men)*	*longer, others (some)*	*betook*

se	in montem,	ut cœpĕrant ;	altĕri
themselves	*unto the mountain,*	*as they had begun ;*	*others*

contulerunt	se	ad	impedimenta et sŭos
brought-together	*themselves*	*to*	*the baggages and their*

carros.	Nam hoc	toto	prœlio,	quum
waggons.	*For in this*	*whole*	*battle,*	*when* (although)

pugnatum-sit (perf. subj.)	ab septĭmâ	horâ
it was fought	*from the seventh*	*hour* (one o'clock)

ad vespĕram,	nemo potŭit videre hostem	aversum.
to evening,	*no one was able to see the enemy*	*turned-away.*

Pugnatum-est etĭam ad multam noctem ad impedimenta:
It was fought also to much night at the baggages:

proptereă quòd objecĕrant carros pro vallo,
because that they had opposed waggons for rampart,

et conjiciebant tela è superiore lŏco in
and did throw weapons from a higher place upon

nostros venientes, et nonnulli subjiciebant matăras
our (men) coming, and some did throw-under spears

ac tragŭlas inter carros que rŏtas, que
and darts between the waggons and wheels, and

vulnerabant nostros. Quum pugnatum-esset
did wound our (men). When it had been fought

(pl. perf. subj.) diu, nostri potiti-sunt
a long-time, our (men) gained

impedimentis que castris. Ibi filĭa Orgetorĭgis,
the baggages and camps. There a daughter of Orgetorix,

atque unus è filiis captus-est. Superfuerunt
and one out of (his) sons was taken. There survived

ex eo prœlio circiter centum et triginta millĭâ
out of that battle about a hundred and thirty thousands

hominum, que ierunt continenter eâ totâ nocte;
of men, and they went incessantly in that whole night;

itinĕre intermisso nullam partem noctis,
the journey being intermitted no part of the night,

quarto die pervenerunt in fines Lingŏnum:
in the fourth day they arrived into the borders of the Lingones;

quum nostri morati tridŭum
when our (men) having delayed the space-of-three-days

et propter vulnĕra militum et
both on-account of the wounds of the soldiers and

propter	sepulturam	occisorum,	potuissent
on-account-of	*the burial*	*of the slain,*	*had been able*

(pl. perf. subj.) non sĕqui ĕos. Cæsar misit litĕras
　　　　　　　　not to follow them. Cæsar sent letters

que nuntĭos ad Lingŏnes, ne-juvarent
and messengers to the Lingones, that they should not-assist

ĕos frumento neve alĭâ re: qui si
them with corn nor with other thing: who if

　　　juvissent, se habiturum illos
they should have assisted (them), himself about-to-have them

eodem lŏco, quo Helvetĭos. Ipse,
in the same place (light), *in which the Helvetii. Himself,*

trĭdŭo intermisso, cœpĭt sĕqui
the space-of-three-days being intermitted, began to follow

ĕos cum omnĭbus copĭis.
them with all (his) forces.

27. Helvetĭi, adducti ĭnopĭâ omnĭum rerum,
　　The Helvetii, induced by want of all things,

miserunt legatos ad ĕum de deditione:
sent ambassadors to him concerning a surrender:

qui cum convenissent (pl. perf. subj.) ĕum in itinĕre,
who when they had met *him in (his) journey,*

que projecissent (pl. perf. subj.) se ad pĕdes,
and had thrown-down *themselves at (his) feet,*

que locuti supplicĭter, flentes petîssent
and having spoken suppliantly, weeping had sought

(pl. perf. subj.) pacem, atque jussisset (pl. perf. subj.)
　　　　　　　peace, and he had ordered

ĕos expectare sŭum adventum in ĕo lŏco, quo
them to await his arrival in that place, in which

tum essent (imp. subj.), paruerunt. Postquam Cæsar
then they were, they obeyed. After-that Cæsar

pervenit ĕò, poposcit obsĭdes, arma, servos, qui
arrived there, he demanded hostages, arms, slaves, who

perfugissent (pl. perf. subj.) ad ĕos. Dum ĕa
had fled *to them. Whilst those*

conquiruntur	et	conferuntur,
(*things*) *are sought-for*	*and*	*are brought-together,*

nocte intermissâ, circĭter sex
a night being intermitted (having intervened), *about six*

millĭa homĭnum ejus pagi, qui appellatur
thousands of men of that district, which is named

Verbigenus, sive perterrĭti timore, ne, armis
Verbigenus, either frightened by fear, lest, (their) arms

tradĭtis, afficerentur supplicĭo; sive
being delivered, they should be affected with punishment; or

inducti spe salutis, quòd in tantâ multitudĭne
induced by hope of safety, because in so-great multitude

dedititiorum, existimarent (imp. subj.) sŭam fŭgam
of (those) surrendered they did think their flight

posse aut occultari aut ignorari
to be able either to be concealed or to be unknown

omnino; primâ vigilĭâ noctis, egressi ex
altogether; in first watch of night, having gone-out from

castris Helvetiorum, contenderunt ad Rhenum que
the camps of the Helvetii, hastened to the Rhine and

fines Germanorum.
borders of the Germans.

28. Quod ŭbi Cæsar rescivit, imperavit his,
Which when Cæsar knew, he ordered to these,

per fines quorum iĕrant, ŭtĭ
through the borders of whom they had gone, that

conquirĕrent et reducĕrent, si
they should search-for and should lead-back, if

vellent (imp. subj.) esse purgati sĭbi. Habŭit
they did will- to be cleared to himself. He had

reductos in numĕro hostĭum: Accepit omnes
(those) led-back in the number of enemies; he received all

relĭquos in deditionem, obsidĭbus, armis, perfŭgis
remaining into surrender, hostages, arms, deserters

tradĭtis. Jussit Helvetĭos, Tulingos,
being delivered-up. He ordered the Helvetii, Tulingi,

Latobrĭgos,   reverti   in   sŭos   fines,   unde
Latobrigi,   to return   into   their   borders,   whence

profecti-ĕrant;   et   quòd,   omnĭbus frugĭbus amissis,
they had set-out;   and because,   all   fruits   being lost,

nĭhil   ĕrat   dŏmi,   quo   tolerarent   fămem,
nothing   was   at-home,   by which   they might bear   hunger,

imperavit   Allobrogĭbus,   ut   facĕrent
he ordered   to the Allobroges,   that   they should make (supply)

copĭam frumenti   his ;   jussit   ipsos   restituĕre
plenty   of corn   to them ;   he ordered   themselves   to restore

oppĭda   que   vicos,   quos   incĕndĕrant.   Fecit
the towns   and   villages,   which   they had burned.   He did

id   maxĭme   eâ   ratione,   quòd   nolŭit
that   chiefly   with that   reason,   because   he willed-not

ĕum   lŏcum,   unde   Helvetĭi   discessĕrant,   vacare;
that   place,   whence   the Helvetii   had departed,   to be-void;

ne   propter   bonitatem   agrorum,   Germani,
lest   on-account-of   the goodness   of the lands,   the Germans,

qui   incŏlunt   trans   Rhenum,   transirent   è
who   inhabit   beyond   the Rhine,   should pass-over   from

sŭis finĭbus   in   fines   Helvetiorum,   et   essent
their borders   into   the borders   of the Helvetii,   and   should be

finitĭmi   provincĭæ Gallĭæ   que   Allobrogĭbus.
neighbouring   to the province   of Gaul   and   to the Allobroges

Concessit   Ædŭis   petentĭbus,   ut   collocarent
He granted   to the Ædui   asking,   that   they might place

Boïos   in   sŭis finĭbus,   (quòd   cognĭti-erant
the Boii   in   their borders,   (because   they had been known

egregĭâ   virtute):   quĭbus   illi   dederunt agros, que
by excellent   valour):   to whom   they   gave   lands, and

quos   receperunt   postĕa   in   părem conditionem
whom   they received   afterwards   into   equal   condition

juris   que libertatis   atque   ipsi   ĕrant.
of right   and of liberty   as   they themselves   were.

29.   In   castris   Helvetiorum   tabŭlæ   confectæ
In   the camps   of the Helvetii   tablets   made

Graecis	litĕris	repertae-sunt,	et perlatae ad	Caesarem;
in Greek	letters	were found,	and brought to	Cæsar;

in	quĭbus	tabŭlis	ratĭo confecta-ĕrat
in	which	tablets	a computation had been made

nominatim,	qui numĕrus	eorum	exîsset (pl. perf.
name-by-name,	what number	of them	had gone-forth

subj.)	dŏmo,	qui possent (imp. subj.)	ferre arma,
	from-home,	who were-able	to bear arms,

et	ĭtem	separatim	puĕri, sĕnes	que mulĭeres.
and	likewise	separately	boys, old-men	and women.

Summa	omnĭum	quarum	rerum ĕrat,	ducenta
The sum	of all	which	things was,	two hundred

sexaginta	et trĭa	millĭa	capĭtum	Helvetiorum;
sixty	and three	thousands	of heads	of the Helvetii;

triginta	et sex	millĭa	Tulingorum;	quatuordĕcim
thirty	and six	thousands	of the Tulingi;	fourteen

Latobrigorum;	Rauracorum viginti	et trĭa;	Boiorum
of the Latobrigi;	of the Rauraci twenty	and three;	of the Boii

triginta	et dŭo.	Ex his, qui	possent (imp. subj.)
thirty	and two.	Of this, who	were able

ferre	arma ad	nonaginta et	dŭo millĭa.	Summa
to bear	arms to	ninety and	two thousands.	The sum

	omnĭum	fuĕrat ad	trecenta	sexaginta et
(total)	of all	had been at	three-hundred	sixty and

octo	millĭa.	Censu	habĭto,	ut Caesar
eight	thousands.	Registering	being had,	as Cæsar

imperavĕrat,	numĕrus eorum,	qui redierunt	dŏmum,
had ordered,	the number of those,	who returned	home,

repertus-est	centum et	dĕcem	millĭa.
was found	a hundred and	ten	thousands.

30. | Bello | Helvetiorum | confecto, | legati |
|---|---|---|---|
| The war | of the Helvetii | being finished, | ambassadors |

fĕrè	totius Gallĭae,	princĭpes civitatum,	convenerunt
almost	of the whole Gaul,	chiefs of states,	came together

ad	Caesărem	gratulatum:	" sese, intelligĕre,
to	Cæsar	to congratulate:	" themselves, to understand,

tametsi	Romanus	popŭlus	repetîsset (pl. perf. subj.)		
although	*the Roman*	*people*	*had required*		

pœnas	ab	iis	bello	pro	vetĕrĭbus injurĭis
penalties	*from*	*them*	*in war*	*for*	*ancient injuries*

Helvetiorum;	tămen	ĕam	rem	accidisse	non
of the Helvetii;	*yet*	*that*	*thing*	*to have happened*	*not*

mĭnùs	ex	usu	terræ	Gallĭæ,
less	*out-of*	*use* (to the advantage)	*of the land*	*of Gaul,*

quàm	Romani	popŭli;	proptereă	quòd	ĕo
than	*of the Roman*	*people;*	*because*	*that*	*with that*

consilĭo,	florentissĭmis	rebus,	Helvetĭi reliquissent
counsel,	*in most-flourishing*	*affairs,*	*the Helvetii had left*

(pl. perf. subj.)	sŭas	dŏmos,	ut inferrent
	their	*houses,*	*that they might bring-on*

bellum	toti	Gallĭæ que	potirentur imperĭo (abl.);
war	*to the whole*	*Gaul and*	*might gain empire;*

que	deligĕrent	lŏcum	domicilĭo	ex magnâ copĭâ,
and	*might choose*	*a place*	*for abode*	*out-of great plenty,*

quem	judicâssent	opportunissĭmum ac
which	*they might have judged*	*most convenient and*

ľructuosissĭmum	ex	omni Gallĭâ;	que haberent
most-fruitful	*out-of*	*all Gaul;*	*and might have*

relĭquas	civitates	stipendiarĭas."	Petierunt, ŭtĭ
the remaining	*states*	*tributary."*	*They asked, that*

"liceret	sĭbi	indicĕre concilĭum
" it might be-lawful	*to themselves*	*to proclaim a council*

totĭus	Gallĭæ	in	certam	dĭem, que facĕre id
of whole	*Gaul*	*upon*	*a certain*	*day, and to do that*

voluntate	Cæsăris.	Sese	habere quasdam res,
with will	*of Cæsar.*	*Themselves*	*to have certain things,*

quas	vellent (imp. subj.)	petĕre	ab	ĕo è
which	*they did will**	*to ask*	*from*	*him out-of*

communi	consensu."	Eâ re	permissâ,
common	*consent."*	*That thing*	*being permitted,*

constituerunt	dĭem	concilĭo,	et sanxerunt
they appointed	*a day*	*for a council,*	*and ratified*

LIBER I.

jurejurando	inter	se,		ne	quis
by oath	*between*	*themselves,*		*(that) not*	*any-one*

enúntiaret		nĭsi	quĭbus	mandatum-esse (pl.
should divulge (it),		*unless*	*to whom*	*it had been enjoined*

perf. subj.) communi consilĭo.
       by common consent.

31. Eo concilĭo dimisso, iidem princĭpes
    That council being dismissed, the same chiefs

civitatum, qui fuĕrant antè, reverterunt ad
of states, who had been before, returned to

Cæsărem; que petierunt, ŭtì "liceret
Cæsar; and asked, that " it might be lawful

sĭbi agĕre secretò cum ĕo de
to themselves to act (treat) secretly with him about

sŭâ salute que omnĭum." Eâ re
their safety and (that) of all That thing

impetratâ, omnes flentes projecerunt sese
being obtained, all weeping cast themselves

ad pĕdes Cæsări; "se non mĭnùs
at the feet to (of) Cæsar; " themselves not less

contendĕre et laborare id, ne ĕa
to strive-after and to labour-for that, lest those (things)

quæ dixissent (pl. perf. subj.) enuntiarentur,
which they had said should be divulged,

quàm ŭtì impetrarent ĕa, quæ
than that they might obtain those (things), which

vellent (imp. subj.); proptereà quòd si enī
they did will; because that if it

tiatum-esse, viderent (imp. subj.) selves
have been divulged, they did see vitiăcus

venturos in summum cruciatur Divitiacus
about-to-come into the highest tortu _{to be} dŭas

Æduus locutus-est pro ĭos *two*
the Æduan spoke for Ædui tenere

factiones totius Gall *to hold*
factions of the whole

principatum	alterĭus	harum,	Arvernos
sovereignty	*of the other* (one)	*of these,*	*the Arverni*

alterĭus.	Quum	hi	contendĕrent (imp. subj.)
of the other.	*When*	*these*	*did contend*

tantopĕre	inter	se	de	potentatu	multos
so greatly	*between*	*themselves*	*about*	*dominion*	*many*

annos,	factum-esse,	ŭtì	Germani	accerserentur
years,	*to have been done,*	*that*	*the Germans*	*were sent-for*

(imp. subj.) ab Arvernĭs que Sequàmis mercede.
by the Arverni ind Sequani by hire (as

Primò circĭter quindĕcim millĭa horum
mercenaries). *At first about fifteen thousands of these*

transîsse	Rhenum;	posteàquam	fĕri	ac
to have crossed	*the Rhine;*	*after-that*	*the wild*	*and*

barbări	homĭnes	adamâssent (pl. perf. subj)
barbarous	*men*	*had fallen-in-love-with*

agros,	et	cultum,	et	copĭas	Gallorum,
the lands,	*and*	*cultivation,*	*and*	*stores*	*of the Gauls,*

plures	transductos:	nunc	esse	in	Gallĭâ
more (to have been)	*led-over:*	*now*	*to be*	*in*	*Gaul*

ad	numĕrum	centum	et	vigĭnti	millĭum :
to	*the number*	*of a hundred*	*and*	*twenty*	*thousands :*

Æduos,	que	clientes	eorum,	sĕmel
the Ædui,	*and*	*clients* (dependants)	*of them,*	*once*

atque	itĕrum	contendisse	armis	cum	his ;
and	*again*	*to have contended*	*in arms*	*with*	*these ;*

ulsos	accepisse	magnam	calamitatem ;
lsed	*to have received*	*a great*	*calamity ;*

to ese	omnem	nobilitatem,	omnem	senatum,
omnęt	all	*(their) nobility,*	all	*the senate,*

all	equitatum.	Fractos	quĭbus	prœliis
que	cĕr) *cavalry.*	*Broken*	*by which*	*battles.*
and	c			

perf. subj.)	us,	qui	antè	potuissent (pl.
		(they) who	*before*	*ad been able*

	in	Gallĭâ,	et		sŭâ
	in	*Gaul,*	*and* (both)		*by their-own*

LIBER I.

virtute	et	hospitio	atque	amicitiâ
valour	*and*	*by the alliance*	*and*	*friendship*

Romani	populi,	coactos-esse	dare	obsides
of the Roman	*people,*	*to have been forced*	*to give*	*hostages*

Sequanis,	nobilissimos	civitatis,	et obstringere
to the Sequani,	*the most-noble (men)*	*of the state,*	*and to bind*

civitatem	jurejurando,	sese	neque	repetituros
the state	*by oath,*	*themselves*	*neither*	*about-to-ask-back*

obsides,	neque	imploraturos	auxilium	à
the hostages,	*nor*	*about-to-implore*	*aid*	*from*

Romano	populo,	neque	recusaturos,	quò
the Roman	*people,*	*nor*	*about-to-refuse,*	*that*

minùs-essent	perpetuò	sub	ditione
they might not be	*perpetually*	*under*	*the dominion*

atque	imperio	illorum.	Se	esse	unum
and	*empire*	*of them.*	*Himself*	*to be*	*the only-one*

ex	omni	civitate	Æduorum,	qui	potuerit (perf.
out-of	*all*	*the state*	*of the Ædui,*	*who*	*has been able*

subj.)	non	adduci	ut	juraret,	aut
	not	*to be brought*	*that*	*he should swear,*	*or*

daret	suos	liberos	obsides:	ob	eam	rem
should give	*his*	*children*	*(as) hostages:*	*for*	*that*	*thing*

se	profugisse	ex	civitate,	et	venisse
himself	*to have fled*	*from*	*the state,*	*and*	*to have come (to)*

Romam	ad	Senatum	postulatum	auxilium,	quòd
Rome	*to*	*the Senate*	*to request*	*aid,*	*because*

solus	teneretur (imp. subj.)	neque	jurejurando,
(he) alone	*was held*	*neither*	*by oath,*

neque	obsidibus.	Sed	accidisse	pejus
nor	*by hostages.*	*But*	*to have happened*	*worse*

Sequanis	victoribus,	quàm	Æduis	victis:
to the Sequani	*conquerors,*	*than*	*to the Ædui*	*conquered:*

proptereà	quòd	Ariovistus,	rex	Germanorum,
because	*that*	*Ariovistus,*	*king*	*of the Germans,*

consedisset (pl. perf. subj.)	in	finibus	eorum,
had settled	*in*	*the borders*	*of them*

que	occupavisset	(pl. perf. subj.)		tertiam	partem
and	*had occupied*			*the third*	*part*

Sequăni	agri,	qui	esset (imp. subj.)	optĭmus,
of the Sequanian	*land,*	*which*	*was*	*the best*

totius	Gallĭæ ;	et	nunc	juberet (imp. subj.)
of the whole	*Gaul ;*	*and*	*now*	*did order*

Sequănos	decedĕre	de	altĕrâ	tertĭâ	parte ;
the Sequani	*to depart*	*from*	*the other*	*third*	*part ;*

proptereă	quòd,	paucis	mensĭbus (abl.)	antè,
because	*that,*	*a few*	*months*	*before,*

viginti	et	quatŭor	millĭa	hommum	Harudum
twenty	*and*	*four*	*thousands*	*of men*	*of Harudes*

venissent (pl. perf. subj.)	ad ĕum,	quĭbus	lŏcus
had come	*to him,*	*to whom*	*a place*

et	sedes	pararentur :	futurum-esse
and	*seats*	*should be prepared :*	*to-be-about-to-be*

paucis	annis,	ŭtĭ	omnes	pellerentur è
in a few	*years,*	*that*	*all*	*would be driven out-of*

finĭbus	Gallĭæ,	atque	omnes	Germani
the borders	*of Gaul,*	*and*	*all*	*the Germans*

transirent	Rhenum :	ĕnim	nĕque	Gallĭcum
would pass	*the Rhine :*	*for*	*neither*	*the Gallic (land)*

esse	conferendum		cum agro
to be	*to be brought-together* (compared)		*with the land*

Germanorum,	nĕque	hanc	consuetudĭnem	victûs
of the Germans,	*nor*	*this*	*custom*	*of sustenance*

	comparandam	cum	illâ. Autem	Ariovistum,
(living)	*to-be-compared*	*with*	*that. But*	*Ariovistus,*

ut	sĕmel	vicĕrit (perf subj.)	copĭas	Gallorum
when	*once*	*he conquered*	*the forces*	*of the Gauls*

prœlĭo,	quod	prœlĭum	factum-sit (perf. subj.)
in battle,	*which*	*battle*	*was made*

Amagetobrĭæ (gen.),		imperare	superbè et
(at) *Amagetobria,*		*to command*	*proudly and*

crudelĭter,	poscĕre	libĕros	cujusque	nobilissĭmi
cruelly,	*to require*	*the children*	*of every-one*	*most-noble*

LIBER I.

obsĭdes, et edĕre omnĭa exempla cruciatûs in
(as) hostages, and to exhibit all examples of torture upon

ĕos, si qua res facta-sit (perf. subj.) non ad nutum
them, if any thing has been done not at the nod

aut ad voluntatem ejus: homĭnem esse barbărum,
or at the will of him: the man to be barbarous,

iracundum, temerarĭum: imperĭa ejus non posse
irascible, rash: the commands of him not to be-able

sustineri diutĭùs: nisi quid auxilĭi sit
to be sustained longer: unless some (thing) of aid may be

in Cæsăre que Romano popŭlo, ĭdem esse
in Cæsar and the Roman people, the same to be

faciendum omnĭbus Gallis, quod Helvetĭi fecĕrant,
to-be-done to (by) all the Gauls, which the Helvetii had done,

ut emĭgrent dŏmo; pĕtant alĭud
that they may emigrate from home; they may seek another

domicilĭum, alĭas sedes remotas à Germanis, que
abode, other seats remote from the Germans, and

experiantur fortunam, quæcunque accĭdat. Si
may try fortune, whatsoever may happen. If

hæc enunciata-sint Ariovisto, non dubitare,
these (things) may have been told to Ariovistus, not to doubt,

quin sumat gravissĭmum supplicĭum de omnĭbus
but-that he may take the heaviest punishment of all

obsĭdĭbus, qui sint (pres. subj.) ăpud ĕum. Cæsărem,
the hostages, who are with him. Cæsar,

vel sŭâ auctoritate atque exercĭtûs, vel
either by his authority and (that) of (his) army, or

recenti victorĭâ, vel nomĭne Romani popŭli,
by (his) recent victory, or by the name of the Roman people,

posse deterrere, ne major multitudo Germanorum
to be-able to deter, lest a greater multitude of Germans

transducatur Rhenum, que posse defendĕre omnem
may be led-over Rhine, and to be able to defend all

Gallĭam ab injurĭâ Ariovisti.
Gaul from the injury of Ariovistus.

32. Hâc   oratione   habĭtâ   à   Divitiăco,
    This   speech   being had (delivered) *by Divitiacus,*

omnes, qui   adĕrant,   cœperunt petĕre auxilĭum à
all,   who were present, began   to ask   aid   from

Cæsăre magno   fletu.   Cæsar animadvertit Sequănos
Cæsar with great weeping. Cæsar observed the Sequani

unos   ex   omnĭbus   facĕre   nĭhil   earum   rerum,
alone out-of   all   to do   nothing of those things,

quas   cætĕri   facĕrent (imp. subj.); sed tristes, capĭte
which the rest did do;   but sad,   head

  demisso,   intueri   terram.   Miratus,
being cast-down, to look-upon the earth. Having wondered,

quæ   esset   caussa   ejus   rĕi,   quæsivit   ex
what might be the cause of that thing, he inquired from

ipsis.   Sequăni   respondêre   nĭhil,   sed
themselves. The Sequani answered   nothing, but

permansêre tacĭti in eâdem tristitĭâ. Quum quærĕret
remained silent in the same sadness. When he did ask

(imp. subj.) sæpĭùs ab ĭis, nĕque posset (imp.
           more-often from them, nor   was-able

subj.) exprimĕre   ullam vocem omnino;
      to express (draw forth) *any   voice at-all;*

idem   Ædŭus Divitiăcus   respondit, "Fortunam
the same Æduan Divitiacus answered, "The fortune

Sequanorum   esse   hôc   miseriorem que graviorem,
of the Sequani to be by this more-wretched and more-heavy,

quàm reliquorum, quòd   soli   audĕrent (imp.
than of the rest, because (they) alone did dare

subj.) nec quĭdem   quĕri   in   occulto,
       neither indeed to complain in hidden (secretly),

nec implorare auxilĭum; que horrerent (imp. subj.)
nor to implore   aid;   and   did dread

crudelitatem absentis Ariovisti, vĕlut si adesset
the cruelty of the absent Ariovistus, as if he was present

(imp. subj.) coràm;   proptereä quòd   tămen
            before (them); *because that notwithstanding*

facultas	fugæ	daretur (imp. subj.)	reliquis ;
an opportunity	of flight	was given	to the rest;
vero	omnes	cruciatus essent (imp. subj.)	perferendi
but	all	tortures were	to be endured

Sequănis, qui recepissent (pl. perf. subj.)
to (by) the Sequani, who had received

Ariovistum intra suos fines, omnia oppida quorum
Ariovistus within their borders, all the towns of whom

essent (imp. subj.) in potestate ejus."
were in the power of him."

33. His rebus cognitis, Cæsar confirmavit
These things being known, Cæsar confirmed (cheered)

animos Gallorum verbis, que pollicitus-est
the minds of the Gauls with words, and promised

"eam rem futuram curæ sibi: se
'that thing about-to-be for a care to himself: himself

habere magnam spem, Ariovistum adductum suo
to have great hope, Ariovistus induced by his

beneficio et auctoritate, facturum finem
kindness and authority, about-to-make an end

injuriis." Hâc oratione habitâ, dimisit
to injuries." This speech being had, he dismissed

concilium. Et secundùm ea multæ res
the council. And next-to those (things) many things

hortabantur eum, quare putaret eam rem
did exhort him, wherefore he should think that thing

cogitandum et suscipiendum sibi:
to be considered and to be undertaken to (by) himself:

imprimis, quòd videbat Æduos, sæpenuměro
in-the-first, because he did see the Ædui, oftentimes

appellatos fratres que consanguineos ab
having been named brothers and kinsmen by

Senatu, teneri in servitute atque in ditione
the Senate, to be held in slavery and in dominion

Germanorum, que intelligebat obsides
of the Germans, and he did understand the hostages

eorum	esse	ăpud	Ariovistum	ac	Sequănos;
of them	*to be*	*with*	*Ariovistus*	*and*	*the Sequani;*

quod,	in	tanto	imperĭo	Romani popŭli,
which,	*in*	*so-great*	*empire*	*of the Roman people,*

arbitrabatur	esse	turpissĭmum	sĭbi	et
he did deem	*to be*	*most-disgraceful*	*to himself*	*and*

reipublĭcæ.	Autem	Germanos	consuescĕre
to the republic.	*But*	*the Germans*	*to be accustomed.*

paullatim	transire	Rhenum,	et	magnam
gradually	*to pass-over*	*the Rhine,*	*and*	*a great*

multitudĭnem	eorum	venire	in	Gallĭam, videbat
multitude	*of them*	*to come*	*into*	*Gaul, he did see*

periculosum	Romano	popŭlo:	nĕque	existimaba
dangerous	*to the Roman*	*people:*	*nor*	*did he think*

fĕros	ac	barbăros	..mĭnes	temperaturos
wild	*and*	*barbarous*	*men*	*about-to-moderate*

sĭbi,	quin,	quum	occupâssent
to themselves,	*but-that,*	*when*	*they had occupied*

(pl. perf. subj.)	omnem	Gallĭam,	ut	Cimbri que
	all	*Gaul,*	*as*	*the Cimbri and*

Teutŏni	fecissent (pl. perf. subj.)	antè,	exirent
Teutoni	*had done*	*before,*	*they would go-out*

in	Provincĭam,	atque	inde	contendĕrent in
into	*the Province,*	*and*	*thence*	*would proceed into*

Italĭam;	præsertim	quum	Rhodănus	dividĕret (imp.
Italy;	*especially*	*since*	*the Rhone*	*did divide*

subj.)	Sequănos	à	nostrâ	provincĭâ. Quĭbus
	the Sequani	*from*	*our*	*province. To which*

rebus	putabat occurrendum
things	*he did think to be met (he ought to prevent)*

quàm-maturĭmè.	Autem Ariovistus	ipse	sumsĕrat
as-early-as-possible.	*But Ariovistus*	*himself*	*had taken*

sĭbi	tantos	spirĭtus,	tantam arrogantĭam,
to himself	*so-great*	*spirits (pride),*	*so-great arrogance,*

ut	videretur (imp. subj.)	non	ferendus.
that	*he did seem*	*not*	*to be borne.*

LIBER I.

34. Quamobrem placuit ei, ut mitteret
Wherefore it pleased to him, that he should send

legatos ad Ariovistum, qui postularent ab
ambassadors to Ariovistus, who should demand from

eo, "ut deligeret aliquem locum medium
him, "that he should choose some place midale

utriusque colloquio; sese velle agere
of each for a conference; himself to will to act (treat)

cum eo de Republicâ et summis rebus
with him about the Republic and the highest affairs

utriusque." Ariovistus respondit ei legationi: "Si
of each." Ariovistus answered to that embassy: "If

quid esset (imp. subj.) opus ipsi à
any (thing) was needful to himself from

Cæsare, sese fuisse venturum ad eum;
Cæsar, himself to have been about to come to him;

si ille velit (pres. subj.) quid à se,
if he wills any (thing) from himself,

oportere illum venire ad se: præterea, se
to behove him to come to himself. besides, himself

neque audere venire sine exercitu in eas
neither to dare to come without an army into those

partes Galliæ, quas Cæsar possideret (imp. subj.);
parts of Gaul, which Cæsar did possess;

neque posse contrahere exercitum in unum
nor to be able to draw-together an army into one

locum sine magno commeatu atque molimento:
place without great provision and trouble·

autem videri mirum sibi, quid negotii
but to seem wonderful to himself, what of business

esset aut Cæsari aut omnino Romano
might be either to Cæsar or at-all to the Roman

populo, in suâ Galliâ, quam vicisset (pl. perf.
people, in his Gaul, which he had conquered

subj.) bello.
in war.

35. His responsis relatis ad Cæsărem,
These answers being brought-back to Cæsar,

Cæsar itĕrum mittit legatos ad ĕum cum his
Cæsar again sends ambassadors to him with these

mandatis: "Quoniam affectus tanto beneficĭo
commands: "Since being affected with so-great kindness

sŭo que Romani popŭli (quum
his own (Cæsar's) and (that) of the Roman people (since

appellatus-esset (pl. perf. subj.) in sŭo consulatu rex
he had been named in his-own consulship king

atque amicus à Senatu,) referret (imp. subj.) hanc
and friend by the Senate,) he did return this

gratĭam sĭbi que Romano popŭlo, ut
gratitude to himself and to the Roman people, that

gravaretur invitatus venire in
he should be-reluctant (though) invited to come into

colloquĭum, nĕque putaret dicendum
a conference, nor should think (it) to-be-spoken

sĭbi et cognoscendum de communi
to (by) himself and to-be-known concerning the common

re; hæc esse, quæ postularet (imp. subj.)
thing; these to be, (things) which he did demand

ab ĕo: primùm, ne-transducĕret quam
from him: first, he should not-lead-over any

multitudĭnem homĭnum amplĭùs trans Rhenum in
multitude of men more 'ver the Rhine into

Gallĭam: deinde reddĕret obsĭdes quos
Gaul: then he should restore the hostages which

haberet (imp. subj.) ab Æduis; que permittĕret
he did have from the Ædui; and should permit

Sequănis, ut licĕret voluntate
to the Sequani, that it should be allowed by the will

ejus reddĕre illis quos illi
of him to restore to them (the Ædui) (those) whom they

haberent (imp. subj.); nève lacessĕret Æduos
did have; nor he should attack the Ædui

injurĭā;	nĕve	inferret	bellum	his	ve
by injury (unjustly);	*nor*	*should bring-on*	*war*	*to these,*	

socĭis	eorum;	si	fecisset	id	ĭtā,
to the allies	*of them;*	*if*	*he might have done*	*that*	*thus,*

perpetŭam	gratĭam	atque	amicĭtĭam	futuram
perpetual	*favour*	*and*	*friendship*	*about-to-be*

sĭbi	que	Romano	popŭlo	cum	ĕo.	Si
to himself	*and*	*to the Roman*	*people*	*with*	*him.*	*If*

impetraret (imp. subj.)	non,	quonĭam,	Marco	Messalā,
he did obtain (it)	*not,*	*since,*	*Marcus*	*Messala,*

Marco	Pisone	consulĭbus,	Senatus	censuisset
Marcus	*Piso*	*(being) consuls,*	*the Senate*	*had resolved*

(pl. perf. subj.)	ŭtĭ	quicunque	obtineret	Gallĭam
	that	*whosoever*	*should obtain*	*Gaul*

provincĭam,	defendĕret	Ædŭos	que
(as a) province,	*should defend*	*the Ædui*	*and*

cætĕros	amicos	Romani	popŭli,	quod
other	*friends*	*of the Roman*	*people,*	*which* (as far as)

posset	facĕre	commŏdo	Reipublĭcæ,
he might be able	*to do*	*to the advantage*	*of the Republic,*

se	non	neglecturum	injurias	Æduorum."
himself	*not*	*about-to-neglect*	*the injuries*	*of the Ædui."*

36. Ariovistus respondit ad hæc : "esse
Ariovistus answered to these (things): "to be

jus	belli,	ut	qui	vicissent (pl. perf. subj.),
the right	*of war,*	*that*	*(they) who*	*had conquered,*

imperarent	iis (dat.),	quos	vicissent (pl. perf. subj.),
should rule	*those,*	*whom*	*they had conquered,*

quemadmŏdum	vellent:	itĭdem	Romanum
as	*they might will:*	*likewise*	*the Roman*

popŭlum	consuēsse	imperare	victis (dat.)
people	*to have been accustomed*	*to rule*	*the conquered*

non	ad	præscriptum	alterĭus,	sed	ad	sŭum
not	*at*	*the prescription*	*of another,*	*but*	*at*	*their-own*

arbitrĭum.	Si	ipse	præscribĕret (imp. subj.)
will.	*If*	*he (himself)*	*did prescribe*

non	Romano	popŭlo,	quemadmŏdum	uteretur
not	*to the Roman*	*people,*	*how*	*it should use*

sŭo	jure,	non	oportere	se	impediri
with its	*right,*	*not*	*to behove*	*himself*	*to be hindered*

à	Romano	popŭlo	in	sŭo	jure:	Ædŭos
by	*the Roman*	*people*	*in*	*his*	*right:*	*the Ædui*

factos-esse	stipendarios	sĭbi,	quoniam
to have been made	*tributary*	*to himself,*	*since*

tentâssent (pl. perf. subj.)	fortunam	belli,	et
they had tried	*the fortune*	*of war,*	*and*

congressi-essent (pl. perf. subj.)	armis	ac
had engaged	*in arms*	*and (had been)*

superati:	Cæsărem	facĕre	magnam	injurĭam,	qui
overcome:	*Cæsar*	*to do*	*great*	*injury,*	*who*

sŭo	adventu	facĕret (imp. subj:)	vectigalia	deteriora
by his	*arrival*	*did make*	*the taxes*	*worse*

sĭbi:	se	esse	non	redditurum	obsĭdes
to him:	*himself*	*to be*	*not*	*about-to-restore*	*the hostages*

Ædúis;	nĕque	illaturum	bellum	injuriâ
to the Ædui;	*nor*	*about-to-bring-on*	*war*	*by injury*

ĭis,	nĕque	socĭis	eorum,	si
(unjustly) to them,	*nor*	*to the allies*	*of them*	*if*

manerent	in	ĕo,	quod	convenisset (pl.
they should remain	*in*	*that,*	*which*	*had been agreed-upon,*

perf. subj.),	que	pendĕrent	stipendĭum	quotannis:
	and	*should weigh* (pay)	*tribute*	*yearly:*

si	fecissent	non	id,	fraternum	nomen
if	*they might have done*	*not*	*that,*	*the fraternal*	*name*

Romani	popŭli	abfuturum	longè	ab
of the Roman	*people*	*about-to-be-absent*	*far*	*from*

his:	quòd	Cæsar	denuntiaret (imp.
these (useless to them):	*that*	*Cæsar*	*did declare*

subj.)	sĭbi,	se	non	neglecturum	injurĭas
	to him,	*himself*	*not*	*about-to-neglect*	*the injuries*

Æduorum,	nemĭnem	contendisse	cum	se
of the Ædui,	*no-one*	*to have contended*	*with*	*himself*

sĭne sŭâ pernicĭe : congrederetur, quum
without his-own destruction : he might engage, when

vellet; intellecturum, quid invicti
he might will ; about-to-understand, what the unconquered

Germani, exercitatissĭmi in armis, qui subîssent
Germans, most-exercised in arms, who had gone-under

(pl. perf. subj.) non tectum intra quatuordĕcim annos,
not a roof within fourteen years,

possent virtute.
might be able (to effect) by valour.

37. Eodem tempŏre hæc mandata
In (at) the same time these charges

referebantur Cæsări ; et legati veniebant
were brought-back to Cæsar ; and ambassadors did come

ab Ædŭis et Trevĭris : Ædŭi, questum,
from the Ædui and Treviri : the Ædui, (came) to complain,

quòd "Harudes, qui nuper transportati-essent (pl.
that "the Harudes, who lately had been carried-over

perf. subj.) in Gallĭam, popularentur (imp. subj.)
into Gaul, did lay-waste

fines eorum ; sese potuisse redimĕre
the borders of them ; themselves to have-been-able to purchase

pacem Ariovisti, ne quĭdem obsidĭbus
peace of Ariovistus, not indeed (even) hostages

dătis." Autem Trevĭri, "centum pagos
being given." But the Treviri, " a hundred districts

Suevorum consedisse ad ripam Rheni, qui
of the Suevi to have settled at the bank of the Rhine, who

conarentur (imp. subj.) transire Rhenum ; fratres
did endeavour to pass-over the Rhine ; the brothers

Nasŭam et Cimberĭum præesse ĭis (dat.)" Quĭbus
Nasua and Cimberius to be-over these." By which

rebus Cæsar commotus vehementer
things Cæsar being moved violently (strongly impressed)

existimavit maturandum sĭbi, ne, si nŏva mănus
thought to-be-hastened to (by) himself, lest, if a new band

Suevorum	conjunxisset (pl. perf. subj.)	sese	cum
of the Suevi	*had joined*	*itself*	*with*

veterĭbus	copiis	Ariovisti,	posset	mĭnùs
the old	*forces*	*of Ariovistus,*	*it might be-able*	*less*

facĭlè	resisti.	Ităque,	frumentariâ	re
easily	*to be withstood.*	*Therefore,*	*corn*	*affair*

	comparatâ,	quàm-celerrĭmè	potŭit,
(provisions)	*being procured,*	*as-quickly-as*	*he could,*

contendit	magnis	itinerĭbus	ad	Ariovistum.
he hastened	*by great*	*journies*	*to*	*Ariovistus.*

38. | Quum | jam | processisset (pl. perf. subj.) |
|---|---|---|
| *When* | *now* | *he had proceeded* |

vĭam	tridŭi,	nuntiatum-est	ĕi,
a way (journey)	*of three days,*	*it was told*	*to him,*

Ariovistum	cum	omnĭbus	sŭis	copiis	contendĕre	ad
Ariovistus	*with*	*all*	*his*	*forces*	*to hasten*	*to*

occupandum	Vescontionem,	quod	est	maxĭmum
occupy	*Vescontio,*	*which*	*is*	*the greatest*

oppĭdum	Sequanorum,	que	processisse	vĭam
town	*of the Sequani,*	*and*	*to have proceeded*	*a way*

	tridŭi	à	sŭis	finĭbus.	Cæsar
(journey)	*of three days*	*from*	*his*	*borders.*	*Cæsar*

existimabat	præcavendum	sĭbi	magnopĕre,	ne
did think	*o be provided*	*to* (by) *himself*	*greatly,*	*lest*

id	accidĕret:	namque	ĕrat	summa	facultas
that	*should happen:*	*for*	*there was*	*the highest*	*means*

in	ĕo	oppĭdo	omnĭum	rerum,	quæ	ĕrant	usŭi	ad
in	*that*	*town*	*of all*	*things,*	*which*	*were*	*for use*	*to*

bellum,	que	id	muniebatur	sic	naturâ
war,	*and*	*that*	*was fortified*	*so*	*by the nature*

lŏci,	ut	dăret (imp. subj.)	magnam	facultatem
of the place,	*that*	*it did give*	*great*	*means*

ad	ducendum	bellum;	proptereă	quòd	flumen
to	*lead* (protract)	*the war;*	*because*	*that*	*the river*

Dubis,	ut	circumductum	circĭno,	cingit
Dubis (Doux),	*as* (if)	*led-around*	*by a compass,*	*girds*

pene   totum   oppĭdum;   reliquum   spatĭum,   quod
almost the whole town ;   the remaining space,   which

est   non   amplĭus   sexcentorum   pĕdum,
is   not   more (than the space)   of six-hundred feet,

quâ   flumen   intermittit,   mons   contĭnet,
where the river intermits (discontinues), a mountain contains,

magnâ   altitudĭne,   ĭta ut   radices   ejus   montis
with (of) great height,   so that the roots of that mountain

contingant (pres. subj.)   ripæ   flumĭnis   ex
reach   to the bank of the river out-of (on)

utrâque   parte.   Murus   circumdătus   efficit   hunc
each   part.   A wall   thrown-around makes   this

      arcem   et   conjungit   cum   oppĭdo.
(mountain) a citadel and   joins (it)   with   the town.

Huc   Cæsar   contendit   magnis   diurnis   que   nocturnis
Hither Cæsar   hastens   by great diurnal   and   nocturnal

itinerĭbus,   que   oppĭdo   occupato,   collŏcat
journies,   and   the town being occupied, he places

præsidĭum   ĭbi.
a garrison   there.

39. Dum   moratur   paucos   dĭes   ad   Vescontionem
Whilst he delays a few   days   at   Vescontio

caussâ   frumentarĭæ   rĕi   que   commeatûs,
by cause (for the sake) of corn affair and of provision,

ex   percunctatione   nostrorum   que   vocĭbus
out-of the inquiry   of our (men)   and   the expressions

Gallorum   et   mercatorum   (qui   prædicabant
of the Gauls and   of the merchants (who   did proclaim

"Germanos   esse   ingenti   magnitudĭne   corpŏrum,
"the Germani to be   with (of) vast   size   of bodies,

incredibĭli   virtute atque exercitatione in armis,
with (of) incredible valour and   exercise   in arms,

sese   sæpenumĕro   congressos   cum   iis,
themselves oftentimes   having engaged   with   them.

potuisse   ne   quĭdem   ferre   vultum   atque
to have been-able not indeed (even) to bear the look   and

DE BELLO GALLICO.

aciem oculorum,") tantus timor subitò
edge (glance) *of (their) eyes,")* *so great fear suddenly*

occupavit omnem exercitum, ut perturbaret (imp.
occupied all the army, that it did disturb

subj.) non mediocriter mentes que animos omnium.
not moderately the minds and spirits of all.

Hic primùm ortus-est à tribunis militum,
This (fear) first arose from the tribunes of soldiers,

ac præfectis, que reliquis, qui caussâ
and prefects, and remaining (persons), who by cause

amicitiæ secuti Cæsarem
(for the sake) of friendship having followed Cæsar

ex urbe, miserebantur magnum periculum,
out-of the city, did deplore the great danger,

quòd habebant non magnum usum in
because they did have not great experience in

militari re: quorum alius, aliâ caussâ
military affair: of whom another, another cause

illatâ, quam diceret (imp. subj.) esse
being brought (alleged), which he did say to be

necessariam sibi ad proficiscendum, petebat, ut
necessary to himself to set-out, did ask, that

liceret discedere voluntate ejus: nonnulli
it might be-allowed to depart by the will of him: some

adducti pudore, ut vitarent suspicionem
induced by shame, that they might avoid the suspicion

timoris, remanebant. Hi poterant neque fingere
of fear, did remain. These were able neither to feign

vultum neque interdum tenere lacrymas; abditi
countenance nor sometimes to hold tears; hidden

in tabernaculis, aut querebantur suum
in tents, either they did complain-of their-own

fatum, aut cum suis familiaribus miserebantur
fate, or with their intimates did deplore (their)

commune periculum. Vulgò testamenta obsignabantur
common danger. Generally wills were sealed

totis	castris (pl.).	Vocibus ac timore	horum
in the whole	*camp.*	*By words and fear*	*of these*

paullatim	etiam	ii,	qui habebant magnum	usum
gradually	*also*	*they,*	*who did have great*	*experience*

in castris (pl.),	milites que centuriones,	que	qui
in camp,	*soldiers and centurions,*	*and*	*those who*

præerant	equitatui,	perturbabantur.	Qui ex
were-over	*to the cavalry,*	*were disturbed.*	*(They) who of*

his volebant	se	existimari minùs	timidos,
these did will	*themselves*	*to be thought less*	*fearful,*

dicebant	se	non vereri hostem, sed	timere
did say	*themselves*	*not to dread the enemy, but*	*to fear*

angustias	itineris et magnitudinem	sylvarum,
the straits	*of the journey and the greatness*	*of the woods,*

quæ	intercederent (imp. subj.)	inter eos	et
which	*did intervene*	*between them*	*and*

Ariovistum,	aut	frumentariam rem,	ut
Ariovistus,	*or*	*the corn affair* (supply),	*that*

posset	commodè satis	supportari.
it might be-able	*(not) conveniently enough*	*to be carried-up.*

Etiam	nonnulli renuntiabant	Cæsari,	cùm
Also	*some did relate*	*to Cæsar,*	*when*

jussisset (pl. perf. subj.)	castra (pl.)	moveri, ac
he had ordered	*camp*	*to be moved, and*

signa	ferri,	milites non	fore
the standards	*to be borne,*	*the soldiers not*	*to be-about-to-be*

audientes	dicto,	neque	laturos
hearing (obedient)	*to word,*	*nor*	*about-to-bear*

signa propter	timorem.
the standards on-account-of	*fear.*

40. Quum	Cæsar	animadvertisset (pl. perf. subj.)
When	*Cæsar*	*had observed*

hæc,	concilio	convocato, que
these (things),	*a council*	*being called together, and*

centurionibus	omnium	ordinum adhibitis	ad
the centurions	*of all*	*ranks being admitted*	*to*

id	concilium,	incusavit	ĕos	vehementer; primùm,
that	*council,*	*he blamed*	*them*	*vehemently; first,*

quòd	putarent (imp. subj.)	quærendum	aut
that	*they did think*	*to-be-inquired*	*or*

cogitandum	sĭbi,	aut	in	quam
to-be-considered	*to (by) themselves,*	*either*	*into*	*what*

partem,	aut	quo	consilio	ducerentur (imp. subj.).
part,	*or*	*with what*	*design*	*they were led.*

Ariovistum,	se	consŭle,	cupidissimè
Ariovistus,	*himself*	*(being) consul,*	*most-eagerly*

appetîsse	amicitĭam	Romani	popŭli: cur
to have sought	*the friendship*	*of the Roman*	*people: why*

quisquam	judicaret	hunc	discessurum tam
any-one	*should judge*	*this (man)*	*about-to-depart so*

temĕrè	ab officio?	Quĭdem persuaderi	sĭbi,
rashly	*from duty?*	*Indeed to be persuaded*	*to himself,*

sŭis	postulatis	cognĭtis,	atque	æquitate con-
his	*demands*	*being known,*	*and*	*the equity of the*

ditionum	perspectâ,	ĕum nĕque	repudiaturum
conditions	*being clearly-seen,*	*him neither*	*about-to-reject*

sŭam	gratĭam nĕque	Romani	popŭli: quòd
his	*favour nor*	*(that) of the Roman*	*people: but*

si,	impulsus	furore atque	amentĭâ, intu-
if,	*impelled*	*by rage and*	*by madness; he might have*

lisset	bellum,	quid tandem	vererentur?
brought-on	*war,*	*what at length*	*should they fear?*

aut	cur	desperarent	de suâ
or	*why*	*should they despair*	*concerning their-own*

virtute,	aut	de diligentĭâ	ipsius?
valour,	*or*	*concerning the diligence*	*of himself (Cæsar)?*

Pericŭlum	ejus	hostis	factum me-
Danger (trial)	*of that*	*enemy*	*(was) made in the me-*

morĭâ	nostrorum	patrum,	quum,	Cimbris et
mory	*of our*	*fathers,*	*when,*	*the Cimbri and*

Teutŏnis	pulsis	à	Caio Marĭo,	exercĭtus
Teutoni	*being routed*	*by*	*Caius Marius,*	*the army*

videbatur	merĭtus	non	minorem	laudem,	quàm
did seem	*having deserved*	*not*	*less*	*praise,*	*than*

imperator	ipse:	etĭam	factum	nuper in
the general	*himself:*	*also*	*(it was) made*	*lately in*

Italĭâ,	servili	tumultu,	quos tămen	alĭquis
Italy,	*in the servile*	*commotion,*	*whom however*	*some*

usus	ac	disciplina,	quam	accepissent
experience	*and*	*discipline,*	*which*	*they had received*

(pl. perf. subj.)	à	nobis,	sublevarent.	Ex quo
	from	*us,*	*did assist.*	*From which*

posset (imp. subj.)	judicari,	quantum	bŏni
it was able	*to be judged,*	*how-much*	*of good*

constantĭa	haberet (imp. subj.)	in se;	proptereă
firmness	*did have*	*in itself;*	*because*

quòd	quos	aliquandĭu	timuissent (pl. perf.
that	*(those) whom*	*some-while*	*they had feared*

subj.)	sine caussâ	inermes,	superâssent (pl.
	without cause	*unarmed,*	*they had conquered,*

perf. subj.),	hos postea	armatos ac	victores.
	these afterwards	*armed and*	*conquerors*

Denĭque,	hos	esse	Germanos	cum quĭbus
Lastly,	*these*	*to be*	*the Germani*	*with whom*

Helvetĭi	sæpenumĕro	congressi	non solùm
the Helvetii	*oftentimes*	*having engaged*	*not only*

in	sŭis,	sed etĭam in	finĭbus	illorum
in	*their-own,*	*but also in*	*the borders*	*of them*

plerumque superâssent (pl. perf. subj.); qui	tămen
generally had overcome;	*who notwithstanding*

potuĕrint (perf. subj.)	non	esse	păres	nostro
have been able	*not*	*to be*	*equal*	*to our*

exercitŭi. Si	adversum	prœlĭum et	fŭga	Gallorum
army. If	*the adverse*	*battle and*	*flight*	*of the Gauls*

commoveret	quos,	hos	posse	reperire,
might move (affect)	*any,*	*these*	*to-be-able*	*to find,*

si	quærĕrent (imp. subj.),	Gallis defatigatis
if	*they did inquire.*	*the Gauls being wearied*

diuturnitāte	belli,	Ariovistum,	quum
by the long-continuance	*of the war,*	*Ariovistus,*	*when*

continuisset (pl. perf. subj.)		se	multos menses
he had kept		*himself*	*many months*

castris	ac paludĭbus,	nĕque	fecisset (pl. perf. subj.)
in camps	*and marshes,*	*nor*	*had made*

potestatem	sŭi,	adortum
power	*of himself* (given opportunity),	*having attacked*

subĭtò	jam	desperantes	de	pugnâ et
suddenly	*(those) now*	*despairing*	*of*	*battle and*

dispersos,	vicisse	măgis	ratione
scattered,	*to have conquered*	*more*	*by reason* (plan)

ac	consilĭo	quàm	virtute :	cui rationi
and	*by counsel*	*than*	*by valour :*	*for which reason*

lŏcus	fuisset	contra	barbăros atque
(plan) *place*	*might have been*	*against*	*barbarous and*

imperitos	homĭnes :	hâc	ne quĭdem
unskilled	*men :*	*by this* (plan)	*not indeed* (even)

ipsum	sperare	nostros exercĭtus	posse	căpi.
himself	*to hope*	*our armies*	*to be able*	*to be taken.*

Qui	conferrent (imp. subj.)	sŭum timorem	in
(*They*) *who*	*did confer* (attribute)	*their fear*	*upon*

simulationem	frumentarĭæ	rĕi que	angustĭas
pretence	*of corn*	*affair and*	*the straits*

itinĕrum,	facĕre	arroganter,	quùm
of the journeys,	*to do*	*assumingly,*	*when* (since)

viderentur (imp. subj.)	aut	desperare	de officĭo
they did seem	*either*	*to despair*	*of the duty*

imperatoris,	aut præscribĕre	ĕi :	hæc
of the commander,	*or to prescribe*	*to him :*	*these* (things)

esse	curæ	sĭbi ;	Sequănos, Leucos,
to be	*for a care*	*to himself ;*	*the Sequani, Leuci,*

Lingönes	subministrare	frumentum ;	que jam
Lingones	*to supply*	*corn ;*	*and now*

frumenta (pl.) esse	matura	in agris.	De itinĕre
corn to be	*ripe*	*in the lands.*	*Of the journey*

ipsos	judicaturos	brĕvi	tempŏre.	Quòd
themselves	*about-to-judge*	*in a short*	*time.*	*That*

milĭtes	dicantur (pres. subj.)	non	fŏre
the soldiers	*are said*	*not*	*to be-about-to-be*

audientes dicto, nĕque laturi
hearing to word (obedient to command), *nor about-to-bear*

signa,	se	commoveri
the standards (about to advance),	*himself*	*to be moved*

nĭhil ĕâ re; enim scire, quibuscunque
nothing by that thing; for to know (he knew), *to whomsoever*

exercĭtus fuĕrit (perf. subj.) non audĭens dicto,
an army has been not hearing to word (obedient),

aut,	re	gestâ	mălè,	fortunam
either,	*an affair*	*being carried-on*	*ill,*	*fortune*

defuisse;	aut	alĭquo	facinŏre	comperto,
to have failed;	*or*	*some*	*crime*	*being found-out,*

avaritĭam	convictam-esse:	sŭam	innŏcentĭam
(their) avarice	*to have been proved:*	*his*	*innocence*

perpetŭâ vitâ, felicitatem bello Helvetiorum
in perpetual life, success in the war of the Helvetii

perspectam-esse. Ităque, se repræ-
to have been clearly-seen. Therefore, himself about-to-

sentaturum quod esset (imp. subj.)
do-presently (that) which he was (otherwise)

collaturus	in	longiorem	dĭem;	et
about-to-confer (defer)	*into*	*a more-distant*	*day;*	*and*

proxĭmâ	nocte	de	quartâ	vigilĭâ
in the nearest (next)	*night*	*from* (at)	*the fourth*	*watch*

moturum	castra (pl.),	ut	quam	primùm
about-to-move	*the camp,*	*that*	*as*	*soonest*

posset intelligĕre,
(as soon as possible) *he might be-able to understand,*

utrùm pŭdor atque officĭum, an tĭmor valeret
whether shame and duty, or fear might prevail

plùs ăpud ĕos. Quòd si nemo præterĕa sequatur
more with them. But if no-one beside follow,

(pres. subj.), tămen   se   iturum   cum   decĭmâ
                yet   himself about-to-go with the tenth

legione solâ, de   quâ   dubĭtaret (imp. subj.) non;
legion   alone, of   which   he did doubt   not;

que ĕam   futuram   Prætorĭam   cohortem   sĭbi."
and that about-to-be a Prætorian cohort   to himself."

Cæsar et   indulsĕrat   præcĭpŭè huic   legioni   et
Cæsar both had indulged especially to this legion   and

confidebat maxĭmè   propter   virtutem.
did trust   chiefly   on-account-of (its) valour.

41. Hâc   oratione   habĭtâ,   mentes   omnĭum
    This   speech   being had,   the minds of all

conversæ-sunt   in   mirum   mŏdum,   que
were changed   into (in) a wonderful manner, and

summa   alacrĭtas et   cupidĭtas   belli   gerendi
the highest alacrity   and   eagerness   of war   to be carried-on

innata-est: que   decĭma   legĭo   prĭnceps
was born-in (inspired): and   the tenth legion   first

egit   gratĭas ĕi   per   Tribunos
acted (returned) thanks   to him through   the Tribunes

milĭtum,   quòd   fecisset (pl. perf. subj.)   optĭmum
of soldiers, that   he had made   the best

judicĭum   de   se,   que   confirmavit   se   esse
judgment   of   itself, and   confirmed   itself to be

paratissĭmam   ad   bellum   gerendum.   Inde
most-prepared to   war   to be carried on. Then

relĭquæ   legiones   egerunt   per   Tribunos
the remaining   legions   acted   through   the Tribunes

milĭtum   et   centuriones primorum   ordĭnum,   ŭtì
of soldiers and   centurions   of the first ranks,   that

satisfacĕrent   Cæsări;   "se   nĕque unquam
they might satisfy to Cæsar; "themselves neither ever

dubitâsse,   nĕque   timuisse,   nĕque   existimavisse
to have doubted, nor   to have feared, nor   to have thought

judicĭum   de   summâ   belli   esse
the judgment of   the sum (highest concerns) of war   to be

sŭum	their-own (appertaining to them)
sed	but
imperatoris."	of the commander."

Satisfactione eorum acceptâ, et itinĕre
The satisfaction of them being received, and the journey

exquisito per Divitiăcum, (quòd habebat
being reconnoitred by Divitiacus, (because he did have

maxĭmam fĭdem ĕi ex aliis Gallis) ut
greatest faith to him out-of the other Gauls) that

ducĕret exercĭtum apertis lŏcis, circuĭtu
he might lead the army in the open places, by a circuit

amplĭus quadraginta millĭum, profectus-est de
of more (than) forty miles, he set-out from (at)

quartâ vigiliâ, ŭtì dixĕrat. Septĭmo dĭe,
the fourth watch, as he had said. On the seventh day,

quum intermittĕret (imp. subj.) non ĭter,
when he did intermit not the journey,

factus-est certĭor ab exploratorĭbus, copĭas
he was made more-certain by scouts, the forces

Ariovisti abesse à nostris quatŭor et
of Ariovistus to be-distant from our (forces) four and

viginti millĭbus (abl.) passŭum.
twenty thousands of paces.

42. Adventu Cæsăris cognĭto, Ariovistus
The arrival of Cæsar being known Ariovistus

mittit legatos ad ĕum; "id licere
sends ambassadors to him; "that to be-lawful

fĭĕri per se, quod antĕa postulâsset
to be done by himself, which before he had demanded

(pl. perf. subj.) de colloquĭo, quonĭam
concerning a conference, since

accessisset (pl. perf. subj.) propĭùs; que existimaret
he had approached nearer; and he did think

(imp. subj.) se posse facĕre id sĭne
himself to be able to do that without

pericŭlo." Cæsar respŭit non conditionem, que
danger." Cæsar rejected not the condition, and

DE BELLO GALLICO.

arbitrabatur ĕum jam reverti ad sanitatem, quum
did imagine him now to return to soundness (reason), *when*

polliceretur (imp. subj.) ultrò id, quod
he did promise *spontaneously that, which*

antĕa denegässet (pl. perf. subj.) petenti;
before he had denied to (him) asking:

que veniebat in magnam spem, pro sŭis
and he did come into great hope, for his

tantis beneficĭis que Romani popŭli
so-great benefits and (those) of the Roman people

in ĕum, sŭis postulatis cognĭtis, fŏre
towards him, his demands being known, to be-about-to-be

ŭtì desistĕret pertinaciâ. Quintus dĭes
that he would desist from obstinacy. The fifth day

ex ĕo dĭe dictus-est colloquĭo.
from that day was said (appointed) for the conference.

Intĕrim, quum legati mitterentur (imp. subj.)
Meanwhile, when ambassadors were sent

sæpe ultrò que citro inter ĕos, Ariovistus
often thither and hither between them, Ariovistus

postulavit; " Cæsar ne-adducĕret quem pedĭtem
requested: " Cæsar should not-lead-up any foot-soldier

ad colloquĭum, se vereri ne circum-
to the conference, himself to dread lest he should

veniretur ab ĕo per insidĭas (pl.): uterque
be circumvented by him by ambush: each

veniret cum equitatu, aliâ ratione se
should come with cavalry, in other method himself

esse non venturum." Cæsar, quòd volebat
to be not about-to-come." Cæsar, because he did will

nĕque colloquĭum tolli, caussâ
neither the conference to be taken-away, cause

interpositâ; nĕque audebat committĕre sŭam
being interposed: nor did dare to commit his

salutem equitatu (*for* equitatŭi) Gallorum; statŭit
safety to the cavalry of the Gauls; determined

esse	commodissĭmum,	omnĭbus	Gallis		equitĭbus
to be	most-convenient,	all	the Gallic		horsemen

˙detractis	ĕquis,	imponĕre	eŏ
being withdrawn	from the horses,	to set-on	there (them)

legionarĭos	milĭtes	decĭmæ	legionis,	cui
the legionary	soldiers	of the tenth	legion,	to which

confidebat	quàm-maxĭmè;	ut	haberet
he did confide	as-much-as-possible;	that	he might have

quàm-amicissĭmum	præsidĭum,	si	quid	ŏpus
as-friendly-as-possible	guard,	if	any	need

esset	facto (abl.).	Quum quod fĭĕret (imp. subj.),	
should be	of deed.	When which was done,	

quidam	ex	milĭtĭbus	decĭmæ	legionis
a certain-one	of	the soldiers	of the tenth	legion

dixit	non	irridĭcŭlè,	"Cæsarem. facĕre plus	quàm
said	not	unwittily,	"Cæsar to do more	than

pollicĭtus-esset (pl. perf. subj.);	pollicĭtum habĭ-
he had promised;	having promised about-

turum	decĭmam	legionem	in lŏco	prætorĭæ
to-have	the tenth	legion	in place	of a prætorian

cohŏrtis;	nunc	rescribĕre ad	ĕquum."
cohort;	now	to write to	a horse (that he now en

rolled them with the horse)."

43. . . Erat magna planitĭes et in ĕâ terrĕus
(There) was a great plain and in `it an earthy

tumŭlus	sătis	grandis.	Hic	lŏcus	abĕrat
hillock	sufficiently	large.	This	place	was distant

spatĭo	fĕrè	æquo ab	utrisque	castris (pl.).
by a space	nearly	equal from	each	camp.

Eò,	ut dictum-ĕrat,	venerunt	ad
Thither,	as had been said (appointed),	they came	to

colloquĭum.	Cæsar	constitŭit legionem,	quam
the conference.	Cæsar	arranged the legion,	which

devexĕrat	ĕquis,	ducentis passĭbus (abl.)
he had carried-down	with horses,	two-hundred paces

ab	ĕo	tumŭlo:	que	ĭtem	equĭtes
from	*that*	*hillock:*	*and*	*likewise*	*the horsemen*

Ariovisti	constiterunt	pări	intervallo.
of Ariovistus	*stood*	*with equal*	*interval.*

Ariovistus	postulavit,	ut	colloquerentur	ex
Ariovistus	*demanded,*	*that*	*they should converse*	*from*

ĕquis	et	ut	adducĕrent	denos	præter
horses	*and*	*that*	*they should lead-up*	*ten*	*besides*

se	ad	colloquĭum.	Ubi	ventum-est	ĕo,
themselves	*to*	*the conference.*	*When*	*it was come*	*thither,*

Cæsar,	initĭo	orationis,	commemoravit
Cæsar,	*in the beginning*	*of (his) speech,*	*recounted*

sŭa	que	beneficĭa	Senatûs	in	ĕum,
his-own	*and*	*the benefits*	*of the Senate*	*towards*	*him,*

" quòd	appellatus-esset (pl. perf. subj.)	rex	à
" that	*he had been called*	*king*	*by*

Senatu,	quòd	amicus,	quòd
the Senate,	*that (he had been called)*	*a friend,*	*that*

amplissĭma	munĕra	missa;	quam	rem,"
most-ample	*gifts*	*(had been) sent;*	*which*	*thing,"*

docebat,	"et	contigisse
he did teach (he informed him),	*" both*	*to have happened*

paucis,	et	consuevisse	tribŭi	à
to few,	*and*	*to have been accustomed*	*to be granted*	*by*

Romanis	pro	maxĭmis	officĭis	homĭnum;
the Romans	*for*	*the greatest*	*services*	*of men;*

illum,	quum	haberet (imp. subj.)	nĕque	adĭtum,
him,	*when*	*he did have*	*neither*	*access,*

nĕque	justam	caussam	postulandi,	beneficio
nor	*just*	*cause*	*of demanding,*	*by (his) bounty*

ac	sŭâ	liberalitate	ac	Senatûs,
and	*by his*	*liberality*	*and (that)*	*of the Senate,*

consecutum	ĕa	præmĭa."	Docebat
having obtained	*those*	*rewards (honours)."*	*He did teach*

	etiam,	"quàm	vetĕres,	que	quàm	justæ
(inform him)	*also,*	*"how*	*old,*	*and*	*how*	*just*

caussæ	necessitudĭnis	intercedĕrent (imp. subj.)
causes	of close-alliance	did intervene (subsist)

ipsis	cum	Ædŭis;	quæ consulta Senatûs,
to themselves	with	the Ædui;	what decrees of the Senate,

quotĭes,	que	quàm	honorifica	facta-essent (pl.
how often,	and	how	honourable	had been made

perf. subj.)	in	ĕos; ut	omni tempŏre,
	towards	them; that	in all time,

Ædŭi	tenuissent (pl. perf. subj.)	principatum
Ædui	had held	supremacy

totius	Gallĭæ,	etĭam	prĭusquàm
of the whole	Gaul,	also (even)	before-that

appetîssent (pl. perf. subj.)	nostram	amicitĭam:
they had sought	our	friendship:

hanc	esse consuetudĭnem	Romani	popŭli,
this	to be the custom	of the Roman	people,

ut	vĕlit	socĭos	atque amicos	non
that	it may will	(its) allies	and friends	not

mŏdò	deperdĕre	nihil	sŭi,	sed esse
only	to lose	nothing	of their-own,	but to be

auctos	gratĭâ,	dignitate,	honore:	verò
increased	in favour,	in dignity,	in honour:	but

quis	posset	păti id	erĭpi
who	would be able	to suffer that	to be snatched

iis (dat.),	quod	attulissent (pl. perf. subj.)	ad
from them,	which	they had brought	to

amicitĭam	Romani	popŭli?"	Deinde
the friendship	of the Roman	people?"	Afterwards

postulavit	eădem,	quæ	dedĕrat in
he demanded	the same (things),	which	he had given in

mandatis	legatis	"ne-inferret
charges	to ambassadors	"that-he-should-not-bring-on

bellum	aut	Ædŭis, aut	socĭis eorum;
war	either	to the Ædui, or	to the allies of them;

reddĕret	obsĭdes;	si	posset (imp. subj.)
he should restore	the hostages;	if	he was able

remittĕre	dŏmum	nullam	partem	Germanorum;
to send-back	*home*	*no*	*part*	*of the Germani;*

at	ne-pateretur	quos	amplĭùs transire
but	*that-he-should-not-suffer*	*any*	*more to pass*

Rhenum."
the Rhine."

44. Ariovistus respondit pauca ad postulata
    Ariovistus answered few (things) to the demands

Cæsăris: prædicavit multa de sŭis virtutĭbus;
of Cæsar: declaimed many (things) of his-own virtues;

sese transîsse Rhenum non suâ sponte,
himself to have passed the Rhine not by his-own accord,

sed rogatum et accersitum à Gallis: reliquisse
but asked and sent-for by the Gauls: to have left

dŏmum que propinquos non sĭne magnâ spe
home and relations not without great hope

que magnis præmĭis: habere sedes in Gallĭâ
and great rewards: to have settlements in Gaul

concessas ab ipsis, obsĭdes dătos voluntate
granted by themselves, hostages given by the will

eorum; capĕre stipendĭum jure belli, quod
of them; to take tribute by right of war, which

victores consueverint (perf. subj.) imponĕre
conquerors have been accustomed to impose

victis; se non intulisse bellum
to the conquered; himself not to have brought-on war

Gallis, sed Gallos sĭbi; omnes civitates
to the Gauls, but the Gauls to himself; all the states

Gallĭæ venisse ad oppugnandum se, ac
of Gaul to have come to to oppose himself, and

habuisse castra contra se; omnes ĕas copĭas
to have had camps against himself; all those forces

fusas-esse ac superatas abs se uno
to have been routed and overcome by himself in one

prœlĭo. Si velint (pres. subj.) experiri iterum,
battle. If they will to try again,

se	paratum	decertare:	sin		malint (pres.
himself	*prepared*	*to contend:*	*but-if*		*they will-rather*
subj.)	uti	pace (abl.),	esse	iniquum	recusare
	to use	*peace,*	*to be*	*unjust*	*to refuse*
		de	stipendio,	quod	pependerint (perf.
(complain)		*about*	*the tribute,*	*which*	*they payed*
subj.)	suâ		voluntate	ad	id	tempus:
	by their own		*will*	*at*	*that*	*time:*
oportere	amicitiam		Romani		populi	esse
to behove	*the friendship*		*of the Roman*		*people*	*to be*
ornamento	et		præsidio	sibi,		non
for an ornament	*and*		*guard*	*to himself,*		*not*
detrimento;	que	se	petîsse		id	eâ
for detriment;	*and*	*himself*	*to have sought*		*it*	*in that*
spe.	Si	stipendium	remittatur (pres. subj.)			per
hope.	*If*	*the tribute*	*be remitted*			*by*
Romanum	populum,	et	dedititii		subtrahantur
the Roman	*people,*	*and*	*the surrendered*		*be withdrawn,*
(pres. subj.),	sese	recusaturum	non	minùs	libenter
	himself	*about-to-refuse*	*not*	*less*	*willingly*
amicitiam	Romani	populi,	quàm		appetiêrit
the friendship	*of the Roman*	*people,*	*than*		*he sought (it).*
(perf. subj.).	Quòd	transducat (pres. subj.)		multitudinem
	That	*he leads-over*		*a multitude*
Germanorum	in	Galliam,	se	facere	id
of the Germani	*into*	*Gaul,*	*himself*	*to do*	*that*
caussâ	sui	muniendi,	non		Galliæ
for the sake	*of himself*	*to-be-fortified,*	*not*		*of Gaul*
impugnandæ:	esse	testimonium			ejus
to be fought-against:	*to be*	*a testimony* (proof)			*of that*
rei	quòd	venerit (perf. subj.)	non		nisi
thing	*that*	*he came*	*not*		*unless* (until)
rogatus,	et	quòd	intulerit (perf. subj.)		non
asked,	*and*	*that*	*he has brought-on*		*not*
bellum,	sed	defenderit (perf. subj.):	se		venisse
war,	*but*	*has defended (himself):*	*himself*		*to have come*

in	Galliam	prius	quàm	Romanum	popŭlum.
into	Gaul	before	than	the Roman	people.

Nunquam	ante	hoc	tempus	exercĭtum	Romani
Never	before	this	time	an army	of the Roman

popŭli	egressum	fines	provincĭæ
people	(to have) gone-out-of	the borders	of the province

Gallĭæ:	quid	vellet (imp. subj.)	sĭbi?	cur
of Gaul:	what	did he will	to himself?	why

veniret (imp. subj.)	in	sŭas	possessiones? hanc
did he come	into	his	possessions? this

Gallĭam	esse	sŭam provincĭam,	sicŭti illam	nostram:
Gaul	to be	his province,	as that	our:

ut	oporteret (imp. subj.)	non	concedi	sĭbi,
as	it did behove (it ought)	not	to be conceded	to himself,

si	facĕret	impĕtum	in	nostros fines;	sic
if	he should make	an attack	upon	our borders;	so

itĕrum,	nos	esse iniquos,	quòd	interpellaremus
again,	us	to be unjust,	because	we did interrupt

(imp. subj.)	se	in sŭo jure:	quòd	dicĕret
	himself	in his right:	that	he did say

(imp. subj.)	Ædŭos	appellatos amicos	ex	consulto
	the Ædui	named friends	from	a decree

Senatûs,	se	esse non tam	barbărum,	nĕque
of the Senate,	himself	to be not so	barbarous,	nor

tam	imperitum	rerum, ut	sciret (imp. subj.)
so	inexperienced	of things, that	he did know

non,	Ædŭos	nĕque	tulisse auxilĭum
not,	the Ædui	neither	to have brought aid

Romanis	proxĭmo	bello Allobrŏgum,
to the Romans	in the nearest (latest)	war of the Allobroges,

nĕque	ipsos	in	his contentionĭbus,	quas
nor	themselves	in	these contentions,	which

Ædŭi	habuissent (pl. perf. subj.)	cum	se	et
the Ædui	had had	with	himself	and

cum Sequănis,	usos-esse	auxilĭo (abl.)	Romani
with the Sequani,	to have-used	the aid	of the Roman

popŭli:	se	debere	**suspicari,**	amicitiâ
people:	*himself*	*to owe* (ought)	*to suspect,*	*friendship*

simulatâ,	Cæsărem,	quòd	habĕat (pres. subj.)
being pretended,	*Cæsar,*	*because*	*he has*

exercĭtum	in	Galliâ,	habere	caussâ	sŭi
an army	*in*	*Gaul,*	*to have* (it)	*for the sake*	*of himself*

opprimendi:	quòd	nĭsi	decedat (pres. subj.)	aut
to-be-oppressed:	*that*	*unless*	*he depart*	*or*

deducat (pres. subj.)		exercĭtum	ex	his	regionĭbus,
lead-away		(his) army	from	these	regions,

sese	habiturum	illum	non	pro	amico,	sed
himself	*about-to-have*	*him*	*not*	*for*	*a friend,*	*but*

pro	hoste:	quòd si	interfecĕrit (perf. subj.)	ĕum,
for	*an enemy:*	*that if*	*he killed*	*him,*

sese	esse	facturum	gratum	multis
himself	*to be*	*about-to-do*	*a grateful* (thing)	*to many*

nobilĭbus	que	principĭbus	Romani	popŭli:
nobles	*and*	*chiefs*	*of the Roman*	*people:*

se	habere	id	compertum	ab	ipsis
himself	*to have*	*that*	*found-out*	*from*	*themselves*

per	nuntĭos	eorum;	gratĭam	atque	amicitĭam
by	*messengers*	*of them;*	*the favour*	*and*	*friendship*

omnĭum	quorum	posset (imp. subj.)	redimĕre
of all	*of whom*	*he was-able*	*to purchase*

morte	ejus:	quòd si	discessisset (pl. perf. subj.)
by the death	*of him:*	*that if*	*he had departed*

ac	tradidisset (pl. perf. subj.)	libĕram	possessionem
and	*had delivered*	*free*	*possession*

Gallïæ	sĭbi,	se	remuneraturum	illum
of Gaul	*to himself,*	*himself*	*about-to-remunerate*	*him*

magno	præmĭo,	et	confecturum,	quæcunque
with great	*reward,*	*and*	*about-to-dispatch,*	*whatever*

bella	vellet (imp. subj.)	gĕri	sĭne	ullo
wars	*he did will*	*to be carried-on*	*without*	*any*

labore	et	pericŭlo	ejus.
labour	*and*	*danger*	*of him.*

45. Multa   dicta-sunt à Cæsăre in ĕam
 Many (things) were said by Cæsar upon that

sententĭam, quare   posset (imp. subj.) non
 opinion, wherefore he was-able   not

desistĕre negotĭo, et nĕque sŭam nĕque
to desist from the business, and neither his nor

consuetudĭnem Romani popŭli păti, ŭtĭ
 the custom of the Roman people to suffer, that

desererēt socĭos merĭtos optĭmè; nĕque
he should desert allies having deserved best; nor

se judicare Gallĭam esse potĭùs
himself to judge Gaul to be rather (the property)

Ariovisti, quàm Romani popŭli. Arvernos
of Ariovistus, than of the Roman people. The Arverni

et Rutenos superatos-esse bello à Quinto
and Ruteni to have been overcome in war by Quintus

Fabĭo Maxĭmo; quĭbus Romanus popŭlus
Fabius Maximus; to whom the Roman people

ignovisset (pl. perf. subj.), nĕque redegisset (pl. perf.
had pardoned,   nor had reduced (them)

subj.) in provincĭam nĕque imposuisset (pl. perf.
  into a province nor had imposed

subj.) stipendĭum: quòd si oporteret (imp. subj.)
  tribute: that if it did behove

quodque antiquissĭmum tempus spectari, imperĭum
every most-ancient time to be regarded, the empire

Romani popŭli in Gallĭâ esse justissĭmum; si
of the Roman people in Gaul to be most-just; if

oporteret (imp. subj.) judicĭum Senatûs
it did behove   the judgment of the Senate

servari, Gallĭam debere esse libĕram,
to be kept, Gaul to owe (ought) to be free.

quam victam bello voluisset (pl. perf.
which (though) conquered in war it had willed.

subj.) uti sŭis legĭbus" (abl.).
  to use its-own laws."

LIBER I.

46. Dum haec geruntur in collo-
Whilst these (things) are carried-on in the confe-

quio, nuntiatum-est Caesari, equites Ariovisti
rence, it was-told to Caesar, the horsemen of Ariovistus

accedere propius tumulum, et adequitare ad
to approach nearer the hillock, and to ride-up to

nostros, conjicere lapides que tela in
our (men) to throw stones and darts against

nostros. Caesar fecit finem loquendi que
our (men). Caesar made an end of speaking and

recepit se ad suos, que imperavit
betook himself to his-own (men), and ordered

suis ne-rejicerent quod
to his-own (men) that they should not throw-back any

telum omnino in hostes: nam etsi
dart at-all against the enemies: for although

videbat proelium fore cum equitatu
he did see a battle to be-about-to-be with the cavalry

sine ullo periculo delectae legionis; tamen
without any danger of (his) chosen legion; yet

putabat committendum non, ut, hostibus
he did think to be committed not, that, the enemies

pulsis, posset dici, eos
being driven-away, it might be-able to be said, them

circumventos à se per fidem in collo-
circumvented by himself through faith in the con-

quio. Posteaquam elatum-est in
ference. After-that it was carried-out (reported) into

vulgus militum, quâ arrogantiâ (abl.)
(among) the common-sort of soldiers, what arrogance

Ariovistus usus interdixisset (pl. perf. subj.)
Ariovistus having used had interdicted

Romanis (dat.) omni Galliâ; que equites
the Romans from all Gaul; and the horsemen

ejus fecissent (pl. perf. subj.) impetum in nostros;
of him had made an attack upon our (men);

que	ĕa	res	diremisset (pl. perf. subj.)
and	*that*	*thing*	*had broken-off*

colloquĭum ;	multò	major	alacrĭtās	que	majus
the conference ;	*by-much*	*greater*	*alacrity*	*and*	*greater*

studĭum	pugnandi	injectum-est	exercitŭi.
desire	*of fighting*	*was thrown-in*	*to the army.*

47.
Bidŭo	pòst	Ariovistus	mittit
In two-days	*afterwards*	*Ariovistus*	*sends*

legatos	ad	Cæsărem,	"se	velle	agĕre
ambassadors	*to*	*Cæsar (to say),*	*"himself*	*to will*	*to act*

cum	ĕo	de	his	rebus,	quæ	cœptæ-essent
(treat)	*with him*	*about*	*these*	*things,*	*which*	*had been-begun*

(pl. perf. subj.)	ăgi	inter	ĕos,
	to be acted (treated)	*between*	*them,*

nĕque	perfectæ-essent (pl. perf. subj.) :	ŭti	aut
nor	*had been perfected*	*that*	*either*

constituĕret	itĕrum	dĭem	colloquĭo,	aut
he would determine	*again*	*a day*	*for a conference,*	*or*

si	vellet (imp. subj.)	mĭnùs	id,	mittĕret
if	*he did will*	*less (not)*	*that,*	*he would send*

alĭquem	ex	sŭis	legatis	ad	se.	Caussa
some-one	*out-of*	*his*	*ambassadors*	*to*	*himself.*	*A cause*

colloquendi	visa-est	non	Cæsari;	et
of conferring	*seemed*	*not (was not evident)*	*to Cæsar;*	*and*

ĕò-măgis,	quòd	pridĭe	ejus diei,	Germani
by that-more,	*that*	*the-day-before*	*of that day*	*the Germani*

potuĕrant	non	retineri,	quin	conjicĕrent
had been-able	*not*	*to be restrained,*	*but-that*	*they would throw*

tela	in	nostros.	Existimabat	sese	missurum
darts	*against*	*our (men).*	*He did think*	*himself*	*about-to-send*

legatum	ex	sŭis	cum	magno	perĭcŭlo	ad
an ambassador	*out-of*	*his-own*	*with*	*great*	*danger*	*to*

ĕum,	et	objecturum	fĕris	homĭnibus
him,	*and*	*about-to-expose*	*to savage*	*men.*

Visum-est	commodissĭmum	mittĕre	ad	ĕum	Caĭum
It seemed	*most-convenient*	*to send*	*to*	*him*	*Caius*

Valerĭum	Procillum,	filĭum	Caĭi	Valerĭi
Valerius	*Procillus,*	*a son*	*of Caius*	*Valerius*

Caburi,	adolescentem	summâ	virtute	et
Caburus,	*a young-man*	*with highest*	*virtue*	*and*

humanitate,	(păter	cujus	donatus-ĕrat
politeness,	*(the father*	*of whom*	*had been presented*

cīvitate	à	Caĭo	Valerĭo Flacco)	et
with citizenship	*by*	*Caius*	*Valerius Flaccus)*	*and* (both)

propter	fĭdem	et	propter	scientĭam
on-account-of	*(his) fidelity*	*and*	*on-account-of*	*(his) knowledge*

Gallĭcæ	linguæ,	quâ (abl.)	Ariovistus	utebatur
of the Gallic	*tongue,*	*which*	*Ariovistus*	*did use*

multâ (adj.)	jam	longinquâ	consuetudĭne,	et	quòd
much (fluently)	*now*	*by long*	*custom,*	*and*	*because*

caussa	peccandi	esset (imp. subj.)	non
a cause	*of transgressing*	*was*	*not*

Germanis	in	ĕo;	et	Marcum	Mettĭum,	qui
to the Germani	*in*	*him;*	*and*	*Marcus*	*Mettius,*	*who*

usus-ĕrat	hospitĭo (abl.)	Ariovisti.	Mandavit
had used	*the hospitality*	*of Ariovistus.*	*He charged*

his,	ut	cognoscĕrent,	quæ	Ariovistus
to these,	*that*	*they should know,*	*what* (things)	*Ariovistus*

dicĕret,	et	referrent	ad	se.	Quos
might say,	*and*	*should bring-back*	*to*	*himself.*	*Whom*

quum	Ariovistus	conspexisset (pl. perf. subj.)	in
when	*Ariovistus*	*had beheld*	*in*

castris (pl.)	ăpud	se,	sŭo	exercĭtu
(his) camp	*with*	*himself,*	*his*	*army* (being)

præsente,	conclamavit:	"Quid	venirent (imp. subj.)
present,	*he cried-out:*	*"Why*	*did they come*

ad	se?	an	caussâ	speculandi?"	Prohibŭit
to himself?		*whether*	*by reason*	*of spying?"*	*He prevented*

conantes	dicĕre,	et	conjecit	in
(them) endeavouring	*to speak,*	*and*	*cast* (them)	*into*

catenas.
chains.

48. Eodem   die   promovit   castra (pl.),
In the same day he moved-forward (his) camp,

et consedit sub monte sex millĭbus (abl.)
and sat-down under a mountain six thousands

passŭum à castris (pl.) Cæsăris. Postridĭe
of paces from the camp of Cæsar The day-after

ejus diei transduxit sŭas copĭas præter castra (pl.)
of that day he led-over his forces beyond the camp

Cæsăris et fecit castra (pl.) duobus
of Cæsar and made camp (encamped) by two

millĭbus (abl.) passŭum ultra ĕum, ĕo
thousands of paces beyond him, with this

consilĭo, ŭtĭ intercludĕret Cæsărem frumento
design, that he might shut-in Cæsar from corn

que commeatu, qui supportaretur ex
and provision, which might be carried-u͵ from

Sequănis et Ædŭis. Ex ĕo dĭe Cæsar
the Sequani and the Ædui. From that day Cæsar

produxit sŭas copĭas quinque continŭos
led-forth his forces five continual (successive)

dĭes pro castris (pl.), et habŭit aciem
days before the camp, and had ⸲ (his) battle-line

instructam, ut si Ariovistus vellet contendĕre
arrayed, that if Ariovistus might will to contend

prœlĭo, potestas deesset non ĕi.
in battle, the power might be-wanting not to him.

Ariovistus omnĭbus his diebus continŭit exercĭtum
Ariovistus in all these days retained (his) army

castris (pl.); contendit quotidĭe prœlĭo equestri (adj.).
in camp; he contended daily in battle of-horse.

Hoc ĕrat gĕnus pugnæ, quo Germani
This was the kind of battle, in which the Germans

exercuĕrant se. Erant sex millĭa
had exercised themselves. (There) were six thousands

equĭtum, totĭdem numĕro pedĭtes velocissĭmi
of horsemen, as many in number foot-soldiers most-swift

ac	fortissimi,	singŭlos	quos	singŭli
and	*most-brave,*	*each*	*whom*	*each*

delegĕrant	ex	omni	copiâ,	caussâ
had chosen	*from*	*all*	*the force,*	*by reason (for the*

	sŭæ	salutis.	Versabantur	cum
sake)	*of-their-own*	*safety.*	*They were employed*	*with*

his	in	prœliis;	equĭtes	recipiebant
these	*in*	*battles;*	*the horsemen*	*did betake*

se	ad	hos:	hi,	si	quid
themselves	*to*	*these:*	*these,*	*if*	*any (thing)*

ĕrat	durĭus,	concurrebant:	si	qui,
was	*more-hard,*	*did run-together (to succour):*	*if*	*any,*

graviore	vulnĕre	accepto,	decidĕrant
a heavier (very severe)	*wound*	*being received,*	*had fallen-down*

ĕquo,	circumsistebant:		si ĕrat
from horse,	*they did stand-around:*		*if it was*

prodeundum	longĭus	aut	recipiendum
to-be-advanced	*farther*	*or*	*to-be-retreated*

celerĭus	quò,	tanta	ĕrat	celerĭtas
more-quickly	*any-where,*	*so great*	*was*	*the speed*

horum	exercitatione,	ut,	sublevati	jŭbis
of these	*by exercise,*	*that,*	*lifted-up*	*by the manes*

equorum,	adæquarent	cursum.
of the horses,	*they would equal*	*(their) course.*

49. Ubi	Cæsar	intellexit	ĕum	tenere	sese
When	*Cæsar*	*understood*	*him*	*to hold*	*himself*

castris,	ne-prohiberetur	diutiùs
in camps,	*that he might not be prohibited*	*longer*

commeatu,	delegit	lŏcum	idonĕum	castris,
from provision,	*he chose*	*a place*	*suitable*	*for camps,*

circĭter	sex-centos	passus	ultra	ĕum lŏcum,	in quo
about	*six hundred*	*paces*	*beyond*	*that place,*	*in which*

lŏco	Germani	consedĕrant,	que triplĭci
place	*the Germans*	*had sat-down* (encamped)	*and a triple*

acĭe	instructâ,	venit ad ĕum lŏcum.		Jussit
line	*being arrayed,*	*he came to that place.*		*He ordered*

K

primam et secundam aciem esse in armis, tertiam
the first and second line to be in arms, the third

munire castra (pl.). Hic locus, uti dictum-est,
to fortify the camp. This place, as has been said,

aberat ab hoste circiter sex-centos passus.
was-distant from the enemy about six-hundred paces.

Eò Ariovistus misit numerum hominum circiter
Thither Ariovistus sent a number of men about

sexdecim millia expedita, cum omni equitatu;
sixteen thousands light-armed, with all the cavalry;

quæ copiæ perterrerent nostros, et prohiberent
which forces should alarm our (men), and should prohibit

munitione. Nihilo secius Cæsar,
from fortifying. By nothing less (nevertheless) Cæsar,

ut constituerat antè, jussit duas acies
as he had determined before, ordered the two lines

propulsare hostem, tertiam perficere opus.
to repel the enemy, the third to complete the work.

Castris munitis, reliquit ibi duas legiones
The camps being fortified, he left there two legions

et partem auxiliorum; reduxit quatuor
and part of the auxiliaries; he led-back the four

reliquas in majora castra (pl.).
remaining (legions) into the greater camp.

50. Proximo die, Cæsar suo instituto
In the next day, Cæsar in his institution (custom)

eduxit suas copias ex utrisque castris; que
led-forth his forces out-of each camps; and

progressus paullulum à majoribus, instruxit
having advanced very-little from the greater, arrayed

aciem que fecit hostibus potestatem pugnandi.
(his) line and made to the enemies power of fighting.

Ubi intellexit eos ne tum quidem
When he understood them not then indeed (even)

prodire, circiter meridiem reduxit exercitum
to come-forth, about mid-day he led-back the army

in	castra (pl.).	Tum	demum	Ariovistus	misit
into	*camp.*	*Then*	*at-last*	*Ariovistus*	*sent*

partem	suarum	copiarum,	quæ	oppugnaret	minora
part	*of his*	*forces,*	*which*	*might assault*	*the less*

castra (pl.).	Pugnatum-est	acriter	utrinque	usque
camp.	*It was fought*	*sharply*	*on-both-sides*	*until*

ad vesperum.	Occasu	solis	Ariovistus	reduxit
to evening.	*With setting*	*of the sun*	*Ariovistus*	*led-back*

suas	copias	in	castra (pl.),	multis	vulneribus et
his	*forces*	*into*	*camp,*	*many*	*wounds both*

illatis	et	acceptis.	Quum Cæsar
being brought-on (given)	*and*	*received.*	*When Cæsar*

quæreret (imp. subj.)	ex	captivis,	quamobrem
did inquire	*from*	*the captives,*	*wherefore*

Ariovistus	decertaret (imp. subj.)	non prœlio,
Ariovistus	*did contend*	*not in battle,*

reperiebat	hanc	caussam:	Quòd	ea consuetudo
he did find	*this*	*the cause:*	*Because*	*that custom*

esset (imp. subj.)	apud	Germanos,	ut matres-
was	*with*	*the Germans,*	*that the mothers-*

familias	eorum	declararent	sortibus	et
of family	*of them*	*should declare*	*by lots*	*and*

vaticinationibus,	utrùm	esset	ex	usu (ad-
by prophecies,	*whether*	*it might be*	*out-of*	*use (ad-*

prœlium	committi	necne:	eas	dicere
vantageous) *battle*	*to be engaged*	*or-not:*	*them*	*to say*

ita,	"Non	esse	fas	Germanos	superare, si
thus,	*"Not*	*to be*	*lawful*	*the Germans*	*to conquer, if*

contendissent	prœlio	ante	novam
they might have contended	*in battle*	*before*	*the new*

lunam."
moon."

51. | | | | |
|---|---|---|---|
| Postridie | ejus | diei, | præsidio relicto |
| *The day-after* | *of that* | *day,* | *a guard being left* |

utrisque	castris,	quod	visum-est	satis, constituit
to each	*camps,*	*which*	*seemed*	*sufficient, he arranged*

K 2

omnes	alārios	in	conspectu	hostĭum	pro
all	the flankers	in	sight	of the enemies	before

minorĭbus	castris (plur.),	(quod	valebat	
the less	camp,	(because	he did avail (was strong)	

mĭnùs	multitudĭne	legionariorum	milĭtum	pro
less	in the multitude	of legionary	soldiers	for

	numĕro	hostĭum ;)	ut	uterctur
(considering)	the number	of the enemies;)	that	he might use

alariis (abl.)	ad	specĭem.	Ipse,	triplĭci
the flankers	to (for)	appearance.	(He) himself,	a triple

acĭe	instructâ,	accessit	usque ad	castra
line	being arrayed.	approached	as-far-as to	the camps

hostĭum.	Tum	demum	necessariò	Germani
of the enemies.	Then	at-last	necessarily	the Germans

eduxerunt	sŭas	copĭas	è castris:	que
led-out	their	forces	from the camps:	and

constituerunt	generatim ;	que	parĭbus
arranged (them)	by-sorts (tribes);	and	at equal

intervallis,	Harudes,	Marcomanos,	Triboccos,
intervals,	the Harudes,	Marcomani,	Tribocci,

Vangiŏnes,	Nemetes,	Sedusĭos,	Suevos; que
Vangiones,	Nemetes,	Sedusii,	Suevi; and

circumdederunt	omnem	sŭam	acĭem	rhedis
surrounded	all	their	line	with carriages

et carris.	Eò	imposuerunt	mulĭeres,	quæ,
and waggons.	There	they placed-on	the women,	who,

crinĭbus	passis,	flentes
(their) hairs (locks)	being spread (dishevelled),	weeping

implorabant	milĭtes	proficiscentes	in	prœlium,
did implore	the soldiers	setting-out	into	battle,

ne-tradĕrent	se	in	servitutem
that they would not deliver	themselves	into	slavery

Romanis.
to the Romans.

52. Cæsar	præfecit	singúlos	legatos
Cæsar	set-over	each (separate)	lieutenants

et	quæstorem	singŭlis	legionĭbus,	ŭtì	quisque
and	*a quæstor*	*to each*	*legions,*	*that*	*every-one*

haberet	ĕos	testes	sŭæ	virtutis.	Ipse
might have	*them*	*witnesses*	*of his*	*valour.*	*(He) himself*

à	dextro	cornu,	quòd	animadvertĕrat
from	*the right*	*horn (wing),*	*because*	*he had observed*

ĕam	partem	hostĭum	esse	minĭmè	firmam,
that	*part*	*of the enemies*	*to be*	*least*	*firm,*

commisit	prœlium.	Nostri,	signo	dăto,
engaged	*battle.*	*Our (men),*	*the sign*	*being given,*

fecerunt	impĕtum	ĭta	acrĭter	in	hostes:	que
made	*an attack*	*so*	*sharply*	*upon*	*the enemies:*	*and*

hostes	procurrerunt	ĭta	repentè	que	celerĭter,	ut
the enemies	*ran-forward*	*so*	*suddenly*	*and*	*quickly,*	*that*

spatĭum	conjiciendi	pila	in	hostes
space	*of throwing*	*the javelins*	*against*	*the enemies*

daretur	non.	Pilis	rejectis,
might be given	*not.*	*The javelins*	*being thrown-away,*

pugnatum-est	comĭnus	gladĭis.	At	Germani
it was fought	*hand-to-hand*	*with swords.*	*But*	*the Germans*

celerĭter	ex	sŭâ	consuetudĭne,	phalange
quickly	*according-to*	*their*	*custom,*	*a phalanx*

factâ,	exceperunt	impĕtus	gladiorum.	Complures
being made,	*received*	*the attacks*	*of the swords.*	*Very-many*

nostri	milĭtes	reperti-sunt,	qui	insilirent	in
our	*soldiers*	*were-found,*	*who*	*would leap-up*	*upon*

phalanges	et	revellĕrent	scuta
the phalanxes	*and*	*would pull-back*	*the shields*

manĭbus,	et	vulnerarent	desŭper.	Quum
with (their) hands,	*and*	*would wound*	*from above.*	*When*

acĭes	hostĭum	pulsa-esset (pl. perf. subj.)	à
the line	*of the enemies*	*had been repulsed*	*from (on)*

sinistro	cornu,	atque	conversa	in	fŭgam,
the left	*horn (wing),*	*and*	*turned*	*into*	*flight,*

premebant	nostram	acĭem	vehementer	à
they did press	*our*	*line*	*vehemently*	*from (on)*

dextro	cornu	multitudĭne	suorum.
the right	horn (wing),	by the multitude	of their (men).

Quum	Publĭus	Crassus	adolescens,	qui	præĕrat
When	Publius	Crassus	a young-man,	who	was-over

equitatŭi,	animadvertisset (pl. perf. subj.)	id,
to the cavalry,	had perceived	that,

quòd	ĕrat	expeditĭor	quàm	hi,	qui
because	he was	more-disengaged	than	these,	who

versabantur	inter	acĭem,	misit	tertĭam	acĭem
were engaged	amid	the line,	he sent	the third	line

nostris	laborantĭbus	subsidĭo.
to our (men)	labouring (distressed)	for a reserve.

53.
Ita	prœlĭum	restitutum-est	atque	omnes
Thus	the battle	was restored	and	all

hostes	verterunt	terga,	nĕque	destiterunt
the enemies	turned	(their) backs,	nor	desisted

fugĕre,	priùs	quàm	pervenerunt	ad	flumen
to flee,	before	than	they arrived	at	the river

Rhenum,	circĭter	quinquaginta	millĭa	passŭum	ex
Rhine,	about	fifty	thousands	of paces	from

ĕo	lŏco.	Ibi	perpauci,	aut	confisi
that	place.	There	very-few,	either	having trusted

virĭbus (pl.),	contenderunt	transnatare;	aut,
to strength,	strained (endeavoured)	to swim-over;	or,

lintrĭbus	inventis,	petierunt	salutem	sĭbi.
barks	being found,	sought	safety	to themselves.

In	his	fŭit	Ariovistus,	qui,	nactus
In	these	was	Ariovistus,	who,	having obtained

navicŭlam	deligatam	ad	ripam,	profugit	ĕâ:
a little-ship	bound	at	the bank,	escaped	in it:

nostri	equĭtes	consecuti	interfecerunt	omnes
our	horsemen	having overtaken	killed	all

relĭques.	Uxores	Ariovisti	fuerunt	dŭæ,
the remaining.	The wives	of Ariovistus	were	two,

una	Sueva	natione,	quam	adduxĕrat
one	a Suevian	by nation,	whom	he had led-up

LIBER I.

secum	dŏmo;	altĕra	Norĭca,	sŏror
with himself	from home;	the other	a Norican,	sister

regis	Vocionis,	quam	duxĕrat	Gallĭâ,
of king	Vocio,	whom	he had led (married)	in Gaul,

missam	à	fratre:	utrăque	perĭit	in	ĕâ
sent	by	(her) brother:	each	perished	in	that

fŭgâ:		dŭæ	filĭæ	harum,	altĕra
flight:	(there were) two	daughters	of these,	the other

occisa-est,	altĕra	capta.	Caĭus	Valerĭus
(one) was slain,	the other	taken.	Caius	Valerius

Procillus,	quum	traheretur (imp. subj.)	in
Procillus,	when	he was dragged	in (their)

fŭgâ	vinctus	trinis	catenis	à	custodĭbus,
flight	bound	with three	chains	by	(his) keepers,

incĭdit	in		Cæsărem	ipsum	persequentem
fell	upon	(fell in with)	Cæsar	himself	pursuing

equitatum	hostĭum.	Quæ	res	quĭdem
the cavalry	of the enemies.	Which	thing	indeed

attŭlit	non	minorem	voluptatem	Cæsări,	quàm
brought	not	less	pleasure	to Cæsar,	than

victorĭa	ipsa;	quòd	videbat	honestissĭmum
the victory	itself;	because	he did see	a most-honourable

homĭnem	provincĭæ	Gallĭæ,	sŭum	familiarem
man	of the province	of Gaul,	his	acquaintance

et	hospĭtem,	ereptum	è	manĭbus	hostĭum,
and	host,	rescued	out-of	the hands	of the enemies,

restitutum	sĭbi:	nĕque	fortuna	diminuĕrat
restored	to himself:	nor	fortune	had diminished

quidquam	de	tantâ	voluptate	et	gratulatione
any-thing	from	so-great	pleasure	and	congratulation

calamitate	ejus.	Is	dicebat	consultum (-esse)
by the calamity	of him.	He	did say	to have been consulted

sortĭbus	ter,	se	præsente,	de
by lots	thrice,	himself	(being) present,	about

se,	utrùm	necaretur	stătim	igni,
himself,	whether	he should be killed	immediately	with fire,

an	reservaretur	in	aliud	tempus:	se
or	should be reserved	unto	another	time:	himself

esse	incolúmen	beneficio	sortium.	Item
to be	safe	by the kindness	of the lots.	Likewise

Marcus	Mettius	repertus-est	et	reductus	ad	eum.
Marcus	Mettius	was found	and	led back	to	him.

54. | Hoc | prœlio | nuntiato | trans | Rhenum, |
| --- | --- | --- | --- | --- |
| This | battle | being announced | beyond | the Rhine, |

Suevi,	qui	venerant	ad	ripas	Rheni,
the Suevi,	who	had come	to	the banks	of the Rhine,

cœperunt	reverti	domum ·	quos	Ubii,	qui
began	to return	home:	whom	the Ubii,	who

incolunt	proxime	Rhenum,	insecuti
inhabit	nearest	the Rhine,	having followed-up

perterritos,	occiderunt	magnum	numerum	ex	his.
dismayed,	slew	a great	number	out-of	these.

Cæsar,	duobus	maximis	bellis	confectis	unâ
Cæsar,	two	greatest	wars	being finished	in one

æstate,	deduxit	paullo	maturiùs,	quàm	tempus
summer,	led-away	a little	earlier,	than	the time

anni	postulabat,	exercitum	in	hiberna
of the year	did demand,	the army	into	winter-quarters

in	Sequanos:	præposuit	Labienum	hibernis:
into the Sequani:	he set-over	Labienus	to the winter-quarters:

ipse	profectus-est	in	citeriorem	Galliam	ad
himself	departed	into	hither	Gaul	to

conventus	agendos.
assemblies	be-acted (held).

LIBER SECUNDUS.
BOOK SECOND.

ARGUMENTUM.

ARGUMENT.

Secundus liber continet quatuor bellicas expeditiones;
The second book contains four warlike expeditions;

nempe, bellum contra Belgas, contra Nervios;
namely, the war against the Belgæ, against the Nervii;

contra Atuaticos; contra Armoricos, quos
against the Atuatici; against the Armorici, whom

postremos P. Crassus legatus ejus debellavit
last P. Crassus lieutenant of him vanquished

sub auspiciis ejus. Hæc gesta-sunt
under the auspices of him. These (things) were done

sexcentesimo nonagesimo septimo anno ab
in the six hundredth ninetieth seventh year from

urbe conditâ.
the city being built.

1. Quum Cæsar esset (imp. subj.) in citeriore
When Cæsar was in hither

Galliâ in hibernis, ita uti demonstravimus
Gaul in winter-quarters, so as we have shown

suprà, crebri rumores afferebantur ad eum, que
above, frequent rumours were brought to him, and

DE BELLO GALLICO.

ĭtem	fiebat	certĭor	litĕrıs (pl.)	Labieni,
likewise	*he was made*	*more-sure*	*by letters*	*of Labienus,*

omnes Belgas, quam dixeramus esse tertĭam
all the Belgæ, which we have said to be the third

partem Gallĭæ, conjurare contra Romanum popŭlum,
part of Gaul, to conspire against the Roman people,

que dăre obsĭdes inter se. Has esse
and to give hostages between themselves. These to be

caussas conjurandi: primùm, quòd vererentur
the causes of conspiring: first, because they did fear

(imp. subj.) ne, omni Gallĭâ pacatâ, noster
lest, all Gaul being subdued, our

exercĭtus adduceretur ad ĕos: deinde, quòd
army should be led-up to them: next, because

sollicitarentur (imp. subj.) ab nonnullis Gallis, partim
they were solicited by some Gauls, partly

qui, ut nollent (imp. subj.) Germanos versari
who, as they were-unwilling the Germani to be engaged

diutĭùs in Gallĭâ, ĭta ferebant molestè exercĭtum
longer in Gaul, so they did bear uneasily the army

Romani popŭli hiemare atque inveterascĕre in
of the Roman people to winter and to grow-old in

Gallĭâ; partim qui, mobilitate et levitate anĭmi,
Gaul; partly who, by fickleness and lightness of mind,

studebant novis imperiis; etiam
uid study (were favourable) to new governments; also

ab nonnullis, quòd in Gallĭâ regna vulgò
by some, because in Gaul kingdoms commonly

occupabantur à potentiorĭbus atque iis, qui
were occupied by the more-powerful and by those, who

habebant facultates ad homĭnes conducendos; qui
did have means to men to-be-hired; who

potĕrant mĭnùs facĭlè consĕqui ĕam rem nostro
were-able less easily to attain that thing (under) our

imperĭo.
government.

LIBER II.

2. Cæsar   commotus   iis   nuntiis   que
   Cæsar   *moved*   *by those*   *announcements*   *and*

literis   conscripsit   duas   novas   legiones   in   citeriore
letters   *levied*   *two*   *new*   *legions*   *in*   *hither*

Galliâ,   et   æstate   initâ,   misit   Quintum
Gaul,   *and*   *summer*   *being entered,*   *he sent*   *Quintus*

Pedium   legatum   qui   deduceret   in
Pedius   *(his) lieutenant*   *who*   *might lead (them) down*   *into*

interiorem   Galliam.   Ipse,   quum   primùm   copia
inner   *Gaul.*   *Himself,*   *when*   *first*   *plenty*

pabuli   inciperet (imp. subj.)   esse,   venit ad exercitum.
of forage   *did begin*   *to be,*   *came to the army.*

Dat   negotium   Senonibus   que
He gives   *business (he commissions)*   *to the Senones*   *and*

reliquis   Gallis,   qui   erant   finitimi   Belgis,
to the remaining   *Gauls,*   *who*   *were*   *bordering*   *to the Belgæ,*

uti   cognoscant   ea,   quæ   gerantur
that   *they may learn*   *those (things),*   *which*   *are carried-on*

(pres. subj.)   apud   eos,   et   faciant   se
   with   *them,*   *and*   *may make*   *himself*

certiorem   de   his   rebus.
more-certain (may inform him)   *about*   *these*   *things.*

Omnes   hi   constanter   nunciaverunt,   manus
All   *these*   *constantly*   *announced,*   *bands*

cogi,   exercitum   conduci
to be brought-together (collected),   *an army*   *to be led-together*

in   unum   locum.   Tum   verò   existimavit   non
into   *one*   *place.*   *Then*   *indeed*   *he thought*   *not*

dubitandum,   quin   proficisceretur   ad   eos
to-be-doubted,   *but-that*   *he should set-out*   *to*   *them*

duodecimo   die.   Re   frumentariâ
on the twelfth   *day.*   *The affair relating-to-corn (the supplies)*

provisâ,   movet   castra (pl.)   que   diebus
being provided,   *he moves*   *camp*   *and*   *in days*

circiter   quindecim   pervenit   ad   fines   Belgarum.
about   *fifteen*   *arrives*   *to*   *the borders*   *of the Belgæ.*

3. Quum venisset (pl. perf. subj.) eŏ de
When he had come thither from

improviso que celerĭus opinione
unexpected (unexpectedly) *and more-quickly than the opinion*

omnĭum, Rhemi, qui sunt proxĭmi ex Belgis
of all, the Rhemi, who are nearest out-of the Belgæ

Galliæ, miserunt ad ĕum legatos, Iccĭum et
to Gaul, ' *sent to him ambassadors, Iccius and*

Antebrogĭum primos sŭæ civitatis, qui dicĕrent,
Antebrogius first (men) *of their state, who might say,*

"permittĕre se que omnĭa sŭa
" to permit (to yield) *themselves and all their* (effects)

in fĭdem atque potestatem Romani popŭli,
into the faith and power of the Roman people,

nĕque se consensisse cum relĭquis
nor themselves to have consented with the remaining

Belgis, nĕque conjurâsse omnino contra
Belgæ, nor to have conspired at all against

Romanum popŭlum, que esse paratos et dăre
the Roman people, and to be prepared both to give

obsĭdes, et facĕre imperata, et recipĕre
hostages, and to do (things) *commanded, and to receive*

oppĭdis et juvare frumento que cætĕris
(them) *in towns and to aid with corn and with other*

rebus; omnes relĭquos Belgas esse in armis:
things; all the remaining Belgæ to be in arms:

que Germanos, qui incŏlunt cis Rhenum
and the Germans, who inhabit on-this-side the Rhine

conjunxisse sese cum his; que
to have joined-together themselves with these (Belgæ); *and*

tantum esse furorem omnĭum eorum, ut
so-great to be the fury of all of them, that

potuĕrint (perf. subj.) deterrere ne quĭdem
they have been able to deter not indeed (even)

Suessiones, sŭos fratres que consanguinĕos, qui
the Suessiones, their brothers and kinsmen, who

LIBER II.

utantur (pres. subj.)	eodem	jure,	iisdem
use	with the same	right,	with the same

legĭbus,	habĕant (pres. subj.)	unum	imperĭum,	que
laws,	have	one	government,	and

unum	magistratum	cum	ipsis,	quin
one	magistracy	with	themselves,	but-that

consentirent	cum	his.
they would consent	with	these.

4.
Quum	quærĕret (imp. subj.)	ab	his,	quæ
When	he did inquire	from	these,	what

civitates	que	quantæ	essent (imp. subj.)	in	armis,
states	and	how-great	were	in	arms,

et	quid	possent (imp. subj.)	in	bello,	reperiebat
and	what	they were-able	in	war,	he did find

sic:	plerosque	Belgas	ortos-esse	. from
thus;	the most-of	the Belgæ	to have sprung	from

Germanis	que	antiquĭtùs	transductos	Rhenum,
the Germans	and	anciently	led-over	the Rhine,

consedisse	ĭbi	propter	fertilitatem
to have sat-down (settled)	there	on-account-of	the fertility

agri;	que	expulisse	Gallos,	qui
of the land;	and	to have driven-out	the Gauls,	who

incolĕrent (imp. subj.)	ĕa"	lŏca;	que	esse	solos,
did inhabit	those	places;	and	to be	alone,

qui,	memoriâ	nostrorum	patrum,	omni	Galliâ
who,	in the memory	of our	fathers,	all	Gaul

vexatâ,	prohibuĕrint (perf. subj.)	Teutŏnes	que
being harassed,	prohibited	the Teutones	and

Cimbros	ingrĕdi	intra	sŭos	fines.	Ex	quâ
Cimbri	to enter	within	their	borders.	Out-of	which

re	fiĕri	ŭtì	sumĕrent (imp. subj.)
thing	to be made (it happened)	that	they did take

magnam	auctoritatem	que	magnos	spirĭtus	in
great	authority	and	great	spirits	in

militari	re	sĭbi,	memoriâ	earum
military	affair	to themselves,	by the memory	of those

rerum.	things.
Rhemi	The Rhemi
dicebant	did say
se	themselves
habere	to have
omnia	all (things)
explorata	explored
de	about
numero	the number
eorum,	of them,
propterea	because
quòd	that
conjuncti	joined-together
propinquitatibus (pl.)	by kindred
atque	and
affinitatibus,	by marriage-alliances,
cognoverint (perf. subj.)	they knew
quantam	how-great
multitudinem	a multitude
quisque	each
pollicitus-sit (perf. subj.)	promised
in	in
communi	the common
concilio	council
Belgarum	of the Belgæ
ad id	to that
bellum.	war.
Bellovacos	The Bellovaci
valere	to prevail
plurimum	most
inter	among
eos,	them,
et	both
virtute, et	in valour, and
auctoritate,	in authority,
et	and
numero	in the number
hominum;	of men;
hos	these
posse	to-be-able
conficere	to accomplish (raise)
centum	a hundred
millia	thousands
armata;	armed (men);
pollicitos	having promised
sexaginta	sixty
millia	thousands
lecta	chosen
ex eo	out-of that
numero,	number,
que	and
postulare	to demand
imperium	the supreme-authority
belli	of the war
sibi.	to themselves.
Suessiones	The Suessiones
esse	to be
suos	their
finitimos;	neighbours ·
possidere	to possess
latissimos	the most-wide
que	and
feracissimos	most-productive
agros;	lands;
Divitiacum	Divitiacus
fuisse	to have-been
regem	king
apud	with (over)
eos,	them,
potentissimum	the most-powerful
totius	of the whole
Galliæ,	Gaul,
etiam	even
nostrâ	in our
memoriâ,	memory,
qu	who
cùm	when (both)
obtinuerit (perf. subj.)	obtained
imperium	the empire
magnæ	of great
partis	part
harum	of these
regionum,	regions,
tum	then (as)
etiam	also
Britanniæ;	of Britain;
Galbam	Galba
nunc	now
esse	to be
regem;	(their) king;

LIBER II. [95

summam		totius	belli deferri
the sum (chief command)		*of the whole*	*war to be conferr'd*

ad	hunc	voluntate	omnium;	habere	duodecim
to	*this* (*man*)	*by the will*	*of all;*	*to have*	*twelve*

oppida	numero:	polliceri	quinquaginta	millia
towns	*in number;*	*to promise*	*fifty*	*thousands*

armata:	Nervios,	totidem,	qui habeantur (pres.
armed:	*the Nervii,*	*just-as-many,*	*who are-had* (deemed)

subj.)	maxime-feri	inter	ipsos	que	absint (pres. subj.)
	the most-fierce	*among*	*them*	*and*	*are-distant*

longissime;	Atrebates,	quindecim	millia;
farthest;	*the Atrebates,*	*fifteen*	*thousands;*

Ambianos,	decem	millia;	Morinos,	viginti
the Ambiani,	*ten*	*thousands;*	*the Morini,*	*twenty*

quinque	millia;	Menapios,	novem	millia;
five	*thousands;*	*the Menapii*	*nine*	*thousands;*

Caletes	decem	millia;	Velocasses	et
the Caletes	*ten*	*thousands;*	*the Velocasses*	*and*

Veromanduos	totidem;	Aduaticos,	viginti	novem
Veromandui	*just-as-many;*	*the Aduatici,*	*twenty*	*nine*

millia;	arbitrari	Condrusos,	Eburones,	Cæresos,
thousands;	*to deem*	*the Condrusi,*	*Eburones,*	*Cæresi,*

Pæmanos,	qui	appellantur	uno	nomine	Germani,
Pæmani,	*who*	*are called*	*by one*	*name*	*Germans,*

ad	quadraginta	millia.
to	*forty*	*thousands.*

5.
Cæsar,	cohortatus	Rhemos,	que
Cæsar,	*having encouraged*	*the Rhemi,*	*and*

prosecutus	liberaliter	oratione,	jussit
having followed-up	*liberally* (kindly)	*with speech,*	*ordered*

omnem	senatum	convenire	ad	se,	que
all	(*their*) *senate*	*to come-together*	*to*	*himself,*	*and*

liberos	principum	adduci	obsides	ad
the children	*of chiefs*	*to be brought*	(*as*) *hostages*	*to*

se.	Omnia	quæ	facta-sunt	diligenter
himself.	*all*	*which* (*things*)	*were-done*	*diligently*

ab	his	ad	diem.	Ipse	cohortatus
by	*these*	*to*	*the day.*	*Himself*	*having encouraged*

magnopĕre	Æduum	Divitiăcum,	que	dŏcet
earnestly	*the Æduan*	*Divitiacus,*	*both*	*teaches*

quantopĕre	intersit (pres. subj.)	Reipublĭcæ (gen.)	que
how-greatly	*it concerns*	*the Republic*	*and*

communis salutis, mănus hostium distineri,
the common safety, the bands of the enemies to be separated,

ne	sit	confligendum	uno	tempŏre	cum
lest	*it may be*	*to be fought*	*in one*	*time*	*with*

tantâ	multitudĭne;	id	posse	fiĕri,	si
so-great	*a multitude;*	*that*	*to be able*	*to be done,*	*if*

Ædŭi	introduxĕrint	sŭas	copĭas	in
the Ædui	*shall have introduced*	*their*	*forces*	*into*

fines	Bellovacorum	et	cœpĕrint (fut. subj.)
the borders	*of the Bellovaci*	*and*	*begun*

populari	agros	eorum. His	mandatis,
to ravage	*the lands*	*of them. These (things)*	*being enjoined,*

dimittit	ĕum	ab	se.	Postquam cognovit
he dismisses	*him*	*from*	*himself.*	*After-that he knew*

ab	his	exploratorĭbus,	quos	misĕrat,	et
from	*these*	*scouts,*	*whom*	*he had sent,*	*and*

ab	Rhemis,	omnes	copĭas	Belgarum	coactas
from	*the Rhemi,*	*all*	*the forces*	*of the Belgæ*	*collected*

in	unum	lŏcum	venire	ad	se,	nĕque	jam
into	*one*	*place*	*to come*	*to*	*himself.*	*nor*	*now*

abesse	longê;	maturavit transducĕre	flumen
to be-distant	*far;*	*he hastened to lead-over (cross)*	*the river*

Axŏnam,	quod	est in	extremis	finĭbus	Rhemorum,
Axona,	*which*	*is in*	*the extreme*	*borders*	*of the Rhemi,*

exercĭtum,	atque	ĭbi	posŭit	castra (pl.).	Quæ
the army,	*and*	*there*	*placed*	*(his) camp.*	*Which*

res	et	muniebat	unum	lătus	castrorum (pl.)
thing	*both*	*did fortify*	*one*	*side*	*of the camp*

ripis	flumĭnis	et	reddebat	ĕa
by the banks	*of the river*	*and*	*did render*	*those (things)*

quæ ĕrant pòst, tuta ab hostĭbus, et	which were behind, safe from the enemies, and
efficiebat, ut commeatus posset portari	did effect, that provision might-be-able to be carried
ad ĕum ab Rhemis, que relĭquis civitatĭbus	to him from the Rhemi, and the remaining states
sĭne pericŭlo. Pons ĕrat in ĕo flumĭne;	without danger. A bridge was in (on) that river;
ĭbi ponit præsidĭum, et reliquit Quintum	there he places a guard, and left Quintus
Titurĭum Sabinum legatum in altĕrâ parte	Titurius Sabinus (his) lieutenant in the other part (side)
flumĭnis cum sex cohortĭbus; jŭbet	of the river with six cohorts; he orders (them)
munire castra (pl.) vallo in altitudĭnem	to fortify the camp with a rampart into height
duodĕcim pĕdum que fossâ duodeviginti	of twelve feet and with a trench of eighteen
pĕdum.	feet.

6. Oppĭdum Rhemorum, nomĭne Bibrax, abĕrat
   A town of the Rhemi, by name Bibrax, was-distant

octo millĭa passŭum ab castris ipsis;
eight thousands of paces from the camps themselves;

Belgæ cœperunt oppugnare id magno impĕtu
the Belgæ began to assault it with great violence

ex itinĕre: sustentatum est
out-of (on) (their) journey (march): it (the assault) was sustained

ægrè ĕo die. Oppugnatĭo Gallorum et
hardly in that day. The assault of the Gauls and

Belgarum est eădem. Hi, ŭbi, multitudĭne
of the Belgæ is the same. These, when, a multitude

homĭnum circumjectâ totis mœnĭbus (dat.)
of men being thrown-around the whole walls

lapĭdes cœpti-sunt jăci in murum
stones were-begun to be thrown against the wall

undīque que murus nudatus-est defensorĭbus;	on-all-sides and the wall was-stripped from defenders:
testudĭne factâ, succedunt	a tortoise (a military covering) being made, approach
portis (dat.) que subruunt murum. Quod tum	the gates and undermine the wall. Which then
fiebat facĭlè; nam tanta multitudo conjiciebant	was done easily; for so-great a multitude did throw
lapĭdes ac tela, ut potestas consistendi in	stones and darts, that a power of standing in (on)
muro esset (imp. subj.) nulli. Quum nox fecisset	wall was to none. When night had made
(pl. perf. subj.) finem oppugnandi, Rhemus Iccĭus,	an end of assaulting, the Rhemian Iccius,
summâ nobilitate et gratĭâ inter	with (of the) highest nobility and favour among
sŭos, qui tum præĕrat oppĭdo; unus ex	his-own, who then was-over to the town; one out-of
iis, qui venĕrant ad Cæsărem legati	those, who had come to Cæsar (as) ambassadors
de pace, mittit nuntĭos ad ĕum, nĭsi	about peace, sends messengers to him, unless
subsidĭum mittatur (pres. subj.) sĭbi, se	a succour is sent to himself, himself
posse non sustinere diutĭùs.	to be-able not to sustain (hold out) longer.

7. Eò de medĭâ nocte, Cæsar usus
Thither about middle night, Cæsar having used

iisdem ducĭbus, qui venĕrant nuntĭi
with the same guides, who had come (as) messengers

ab Iccĭo, mittit Numĭdas et Cretas sagittarĭos
from Iccius, sends Numidian and Cretan archers

et Baleares funditores subsidĭo oppidanis.
and Balearic slingers for a succour to the townsmen.

Adventu quorum, et studĭum propugnandi
By the arrival of whom, both eagerness of resisting

cum spe defensionis accessit	with hope of defence approached (was added)
Rhemis, et de eâdem caussâ spes	to the Rhemi, and from the same cause the hope
potiundi oppĭdi discessit hostĭbus.	of gaining the town departed from the enemies.
Itáque morati paulisper ăpud oppĭdum	Therefore having delayed a little-while at the town
que depopulati agros Rhemorum, omnĭbus	and having laid-waste the lands of the Rhemi, all
vicis que ædificĭis incensis, quò	the villages and edifices having been burnt, where
potĕrant adire, contenderunt	they were able to approach, they strained (hastened)
ad castra Cæsăris cum omnĭbus copĭis,	to the camps of Cæsar with all (their) forces,
et posuerunt castra (pl.) à mĭnùs duobus	and placed camp from (at) less than two
millĭbus passŭum, quæ castra (pl.), ut significabatur	thousands of paces, which camp as was signified
fumo atque ignĭbus, patebant in latitudĭnem	by smoke and by fires, did extend into breadth
amplĭus octo millĭbus passŭum.	more (than) eight thousands of paces.

8. Cæsar primò statŭit supersedĕre — Cæsar at-first determined to supersede (abstain
prœlio (abl.) et propter multitudĭnem — from) battle both on-account-of the multitude
hostĭum et propter eximĭam opinionem — of the enemies and on-account-of the eminent opinion
virtutis; tămen periclitabatur quotidie — of (their) valour; yet he did hazard (make trial) daily
equestrĭbus prœlĭis, quid hostis posset — in cavalry battles, what the enemy might-be-able
virtute, et quid nostri auderent. Ubi — in valour, and what our (men) might-dare. When

intellexit	nostros	esse	non	inferiores,	lŏco
he understood	*our (men)*	*to be*	*not*	*inferior,*	*the place*

pro	castris (pl.)		opportuno	atque idonĕo
before	*the camp*	*(being)*	*opportune*	*and fit*

naturâ	ad	acĭem	instruendam;	quŏd	is
by nature	*to*	*the line*	*to-be-arrayed;*	*because*	*that*

collis	ŭbi	castra (pl.)	posita-ĕrant,	edĭtus
hill	*where*	*the camp*	*had been placed,*	*being raised*

paullŭlum	ex	planitĭe,	patebat	in
a little	*out-of*	*the plain,*	*did lie-open (extend)*	*into*

latitudĭnem	adversus	antum	lŏci,	quantum
breadth	*opposite*	*so-much*	*of place,*	*as-much-as*

acies	instructa	potĕrat	occupare	atque habebat
the line (of battle)	*arrayed*	*was-able*	*to occupy,*	*and did have*

dejectus	latĕris	ex	utrâque	parte, et
descents	*of the side*	*from (on)*	*either*	*part, and*

lenĭter fastigiatus	in fronte,	paullatim	redibat
gently pointed (sloping)	*in front,*	*gradually*	*did return*

ad	planitĭem:	ab utroque	latĕre	ejus collis
to	*a plain:*	*from each*	*side*	*of that hill*

obduxit	transversam	fossam	circĭter	quadringenorum
he led-over	*a transverse*	*trench*	*about*	*of four-hundred*

passŭum,	et ad	extremas	fossas
paces,	*and at*	*the extreme (both ends of)*	*the trenches*

constitŭit	castella,	que	ĭbi	collocavit tormenta;
he erected	*castles,*	*and*	*there*	*placed engines;*

ne,	quum	instruxisset (pl. perf. subj.)	acĭem,
lest,	*when*	*he had arrayed*	*(his) line,*

hostes	(quŏd potĕrant	tantum	multitudĭne)
the enemies	*(because they were-able*	*so-much*	*by multitude)*

possent	circumvenire	à	laterĭbus sŭos
might be-able	*to surround*	*from (on)*	*the flanks his (men)*

pugnantes.	Hoc	facto,	duabus legionĭbus,	quas
fighting.	*This*	*being done,*	*two legions,*	*which*

conscripsĕrat	proxĭmè,	relictis	in castris,
he had levied	*most-nearly (last),*	*being left*	*in camp*

ut,	si	quid	ŏpus	esset	possent
that,	if	any	need	hould be,	they might be-able

duci	subsidĭo,	constitŭit	relĭquas	sex
to be led	for a relief,	he arranged	the remaining	six

legiones	in	acĭe	pro	castris (pl.). Item
legions	in	line	before	the camp. Likewise

hostes	instruxĕrant	sŭas	copĭas eductas	ex
the enemies	had arrayed	their	forces led-out	from

castris (pl.).
the camp.

9. Pălus non magna ĕrat inter nostrum atque
   A marsh not great was between our (men) and

exercĭtum hostĭum; hostes expectabant, si
the army of the enemies; the enemies did await, if

nostri transirent hanc; autem nostri ĕrant
our (men) would pass-over this; but our (men) were

parati in armis ut, si initĭum transeundi
prepared in arms that, if a beginning of passing

fieret ab illis, aggrederentur impeditos.
should be made by them, they might attack (them) entangled.

Intĕrim contendebatur equestri prœlĭo
Meanwhile it was contended in an equestrian battle

inter dŭas acĭes. Ubi neutri facĭunt
between the two lines. When neither make

initĭum transeundi, prœlĭo nostrorum equĭtum
a beginning of passing, the battle of our horsemen

secundiore, Cæsar reduxit sŭos in
(being) more successful, Cæsar led-back his (men) into

castra. Hostes protĭnus contenderunt
the camps. The enemies forthwith strained (hastened)

ex ĕo lŏco ad flumen Axŏnam, quod
from that place to the river Axona, which

demonstratum-est esse post nostra castra (pl.); ibi
has been pointed-out to be behind our camp; there

vadis repertis, conati-sunt transducĕre
fords being found, they endeavoured to lead-over

partem	suarum	copiarum,	ěo	consilĭo,	ut,
part	of their	forces,	with this	design,	that

si	possent,	expugnarent	castellum,
if	they should be-able,	they might storm	the castle,

cui	Q. Titurĭus	legatus	præĕrat,	que
to which	Q. Titurius	the lieutenant	was-over,	and

interscindĕrent	pontem :	si	mĭnùs,	popula-
might cut-down	the bridge :	if	less (not),	they might

rentur	agros	Rhemorum,	qui ěrant	magno
ravage	the lands	of the Rhemi,	which were	for (of) great

usŭi	nobis ad	bellum	gerendum	que sustinebant
use	to us to	the war	to-be-carried-on	and did sustain

nostros	commeatus.
our	provisions.

10.
Cæsar	factus	certior	à	Titurĭo,
Cæsar	being made	more-sure	by	Titurius,

transducit	pontem	omnem equitatum,	et	Numĭdas
leads-over	the bridge	all the cavalry.	and	Numidians

lĕvis	armaturæ,	funditores	que sagittarĭos,	atque
of light	armour,	the slingers	and archers,	and

contendit	ad	ěos.	Pugnatum-est acrĭter in
strains (hastens)	to	them.	It was fought sharply in

ěo	lŏco :	nostri	aggressi hostes
that	place :	our (men)	having attacked the enemies

impeditos	in flumĭne,	occiderunt	magnum	numĕrum
entangled	in the river,	slew	a great	number

eorum ;	repulerunt	multitudĭne	telorum
of them :	they repulsed	with a multitude	of weapons

relĭquos	conantes	audacissĭmè	transire
the remaining (men)	endeavouring	most-boldly	to pass

per	corpŏra	eorum :	interfecerunt primos, qui
through	the bodies	of them :	they killed the first, who

transiĕrant,	circumventos	equitatu.	Hostes,
had passed,	surrounded	with the cavalry.	The enemies,

ŭbi	intellexerunt	spem	fefellisse	se
when	they understood	hope	to have deceived	themselves

LIBER II.

et de oppĭdo expugnando, et de flumĭne
and (both) *of the town to-be-stormed, and of the river*

transeundo, nĕque vidĕrunt nostros progrĕdi
to-be-passed-over, nor saw our (men) *to advance*

in iniquiorem lŏcum caussâ
into more-unequal (disadvantageous) *place by cause* (for

pugnandi, atque frumentarĭa res
the sake) *of fighting, and corn thing* (provisions)

cœpit deficĕre ĕos; concilĭo convocato,
began to fail them; a council being called-together,

ccnstituerunt esse optĭmum quemque reverti sŭam
they resolved to be best each to return (to) *his*

dŏmum: et convenire undĭque ad ĕos
home: and to assemble from-all-sides to them

defendendos, in fines quorum Romani
to-be-defended. into the borders of whom the Romans

primùm introduxissent exercĭtum; ut decertarent
first might have led-in the army; that they might contend

potĭùs in sŭis, quàm alienis finĭbus, et
rather in their-own, than in foreign borders, and

uterentur domesticis copĭis (abl.) frumentarĭæ rĕi.
might use domestic supplies of corn thing

Quŏque hæc ratĭo, cum relĭquis
(provisions). *Also this reason, with the remaining*

caussis, deduxit ĕos ad ĕam sententĭam,
causes, brought them to that opinion (resolution),

quòd cognovĕrant Divitiăcum atque Ædŭos
because they had known Divitiacus and the Ædui

appropinquare finĭbus Bellovacorum. Potĕrat
to approach to the borders of the Bellovaci. It-was-able

non persuaderi his, ut morarentur
not to be persuaded to those, that they should delay

diutĭùs, nĕque ferrent auxilĭum suis.
longer, nor should bring assistance to their (countrymen).

11. Eâ re constitutâ, secundâ vigilĭâ,
That thing being resolved, in the second watch,

egressi castris cum magno strepitu
having gone-out from the camps with great noise

ac tumultu, nullo certo ordine neque imperio,
and tumult, in no certain order neither command,

quum quisque peteret (imp. subj.) primum locum
when each did seek the first place

itineris sibi, et properaret (imp. subj.)
of the journey to himself, and did-hasten

pervenire domum, fecerunt, ut profectio
to arrive (to) home, they made, that (their) departure

videretur (imp. subj.) consimilis fugæ. Hâc
did seem like to a flight. This

re statim cognita per speculatores, Cæsar
thing immediately being known by scouts. Cæsar

veritus insidias, quòd perspexerat nondum
having feared snares, because he had seen-clearly not-yet

de quâ caussâ discederent (imp. subj.) continuit
from what cause they did depart held

exercitum, que equitatum castris. Primâ luce,
the army, and cavalry in camp. In first light,

re confirmatâ ab exploratoribus,
the thing being confirmed by scouts,

præmisit omnem equitatum, qui moraretur
he sent-before all the cavalry, which should delay

novissimum agmen; que præfecit
(detain) the last troop (rear); and he appointed

Quintum Pedium, et Lucium Aurunculeium Cottam
Quintus Pedius, and Lucius Aurunculeius Cotta

legatos ei: jussit Titum Labienum
lieutenants to it: he ordered Titus Labienus

legatum subsequi cum tribus legionibus.
the lieutenant to follow-close with three legions.

Hi adorti novissimos et prosecuti
These having attacked the last (rear) and having pursued

multa millia passuum, conciderunt magnam
(them) many thousands of paces, cut-up a great

multitudĭnem eorum fugentĭum.	multitude of them fleeing.
Quum hi ab extremo agmĭne,	When those from (on) the last troop (rear),
ad quos ventum-ĕrat,	to whom it had been come,
consistĕrent (imp. subj.), que	did stand-together, and
sustinerent (imp. subj.)	did sustain
fortĭter impĕtum nostrorum milĭtum;	bravely the attack of our soldiers;
priores, quòd viderentur (imp. subj.)	the former (the van), because they did seem
abesse à perĭcŭlo,	to be distant from danger,
nĕque continerentur (imp. subj.)	nor were held-together
ullâ necessitate nĕque imperĭo,	by any necessity nor command,
clamore exaudito,	the noise being heard,
ordinĭbus perturbatis,	the ranks being disturbed (confused),
omnes posuerunt præsidĭum sĭbi in fŭgâ.	all placed safe-guard to themselves in flight.
Ita sĭne ullo perĭcŭlo nostri interfecerunt	Thus without any danger our (men) killed
tantam multitudĭnem eorum,	so-great a multitude of them,
quantum spatĭum diei fŭit;	as the space of the day was;
que sub occasum solis	and under (about) the going-down of the sun
destiterunt sĕqui,	they desisted to follow,
que receperunt se in castra,	and betook themselves into camps,
ŭti imperatum-ĕrat.	as it had been commanded.

12. Postridĭe ejus diei, priùs-quàm hostes recipĕrent se ex terrore ac fŭgâ, Cæsar duxit exercĭtum in fines Suessi-onum, qui ĕrant proxĭmi Rhemis; et

The day after of that day, before-that the enemies might recover themselves out-of terror and flight, Cæsar led (his) army into the borders of the Sues-siones, who were nearest to the Rhemi, and

magno	itinĕre	confecto,	contendit	ad
a great	*journey*	*being accomplished,*	*he hastened*	*to*

oppĭdum,	Noviodunum.	Conatus	oppugnare
the town,	*Noviodunum.*	*Having attempted*	*to storm*

id	ex	itinĕre,	quòd	audiebat
that	*out-of*	*the journey* (in his march),	*because*	*he did hear*

	esse	vacŭum	ab	defensorĭbus,	potŭit
	(it) to be	*void*	*from* (of)	*defenders,*	*he was-able*

non	expugnare	propter	latitudĭnem	fossæ,
not	*to storm* (it)	*on-account-of*	*the breadth*	*of the ditch,*

que	altitudĭnem	muri,	paucis	defendentĭbus.
and	*the height*	*of the wall,*	*few* (men)	*defending* (it).

Castris	munitis,	cœpit	agĕre
The camps	*being fortified*	*he began*	*to act* (to apply)

vinĕas,	que	comparare	quæ	ĕrant
mantlets,	*and*	*to prepare* (the things)	*which*	*were*

usŭi	ad	oppugnandum.	Intĕrim	omnis multitudo
to use	*to*	*to-storming.*	*Meanwhile*	*all the multitude*

Suessionum	ex	fŭgâ	convĕnit	in
of the Suessiones	*out-of*	*flight*	*comes-together*	*into*

oppĭdum	proxĭmâ	nocte.	Vinĕis actis
the town	*in the nearest* (next)	*night.*	*Mantlets being applied*

celerĭter	ad	oppĭdum,	aggĕre	jacto, que
quickly	*to*	*the town,*	*a mound*	*being thrown-up, and*

turrĭbus	constitutis,	Galli	permoti
towers	*erected,*	*the Gauls*	*much-moved* (alarmed)

magnitudĭne	opĕrum,	quæ	nĕque	vidĕrant
by the greatness	*of the works,*	*which*	*neither*	*they had seen*

antè	nĕque	audiĕrant,	et	celeritate
before	*nor*	*had heard,*	*and*	*by the quickness*

Romanorum,	mittunt	legatos	ad	Cæsărem
of the Romans,	*send*	*ambassadors*	*to*	*Cæsar*

de	deditione;	et,	Rhemis petentĭbus,
about	*a surrender;*	*and,*	*the Rhemi seeking* (asking),

ut	conservarentur,	impĕtrant.
that	*they might be preserved,*	*they obtain* (safety)

LIBER II.

13.	Primis		civitatis,	atque	duobus	filiis
The first (*men*)		*of the state,*	*and*	*two*	*sons*

regis	Galbæ	ipsius	acceptis	obsidibus,	que
of king	*Galba*	*himself*	*being received*	*(as) hostages,*	*and*

omnibus	armis	transditis	ex	oppido,	Cæsar
all	*arms*	*being delivered*	*out-of*	*the town,*	*Cæsar*

accepit	Suessiones	in	deditionem;	que	duxit
received	*the Suessiones*	*into*	*a surrender;*	*and*	*led*

exercitum	in	Bellovacos:	qui	quum	contu-
the army	*into*	*the Bellovaci:*	*who*	*when*	*they had*

lissent (pl. perf. subj.)		se	que	omnia
brought-together		*themselves*	*and*	*all*

sua	in	oppidum Bratuspantium,	atque	Cæsar,
their (things)	*into*	*the town Bratuspantium,*	*and*	*Cæsar,*

cum exercitu,	abesset (imp. subj.)	ab	eo	oppido
with the army,	*was-distant*	*from*	*that*	*town*

circiter	quinque	millia	passuum,	omnes
about	*five*	*thousands*	*of paces,*	*all (those)*

majores	natu	egressi	ex	oppido,
greater	*by birth* (elders)	*having gone-out*	*from*	*the town,*

cœperunt	tendere	manus	ad	Cæsarem,
began	*to stretch*	*(their) hands*	*to*	*Cæsar,*

significare	voce,	sese	venire	in	fidem
to signify	*by voice,*	*themselves*	*to come*	*into*	*the faith*

ac	potestatem	ejus	neque	contendere	contra
and	*power*	*of him*	*nor*	*to contend*	*against*

Romanum	populum	armis:	item,	quum
the Roman	*people*	*with arms:*	*also,*	*when*

accessisset (pl. perf. subj.)	ad	oppidum,	que
he had approached	*to*	*the town,*	*and*

poneret (imp. subj.)	castra	ibi,	pueri	que
did place	*camps*	*there,*	*the boys*	*and*

mulieres	ex	muro,	manibus	passis,
women	*out-of* (from)	*the wall,*	*with hands*	*stretched-out,*

suo	more,	petierunt	pacem	à	Romanis.
by their	*custom,*	*sought*	*peace*	*from*	*the Romans.*

14. Divitiācus făcit verba pro his
    Divitiacus makes words (a speech) for these

(nam post discessum Belgarum, copiis
(for after the departure of the Belgæ, the forces

Æduorum dimissis, reverterat ad
of the Ædui being sent-away, he had returned to

ĕum): Bellovācos omni tempŏre fuisse
him (Cæsar)): the Bellovaci in all time to have been

in fĭde atque amicitĭâ Ædŭæ civitatis;
in the faith and friendship of the Æduan state:

impulsos à sŭis principĭbus, qui dicĕrent (imp.
impelled by their chiefs, who did say

subj.) Ædŭos redactos in servitutem à Cæsăre,
the Ædui reduced into servitude by Cæsar,

perferre omnes indignitates que contumelĭas, et
to endure all indignities and affronts, and

defecisse ab Ædŭis, et intulisse
(both) to have revolted from the Ædui, and to have brought-on

bellum Romano popŭlo. Qui fuissent
war to the Roman people. (Those) who had been

(pl. perf. subj.) princĭpes hujus consilĭi, quòd
chiefs (authors) of this counsel, because

intelligĕrent (imp. subj.) quantam calamitatem
they did understand how-great a calamity

intulissent (pl. perf. subj.) civitati, profugisse
they had brought-on to the state, to have fled

in Britannĭam. Non solŭm Bellovăcos petĕre,
into Britain. Not only the Bellovaci to entreat

sed etiam Ædŭos, pro his, ut utatur
but also the Ædui, for these, that he may use

sŭâ clementĭâ ac mansuetudĭne in ĕos:
with his clemency and mildness towards them,

quod si fecĕrit, amplificaturum auctoritatem
which if he shall have done. about-to-enlarge the authority

Æduorum apud omnes Belgas, auxilĭs
of the Ædui at (among) all the Belgæ, by aids

atque	opĭbus	quorum	consuevĕrint (perf. subj.)
and	*resources*	*of whom*	*they have been-accustomed*

sustentare,	si	qua bella	incidĕrint.
to sustain,	*if*	*any wars*	*may have happened.*

15.
Cæsar,	caussâ	honoris
Cæsar,	*by cause* (for the sake)	*of the honour*

Divitiăci	atque	Æduorum,	dixit sese
of Divitiacus	*and*	*of the Ædui,*	*said himself*

recepturum	ĕos in	fĭdem et	conservaturum ;
about-to-receive	*them into*	*faith and*	*about-to-preserve*

et	quòd	civĭtas	ĕrat	magna	et
(them) ;	*and because*	*the state*	*was*	*great*	*and*

præstabat inter	Belgas	auctoritate ac	multitudĭne
did excel among	*the Belgæ*	*in authority and*	*in multitude*

homĭnum,	poposcit	sex-centos	obsĭdes : his
of men,	*he required*	*six-hundred*	*hostages : these*

tradĭtis	que omnĭbus	armis	collatis
being delivered	*and all*	*(their) arms*	*brought-together*

ex	oppĭdo,	pervenit ab	ĕo lŏco	in
out-of	*the town,*	*he arrived from*	*that place*	*into*

fines	Ambianorum, qui	dediderunt se
the borders	*of the Ambiani, who*	*surrendered themselves*

que omnĭa	sŭa	sĭne mŏrâ.	Nervii
and all	*their (things)*	*without delay.*	*The Nervians*

attingebant	fines	eorum : de	naturâ que
did reach-to	*the borders*	*of them : of*	*the nature and*

morĭbus	quorum, quum	Cæsar	quærĕret (imp. subj.),
manners	*of whom, when*	*Cæsar*	*did inquire,*

reperiebat	sic ; nullum	adĭtum esse	mercatorĭbus
he did find	*thus ; no*	*access to be*	*to merchants*

ad ĕos :	păti	nĭhil vini,	que reliquarum
to them ;	*to suffer*	*nothing of wine,*	*and of remaining*

rerum	pertinentĭum ad	luxurĭam,	inferri :
things	*tending to*	*luxury,*	*to be brought-in :*

quòd	existimarent (imp. subj.)	animos eorum
because	*they did think*	*the minds of them*

relanguescĕre,	to grow-feeble,
que	and
virtutem	(their) virtue
remitti	to be relaxed
his	by these
rebus:	things:
homĭnes	the men
esse	to be
fĕros,	fierce,
que	and
magnæ	of great
virtutis:	virtue
(valour):	(valour):
increpitare	to chide
atque	and
incusare	to blame
relĭquos	the remaining
Belgas,	Belgæ,
qui	who
dedissent (pl. perf. subj.)	had surrendered
se	themselves
Romano	to the Roman
popŭlo,	people,
que	and
projecissent (pl. perf. subj.)	had cast-off
patrĭam	(their) native
virtutem;	virtue;
confirmare,	to affirm,
se	themselves
nĕque	neither
missuros	about-to-send
legatos,	ambassadors,
nĕque	nor
accepturos	about-to-receive
ullam	any
conditionem	condition
pacis	of peace.

16. Quum fecisset (pl. perf. subj.) iter
When he had made a journey

tridŭo	for three-days
per	through
fines	the borders
eorum,	of them,
inveniebat	he did find
ex	from
captivis,	the captives,
flumen	the river
Sabin	Sabis
abesse	to be-distant
ab	from
sŭis	his
castris	camps
non	not
amplĭùs	more
decem	(than) ten
millĭa	thousands
passŭum:	of paces:
omnes	all
Nervĭos	the Nervii
consedisse	to have sat-down (were posted)
trans	beyond
id	that
flumen,	river,
que	and
ĭbi	there
unà	together
cum	with
Atrebatĭbus	the Atrebates
et	and
Veromandŭis,	Veromandui,
sŭis	their
finitĭmis,	neighbours,
expectare	to await
adventum	the arrival
Romanorum;	of the Romans;
nam	for
persuasĕrant	they had persuaded
utrisque	to both
his,	these,
ut	that
experirentur	they should try
eandem	the same
fortunam	fortune
belli;	of war;
etĭam	also
copĭas	the forces

LIBER II.

Aduaticorum	expectari	ab	his,	atque	esse
of the Aduatici	to be waited-for	by	these,	and	to be

in	itinere :		conjecisse	mulieres,
in	way (march):		to have thrown-together	the women,

que	qui	per	ætatem	viderentur (imp. subj.)
and	(those) who	through	age	did seem

inutiles	ad	pugnam,	in	eum	locum,	quò
useless	to	fight,	into	that	place,	whither

propter	paludes	aditus	esset	non	exercitui.
on-account-of	the marshes	access	might be	not	to an army.

17.
His	rebus	cognitis,	Cæsar	præmittit
These	things	being known,	Cæsar	sends-before

exploratores,	que	centuriones,	qui	deligant	locum
scouts,	and	centurions,	who	may choose	a place

idoneum	castris :	que	quum	complures	ex
fit	for camps:	and	when	many	out-of

Belgis	que	reliquis	Gallis	dedititiis,
the Belgæ	and	remaining	Gauls	surrendered,

secuti	Cæsarem,	facerent (imp. subj.)	
having followed	Cæsar,	did make	(their)

iter	unà :	quidam	ex	his,	ut
journey	together :	certain-ones	out-of	these,	as

posteà	cognitum-est	ex	captivis,	consuetudine
afterwards	it was known	from	the captives,	the custom

itineris	nostri	exercitûs	eorum	dierum
of the journey (march)	of our	army	of those	days

perspectâ,	pervenerunt	nocte	ad	Nervios
being fully-seen,	arrived	by night	to	the Nervii

atque	demonstraverunt	iis	magnum	numerum
and	shewed	to those	a great	many

impedimentorum	intercedere	inter	singulas
of baggage-waggons	to come-between	between	each

	legiones;	neque	esse	quidquam	negotii,
(the several)	legions;	nor	to be	any-thing	of business

	cùm	prima	legio	venisset	in
difficulty),	when	the first	legion	might have come	into

castris,	que	relĭquæ	legiones	abessent
camps,	and	the remaining	legions	might be-distant

magnum	spatĭum,	adoriri	hanc	sub	sarcĭnis:
a great	space,	to attack	this	under	packs

	quâ	pulsâ,	que	impedimentis
(baggage):	which	oeing routed,	and	the baggage-waggons

direptis,	futurum,	ut	relĭquæ
being plundered,	about-to-be,	that	the remaining (legions)

auderent	non	consistĕre	contrà.	Etĭam	adjuvabit
would dare	not	to stand	against.	Also	it did assist

consilĭum	eorum,	qui	deferebant		rem,
the counsel	of those,	who	did bring (report)		the thing,

quòd	Nervĭi	antiquĭtùs,	quum	possent
because	the Nervii	anciently,	when	they were able (to do)

(imp. subj.)	nĭhil	equitatu,	(ĕnim	nĕque	ad	hoc
	nothing	in cavalry,	(for	neither	to	this

tempus	stŭdent	ĕi	rĕi,	sed,	quidquid
time	they study	to that	thing,	but,	whatever

possunt,	vălent	pedestrĭbus copĭis,)	quò
they are-able,	they are-strong	in foot forces,)	that

impedirent	facilĭùs	equitatum	fini-
they might hinder	more-easily	the cavalry	of (their)

timorum,	si	venisset	ad	ĕos	caussâ
neighbours,	if	it might have come	to	them	by cause

	prædandi,	tenĕris	arborĭbus	incisis
(for the sake)	of robbing,	tender	trees	being cut

atque	inflexis,	que	crebris	ramıs	enatis	in
and	bent-in,	and	thick	boughs	sprung-forth	into

latitudĭnem,	et	rŭbis	que	sentĭbus	inter-
breadth,	and	brambles	and	thorns	being cast-

jectis,	effecĕrant,	ut	hæ	sepes	præberent
between,	they had effected,	that	these	hedges	did afford;

(imp. subj.)	munimenta	instar	muri;	quò
	fortifications	like	of a wall;	whither

posset (imp. subj.)	non	mŏdò	non	intrari,	sed
it was able	not	only	not	to be entered,	but

ne	quĭdem	perspíci.	Quum	ĭter
not	indeed	to be seen-through.	When	the journey

	nostri	agmĭnis	impediretur (imp. subj.)	his
(march)	of our	army	was hindered	by these

rebus	Nervĭi	existimaverunt	consilium	non
things	the Nervii	thought	the advice	not

omittendum	sĭbi.
to-be-omitted (neglected)	to (by) themselves.

18.
Hæc	ĕrat	natura	lŏci,	quem
This	was	the nature	of the place,	which

nostri	delegĕrant	castris.	Collis æqualĭter
(our) men	had chosen	for camps.	A hill equally

declivis	ab	summo	vergebat ad
slanting	from	the highest (place)	did decline to

flumen	Sabim,	quod nominavĭmus	suprà :
the river	Sabis (Sambre),	which we have named	above :

ab	ĕo	flumĭne	pări acclivitate	collis
from	that	river	with equal acclivity	a hill

nascebatur	adversus	et contrarĭus huic,	infĭmus
did rise	opposite	and facing to this,	the lowest

	circĭter ducentos	passus apertus,
(the bottom of the hill) about two-hundred	paces open,

silvestris	ab	superiore parte ;	ut posset (imp.
woody	from (on)	the higher part ;	that it was able

subj.) non	perspĭci	facĭlè	introrsus.	Intra
not	to be seen-through	easily	inwardly.	Within

ĕas	silvas	hostes	continebant	se in
those	woods	the enemies	did hold	themselves in

occulto.	In	aperto	lŏco, secundùm	flumen,
secret.	In	the open	place, near (along)	the river,

paucæ	stationes	equĭtum	videbantur.	Altitudo
a few	stations	of horsemen	were seen.	The depth

flumĭnis	ĕrat	circĭter	trĭum	pĕdum.
of the river	was	about	of three	feet.

19.
Cæsar,	equitatu	præmisso,	subsequebatur
Cæsar,	the cavalry	being sent before,	did follow-closely

L 3

omnĭbus	copĭis:	sed	ratĭo	que	ordo
with all	(his) forces:	but	the manner	and	order

agmĭnis		habebat	se	alĭter	ac
of the troop	(on the march)	did have	itself	otherwise	and

	Belgæ	detulĕrant		ad	Nervĭos.
(than)	the Belg	had carried	(reported)	to	the Nervii.

Nam,	quòd	hostis	appropinquabat,	Cæsar	sŭâ
For,	because	the enemy	did approach,	Cæsar	by his

consuetudĭne	ducebat	sex	expedĭtas	legiones:	post
custom	did lead	six	light-armed	legions:	after

	ĕas	collocabat		impedimenta	
(behind)	those	he did place		the baggage-waggons

totius	exercĭtûs:	inde	dŭæ	legiones,	quæ
of the whole	army:	then	two	legions,	which

conscriptæ-ĕrant	proxĭmè,	claudebant		totum
had been enrolled	last,	did shut (close)		the whole

agmen,	que	ĕrant	præsidĭo		impedi-
army (march),	and	were	for safeguard	to the baggage-

mentis.	Nostri	equĭtes	cum	funditorĭbus	que
waggons.	Our	horsemen	with	the slingers	and

sagittarĭis	transgressi	flumen,	commiserunt	prœlĭum
archers	having passed	the river,	joined	battle

cum	equitatu	hostĭum.	Quum	illi	identĭdem
with	the cavalry	of the enemies.	When	they	now-and-then

recipĕrent (imp. subj.)		se	in	silvas	ad	sŭos,
did betake		themselves	into	the woods	to	their

	ac	rursus	facĕrent (imp. subj.)	impĕtum	in
(men),	and	again	did make	an attack	upon

nostros	ex	silvâ;	nĕque	nostri	auderent
our (men)	out-of	the wood;	nor	our (men)	did dare

(imp. subj.)	insĕqui	cedentes	longĭŭs,	quam	ad
	to pursue	(those) yielding	farther,	than	to

quem	finem	porrecta	ac	aperta	lŏca	pertinebant:
what	end	the extended	and	open	places	did reach:

intĕrim	sex	legiones,	quæ	venĕran	primæ,
meanwhile	the six	legions,	which	had come	first.

LIBER II.

opĕre dimenso, cœperunt munire castra.
the work being measured, began to fortify camps.

Ubi prima impedimenta nostri exercĭtûs visa-
When the first baggage-waggons of our army were-

sunt ab iis, qui latebant abdĭti in silvis,
seen by those, who did lie-hid concealed in the woods,

quod tempus convenĕrat inter ĕos
which time had been agreed-upon between them

committendi prœlĭum: ut constituĕrant intra
of joining battle: as they had placed within

silvas acĭem que ordĭnes, atque
the woods the line (of battle) and ranks, and

ipsi confirmavĕrant sese, subĭtò
themselves had strengthened themselves, suddenly

provolaverunt omnĭbus copĭis, que fecerunt
they flew-forth with all (their) forces, and made

impĕtum in nostros equĭtes. His pulsis
an attack upon our horsemen. These being routed

facĭlè ac proturbatis, decucurrerent incredibĭli
easily and disordered, they ran-down with incredible

celeritate ad flumen; ut penè uno tempŏre
quickness to the river; so-that almost in one time

hostes viderentur (imp. subj.) et ad
the enemies did seem and (both) at

silvas, et in flumĭne, et jam in nostris
the woods, and in the river, and now in our

manĭbus. Autem contenderunt eâdem
hands (close at hand). But they hastened with the same

celeritate adverso colle at nostra castra, atque ĕos
quickness in (up) the opposite hill to our camps, and those

qui ĕrant occupati in opĕre.
who were occupied in the work.

20. Omnĭa ĕrant agenda Cæsări uno
All (things) were to-be-acted to (by) Cæsar in one

tempŏre; vexillum proponendum, quod ĕrat
time; the standard to-be-set-up, which was

insigne,	quum	oporteret	concurri	ad
the sign,	*when*	*it might behove*	*to be run-together*	*to*
arma:	signum	dandum	tŭbâ:	milĭtes
arms:	*the signal*	*to-be-given*	*with trumpet:*	*the soldiers*

revocandi	ab	opĕre:	qui processĕrant
to-be-recalled	*from*	*the work:*	*(those) who had proceeded*

paullò	longiùs,	caussâ	aggĕris
a little	*farther,*	*by cause* (for the sake)	*of the rampart*

	petendi,	accersendi,	acies
(materials)	*to-be-sought*	*(were) to-be-sent-for;*	*the line*

	instruenda:	milĭtes	cohortandi:
(of battle)	*to be arranged:*	*the soldiers*	*to-be-exhorted:*

signum	dandum.	Magnam	partem	quarum rerum
the signal	*to-be-given.*	*A great*	*part*	*of which things*

brevĭtas	tempŏris,	et	successus	et incursus
the shortness	*of the time,*	*and*	*the coming-up*	*and charge*

hostĭum	impediebat.	Dŭæ	res	ĕrant subsidĭo
of the enemies	*did hinder.*	*Two*	*things*	*were for aid*

his	difficultatĭbus,	scientĭa	atque	usus
to these	*difficulties,*	*the knowledge*	*and*	*experience*

milĭtum,	quòd,	exercitati	superiorĭbus
of the soldiers,	*because,*	*being exercised*	*in former*

prœlĭis,	potĕrant	ipsi	præscribĕre
battles,	*they were-able*	*themselves*	*to prescribe*

sĭbi	quid	oporteret	fĭĕri,	non mĭnùs
to themselves	*what*	*it might behove*	*to be done,*	*not less*

commŏdè,	quàm	doceri	ab aliis;
conveniently (properly),	*than*	*to be taught*	*by others:*

et	quòd	Cæsar	vetuĕrat	singŭlos	legatos
and	*because*	*Cæsar*	*had forbid*	*the several*	*lieutenants*

discedĕre	ab	opĕre	que	singŭlis legionĭbus,
to depart	*from*	*the work*	*and*	*(their) several legions,*

nĭsi	castris	munitis.	Hi,	propter
unless	*the camps*	*being fortified.*	*These,*	*on-account-of*

propinquitatem	et	celeritatem	hostĭum,
the nearness	*and*	*swiftness*	*of the enemies,*

spectabant	nihil	jam	imperium	Cæsăris;
did regard (await)	*not-at-all*	*now*	*the command*	*of Cæsar:*

sed	per	se,	administrabant	quæ
but	*by*	*themselves,*	*did manage*	*what (things)*

videbantur.
did seem (fit).

21. Necessariis rebus imperatis, Cæsar
The necessary things being commanded, Cæsar

decucurrit	ad	milites	cohortandos	in partem,
ran-down	*to*	*the soldiers*	*to-be-encouraged*	*into a part,*

quam	fors	obtulit;	et devenit	ad decimam
which	*chance*	*presented;*	*and came-down*	*to the tenth*

legionem.	Cohortatus-est	milites	non	longiore
legion.	*He encouraged*	*the soldiers*	*not*	*with longer*

oratio,	quàm	uti	retinerent	memoriam
speech,	*than*	*that*	*they should retain*	*the memory*

suæ	pristinæ	virtutis,	neu perturbarentur	animo
of their	*former*	*valour,*	*nor should be troubled*	*in mind*

que	sustinerent	fortiter	impetum	hostium;
and	*should sustain*	*bravely*	*the attack*	*of the enemies:*

et,	quòd	hostes	aberant	non longius,
and,	*because*	*the enemies*	*were-distant*	*not farther,*

quàm	quò	telum	posset adjici,	dedit
than	*whither*	*a dart*	*might be-able to be cast,*	*he gave*

signum	prœlii committendi:	atque	profectus
the signal	*of battle to be engaged:*	*and*	*having set-out*

item	in	alteram	partem,	caussâ
likewise	*into*	*another*	*part,*	*by cause (for the sake*

cohortandi,	occurrit	pugnantibus.	Tanta
of encouraging,	*he meets (them)*	*fighting.*	*So-great (such*

fuit	exiguitas	temporis,	que tam paratus	animus
was	*the smallness*	*of the time,*	*and so prepared*	*the mind*

hostium	ad	dimicandum,	ut tempus	defuerit
of the enemies	*to*	*contending,*	*that time*	*was wanting*

(perf. subj.)	non	modò ad	insignia	accommodanda,
	not	*only to*	*the ensigns*	*to-be-arranged,*

DE BELLO GALLICO. [22

sed	etïam	ad	galĕas	induendas,	que	tegmenta
but	even	to	the helmets	to-be-put-on,	and	the coverings

detrahenda	scutis.	In	quam	partem
to-be-drawn-off	from the shields.	Into	what	part

quisque	devenit	casu	ab	opĕre,	que	quæ
each	came-down	by chance	from	the work,	and	what

signa	conspexit	prima,	constĭtit	ad	'.æc,	ne
standards	he beheld	first,	he stood	at	these,	lest

dimittĕret	tempus	pugnandi	in	quærendo
he might let-slip	the time	of fighting	in	seeking

suos.
his-own (comrades).

22. | Exercĭtu | instructo, | măgis | ut | natura |
|---|---|---|---|---|
| The army | being arranged, | rather | as | the nature |

lŏci	que	dejectus	collis,	et	necessĭtas
of the place	and	the declivity	of the hill,	and	the necessity

tempóris	postulabat,	quàm	ut	ratĭo	atque
of the time	did require,	than	as	the plan	and

ordo	militaris	rĕi ;	quum	alïæ	legiones
arrangement	of military	affair ;	when	other	legions

in	aliâ	parte	resistĕrent (imp. subj.)
in	another	part	did resist (i. e. some in one part, some

hostĭbus	diversis	lŏcis,	que
in another)	to the enemies	in different	places,	and

densissĭmis	sepĭbus	interjectis,	ut	demon-
very-thick	hedges	being thrown-between,	es	we have

stravĭmus	antè,	prospectus	impediretur (imp. subj.) :
shown	before,	the view	was impeded :

nĕque	certa	subsidia	potĕrant	collocari,	nĕque
neither	sure	reserves	were able	to be placed,	nor

provideri,	quid	esset	ŏpus	in	quâque
to be foreseen,	what	might be	needful	in	each

parte ;	nĕque	omnĭa	imperĭa	administrari	ab
part ;	nor	all	the orders	to be managed	by

uno.	Ităque,	in	tantâ	iniquitate
one,	Therefore,	in	so-great	unfavourableness

23] LIBER II. 119

rerum,	varii	eventus	fortunae	quŏque	sequebantur.
of things,	*various*	*events*	*of fortune*	*also*	*did follow.*

23. Milites nonæ et decĭmæ legionis,
The soldiers of the ninth and tenth legion,

ut constitĕrant in sinistrâ parte aciei,
as they had stood in the left part of the line, (their)

pilis emissis, celerĭter compulerunt ex
jacelins being thrown, quickly forced from

superiore lŏco in flumen. Atrebates, (nam
the higher place into the river the Atrebates, (for

ĕa pars obvenĕrat his) exanimatos cursu
that part had chanced to these) spent with running

ac lassitudĭne, que confectos vulnerĭbus;
and fatigue, and finished (exhausted) with wounds ;

et insecuti gladĭis conantes
and having pursued with swords (them) endeavouring

transire, interfecerunt magnam partem eorum
to cross-over, they killed a great part of them

impeditam. Ipsi dubitaverunt non transire flumen;
encumbered. They hesitated not to cross the river ;

et progressi in iniquum lŏcum,
and having advanced into an unfavourable place,

dederunt in fŭgam hostes regressos
gave (put) into flight the enemies having returned

rursus ac resistentes, proelĭo redintegrato. Item
again and resisting, the battle being renewed. Also

in alĭâ parte, dŭæ diversæ legiones, undecĭma
in another part, two different legions, the eleventh

et octava, Veromandŭis profligatis, cum quĭbus
and eighth, the Veromandui being routed, with whom

congressi-ĕrant, proeliabantur ex superiore
they had encountered, did fight from the higher

lŏco in ripis ipsis flumĭnis. At
place in (on) the banks themselves of the river But

totis castris fĕrè nudatis à fronte
the whole camps nearly being exposed from the front

et	à	sinistrâ	parte,	cùm	duodecīma	legĭo
and	from	the left	part (side),	when	the twelfth	legion,

et	septĭma	non	magno	intervallo	ab	ĕâ,
and	the seventh	not	in great	distance	from	it

constitisset (pl. perf. subj.)	in	dextro	cornu
had stood-together	in	the right	wing,

omnes	Nervĭi	confertissĭmo	agmĭne,	duce
all	the Nervii	in closest	troop (array),	the leader

Boduognato,	qui	tenebat	summam
(being) Boduognatus,	who	did hold	the chief-place

imperĭi,	contenderunt	ad	ĕum	lŏcum:	pars
of command,	hastened	to	that	place:	part

quorum	cœpit	circumvenire	legiones	aperto
of whom	began	to surround	the legions	(on) the open

latĕre	pars petĕre	summum lŏcum castrorum.
flank,	part to seek (attack)	the highest place of the camps.

24. Eodem	tempŏre	nostri	equĭtes	que	pedĭtes
In the same	time	our	cavalry	and	infantry

lĕvis	armaturæ,	qui	iuĕrant	unà	cum	his,
of light	armour,	who	had been	together	with	these,

quos	dixĕram	pulsos(-esse)	primo	impĕtu
whom	I had said	to have been routed	in the first	attack

hostĭum,	cùm	recipĕrent (imp. subj.)	se
of the enemies,	when	they did betake	themselves

in	castra,	occurrebant	hostĭbus	adversis
into	camps,	did meet	to the enemies	opposite (in front)

ac	rursus	petebant	fŭgam	in	alĭam	partem.
and	again	did seek	flight	into	another	part.

Et	calones,	qui	conspexĕrant	à
And	the soldiers'-servants,	who	had beheld	from

Decumanâ	portâ,	ac	summo	jŭgo	collis
the Decuman	gate,	and	the highest	ridge	of the hill

nostros	victores	transire	flumen,	egressi
our (men)	conquerors	to cross	the river,	having gone-out

caussâ	prædandi,	quum	respex-
by cause (for the sake)	of plundering,	when	they had

issent (pluperf. subj.)	et	vidissent	(pluperf. subj.)
looked-back	*and*	*had seen*	

hostes	versari	in	nostris castris,	præcipites
the enemies	*to be engaged*	*in*	*our camps,*	*hasty*

mandabant	sese	fugæ:	simul
did commit	*themselves*	*to flight:*	*at the same-time*

clamor	que	fremitus	eorum	qui veniebant	cum
the cry	*and*	*uproar*	*of those*	*who did come*	*with*

impedimentis	oriebatur,	que	alii
the baggage-waggons	*did arise,*	*and*	*others* (some)

perterriti	ferebantur	in aliam	partem.
dismayed	*were borne*	*into another* (one)	*part,* (*others*

	Omnibus	quibus rebus	Treviri
into another part).	*By all*	*which things,*	*the Trevirian*

equites	permoti,	virtutis	quorum est
cavalry	*being alarmed,*	*of the valour*	*of whom there is*

singularis	opinio	inter	Gallos, qui
a singular (very high)	*opinion*	*among*	*the Gauls, who*

missi	caussâ	auxilii à	civitate,
being sent	*by cause* (for the sake)	*of aid by*	*the state,*

venerant ad Cæsarem,	quum	vidissent (pluperf. subj.)
had come to Cæsar,	*when*	*they had seen*

nostra castra	compleri	multitudine hostium,
our camps	*to be filled*	*with a multitude of the enemies,*

legiones	premi,	et teneri	penè
the legions	*to be pressed,*	*and to be held*	*almost*

circumventas,	calones,	equites,	Numidas
surrounded,	*the soldiers'-servants,*	*cavalry,*	*Numidian*

funditores,	diversos que dissipatos	fugere	in omnes
slingers,	*apart and scattered*	*to flee*	*into all*

partes, nostris rebus	desperatis,	contenderunt
parts, our things (affairs)	*being despaired of*	*hastened*

domum;	renuntiaverunt	civitati,	Romanos pulsos
home;	*they announced*	*to the state,*	*the Romans routed*

que	superatos,	hostes potitos	castris
and	*overcome,*	*the enemies having possessed*	*the camps*

que	impedimentis	eorum.
and	*baggage-waggons*	*of them.*

25. Caesar   profectus   ab   cohortatione
    Caesar   *having set-out*   *from*   *the exhortation*

decimae   legionis   ad   dextrum   cornu,   ubi   vidit
f the tenth *legion*   *to*   *the right*   *wing,*   *when*   *he saw*

suos   urgeri,   que   signis
his (men)   *to-be-pressed-hard,*   *and*   *the standards*

collatis   in   unum   locum,   milites
being brought-together   *into* *one*   *place,*   *the soldiers*

duodecimae   legionis   confertos   esse   impedi-
of the twelfth *legion*   *close-together*   *to-be*   *for an impe-*

mento   sibi-ipsis   ad   pugnam,   omnibus   centurionibus
diment   *to themselves*   *to* *battle;* *all*   *the centurions*

quartae   cohortis   occisis,   que   signi-
of the fourth *cohort*   *being killed,*   *and*   *the standard*

fero   interfecto,   signo   amisso,   fere   omnibus
bearer   *being slain,*   *the standard*   *being lost,*   *almost* *all*

centurionibus   reliquarum   cohortium,   aut
the centurions   *of the remaining*   *cohorts,*   *either*

vulneratis   aut   occisis,   in   his
being wounded   *or*   *killed,*   *in* (among)   *these*

primopilo   Publio   Sextio   Baculo,   fortissimo
the first-centurion *Publius*   *Sextius*   *Baculus,*   *a very-brave*

viro,   confecto   multis   que   gravibus   vulneribus,
man,   *being spent*   *with many*   *and*   *heavy*   *wounds,*

ut   jam   posset (imp. subj.)   non   sustinere
(so) that *now*   *he was able*   *not*   *to support*

se;   reliquos   esse   tardiores,   et   nonnullos
himself;   *the rest*   *to be*   *more-slow,*   *and*   *some*

desertos   à   novissimis   excedere   prœlio,
being deserted   *by*   *the rear*   *to depart*   *from the battle,*

ac   vitare   tela;   hostes   neque   inter
and   *to avoid*   *the weapons;*   *the enemies*   *neither*   *to inter-*

mittere,   subeuntes   à   fronte   ex
mit,   *going-up* (advancing)   *from*   *the front*   *from*

inferiore   loco,   et   instare   ab   utroque
the lower   *place* (ground),   *and*   *to press-on*   *from*   *either*

LIBER II.

latĕre,	et	rem	esse	in	angusto,
flank,	and	the affair	to be	in	a narrow (critical state)

nĕque	esse	ullum	subsidĭum,	quod	posset
neither	to be	any	aid,	which	might be-able

submitti;	scuto	detracto	uni
to be sent-up;	a shield	being drawn-away	to (from) one

milĭti	ab	novissĭmis	(quòd	ipse	venĕrat
soldier	from	the latest (rear)	(because	himself	had come

ĕò	sĭne	scuto)	processit	in	primam
thither	without	a shield)	he advanced	into	the first

aciem;	que	centurionĭbus	appellatis	nominatim,
line;	and	the centurions	being called	by-name,

cohortatus	relĭquos,	jussit	milĭtes
having encouraged	the rest,	he commanded	the soldiers

inferre	signa,	et	laxare
to bear-on	the standards,	and	to loosen (widen)

manipŭlos,	quò	possent	uti
the companies.	in-order-that	they might be-able	to use

gladĭis (abl.)	facilĭùs.	Spe	illatâ
(their) swords	more-easily.	Hope	being brought-in

militĭbus	adventu	ejus,	ac	anĭmo
to the soldiers	by the arrival	of him,	and	mind (spirit)

redintegrato,	quum	quisque	pro	se	cupĕret
being renewed,	when	every-one	for	himself	did desire

(imp. subj.)	navare	opĕram
	to ply	(his) endeavour (to act with vigour)

in	conspectu	Imperatoris,	etĭam	in	sŭis	extremis
in	sight	of the General,	even	in	his	extreme

rebus.	impĕtus	hostĭum	tardatus-est paullùm.
affairs (danger),	the violence of the enemies was retarded a-little.

26. | Quum | Cæsar | vidisset (pluperf. subj.) | septĭmam |
|---|---|---|---|
| When | Cæsar | had seen | the seventh |

legionem,	quæ	constitĕrat	juxtà,	urgeri
legion,	which	had stood	near,	to be pressed

ĭtem	ab	hoste,	monŭit	tribunos	milĭtum,
likewise	by	the enemy,	he advised	the tribunes	of soldiers,

ut	legiones	conjungĕrent	sese	paullatim,	et
that	*the legions*	*should join*	*themselves*	*gradually,*	*and*

inferrent	signa	conversa
should-bear-on	*the standards*	*turned (on different sides. i. e.*

	in	hostes.	Quo	facto,
with double front)	*against*	*the enemies.*	*Which*	*being done,*

quum	alii		ferrent (imp. subj.)	subsidium
when	*others* (some)		*did bring*	*aid*

aliis	nĕque	timerent (imp. subj.)	ne	aversi
to others	*nor*	*did fear*	*lest*	*being turned*

circumvenirentur	ab	noste,	cœperunt
they might be surrounded	*by*	*the enemy,*	*they began*

resistĕre	audaciŭs	ac	pugnare	fortius.
to resist	*more-boldly*	*and*	*to fight*	*more-bravely.*

Intĕrim	milĭtes	duarum	legionum,	quæ
Meanwhile	*the soldiers*	*of the two*	*legions,*	*which*

fuĕrant	in	novissimo	agmine	præsidio
had been	*in*	*the last*	*troop* (rear)	*for protection*

impedimentis,	prœlio	nuntiato,	cursu
to the baggages,	*the battle*	*being announced,*	*(their) course*

incitato,	conspiciebantur	in	summo
being accelerated,	*were beheld*	*on*	*the highest* (the top

	colle	ab	hostibus:	et	Titus	Labienus
of)	*the hill*	*by*	*the enemies:*	*and*	*Titus*	*Labienus*

potitus	castris (abl.)	hostium,	et
having possessed	*the camps*	*of the enemies,*	*and*

conspicatus	ex	superiore	lŏco,	quæ	res
having beheld	*from*	*the higher*	*place,*	*what*	*things*

gererentur (imp. subj.)	in	nostris	castris,	misit
were carried-on	*in*	*our*	*camps.*	*sent*

decĭmam	legionem	subsidio	nostris;	qui
the tenth	*legion*	*for* (as) *aid*	*to our* (men);	*who*

quum	cognovissent (pl. perf. subj.)	ex	fŭgâ
when	*they had known*	*from*	*the flight*

equitum	et	calonum,	in	quo
of the cavalry	*and*	*of the soldiers'-servants,*	*in*	*what*

LIBER II.

lŏco	res	esset (imp. subj.),	que
place (situation)	*the affair*	*was,*	*and*

quanto	pericŭlo	et	castra	et	legiones
in how-great	*danger*	*both*	*the camps*	*and*	*legions*

et	Imperator	versaretur,	fecerunt	nĭhil
and	*the Commander*	*might-be,*	*made*	*nothing*

relĭqui	sĭbi	ad	celeritatem.
of left (left nothing undone)	*for themselves*	*to*	*speed.*

27 Tanta	commutatĭo	rerum	facta-est
So-great	*a change*	*of things*	*was made*

adventu	horum,	ut	nostri	etĭam	qui
by the arrival	*of these,*	*that*	*our (men)*	*even*	*who*

procubuissent (pluperf. subj.)	confecti	vulnerĭbus,
had lain-down	*spent*	*with wounds,*

innixi	scutis,	redintegrarent (imp. subj.)
having leaned	*to* (on) *the shields,*	*did renew*

prœlĭum.	Tum	calones	conspicati
the battle.	*Then*	*the soldiers'-servants*	*having beheld*

hostes	perterrĭtos,	etĭam	inermes	occurrĕrent
the enemies	*dismayed,*	*even*	*unarmed*	*did oppose*

(imp. subj.)	armatis:	equĭtes	vero,
	the armed (enemies):	*the cavalry*	*indeed,*

ut	delerent	turpitudĭnem	fugæ	virtute,
that	*they might blot-out*	*the disgrace*	*of flight*	*by valour,*

pugnabant in omnĭbus lŏcis,	quò	præferrent
did fight in all places,	*in-order-that*	*they might prefer*

se	legionarĭis	militĭbus.	At
themselves (surpass)	*to the legionary*	*soldiers.*	*But*

hostes,	etĭam	in	extremâ	spe	salutis,
the enemies,	*even*	*in*	*extreme* (last)	*hope*	*of safety*

præstiterunt	tantam	virtutem,	ut,	quum
performed (exhibited)	*so-great*	*valour,*	*that,*	*when*

primi	eorum	cecidissent	proxĭmi	insis-
the first	*of them*	*might have-fallen*	*the nearest*	*would*

tĕrent	jacentĭbus,	atque	pugnarent
stand-on	*(those) lying-down* (the slain),	*and*	*would fight*

ex corporibus eorum: his dejectis, et
from the bodies of them: these being prostrated, and

cadaveribus coacervatis qui
the dead-bodies being heaped-up (so that) (those) who

superessent, conjicĕrent tela in nostros ac ex
might remain, would hurl the darts upon our (men) as from

tumŭlo, que remittĕrent intercepta pila:
a hillock, and would hurl-back the intercepted javelins:

ut deberet (imp. subj.) judicari non nequidquam
so-that it ought to be judged not in vain

homĭnes tantæ virtutis ausos-esse transire
men of so-great valour to have dared to cross

latissĭmum flumen, ascendĕre altissĭmas ripas,
a very-broad river, to ascend very-high banks,

subire iniquissĭmum lŏcum; quæ
to go-up a most-unfavourable place: which (things)

magnitudo anĭmi redegĕrat
the greatness of (their) mind had reduced (had rendered)

facilia ex difficillĭmis.
easy from most-difficult.

28. Hoc prœlio facto, et gente
This battle being made (fought), and the nation

ac nomĭne Nerviorum redacto prŏpè ad
and name of the Nervii being reduced nearly to

internecionem: majores natu,
utter-destruction: (those) greater by birth (the elders),

quos dixeramus collectos unà cum puĕris
whom we had said being collected together with the boys

que mulierĭbus in æstuariâ ac paludes, ha
and women into the estuaries (swamps) and marshes, thi

pugnâ nuntiatâ, quum arbitrarentur (imp. subj.)
battle being announced, when they did think

nihil impeditum victorĭbus, nihil
nothing entangled (an obstacle) to the conquerors, nothing

tutum victis; consensu omnium, qui
safe to the conquered; by consent of all, who

superĕrant,	miserunt	legatos	ad	Caesărem	que
did remain,	sent	ambassadors	to	Caesar	and

dediderunt	se	ĕi:	et	in	calamitate
surrendered	themselves	to him:	and	in	the calamity

civitatis	commemorandâ,	dixerunt:	sese
of the state	to-be-recounted,	they said:	themselves

esse	redactos	ex	sexcentis	ad tres	senatores;
to be	reduced	out-of	six-hundred	to three	senators;

ex	sexaginta	millĭa	homĭnum,	ad	vix
out-of	sixty	thousands	of men,	to	scarcely

quingentos,	qui	possent	ferre arma;	quos
five-hundred,	who	might be-able	to bear arms;	whom

Caesar	conservavit	diligentissĭmè,	que jussit
Caesar	preserved	most-carefully,	and commanded

uti	súis	finĭbus	atque oppĭdis,	ut
to use	with their-own	territories	and towns,	that

videretur	usus	misericordĭâ	in
he might seem	having used	with compassion	unto

misĕros	ac	supplĭces;	et imperavit
the wretched	and	suppliant;	and ordered

finitĭmus	ut	prohiberent
to the neighbouring (people)	that	they would prohibit (restrain)

se	que	súos	ab	injurĭâ	et
themselves	and	their-own (people)	from	injury	and

maleficĭo.
malice.

29. | | | | | |
|---|---|---|---|---|
| Aduatĭci, | de | quĭbus | scripsĭmus | supra, |
| The Aduatici, | of | whom | we have written | above, |

quum	venirent (imp. subj.)	omnĭbus	copĭis
when	they did come	with all	(their) forces

auxilĭo	Nervĭis,	hâc pugnâ	nuntiatâ,
for (as) aid	to the Nervii,	this battle	being announced,

reverterunt	dŏmum	ex itinĕre;	cunctis
returned	home	from the journey (march);	all

oppĭdis	que castellis	desertis,	ontulerunt
the towns	and castles	being deserted,	they brought-together

omnĭa	sŭa	in	unum	oppĭdum	egregĭè
all	*their (effects)*	*into*	*one*	*town*	*excellently*

munitum	naturâ:	quum	quod	haberet
fortified	*by nature:*	*when*	*which (town)*	*aid have*

(imp. subj.) altissĭmas rupes que despectus
very-high rocks and views (precipices)

ex	omnĭbus	partĭbus	in circuĭtu,
out-of	*all*	*parts*	*in compass* (all round).

adĭtus	lenĭter	acclivis	relinquebatur,	ex unâ
an access	*gently*	*steep*	*was left,*	*from one*

parte, non amplĭùs ducentis pĕdum in
part, not more (than) two-hundred of feet into (in)

latitudĭnem:	quem	lŏcum	munĭerant
breadth:	*which*	*place*	*they had fortified*

altissĭmo duplĭci muro: tum collocârant
with a very-high double wall: then they had placed

saxa	magni	pondĕris,	et	præacutas trăbes
stones	*of great*	*weight,*	*and*	*sharp-pointed beams*

in muro. Ipsi ĕrant prognati ex Cimbris
on the wall. They were descended from the Cimbri

que Teutŏnis. qui, quum facĕrent (imp. subj.)
and Teutoni: who, when they did make

ĭter in nostram Provincĭam atque Italĭam,
(their) march into our Province and Italy,

his impedimentis, quæ potĕrant non agĕre
those baggages, which they were-able not to act

ac portare secum, deposĭtis
(manage) *and to carry with them, being deposited*

citra flumen Rhenum, reliquerunt unà
on-this-side the river Rhine, they left together

sex	millĭa	homĭnum	ex	sŭis custodĭæ
six	*thousands*	*of men*	*out-of*	*their-own for a guard*

ac præsidĭo. Hi, post obĭtum eorum,
and protection. These, after the death of them,

exagitati multos annos à finitĭmis,
being harassed many years by (their) neighbours,

| quum | alĭas | | inferrent (imp. subj.) |
| when | otherwise (sometimes) | | they did bring on |

| bellum, | alĭas | | defendĕrent (imp. |
| war, | otherwise (at another time) | | did repel (it) |

| subj.) | illatum, | pace | factâ | consensu |
| | brought-on, | a peace | being made | by consent |

| omnĭum, | delegerunt | hunc | lŏcum | domicilĭo. |
| of all, | chose | this | place | for an abode. |

30. | Ac | primo | adventu | nostri | exercĭtûs, |
| And | in the first | arrival | of our | army, |

| faciebant | crebras | excursiones | | ex |
| they did make | frequent | excursions (sallies) | | from |

| oppĭdo, | que | contendebant | parvŭlis | prœliis |
| the town, | and | did contend | in trifling | battles |

| cum | nostris. | Postĕa | | circummuniti |
| with | our (men). | Afterwards | | being fortified-around |

| vallo | duodĕcim | pĕdum, | quindĕcim | millĭum |
| with a rampart | of twelve | feet, | fifteen | thousand |

| | in | circuĭtu, | que | crebris | |
| (feet) | in | compass, | and | with frequent (numerous) |

| castellis, | continebant | sese | oppĭdo. |
| castles, | they did contain | themselves | in the town. |

| Ubi, | , vinĕis | actis, | | aggĕre |
| When, | the mantelets | being acted (advanced), | | a mound |

| exstructo, | viderunt | turrim | constitŭi |
| being constructed, | they saw | a tower | to be erected |

| prŏcul, | | primùm | irridere | ex |
| at-a-distance, | (they began) | firstly | to mock | from |

| muro | atque | increpitare | vocĭbus : | quò |
| the wall | and | to chide | by sayings : | whither (to |

| | tanta | machinatĭo | institueretur |
| what purpose) | so-great | a machine | might be constructed |

| ab | tanto | spatĭo! | quibusnam | manĭbus, |
| from | so-great | a space (distance)! | with what | hands, |

| aut | quĭbus | virĭbus, | confidĕrent | sese |
| or | with what | forces, | might they trust | themseives |

M

collocare	turrim	tanti	onĕris	in	muros,
to place	*a tower*	*of so-great*	*burden*	*against*	*the walls,*

præsertim	homĭnes	tantŭlæ	staturæ,	(nam nostra
especially	*men*	*of so-little*	*stature,*	*(for our*

brevĭtas	est	contemptŭi	plerisque	Gallis hominĭbus,
shortness	*is*	*for contempt*	*to most*	*Gallic men,*

præ   magnitudĭne   suorum
before (in comparison with) *the magnitude*   *of their-own*

corpŏrum).
bodies).

31.

Verò	ŭbi	viderunt	moveri,	et
But	*when*	*they saw (it)*	*to be moved,*	*and*

appropinquare	mœnĭbus,	commoti	nŏvâ
to approach	*to the walls,*	*being alarmed*	*by the new*

et	inusitatâ	specĭe,	miserunt	legatos ad
and	*unusual*	*appearance,*	*they sent*	*ambassadors to*

Cæsărem	de	pace:	qui locuti (-sunt)	ad hunc
Cæsar	*about*	*peace:*	*who spoke*	*to this*

mŏdum:	Se	existimare	Romănos gerĕre
manner:	*Themselves*	*to think*	*the Romans to carry-on*

bellum	non	sĭne	ŏpe	Deorum, qui
war	*not*	*without*	*the assistance*	*of the Gods, who*

possent	promovere	machinationes tantæ
might be able	*to move-forward*	*machines of so-great*

altitudĭnis	tantâ	celeritate,	et pugnare	ex
height	*with so-great*	*speed,*	*and to fight*	*from*

propinquitate:	dixerunt	permittĕre se que
nearness (close quarters):	*they said*	*to give-up themselves and*

omnĭa	sŭa	potestati	eorum:	petĕre
all	*their (effects)*	*to the power*	*of them:*	*to seek*

ac	deprecari	unum,	si pro	sŭâ
and	*to beg*	*one (thing),*	*if for* (according-to)	*his*

clementĭâ	ac	mansuetudĭne,	quam ipsi	audîssent
clemency	*and*	*mildness,*	*which they*	*had heard*

(pluperf. subj.)	ab	aliis, statuisset
	from	*others,* *he might have determined*

| 32] | | LIBER II. | | 131 |

| fortè | Aduaticos | esse | conservandos, |
| by-chance (perhaps) | the Aduatici | to be | to-be-preserved. |

| ne-despoliaret | se | armis : | omnes |
| he would not-deprive | themselves | from (of) arms : | all |

| finitimos | fĕrè | esse | inimicos | sĭbi, | ac |
| the neighbours | nearly | to be | hostile | to themselves, | and |

| invidere | sŭæ | virtuti, | à | quĭbus | possent |
| to envy | to their | valour, | from | whom | they might be-able |

| non | defendĕrc | se, | armis | tradĭtis ; |
| not | to defend | themselves, | (their) arms | being delivered ; |

| præstare | sĭbi | păti | quamvis |
| to excel (to be better) | for themselves | to endure | any |

| fortunam | à | Romano | popŭlo, | si | deducerentur |
| fortune | from | the Roman | people, | if | they should be led |

| in | ĕum | casum, | quàm | interfĭci | ab | his | inter |
| into | that | calamity, | than | to be slain | by | those | among |

| quos | consuêssent (pluperf. subj.) | dominari. |
| whom | they had been accustomed | to rule. |

32. Caesar respondit ad hæc : Se
 Cæsar answered to these (words): Himself

| conservaturum | civitatem | măgis | sŭâ | consuetudĭne |
| about-to-preserve | the state | rather | by his | custom |

| quàm | merĭto | eorum, | si | dedidissent |
| than | by the merit | of them, | if | they might have surrendered |

| se, | priùs-quàm | aries | attigisset |
| themselves, | before-that | the battering-ram | might have touched |

| murum : | sed | nullam | conditionem | deditionis | esse, |
| the wall : | but | no | condition | of surrender | to be, |

| nĭsi | armis | tradĭtis : | se | facturum |
| unless | the arms | being delivered-up : | himself | about-to-do |

| id, | quod | fecisset (pluperf. subj.) | in | Nervĭos ; |
| that, | which | he had done | | unto | the Nervii ; |

| que | imperaturum | finitĭmis, |
| and | about-to-order | to the neighbouring (people), |

| ne-inferrent | quam | injurĭam | deditĭtĭis |
| that they should not-bring | any | injury | to the surrendered |

M 2

	Romani	popŭli.	Re	nuntiatâ
(subjects)	of the Roman	people.	The thing	being announced

ad	sŭos,	illi	dixerunt	se	facĕre,	quæ
to	their-own,	they	said	themselves	to do,	what

	imperarentur.	Magnâ	multitudĭne	armorum
(things)	might be ordered.	A great	multitude	of arms

jactâ	de	muro	in	fossam,	quæ	ĕrat
being thrown	from	the wall	into	the ditch	which	was

ante	oppĭdum,	sic	ut	acervi	armorum
before	the town,	so	that	the heaps	of arms

adæquarent (imp. subj.)	propè	summam	altitudĭnem
did equal	nearly	the highest	height

muri	que	aggĕris :	et	tămen	circĭter
of the wall	and	of the mound :	and	however	about

tertĭâ	parte	celatâ,	(ut	perspectum-est
a third	part	being concealed,	(as	was clearly-seen

posteă,)	atque	retentâ	in	oppĭdo,	portis
afterwards,)	and	being retained	in	the town,	the gates

patefactis,	usi-sunt	pace (abl.)	ĕo
being thrown-open,	they used (enjoyed)	peace	on that

die.
day.

33. | Sub | | vespĕrum | Cæsar | jussit |
|---|---|---|---|---|
| Under (towards) | | evening | Cæsar | ordered |

portas	claudi,	que	milĭtes	exire
the gates	to be shut,	and	the soldiers	to go-out

ex	oppĭdo,	ne	oppidani	accipĕrent	quam
from	the town,	lest	the townsmen	might receive	any

injurĭam	à	militĭbus	noctu.	Illi,	consilio
injury	from	the soldiers	by night.	They,	a plan

inĭto	antè,	ut	intellectum-est,	quòd,
being entered-into	before,	as	it was understood,	because,

deditione	factâ,	credidĕrant	nostros
the surrender	being made,	they had believed	our (people)

non	inducturos	præsidia,	aut	denĭque
not	about-to-introduce	garrisons,	or	in-fine

LIBER II.

servaturos	indiligentius:	partim	cum
about-to-keep (watch)	*very-carelessly:*	*partly*	*with*

his	armis,	quæ	retinuerant	et	celaverant,
those	*arms,*	*which*	*they had retained*	*and*	*had concealed,*

partim	scutis	factis	ex	cortice,	aut	intextis
partly	*with shields*	*made*	*out-of*	*bark,*	*or*	*woven*

viminibus,	quæ	induxerant	pellibus
twigs,	*which*	*they had laid-on (covered)*	*with hides*

subito	(ut	exiguitas	temporis,	postulabat),
suddenly	*(as*	*the smallness*	*of the time*	*did require),*

fecerunt	eruptionem	repente	ex	oppido	omnibus
made	*a sally*	*suddenly*	*from*	*the town*	*with all*

copiis,	tertia	vigilia,	qua	ascensus	ad
the forces,	*in the third*	*watch,*	*where*	*the ascent*	*to*

nostras	munitiones	videbatur	minime	arduus.
our	*fortifications*	*did seem*	*least*	*difficult.*

Significatione	factâ	celeriter	ignibus,	ut	Cæsar
A signal	*being made*	*quickly*	*by fires,*	*as*	*Cæsar*

imperaverat	ante,	concursum-est	eo	ex
had ordered	*before,*	*it was run-together*	*thither*	*from*

proximis	castellis;	que	pugnatum (-est)	ab
the nearest	*castles;*	*and*	*it was fought*	*by*

hostibus	ita	acriter,	ut	debuit	pugnari
the enemies	*so*	*vigorously,*	*as*	*it ought*	*to be fought*

à	fortibus	viris	in	extremâ	spe	salutis,
by	*brave*	*men*	*in*	*the last*	*hope*	*of safety,*

iniquo	loco,	contra	eos,	qui	jacerent (imp.
in an unfavorable	*place,*	*against*	*those,*	*who*	*did cast*

subj.)	tela	ex	vallo	que	turribus,	quum
	weapons	*from*	*the rampart*	*and*	*towers,*	*when*

omnis	spes	salutis	consisteret (imp. subj.)	in
all	*hope*	*of safety*	*did consist*	*in*

virtute	unâ.	Ad	quatuor	millibus	hominum
valour	*alone.*	*To (about)*	*four*	*thousands*	*of men*

occisis,	reliqui	rejecti-sunt	in	oppidum.
being killed	*the rest*	*were thrown-back*	*into*	*the town.*

Postridĭe	ejus	diei,	portis	refractis, quum
The-day-after	*of that*	*day,*	*the gates*	*being broken, when*

nemo	jam	defendĕret (imp. subj.),	atque	nostris
no-one	*now*	*did defend,*	*and*	*our*

militĭbus	intromissis,	Cæsar	vendĭdit	universam
soldiers	*being let-in,*	*Cæsar*	*sold*	*the entire*

sectionem	ejus	oppĭdi.	Numĕrus quinquaginta
section (allotment)	*of that*	*town.*	*The number of fifty*

trĭum	millĭum	capĭtum	relatus-est	ab
three	*thousands*	*of heads*	*was brought back* (reported)	*by*

his	qui	emĕrant.
those	*who*	*had bought (them).*

34. Eodem tempŏre factus-est certĭor
In the same time he was made more-sure (was

à	Publio	Crasso,	quem	misĕrat	cum
ınformed) *by*	*Publius*	*Crassus,*	*whom*	*he had sent*	*with*

unâ	legione	ad	Venĕtos,	Unellos, Osismĭos,
one	*legion*	*to*	*the Veneti,*	*Unelli, Osismii,*

Curiosolitas,	Sesuvĭos,	Aulercos,	Rhedŏnes,	quæ
Curiosolitæ,	*Sesuvii,*	*Aulerci,*	*Rhedones,*	*which*

sunt	maritĭmæ	civitates,	que attingunt	oceănum,
are	*maritime*	*states,*	*and touch-on*	*the ocean,*

omnes	ĕas	civitates	redactas-esse	in ditionem
all	*those*	*states*	*to have been-reduced*	*into the authcrity*

que	potestatem	Romani	popŭli.
and	*power*	*of the Roman*	*people.*

35. His rebus gestis, omni Gallĭâ
These things being carried-on, all Gaul

pacatâ,	tantâ	opinĭo	hujus belli
being subdued,	*so-great*	*an opinion*	*of this war*

perlata-est	ad	Barbăros,	ut	legati
was-carried	*to*	*the Barbarians,*	*that*	*ambassadors*

mitterentur (imp. subj.)	ad	Cæsărem	ab nationĭbus,
were-sent	*to*	*Cæsar*	*by the nations,*

quæ	incolĕrent (imp. subj.)	trans	Rhenum, quæ
which	*did inhabit*	*across*	*the Rhine, which*

LIBER II.

pollicerentur (imp. subj.)	se	daturas	obsides,
did promise	*themselves*	*about-to-give*	*hostages,*

facturas		imperata:	quas legationes
about-to-do (the things)		*commanded:*	*which embassies*

Cæsar jussit reverti ad se, proximâ
Cæsar commanded to return to himself, the next

æstate inïtâ, quòd properabat in
summer being entered-on, because he did hasten into

Italïam, que Illyrĭcum. Ipse profectus-est in
Italy, and Illyricum. Himself set-out into

Italïam, legionĭbus deductis in hiberna
Italy, the legions being led-down into winter-quarters

in Carnutes, Andes, Turŏnes, quæ civitates
into the Carnutes, Andes, Turones, which states

ĕrant propinquæ his lŏcis, ŭbi gessĕrat
were neighbouring to those places, where he had carried-on

bellum. Ex litĕris Cæsăris, supplicatĭo
war. From the letters of Cæsar, a general-thanksgiving

quindĕcim dĭes decreta-est ob ĕas
(for) fifteen days was decreed on-account-of those

res: quod accidĕrat nulli ante id
things: which had happened to no-one before that

tempus.
time.

TERTIUS LIBER.
THIRD BOOK.

ARGUMENTUM.
ARGUMENT.

Quinque   bella   gesta   adversus   varias   gentes
Five   wars   carried-on   against   various   nations

Galliæ describuntur hoc libro: primum adversus
of Gaul are described in this book: the first against

Veragros et Sedunos, quod gestum-fuit,
the Veragri and Seduni, which was carried-on,

ipso quidem absente, sed auspiciis
himself indeed (being) absent, but (under his) auspices

à Galbâ legato: secundum, contra
by Galba (his) lieutenant: the second, against

Venetos, quod ipse confecit navali prœlio:
the Veneti, which himself finished by a naval battle:

tertium, quod à legato
the third, which (was carried on) by (his) lieutenant

Titurio Sabino contra Unellos, Aulercos,
Titurius Sabinus against the Unelli, Aulerci,

Eburovices, et Lexovios: quartum, quo
Eburovices, and Lexovii: the fourth, in which

Sontiates et cæteri Aquitani debellati-sunt
the Sontiates and the other Aquitani were subdued

à Publio Crasso: quintum, adversus Morinos
by Publius Crassus: the fifth, against the Morini

et	Menapios,	quod	coactus-est	relinquĕre
and	*Menapii,*	*which*	*he was compelled*	*to leave*
infectum	propter	tempus	anni	Omnia
unfinished	*on-account-of*	*the time*	*of the year.*	*All*
quæ	peracta-sunt	tertio	anno	Gallĭci
which	*were accomplished*	*in the third*	*year*	*of the Gallic*
belli,	qui	fŭit	sexcentesĭmus	nonagesĭmus
war,	*which*	*was*	*the six-hundredth*	*ninetieth*
octavus	ab	urbe	condĭtâ,	Cneïo Lentŭlo
eighth	*from*	*the city*	*being built,*	*Cneius Lentulus*
Marcellino,	Lucio	Marcello	Philippo
Marcellinus,	*Lucius*	*Marcellus*	*Philippus*

Consulĭbus.
(being) Consuls.

1. Quum Cæsar proficisceretur (imp. subj.) in
   When *Cæsar* *did set-out* *into*

Italiam,	misit	Sergium	Galbam	cum duodecĭmâ
Italy,	*he sent*	*Sergius*	*Galba*	*with the twelfth*
legione	et	parte	equitatûs	in Nantuates,
legion,	*and*	*part*	*of the cavalry*	*into the Nantuates,*
Veragros,	que	Sedunos;	qui	pertinent à
Veragri,	*and*	*Seduni;*	*who*	*reach from*
finibus	Allobrŏgum,	et	lăcu	Lemano
the borders	*of the Allobroges,*	*and*	*the lake*	*Lemanus*
et	flumĭne	Rhodăno,	ad	summas
and	*the river*	*Rhone,*	*to*	*the highest (top of the)*
Alpes.	Caussa	mittendi	fŭit,	quòd
Alps.	*The cause*	*of sending (him)*	*was,*	*because*
volebat	ĭter	patefiĕri	per	Alpes,
he did will	*a passage*	*to be laid-open*	*through*	*the Alps,*
quo	mercatores	consueverant	ire	cum
by which	*merchants*	*had been accustomed*	*to go*	*with*
magno	periculo	que magnis	portoriis,	Permisit
great	*danger,*	*and great*	*tolls.*	*He permitted*
huic,	si	arbitraretur	esse	ŏpus,	ŭti
to him,	*if*	*he should think (it)*	*to be*	*necessary,*	*that*

collocaret	legionem	in	iis	locis,	caussâ
he might place	*a legion*	*in*	*those*	*places,*	*by cause*
	hiemandi.	Galba,	aliquot	secundis	
(for the sake)	*of wintering.*	*Galba,*	*some*	*successful*	
prœliis	factis,	que	compluribus	castellis	eorum
battles	*being made,*	*and*	*several*	*castles*	*of them*
expugnatis,	legatis	missis	undique	ad	
being stormed,	*ambassadors*	*being sent*	*from-every-side*	*to*	
eum,	que	obsidibus	datis,	et	pace	factâ,
him,	*and*	*hostages*	*being given,*	*and*	*peace*	*being made,*
constituit	collocare	duas	cohortes	in	
resolved	*to place*	*two*	*cohorts*	*in*	*(among)*
Nantuatibus;	ipse	hiemare	cum	reliquis	
the Nantuates;	*himself*	*to winter*	*with*	*the rest*	
	cohortibus	ejus	legionis,	in	vico
(remaining)	*cohorts*	*of that*	*legion,*	*in*	*a village*
Veragrorum,	qui	appellatur	Octodurus:	qui	
of the Veragri,	*which*	*is called*	*Octodurus:*	*which*	
vicus	positus	in	valle,	non	magnâ	planitie
village	*being placed*	*in*	*a valley,*	*not*	*a great*	*plain*
adjectâ,	continetur	undique	altissimis	
being added,	*is bounded*	*on-every-side*	*by very-high*	
montibus.				
mountains.				

2.
Quum	hic	divideretur (imp subj.)	in	duas
Since	*this*	*was divided*	*into*	*two*
partes	flumine,	concessit	alteram	partem
parts	*by the river,*	*he granted*	*the other* (one)	*part*
ejus	vici	Gallis;	attribuit	alteram
of that	*village*	*to the Gauls;*	*he assigned*	*the other*
relictam vacuam	ab	illis	cohortibus	ad-hiemandum:
left vacant	*by*	*them*	*to the cohorts*	*to-winter:*
munivit	eum locum	vallo	que	fossâ.
he fortified	*that place*	*with a rampart*	*and*	*with a trench.*
Quum	complures	dies	hibernorum	transisset
When	*several*	*days*	*of the winter-quarters*	*had passed*

LIBER III.

(pluperf. subj.)	que	jussisset (pluperf. subj.)	frumentum
	and	he had ordered	corn

comportari	eŏ,	factus-est	certior
to be brought	thither,	he was made	more sure (was in-

	subĭtò	per	exploratores,	omnes
formed)	suddenly	by	scouts,	all (the people)

discessisse	noctu	ex	eâ	parte	vici,
to have departed	by night	from	that	part	of the village,

quam	concessĕrat	Gallis;	que	montes,
which	he had granted	to the Gauls;	and	the mountains,

qui	impenderent (imp. subj.),	teneri	à	max-
which	did impend,	to be held	by	a very-

ĭmâ	multitudĭne	Sedunorum	et	Veragrorum.
great	multitude	of the Seduni	and	of the Veragri.

Id	accidĕrat	de	alĭquot	caussis,	ut
That	had happened	from	some	causes,	that

Galli	capĕrent (imp. subj.)	subĭtò	consilĭum
the Gauls	did take	suddenly	the design

belli	renovandi	que	legionis	opprimendæ.
of the war	to-be-renewed	and	of the legion	to-be-overwhelmed.

Primùm,	quòd	despiciebant	legionem,	propter
First,	because	they did despise	the legions,	on-account-of

paucitatem,	nĕque	ĕam	plenissĭmam,	duabus
(its) fewness,	neither	that	very-full,	two

cohortĭbus	detractis		et	complurĭbus
cohorts	having been drawn-out (of it)	and	many (men)

sigillatim	absentĭbus,	qui	missi-ĕrant	caussâ
individually	(being) absent,	who	had been sent	by cause

	commeatûs	petendi:	tum	etĭam,
(for the purpose)	of provision	to-be-sought:	then	also,

quòd	existimabant	ne	quĭdem	primum
because	they did think	not	indeed (even)	the first

impĕtum	posse	sustineri,		quum
shock	to be able	to be withstood (by the Romans),	when

ipsi	decurrĕrent	ex	montĭbus	in	vallem,
themselves	might run-down	from	the mountains	into	the valley

et	conjicĕrent	tela.	Accedebat,
and	*they might hurl*	*(their) darts.*	*It did approach*

	quòd	dolebant	sŭos	libĕros
(added to this),	*because*	*they did grieve*	*their*	*children*

abstractos	ab	se		nomĭne
being drawn-away	*from*	*themselves*	*(under)*	*the name*

obsĭdum;	et	habebant	persuasum
of hostages;	*and*	*they did have (it)*	*persuaded*

sĭbi	Romanos	conari	occupare	culmĭna
to themselves	*the Romans*	*to endeavour*	*to occupy*	*the tops*

Alpĭum	non	solùm	caussâ	
of the Alps	*not*	*only*	*by cause (for the sake)*	

itinĕris,	sed	etĭam	perpetŭæ	possessionis,
of a way (passage),	*but*	*also*	*of perpetual*	*possession,*

et	adjungĕre	ĕa	lŏca	finitĭmæ
and	*to unite*	*those*	*places*	*to the neighbouring*

provincĭæ.
province.

3. His	nuncĭis	acceptis,	quum
These	*messages (news)*	*being received,*	*when*

nĕque	ŏpus	hibernorŭm,	que	muni-
neither	*the work*	*of the winter-quarters,*	*and*	*the for-*

tiones	essent (imp. subj.)	plenè	perfectæ,	nĕque
tifications	*were*	*fully*	*finished,*	*nor*

esset (imp. subj.)	provisum	sătis	de	frumento,
it was	*provided*	*sufficiently*	*about*	*corn,*

que	relĭquo	commeatu,	quòd,	deditione
and	*the rest (other)*	*provision,*	*because,*	*a surrender*

factâ,	que	obsĭdibus	acceptis,	Galba
being made,	*and*	*hostages*	*being received,*	*Galba*

existimavĕrat	nĭhil	timendum	dè	bello:
had thought	*nothing*	*to-be-feared*	*about*	*war:*

concilĭo	convocato	celerĭter,	cœpit	exquirĕre
council being called-together		*quickly,*	*he began*	*to seek*

sententĭas.	In	quo	concilĭo,	quum
(its) opinions.	*In*	*which*	*council,*	*when (since)*

| tantum | repentini | periculi | accidisset (plup. |
| *so-great* (so much) | *of sudden* | *danger* | *had happened* |

subj.) præter opinionem, ac jam fèrè omnia
contrary-to opinion, and now nearly all

superiora loca conspicerentur (imp. subj.) completa
the higher places were seen filled

multitudine armatorum, neque posset (imp.
with a multitude of armed (men), *neither it was-able*

subj.) veniri subsidio, neque commeatus
to become to aid (secure re-inforcements), *neither provision*

supportari, itineribus interclusis: jam salute
to be brought-up, the ways being shut-up: now safety

prope desperata, nonnullæ sententiæ hujusmodi
nearly being despaired-of, some opinions of this kind

dicebantur; ut, impedimentis relictis, eruptione
were said; that, the baggages being left, a sally

factâ, contenderent ad salutem, iisdem
being made, they should set-out to safety, by the same

itineribus, quibus pervenissent (plup. subj.) eò.
ways, by which they had arrived thither.

Tamen placuit majori parti, hoc consilio
However it pleased to the greater part, this counsel

reservato ad extremum, experiri eventum
being reserved to the last, to try the issue

rēi interim, et defendere castra.
of the thing meanwhile, and to defend the camps.

4. Brevi spatio interjecto,
A short space being cast-between (having elapsed),

vix ut tempus daretur his rebus,
scarcely that time might be given for these things,

quas constituissent (pluperf. subj.), collocandis
which they had resolved, to-be-arranged

atque administrandis, hostes decurrere
and to-be-managed, the enemies (began) *to run-down*

ex omnibus partibus, signo dăto,
from all parts, a sign being given, (und)

conjicĕre lapĭdes que gæsa in vallum.
to hur' stones and heavy darts into the rampart.

Nostri primò repugnare fortĭter intĕgris
Our (men) at first to (did) repulse (resisted) bravely with entire

virĭbus nĕque mittĕre
forces (while their strength was fresh), nor to (did they) cast

ullum telum frustrà ex superiore lŏco: ut
any weapon in-vain from the higher place: as

quæque pars castrorum nudata defensorĭbus
each part of the camps stripped from (of) defenders

videbatur prĕmi, occurrĕre eò, et ferre
did seem to be pressed, to run thither, and to bring

auxilium: sed superari hoc, quòd hostes
aid: but to be surpassed in this, because the enemies

defessi diuturnitate pugnæ excedebant prœlio,
wearied by the length of the fight did retire from battle,

alii succedebant intĕgris virĭbus:
others did succeed with entire (fresh) forces (strength):

nĭhil quarum rerum potĕrat fiĕri à
nothing of which things was-able to be done by

nostris propter paucitatem; ac non
our (men) on-account-of (their) fewness; and not

mŏdò facultas dabatur defesso excedendi
only (no) power was given to a wearied (man) of retiring

ex pugnâ, sed ne quĭdem saucĭo
from the fight, but not indeed (even) to a wounded (man)

relinquendi ejus lŏci, ŭbi constitĕrat, ac
of leaving of that place, where he had stood, and

recipiendi sŭi.
of taking-away of himself.

5. Quum pugnaretur jam continenter amplĭùs
When it was fought now unceasingly more (than)

sex horis, ac non solùm vires sed etĭam
six hours, and not only forces (strength) but also

tela deficĕrent (imp. subj.) nostris, atque
weapons did fail to our (men), and

LIBER III.

hostes	instarent (imp. subj.)	acrius,	que
the enemies	*did press-on*	*more-vigorously,*	*and*

nostris	languidioribus,	cœpissent (pluperf. subj.)
our (men)	*(being) more-faint,*	*had begun*

scindere	vallum	et	complere	fossas,	que
to tear	*the rampart*	*and*	*to fill-up*	*the ditches,*	*and*

res	esset (imp. subj.)	jam	deducta	ad
the affair	*was*	*now*	*led* (brought)	*to*

extremum	casum;	Publius Sextius Baculus,	centurio
the last	*chance;*	*Publius Sextius Baculus,*	*a centurion*

primipili	quem	diximus	confectum (-esse)
of the first-rank	*whom*	*we have said*	*to have been finished*

	compluribus	vulneribus	Nervico
(exhausted)	*with many*	*wounds*	*in the Nervian*

prœlio,	et	item	Caius Volusenus,	tribunus	militum,
battle,	*and*	*also*	*Caius Volusenus,*	*a tribune*	*of soldiers,*

vir	et	magni	consilii	et	virtutis,	accurrunt	ad
a man	*both*	*of great*	*counsel*	*and*	*valour,*	*run-up*	*to*

Galbam,	atque	docent		unam	spem
Galba,	*and*	*teach* (inform him)		*one* (the only)	*hope*

salutis	esse,	si	eruptione	facta,	experirentur
of safety	*to be,*	*if*	*a sally*	*being made,*	*they should try*

extremum	auxilium.	Itaque	centurionibus
the last	*aid.*	*Therefore*	*the centurions*

convocatis,	facit	milites	certiores
being called-together,	*he makes*	*the soldiers*	*more-sure*

	intermitterent	prœlium	paullisper,
(informs them)	*they should intermit*	*the battle*	*a little-while,*

ac	exciperent	tantummodo	tela	missa,
and	*should receive*	*only*	*the weapons*	*sent*

	que	reficerent	se	ex	labore;
(thrown),	*and*	*should refresh*	*themselves*	*from*	*labour;*

post,	signo	dato,	erumperent
afterwards,	*a sign*	*being given,*	*they should burst-forth*

è	castris,	atque	ponerent	omnem	spem
from	*the camps,*	*and*	*should place*	*all*	*hope*

salutis	in	virtute.
of safety	*in*	*valour.*

6. Faciunt, quod jussi-sunt; ac eruptione
   They do, what they were-ordered; and a sally

facta subito omnibus portis, relinquunt
being made suddenly from all the gates, they leave

facultatem hostibus neque cognoscendi quid
power to the enemies neither of knowing what

fieret, neque sui colligendi.
might be done, nor of themselves to-be-collected (of

       Ita, fortuna commutata,
collecting themselves). Thus, fortune being changed,

interficiunt eos circumventos undique, qui
they slay those surrounded on-every-side, who

venerant in spem castrorum potiundorum; et
had come into hope of the camps to-be-possessed; and

ex amplius triginta millibus hominum, (quem
out-of more (than) thirty thousands of men, (which

numerum barbarorum constabat venisse
number of the barbarians it was-manifest to have come

ad castra) plus tertia parte interfecta,
to the camps) more (than) the third part being killed,

conjiciunt in fugam reliquos perterritos; ac
they throw into flight the rest affrighted; and

patiuntur consistere ne quidem in superioribus
suffer (them) to stand not indeed (even) in the higher

locis. Sic omnibus copiis hostium
places. Thus all the forces of the enemies

fusis, que exutis armis, recipiunt
being routed, and stripped-of (their) arms, they betake

se in castra que suas munitiones.
themselves into the camps and their fortifications.

Quo prœlio facto, quòd Galba nolebat
Which battle being made, because Galba was unwilling

tentare fortunam sæpius, atque meminerat
to try fortune too-often, and he had remembered

sese venisse alio consilio
himself to have come with another (different) intention

LIBER III.

in	hiberna,	videbat	occurrisse
into	*winter-quarters,*	*he did see (himself)*	*to have met*

aliis	rebus;	permotus	maxime	inopiâ
to other	*things;*	*being moved*	*chiefly*	*with the want*

frumenti	que	commeatûs:	postero	die,
of corn	*and*	*of provision:*	*on the following*	*day,*

omnibus	ædificiis	ejus	vici	incensis,
all	*the buildings*	*of that*	*village*	*being burned,*

contendit	reverti	in	provinciam:	ac	nullo
he hastened	*to return*	*into*	*the province:*	*and*	*no*

hoste	prohibente,	aut	demorante	iter,	perduxit
enemy	*preventing,*	*or*	*delaying*	*(his) journey,*	*he led*

legionem	incolumem	in	Nantuates,	inde	in
the legion	*safe*	*into*	*the Nantuates,*	*thence*	*into*

Allobroges,	que	hiemavit	ibi.
the Allobroges,	*and*	*he wintered*	*there.*

7. | His | rebus | gestis, | quum | Cæsar |
| *These* | *things* | *being carried-on,* | *when* | *Cæsar* |

existimaret (imp. subj.)	Galliam pacatam	de	omnibus
did think	*Gaul subdued*	*from*	*all*

caussis;	Belgis	superatis,	Germanis
(these) reasons;	*the Belgæ*	*being overcome,*	*the Germans*

expulsis,	Sedunis	in	Alpibus	victis,
being expelled,	*the Seduni*	*in*	*the Alps*	*being conquered,*

atque	ita	hieme	initâ	profectus-esset
and	*thus*	*the winter*	*being entered-on*	*had set-out*

(plup. subj.)	in	Illyricum,	quòd	volebat
	into	*Illyricum,*	*because*	*he did wish*

adire	eas	nationes quoque	et	cognoscere
to go-to	*those*	*nations also*	*and*	*to know (become*

		regiones;	subitum	bellum
acquainted with)		*the countries;*	*a sudden*	*war*

coortum-est	in	Galliâ	Hæc	fuit	caussa	ejus
arose	*in*	*Gaul.*	*This*	*was*	*the cause*	*of that*

belli.	Publius	Crassus	adolescens	hiemabat	cum
war.	*Publius*	*Crassus*	*a young-man*	*did winter*	*with*

septĭmâ	legione	in	Andĭbus	proxĭmus	Oceănum
the seventh	legion	in	the Andes	nearest	the Ocean

măre.	Is	dimisit	complures	præfectos	que
sea.	He	dismissed	many	prefects	and

tribunos	milĭtum	in	finitĭmas	civitates,
tribunes	of soldiers	into	the neighbouring	states,

caussâ		frumenti que	commeatûs
by cause (for the sake)		of corn and	of provision

petendi,	quòd	inopĭa frumenti	ĕrat	in his
to-be-sought,	because	a want of corn	was	in these

lŏcis:	in	quo	numĕro	Titus Terrasidĭus
places:	in	which	number	Titus Terrasidius

missus-ĕrat	in	Eusubĭos;	Marcus Trebĭus
had been sent	unto	the Eusubii;	Marcus Trebius

Gallus	in	Curiosolitas;	Quintus Velanĭus	cum
Gallus	unto	the Curiosolitæ,	Quintus Velanius	with

Tito	Silĭo	in	Venĕtos.
Titus	Silius	unto	the Veneti.

8.

Auctorĭtas	hujus	civitatis	est	longè
The authority	of this	state	is	by-far

amplissĭma	omnis	maritĭmæ	oræ	earum
the most-extensive	of all	the maritime	coast	of those

regionum;	quòd	Venĕti habent	et	plurĭmas
countries;	because	the Veneti have	both	very-many

naves,	quĭbus	consueverunt	navigare	in
ships,	with which	they have been accustomed	to sail	into

Britannĭam;	et	antecedunt	cætĕros	scientĭâ
Britain;	and	they excel	the rest	in the knowledge

atque	usu	nauticarum rerum;	et	in	magno atque
and	use	of naval things;	and	in	a great and

aperto	impĕtu	măris, paucis	portŭbus	interjectis,
open	violence	of sea, few	harbours	being cast-between

(intervening),	quos	ipsi	tĕnent,	hăbent fĕrè
	which	themselves	hold,	they have nearly

omnes	vectigales,	qui	consueverunt uti
all	tributary,	who	have been accustomed to use

LIBER III.

eodem	mări.	Initĭum	Silĭi	atque
with the same	*sea.*	*The beginning*	*of Silius*	*and*

Velanĭi	retinendi	fŭit	ab	ĭis,	quòd	per
of Velanius	*to be retained*	*was*	*from*	*those,*	*because*	*through*

ĕos	existimabant	se	recuperaturos	sŭos
them	*they did think*	*themselves*	*about-to-recover*	*their*

obsĭdes,	quos	dedissent (pluperf. subj.)	Crasso.
hostages,	*whom*	*they had given*	*to Crassus.*

Finitĭmi	adducti	auctoritate
The neighbouring (people)	*induced*	*by the authority*

horum	(ut	consilĭa	Gallorum	sunt subĭta	et
of these	*(as*	*the counsels*	*of the Gauls*	*are sudden*	*and*

repentina)	retĭnent	Trebĭum	que	Terrasidĭum	de
immediate)	*detain*	*Trebius*	*and*	*Terrasidius*	*from*

eâdem	caussâ:	et	legatis	missis	celerĭter,
the same	*cause:*	*and*	*ambassadors*	*being sent*	*quickly,*

conjurant	inter	se	per	sŭos	princĭpes ;
they conspire	*among*	*themselves*	*through*	*their*	*chiefs ;*

esse acturos	nĭhil	nĭsi communi consilĭo,
to be about-to-act (would do)	*nothing*	*unless by common counsel,*

que	laturos	eundem exĭtum omnis fortunæ ;	que
and	*about-to-bear*	*the same issue of all fortune ;*	*and*

sollicĭtant	relĭquas	civitates,	ut	mallent
they solicit	*the remaining*	*states,*	*that*	*they would-rather*

permanere	in	ĕâ	libertate,	quam	accepĕrant
to remain	*in*	*that*	*liberty,*	*which*	*they had received*

à	majorĭbus,	quàm	perferre	servitutem
from	*(their) ancestors,*	*than*	*to endure*	*the slavery*

Romanorum.	Omni	maritĭmâ	orâ	perductâ
of the Romans.	*All*	*the maritime*	*coast*	*being led-over*

celerĭter	ad	sŭam	sententĭam,	mittunt	communem
quickly	*to*	*their*	*opinion,*	*they send*	*a common*

legationem	ad	Publĭum	Crassum,	"Si
(general) embassy	*to*	*Publius*	*Crassus,*	*" If*

vĕlit	recipĕre	sŭos,	remittat
he may will	*to receive*	*his (ambassadors),*	*he may send-back*

obsĭdes	sĭbi."
(their) hostages	*to themselves."*

148 DE BELLO GALLICO. [9

9. De quibus rebus Cæsar factus
Concerning which things Cæsar being made

certior à Crasso, jubet
more-sure (being informed) by Crassus, he orders

longas naves ædificari interim in
long ships (ships of war) to be built meanwhile on

flumine Ligeri, quod influit Oceanum,
the river Liger (Loire), which flows-into the Ocean,

remiges institui ex Provinciâ, nautas
rowers to be prepared from the Province, sailors

que gubernatores comparari, quòd ipse
and pilots to be procured, because himself

aberat longius. His rebus administratis
was-distant farther (too far). These things being managed

celeriter, ipse contendit ad exercitum, quàm-primùm
quickly, himself hastened to the army, as-soon-as

potuit per tempus anni. Veneti
he was-able through the time of the year. The Veneti

que item reliquæ civitates, adventu Cæsaris
and also the rest (other) states, the arrival of Cæsar

cognito, simul quòd intelligebant
being known, at the same-time because they did understand

quantum facinus admisissent (pluperf. subj.) in
how-great a crime they had admitted unto

se legatos, nomen quod semper fuisset
themselves, the ambassadors, a name which always had been

(pluperf. subj.) sanctum que inviolatum apud
holy and inviolate at (among)

omnes nationes, retentos ab se et
all nations, being detained by themselves and

conjectos in vincula; instituunt parare bellum
cast into chains; resolve to prepare war

pro magnitudine periculi, et
for (in proportion to) the greatness of the danger, and

maximè providere ea quæ pertinerent
chiefly to provide those (things) which did relate

LIBER III.

(imp. subj.)	ad	usum	navĭum;	hôc,
	to	the use	of ships;	from this (on this

account),	majore	spe,	quòd	confidebant
	with greater	hope,	because	they did trust

multùm	naturâ	lŏci.	Sciebant
much	in the nature	of the place.	They did know

pedestrĭa	itinĕra	concisa-esse	æstuarĭis;
the foot (land)	ways	to have been cut-up	by æstuaries

navigationem	impeditam	propter	inscientĭam
navigation	prevented	on-account-of	(our) ignorance

locorum	que paucitatem	portŭum:	confidebant
of the places	and the fewness	of the harbours:	they did trust

nostros	exercĭtus	nĕque	posse	morari	diutĭùs
our	armies	neither	to be able	to delay	longer

ăpud	se,	propter	inopĭam	frumenti.
at (among)	themselves,	on-account-of	the want	of corn.

Ac	jam,	ut	omnĭa	accidĕrent	contra
And	now,	though	all (things)	might-happen	against

opinionem,	tămen	se	posse
(their) opinion,	yet	themselves	to be able (to do)

plurĭmum	navĭbus:	Romanos	habere	nĕque	ullam
very much	in ships:	the Romans	to have	neither	any

facultatem	navĭum,	nĕque	novisse	văda,
power	of ships,	nor	to have-known	the shallows,

portus,	insŭlas	eorum	locorum,	ŭbi	essent (imp.
harbours,	islands	of those	places,	where	they were

subj.)	gesturi	bellum:	ac	perspiciebant
	about-to-carry-on	war:	and	they did clearly-see

navigationem	in	concluso	mări,	atque	in
navigation	in	an inclosed	sea,	and	in

vastissĭmo	atque	apertissĭmo	Oceăno,	esse	longè
a most-immense	and	most-open	Ocean,	to be	far

alĭam.	His	consilĭis	initis,
other (different).	These	counsels	being entered-into,

munĭunt	oppĭda,	comportant	frumenta (pl.)
they fortify	the towns,	they bring-together	corn

ex	agris	in	oppida;	cogunt	naves
from	*the lands*	*into*	*the towns;*	*they collect*	*(their) ships*

quàm-plurimas		possunt,	in	Venetiam,	ŭbi
as-many-as		*they can,*	*into*	*Venetia,*	*where*

constabat	Cæsărem	primum	gesturum
it was-evident	*Cæsar*	*(to be) first*	*about to carry-on*

bellum.	Adsciscunt	socios	sĭbi	ad id
the war.	*They unite*	*(as) allies*	*to themselves*	*to that*

bellum	Osismios,	Lexovios,	Nannetes,	Ambialites,
war	*the Osismii,*	*Lexovii,*	*Nannetes,*	*Ambialites,*

Morinos,	Diablintes,	Menapios;	accersunt auxilia
Morini,	*Diablintes,*	*Menapii;*	*they send-for auxiliaries*

ex	Britannĭâ,	quæ est	posita	contra
from	*Britain,*	*which is*	*placed*	*against* (opposite)

eas	regiones.
those	*countries.*

10. Hæ ĕrant difficultates belli gerendi,
These were the difficulties of a war to-be-carried-on,

quas	ostendimus	suprà:	sed tămen	multa
which	*we have shown*	*above:*	*but however*	*many (things)*

incitabant	Cæsărem	ad	id	bellum: injuriæ
did urge	*Cæsar*	*to*	*that*	*war: the injuries*

Romanorum	equitum	retentorum:	rebellio
of Roman	*knights*	*being detained:*	*the rebellion*

facta	post	deditionem:	defectio,	obsidibus
being made	*after*	*a surrender:*	*the revolt,*	*hostages*

dătis:		conjuratio tot	civitatum:
having been given:	*the conspiracy of so-many*	*states:*

in-primis,	ne,	hâc parte	neglectâ,	reliquæ
in-particular,	*lest,*	*this part*	*being neglected,*	*the rest*

nationes	arbitrarentur ĭdem	licere
(other) nations	*might think the same (thing)*	*to-be-lawful*

sĭbi.	Ităque	quum	intelligĕret (imp. subj.)
for themselves.	*Therefore*	*when*	*he understood*

fĕrè	omnes	Gallos	studere	novis
nearly	*all*	*the Gauls*	*to study* (to be desirous)	*for new*

LIBER III. 151

rebus,	et	excitari	mobiliter que
things (revolution),	*and*	*to-be-roused*	*changeably and*

celeriter ad bellum; autem omnes homines naturâ
quickly to war; but all men by nature

studere libertati, et odisse
to study for liberty, and to have hated (to hate)

conditionem servitutis; priùs-quam plures civitates
the condition of slavery; before-that more states

conspirarent, putavit exercitum partiendum, ac
should conspire, he thought the army to-be-divided, and

distribuendum latiùs sibi.
to-be-distributed more-widely to (by) *himself.*

11. Itaque mittit Titum Labienum legatum
Therefore he sends Titus Labienus (his) *lieutenant*

cum equitatu in Treviros, qui sunt proximi
with the cavalry unto the Treviri, who are nearest

flumini Rheno. Mandat huic, adeat
to the river Rhine. He charges to him, (that) *he may go-to*

Rhemos que reliquos Belgas, atque contineat
the Rhemi and the rest-of the Belgæ, and may constrain

in officio; que prohibeat Germanos, qui
(them) *in duty; and may prevent the Germans, who*

dicebantur accersiti auxilio à Belgis, si
were-said being sent-for to aid by the Belgæ, if

conentur per vim transire flumen
they may attempt by force to cross the river

navibus. Jubet Publium Crassum cum
with ships. He orders Publius Crassus with

duodecim legionariis cohortibus, et magno numero
twelve legionary cohorts, and a great number

equitatûs proficisci in Aquitaniam, ne auxilia
of cavalry to set-out into Aquitania, lest auxiliaries

mittantur ex his nationibus in Galliam, ac
may be sent out-of these nations into Gaul, and

tantæ nationes conjungantur. Mittit Quintum
so-great nations may be united. He sends Quintus

Titurĭum	Sabinum	legatum	cum	trĭbus	legionĭbus
Titurius	*Sabinus*	*(his) lieutenant*	*with*	*three*	*legions*

in	Unellos,	Curiosolitas,	que	Lexovĭos;	qui
unto	*the Unelli,*	*the Curiosolitæ,*	*and*	*the Lexovii;*	*who*

curet	ĕam	mănum	distinendam.
may take-care	*that*	*band (of people)*	*to-be-checked.*

Præfecit	Decĭum	Brutum	adolescentem	classi,
He appointed	*Decius*	*Brutus*	*a young-man*	*to the fleet,*

que	Gallĭcis	navĭbus,	quas	jussĕrat
and	*to the Gallic*	*ships,*	*which*	*he had ordered*

convenire	ex	Pictonĭbus	que	Santŏnis,	et
to assemble	*from*	*the Pictones*	*and*	*Santoni,*	*and*

relĭquis	pacatis	regionĭbus;	et	jŭbet
the rest (other)	*subdued*	*countries;*	*and*	*he orders*

proficisci	quàm-primùm	posset,	in
(him) to set-out	*as-soon-as*	*he might be-able,*	*unto*

Venĕtos.	Ipse	contendit	ĕò	pedestrĭbus
the Veneti.	*Himself*	*hastens*	*thither*	*with the foot*

copĭis.
forces.

12.
Sĭtus	oppidorum	ĕrant	fĕrè
The situations	*of (their) towns*	*were*	*nearly*

ejusmŏdi,	ut	posĭta	in	extremis	lingŭlis
of this-sort,	*that*	*being placed*	*in*	*extreme*	*little-tongues*

que	promontorĭis,	haberent (imp. subj.)	nĕque	aditum
and	*promontories,*	*they had*	*neither*	*access*

pedĭbus,	quum	æstus	incitavisset	se	ex
by feet,	*when*	*the tide*	*might have urged*	*itself*	*from*

alto,	quod	accĭdit	semper	bis	spatĭo
the deep,	*which*	*happens*	*always*	*twice*	*in the space*

duodĕcim	horarum:	nĕque	navĭbus,	quòd
of twelve	*hours:*	*neither*	*by ships,*	*because*

æstu	rursus	minuente	naves	afflicta-
the tide	*again*	*diminishing (ebbing)*	*the ships*	*might be*

rentur	in	vădis.	Ita	utrâque	re
dashed	*on*	*the shallows.*	*Thus*	*from each*	*thing*

LIBER III.

oppugnatĭo	oppidorum	impediebatur.	Ac,	si
an assault	*of the towns*	*was prevented.*	*And,*	*if*

quando	fortè	superati	magnitudĭne
any-time	*by-chance*	*being overcome*	*by the greatness*

opĕris,	mărì	extruso	aggĕre	ac
of a work,	*the sea*	*being shut-out*	*by a mound*	*and*

molĭbus,	atque	his	adæquatis	fermè	mœnĭbus
by moles,	*and*	*these*	*being equalled*	*nearly*	*to the walls*

oppĭdi,	cœpĕrant	desperare	sŭis fortunis;
of the town,	*they had begun*	*to despair-of*	*their fortunes;*

magno	numĕro	navĭum	appulso,
a great	*number*	*of ships*	*being brought-into-harbour,*

cujus	rĕi	habebant	summam	facultatem,
of which	*thing*	*they did have*	*the highest*	*power,*

deportabant	omnĭa	sŭa	que	recipiebant
they did carry-away	*all*	*their (effects)*	*and*	*did betake*

se	in	proxĭma	oppĭda:	ĭbi	defendebant
themselves	*into*	*the nearest*	*towns:*	*there*	*they did defend*

se	rursus	iisdem	opportunitatĭbus	lŏci.
themselves	*again*	*by the same*	*opportunities*	*of place.*

Faciebant	hæc	ĕò	facilĭùs	magnam
They did do	*these (things)*	*therefore*	*more-easily*	*a great*

partem	æstatis,	quòd	nostræ naves	detinebantur
part	*of the summer,*	*because*	*our ships*	*were detained*

tempestatĭbus;	que	ĕrat	summa	difficultas
by tempests;	*and*	*(there) was*	*the highest*	*difficulty*

navigandi	vasto	atque aperto	mări,	magnis
of sailing	*in an immense*	*and open*	*sea,*	*with great*

æstĭbus,	raris	ac	prŏpè nullis	portŭbus,
tides,	*with few*	*and*	*nearly no*	*harbours.*

13. | Namque | naves | ipsorum | factæ-ĕrant | que |
|---|---|---|---|---|
| *For* | *the ships* | *of them* | *had been-made* | *and* |

armatæ	ad	hunc	mŏdum:	carinæ
armed (furnished)	*to (in)*	*this*	*manner:*	*the keels (were)*

aliquanto	planiores	quàm	nostrarum navĭum;
by something	*more-flat*	*than*	*(those) of our ships.*

quò	possent	excipĕre
in-order-that	*they might be-able*	*to receive* (sustain)

văda	ac	decessum	æstûs	faciliùs:
the shallows	*and*	*the departure*	*of the tide*	*more-easily:*

proræ	admŏdum	erectæ,	atque	ĭtem	puppes,
the prows (were)	*very*	*upright,*	*and*	*also*	*the poops,*

accommodatæ	ad	magnitudĭnem	fluctŭum	que
fitted	*to*	*the greatness*	*of the waves*	*and*

tempestatum.	Totæ	naves	factæ	ex
tempests.	*The whole*	*ships*	(were) *made*	*out-of*

robŏre,	ad	quamvis	vim	et	contumelĭam
oak.	*at* (with a view to)	*any*	*force*	*and*	*injury*

perferendam:	transtra	ex	pedalĭbus
to-be-borne:	*the benches* (were made)	*out-of*	*foot*

trabĭbus	in	latitudĭnem,	confixa	ferrĕis
beams	*into*	*width,*	*fixed-together*	*with iron*

clavis,	crassitudĭne	pollĭcis	digĭti:
nails,	*with* (of) *the thickness*	*of the thumb*	*finger:*

anchŏræ	revinctæ	ferrĕis	catenis,	pro
the anchors	(were) *fastened*	*with iron*	*chains,*	*instead-of*

funĭbus.	Pelles	que	alutæ (pl.)	tenuĭter	confectæ
ropes.	*Hides*	*and*	*thin-leather*	*slenderly*	*made-up*

pro	velis;	sive	propter	inopĭam
(were) *instead-of*	*sails;*	*whether*	*on-account-of*	*the want*

lini,	atque	inscientĭam	usûs	ejus;	sive,
of linen,	*and*	*ignorance*	*of the use*	*of it;*	*or,*

quod	est	măgis	verisimĭle,	quòd	arbitrabantur
what	*is*	*more*	*likely,*	*because*	*they did think*

tantas	tempestates	oceăni	que	tantos	impĕtus
so-great	*tempests*	*of the ocean*	*and*	*so-great*	*violence*

ventorum	non	posse	sustineri,	ac	tanta
of winds	*not*	*to be-able*	*to be supported,*	*and*	*so-great*

onĕra	navĭum	rĕgi	velis	sătis
burdens	*of ships*	*to be governed*	*by sails*	*sufficiently*

commŏdè.	Congressus	nostræ	classi	cum	his
conveniently.	*The encounter*	*to our*	*fleet*	*with*	*these*

năvĭbus	ĕrat	ejusmŏdi	ut	præstaret	(imp. subj.)
ships	was	of this kind	that	it did excel	

celeritate	unâ,	et	pulsu	remorum; reliqua
in speed	alone,	and	the beat (stroke)	of oars; the rest

	essent (imp. subj.)	aptiora	et
(other things)	were	more suitable	and

accommodatiora	illis	pro	naturâ
more-accommodated	to them	for (regarding)	the nature

lŏci,	pro	vi	tempestatum:	ĕnim
of the place,	for	the violence	of the tempests:	for

nostræ	nĕque	potĕrant	nocere his
our (ships)	neither	were-able	to injure to them

rostro,	(tanta	ĕrat firmitudo	in his)	nĕque
with the beak,	(so-great	was the strength	in them)	neither

telum	adjiciebatur	făcĭlè propter	altitudĭnem;
a weapon	was hurled	easily on-account-of	(their) height;

et	de	eâdem caussâ	continebantur
and	from	the same cause	they were kept (close

scopŭlis	mĭnùs	incommŏdè. Accedebat
to the rocks	less	inconveniently. It did approach (was

	ut	quum ventus	cœpisset (pluperf. subj.)
added),	that	when the wind	had begun

sævire	et	dedidissent (pluperf. subj.)	se
to rage	and	they had given	themselves

vento,	et	ferrent	tempestatem faciliùs,
to the wind,	both	they might bear	a tempest more-easily,

et	consistĕrent	tutĭùs	in	vădis, et
and	might stop	more-safely	in	the shallows, and

derelictæ	ab	æstu, timerent	nĭhil
being left	by	the tide, they might fear	nothing (not)

saxa	et	cautes:	casus omnĭum	quarum
the rocks	and	reefs:	the accidents of all	which

rerum	ĕrant	extimescendi	nostris navĭbus.
things	were	to-be-dreaded	to (by) our ships.

14. Complurĭbus oppĭdis expugnatis, ŭbi Cæsar
      Several towns being stormed, when Cæsar

intellexit	tantum	laborem	sumi	frustrà,	neque
understood	so-great	labour	to be taken	in vain,	nor

fugam	hostium	reprimi,	oppidis	captis,
the flight	of the enemies	to be checked,	the towns	being taken,

neque	posse	noceri	his,	statuit
neither	to be able	to be injured	to them,	he resolved

classem	exspectandam.	Ubi	quæ	convenit
the fleet	to-be-awaited.	When	which (fleet)	assembled

ac	primùm	visa-est	ab	hostibus,	circiter
and	first	was-seen	by	the enemies,	about

ducentæ	viginti	paratissimæ	naves	eorum,
two-hundred	twenty	most-prepared	ships	of them,

atque	ornatissimæ	omni	genere	armorum,
and	most-furnished	with every	kind	of arms,

profectæ	è	portu,	constiterunt	adversæ
having set-out	from	port,	stood	opposite

nostris.	Neque	satis-constabat	Bruto,
to our (ships).	Neither	was it sufficiently-evident	to Brutus,

qui	præerat	classi,	neque	tribunis
who	was-over (commanded)	to the fleet,	nor	to the tribunes

militum	que	centurionibus,	quibus	singulæ
of soldiers	and	to the centurions,	to whom	single

	naves	attributæ-erant,	quid	agerent,
(particular)	ships	had been-assigned,	what	they should act

aut	quam	rationem	pugnæ	insist-
(do), or	what	plan	of battle	they should

erent :	enim	cognoverant	non	posse
determine on:	for	they had known	not	to be able

noceri	rostro :	autem	turribus	excitatis,
to be injured	by the beak:	but	towers	being raised,

tamen	altitudo	puppium	ex	barbaris
yet	the height	of the poops	out-of	the barbarian

navibus	superabat	has;	ut	neque	tela
ships	did over-top	these;	(so) that	neither	darts

possent	adjici	commodè	satis	ex
might be-able	to be thrown	conveniently	enough	from

inferiore	lŏco,	et	missa	à	Gallis
a lower	*place,*	*and*	*(those) sent*	*by*	*the Gaul*

accidĕrent	graviŭs.	Una	res	præparata	à
might fall	*more-heavily.*	*One*	*thing*	*prepared*	*by*

nostris ĕrat magno usŭi; præacutæ falces,
our (men) was for great use; sharp-pointed scythes,

insertæ que affixæ longurĭis, non absimĭli
inserted and fastened to long-poles, not with unlike

formâ muralĭum falcĭum: quum funes, qui
form of mural scythes: when the ropes, which

destinabant antennas ad malos, comprehensi-ĕrant
did brace the yards to the masts, had been-seized

que adducti his, navigĭo incitato
and drawn-to by these, the vessel being urged-forward

remis, præræmpebantur: quĭbus
with the oars, they were broken-asunder: which

abscissis, antennæ necessarĭò concidebant;
being cut-away, the yards necessarily did fall;

ut quum omnis spes consistĕret (imp. subj.)
(so) that when all hope did consist

Gallĭcis navĭbus in velis que armamentis,
to the Gallic ships in (their) sails and riggings,

his ereptis, omnis usus navĭum
these being torn-away, all use of (their) ships

eriperetur (imp. subj.) uno tempŏre.
was torn-away in one time (at the same time).

Relĭquum certamen ĕrat posĭtum in virtute;
The rest-of the contest was placed in valour,

quâ nostri milĭtes facĭlè superabant; atque
in which our soldiers easily did excel; and

măgis ĕò, quòd res gerebatur in
the more therefore, because the affair was carried-on in

conspectu Cæsăris atque omnis exercĭtûs, ut
sight of Cæsar and of all the army, that

nullum factum paullò fortius posset latere;
no deed a little more-brave might be-able to lie-hid,

ĕnim	omnes	colles	et	superiora	lŏca,	unde
for	*all*	*the hills*	*and*	*higher*	*places,*	*whence*

propinquus	despectus	ĕrat	in	măre,	tenebantur
a near	*view*	*was*	*unto*	*the sea,*	*were held*

ab exercĭtu.
by the army.

15. Antennis disjectis, ut, dixĭmus,
The yards being thrown-down, as we have said,

quum binæ aut ternæ naves circumsisterent (imp.
when two or three ships did surround

subj.) singŭlas naves, milĭtes contendebant
each (of our) ships, the soldiers did strive

summâ vi transcendĕre in naves
with highest (utmost) force to climb-over into the ships

hostĭum. Quod postquam barbări
of the enemies. Which after-that the barbarians

animadverterunt fiĕri, complurĭbus navĭbus
perceived to be done, several ships

expugnatis, quum nullum auxilĭum
being stormed (boarded), when no aid

reperiretur ĕi rĕi, contenderunt petere
might be found for that thing, they hastened to seek

salutem fŭgâ: ac jam navĭbus conversis in
safety by flight: and now the ships being turned unto

ĕam partem, quò ventus ferebat, tanta
that part, whither the wind did bear, so-great

malacĭa ac tranquillĭtas subĭtò exstĭtit, ut
a calm and stillness suddenly existed, that

possent (imp. subj.) non movere se ex
they were-able not to move themselves from

lŏco: quæ res quĭdem fŭit maxĭmè opportuna
the place: which thing indeed was most seasonable

ad negotĭum conficiendum: nam nostri
to the business to be finished: for our (men)

consectati singŭlas expugnaverunt, ut
having pursued single (ships) stormed (them), so-that

perpaucæ	ex	omni	numĕro	pervenĕrint	ar
very-few	out-of	all	the number	may have arrived	to

terram,	interventu		noctis,	quum pugnaretur
land,	by interposition		of the night,	when it was fought

(imp. subj.) ab quartâ horâ usque ad occasum
from the fourth hour until to the setting

solis.
of the sun.

16. Quo prœlio bellum Venetorum que
By which battle the war of the Veneti and

totius maritĭmæ oræ confectum-est. Nam quum
of the whole maritime coast was finished. For when

omnis juventus, etiam omnes gravioris
all (their) youth, also all of more serious

ætatis, in quĭbus alĭquid consilii aut dignitatis
age, in whom something of counsel or of dignity

fŭit, convenĕrant ĕò; tum coëgĕrant
was, had assembled thither; then (also) they had collected

in unum lŏcum, quod navĭum fuĕrat ubique:
into one place, what of ships had been everywhere:

quĭbus amissis, relĭqui habebant nĕque quò
which being lost, the rest did have neither whither

recipĕrent se, nĕque quemadmŏdum
they might betake themselves, nor how

defendĕrent oppĭda. Ităque dediderunt
they might defend (their) towns. Therefore they surrendered

se que omnĭa sŭa Cæsări: in
themselves and all their (effects) to Cæsar: against

quos Cæsar statŭit vindicandum gravĭùs
whom Cæsar resolved to-be-avenged more-severely

ĕò, quò jus legatorum con-
therefore, in-order-that the right of ambassadors might be

servaretur diligentiùs à barbăris in
preserved more-carefully by the barbarians unto

reliquum tempus. Ităque, omni senatu
the rest (future) time. Therefore, all the senate

necato,	vendĭdĭt	relĭquos	sub	co-
being put-to-death,	*he sold*	*the rest*	*under*	*the*

ronâ.
crown (by auction).

17. | Dum | hæc | | geruntur | in |
|---|---|---|---|---|
| *Whilst* | *these* (*things*) | | *are carried-on* | *in* (among) |

Venĕtis,	Quintus	Titŭrĭus	Sabinus	pervenit	in
the Veneti,	*Quintus*	*Titurius*	*Sabinus*	*arrived*	*into*

fines	Unellorum,	cum	his	copĭis,	quas
the borders	*of the Unelli,*	*with*	*these*	*forces,*	*which*

accepĕrat	à	Cæsăre.	Viridŏvix	præĕrat
he had received	*from*	*Cæsar.*	*Viridovix*	*was-over*

his,	ac	tenebat	summam		imperĭi
to these,	*and*	*did hold*	*the height*	(presidency)	*of power*

omnĭum	earum	civitatum,	quæ	defecĕrant;	ex
of all	*of those*	*states,*	*which*	*had revolted;*	*out-of*

quĭbus	coëgĕrat	exercĭtum	que	magnas
which	*he had collected*	*an army*	*and*	*great*

copĭas.	Atque	his	paucis	diebus,	Aulerci,
resources.	*And*	*in these*	*few*	*days,*	*the Aulerci,*

Eburovices,	que	Lexovĭi,	sŭo	senatu	interfecto,
Eburovices,	*and*	*Lexovii,*	*their*	*senate*	*being put-to-death,*

quòd	nolebant	esse	auctores	belli,
because	*they were-unwilling*	*to be*	*advisers*	*of war,*

clauserunt	portas,	que	conjunxerunt	se
shut	(*their*) *gates,*	*and*	*joined*	*themselves*

cum	Virĭdovice:	que	præterĕa	magna	multitudo
with	*Viridovix:*	*and*	*besides*	*a great*	*multitude*

perditorum	homĭnum	que	latronum	convenĕrat
of abandoned	*men*	*and*	*robbers*	*had assembled*

undĭque	ex	Gallĭâ,	quos	spes
from-every-side	*out-of*	*Gaul,*	*whom*	*the hope*

prædandi	que	studĭum	bellandi	revocabat
of plundering	*and*	*an inclination*	*of warring*	*did call-away*

ab	agriculturâ	et	quotidiano	labore.	Sabinus
from	*agriculture*	*and*	*daily*	*labour.*	*Sabinus*

| tenebat | sese | castris (pl.) | lŏco | idonĕo | omnĭbus |
| did keep | himself | in camp | in a place | fit | for all |

| rebus: | quum | Viridŏvix | consedisset (pluperf. subj.) |
| things: | when | Viridovix | had sat-down (had encamped) |

| contra | ĕum | spatĭo | dŭûm | millĭum, | que |
| opposite | him | (at) a space | of two | miles, | and |

| copĭis | productis | quotidĭe | facĕret (imp. subj.) |
| (his) forces | being led-forth | daily | did make |

| potestatem | pugnandi; | ut | Sabinus | jam |
| power (opportunity) | of fighting; | so-that | Sabinus | now |

| veniret (imp. subj.) | in | contemptionem | non | solùm |
| did come | into | contempt | not | only |

| hostĭbus, | sed | etĭam | carperetur (imp. subj.) |
| to the enemies, | but | also | was censured |

| nonnĭhil | vocĭbus | nostrorum | milĭtum: | que |
| somewhat | by expressions | of our | soldiers: | and |

| præbŭit | tantam | opinionem | timoris, | ut | hostes |
| he afforded | so-great | an opinion | of fear, | that | the enemies |

| audĕrent | jam | accedĕre | ad | vallum | castrorum |
| would dare | now | to approach | to | the rampart | of the camp. |

| (pl.). | Faciebat | id | ĕâ | caussâ, | quòd |
| | He did do | that | from that | cause, | because |

| existimabat | non | dimicandum | legato |
| he did think (it) | not | to-be-contended | (by) a lieutenant |

| cum | tantâ | multitudĭne | hostĭum, | præsertim | ĕo |
| with | so-great | a multitude | of enemies, | especially | he |

| absente, | qui | tenĕret (imp. subj.) | summam |
| (being) absent, | who | did hold | the height (chief) |

| imperĭi, | nĭsi | æquo | lŏco, | aut | alĭquâ |
| of command, | unless | on equal | place, | or | some |

| opportunitate | dătâ. |
| opportunity | being given. |

18. | Hâc | opinione | timoris | confirmatâ, |
| This | opinion | of fear | being strengthened, |

| delegit | quendam | Gallum | idonĕum | et | callĭdum |
| he selected | a certain | Gaul | a fit | and | shrewd |

hominum, ex iis, quos habebat secum	man, out-of those, whom he did have with-him
caussâ auxiliî. Persuadet	by cause (for the purpose) of aid (as auxiliaries) He persuades
huic magnis præmiis que pollicitationibus, ŭtĭ	to him by great rewards and promises, that
transĕat ad hostes: edŏcet quod	he may go-over to the enemies: he instructs (him) what
vĕlit fieri. Qui, ŭbi venit ad ĕos	he may will to be done Who, when he came to them
pro perfŭgâ, proponit timorem Romanorum:	for a deserter, sets-forth (describes) the fear of the Romans:
dŏcet quĭbus angustiis Cæsar	he informs (them) in what straits (difficulties) Cæsar
ipse prematur (pres. subj.) à Venĕtis: nĕque	himself is pressed by the Veneti: neither
abesse longĭus, quin Sabinus educat	to be-distant farther, but-that Sabinus may lead-out
exercĭtum clàm ex castris (pl.) proxĭmâ	(his) army secretly out-of the camp in the next
nocte, et proficiscatur ad Cæsărem, caussâ	night, and may set-out to Cæsar, by cause (for the
auxilii ferendi. Ubi quod	sake) of aid to-be-brought. When which (report)
audĭtum-est, omnes conclamant, occasionem ne-	was-heard, all cry-out, an opportunity of the
gotii gerendi bĕnĕ non amittendam-esse:	business to be carried-on well not to-be-lost:
oportere iri ad castra (pl.). Multæ	to behove (it ought) to be gone to the camp. Many
res hortabantur Gallos ad hoc consilium:	things did encourage the Gauls to this plan:
cunctatĭo Sabini superiorum dierum;	the delay of Sabinus of (on) the former days;
confirmatĭo perfŭgæ; inopĭa cibariorum,	the assertion of the deserter; the want of provisions,

LIBER III.

cui provisum-erat ab his parùm diligenter:
to (for) which it had been provided by these little carefully

spes Venetici belli; et quòd
(inadequately) the hopes of the Venetian war; and because

homines ferè credunt libenter id quod
men generally believe willingly that which

volunt. Adducti iis rebus, dimittunt
they will. Induced by those things, they dismiss

Viridovicem que reliquos duces ex concilio
Viridovix and the rest-of the generals from the council

non priùs quàm concessum-sit ab his,
not before than it may have-been-granted by them,

uti capiant arma et contendant ad castra (pl.)
that they may take arms and may hasten to the camp.

Quâ re concessâ, læti, vëlut victoriâ
Which thing being granted, (they) joyful, as-if the victory

exploratâ, sarmentis que virgultis
being discovered (certain), faggots and twigs

collectis, quibus compleant fossas
being collected. with which they may fill-up the ditches

Romanorum, pergunt ad castra (pl.).
of the Romans, proceed to the camp.

19. Locus castrorum (pl.) erat editus, et
The situation of the camp was elevated, and

paullatim acclivis ab imo, circiter
gradually steep from the lowest (the bottom), about

mille passus: huc contenderunt magno
a thousand paces: hither they hastened with great

cursu, ut quàm minimum spatii
course (speed), that as least of space (as little

daretur Romanis ad
time as possible) might be given to the Romans to

se colligendos que armandos, que exanimati
themselves to-be-collected and to-be-armed, and breathless

pervenerunt. Sabinus, hortatus suos,
they arrived (there). Sabinus, having encouraged his (men),

dat	signum	cupientĭbus:	hostĭbus
gives	*the signal*	*to (them) desiring (it.):*	*the enemies*

	impedĭtis	propter	ĕa	onĕra,	quæ
	being encumbered	*on-account-of*	*those*	*burdens,*	*which*

ferebant,	jŭbet	eruptionem	fĭĕri	subĭtò
they did bear,	*he orders*	*a sally*	*to be made*	*suddenly*

duabus	portis.	Factum-est	opportunitate
from the two	*gates.*	*It-was-done*	*by the convenience*

lŏci,	inscientĭa	ac	defatigatione	hostĭum,
of the place,	*by the ignorance*	*and*	*fatigue*	*of the enemies,*

virtute	milĭtum	ac	exercitatione	superiorum
by the valour	*of the soldiers*	*and*	*the exercise*	*of former*

pugnarum,	ut	ferrent (imp. subj.)	ne
battles,	*that*	*(the enemy) bore*	*not*

quĭdem	unum	impĕtum	nostrorum;	ac
indeed (even)	*one*	*charge*	*of our (men);*	*and*

stătim	vertĕrent (imp. subj.)	terga:	quos
immediately	*turned*	*(their) backs:*	*whom*

impedĭtos	nostri	milĭtes	consecuti	intĕgris
encumbered	*our*	*soldiers*	*having pursued*	*with entire*

virĭbus,	occiderunt	magnum	numĕrum
(fresh) forces (strength),	*killed*	*a great*	*number*

eorum:	equĭtes	consectati	relĭquos	reliquerunt
of them:	*the cavalry*	*having pursued*	*the rest*	*left*

paucos,	qui	evasĕrant	ex	fŭgâ.	Sic	Cæsar
few,	*who*	*had escaped*	*from*	*flight*	*Thus*	*Cæsar*

factus-est	certĭor		uno	tempŏre	et
was-made	*more-sure (was informed)*		*in one*	*time*	*both*

de	navali	pugnâ,	et	de	victoriâ	Sabini:
of	*the naval*	*battle,*	*and*	*of*	*the victory*	*of Sabinus:*

que	omnes	civitates	dediderunt	se	stătim
and	*all*	*the states*	*surrendered*	*themselves*	*immediately*

Titurĭo.	Nam	ut	anĭmus	Gallorum	est
to Titurius.	*For*	*as*	*the mind (spirit)*	*of the Gauls*	*is*

alăcer	ac	promptus	ad	bella	suscipienda,	sic
eager	*and*	*ready*	*to*	*wars*	*to-be-undertaken.*	*so*

mens	eorum	est	mollis	ac	minĭmè resistens
the mind	*of them*	*is*	*soft*	*and*	*by-no-means resisting*

ad	calamitates	perferendas.
to	*misfortunes*	*to-be-borne.*

20. Fĕrè eodem tempŏre, quum Publĭus Crassus
 Nearly in the same time, when Publius Crassus

pervenisset (pluperf. subj.) in Aquitanĭam, quæ pars,
had arrived in Aquitania, which part,

ut	dictum-est	antè,	est	æstimanda	ex
as	*has been-said*	*before,*	*is*	*to-be-esteemed*	*from*

tertĭâ	parte	Gallĭæ,	et	latitudĭne
the third	*part*	*of Gaul,*	*both*	*in breadth* (extent)

regionum	et	multitudĭne	homĭnum ;	quum
of countries	*and*	*by the multitude*	*of men ;*	*when*

intelligĕret (imp. subj.)		bellum	gerendum
he understood		*war*	*to be carried-on*

sĭbi	in	illis	lŏcis,	ŭbi paucis (abl.)
to (by) himself	*in*	*those*	*places,*	*where a few*

annis	ante	Lucĭus Valerĭus Præconinus	legǎtus
years	*before*	*Lucius Valerius Præconinus*	*the lieutenant*

interfectus-esset (pluperf. subj.),	exercĭtu	pulso ;
had been killed,	*(his) army*	*being routed ,*

atque	unde	Lucĭus Manilĭus	Proconsul,
and	*whence*	*Lucius Manilius*	*the Proconsul,*

impedimentis	amissis,	profugisset (pluperf. subj.),
(his) baggages	*being lost,*	*had escaped,*

intelligebat	non	mediocrem	diligentĭam	adhi-
he did understand	*not*	*moderate*	*diligence*	*to-be-*

bendam	sĭbi.	Ităque,	frumentarĭâ re
applied	*to (by) himself.*	*Therefore,*	*corn affair*

provisâ,	auxilĭis	que equitatu	comparato,
being provided,	*auxiliaries*	*and cavalry*	*being prepared,*

præterĕa multis	fortĭbus	vĭris	Tolosâ, Carcasone,
moreover many	*brave*	*men*	*from Tolosa, Carcaso,*

et	Narbone	(quæ	sunt	civitates provinciæ
and	*Narbo*	*(which*	*are*	*cities of the province*

Galliæ,	finitĭmæ	his	regionĭbus)	evocatis
of Gaul,	*neighbouring*	*to these*	*countries)*	*being called-out*

nominatim,	introduxit	exercĭtum	in	fines
by name,	*he introduced*	*(his) army*	*into*	*the territories*

Sotiatĭum.	Cujus adventu	cognĭto,	Sotiates,
of the Sotiates.	*Whose arrival*	*being known,*	*the Sotiates,*

magnis copiis	coactis,	que equitatu,	quo
great forces	*being collected,*	*and cavalry,*	*in which*

valebant	plurĭmum,	adorti	nostrum agmen
they did prevail	*most,*	*having attacked*	*our army*

in	itinĕre,	primùm commiserunt	equestre prœlĭum;
on	*the march,*	*first engaged (in)*	*a cavalry fight;*

deinde	sŭo equitatu	pulso,	atque nostris
afterwards	*their cavalry*	*being routed,*	*and our (men)*

insequentĭbus,	ostenderant	subĭtò	pedestres	copĭas,
pursuing,	*they showed*	*suddenly*	*the foot*	*forces,*

quas	collocavĕrant	in	convalle	in	insidĭis.
which	*they had placed*	*in*	*a valley*	*in*	*ambuscades.*

Hi	adorti	nostros	disjectos,	renovârunt
These	*having attacked*	*our (men)*	*scattered,*	*renewed*

prœlĭum.
the battle.

21.
Pugnatum-est	dĭu	atque	acrĭter,	quum
It was-fought	*long*	*and*	*sharply,*	*when*

Sotiates,	freti	superiorĭbus	victorĭis,
the Sotiates,	*having relied*	*on former*	*victories,*

putarent (imp. subj.)	salutem	totius	Aquitanĭæ
did think	*the safety*	*of the whole*	*of Aquitania*

posĭtam	in	sŭâ	virtute;	autem	nostri
placed	*in*	*their-own*	*valour;*	*but*	*our (men)*

cupĕrent (imp. subj.)	perspĭci,	quid	possent
did desire	*to be seen,*	*what*	*they might be-able*

efficĕre	sine	imperatore,	et	sine
to perform	*without*	*the commander-in-chief,*	*and*	*without*

reliquis	legionĭbus,	adolescentŭlo	duce.
the rest (other)	*legions,*	*a very-young-man*	*(being) general.*

Tămen	hostes	tandem	confecti	vulnerĭbus
However	the enemies	at-length	being spent	with wounds

vertêre	terga :	magno	numĕro	quorum
turned	(their) backs :	a great	number	of whom

interfecto, Crassus cœpit oppugnare oppĭdum
being slain, *Crassus* *began* *to storm* *the town*

Sotiatium ex itinĕre; quĭbus resistentĭbus
of the Sotiates *from* *(his) march;* *who* *opposing*

fortĭter, egit vinĕas que
bravely, *he acted* (put in motion) *the mantelets* *and*

turres. Illi, aliàs eruptione tentatâ,
towers. *They* *otherwise* (one time) *a sally* *being tried,*

aliàs cunicŭlis actis ad
otherwise (another time) *mines* *being carried-on* *to*

aggĕrem que vinĕas; cujus rĕi Aquitani
the rampart *and* *mantelets;* *of which thing* *the Aquitani*

sunt longè peritissĭmi, propterĕa-quòd ærariæ secturæ
are *by-far most-skilful,* *because-that* *copper veins*

sunt ăpud ĕos multis lŏcis; ŭbi intellexerunt
are *among them* *in many places;* *when* *they understood*

nihil posse profici his rebus,
nothing *to be-able* *to be profited* *by these* *things,*

diligentïâ nostrorum, mittunt legatos ad
from the diligence *of our* (men), *they send* *ambassadors* *to*

Crassum que pĕtunt, ut recipĭat se
Crassus *and* *request,* *that* *he may receive* *themselves*

in dedicionem. Quâ re impetratâ,
into *a surrender.* *Which* *thing* *being obtained,*

jussi tradĕre arma, facïunt.
being ordered *to deliver* *(their) arms,* *they do* (it.)

22. Atque anĭmis omnĭum nostrorum intentis
And *the minds* *of all* *our* (men) *being intent*

in ĕâ re, Adiatŏmus qui tenebat summam
in that thing, *Adiatomus* *who* *did hold* *the height* (chief)

imperïi, ex alĭâ parte oppĭdi, cum
of command, *from* *another* *part* *of the town,* *with*

sexcentis	devotis,	quos	illi	appellant
six-hundred	devoted (men).	whom	they	call

Soldurios:	quorum	hæc est conditio	ut
Soldurii:	of whom	this is the condition (of life),	that

fruantur (pres. subj.)	omnibus	commodis	in vitâ
they enjoy	with all	advantages	in life

unà	cum	his,	amicitiæ	quorum
together	with	those,	to the friendship	of whom

dediderint	se:	si quid
they may have given-up (engaged)	themselves:	if any (thing)

accidat	iis	per vim, aut	ferant
may happen	to them	through violence, either	they may bear

eundem	casum	unà, aut consciscant	mortem
the same	calamity	together, or may inflict	death

sibi:	neque	quisquam	repertus-est
to (on) themselves:	neither	any-one	has been-found

adhuc	memoriâ	hominum, qui	recusaret
as-yet	in the memory	of men, who	would refuse

mori,	eo	interfecto, amicitiæ	cujus
to die,	he	being killed, to the friendship	of whom

devovisset	se.	Cum his Adiatomus
he might have devoted	himself.	With these Adiatomus

conatus	facere	eruptionem, clamore
having endeavoured	to make	a sally, a shout

sublato	ab eâ	parte munitionis,	quum
being raised	from that	part of the fortification,	when

milites	concurrissent (pluperf. subj.)	ad arma,
the soldiers	had run-together	to arms,

que	pugnatum-esset (pluperf. subj.)	ibi vehementer,
and	it had been-fought	there violently,

repulsus-est	in	oppidum; tamen	impetravit
he was-repulsed	into	the town; however	he obtained

à Crasso,	uti	uteretur eâdem
from Crassus,	that	he might use (possess) the same

conditione (abl.)	deditionis.
condition	of surrender.

LIBER III.

23. Armis que obsidĭbus acceptis, Crassus
The arms and hostages being received, Crassus

profectus-est in fines Vocatĭum et
set-out into the territories of the Vocates and

Tarusatĭum. Tum verò barbări
of the Tarusates. Then indeed the barbarians (were)

commoti, quòd cognovĕrant oppĭdum munitum
alarmed, because they had known a town fortified

et naturâ lŏci et mănu
both by the nature of the place and by hand (by art)

expugnatum paucis diebus, quĭbus
having been-overthrown (by the Romans), in a few days, in which

ventum-fuĕrat ĕò; cœpĕrunt
it had been-come thither (after their arrival); they began

dimittĕre legatos quoquoversum, conjurare, dăre
to send-about ambassadors in-every-direction, to conspire, to give

obsĭdes inter se, parare copĭas. Legati
hostages between themselves, to prepare forces. Ambassadors

mittuntur etĭam ad ĕas civitates, quæ sunt
are sent also to those states, which are

citerioris Hispanĭæ, finitĭmæ Aquitanĭæ: inde
of the nearer Spain, bordering to Aquitania: thence

auxilĭa que dŭces accersuntur; adventu
auxiliaries and generals are sent-for; by arrival

quorum conantur gerĕre bellum cum magnâ
of whom they endeavour to wage war with great

auctoritate et cum magnâ multitudĭne homĭnum.
authority and with a great multitude of men.

Verò ii deliguntur dŭces, qui fuĕrant unà
But those are chosen generals, who had been together

cum Quinto Sertorĭo omnes annos, que existimabantur
with Quintus Sertorius all years, and were thought

habere summam scientĭam militaris rĕi. Ii
to have the highest knowledge of military affair. Those

consuetudĭne Romani popŭli instituunt capĕre
by custom of Roman people resolve to take

DE BELLO GALLICO. [24

lŏca,	munire	castra (pl.),
(choose) (*their*) *places* (*ground*),	*to fortify*	*the camp,*

intercludĕre	nostros	commeatĭbus.	Quod	ŭbi
to shut-in	*our* (*men*)	*from provisions.*	*Which*	*when*

Crassus	animadvertit,	sŭas	copĭas	non	facĭlè
Crassus	*perceived,*	(*and*) *his-own*	*forces*	*not*	*easily*

diduci	propter	exiguitatem,	et
to be divided	*on-account-of*	(*their*) *smallness* (*fewness*),	*and*

.hostem	vagari	et	obsidere	vĭas,
the enemy	*to wander-about*	*and*	*to block-up*	*the ways,*

et	relinquĕre	sătis	præsidĭi	castris (pl.) ;
and	*to leave*	*enough*	*of protection*	*to* (*their*) *camp ;*

ob	ĕam caussam,	frumentum	que	commeatum
on-account-of	*that cause*	*corn*	*and*	*provision*

supportari	sĭbi	mĭnùs	commŏdè,	numĕrum
to-be-brought-up	*to himself*	*less*	*conveniently,*	*the number*

hostĭum	augeri	in-dĭes ;	existimavit	non
of the enemies	*to be increased*	*daily ;*	*he thought*	*not*

cunctandum,	quin	decertaret	pugnâ.	Hâc
to-be-delayed,	*but-that*	*he should contend*	*in battle.*	*This*

re	delatâ	ad concilĭum,	ŭbi	intellexit
thing	*being referred*	*to a council,*	*when*	*he understood*

omnes	sentire	ĭdem,	constitŭit	postĕrum
all	*to think*	*the same,*	*he appointed*	*the following*

dĭem	pugnæ.
day	*for the battle.*

24. | Omnĭbus | copĭis | productis | primâ |
|---|---|---|---|
| *All* | (*his*) *forces* | *being drawn-out* | *in the first* |

luce,	duplĭci	acĭe	institutâ,	que	auxilĭis
light,	*a double*	*line*	*being formed,*	*and*	*the auxiliaries*

conjectis	in	medĭam	acĭem,	exspectabat	quid
being thrown	*into*	*the middle*	*line,*	*he did wait*	*what*

consilĭi	hostes	capĕrent.	Illi,	etsi
of plan	*the enemies*	*might take.*	*They,*	*although*

propter	multitudĭnem,	et	vetĕrem	glorĭam
on-account-of	(*their*) *multitude,*	*and*	*ancient*	*glory*

LIBER III.

belli que paucitatem nostrorum existimabant
of war and the fewness of our (men) they did think

se dimicaturos tutò; tamen arbitrabantur
themselves about-to-contend safely; however did think (it,

esse tutius potiri victoriâ sine ullo
to be safer to possess a victory without any

vulnere, viis obsessis, commeatu
wound, the ways (roads) being blocked-up, provision

intercluso: et si Romani cœpissent (plup.
being intercepted: and if the Romans had begun

subj.) recipere sese, cogitabant
to take-away themselves (to retreat), they did think

adoriri impeditos agmine et sub
to attack (them) encumbered on the march and under

sarcinis (pl.), inferiores animo. Hoc consilio
baggage, inferior in mind (spirit). This plan

probato ab ducibus, copiis Romanorum
being approved by (their) generals, the forces of the Romans

productis, tenebant sese castris (pl.),
being drawn-out, they did keep themselves in camp.

Hâc re perspectâ, quum Crassus effecisset
This thing being clearly-seen, when Crassus had rendered

(pluperf. subj.) hostes timidiores suâ
the enemies more-fearful by their

cunctatione atque opinione, nostros milites
delay and expectation, our soldiers

alacriores ad-pugnandum, atque voces
more-cheerful to-fight, and the expressions

omnium audirentur (imp. subj.), non oportere
of all were heard, not to behove

exspectari diutius, quin
to be waited (that they ought not to wait) longer, but-that

iretur ad castra (pl.);
it should be gone (they should go) to the camp;

cohortatus suos, omnibus cupientibus,
having exhorted his (men), all desiring (it),

contendit ad castra (pl.) hostium.
he hastens to the camp of the enemies.

25. Ibi quum alii complerent (imp. subj.)
There when others (some) *did fill*

fossas, alii depellĕrent (imp. subj.) defensores
the ditches, others did drive-off the defenders

vallo que munitionĭbus, multis telis
from the rampart and fortifications, many weapons

conjectis, que auxiliares, quĭbus Crassus
being thrown, and the auxiliaries, to whom Crassus

confidebat non multùm ad pugnam, præberent (imp.
did confide not much to battle, did exhibit

subj.) speciem atque opinionem pugnantĭum
an appearance and supposition of fighting (men)

lapidĭbus que telis subministrandis, et cespitĭbus
in stones and weapons to-be-supplied, and turfs

comportandis ad aggĕrem; quum ĭtem
to-be-brought to (for) *a mound; when likewise*

pugnaretur (imp. subj.) constanter ac non timĭdè
it was fought resolutely and not fearfully

ab hostĭbus, que tela missa ex
by the enemies, and the weapons sent (thrown) *from*

superiore lŏco, accidĕrent (imp. subj.) non frustrà;
the higher place, did fall not in-vain;

equĭtes, castris (pl.) hostĭum circumĭtis,
(some) *horsemen, the camp of the enemies being gone-round,*

renuntiaverunt Crasso castra (pl.) non esse
announced to Crassus the camp not to be

munita eâdem diligentïâ ab Decumanâ
fortified with the same diligence from (at) *the Decuman*

portâ, que habere facĭlem adĭtum.
gate, and to have an easy access.

26. Crassus cohortatus præfectos equĭtum
Crassus having encouraged the prefects of the horse

ut excitarent sŭos magnis præmiis
that they should rouse their (men) *by great rewards*

que pollicitationĭbus, ostendit quid vĕlit
and promises, shows (them) *what he may will*

fiĕri. Illi, ut imperatum-ĕrat, quatŭor	to be done. They, as it had been-commanded, four
cohortĭbus eductis, quæ relictæ præsidĭo	cohorts being led-out, which being left for a guard
castris (pl.), ĕrant intĕgræ ab labore: et	to the camp, were whole (fresh) from labour: and
circumductis longiore itinĕre, ne possent	being led-round by a longer route, lest they might be-able
conspĭci ex castris hostĭum; ocŭlis que	to be seen from the camps of the enemies; the eyes and
mentĭbus omnĭum intentis ad pugnam,	minds of all being engaged to (on) the fight,
pervenerunt celerĭter ad ĕas munitiones, quas	they arrived quickly to those fortifications, which
dixĭmus; atque his proruptis, constiterunt	we have said; and these being thrown-down, they stood
in castris (pl.) hostĭum priŭs quàm posset	in the camp of the enemies before than it might be-able
videri planè ab his aut cognosci, quid	to be seen plainly by these or to be known, what
rĕi gereretur. Tum verò clamore audito	of thing might be carried-on. Then truly a shout being heard
ab ĕâ parte, nostri, virĭbus	from that part, our (men), their forces (strength)
redintegratis, quod plerumque consuevit	being renewed, which generally has been-accustomed
accidĕre in spe victorĭæ, cœperunt impugnare	to happen in the hope of victory, began to assault
acriŭs. Hostes circumventi undĭque,	more-vigorously. The enemies surrounded on-every-side,
omnĭbus rebus desperatis, contenderunt dejicĕre	all things being despaired-of, hastened to cast-out
se per munitiones, et petĕre salutem	themselves through the fortifications, and to seek safety
fŭgâ. Quos equitatus consectatus apertissĭmis	by flight. Whom the cavalry having pursued in most-open

campis,	recepit	se	in	castra (pl.)	multâ
plains,	*betook*	*itself*	*into*	*camp*	*in much*

nocte,		vix	quartâ	parte	relictâ
night (late at night),		*scarcely*	*a fourth*	*part*	*being left*

ex	numěro	quinquaginta	millĭum,	quæ
out-of	*the number*	*of fifty*	*thousands,*	*which*

constabat	venisse	ex	Aquitaniâ	que
it was-evident	*to have come*	*out-of*	*Aquitania*	*and,*

Cantăbris.
the Cantabri.

27. Hâc pugnâ auditâ, maxĭma pars
    This battle being heard, the greatest part

Aquitanïæ dedĭdit sese Crasso, que misit
of Aquitania surrendered itself to Crassus, and sent

obsĭdes ultrò: in quo numěro fuerunt
hostages voluntarily: in which number were

Tarbelli, Bigerriŏnes, Preciani, Vocates, Tarusates,
the Tarbelli, Bigerriones, Preciani, Vocates, Tarusates,

Elusătes, Garītes, Ausci, Garumni, Sibutzates, que
Elusates, Garites, Ausci, Garumni, Sibutzates, and

Cocosates. Paucæ ultĭmæ .iationes, confisæ
Cocosates. A few remotest nations, having relied

tempŏre anni, quòd hĭems subĕrat,
in (on) *the time of the year, because winter was-near*

neglexerunt facĕre id.
neglected to-do that.

28. Fĕrè eodem tempŏre, etsi æstas
    Nearly in the same time, although the summer

ĕrat jam prŏpè exacta, tămen quòd, omni
was already nearly finished, however because, all

Galliâ pacatâ, Morĭni que Menapĭi superĕrant,
Gaul being subdued, the Morini and Menapii did remain,

qui essent (imp. subj.) in armis nĕque misissent (plu-
who were in arms nor had sent

perf. subj.) unquam ad ĕum legatos de pace,
ever to him ambassadors about peace;

LIBER III.

Cæsar   arbitratus   id   bellum   posse
Cæsar   *having thought* *that* *war*   *to be-able*

confici   celeriter,   adduxit   exercitum   eò :   qui
to be finished *quickly,*   *led-on* *the army*   *thither:* *who*

instituerunt   agĕre   bellum   ratione   longè
resolved   *to act (conduct)*   *war*   *in a manner*   *far*

aliâ   ac   reliqui   Galli :   nam,
other (different) *and (than)*   *the rest (other)* *Gauls :* *for,*

quòd   intelligebant   maximas   nationes,   quæ
because   *they did understand*   *the greatest* *nations,* *which*

contendissent (pluperf. subj.)   prœlio   pulsas-esse
had contended   *in battle*   *to have been routed*

que   superatas,   que   habebant   continentes   silvas
and   *overcome,*   *and* *they did have* *extended*   *woods*

ac   paludes,   contulerunt   eò   se   que
and   *marshes,*   *they bore-away*   *thither*   *themselves*   *and*

omnia   sua.   Ad   initium   quarum
all   *their (effects).*   *To*   *the beginning*   *of which*

silvarum,   quum   Cæsar   pervenisset (pluperf. subj.),
woods,   *when*   *Cæsar*   *had arrived,*

que   instituisset (pluperf. subj.)   munire   castra (pl.),
and   *had resolved*   *to fortify*   *the camp,*

nĕque   intĕrim   hostis   visus-esset (pluperf. subj.) ;
nor   *meanwhile*   *the enemy*   *had been seen ;*

nostris   dispersis   in   opĕre,   evolaverunt
our (men)   *being scattered*   *in*   *the work,*   *they flew-out*

subitò   ex   omnibus   partibus   silvæ,   et
suddenly   *from*   *all*   *parts*   *of the wood,* *and*

fecerunt   impĕtum   in   nostros.   Nostri   celeriter
made   *an attack* *upon* *our (men).*   *Our (men)*   *quickly*

ceperunt   arma,   que   repulerunt   eos   in   silvas ;
took   *arms,*   *and*   *repulsed*   *them*   *into*   *the woods ;*

et   compluribus   interfectis,   secuti
and   *many*   *being killed,*   *having followed (them)*

longius   impeditioribus   locis,   deperdiderunt
farther (too far) *in more-entangled*   *places,*   *they lost*

paucos   ex   suis.
a few *out-of*   *their-own.*

DE BELLO GALLICO. [29

29. Caesar   instituit   caedere   silvas   deinceps
    Cæsar   *resolved*   *to cut*   *the woods*   *afterwards*

reliquis   diebus;   et   ne   quis   impetus
on the rest (remaining)   *days;*   *and*   *lest*   *any*   *attack*

posset   fieri   ab   latere   militibus
might be-able *to be made*   *from*   *the flank*   *to* (on) *the soldiers*

inermibus   que   imprudentibus,   collocabat   omnem
unarmed   *and*   *unaware,*   *he did place* *all*

eam   materiam,   quae   caesa-erat,   conversam
that   *material* (timber),   *which*   *had been-cut,* *turned*

ad   hostem,   que   exstruebat   pro   vallo
to   *the enemy,* *and*   *did construct* (it) *for*   *a rampart*

ad   utrumque   latus.   Magno   spatio   confecto
to (on) *each*   *flank.*   *A great*   *space*   *being finished*

paucis   diebus   incredibili   celeritate,   quum
in a few   *days*   *with incredible*   *speed,*   *when*

pecus   atque   extrema   impedimenta   tenerentur
the cattle   *and*   *the farthest*   *baggages*   *were possessed*

(imp. subj.)   jam   ab   nostris,   ipsi   peterent
               now   *by*   *our* (men),   *themselves*   *did seek*

(imp. subj.)   densiores   silvas;   tempestates   ejusmodi
               the thicker   *woods;*   *tempests*   *of this-kind*

consecutae-sunt,   uti   opus   intermitteretur   (imp.
followed,   *that*   *the work*   *was intermitted*

subj.)   necessario;   et·   continuatione   imbrium,
             necessarily;   *and*   *from continuance* *of the rains,*

milites   possent (imp. subj.)   non   contineri   diutius
the soldiers   *were able*   *not*   *to be kept*   *longer*

sub   pellibus.   Itaque,   omnibus   agris
under   *hides* (tents).   *Therefore,*   *all*   *the lands*

eorum   vastatis,   vices   que   aedificiis
of them   *being ravaged,*   *the villages*   *and*   *buildings*

incensis,   Caesar   reduxit   exercitum   et   collocavit
being burnt,   *Cæsar*   *led-back*   *the army*   *and*   *placed* (it)

in   hibernis   in   Aulercis   que   Lexoviis,
in winter-quarters   *in* (among)   *the Aulerci*   *and*   *the Lexovii*

Item	relĭquis	cīvĭtātĭbus,	quæ	fecerant
also	*the rest* (remaining)	*states,*	*which*	*had made*

bellum	proxĭmè.
war	*last.*

QUARTUS LIBER.
FOURTH BOOK.

ARGUMENTUM.
ARGUMENT.

Bellum	contra	Usipĕtes	et Tenchthĕros
The war	*against*	*the Usipetes*	*and Tenchtheri*

continetur	hôc	libro,	atque	obĭter
is contained	*in this*	*book,*	*and*	*by-the-way*

mores	Suevorum	que	Germanorum
the manners	*of the Suevi*	*and*	*of the Germans*

describuntur	generatim :	deinde	trajectus
are described	*generally :*	*afterwards*	*the crossing*

Rheni,	ut transiret	in	Germanĭam;
of the Rhine,	*that he might pass-over*	*into*	*Germany ;*

et	trajectus	in Britannĭam:	utrumque	quem
and	*the crossing*	*into Britain :*	*each*	*which*

nemo	Romanus	ausus-fuĕrat	ante	illum.
no-one	*Roman*	*had dared*	*before*	*him.*

1.
Eâ	hiĕme	quæ secuta-est,	qui fŭit annus,
In that	*winter*	*which followed,*	*which was the year,*

Cneĭo	Pompeĭo,	Marco Crasso consulĭbus,
Cneius	*Pompey,*	*Marcus Crassus (being) consuls.*

Germani Usipētes, et ĭtem Tenchthĕri transiêrunt
the German Usipetes, and also the Tenchtheri crossed

flumen Rhenum cum magnâ multitudĭne homĭnum,
the river Rhine with a great multitude of men,

non longè à mări, quò Rhenus influit.
not far from the sea, where the Rhine flows-in (to it).

Caussa transeundi fuit, quòd exagitati ab
The cause of crossing was, because being harassed by

Suevis complures annos, premebantur bello,
the Suevi many years, they were oppressed by war,

et prohibebantur agriculturâ. Gens
and were prevented from agriculture. The nation

Suevorum est longè maxĭma et bellicosissĭma
of the Suevi is by-far the greatest and most-warlike

omnĭum Germanorum. Ii dicuntur habere
of all the Germans. Those are said to have

centum pagos; ex quĭbus educunt
a hundred villages; out-of which they lead-out

quotannis singŭla (pl.) millĭa armatorum
yearly single thousands of armed (men) (i. e. a

ex sŭis finĭbus, caussâ
thousand from each) out-of their borders, by cause (for

bellandi: relĭqui mănent dŏmi,
the sake) of warring: the rest remain of (at) home,

cŏlunt pro se atque illis. Hi rursus
they till for themselves and them. These again

sunt in armis invĭcem anno pòst; illi
are in arms in-turn in the year after; they

remănent dŏmi. Sic nĕque agricultura, nĕque
remain of (at) home. Thus neither agriculture, nor

ratĭo atque usus belli intermittĭtur.
the method and experience of war is interrupted.

Sed est nĭhil privati ac separati agri
But (there) is nothing of private and separate land

ăpud ĕos: nĕque lĭcet remanere
at (among) them: neither is it lawful to remain

LIBER IV.

longĭus	anno	in	uno	lŏco,	caussā
longer	*(than) a year*	*in*	*one*	*place,*	*by cause (for the sake)*

incolendi :	nĕque	vivunt	multum	frumento,
of inhabiting :	*neither*	*do they live*	*much*	*by (on) corn,*

sed	maxĭmam	partem	lacte	atque	pecŏre ;
but	*the greatest*	*part*	*by (on) milk*	*and*	*cattle ;*

que	sunt	multum	in	venationĭbus :	quæ	res
and	*they are*	*much*	*in*	*huntings :*	*which*	*thing*

et	ălit	vires	et	efficit
both	*nourishes*	*the forces (strength)*	*and*	*renders (them)*

immani	magnitudĭne	corpŏrum	et	genĕre
with huge	*size*	*of bodies*	*both*	*from the kind*

cĭbi,	et	quotidianâ	exercitatione,	et	libertate
of food	*and*	*daily*	*exercise,*	*and*	*freedom*

vitæ,	(quòd	assuefacti	nullo	officĭo	aut
of life,	*(because*	*being accustomed*	*in no*	*-duty*	*or*

disciplinâ	à	puĕris,	facĭant (pres. subj.)
discipline	*from*	*boys (boyhood),*	*they do*

nĭhil	omnino	contra	voluntatem) :	atque	addux-
nothing	*at-all*	*against*	*(their) will) :*	*and*	*they*

erunt	se	in	ĕam	consuetudĭnem,	ut
have brought	*themselves*	*into*	*that*	*habit,*	*that*

habĕant (pres. subj.)	nĕque	quidquam	vestitûs	frigid-
they have	*neither*	*any (thing)*	*of clothing*	*in the*

issĭmis	lŏcis,	præter	pelles ;	propter	exiguitatem
coldest	*places,*	*except*	*skins ;*	*on-account-of*	*the smallness*

quarum,	magna	pars	corpŏris	est	aperta ;	et
of which,	*great*	*part*	*of the body*	*is*	*uncovered ;*	*and*

laventur (pres. subj.)	in	fluminĭbus.
they are washed	*in*	*the rivers.*

2. | Adĭtus | est | mercatorĭbus | ad | ĕos, | măgis |
|---|---|---|---|---|---|
| *Access* | *is* | *for merchants* | *to* | *them,* | *more* |

ĕò,	ut	habĕant
therefore (on this account),	*that*	*they may have (those)*

quĭbus	vendant,	quæ	cepĕrint	bello,
to whom	*they may sell,*	*what*	*they may have taken*	*in war,*

quàm	quò	desiderent	ullam	rem	importari
than	that	they may desire	any	thing	to be imported

ad	se.	Quinetiam	Germani	utuntur	non
to	themselves.	Moreover	the Germans	use	not

importatis	jumentis,	quibus	Gallia	delectatur
imported	beasts-of-burden,	with which	Gaul	is delighted

maxime	que	quæ	parat	impenso	pretio;
most	and	which	it procures	with expensive	price;

sed	efficiunt	hæc,	quæ	sunt	nata	prava
but	they render	these,	which	are	born	mis-shapen

atque	deformia	apud	eos,	quotidianâ	exercitatione,
and	deformed	among	them,	by daily	exercise,

ut	sint		summi	laboris.	Equestribus
that	they may be (capable)		of the highest	labour.	In cavalry

prœliis	desiliunt	sæpe	ex	equis,	ac
fights	they leap-down	often	from	the horses,	and

prœliantur	pedibus;	que	assuefaciunt	equos
fight	with (on) feet;	and	they accustom	the horses

remanere	eodem	vestigio,	ad	quos
to remain	in the same	footstep (spot),	to	which

recipiunt	se	celeriter,	quum	usus	poscit:
they betake	themselves	quickly.	when	need	requires:

neque	quidquam	habetur	turpius	aut
neither	any (thing)	is held	more-shameful	or

inertius	moribus	eorum,	quàm	uti
more-lazy	by the customs	of them,	than	to use

ephippiis (abl.).	Itaque,	quamvis		pauci
saddles.	Therefore,	although (however)		few

audent	adire	ad	quemvis	numerum	equitum
they dare	to approach	to	any	number	of horsemen

ephippiatorum.	Sinunt	non	vinum	importari
using-saddles.	They permit	not	wine	to be imported

omnino	ad	se,	quòd	arbitrantur	homines
at-all	to	themselves,	because	they think	men

remollescere	eâ	re	ad	laborem	ferendum,
to become-relaxed	by that	thing	to	labour	to-be-borne,

atque	effœminari.
and	to be rendered-effeminate.

LIBER IV.

3. Publĭcè   pŭtant   esse   maximam
  Publicly (as a nation) *they think* (*it*) *to be* *the greatest*

laudem,   agros   vacare   quàm   latissĭmè
praise, *the lands* *to be-vacant* *as*   *most-extensively* (*as*

                    à   sŭis finĭbus.   Sig-
extensively as possible) *from their borders.* (*They think it*) *to*

nificari   hâc   re,   magnum   numĕrum   civitatum
be signified *by this* *thing,* *a great* *number* *of states*

non potuisse   sustinere   sŭam   vim.   Ităque
not *to have been-able* *to withstand* *their* *force.* *Therefore*

arcĭter sexcenta   millĭa passŭum agri   dicuntui
about six hundred thousands of paces of land (*country*) *are said*

   vacare   à   Suevis   ex   unâ parte. Ubĭi
to be-vacant *from* *the Suevi* *from* *one* *part.* *The Ubii*

succedunt   ad   altĕram partem,   quorum civitas
come-next *at* *the other* *part,* *whose* *state*

fŭit   ampla   atque   florens, ut captus
has been *extensive* *and* *flourishing,* *as* *the capacity*

Germanorum   est ;   et qui sunt   paullò huma-
of the Germans *is ;* *and* *who* *are* *a little* *more-*

niores   etĭam caetĕris,   qui sunt ejusdem
civilized *also* *than the rest,* *who* *are* *of the same*

genĕris ; propterĕa quòd attingunt   Rhenum, que
race ;   *because* *that* *they touch-on* *the Rhine,* *and*

mercatores ventĭtant   multùm ad   ĕos, et ipsi
merchants *often-come* *much* *to* *them,* *and* *they*

sunt   assuefacti   Gallĭcis   morĭbus   propter
are *accustomed* *to Gallic* *manners* *on-account-of*

propinquitatem. Quum   Suevi,   experti   hos
(*their*) *nearness.* *When* *the Suevi,* *having tried* *these*

saepè multis bellis,   potuissent (pluperf. subj.) non
often *in many* *wars,* *had been-able*   *not*

expellĕre   finĭbus,   propter
to expel (*them*) *from* (*their*) *borders,* *on-account-of*

amplitudĭnem que gravitatem   civitatis,
the extent *and* *weight* (consequence) *of the state,*

támĕn	fecerunt	vectigales	sĭbi,
however	*they made*	*(them) tributary*	*to themselves,*

ac	redegerunt	multò	humiliores	que
and	*reduced* (brought them)	*by-much*	*lower*	*and*

infirmiores.
weaker.

4. Usĭpĕtes et Tenchthĕri, quos dixĭmus
    The Usipetes and Tenchtheri, whom we have said

suprà, fuerunt in eâdem caussâ; qui sustinuerun*
above, were in the same cause (condition); *who supported*

vim	Suevorum	complures	annos:	tămen
the violence	*of the Suevi*	*many*	*years:*	*however*

ad	extremum	expulsi	agris,	et
at	*last*	*being driven-out*	*from (their) lands,*	*and*

vagati	multis	lŏcis	Germanĭæ
having wandered	*in many*	*places*	*of Germany (during)*

triennĭum,	pervenerunt ad	Rhenum:	quas
three-years'-space,	*they arrived at*	*the Rhine:*	*which*

regiones	Menapĭi	incolebant,	et	habebant
countries	*the Menapii*	*did inhabit,*	*and*	*did have*

agros,	ædificĭa,	que	vicos	ad utramque	ripam
lands,	*buildings,*	*and*	*villages*	*at each*	*bank*

flumĭnis:	sed	perterrĭti	adventu	tantæ
of the river:	*but*	*affrighted*	*by the arrival*	*of so-great*

multitudĭnis,	demigraverunt	ex	his	ædificĭis,
a multitude,	*they emigrated*	*from*	*these*	*buildings,*

quæ	habuĕrant	trans	flumen:	et	præsidĭis
which	*they had had*	*beyond*	*the river:*	*and*	*garrisons*

dispositis	cis	Rhenum,	prohibebant
being arranged	*on-this-side*	*the Rhine,*	*they did hinder*

Germanos	transire.	Illi	experti	omnĭa,
the Germans	*to cross-over.*	*They*	*having tried*	*all (things)*

quum	possent (imp. subj.)	nĕque	contendĕre
when	*they were able*	*neither*	*to contend*

vi,	propter	inopĭam	navĭum,	nĕque
by force,	*on-account-of*	*the want*	*of ships,*	*neither*

LIBER IV.

transire	clàm,	propter	custodias
to cross-over	*secretly,*	*on-account-of*	*the watches*

Menapiorum,	simulaverunt	se	reverti	in
of the Menapii,	*pretended*	*themselves*	*to return*	*into*

súas	sedes	que	regiones;	et	pro-
their	*seats* (settlements)	*and*	*countries;*	*and*	*having*

gressi	vïam	tridŭi,	reverterunt
advanced	*a way* (distance)	*of three-days,*	*they returned*

rursus;	atque	omni	hoc	itinĕre	confecto	unâ
again;	*and*	*all*	*this*	*journey*	*being finished*	*in one*

nocte	equitatu,	oppresserunt	Menapios	inscïos
night	*by cavalry,*	*they overwhelmed*	*the Menapii*	*ignorant*

que	inopinantes;	qui	facti	certiores	de	dis-
and	*unaware;*	*who*	*being made*	*more-sure*	*of*	*the de-*

cessu	Germanorum	per exploratores,	remigravĕrant
parture	*of the Germans*	*by spies,*	*had re-emigrated*

sine	mětu	in	súos	vicos	trans	Rhenum.
without	*fear*	*into*	*their*	*villages*	*beyond*	*the Rhine.*

His	interfectis	que	navïbus	eorum	occupatis,
These	*being slain*	*and*	*the ships*	*of them*	*being seized,*

priùs-quam	ĕa	pars	Menapiorum,	quæ	ĕrat
before-that	*that*	*part*	*of the Menapii,*	*which*	*was*

citra	Rhenum,	fiĕret (imp. subj.)	certïor,
on-this-side	*the Rhine,*	*was made*	*more-sure,*

transierunt	flumen;	atque	omnïbus	ædificïis
they crossed	*the river;*	*and*	*all*	*the buildings*

eorum	occupatis,	aluerunt	se	copïis
of them	*being seized,*	*they supported*	*themselves*	*with the stores*

eorum	relíquam	partem	hiĕmis.
of them	(*during*) *the rest* (remaining)	*part*	*of the winter.*

5. Cæsar	factus	certior	de	his	rebus,
Cæsar	*being made*	*more-sure*	*of*	*these*	*things,*

et	verïtus	infirmitatem	Gallorum,	quòd
and	*having feared*	*the weakness*	*of the Gauls,*	*because*

sunt	mobïles	in	consilïis	capiendis,	et
they are	*changeable*	*in*	*counsels*	*to-be-taken,*	*and*

184 DE BELLO GALLICO. [6

pierumque	student	novis	rebus,	existimavit	nihil
generally	*study*	*for new*	*things,*	*thought*	*nothing*

committendum	his.	Autem	hoc	est	Gallicæ
to-be-entrusted	*to these.*	*But*	*this*	*is*	*of Gallic*

consuetudinis;	ut	et	cogant (pres. subj.)	viatores,
custom;	*that*	*both*	*they compel*	*travellers,*

etiam	invitos,	consistere;	et	quærant (pres. subj.)
even	*unwilling,*	*to stop;*	*and*	*inquire*

quod	quisque	eorum	audierit	aut
what	*each*	*of them*	*may have heard*	*or*

cognoverit	de	quâque	re:	et
may have known	*about*	*each*	*thing:*	*and*

vulgus	circumsistat (pres. subj.)	mercatores
the common-people	*stands-round*	*the merchants*

in	oppidis:	cogant (pres. subj.)	pronuntiare	ex
in	*the towns:*	*compel (them)*	*to declare*	*from*

quibus	regionibus	veniant,	que	quas	res
what	*countries*	*they may come,*	*and*	*what*	*things*

cognoverint	ibi.	Permoti	his
they may have known	*there.*	*Moved-much*	*by these*

rumoribus	atque	auditionibus,	ineunt	consilia
reports	*and*	*hear-says,*	*they enter-on*	*counsels*

sæpè	de	summis	rebus:	quorum
often	*concerning*	*the most-important*	*things:*	*of which*

est	necesse	pœnitere	eos	è-vestigio,	quum
it is	*necessary*	*to repent*	*them*	*immediately,*	*when*

	serviant (pres. subj.)	incertis	rumoribus,
(since)	*they are-slaves*	*to uncertain*	*reports,*

et	plerique	respondeant (pres. subj.)	ficta
and	*most (travellers)*	*answer*	*feigned*

	ad	voluntatem	eorum.
(things)	*to*	*the will*	*of them.*

6. Quâ consuetudine cognitâ, Cæsar proficiscitur
Which custom being known, Cæsar sets-out

ad	exercitum	maturiùs	quàm	consueverat,
to	*the army*	*sooner*	*than*	*he had been-accustomed,*

ne	occurrĕret	graviori	bello.	Quum	venisset
lest	*he might meet*	*to a heavier*	*war.*	*When*	*he had come*

(pluperf. subj.) eò cognovit ea
thither he knew (learned) *those* (*things*)

facta,	quæ	suspicatus-ĕrat	fŏre :
done,	*which*	*he had suspected*	*to be-about-to-be :*

legationes	missas	à	nonnullis	civitatĭbus	ad
embassies	*being sent*	*by*	*some*	*states*	*to*

Germanos,	que	eos	invitatos	ŭtì	discedĕrent
the Germans,	*and*	*those*	*being invited*	*that*	*they should depart*

ab	Rheno :	que	omnĭa	quæ
from	*the Rhine :*	*and*	*all* (*things*)	*which*

postulâssent fŏre parata ab
they might have demanded to be-about-to-be prepared by

se.	Quâ	spe	Germani	adducti,
themselves.	*By which*	*hope*	*the Germans*	*being induced,*

vagabantur	jam	latĭùs,	et	pervenĕrant	in
did wander	*now*	*more-widely,*	*and*	*had arrived*	*into*

fines	Eburonum	et	Condrusorum,	qui
the borders	*of the Eburones*	*and*	*of the Condrusi,*	*who*

sunt	clientes	Trevirorum.	Principĭbus	Gallĭæ
are	*dependants*	*of the Treviri.*	*The chiefs*	*of Gaul*

evocatis,	Cæsar	existimavit	ea,	quæ
being summoned,	*Cæsar*	*thought*	*those* (*things*),	*which*

cognovĕrat,	dissimulanda	sĭbi :	que
he had known,	*to-be-dissembled*	*to* (*by*) *himself :*	*and*

anĭmis	eorum	permulsis	et	confirmatis,	que
the minds	*of them*	*being soothed*	*and*	*strengthened,*	*and*

equitatu	imperato,	constitŭit	gerĕre
cavalry	*being ordered* (*to be sent*),	*he resolved*	*to carry-on*

bellum cum Germanis.
war with the Germans.

7. Frumentarĭâ re comparatâ, que equitĭbus
 Corn affair being prepared, and cavalry

delectis,	cœpit	facére	ĭter	in	ea
being chosen,	*he began*	*to make*	(*his*) *march*	*into*	*those*

lŏca,	in	quĭbus	lŏcis	audiebat	Germanos
places	*in*	*which*	*places*	*he did hear*	*the Germans*

esse.	A	quĭbus	quum	abesset (imp. subj.)
to be.	*From*	*whom*	*when*	*he was distant*

ĭter	paucorum	dierum,	legati	venerunt	ab
a journey	*of a few*	*days,*	*ambassadors*	*came*	*from*

ĭis,	quorum	hæc	fŭit	oratĭo:	"Germanos
them,	*of whom*	*this*	*was*	*the speech:*	*"The Germans*

nĕque	inferre	bellum	Romano	popŭlo priores,
neither	*to bring-on*	*war*	*to the Roman*	*people former*

	nĕque	tămen	recusare,	quin contendant
(first),	*nor*	*however*	*to refuse,*	*but-that they may contend*

armis,	si	lacessantur:	quòd	hæc	consuetudo
by arms,	*if*	*they be provoked:*	*because*	*this*	*custom*

Germanorum	tradĭta-sit (perf. subj.)	à	majorĭbus,
of the Germans	*has been delivered*	*by*	*(their) ancestors,*

resistĕre,	nĕque	deprecari,	quicumque
to oppose,	*neither* (and not)	*to beg-off,*	*whosoever*

infĕrant	bellum:	tămen	dicĕre
may bring-on	*war:*	*however*	*to say* (that they must

hoc:	venisse	invitos,	ejectos dŏmo:
say) *this:*	*to have come*	*unwilling,*	*cast-out from home:*

si	Romani	vĕlint	sŭam	gratĭam,	posse esse
if	*the Romans*	*may will*	*their*	*favour,*	*to be-able to be*

utĭles	amicos	ĕis:	vel	attribŭant agros
useful	*friends*	*to them:*	*either*	*they may assign lands*

sibi,	vel	patiantur	tenere	ĕos, quos
to themselves,	*or*	*may allow* (them)	*to hold*	*those, which*

possedĕrint	armis:	sese concedĕre
they may have possessed	*by arms:*	*themselves to yield*

Suevis	unis;	quĭbus	ne quĭdem
to the Suevi	*one* (alone);	*to whom*	*not indeed* (even)

immortales	Dii	possint	esse păres:	nemĭnem
the immortal	*Gods*	*may be-able*	*to be equal:*	*no-one*

relĭquum	esse	quĭdem	in terris,	quem
rest (else)	*to be*	*indeed*	*in the lands* (on earth),	*whom*

non-possint	superare."
they may not-be-able	*to overcome."*

LIBER IV.

8. Cæsar respondit ad hæc, quæ
Cæsar answered to these (words), what (thing.)

visum-est: sed exitus orationis fuit:
seemed (fit): but the conclusion of (his) speech was:

"Nullam amicitiam posse esse sibi cum
"No friendship to-be-able to be for himself with

his, si remanerent in Galliâ: neque esse
them, if they should remain in Gaul: neither to-be

verum occupare alienos, qui
true (proper for them) to seize others' (lands), who

potuerint non tueri suos fines:
may har: been-able not to defend their-own borders:

neque ullos agros vacare in Galliâ, qui
neither any 'lands to-be-vacant in Gaul, which

possint dari sine injuriâ, præsertim
may be-able to be given without injury, especially

tantæ multitudini: sed licere, si velint,
to so-great a multitude: but to-be-lawful, if they may will,

considere in finibus Ubiorum; legati
to settle in the territories of the Ubii; ambassadors

quorum sint (pres. subj.) apud se, et
of whom are at (with) himself, and

querantur (pres. subj.) de injuriis Suevorum, et
complain of the injuries of the Suevi, and

petant (pres. subj.) auxilium à se: se
ask aid from himself: himself

impetraturum hoc ab Ubiis."
about-to-obtain this from the Ubii."

9. Legati dixerunt se relaturos
The ambassadors said themselves about-to-carry-back

hæc ad suos, et re
these (words) to their-own (people), and the thing

deliberatâ, reversuros ad Cæsarem
being considered, (to be) about-to-return to Cæsar

post tertium diem: intereâ petierunt
after the third day: meantime they required

ne-moveret	castra (pl.)	propĭŭs	se.
he would not-move	*(his) camp*	*nearer*	*themselves.*

Cæsar	dixit	ne	id	quĭdem	posse
Cæsar	*said*	*not*	*that*	*indeed (even)*	*to be-able*

impetrari	ab	se.	Enim	cognovĕrat
to be obtained	*from*	*himself.*	*For*	*he had known*

magnam	partem	equitatûs	missam	ab
a great	*part*	*of (their) cavalry*	*having been sent*	*by*

iis	ad	Ambivaritos	trans	Mŏsam, aliquot
them	*to*	*the Ambivariti*	*across*	*the Meuse,* *some*

diebus	antè,	caussâ	prædandi	que
days	*before,*	*by cause (for the sake)*	*of plundering*	*and*

frumentandi :	arbitrabatur	hos	equĭtes
of providing-corn :	*he did think*	*these*	*horsemen*

expectari,	atque	mŏram	interponi	caussâ
to be waited-for,	*and*	*the delay*	*to be interposed*	*by cause*

ejus	rĕi.
(for the sake) of that	*thing.*

10.
Mŏsa	proflŭit	ex	monte	Vogĕso,
The Mosa (Meuse)	*flows*	*from*	*mount*	*Vogesus*

	qui	est	in	finĭbus Lingŏnum ;
(Vosges),	*which*	*is*	*in*	*the territories of the Lingones ;*

et	quâdam	parte	Rheni	receptâ,	quæ
and	*a certain*	*part*	*of the Rhine*	*being received,*	*which*

	appellatur	Vahălis,	efficit	insŭlam
(part)	*is called*	*Vahalis (Waal),*	*it forms*	*the island*

Batavorum :	nĕque-lorgĭŭs	ab	ĕo
of the Batavi :	*and-not-farther*	*from*	*that (than)*

octoginta	millĭbus	passŭum	transit	in Oceănum.
eighty	*thousands*	*of paces*	*it passes*	*into the Ocean.*

Autem	Rhenus	orĭtur	ex	Lepontĭis, qui
But	*the Rhine*	*arises*	*out-of*	*the Lepontii,* *who*

incŏlunt	Alpes,	et	fertur citatus	longo spatĭo
habit	*the Alps,*	*and*	*is borne rapid*	*in a long distance*

per	fines	Nantuatĭum,	Helvetiorum,
through	*the territories*	*of the Nantuates,*	*of the Helvetii,*

Sequanorum,	Mediomatricorum,	Triboccorum,	que
of the Sequani,	*of the Mediomatrici,*	*of the Tribocci,*	*and*

Trevirorum;	et	ŭbi	appropinquat	Oceăno,
of the Treviri ;	*and*	*when*	*it approaches*	*to the Ocean,*

diffiŭit	in	plures	partes;	multis
it flows-dividedly	*into*	*more* (several)	*parts ;*	*many*

que	ingentĭbus	insŭlis	effectis ;	magna	pars
and	*great*	*islands*	*being formed ;*	*a great*	*part*

quarum	incolĭtur	à	fĕris	que	barbăris
of which	*is inhabited*	*by*	*wild*	*and*	*barbarous*

nationĭbus;	(ex	quĭbus		sunt	qui
nations ;	*(out-of*	*which*	(*there*) *are*		(*some*) *who*

existimantur	vivĕre	piscĭbus	atque	ovis
are thought	*to live*	(*on*) *fishes*	*and*	*the eggs*

avĭum) ;	que	inflŭit	in	Oceănum	multis
of birds);	*and*	*it flows-in*	*into*	*the Ocean*	*by many*

capitĭbus.
heads.

11. Quum Caesar abesset (imp. subj.) ab
When Caesar was-distant from

hoste	non	amplĭus	duodĕcim	millĭbus
the enemy	*not*	*more*	(*than*) *twelve*	*thousands*

passŭum,	legati	revertuntur	ad	ĕum,
of paces,	*the ambassadors*	*returned*	*to*	*him,*

ut	constitutum-ĕrat :	qui	congressi	in
as	*it had been-appointed :*	*who*	*having met* (*him*)	*on*

itinĕre,	orabant	magnopĕrè,	ne-progrederetur
the march,	*did pray*	*greatly,*	*that-he would not-advance*

longĭus.	Quum	impetrâssent (pluperf. subj.)	non
farther.	*When*	*they had obtained*	*not*

id,	petebant,	"útì	praemittĕret	ad	ĕos
that,	*they did ask,*	*" that*	*he would send-before*	*to*	*those*

equĭtes,	qui	antecessissent (pluperf. subj.)	agmen,
horsemen,	*who*	*had preceded*	*the troop*

	que	prohiberet	ĕos	pugnâ:	que
(*army*),	*and*	*would prohibit*	*them*	*from battle ;*	*and*

uti	faceret	potestatem	sibi	mittendi
that	he would make	power	to themselves	of sending

legatos	in	Ubios:	si	principes que	senatus
ambassador	unto	the Ubii:	if	the chiefs and	senate

quorum	fecissent	fidem	sibi
of whom	might have made	faith (given security)	to themselves

jurejurando,	ostendebant	se	usuros	eâ
by oath,	they did show	themselves	about-to-use (accept)	that

conditione,	quæ	ferretur	à Cæsare;
condition,	which	might be brought (was offered)	by Cæsar;

daret	sibi	spatium	tridui	ad
he might give	to themselves	the space	of three-days	to

has	res	conficiendas."	Cæsar arbitrabatur
these	things	to-be-accomplished."	Cæsar did think

omnia	hæc	pertinere	eòdem-illò,	ut,
all	these (things)	to tend	to-that-same (point),	that.

morâ	tridui	interposità,	equites
the delay	of three-days	having been interposed,	the cavalry

eorum,	qui abessent (imp. subj.)	reverterentur:
of them,	who were-absent	might return:

tamen	dixit	sese	non	processurum	longiùs
however	he said	himself	not	about-to-advance	farther

	quatuor	millibus	passuum	eo die	caussâ
(than)	four	thousands	of paces	in that day	by cause

	aquationis:	convenirent huc
(for the sake)	of watering:	they should assemble hither

quàm frequentissimi	postero
as most-numerous (as numerous as possible)	on the following

die,	ut cognosceret	de	postulatis
day,	that he might know (learn)	concerning	the requests

eorum.	Interim	mittit	ad præfectos,
of them.	Meanwhile	he sends (persons) to	the commanders,

qui	antecesserant	cum	omni	equitatu,	qui
who	had gone-before	with	all	the cavalry,	who

nuntiarent,	ne-lacesserent	hostes
might announce,	they should not-provoke	the enemies

proelio;	et,	si	ipsi	lacesserentur,
to battle ;	*and,*	*if*	*themselves*	*should be provoked,*

sustinerent	quŏad	ipse	accessisset
they should support (it)	*until*	*himself*	*might have approached*

propius cum exercitu.
nearer with the army.

12. At hostes, ubi primùm conspexerunt
But the enemies, when first they beheld

nostros equites, numerus quorum erat quinque
our cavalry, the number of whom was of five

millium, quum ipsi haberent (imp. subj.) non
thousands, when themselves did have not

amplius octingentos equites, quòd ii,
more (than) eight-hundred cavalry, because those,

qui ierant trans Mosam caussâ
who had gone beyond the Meuse for the sake

frumentandi, redierant nondum; nostris
of foraging, had returned not-yet; our (men)

timentibus nihil, quòd legati eorum
fearing nothing, because the ambassadors of them

discesserant paullò antè à Cæsăre, atque
had departed a little before from Cæsar, and

is dies petitus-erat ab iis induciis (pl.),
that day had been sought by them for a truce,

impetu facto, perturbaverunt celeriter nostros.
an attack being made, confused quickly our (men).

Nostris rursus resistentibus, desilierunt ad
Our (men) again resisting, they leaped-down to

pedes, suâ consuetudine, que equis
(on) feet, by their custom, and the horses

suffossis, que compluribus nostris dejectis,
being stabbed, and many our (men) being thrown-down,

conjecerunt reliquos in fugam; atque egerunt
they threw the rest into flight, and drove (them)

ita perterritos, ut desistĕrent (imp. subj.) non
so affrighted, that they did cease not

fŭgâ,	priŭs	quàm	venissent	(pluperf. sŭbj.)
from flight,	*before*	*than*	*they had come*	

in	conspectum	nostri	agmĭnis.	Quatŭor et
into	*sight*	*of our*	*troop* (army).	*Four and*

septuaginta	ex	nostris	equitĭbus	interficiuntur in
seventy	*out-of*	*our*	*cavalry*	*are killed in*

ĕo	prœlĭo;	in his	Piso,	fortissĭmus vir,
that	*battle;*	*in these*	(was) *Piso,*	*a most-brave man,*

Aquitanus,	natus	amplissĭmo	genĕre,
an Aquitanian,	*born*	*from most-extensive* (noble)	*birth,*

cujus	ăvus	obtinuĕrat	regnum
whose	*grand-father*	*had obtained*	*kingdom* (sovereign

	in	sŭâ	civitate,	appellatus amicus à
power)	*in*	*his-own*	*state,*	*being called a friend by*

nostro	senatu.	Quum	hic	ferret (imp. subj.)
our	*senate.*	*When*	*he*	*did bring*

auxilĭum	fratri	intercluso	ab	hostĭbus,
aid	*to* (his) *brother*	*shut-in*	*by*	*the enemies,*

eripŭit	illum	ex	pericŭlo;	ipse, ĕquo
he rescued	*him*	*from*	*danger;*	*himself,* (his) *horse*

vulnerato,	dejectus	restĭtit fortissĭme
being wounded,	*being thrown-down*	*resisted most-bravely*

quŏad	potŭit.	Quum circumventus
as-long-as	*he was-able.*	*When being surrounded*

cecĭdisset (plup. subj.);	multis vulnerĭbus	acceptis,
he had fallen;	*many wounds*	*being received,*

atque	frater,	qui	jam	excessĕrat
and	(his) *brother,*	*who*	*already*	*had departed*

prœlĭo,	animadvertisset (pluperf. subj.)	id
from the battle,	*had perceived*	*that*

prŏcul,	ĕquo	incitato	obtŭlit sese
at-a-distance,	(his) *horse*	*being urged-on,*	*he offered himself*

hostĭbus,	atque	interfectus-est
to the enemies,	*and*	*was-slain.*

13

Hoc	prœlĭo	facto,	Cæsar jam
This	*battle*	*being made* (fought),	*Cæsar now*

LIBER IV.

arbitrabatur nĕque legatos audiendos
did think *neither* *the ambassadors* *(ought) to-be-heard*

sĭbi, nĕque conditiones accipiendas ab
to (by) himself, *neither* *conditions* *to-be-received* *from*

iis, qui, pace petitâ, intulissent (pluperf.
those, *who,* *peace* *being sought,* *had brought-on*

subj.) bellum ultrò, per dŏlum atque
war *voluntarily,* *through* *deceit* *and*

insidĭas. Verò judicabat esse summæ
snares. *But* *he did judge (it)* *to be* *of the highest*

dementĭæ expectare, dum copĭæ hostĭum
madness *to wait,* *until* *the forces* *of the enemies*

augerentur que equitatus reverteretur
might be increased *and* *(their) cavalry* *might return :*

et infirmitate Gallorum cognĭtâ,
and *the weakness* (levity) *of the Gauls* *being known,*

sentiebat quantum auctoritatis hostes
he did perceive *how-much* *of authority* *the enemies*

consecuti-essent (pluperf. subj.) ăpud ĕos uno
had obtained *among* *them* *by one*

prœlĭo; quĭbus existimabat nĭhil spatĭi
battle; *to whom* *he did think* *nothing* *of space* (time)

dandum ad consilĭa capienda. His rebus
to-be-given *to (for)* *counsels* *to-be-taken.* *These* *things*

constitutis, et consilĭo communicato
being determined, *and* *(his) plan* *being communicated*

cum legatis et quæstore, opportunissĭma
with *the lieutenants* *and* *the quæstor,* *a most-convenient*

res accĭdit, ne-prætermittĕret quem dĭem
thing *happened,* *that-he-might-not-pass-by* *any* *day*

pugnæ, quòd manè postridĭe ejus
of a battle, *because* *in-the-morning* *the day-after* *of that*

diei, Germani usi et eâdem
day; *the Germans* *having used* *both* *the same*

perfidĭâ et simulatione, frequentes, omnĭbus
treachery *and* *pretence,* *numerous,* *all*

   principĭbus   que   majorĭbus-natu
  (their) chiefs   *and*   *(those) greater-by-birth* (elders)

adhibĭtis,   venerunt   ad   ĕum   in   castra (pl.);
being brought,   *came*   *to*   *him*   *into*   *the camp;*

sĭmul,   ut   dicebatur,   caussâ
at-the-same-time,   *as*   *it was said,*   *by cause* (for the sake)

suï   purgandi,   quòd   commisissent
of themselves   *to-be-cleared,*   *because*   *they had engaged*

(pluperf. subj.)   prœlĭum   pridïe,   contrà   atque
                  battle   *the day-before,*   *contrary*   *and*

     dictum-esset (pluperf. subj.),   et   ipsi
(than) it had been-said,   *and*   *themselves*

petîssent (pluperf. subj.) :   sĭmul   ut
had requested: *at-the-same-time*   *that*

impetrarent   quid,   si   possent (imp. subj.),
they might obtain   *some (thing),*   *if*   *they could,*

fallendo   de   induciis.   Quos   oblatos
by deceiving   *concerning*   *the truces.*   *Whom being presented*

sĭbi   Cæsar   gavisus,   jussit   retineri :
to himself   *Cæsar*   *having rejoiced,*   *commanded*   *to be detained:*

ipse   eduxit   omnes   copĭas   castris (pl.);
himself   *led-out*   *all*   *(his) forces*   *from the camp;*

jussit   equitatum   subsĕqui   agmen,
he ordered   *the cavalry*   *to follow-near*   *the troop* (army),

quòd   existimabat   perterrĭtum-esse   recenti
because   *he did think*   *(it) to have been-dismayed*   *by the late*

prœlĭo.
battle.

14. Triplĭci   acĭe   institutâ,   et   itinĕre
    A triple   *line*   *being arranged,*   *and*   *a march*

octo   millĭum   confecto   celerĭter,   pervenit   ad
of eight   *miles*   *being finished*   *quickly,*   *he arrived*   *at*

castra   hostĭum,   priùs   quàm   Germani
the camps   *of the enemies,*   *before*   *than*   *the Germans*

possent   sentire   quid   ageretur :   qui
might be-able   *to perceive*   *what*   *might be done:*   *who*

LIBER IV.

perterrĭti	subĭtò	omnĭbus	rebus,	et
being affrighted	*suddenly*	*by all*	*things,*	*both*

celeritate	nostri	adventûs,	et	discessu
by the quickness	*of our*	*arrival,*	*and*	*by the departure*

suorum,		nĕque	spatĭo	dăto	consilĭi
of their-own (people),		*neither*	*space*	*being given*	*of counsel*

habendi,	nĕque	capiendi	arma,	perturbantur,
to-be-had,	*nor*	*of taking*	*arms,*	*are disturbed,*

ne	præstaret	educĕre	copĭas
whether	*it might be-better*	*to lead-out*	*(their) forces*

adversùs	hostem,	an	defendĕre	castra,	an petĕre
against	*the enemy,*	*or*	*to defend*	*the camps,*	*or to seek*

salutem	fŭgâ.	Quum	tĭmor	quorum	significaretur
safety	*by flight.*	*When*	*the fear*	*of whom*	*was signified*

(imp. subj.)	fremĭtu	et	concursu,	nostri	milĭtes
	by the noise	*and*	*running,*	*our*	*soldiers*

incitati	perfidĭâ	pristĭni	diei,	irruperunt
urged-on	*by the treachery*	*of the former*	*day,*	*burst-in*

in	castra (pl.) :	in	quo	lŏco,	qui
into	*the camp:*	*in*	*which*	*place,*	*(those) who*

potŭerunt	capĕre	arma	celerĭter,	restiterunt	nostris
were-able	*to take*	*arms*	*quickly,*	*resisted*	*to our (men)*

paulisper,	atque	commiserunt	prœlĭum	inter
a little-while,	*and*	*engaged*	*battle*	*between*

carros	que	impedimenta.	At	relĭqua
the waggons	*and*	*baggages.*	*But*	*the rest (remaining)*

multitudo	puerorum	que	mulĭerum	(nam
multitude	*of boys*	*and*	*of women*	*(for*

excessĕrant	'dŏmo	cum	omnĭbus	sŭis
they had departed	*from home*	*with*	*all*	*their*

	que	transiĕrant	Rhenum,)	cœpit	fugĕre
(people)	*and*	*had crossed*	*the Rhine,)*	*began*	*to flee*

passim,	ad-consectandos	quos	Cæsar	misit
every-where,	*to-pursue*	*whom*	*Cæsar*	*sent*

equitatum.
the cavalry.

DE BELLO GALLICO. [15

15. **Germani,** clamore audito post
    The Germans, *a shout* *being heard* *behind*

tergum, quum viderent (imp. subj.) sŭos
the back (rear), *when* *they did see* *their* (*people*)

interfĭci, armis abjectis que
to be slaughtered, (*their*) *arms* *being cast-away* *and*

militarĭbus signis relictis, ejecerunt se
military *standards* *being left,* *cast-out* *themselves*

ex castris (pl.) ; et quum pervenissent
out-of *the camp ;* *and* *when* *they had arrived*

(pluperf. subj.) ad confluentem Mŏsæ et
                 at *the conflux* *of the Meuse* *and*

Rheni, relĭquâ fŭgâ desperatâ, magno
of the Rhine, *the rest-of flight* *being despaired-of,* *a great*

numĕro interfecto, relĭqui præcipitaverunt se
number *being killed,* *the rest* *precipitated* *themselves*

in flumen, atque oppressi ĭbi timore,
into *the river,* *and* *being overpowered* *there* *by fear,*

lassitudĭne, et vi flumĭnis, periêrunt.
by fatigue, *and* *by the force* *of the river,* *they perished.*

Omnes nostri incolŭmes ad unum,
All *our* (*men*) *safe* *to* *one* (to a man),

perpaucis vulneratis, receperunt se in
very few *being wounded,* *betook* *themselves* *into*

castris (pl.) ex timore tanti belli, quum
camp *out-of* *fear* *of so-great* *a war,* *when*

numĕrus hostĭum fuisset quadringentorum
the number *of the enemies* *might have been* *of four-hundred*

triginta millĭum capĭtum. Cæsar fecit
thirty *thousands* *of heads.* *Cæsar* *made* (gave)

potestatem discedendi ĭis, quos retinuĕrat
power *of departing* *to those,* *whom* *he had detaine*

in castris (pl.). Illi verĭti supplicĭa
in *the camp.* *They* *having feared* *the punishments*

que cruciatus Gallorum, quorum agros vexa-
and *tortures* *of the Gauls,* *whose* *lands* *they had*

LIBER IV.

vĕrant, dixerunt se velle remanere ăpud
harassed, said themselves to will to remain at (with)

ĕum. Cæsar concessit libertatem his.
him. Cæsar granted (this) liberty to them.

16. Germanĭco bello confecto, Cæsar de
The German war being finished, Cæsar from

multis caussis statŭit Rhenum transeundum-esse
many causes resolved the Rhine to-be-crossed

sĭbi; quarum illa fŭit justissĭma;
to (by) himself; of which that (this) was the most-just

quòd, quum vidēret (imp. subj.)
(most cogent); because, when he did see

Germanos impelli tam facĭlè, ut veni-
the Germans to be impelled so easily, that they might

rent in Gallĭam, volŭit ĕos timere súis
come into Gaul, he willed them to fear for their-own

rebus quŏque, quum intelligĕrent exercĭtum
things also, when they might understand the army

Romani popŭli et posse et audere
of the Roman people both to-be-able and to dare

transire Rhenum. Accessit etĭam,
to cross the Rhine. It-acceded (added to this) also,

quòd illa pars equitatûs Usipĕtum et
because that part of the cavalry of the Usipetes and

Tenchtherorum, quam commemoravi suprà
of the Tenchtheri, which I have mentioned above

transîsse Mŏsam caussâ
to have crossed the Meuse by cause (for the sake)

prædandi que frumentandi, nĕque inter-
of plundering and of providing-corn, nor to have been-

fuisse prœlĭo, recepĕrat se trans
present to (at) the battle, had betaken itself across

Rhenum, post fŭgam suorum in
the Rhine, after the flight of their-own (people) into

fines Sicambrorum, que conjunxĕrat se
the borders of the Sicambri, and had united itself

cum	iis.	Ad	quos	quum	Cæsar misisset (plu-
with	them.	To	whom	when	Cæsar had sent

perf. subj.) nuncios, qui postularent, "uti
                messengers, who should demand, "that

dederent sibi eos, qui intulissent
they should surrender to himself those, who had brought-on

(pluperf. subj.) bellum sibi que Galliæ,"
                war to himself and to Gaul,'

responderunt: Rhenum finire
they answered: the Rhine to end (that the Rhine terminates)

imperium Romani populi: si existimaret
the empire of the Roman people: if he might think (it)

non æquum Germanos transire in Galliam,
not just the Germans to cross-over into Gaul,

se invito, cur postularet quidquam
himself (being) unwilling, why should he require any

sui imperii aut potestatis esse trans Rhenum?
of his empire or power to be across the Rhine?

Autem Ubii, qui uni ex Transrhenanis
But the Ubii, who one (alone) out-of the Transrhenani

                      miserant legatos ad
(nations across the Rhine) had sent ambassadors to

Cæsarem, fecerant amicitiam, dederant obsides,
Cæsar, had made friendship, had given hostages,

orabant magnopere, "ut ferret auxilium
did pray greatly, "that he would bring aid

sibi, quòd premerentur (imp. subj.)
to themselves, because they were oppressed

graviter ab Suevis: vel, si prohiberetur
grievously by the Suevi: or, if he might be hindered

facere id occupationibus reipublicæ, modò
to do that by the engagements of the state, only

transportaret Rhenum exercitum: id
he would carry-over the Rhine (his) army: that

futurum satis sibi ad auxilium
about-to-be enough for themselves to (for) aid

que	spem	relĭqui		tempŏris :	tantum
and	hope	of the rest (remaining)		time :	so-great

esse	nomen	atque	opinionem	Romani	exercĭtûs,
to be	the name	and	opinion	of a Roman	army,

Ariovisto pulso, et hoc novissĭmo prœlĭo
Ariovistus being routed, and this newest (last) battle

facto, etĭam ad ultĭmas nationes
being made (fought), even to the remotest nations

Germanorum, ŭtĭ possint esse tutɩ
of the Germans, that they may be able to be safe

opinione et amicitiâ Romani popŭli."
by the opinion (prestige) and friendship of the Roman people."

Pollicebantur magnam copĭam navĭum ad
They did promise a great plenty of ships to

exercĭtum transportandum.
the army to-be-carried-over.

17. Cæsar de his caussis, quas commemoravi,
Cæsar from these causes, which I have mĕntioned,

decreverat transire Rhenum : sed arbitrabatur
had resolved to cross the Rhine : but he did think (it)

nĕque esse sătis tutum transire navĭbus,
neither to be sufficiently safe to cross with ships,

nĕque statuebat esse sŭæ
neither did he decide (it) to be (the part) of his-own

dignitatis, nĕque Romani popŭli : ităque,
dignity, nor (that) of the Roman people : therefore,

etsi summa difficultas pontis faciundi
although the highest difficulty of a bridge to-be-made

proponebatur, propter latitudĭnem, rapiditatem,
was set-before (him), on-account-of the breadth, rapidity,

que altitudĭnem flumĭnis ; tămen existimabat id
and depth of the river ; however he did think that

contendendum sĭbi, aut alĭter exercĭtum
to-be-endeavoured to (by) himself, or otherwise the army

non transducendum. Igĭtur institŭit hanc
not to-be-led-over. Therefore he framed this

DE BELLO GALLICO. [17

rationem pontis. Jungebat bina
plan *of the bridge.* *He did join* *double (two)*

sesquipedalia tigna, paullùm præacuta ab
foot-and-half-thick *beams,* *a little* *sharp-pointed* *from*

imo, dimensa ad altitudinem
the lowest (part), *measured* *to (according to)* *the depth*

fluminis, intervallo duorum pedum inter
of the river, *with (at) an interval* *of two* *feet* *between*

se: cùm defixerat hæc demissa in
themselves: *when* *he had fastened* *these* *sent-down* *into*

flumen machinationibus que adegerat
the river *by machines* *and* *had driven (them)*

fistucis, non directa ad perpendiculum
with rammers, *not* *straight* *to* *a perpendicular*

modo sublicæ, sed prona ac fastigiata,
in the manner *of a pile,* *but* *inclined* *and* *pointed;*

ut procumberent secundùm naturam
that *they might incline-forward* *according-to* *the nature*

fluminis: statuebat item duo contraria
of the river: *he did place* *also* *two (beams)* *opposite*

his juncta ad eundem modum intervallo
to these *joined* *to (in)* *the same* *manner* *in (at) an interval*

quadragenûm pedum ab inferiore parte conversa
of forty *feet* *from* *the lower* *part* *turned*

contra vim atque impetum fluminis: utræque
against *the force* *and* *violence* *of the river:* *each-of*

hæc distinebantur binis fibulis utrimque
these *were separated* *by two* *braces* *on-either-side*

ab extremâ parte, bipedalibus trabibus
from *the extreme* *part (the top),* *two-foot-wide* *beams*

immissis, quantum junctura
being let-in (to them), *as-much-as* *the joining* (the space

eorum tignorum distabat: quibus
between) *of those* *beams* *was-distant:* *which*

disclusis, atque revinctis in
being shut-out (pushed out), *and* *being fastened* *on*

LIBER IV.

contrariam partem, tanta. erat firmitudo operis,
the opposite part, so-great was the firmness of the work,

atque ea natura rerum, ut
and that (such) the nature of the things, that

quò-major vis aquæ incitavisset
by how-much-greater the force of the water might have urged

se, hòc arctiùs tenerentur
itself, by this (by so much) more-closely they were kept

(imp. subj.) illigata: hæc directa
fastened: these straight-forward

contexebantur materiâ injectâ,
were interwoven with material (timber) thrown-on (them),

ac consternebantur longuriis que cratibus:
and were strewed with long-stakes and hurdles:

ac nihilo seciùs sublicæ adigebantur obliquè ad
and nevertheless piles were driven obliquely at

inferiorem partem fluminis, quæ subjectæ
the lower part of the river, which being subjoined

pro pariete, et conjunctæ cum omni opere,
for (as) a wall, and united with all the work,

exciperent vim fluminis: et item aliæ
might receive the force of the river: and also other (piles)

mediocri spatio supra pontem, ut si trunci
at a moderate distance above the bridge, that if trunks

arborum sive naves essent missæ à barbaris,
of trees or ships might be 'sent by the barbarians,

caussâ operis dejiciendi,
by cause (for the sake) of the work to-be-thrown-down,

vis earum rerum minueretur his
the force of those things might be diminished by these

defensoribus, neu nocerent ponti.
protectors, nor (lest) they might injure to the bridge.

18. Omni opere effecto decem diebus,
All the work being completed in ten days,

quibus materia cœpta-erat comportari,
in which the material had been-begun to be brought-together,

exercĭtus	transducĭtur.	Cæsar,	firmo	præsidĭc
the army	is led-over.	Cæsar,	a strong	guard

relicto	ad utramque	partem	pontis,
being left	at each	part (side)	of the bridge,

ontendit in	fines	Sicambrorum.	Intĕrim
hastened into	the territories	of the Sicambri.	Meantime

legati	à	complurĭbus	civitatĭbus	venĭunt
ambassadors	from	many	states	come

ad ĕum,	quĭbus	petentĭbus	pacem atque	amicĭtĭam
to him,	to whom	seeking	peace and	friendship

respondit	liberalĭter, que	jŭbet	obsĭdes	adduci
he answered	liberally, and	orders	hostages	to be brought

ad se.	Sicambri,	ex	ĕo	tempŏre,
to himself.	The Sicambri,	from	that	time,

quo	pons	cœptus-est institŭi,	fŭgâ
in which	the bridge	was begun to be framed,	flight

comparatâ,	ĭis	hortantĭbus,	quos ha-
being prepared,	those	exhorting (them),	whom they

bebant	ex	Tenchthĕris atque	Usipetĭbus
did have	out-of	the Tenchtheri and	Usipetes

ăpud	se,	excessĕrant sŭis	finĭbus,
at (among)	themselves,	had departed from their	territories,

que	exportavĕrant	omnĭa sŭa,	que
and	had carried-away	all their (effects),	and

abdidĕrant	se	in solitudĭnem ac	silvas.
had concealed	themselves	into a desert and	woods.

19. Cæsar moratus paucos dĭes in finĭ-
Cæsar having delayed a few days in the terri-

bus	eorum,	omnĭbus vicis	que	ædificĭis
tories	of them,	all the villages	and	buildings

incensis,	que frumentis (pl.)	succisis,	recepit
being burned,	and the corn	being cut-down,	betook

se in	fines	Ubiorum; atque	polli-
himself into	the territories	of the Ubii; and	having

cĭtus	sŭum auxilĭum	his, si	premerentur
promised	his aid	to them, if	they might be oppressed

iter	mare	exercitus	cornu
itineris	maris	exercitus	cornus
itineri	mari	exercitui	cornu
iter	mare	exercitum	cornu
itinere et	mari	exercitu	cornu
itinera	maria	exercitus	cornua
itinerum	marium	exercituum	cornuum
itineribus	maribus	exercitibus	cornibus
itinera	maria	exercitus	cornua
itineribus	maribus	exercitibus	cornibus

puer	templum	sollicitudo
pueri	templi	sollicitudinis
puero	templo	sollicitudini
puerum	templum	sollicitudinem
puerō	templō	sollicitudine
puerī	templa	sollicitudines
puerōrum	templōrum	sollicitudinum
puerīs	templīs	sollicitudinibus
pueros	templa	sollicitudines
pueris	templis	sollicitudinibus

LIBER IV. [19

à	Suevis,	cognovit	hæc	ab
by	*the Suevi,*	*he knew* (learned)	*these (things)*	*from*

iis;	Suevos,	postquam	comperissent (pluperf.
them;	*the Suevi,*	*after-that*	*they had found*

subj.) per	exploratores	pontem	fiĕri,	concilĭo
by	*spies*	*a bridge*	*to be made,*	*a council*

habĭto,	sŭo more,	dimisisse	nuncĭos
being held,	*in their manner,*	*to have sent*	*messengers*

in	omnes	partes, ŭtì	demigrarent	de
into	*all*	*parts, that*	*they might emigrate*	*from*

oppĭdis,	deponĕrent		libĕros,	'uxores, que
the towns,	*might deposit*		*(their) children,*	*wives, and*

omnĭa	sŭa	in	silvas,	atque omnes,
all	*their (effects)*	*into*	*the woods,*	*and all,*

qui	possent	ferre	arma, convenirent	in
who	*might be-able*	*to bear*	*arms, should assemble*	*into*

unum	lŏcum:	hunc	delectum-esse fĕrè
one	*place:*	*this (place)*	*to have been chosen nearly*

medĭum	earum	regionum,	quas	Suevi
the middle	*of those*	*countries,*	*which*	*the Suevi*

obtinerent (imp. subj.):	exspectare	ïbi	adventum
did possess:	*to await*	*there*	*the coming-up*

Romanorum,	atque	constituisse	decertare	ïbi.
of the Romans,	*and*	*to have resolved*	*to contend*	*there.*

Quod	ŭbi	Cæsar	compĕrit,	omnĭbus his	rebus
Which	*when*	*Cæsar*	*discovered,*	*all these*	*things*

confectis,	caussâ	quarum	rerum
being finished,	*by cause* (for the sake)	*of which*	*things*

constituĕrat	transducĕre	exercĭtum,	ut	inji-
he had resolved	*to lead-over*	*(his) army,*	*that*	*he might*

cĕret	mĕtum	Germanis,	ut	ulcis-
cast-in	*fear*	*to the Germans,*	*that*	*he might take-*

ceretur		Sicambros, ut	liberaret
vengeance-on (punish)		*the Sicambri, that*	*he might deliver*

Ubĭos	obsidione,	octodĕcim	diebus	omnino
the Ubii	*from a siege,*	*eighteen*	*days*	*altogether*

P 2

consumptis	trans	Rhenum,	arbitratus		
being spent	*across*	*the Rhine,*	*having thought (himself)*		

profectum (-esse)	sătis	et	ad	laudem	et
to have advanced	*enough*	*both*	*to (for)*	*praise*	*and*

ad	utilitatem,	recepit	se	in	Gallïam que
to	*utility,*	*he betook*	*himself*	*into*	*Gaul and*

rescïdit pontem.
cut-down the bridge.

20. Exigŭâ parte æstatis relïquâ, Cæsar,
   A small part of the summer (being) left, Cæsar,

etsi hiëmes in his lŏcis sunt maturæ,
although the winters in these places are early,

quòd omnis Gallïa vergit ad Septentrionem,
because all Gaul bends (inclines) to the North,

tămen contendit proficisci in Britannïam;
yet hastened to set-out into Britain;

quòd intelligebat auxilïa subministrata (-esse)
because he did understand aids to have been supplied

inde nostris hostïbus, fĕrè omnïbus Gallïcis
thence to our enemies, nearly in all the Gallic

bellis: et, si tempus anni deficĕret ad
wars: and, if the time of the year might fail to

bellum gerendum: tămen arbitrabatur
war to-be-carried-on: yet he did think (it)

fŏre magno usŭi sĭbi, si mŏdò
to-be-about-to-be for great use to himself, if only

adîsset insŭlam; perspexisset
he might have gone-to the island; might have observed

gĕnus homïnum; cognovisset lŏca, portus,
the kind of men; might have known the places, harbours,

adïtus; omnïa quæ fĕrè ĕrant
approaches; all which (things) nearly were

incognïta Gallis. Enim nĕque quisquam ădit
unknown to the Gauls. For neither any-one goes

illò temĕrè præter mercatores; nĕque est
thither rashly except merchants; nor is

LIBER IV.

quidquam	notum	iis	ipsis,	præter	marĭtĭmam
any (thing)	known	to those	selves,	except	the maritime

oram,	atque	ĕas	regiones,	quæ	sunt	contra
coast,	and	those	countries,	which	are	opposite

Gallĭam.	Ităque,	mercatorĭbus	convocatis
Gaul.	Therefore,	the merchants	being called-together

undĭque	ad	se,	potĕrat	reperire	nĕque
from-every-side	to	himself,	he was-able	to find	neither

quanta	esset	magnitudo	insŭlæ,	nĕque
how-great	might be	the size	of the island,	neither

quæ	aut	quantæ	nationes	incolĕrent,	nĕque
what	or	how-great	nations	might inhabit (it),	neither

quem	usum	belli	haberent,	aut	quĭbus
what	method	of warfare	they might have,	or	with what

institutis	uterentur,	nĕque	qui	portus	essent
institutions	they might use,	nor	what	harbours	might be

idonĕi	ad	multitudĭnem	majorum	navĭum.
fit	to (for)	a number	of greater	ships.

21.
Arbitratus	esse	idonĕum,	prĭus	quàm
Having thought (it)	to be	proper,	before	than

facĕret	perĭcŭlum,	præmittit	Caïum
he should make	the trial,	he sends-before (him)	Caius

Volusenum	cum	longâ	navi,	ad
Volusenus	with	a long	ship (a ship of war),	to (for)

hæc	cognoscenda.	Mandat	huic	ut,
these (things)	to-be-known.	He charges	to him	that,

omnĭbus	rebus	exploratis,	revertatur	ad
all	things	being examined,	he may return	to

se	quamprimùm.	Ipse	proficiscĭtur	cum
himself	as-soon-as-possible.	Himself	sets-out	with

omnĭbus	copĭis	in	Morĭnos,	quòd	trajectus
all	(his) forces	into	the Morini,	because	the passage

inde	in	Britannĭam	ĕrat	brevissimus.	Jŭbet
thence	into	Britain	was	the shortest.	He orders

naves	convenire	huc	undĭque	ex
ships	to assemble	hither	from-every-side	from

finitĭmis	regionĭbus,	et	classem,	quam
the neighbouring	*countries,*	*and*	*the fleet,*	*which*

fecĕrat	ad	Venetĭcum	bellum	superiore
he had made	*to (for)*	*the Venetian*	*war*	*in the former*

æstate.	Intĕrim	consilĭo	ejus	cognĭto, et
summer.	*Mean-time*	*the design*	*of him*	*being known, and*

perlato	ad	Britannos	per
being carried (reported)	*to*	*the Britons*	*through*

mercatores,	legati	venĭunt	ad ĕum	à
the merchants,	*ambassadors*	*come*	*to him*	*from*

ccmplurĭbus civitatĭbus	ejus	insŭlæ, qui	polliceantur
very-many states	*of that*	*island, who*	*may promise*

dăre	obsĭdes, atque	obtemperare	imperĭo
to give	*hostages, and*	*to obey*	*to the empire*

Romani	popŭli.	Quĭbus auditis,	polli-
of the Roman	*people.*	*Who being heard,*	*having*

citus	liberalĭter, que	hortatus	ut
promised	*liberally, and*	*having exhorted* (them)	*that*

permanerent	in ĕa	sententĭa	remisit
they should remain-firm	*in that*	*determination*	*he sent-back*

ĕos	dŏmum :	et una cum	his	mittit
them	*home :*	*and together with*	*these*	*he sends*

Comĭum,	quem	ipse constituĕrat	regem	ĭbi,
Comius,	*whom*	*himself had appointed*	*king*	*there,*

Atrebatĭbus	superatis,	et cujus	virtutem et
the Atrebates	*being overcome,*	*and whose*	*valour and*

consilĭum	probabat,	et quem	arbitrabatur
counsel	*he did approve,*	*and whom*	*he did think*

fidelem	sĭbi,	que cujus auctorĭtas	habebatur
faithful	*to himself,*	*and whose authority*	*was accounted*

magna	in his	regionĭbus :	impĕrat	huic,
great	*in these*	*countries :*	*he commands*	*to him,*

adĕat	quas civitates	possit,	que hortetur
(that) he may go-to	*what states*	*he may be-able,*	*and may exhort*

ut sequantur	fĭdem
(them) that they may follow	*the faith* (secure the protection)

LIBER IV.

Romani	popŭli,	que	nuntĭet	se
of the Roman	people,	and	he may announce	himself

venturum	ĕŏ	celerĭter.	Volusenus,	regionĭbus
about-to-come	thither	quickly.	Volusenus,	the countries

perspectis,	quantum	facultatis	potŭit	dări
being observed,	as-much	of power	was-able	to be given

ĕi,	qui	auderet	non	egrĕdi	navi,
to him,	who	might dare	not	to go-out	from the ship,

ac	committĕre	se	barbăris,	revertĭtur
and	to entrust	himself	to the barbarians,	returns

quinto	dĭe	ad	Cæsărem,	que	renuntĭat	quæ
on the fifth	day	to	Cæsar,	and	announces	what

	perspexisset (pluperf. subj.)	ĭbi.
(things)	he had seen	there.

22.
Dum	Cæsar	commoratur	in	his	lŏcis
Whilst	Cæsar	delays	in	these	places

caussâ	navĭum	parandarum,	legati
by cause (for the sake)	of ships	to-be-prepared,	ambassadors

venerunt	ad	ĕum	ex	magnâ	parte	Morinorum,
came	to	him	from	a great	part	of the Morini,

qui	excusarent	se	de	consilĭo
who	might excuse	themselves	concerning	the counsel

superioris	tempŏris;	quòd	barbări
of the foregoing	time;	because	(being) barbarous

homĭnes	que	imperiti	nostræ	consuetudĭnis,
men	and	unacquainted	of (with) our	custom,

fecissent (pluperf. subj.)	bellum	Romano	popŭlo;
they had made	war	to the Roman	people;

que	pollicerentur	se	facturos	ĕa,
and	might promise	themselves	about-to-do	those (things),

quæ	imperâsset.	Cæsar	arbitratus
which	he might have commanded.	Cæsar	having thought

hoc	accidisse	opportunè	sătis	sĭbi;
this	to have happened	conveniently	enough	to himself;

quòd	volébat	nĕque	relinquĕre	hostem	post
because	he did will	neither	to leave	an enemy	after

(behind)	tergum, (his) rear,	nĕque neither	habebat did he have	facultatem the power
belli of war	gerendi to-be-carried-on	propter on-account-of	tempus the time	anni ; of the year;
nĕque nor	judicabat did he judge	has these	occupationes engagements	tantularum of so-very-little
rerum things	anteponendas to-be-preferred	sĭbi to (by) himself		Britanniæ : to Britain :
impĕrat commands	his to them		magnum (to furnish) a great	numĕrum number
obsĭdum. of hostages.	Quĭbus Which	adductis, being brought-to (him),		recepit he received
eos them	in into	fĭdem. allegiance.	Circĭter About	octoginta eighty	onerarĭis burden (transport
navĭbus ships	coactis being collected	que and	contractis, brought-together,	quod which
existimabat he did think	esse to be	'satis sufficient	ad to (for)	dŭas two	legiones legions
transportandas ; to-be-carried-over ;		distribŭit he distributed		quæstori, to the quæstor,
legatis to the lieutenants	que and	præfectis prefects	quidquid whatever	prætcrĕa besides
longarum of long	navĭum ships (ships of war)		habebat : he did have.	huc hither
accedebant did approach (were added)		octodĕcim eighteen	onerarĭæ burden (transport)
naves, ships,	quas which	tenebantur were detained	vento by the wind	octo eight	millĭbus thousands
passŭum of paces	ex from	ĕo that	lŏco, place,	quò that	mĭnùs-possent they might not-be-able
pervenire to arrive	in into	eundem the same	portum : harbour :	distribŭit he distributed	has these
equitĭbus ; to the cavalry ;	dĕdit he gave	relĭquum the rest-of	exercĭtum the army	Quinto to Quintus
Titurĭo Titurius	Sabino, Sabinus,	et and	Lucĭo to Lucius	Aurunculeĭo Aurunculeius	Cottæ, Cotta,

legatis,	deducendum	in	Menapios	atque
(his) lieutenants,	to-be-led-down	unto	the Menapii	and
in	eos	pagos	Morinorum,	ab	quibus
unto	those	districts	of the Morini,	from	which
legati	venerant	non	ad	eum :	jussit
ambassadors	had come	not	to	him :	he ordered
Publium	Sulpicium	Rufum	legatum	tenere
Publius	Sulpicius	Rufus	(his) lieutenant	to keep
portum	cum	eo	præsidio,	quod	arbitrabatur
the harbour	with	that	guard,	which	he did think
esse	satis.				
to be	sufficient				

23. His rebus constitutis, nactus idoneam
    These things being arranged, having got a proper

tempestatem ad-navigandum, solvit
    time (weather) to-sail, he loosed (set sail)

fere tertia vigilia, que jussit equites
nearly in the third watch, and commanded the cavalry

progredi in ulteriorem portum, et conscendere
to proceed unto the further harbour, and to mount

naves, ac sequi se : ab quibus
the ships (embark), and to follow himself : by whom

cum administratum-esset (pluperf. subj.) paullo tar-
when it had been executed a little more-

dius, ipse attigit Britanniam cum
slowly, himself touched (reached) Britain with

primis navibus circiter quarta hora diei :
the first ships about in the fourth hour of the day :

atque ibi conspexit copias hostium
and there he beheld the forces of the enemies

firmatas, expositas in omnibus collibus.
confirmed (in position), drawn-out on all the hills.

Cujus loci hæc erat natura : mare con-
Of which place this was the nature : the sea was

tinebatur montibus adeo angustis, ut telum
bounded by mountains so close (to it), that a dart

P 3

posset	adjĭci	ex	superiorĭbus	lŏcis	in
might be-able	to be cast	from	the higher	places	unto

littus.	Arbitratus	hunc	lŏcum	nequaquam
the shore.	Having thought	this	place	by-no-means

idonĕum	ad-egrediendum		expectavit	in
fit	to-go-out (disembark)		he waited	in (at)

anchŏris	ad	nonam	horam,	dum	relĭquæ
anchors	to	the ninth	hour,	until	the rest-of

naves	convenirent	ĕō.	Intĕrim	legatis
the ships	might assemble	there.	Mean-time	the lieutenants

que	tribunis	milĭtum	convocatis,
and	tribunes	of soldiers	being called-together,

ostendit	et	quæ	cognovisset (pluperf.
he showed (them)	both	what (things)	he had known

subj.)	ex	Voluseno,	et	quæ	vellet
	from	Volusenus,	and	what	he might will

fĭĕri:	que	monŭit		omnes	res
to be done:	and	he advised (them that)	all	things

administrarentur	ab	ïis	ad	nutum	et	ad
should be managed	by	them	at	a nod	and	to

tempus	(ut	ratĭo	militaris	rĕi,	maxĭmè
time	(as	the method	of military	affair,	(and) chiefly

ut	maritĭmæ	res	postularent (imp. subj.),	ut
as	maritime	affairs	did require	as (cir-

	quæ	haberent (imp. subj.)	celĕrem	atque
cumstances)	which	did have	a quick	and

instabĭlem	motum.)	His	dimissis,	et
unstable	movement.)	These	being dismissed,	and

nactus	et	secundum	ventum	et	æstum
having got	both	a favourable	wind	and	tide

uno	tempŏre,	signo	dăto,	et	anchŏris
in (at) one	time,	a signal	being given,	and	the anchors

sublatis,	progressus	circĭter	octo
being taken-up (weighed),	having advanced	about	eight

millĭa	passŭum	ab	ĕo	lŏco,	constitŭit
thousands	of paces	from	that	place,	he placed

naves aperto ac plano littŏre.	the ships on an open and level shore.

24. At barbări, consilĭo Romanorum
But the barbarians, the design of the Romans

cognĭto, equitatu præmisso, et
being known, the cavalry being sent-before, and

essedariis; quo genĕre consueverunt
the charioteers; with which kind they have been accustomed

plerumque uti in prœliis, subsecuti
generally to use in battles, having followed-near

relĭquis copĭis, prohibebant nostros
with the rest-of (their) forces, they did hinder our (men)

egrĕdi navĭbus. Erat summa
to come-out from the ships. (There) was the highest

difficultas ob has caussas, quŏd
difficulty on-account-of these reasons, because

naves, propter magnitudĭnem potĕrant non
the ships, on-account-of (their) size were-able not

constitŭi nĭsi in alto: autem ĕrat et
to be placed unless in the deep: but it was both

desiliendum sĭmul de navĭbus, et
to-be-leaped-down at-the-same-time from the ships, and

consistendum fluctĭbus, et pugnandum cum
to-be-stood in the waves, and to-be-fought with

hostĭbus militĭbus, ignotis lŏcis,
the enemies by the soldiers, in unknown places,

impeditis manĭbus, pressis magno et
with encumbered hands, oppressed with a great and

grăvi onĕre armorum; quum illi aut conjicĕrent
heavy load of arms; when they either did hurl

(imp. subj.) tela audacter ex arĭdo aut
darts boldly from dry (ground) or

progressi paullŭlum in ăquam, expediti
having advanced a very-little into the water, unencumbered

omnĭbus membris, notissĭmis lŏcis, et
in all (their) limbs, in very-well-known places, and

incitarent (imp. subj.) ĕquos insuefactos. Quĭbus
did urge-on *horses* *accustomed-to (it).* *By which*

rebus nostri perterrĭti, atque imperiti
things *our (men)* *being dismayed,* *and* *unskilled*

omnino hujus genĕris pugnæ, omnes utebantur
altogether *of this* *kind* *of battle,* *all* *did use*

non eâdem alacritate ac studĭo,
(exhibit) *not* *with the same* *cheerfulness* *and* *zeal,*

quo consuevĕrant uti in pedestrĭbus
with which *they had been accustomed* *to use* *in* *infantry*

prœlĭis.
battles.

25. Quod ŭbi Cæsar animadvertit, jussit
Which *when* *Cæsar* *perceived,* *he ordered*

longas naves, species quarum
the long *ships (ships of war),* *the appearance* *of which*

et ĕrat inusitatĭor barbăris, et motus
both *was* *more-unusual* *to the barbarians,* *and* *the motion*

expeditĭor ad usum, removeri paullŭlum
more-quick *to (for)* *use,* *to be removed* *a very-little*

ab onerarĭis navĭbus, et incitari
from *the burden (transport)* *ships,* *and* *to be pushed-on*

remis, et constituĭ ad apertum lătus
with oars, *and* *to be stationed* *at* *the open* *flank*

hostĭum, atque hostes propelli ac
of the enemies, *and* *the enemies* *to be repulsed* *and*

submoveri inde fundis, tormentis, sagittis;
to be removed *thence* *by slings,* *shooting-engines,* *arrows;*

quæ res fŭit magno usŭi nostris. Nam
which *thing* *was* *for great* *use* *to our (men).* *For*

barbări permoti et figurâ navĭum,
th barbarians *much-alarmed* *both* *by the shape* *of the ships,*

et motu remorum, et inusitato
and *by the motion* *of the oars,* *and* *by the unusual*

genĕre tormentorum, constiterunt, ac mŏdò
kind *of shooting-engines,* *halted,* *and* *now*

LIBER IV.

retulerunt	pědem	paullùm.	Ac,	nostris
carried-back	foot (retreated)	a little.	And,	our

militĭbus	cunctantĭbus,	maxĭmè	propter	altitudĭnem
soldiers	delaying,	chiefly	on account-of	the depth

măris,	qui	ferebat	aquĭlam	decĭmæ
of the sea,	(he) who	did bear	the eagle	of the tenth

legionis,	contestatus		Děos,	ut	ĕa
legion,	having attested (besought)		the Gods,	that	that

res	eveniret	felicĭter	legioni:	inquit,
thing	might happen	fortunately	to the legion:	says,

Desilite,	milĭtes,	nĭsi	vultis	proděre	aquĭlam
Leap-down,	soldiers,	unless	you will	to betray	the eagle

hostĭbus;	ĕgo	certè	præstitĕro
to the enemies;	I	certainly	shall have performed

měum	officĭum	Reipublĭcæ	atque	Imperatori.
my	duty	to the state	and	(my) Commander.

Quum	dixisset (pluperf. subj.)	hoc	magnâ
When	he had said	this	with a great (loud)

voce,	projecit	se	ex	navi,	atque
voice,	he cast-forth	himself	from	the ship,	and

cœpit	ferre	aquĭlam	in	hostes.	Tum
began	to carry	the eagle	against	the enemies.	Then

nostri	cohortati	inter	se,	universi
our (men)	having encouraged	among	themselves,	the whole

desilierunt	ex	navi,	ne	tantum	deděcus
leaped-down	from	the ship,	lest	so-great	a disgrace

admitteretur.	Quum	alii	ĭtem	ex	proxĭmis
should be allowed.	When	others	also	out-of	the nearest

navĭbus	conspexisset (pluperf. subj.)	hos,	sub-
ships	had beheld	these,	having

secuti	appropinquârunt	hostĭbus.
followed-close	they approached	to the enemies.

26. | Pugnatum-est | acrĭter | ab | utrisque (plur.) |
|---|---|---|---|
| It was fought | vigorously | by | each. |

Tămen	nostri	perturbabantur	magnopěre,	quòd
However	our (men)	were disordered	greatly,	because

potĕrant	nĕque	servare	ordĭnes,	nĕque
they were-able	neither	to keep	(their) ranks,	neither

insistĕre	firmĭter,	nĕque	subsĕqui
to stand	firmly (to get firm footing),	nor	to follow-closely

signa, atque alĭus ex alĭâ
the standards, and another from another (one from

navi aggregabat se
one, another from another) ship did associate himself

quibuscumque signis occurrĕret. Verò hostes,
to whatever standards he might meet. But the enemies,

omnĭbus vădis notis, ŭbi conspexĕrant
all the shallows being known, when they had beheld

ex littŏre alĭquos egredientes singulares
from the shore some coming-out single

ex navi, ĕquis incitatis, adoriebantur
from a ship, (their) horses being urged-on, did attack

impeditos. Plures circumsistebant
(them) encumbered. More (several) did surround

paucos: alĭi conjiciebant tela in
a few: others did hurl (their) darts upon

universos ab aperto latĕre. Quod quum Cæsar
the whole from the open flank. Which when Cæsar

animadvertisset (plup. subj.), jussit scăphas longarum
had observed, he ordered the skiffs of the long

navĭum, ĭtem speculatorĭa-navigĭa
ships (ships of war), likewise the spy-boats

compleri militĭbus; et summittebat subsidĭa
to be filled with soldiers; and he did send-up aids

ĭis, quos conspexĕrat laborantes. Nostri
to those, whom he had beheld labouring. Our (men)

sĭmul-atque constiterunt in arĭdo, omnĭbus
as-soon-as they stood on dry (ground), all

sŭis consecutis, fecerunt impĕtum
their (comrades) having followed, made a charge

in hostes, atque dederunt ĕos in
upon the enemies and gave (put) them into

fŭgam :	nĕque	potuerunt	prosĕqui	longĭus
flight :	nor	were they able	to pursue	farther (very far)

quòd	equĭtes	potuĕrant	non	tenere
because	the horsemen	had been able	not	to hold-on

cursum,	atque	capĕre	insŭlam.	Hoc
(their) course,	and	to take (reach)	the island.	This

unum	defúit	Cæsări	ad	pristĭnam
one (thing)	was-wanting	to Cæsar	to	(his) ancient (former)

fortunam.
fortune.

27. Hostes, superati prœlĭo, miserunt
The enemies, being overcome in the battle, sent

stătim	legatos	ad	Cæsărem	de pace,
immediately	ambassadors	to	Cæsar	about peace,

sĭmul-atque	receperunt	se	ex	fŭgâ ;
as-soon-as	they recovered	themselves	from	flight ;

pollicĭti-sunt	sese	daturos	obsĭdes,	que
they promised	themselves	about-to-give	hostages,	and

facturos	quæ	imperâsset.	Comĭus
about-to-do	what (things)	he might have commanded.	Comius

Atrĕbas	venit	unà	cum	his	legatis,
the Atrebatian	came	together	with	these	ambassadors.

quem	demonstravĕram	suprà	præmissum (-esse)
whom	I had shown	above	to have been sent-before

in	Britannĭam :	illi	comprehendĕrant hunc
into	Britain :	they	had seized him

egressum	è	navi,	quum deferret (imp.
having gone-out	from	the ship,	when he did carry subj.)

mandata	Imperatoris	ad eos,	atque
the commands	of the Commander	to them,	and

conjecĕrant	in	vincŭla.	Tum prœlĭo
had thrown (him)	into	chains.	Then the battle

facto,	remiserunt	et	in pace
being made (fought),	they sent-back	and	in peace

petendâ	contulerunt
to-be-sought (in requesting peace)	they carried-over (imputed;

culpam	the fault
ejus	of that
rĕi	thing
in	unto
multitudĭnem,	the multitude,
et	and
petiverunt,	requested,
ut	that
ignosceretur	it might be pardoned
propter	on-account-of
imprudentĭam.	ignorance.
Cæsar	Cæsar
questus	having complained
quòd	that
quum	when
petîssent (pluperf. subj.)	they had sought
pacem	peace
à	from
se,	himself
legatis	ambassadors
missis	being sent
ultrò	voluntarily
in	unto
continentem,	the continent.
intulissent (pluperf. subj.)	they had brought-on
bellum	war
sĭne	without
caussâ,	cause,
dixit	said
igncscĕre	to pardon
imprudentĭæ,	(their) indiscretion,
que	and
imperavit	commanded to
obsĭdes:	hostages:
partem	part
quorum	of whom
illi	they
dederunt	gave
stātim:	immediately:
dixerunt	they said
sese	themselves
daturos	about-to-give
paucis	in a few
diebus	days
partem	a part
accersitam	sent-for
ex	from
longinquiorĭbus	more distant
lŏcis.	places.
Interĕa	Meantime
jusserunt	they ordered
sŭos	their (people)
remigrare	to return
in	into
agros;	the lands;
que	and
princĭpes	the chiefs
convenêre	assembled
undĭque	from-every-side
et	and
commendârunt	recommended
se	themselves
que	and
sŭas	their
civitates	states
Cæsări.	to Cæsar

28.
Pace	Peace
firmatâ	being confirmed
his	by these
rebus,	things,
oc-	the
todĕcim	eighteen
naves	ships
de	concerning
quĭbus	which
demonstratum-est	it has been shown
suprà,	above,
quæ	which
sustulĕrant	had taken-up
equĭtes,	the cavalry,
solverunt	loosed (set
ex	sail) from
superiore	the upper
portu	harbour
leni	with a gentle
vento,	wind,

post	quartum	diem	quàm	ventum-est	
after	*the fourth*	*day*	*than* (since)	*it was come* (they	
	in	Britanniam :	quum	quæ	appro-
came)	*into*	*Britain:*	*when*	*which (ships)*	*did ap-*
pinquarent (imp. subj.)		Britanniæ,	et	viderentur (imp.	
prouch		*to Britain,*	*and*	*were seen*	
subj.)	ex	castris (pl.),	tanta	tempestas	subitò
	from	*the camp,*	*so-great*	*a tempest*	*suddenly*
coorta-est,	ut	nulla	earum	posset (imp. subj.)	
arose,	*that*	*no-one*	*of them*	*was able*	
tenere	cursum,	sed	aliæ	referrentur (imp. subj.)	
to hold	*the course,*	*but*	*others*	*were carried-back*	
eòdem		unde	profectæ-erant ;		aliæ
to the same (place)		*whence*	*they had set-out,*		*others*
dejicerentur (imp. subj.)		ad	inferiorem	partem	
were thrown		*to*	*the lower*	*part*	
insulæ,	quæ	est	propius	occasum	solis
of the island,	*which*	*is*	*nearer*	*the setting*	*of the sun*
	cum	magno	periculo	sui :	quæ
(the West)	*with*	*great*	*danger*	*of themselves :*	*which*
tamen,	anchoris	jactis,	cùm	complerentur (imp.	
however,	*anchors*	*being cast,*	*when*	*they were filled*	
subj.)	fluctibus,	provectæ		necessariò	in
	with waves,	*borne-forward*		*necessarily*	*unto*
altum	adversâ	nocte,	petiverunt	continentem.	
the deep	*in unfavourable*	*night,*	*sought*	*the continent.*	

29. Accidit eâdem nocte, ut luna
It happened in the same night, that the moon

esset (imp. subj.)	plena,	quæ	dies	consuevit
was	*full,*	*which*	*day*	*has been-accustomed*
efficere	maritimos	æstus	maximos	in oceano ;
to render	*the maritime*	*tides*	*greatest*	*in the ocean ;*
que	id	erat	incognitum	nostris. Ita
and	*that*	*was*	*unknown*	*to our (people). Thus*
æstus	complebat	uno		tempore et
the tide	*did fill*	*in one* (the same)		*time both*

| longas | naves, | quibus | Cæsar |
| *the long* | *ships* (ships of war), | *in which* | *Cæsar* |

| curavĕrat | exercĭtum | transportandum | que | quas |
| *had taken-care* | *the army* | *to-be-carried-over* | *and* | *which* |

| subduxĕrat | in | arĭdum; | et | tempestas |
| *he had drawn-up* | *on* | *dry (ground);* | *and* | *the tempest* |

| afflictabat | onerarĭas, | quæ | deligatæ-ĕrant |
| *did dash* | *the burden (ships),* | *which* | *had been fastened* |

| ad | anchŏras: | nĕque | ulla | facultas | aut |
| *to* | *anchors* | *neither* | *any* | *power* | *either* |

| administrandi | aut | auxiliandi | dabatur | nostris. |
| *of managing* | *or* | *of aiding* | *was given* | *to our (men).* |

| Complurĭbus | navĭbus | fractis, | quum |
| *Very-many* | *ships* | *being broken (wrecked),* | *when* |

| relĭquæ | essent (imp. subj.) | inutĭles | ad-navigandum, |
| *the rest* | *were* | *useless* | *to sail,* |

| funĭbus, | anchŏris, | que | relĭquis |
| *ropes (cables),* | *anchors,* | *and* | *the rest (other)* |

| armamentis | amissis, | magna | perturbatĭo | totius |
| *riggings* | *being lost,* | *a great* | *alarm* | *of the whole* |

| exercĭtûs | facta-est, | id | quod | ĕrat | necesse |
| *army* | *was-made,* | *that* | *which* | *was* | *necessary* |

| | accidĕre. | Enim | nĕque | ĕrant |
| (unavoidable) | *to happen.* | *For* | *neither* | *were (there)* |

| alĭæ | naves, | quĭbus | possent (imp. subj.) |
| *other* | *ships,* | *by which* | *they were-able* |

| reportari; | et | omnĭa | deĕrant, |
| *to be carried-back;* | *and* | *all (things)* | *were-wanting* |

| quæ | essent | usŭi | ad | naves | reficiendas; |
| *which* | *might be* | *for use* | *to* | *the ships* | *to-be-repaired;* |

| et | quòd | constabat | omnĭbus | oportere |
| *and* | *because* | *it was-evident* | *to all* | *to behove (that they* |

| hiemare | in | Galliâ, | frumentum | provisum-ĕrat |
| *ought) to winter* | *in* | *Gaul,* | *corn* | *had been provided* |

| non | in | his | lŏcis | in | hiĕmem. |
| *not* | *in* | *these* | *places* | *unto (for)* | *the winter.* |

LIBER IV.

30. Quĭbus rebus cognĭtis, princĭpes Britannĭæ,
Which things being known, the chiefs of Britain,

qui post prœlĭum convenĕrant ad ĕa
who after the battle had assembled to those (things)

facienda, quæ Cæsar jussĕrat, collocuti
to-be-done, which Cæsar had commanded, having conferred

inter se; quum intelligĕrent (imp. subj.)
between themselves; when they did understand

equĭtes, et naves et frumentum deesse
cavalry, and ships and corn to be-wanting

Romanis, et cognoscĕrent (imp. subj.) paucitatem
to the Romans, and did know the fewness

nostrorum milĭtum ex exiguitate castrorum;
of our soldiers from the smallness of the camps;

quæ etĭam ĕrant angustiora hôc,
which also were more-narrow from this (circumstance),

quòd Cæsar transportavĕrat legiones sĭne
because Cæsar had brought-over the legions without

impedimentis; duxerunt esse optĭmum factu,
baggages; they deemed (it) to be best to be done,

rebellione factâ, prohibere nostros frumento
a rebellion being made, to prevent our (men) from corn

que commeatŭ, et producĕre rem in
and provision, and to prolong the thing unto

hiĕmem; quòd his superatis, aut interclusis
winter; because these being overcome, or intercepted

redĭtu, confidebant nemĭnem postĕa
from a return, they did trust no-one afterwards

transiturum in Britannĭam caussâ
about-to-cross-over into Britain by cause (for the sake)

belli inferendi. Ităque, conjuratione
of war, to-be-brought-on. Therefore, a conspiracy

factâ rursus, cœperunt discedĕre paullatim
being made again, they began to depart by-degrees

ex castris (pl.), ac deducĕre clam sŭos
from the camp, and to lead-down secretly their

	ex	agris.			
(*people*)	*from*	*the lands.*			

31. At	Cæsar,	etsi	cognovĕrat	consilĭa
But	*Cæsar,*	*although*	*he had known*	*the plans*

eorum	nondum,	tămen	suspĭcabatur	id
of them	*not-yet,*	*however*	*did suspect*	*that*

fŏre,	quod	accĭdit,	et	ex	eventu
to-be-about-to-be,	*which*	*happened,*	*both*	*from*	*the event*

	suarum	navĭum;	et	ex	ĕo,
(*disaster*)	*of his*	*ships,*	*and*	*from*	*that (circum-*

	quòd	intermisĕrant	dăre	obsĭdes.
stance),	*because*	*they had omitted*	*to give*	*hostages.*

Ităque	comparabat	subsidĭa	ad	omnes
Therefore	*he did prepare*	*helps*	*to (for)*	*all*

casus:	nam	conferebat	et	frumentum	quotidĭe
chances:	*for*	*he did bring*	*both*	*corn*	*daily*

ex	agris	in	castra;	et	utebatur
from	*the lands*	*into*	*the camps;*	*and*	*did use*

materĭâ		atque	ære	earum,
with the material (*timber*)	*and*	*copper*	*of those (ships),*

quæ	naves	afflictæ-ĕrant	gravissĭmè,	ad
which	*ships*	*had been shattered*	*most-severely,*	*to (for)*

relĭquas	reficiendas;	et	jubebat	
the rest	*to-be-repaired;*	*and*	*he did order (those things)*

comportari	ex	continenti,	quæ	ĕrant	usŭi
to be brought	*from*	*the continent,*	*which*	*were*	*for use*

ad	ĕas	res.	Ităque,	quum	id	administraretur
to	*those*	*things.*	*Therefore,*	*when*	*that*	*was managed·*

(imp. subj.)	summo	studĭo	à	militĭbus,
	with the highest	*zeal*	*by*	*the soldiers,*

duodĕcim	navĭbus	amissis,	effecit,	ut
twelve	*ships*	*being lost,*	*he accomplished,*	*that*

posset	navigari	commŏdè	relĭquis.
it might be-able	*to be sailed*	*conveniently*	*in the rest.*

32. Dum	ĕa	geruntur,	unâ	legione,
Whilst	*those (things)*	*are carried-on,*	*one*	*legion,*

LIBER IV.

quæ	appellabatur	septĭma,	missâ	frumen-
which	was called	the seventh,	being sent	to provide-

tatum	ex	consuetudĭne,	nĕque	ullâ	suspicione
corn	according-to	custom,	neither	any	suspicion

belli	interposĭtâ		ad	id
of war	being interposed	(having intervened)	to	that

tempus,	quum	pars	homĭnum	remaneret (imp.
time,	when	a part	of the men	did remain

subj.)	in	agris,	pars	etĭam	ventitaret (imp.
	in	the lands,	part	also	did come-to-and-fro

subj.)	in	castra (pl.);	ĭi,	qui	ĕrant	in	statione
	into	the camp;	those,	who	were	on	guard

pro	portis	castrorum (pl.),	renunciaverunt
before	the gates	of the camp,	announced

Cæsări,	majorem	pulvĕrem,	quàm	consuetudo
to Cæsar,	a greater	dust,	than	custom

ferret,	viderí	in	ĕâ	parte,	in	quam
might bear,	to be seen	in	that	part,	into	which

partem	legĭo	fecisset (pluperf. subj.)	ĭter.
part	the legion	had made	(their) march.

Cæsar	suspicatus,	id	quod	ĕrat,	alĭquid
Cæsar	having suspected,	that	which	it was,	some

	nŏvi	onsilĭi	inĭtum	à
(thing)	of new	plan	having been entered-on	by

barbăris,	jussit	cohortes,	quæ	ĕrant	in
the barbarians,	ordered	the cohorts,	which	were	on

stationĭbus,	proficisci	secum	in	ĕam	partem,
guards,	to set-out	with himself	into	that	part,

dŭas	succedĕre	in	stationem,	relĭquas
two (cohorts)	to succeed	unto	guard,	the rest

armari,	et	subsĕqui	se	confestim.
to be armed,	and	to follow-closely	himself	immediately.

Quum	processisset (pluperf. subj.)	paullò	longĭùs
When	he had advanced	a little	farther

à	castris,	animadvertit	sŭos	prĕmi
from	the camps,	he perceived	his-own (men)	to be pressed

ab	hostibus,	atque	sustinere	ægrè, et
by	*the enemies,*	*and*	*to withstand*	*hardly, and*

legione	confertâ,	tela	conjici
the legion	*being crowded-together,*	*darts*	*to be thrown*

ex	omnibus	partibus.	Nam, quòd	omni	frumento
from	*all*	*parts.*	*For, because*	*all*	*the corn*

demesso	ex	reliquis	partibus,
being cut-down	*from*	*the rest* (remaining)	*parts,*

una	pars ěrat	reliqua,	hostes,	suspicati
one	*part was*	*left,*	*the enemies,*	*having suspected*

nostros	esse venturos	huc,	delituěrant	noctu
our (men)	*to be about-to-come*	*hither,*	*had lain-hid*	*by night*

in	silvis.	Tum subitò	adorti
in	*the woods.*	*Then suddenly*	*having attacked (them)*

dispersos,	occupatos	in metendo,	armis
dispersed,	*engaged*	*in reaping,*	*(their) arms*

depositis,	paucis interfectis,	perturbavěrant
being laid-aside,	*a few being slain,*	*they had disordered*

reliquos	incertis	ordinibus;
the rest	*in uncertain* (confused)	*ranks;* *at-the-*

simul	circumdeděrant	equitatu	atque
same-time	*they had surrounded (them)*	*with cavalry*	*and*

essědis.
with chariots.

23. Hoc est genus pugnæ ex essědis:
This is the kind of battle from the chariots

primò,	perequitant	per	omnes partes,	et
firstly,	*they ride*	*through*	*all parts,*	*and*

conjiciunt	tela;	atque perturbant	ordines
hurl	*(their) weapons;*	*and they disorder*	*the ranks*

plerumque	terrore	ipso	equorum, et
generally	*by the terror*	*itself*	*of the horses, and*

strepitu	rotarum:	et quum	insinuavêre
rattling	*of the wheels:*	*and when*	*they have introduced*

se	inter turmas	equitum,	desiliunt
themselves	*among the troops*	*of the cavalry,*	*they leap-down*

LIBER IV.

ex	essĕdis	et	prœliantur	pedĭbus.	Intĕrim
from	*the chariots*	*and*	*fight*	*on feet.*	*Meantime*

aurigæ	excedunt	paullùm	è	prœlio,
the charioteers	*retire*	*a little*	*from*	*the battle,*

atque	collŏcant	se	ĭta,	ut	si	illi
and	*place*	*themselves*	*so,*	*that*	*if*	*they*

premantur	à	multitudĭne	hostĭum,	habĕant
be pressed	*by*	*the multitude*	*of the enemies,*	*they may have*

expedĭtum	receptum	ad	sŭos.	Ita
a prepared (ready)	*retreat*	*to*	*their-own.*	*Thus*

præstant	mobilitatem	equĭtum,
they perform (exhibit)	*the changeableness* (activity)	*of cavalry,*

stabilitatem	pedĭtum	in prœliis;	ac	effĭciunt
the firmness	*of infantry*	*in battles;*	*and*	*they accomplish*

tantum	quotidiano	usu	et	exercitatione,	ut
so-much	*by daily*	*practice*	*and*	*exercise,*	*that*

consuevĕrint (perf. subj.)	in	declivi	ac
they have been accustomed	*in*	*a sloping*	*and*

præcipĭti	lŏco,	sustinere	ĕquos	incitatos,	et
steep	*place,*	*to check*	*(their) horses*	*spurred-on,*	*and*

moderari	ac	flectĕre	brĕvì,	et
to govern	*and*	*to turn* (them)	*shortly* (quickly),	*and*

percurrĕre	per	temonem,	et	insistĕre	in
to run-along	*through* (on)	*the pole,*	*and*	*to stand*	*on*

jugo,	et	recipĕre	se	inde	citissĭmè
the yoke,	*and*	*to betake*	*themselves*	*thence*	*most-quickly*

in	currus.
unto	*the chariots.*

34. | Quĭbus | rebus, | nostris | perturbatis |
|---|---|---|---|
| *To which* | *things,* | *our (men)* | *being disordered* |

novitate	pugnæ,	Cæsar	tŭlit
from the unusualness	*of the battle,*	*Cæsar*	*brought*

auxilĭum	opportunissĭmo	tempŏre:	namque	hostes
aid	*in most-seasonable*	*time:*	*for*	*the enemies*

constitĕrunt	adventu	ejus,	nostri	recepērunt
halted	*at the arrival*	*of him.*	*our (men)*	*recovered*

| se | ex | timore. | Quo | facto, |
| *themselves* | *from* | *fear.* | *Which* | *being done,* |

| arbitratus | tempus | esse | alienum | ad | hostem |
| *having thought* | *the time* | *to be* | *improper* | *to (for)* | *the enemy* |

| lacessendum | et | prœlium | committendum, | continuit |
| *to-be-provoked* | *and* | *battle* | *to-be-engaged,* | *he kept* |

| se | suo | loco; | et | brevi | tempore |
| *himself* | *in his-own* | *place;* | *and* | *a short* | *time* |

| intermisso, | reduxit | legiones | in | castra. |
| *being intermitted,* | *he led-back* | *the legions* | *into* | *the camps.* |

| Dum | hæc | geruntur, | omnibus | nostris |
| *Whilst* | *these (things)* | *are carried-on,* | *all* | *our (men)* |

| occupatis, | qui | erant | in | agris, | reliqui |
| *being engaged,* | *who* | *were* | *in* | *the lands,* | *the rest* |

| discesserunt. | Tempestates | secutæ-sunt | complures |
| *departed.* | *Tempests* | *followed* | *many* |

| continuos | dies, | quæ | et | continerent (imp. subj.) |
| *successive* | *days,* | *which* | *both* | *did restrain* |

| nostros | in castris (pl.), | et | prohiberent (imp. subj.) |
| *our (men)* | *in camp,* | *and* | *did hinder* |

| hostem | à | pugnâ. | Interim | barbari |
| *the enemy* | *from* | *battle.* | *Meantime* | *the barbarians* |

| dimiserunt | nuncios | in | omnes | partes, | que |
| *dismissed* | *messengers* | *into* | *all* | *parts,* | *and* |

| prædicaverunt | suis | paucitatem nostrorum |
| *declared* | *to their-own (people)* | *the fewness of our* |

| militum; | et | demonstraverunt | quanta | facultas |
| *soldiers;* | *and* | *showed* | *how-great* | *a power (op-* |

| | daretur (imp. subj.) | prædæ | faciendæ, |
| *portunity)* | *was given* | *of plunder* | *to-be-made,* |

| atque | sui | liberandi | in-perpetuum, | si |
| *and* | *of themselves* | *to-be-freed* | *for-ever,* | *if* |

| | expulissent | Romanos | castris (pl.). |
| *they might have driven* | *the Romans* | *from the camp.* |

| Magnâ | multitudine | peditatûs | que | equitatûs |
| *A great* | *multitude* | *of infantry* | *and* | *of cavalry* |

LIBER IV.

coactâ	celerĭter	his	rebus,	venerunt	ad
being gathered	*quickly*	*by these*	*things.*	*they came*	*to*

castra (pl.).
the camp.

35. Etsi   Cæsar   videbat   ĭdem
    Although   *Cæsar*   *did see*   *the same (thing)*

fŏre,	quod	accidĕrat	superiorĭbus
to-be-about-to-be,	*which*	*had happened*	*in former*

diebus;	ut,	si	hostes	essent	pulsi,
days;	*that,*	*if*	*the enemies*	*might be*	*routed,*

effugĕrent	perīcŭlum	celeritate;	tămen
they would escape	*danger*	*by speed;*	*however*

nactus	circĭter	triginta	equĭtes,	quos	Comĭus
having got	*about*	*thirty*	*horsemen,*	*whom*	*Comius*

Atrĕbas,	de	quo	dictum-est	antè,
the Atrebatian,	*of*	*whom*	*it has been-said*	*before,*

transportavĕrat	secum,	constitŭit	legiones
had brought-over	*with himself,*	*he arranged*	*the legions*

in	acie	pro	castris (pl.).	Prœlio	commisso,
in	*line*	*before*	*the camp.*	*The battle*	*being engaged,*

hostes	potuerunt	non	ferre	impĕtum
the enemies	*were-able*	*not*	*to bear*	*the charge*

nostrorum	milĭtum	diutĭùs	ac	verterunt	terga:
of our	*soldiers*	*longer*	*and*	*turned*	*(their) backs:*

quos	secuti	tanto	spatĭo,	quantum
whom	*having followed*	*in so-much*	*distance,*	*as-much-as*

potuerunt	efficĕre	cursu	et	virĭbus,
they were-able	*to perform*	*by running*	*and*	*by forces*

	occiderunt	complures	ex	iis:	deinde
(endurance),	*they killed*	*many*	*out-of*	*them:*	*then*

omnĭbus	ædificĭis	incensis	longè	que	latè,
all	*the buildings*	*being-burned*	*far*	*and*	*widely,*

receperunt	se	in	castra (pl.).
they betook	*themselves*	*into*	*the camp.*

36. Eodem   die   legati   missi ab hostĭbus
    On the same   *day*   *ambassadors*   *sent*   *by*   *the enemies*

vēnerunt	ad	Cæsărem	de	pace.	Cæsar	duplicavit
came	to	Cæsar	about	peace.	Cæsar	doubled

his	numĕrum	obsĭdum,	quem	imperavĕrat
to these	the number	of hostages,	which	he had ordered

antĕa;	que	jussit	ĕos adduci	in
before;	and	commanded	them to be conducted	unto

continentem;	quòd,	dĭe	æquinoctĭi
the continent,;	because,	the day	of the equinox

propinquâ,	existimabat	navigationem	non
(being) near,	he did think	the voyage	not

subjiciendam	hiĕmi	infirmis	navĭbus:	ipse
to-be-exposed	to winter	with weak	ships:	himself

nactus	idonĕam	tempestatem	solvit
having gained	a proper	season (weather)	loosed

naves	paullò	post	medĭam	noctem;
the ships (set sail)	a little	after	middle	night;

omnes	quæ pervenerunt	incolŭmes	ad	continentem.
all	which arrived	safe	to	the continent.

Ex	his,	dŭæ	onerarĭæ	potuerunt
Out-of	these,	two	burden (transport ships)	were-able

non	capĕre	eosdem	portus,	quos
not	to take (reach)	the same	harbours,	which

relĭquæ;	sed	delatæ-sunt	paullò	infrà.
the rest (did);	but	were carried-down	a little	beneath

(lower down).

37. Ex	quĭbus	navĭbus,	quum	circĭter
Out-of	which	ships,	when	about

trecenti	milĭtes	expositi-essent (pluperf. subj.),
three-hundred	soldiers	had been landed,

atque	contendĕrent (imp. subj.)	in	castra,
and	did proceed	unto	the camps,

Morĭni,	quos Cæsar	reliquĕrat	pacatos
the Morini,	whom Cæsar	had left	subdued,

proficiscens	in	Britannĭam,	adducti	spe prædæ,
setting-out	into	Britain,	induced	by hope of plunder,

primò	circumsteterunt	numĕro	suorum
first	*surrounded (them)*	*with a number*	*of their-own*

	non ĭta magno, ac	jusserunt	ponĕre
(people)	*not so great, and*	*ordered (them)*	*to lay-down*

arma,	si	nollent	sese
(their) arms,	*if*	*they might be unwilling*	*themselves*

interfĭci.	Quum	illi, orbe	facto,
to be slain.	*When*	*they, a circle*	*being formed*

defendĕrent (imp. subj.)	sese,	circĭter sex	millĭa
did defend	*themselves,*	*about six*	*thousands*

celerĭter convenerunt	ad	clamorem homĭnum.	Quâ
speedily assembled	*at*	*the shout of the men.*	*Which*

re	nuntiatâ,	Cæsar misit omnem	equitatum
thing	*being announced,*	*Cæsar sent all*	*the cavalry*

ex	sŭis castris	auxilĭo sŭis.	Intĕrim
out-of	*his camps*	*for aid to his (men).*	*Meantime*

nostri	milĭtes sustinuerunt	impĕtum	hostĭum,
our	*soldiers sustained*	*the attack*	*of the enemies,*

atque	pugnaverunt fortissĭmè	amplĭùs	quatŭor
and	*fought most-bravely*	*more (than)*	*four*

horis;	et, paucis vulnerĭbus	acceptis,	occiderunt
hours;	*and, a few wounds*	*being received,*	*killed*

complures	ex ĭis.	Verò posteăquàm	noster
many	*out-of them.*	*But after-that*	*our*

equitatus	venit in	conspectum,	hostes,
cavalry	*came into*	*sight,*	*the enemies, (their)*

armis	abjectis,	verterunt	terga, que
arms	*being thrown-away,*	*turned*	*(their) backs, and*

magnus	numĕrus eorum	occisus-est.	
a great	*number of them*	*was killed.*	

38. Cæsar	misit	legatum	Titum	Labienum
Cæsar	*sent*	*(his) lieutenant*	*Titus*	*Labienus*

postĕro	dĭe,	cum	ĭis	egionĭbus, quas
in the following	*day,*	*with*	*those*	*legions, which*

reduxĕrat	ex	Britannĭâ,	in	Morĭnos, qui
he had led-back	*from*	*Britain,*	*unto*	*the Morini, who*

fecerant   rebellionem   Qui,   quum   haberent (imp.
had made   a rebellion.   Who,   when   they did have

subj.)   non   quò   recipĕrent   se
          not   whither   they might betake   themselves

    propter   siccitates   paludum,
on-account-of   the droughts (drying-up)   of the marshes,

  quo   perfugĭo   usi-fuĕrant   superiore   anno,
with which   refuge   they had used   in the former   year,

fĕrè   omnes   pervenerunt   in   potestatem   Labieni.
nearly   all   came   into   the power   of Labienus.

At   Quintus   Titurĭus   et   Lucĭus   Cotta,   legati,
But   Quintus   Titurius   and   Lucius   Cotta,   the lieutenants

qui   duxĕrant   legiones   in   fines   Me-
who   had led   the legions   into   the territories   of the

napiorum,   omnĭbus   agris   eorum   vastatis,
Menapii,   all   the lands   of them   being ravaged,

frumentis (plur.)   succisis,   que   ædificĭis
   the corn   being cut-down,   and   the buildings

   incensis,   quòd   omnes   Menapĭi   abdidĕrant
being set-on-fire,   because   all   the Menapii   had hid

  se   in   densissĭmas   silvas,   receperunt   se
themselves   into   the thickest   woods,   betook   themselves

ad   Cæsărem.   Cæsar   constitŭit   hiberna
to   Cæsar.   Cæsar   established   the winter-quarters

omnĭum   legionum   in   Belgis.   Eò   dŭæ
 of all   the legions   among   the Belgæ.   Thither   two

civitates   omnino   ex   Britannĭâ   miserunt   obsĭdes:
 states   in-all   out-of   Britain   sent   hostages:

relĭquæ   neglexerunt.   His   rebus   gestis,
the rest   neglected (it)   These   things   being carried-on,

   supplicatĭo   viginti   dierum   decreta-est   à
a general thanksgiving   of twenty   days   was decreed   by

senatu,   ex   litĕris (pl.)   Cæsăris.
the senate,   from   the letter   of Cæsar.   [upon receipt of

Cæsar's dispatches).

QUINTUS LIBER.
FIFTH BOOK.

ARGUMENTUM.
ARGUMENT.

Hic	liber	continet	aliquos	motus	Pirustarum
This	book	contains	some	disturbances	of the Pirustæ

coërcitos	à	Cæsare:	item	dissidia	Trevirorum
checked	by	Cæsar:	also	the quarrels	of the Trevir

contendentium	inter	se	de	Princi-
contending	among	themselves	about	the supreme

patu:	transitum	in	Britanniam:	bellum
authority:	the crossing-over	into	Britain:	the war

Ambiorigis:	mortem	Indutiomari.
of Ambiorix:	the death	of Indutiomarus.

1. Lucio	Domitio,	Appio	Claudio
Lucius	Domitius,	Appius	Claudius (being)

Consulibus,	Cæsar	discedens	ab	hibernis
Consuls,	Cæsar	departing	from	winter-quarters

in	Italiam,	ut	instituërat	facëre	quotannis,
into	Italy,	as	he had resolved	to do	yearly,

impërat	legatis,	quos	præfecërat
orders	to the lieutenants,	whom	he had set-over

legionibus,	ut	curarent	quam-plurimas
to the legions,	that	they should take-care	as-many-as

possent	naves	ædificandas	hiëme,	que
they might be-able	ships	to-be-built	in the winter,	and

vetëres	reficiendas.	Demonstrat	mödum
the old (ships)	to-be-repaired.	He points-out	the size

que formam	earum;	făcit	paullò	humiliores
and form	*of them;*	*he makes (them)*	*a little*	*lower*

quàm	quĭbus (abl.)	consuevĭmus	uti
than	*(those) which*	*we have been accustomed*	*to use*

in	nostro	mări, ad	celeritatem onerandi,	que
in	*our*	*sea, to (for)*	*quickness of loading,*	*and*

subductionis;		atque id	măgis	eŏ,
of drawing-up (ashore);		*and that*	*the more*	*therefore*

	quòd	cognovĕrat	mĭnùs magnos
(for this reason),	*because*	*he had known*	*less great*

fluctus	fiĕri	ĭbi	propter crebras
waves	*to be made*	*there*	*on-account-of the frequent*

commutationes	æstuum;	paullò latiores
changes	*of the tides;*	*(he makes them) a little wider*

quàm	quĭbus (abl.)	utĭmur in	relĭquis
than	*(those) which*	*we use in*	*the rest (other)*

marĭbus,	ad	onĕra et	ad multitudĭnem
seas,	*to (for)*	*burdens and*	*to a multitude*

jumentorum	transportandam.	Impĕrat omnes
of beasts-of-burden	*to-be-carried-over.*	*He orders all*

has	fiĕri	actuarĭas:	ad quam	rem
these	*to be made*	*fit-to-be-rowed (light):*	*to which*	*thing*

humilĭtas	adjŭvat	multùm. Jŭbet	ea,
lowness	*aids*	*much. He orders*	*those (things),*

quæ	sunt	usŭi ad	naves armandas,	apportari
which	*are*	*for use to*	*ships to-be-rigged,*	*to be brought*

ex	Hispanĭâ. Ipse,	conventĭbus citerioris
out-of	*Spain. Himself,*	*the assemblies of the nearer*

Galliæ	peractis,	proficiscĭtur in	Illyrĭcum;
Gaul	*being finished,*	*sets-out into*	*Illyricum;*

quòd	audiebat	finitĭmam	partem Pro-
because	*he did hear*	*the neighbouring*	*part of the*

vincĭæ	vastari	incursionĭbus	à Pirustis.
Province	*to be ravaged*	*in incursions*	*by the Pirustæ.*

Quum	venisset (pluperf. subj.)	eŏ,	impĕrat
When	*he had come*	*thither.*	*he orders*

LIBER V.

civitatĭbus	to the states (to furnish)
milĭtes:	soldiers:
que	and
jŭbet	commands (them)
convenire	to assemble
in	into
certum	a certain
lŏcum.	place.
Quâ	Which
re	thing
nuntiatâ,	being announced,
Pirustæ	the Pirustæ
mittunt	send
legatos	ambassadors
ad	to
ĕum,	him,
qui	who
docĕant	may teach (him)
"nĭhil	"nothing
earum	of those
rerum	things
factum (-esse)	to have been done
publĭco	by public
concilĭo:"	council:"
que	and
demonstrant	they show
"sese	"themselves
esse	to be
paratos	prepared
satisfacĕre	to satisfy
omnĭbus	by all
rationĭbus	means
de	about
injurĭis."	the injuries."
Oratione	The speech
eorum	of them
acceptâ,	being received (heard),
Cæsar	Cæsar
impĕrat	orders (them to furnish)
obsĭdes,	hostages,
que	and
jŭbet	commands
ĕos	them
adduci	to be brought
ad	to
certam	a certain
dĭem:	day:
nĭsi	unless
fecĕrant	they shall have done
ĭta,	so,
demonstrat	he shows
sese	himself
persecuturum	about-to-pursue
civitatem	the state
bello.	by war.
Iis	Those
adductis	being brought
ad	on-the
dĭem,	day,
ut	as
imperavĕrat,	he had ordered,
dat	he gives
(appoints)	arbĭtros	arbitrators
inter	among
civitates,	the states,
qui	who
æstĭment	may value
litem	the suit (damage)
que	and
constitŭant	may appoint
pœnam.	the penalty.

2. His rebus confectis, que conventĭbus
   These things being finished, and the assemblies

peractis, revertĭtur in citeriorem Gallĭam,
being concluded, he returns into hither Gaul,

atque inde proficiscĭtur ad exercĭtum. Quum
and thence sets-out to the army. When

venisset (plup. subj.) ĕo, omnĭbus hibernis
he had come thither, all the winter-quarters

circuĭtis,	being gone-round,
invenit	he found
circĭter	about
sexcentas	six-hundred
naves	ships
ejus	of that
genĕris,	kind,
cujus	of which
demonstravĭmus	we have shown
supra,	above,
et	and
viginti	twenty
octo	eight
longas	long (ships of war)
constructas;	built,
singu-	by the
lari	singular
studĭo	zeal
milĭtum,	of the soldiers,
in	in
summâ	the highest
inopĭâ	want
omnĭum	of all
rerum,	things,
nĕque	nor
multum	much
abesse	to be absent (to be
wanting)	ab	from
ĕo,	that,
quin	but-that
possent	they might-be-able
deduci	to be led-down (launched)
paucis	in a few
diebus.	days.
Milĭtĭbus	The soldiers
collaudatis,	being praised,
atque	and
iis,	those,
qui	who
præfuĕrant	had presided
negotĭo,	to the business,
ostendit	he shows
quid	what
vĕlit	he may will
fiĕri;	to be done;
atque	and
jŭbet	orders
omnes	all
convenire	to assemble
ad	at
portum	port
Itĭum:	Itius
(Boulogne):	ex	from
quo	which
portu	harbour
cognovĕrat	he had known
trajectum	the passage
in	into
Britannĭam	Britain
esse	to be
commodissĭmum,	most-convenient,
circĭter	about
triginta	thirty
millĭum	of thousands
passŭum	of paces
à	from
continenti.	the continent.
Relinquit	He leaves
quod	what
visum-est	seemed
esse	to be
sătis	enough
milĭtum	of soldiers
huic	for this
rĕi:	thing:
ipse	himself
proficiscĭtur	sets-out
cum	with
quatŭor	four
expedĭtis	lightly-equipped
legionĭbus,	legions,
et	and
octingentis	eight-hundred
equitĭbus,	cavalry,
in	into
fines	the territories
Trevirorum;	of the Treviri;
quòd	because
hi	these
nĕque	neither
veniebant	did come
ad	to
concilĭa,	the councils,
nĕque	nor

parebant	imperio,	que	dicebantur	sollicitari
did obey	*to (his) command,*	*and*	*were said*	*to stir-up*

Germanos	transrhenanos.
the Germans	*beyond-the-Rhine.*

3.
Hæc	civitas	valet	longè	plurimùm
This	*state*	*prevails*	*by far*	*the most*

totius	Galliæ	equitatu,	que	habet	magnas
of the whole	*of Gaul*	*in cavalry,*	*and*	*has*	*great*

copias	peditum;	que	tangit	Rhenum,	ut
forces	*of infantry;*	*and*	*touches-on*	*the Rhine,*	*as*

demonstravimus	suprà.	In	eâ	civitate	duo,
we have shown	*above.*	*In*	*that*	*state*	*two (persons),*

Indutiomarus	et	Cingetorix,	contendebant	inter
Indutiomarus	*and*	*Cingetorix,*	*did contend*	*among*

se	de	principatu:	alter	ex
themselves	*about*	*supreme-authority:*	*the other (one)*	*out-of*

quibus,	simul-atque	cognitum-est	de	adventu
whom,	*as-soon-as*	*it was known*	*concerning*	*the coming*

Cæsaris	que	legionum,	venit	ad eum;	confirmavit
of Cæsar	*and*	*of the legions,*	*came*	*to him;*	*he affirmed*

se	que	omnes	suos	futuros	in officio,
himself	*and*	*all*	*his (people)*	*about-to-be*	*in duty*

	neque	defecturos	ab	amicitiâ
(allegiance),	*nor*	*about-to-revolt*	*from*	*the friendship*

Romani	populi;	que	ostendit,	quæ
of the Roman	*people;*	*and*	*he shows,*	*what (things)*

gererentur (imp. subj.)	in	Treviris.	At
were carried-on	*in*	*the Treviri.*	*But*

Indutiomarus	instituit	cogere	equitatum	que
Indutiomarus	*began*	*to collect*	*cavalry*	*and*

peditatum;	que	iis, qui	per	ætatem	poterant
infantry;	*and*	*those, who*	*through*	*age*	*were-able*

non	esse	in armis,	abditis	in	silvam
not	*to be*	*in arms,*	*being hid*	*into*	*the wood*

Arduennam,	(quæ	ingenti	magnitudine
Arduenna (Ardennes),	*(which*	*with (of) great*	*extent*

pertĭnet	à	flumĭne	Rheno	ad	initĭum
reaches	from	the river	Rhine	to	the beginning

Rhemorum per medĭos fines Trevirorum)
of the Rhemi *through* *the middle* *territories* *of the Treviri*)

parare bellum. Sed posteăquàm nonnulli princĭpes
to prepare *war.* *But* *after-that* *some* *chiefs*

ex ĕâ civitate, et adducti familiaritate
out-of *that* *state,* *both* *induced* *by the acquaintance*

Cingetorĭgis, et perterrĭti adventu nostri
of Cingetorix, *and* *affrighted* *by the coming* *of our*

exercĭtûs, venerunt ad Cæsărem, et cœperunt petĕre
army, *came* *to* *Cæsar,* *and* *began* *to seek*

privatim ab de sŭis rebus, quonĭam
privately *from* *him* *about* *their-own* *affairs,* *since*

possent (imp. subj.) non consulĕre civitati:
they were able *not* *to consult* *for the state:*

Indutiomărus verĭtus ne desereretur
Indutiomarus *having feared* *lest* *he might be abandoned*

ab omnĭbus, mittit legatos ad Cæsărem;
by *all,* *sends* *ambassadors* *to* *Cæsar;* *(to say)*

se discĕdere idcircò à sŭis,
himself *to depart* *for-this-reason* *from* *his-own (people),*

atque noluisse venire ad ĕum, quò
and *to have been-unwilling* *to come to* *him,* *in order-that*

contineret civitatem faciliùs in officĭo;
he might restrain *the state* *more-easily* *in* *duty*

ne discessu omnis nobilitatis,
(allegiance); *lest* *by the departure* *of all* *the nobility,*

plebs laberetur propter
the common-people *might slip* (revolt) *through (their)*

imprudentĭam: ităque civitatem esse in sŭâ
indiscretion: *therefore* *the state* *to be* *in* *his*

potestate; que se venturum ad ĕum
power; *and* *himself (to be)* *about-to-come* *to* *him*

in castra (pl.), si Cæsar permittĕret; et
into *the camp,* *if* *Cæsar* *would permit (him);* *and*

4] LIBER V. **235**

permissurum	sŭas	fortunas	que
(to be) about-to-yield-up	*his-own*	*fortunes*	*and (those)*

civitatis	fidëi	ejus.
of the state	*to the faith*	*of him.*

4. Etsi Cæsar intelligebat de quâ caussâ
Although Cæsar did understand from what cause

ĕa dicerentur (imp. subj.), que quæ res
those (words) were said, and what thing

deterreret (imp. subj.) ĕum ab instituto
did deter him from (his) purposed

consilĭo; tămen, ne cogeretur consumĕre
design; however, lest he might be compelled to waste

æstatem in Trevĭris, omnĭbus rebus comparatis
the summer in the Treviri, all things being prepared

ad Britannĭcum bellum, jussit Indutiomărum
to (for) the Britannic war, he ordered Indutiomarus

venire ad se cum ducentis obsidĭbus. His
to come to himself with two-hundred hostages. These

adductis, et filĭo in ïis, que
being brought, and (his) son in (among) them, and

omnĭbus propinquis ejus, quos evocavĕrat
all the relations of him, whom he had called-out

nominatim, consolatus-est que hortatus (-est)
by-name, he consoled and encouraged

Indutiomărum, ŭtì permaneret in officĭo.
Indutiomarus, that he might continue in duty (alle-

Tămen, nihĭlo-seciùs principĭbus Trevirorum
giance). However, nevertheless the chiefs of the Treviri

convocatis ad se, conciliavit ĕos
being called-together to himself, he reconciled them

sigillatim Cingetorĭgi: quod intelligebat
individually to Cingetorix: which (thing) he did understand

cùm fĭĕri à se merĭto
when (as well) to be done by himself by the desert

ejus, tum arbitrabatur interesse
of him, then (as) he did think (it) to concern (him)

236 DE BELLO GALLICO. [B

magni,	auctoritatem	ejus	valere
of great (greatly),	*the authority*	*of him*	*to prevail.*

quam-plurĭmùm	inter	sŭos,	cujus
ts-much-as-possible	*among*	*his-own (people),*	*whose*

voluntatem	perspexisset (pluperf. subj.)	tam	egregĭam
(good)-will	*he had perceived*	*so*	*excellent*

in	se.	Indutiomăris	tŭlit	ĭd	factum
unto	*himself.*	*Indutiomarus*	*bore*	*that*	*being done* (this act)

gravĭter,	sŭam	gratĭam	minŭi	inter
heavily (bitterly),	*his-own*	*favour*	*to be diminished*	*among*

sŭos:	et	qui	fuisset (pluperf. subj.)
his-own (people):	*and*	*(he) who*	*had been*

inimico	anĭmo	antè	in	nos	exarsit
with (of) unfriendly	*mind*	*before*	*unto*	*us*	*burnt-forth*

multò	gravĭùs	hoc	dolore.
by-much	*more-severely*	*by this*	*grief.*

5.
Iis	rebus	constitutis,	Cæsar	pervenit	ad
Those	*things*	*being settled,*	*Cæsar*	*arrived*	*at*

portum	Itĭum	cum	legionĭbus.	Cognoscit
the harbour	*Itius*	*with*	*the legions.*	*He knows* (learns)

ĭbi,	quadraginta	naves,	quæ	factæ-ĕrant	in
there,	*forty*	*ships,*	*which*	*had been made*	*among*

Meldis,	rejectas	tempestate,	non	potuisse
the Meldi,	*thrown-back*	*by a tempest,*	*not*	*to have been-able*

tenere	cursum,	atque	relatas	eŏdem,
to hold	*(their) course,*	*and*	*being carried-back*	*to the same*

(place),	unde	profectæ-ĕrant:	invĕnit	relíquas
(place),	*whence*	*they had set-out:*	*he finds*	*the rest*

paratas	ad-navigandum,	atque	instructas	omnĭbus
prepared	*to-sail,*	*and*	*furnished*	*with all*

rebus.	Equitatus	totius	Gallĭæ	convenit
things.	*The cavalry*	*of the whole*	*of Gaul*	*assembled*

eòdem,	numĕro	quatŭor	millĭum,	que
in the same (place),	*in number*	*of four*	*thousands,*	*and*

princĭpes	ex	omnĭbus	civitatĭbus;	perpaucos	ex,
the chiefs	*out-of*	*all*	*the states;*	*a very-few*	*out-of*

quĭbus,	quorum	fĭdem in	se	perspexĕrat,
whom,	*whose*	*fidelity unto*	*himself*	*he had clearly-seen,*

decrevĕrat	relinquĕre	in Gallĭâ;	ducĕre
he had resolved	*to leave*	*in Gaul;*	*(and) to conduct*

relĭquos	secum	lŏco	obsĭdum;	quòd
the rest	*with him*	*in the place*	*of hostages;*	*because*

verebatur	motum	Gallĭæ, quum	ipse
he did fear	*a disturbance*	*of Gaul when*	*himself*

abesset.
might be absent.

6. Dumnŏrix Ædŭus ĕrat una cum
Dumnorix the Æduan was together with

cætĕris de quo dictum-est à nobis antĕa.
the rest of whom it has been spoken by us before.

Constituĕrat ducĕre hunc secum inprimis,
He had resolved to conduct him with him in-particular,

quòd -cognovĕrat ĕum cupĭdum novarum rerum,
because he had known him desirous of new things

(revolution), cupĭdum imperii, magni anĭmi, magnæ
desirous of power, of great spirit, of great

auctoritatis inter Gallos. Accedebat huc,
authority among the Gauls. It did approach hither

quòd Dumnŏrix dixĕrat jam in
(added to this), *that Dumnorix had said already in*

concilĭo Æduorum, "regnum civitatis
a council of the Ædui, "*the government of the state*

deferri sĭbi à Cæsăre." Quod
to be conferred to (on) himself by Cæsar." *Which*

dictum Ædŭi ferebant gravĭter, nĕque
saying the Ædui did bear heavily (ill), nor

audebant mittĕre legatos ad Cæsărem
did they dare to send ambassadors to Cæsar

caussâ recusandi nĕque deprecandi.
by cause (for the purpose) of refusing nor of deprecating

Cæsar cognovĕrat id factum (-esse)
(the thing). *Cæsar had known that to have been done*

ex	suis	hospitĭbus.	Ille	primò	contendit petĕre
from	*his*	*guests.*	*He*	*at-first*	*strove to solicit*

omnĭbus	precĭbus,	ut	relinqueretur	in Gallĭâ;
by all	*entreaties,*	*that*	*he might be left*	*in Gaul;*

partim	quòd	insuetus	navigandi	timeret (imp.
partly	*because*	*unused*	*of voyaging*	*he did fear*

subj.)	măre;	partim	quòd	dicĕret (imp. subj.)
	the sea;	*partly*	*because*	*he did say*

sese	impediri	religionĭbus. Posteăquam
himself	*to be hindered*	*by religious-scruples. After-that*

vidit	id	negari	obstinatè	sĭbi, omni
he saw	*that*	*to be denied*	*obstinately*	*to himself, all*

spe impetrandi	ademptâ,	cœpit	sollicitare
hope of obtaining (it)	*being taken-away,*	*he began*	*to stir-up*

princĭpes	Gallĭæ,	sevocare	singŭlos	que
the chiefs	*of Gaul,*	*to call-apart*	*each (of them)*	*and*

hortari,	ut	remanerent	in continenti;
to exhort,	*that*	*they should remain*	*on the continent;*

territare	mĕtu,	"fĭĕri	non	sĭne
to affright (them)	*with fear,*	*"to be done*	*not*	*without*

caussâ,	ut	Gallĭa spoliaretur	omni
reason,	*that*	*Gaul might be stripped*	*from (of) all*

nobilitate.	Id	esse	consilĭum Cæsăris,	ut
the nobility.	*That*	*to be*	*the plan of Cæsar,*	*that*

necaret	omnes	hos	transductos	in
he might destroy	*all*	*these*	*conveyed-over*	*into*

Britannĭam,	quos	vereretur (imp. subj.)	interficĕre
Britain,	*whom*	*he did fear*	*to slay*

in conspectu Gallĭæ."	Interponĕre
in sight of Gaul."	*(He began) to interpose (engage)*

fĭdem	relĭquis;	poscĕre	jusjurandum, ut
faith	*to the rest;*	*to require*	*an oath, that*

administrarent	communi	consilĭo, quod	intel-
they should manage	*by common*	*counsel, what*	*they might*

lexissent	esse	ex	usu	Gallĭæ,
have understood	*to be*	*from (for)*	*the use (advantage)*	*of Gaul*

LIBER V.

7. Hæc   deferebantur   ad   Cæsărem   à
These (matters)   were reported   to   Cæsar   by

complurĭbus.   Quâ   re   cognĭtâ,   Cæsar,   quòd
very-many.   Which thing being known, Cæsar, because

trĭbuebat   tantum   dignitatis   Æduæ   civitati,
he did grant so-much of honour   to the Æduan state,

statuebat   Dumnorĭgem   coërcendum   atque
did determine Dumnorix   to-be-restrained and

deterrendum   quibuscunque   rebus   posset;
to-be-deterred by whatever   things   he might be-able;

quòd   vidēbat   amentĭam   ejus   progrĕdi
because   he did see   the insanity   of him   to proceed

longĭùs,   prospiciendum,   ne   posset
further,   (it was) to-be-provided, lest   he might be-able

nocere   sĭbi   ac   Reipublĭcæ.   Ităque
to injure   to himself and   to the state.   Therefore

commoratus   in   ĕo   lŏco   circĭter   viginti   quinque
having delayed in   that place about   twenty   five

dĭes,   quòd   ventus   Corus   impediebat
days,   because the wind Corus (North-west)   did hinder

navigationem,   qui   consuevit   flare   in
the voyage,   which (wind)   has been-used   to blow   in

his   lŏcis   magnam   partem   omnis   tempŏris,
these places   (during) a great part   of every season,

dăbat   opĕram,   ut   contineret
he did give (use) endeavour, that   he might restrain

Dumnorĭgem   in   officĭo;   tămen   cognoscĕret
Dumnorix   in   duty;   however   he should know

nihĭlò-secĭus   omnĭa   consilia   ejus.   Tandem
nevertheless   all   the designs of him.   At-length

nactus   idoneam   tempestatem,   jŭbet   milĭtes
having got   suitable   weather,   he orders   the soldiers

que   equĭtes   conscendĕre   in   naves.   At   anĭmis
and   cavalry   to embark   into   the ships. But   the minds

omnĭum   impedĭtis,   Dumnorix   cum   equitĭbus
of all   being engaged.   Dumnorix   with   the cavalry

Æduorum,	Cæsăre	insciente,	cœpit
of the Ædui,	*Cæsar*	*(being) ignorant (of it)*	*began*

discedĕre	dŏmum	à	castris.	Quâ	re
to depart	*home*	*from*	*the camps.*	*Which*	*thing*

nuntiatâ,	Cæsar,	profectione	intermissâ
being announced,	*Cæsar,*	*the departure*	*being interrupted*

atque	omnĭbus	rebus	postposĭtis,	mittit	magnam
and	*all*	*thing*	*being postponed,*	*sends*	*a great*

partem	equitatûs	ad-insequendum	ĕum,	que
part	*of the cavalry*	*to-pursue*	*him,*	*and*

impĕrat	retrăhi :	si	faciat
orders (him)	*to be dragged-back :*	*if*	*he may make*

vim,	nĕque	parĕat,	jŭbet	interfĭci :
violence,	*nor*	*may obey,*	*he commands (him)*	*to be killed :*

arbĭtratus	hunc	facturum	nĭhil	pro
having considered	*him*	*about-to-do*	*nothing*	*for* (as)

sano,	qui	neglexisset (pluperf. subj.)
a sound (man),	*who*	*had contemned*

imperĭum	præsentis.	Enim	ille	revocatus
the command	*of (him) present.*	*For*	*he*	*being recalled*

cœpit	resistĕre,	ac	defendĕre	se	mănu,
began	*to resist,*	*and*	*to defend*	*himself*	*by hand* (force),

que	implorare	fĭdem	suorum ;
and	*to entreat*	*the faith* (protection)	*of his-own* (people);

clamĭtans	sæpe,	"se	esse	libĕrum,	que
crying-out	*often,*	*"himself*	*to be*	*a free (-man),*	*and*

libĕræ	civitatis."	Isti	circumsistunt	que	interficĭunt
of a free	*state."*	*They*	*surround*	*and*	*slay*

hŏmĭnem,	ut	imperatum-ĕrat :	at	omnes	Ædŭi
the man,	*as*	*it had been ordered:*	*but*	*all*	*the Æduan*

equĭtes	revertuntur	ad	Cæsărem.
horsemen	*return*	*to*	*Cæsar*

8. | His | rebus | gestis, | Labieno | relicto |
|---|---|---|---|---|
| *These* | *things* | *being carried-on,* | *Labienus* | *being left* |

in	continente	cum	trĭbus	legionĭbus	et	duobus
on the continent	*with*	*three*	*legions*	*and*	*two*

LIBER V.

millĭbus	equĭtum,	ut	tueretur	portus,
thousands	of cavalry,	that	he might defend	the harbours,

et provideret frumentariæ rĕi, que cognoscĕret
and might provide for the corn affair, and might know

quæ gererentur in Gallĭâ, et capĕret
what (things) might be carried-on in Gaul, and might take

consilĭum pro tempŏre et pro
counsel for (according to) time and for

re: ipse cum quinque legionĭbus et
the affair: himself with five legions and

pāri numĕro equĭtum, quem reliquĕrat in
an equal number of cavalry, which he had left on

continente, solvit naves ad occasum
the continent, loosed the ships (set sail) to (at) the setting

solis; et provectus leni
of the sun; and being carried-forward by a gentle

Afrĭco, vento intermisso
South-west-wind, the wind being intermitted (having ceased)

circĭter mediâ nocte, tenŭit non cursum:
about in middle night, he kept not the course:

et delatus longĭùs æstu, luce
and being carried-away farther by the tide, the light (day)

ortâ, conspexit Britannĭam relictam sub
having risen, he beheld Britain left under (on)

sinistrâ. Tum rursus secutus commutationem
the left. Then again having followed the change

æstûs, contendit remis, ut capĕret
of the tide, he strove with oars, that he might take (reach)

ĕam partem insŭlæ, quâ cognovĕrat
that part of the island, in which he had known

superiore æstate optimum egressum esse. In
in the former summer the best landing to be. In

quâ re virtus milĭtum fŭit admŏdum
which thing the excellence of the soldiers was very-much

laudanda, qui, labore remigandi non
to-be-praised, who, the labour of rowing not

intermisso,	being interrupted,
adæquaverunt	equalled
cursum	the course
longarum navium,	of the long ships (ships of war),
vectoriis que	with transport and
gravibus	heavy
navigiis.	vessels.

Accessum-est ad Britanniam omnibus navibus
It was approachedto Britain by all the ships

fere meridiano tempore. Neque hostis visus-est
nearly in the noon time. Neither an enemy was seen

in eo loco. Sed, ut Cæsar postea comperit
in that place. But, as Cæsar afterwards discovered

ex captivis, quum magnæ manus convenissent
from the prisoners, when great bands had assembled

(pluperf. subj.) eo, perterritæ multitudine
there, being affrighted by the multitude

navium, quæ amplius octingentæ
of the ships, which more (than) eight-hundred

visæ-erant una cum annotinis que
had been seen together with last-year's (ships) and

privatis, quas quisque fecerat caussâ
private (ones), which each had made by cause (for the

sui commodi, discesserant timore
sake) of his-own convenience, they had departed by fear

à littore, ac abdiderant se in
from the shore, and had concealed themselves into

superiora loca.
the higher places.

9. Cæsar, exercitu exposito, ac
Cæsar, the army being put-out (landed), and

loco idoneo castris (pl.) capto, ubi
a place fit for a camp being taken, when

cognovit ex captivis, in quo loco copiæ
he learned from the prisoners, in what place the forces

hostium consedissent (pluperf. subj.), decem
of the enemies had encamped, ten

cohortibus relictis ad mare, et trecentis
cohorts being left at the sea, and three-hundred

LIBER V. 243

equitĭbus,	qui	essent	præsidĭo	navĭbus,
horsemen,	*who*	*might be*	*for a guard*	*to the ships,*

contendit	ad	hostes	de	tertĭâ vigilĭâ;
hastened	*to*	*the enemies*	*from* (at)	*the third watch:*

verĭtus	ĕŏ	mĭnŭs	navĭbus,	quòd
having feared	*therefore*	*the less*	*for the ships,*	*because*

relinquebat	deligatas	ad anchŏras	in molli
he did leave (them)	*fastened*	*at anchors*	*on a soft*

atque	aperto littŏre:	et	præfecit Quintum	Atrĭum
and	*open shore:*	*and*	*he set-over Quintus*	*Atrium*

præsidĭo	navĭbus.	Ipse progressus
for protection	*to the ships.*	*Himself having advanced*

noctu	circĭter	duodĕcim	millĭa	passŭum
by night	*about*	*twelve*	*thousands*	*of paces*

conspicatus-est	copĭas	hostĭum.	Illi
espied	*the forces*	*of the enemies.*	*They*

progressi	ad	flumen	equitatu	atque
having advanced	*to*	*the river*	*with the cavalry*	*and*

essĕdis,	cœperunt	prohibere	nostros	ex
chariots,	*began*	*to prevent*	*our (men)*	*from*

superiore lŏco	et	committĕre prœlĭum.	Repulsi
the higher place	*and*	*to engage battle.*	*Being repulsed*

ab	equitatu,	nacti	lŏcum egregĭè	munitum
by	*the cavalry,*	*having got*	*a place excellently*	*fortified*

et	naturâ	et	opĕre,	quem, ut
both	*by nature*	*and*	*by work* (art),	*which (place), as*

videbatur,	præparavĕrant	jam antè,	caussâ
it did seem,	*they had prepared*	*already before,*	*by cause*

	domestĭci	belli, abdiderunt	se
(for the sake)	*of domestic*	*war, they hid*	*themselves*

in	silvas:	nam crebris	arborĭbus
into	*the woods:*	*for frequent* (many)	*trees*

succissis,	omnes	introĭtus	præclusi-ĕrant.
being cut-down,	*all*	*the entrances*	*had been shut-out.*

Ipsi	rari	propugnabant	ex
Themselves	*few* (in parties)	*did fight*	*out-of*

silvis,	que	prohibebant	nostros	ingrĕdi	intra
the woods,	*and*	*did hinder*	*our (men)*	*to enter*	*within*

munitiones.	At	milĭtes	septĭmæ	legionis,
the fortifications.	*But*	*the soldiers*	*of the seventh*	*legion,*

testudĭne	factâ,	et	aggĕre
a covering (with their shields)	*being made,*	*and*	*a mound*

adjecto	ad	munitiones,	ceperunt	lŏcum,
being added	*to*	*the fortifications,*	*took*	*the place,*

que	expulerunt	ĕos	ex	silvis,	paucis	vulnerĭbus
and	*drove-out*	*them*	*from*	*the woods,*	*few*	*wounds*

acceptis.	Sed	Cæsar	vetŭit	persĕqui	ĕos
being received.	*But*	*Cæsar*	*forbade*	*to pursue*	*them*

fugientes	longĭùs,	et	quòd	ignorabat	naturam
fleeing	*farther,*	*both*	*because*	*he did not know*	*the nature*

lŏci,	et	quòd	magnâ	parte	diei
of the place,	*and*	*because*	*a great*	*part*	*of the day*

consumptâ,	volebat	tempus	relinqui	munitioni
being spent,	*he did will*	*time*	*to be left*	*for the fortification*

castrorum (pl.).
of the camp.

10.
Postridĭe	ejus	diei,	misit	manè
The day-after	*of that*	*day,*	*he sent*	*in-the-morning*

milĭtes	que	equĭtes	tripartitò	in
the soldiers	*and*	*cavalry*	*in three-divisions*	*unto*

expeditionem,	ut	persequerentur	ĕos,	qui
the expedition,	*that*	*they might pursue*	*those,*	*who*

fugĕrant.	Iis	progressis	aliquantum	itinĕris,
had fled.	*Those*	*having advanced*	*some-little*	*of the march,*

quum	jam	extremi	essent (imp. subj.)	in	conspectu,
when	*already*	*the last*	*were*	*in*	*sight,*

equĭtes	venerunt	à	Quinto	Atrĭo	ad	Cæsărem,
horsemen	*came*	*from*	*Quintus*	*Atrius*	*to*	*Cæsar,*

qui	nuntiarent	"maxĭmâ	tempestate	coortâ
who	*might announce*	*"a very-great*	*tempest*	*having arisen*

superiori	nocte,	omnes	naves	propè
on the former	*night,*	*all*	*the ships*	*nearly*

11] LIBER V. 245

afflictas-esse	atque	ejectas	in	li tōre;	quòd
to have been dashed	and	cast-out	on	the shore;	because

nĕque	anchŏræ	que	funes	subsistĕrent (imp. subj.),
neither	the anchors	and	ropes	did withstand

nĕque	nautæ	que	gubernatores	possent (imp.
neither	the sailors	and	pilots	were-able

subj.)	păti	vim	tempestatis.	Ităque
	to endure	the violence	of the tempest.	Therefore

magnum	incommŏdum	acceptum-esse	ex	ĕo
great	inconvenience	to have been received	from	that

concursu	navĭum."
collision	of the ships."

11.
His	rebus	cognĭtis,	Cæsar	jŭbet
These	things	being known,	Cæsar	orders

legiones	que	equitatum	revocari,	atque
the legions	and	the cavalry	to be recalled,	and

desiscĕre	itinĕre.	Ipse	revertĭtui	ad
to halt	from the march.	Himself	returns	to

naves:	perspĭcit	coràm	fĕrè	eadem,
the ships:	he observes	in-presence	nearly	the same (things),

quæ	cognovĕrat	ex	nuntĭis	que
which	he had known	from	the messengers	and

litĕris (pl.);	sic	ut,	circĭter	quadragĭnta	navĭbus
the letter;	so	that,	about	forty	ships

amissis,	tămen	relĭquæ	viderentur (imp. subj.)
being lost,	however	the rest	did seem

posse	refĭci	magno	negotĭo.	Ităque
to be-able	to be repaired	with great	trouble.	Therefore

deligit	fabros	ex	legionĭbus,	et	jŭbet	alĭos
he selects	workmen	out-of	the legions,	and	orders	others

accersiri	ex	continenti:	scribit	Labieno,
to be sent-for	from	the continent:	he writes	to Labienus,

ut	instĭtúat	quàm-plurĭmas	naves
that	he may construci	the greatest-number	ships

posset	iis	legionĭbus,	quæ	sunt	ăpud
he might be-able	with those	legions,	which	are	with

eum.	Ipse,	etsi	res	ĕrat	multæ opĕræ
him.	Himself,	although	the thing	was	of much trouble

ac	laboris,	tămen	statŭit	esse com-
and	labour,	however	determined (it)	to be most-

modissĭmum,	omnes	naves	subduci,	et
convenient,	all	the ships	to be drawn-up,	and

conjungi	unâ	munitione	cum	castris (pl.).
to be united	in one	fortification	with	the camp.

Consumit	circĭter	dĕcem	dies	in his	rebus, ne
He spends	about	ten	days	in these	things, not

quĭdem	nocturnis	tempŏrĭbus	intermissis
indeed (even)	the night	times	being intermitted

ad laborem	milĭtum.	Navĭbus	subductis
to the labour	of the soldiers.	The ships	being drawn-up

que	castris (pl.)	egregĭè	munitis, relinquit	easdem
and	the camp	excellently	fortified, he leaves	the same

copĭas	quas	antè,	præsidĭo	navĭbus:
forces	which	(he left) before,	for a guard	to the ships:

ipse	proficiscĭtur	eòdem,	unde
himself	sets-out	to the same (place),	whence

redĭerat.	Quum	venissèt (plup. subj.)	eò,
he had returned.	When	he had come	thither,

majorĕ	copĭæ	Britannorum	jam	convenĕrant
greater	forces	of the Britons	now	had assembled

undĭque	in	ĕum	lŏcum.	Summa
from every-side	into	that	place.	The supreme-authority

imperĭi	que	belli	gerendi	permissa-est,
of command	and	of the war	to-be-carried-on	was entrusted,

communi	consilĭo,	Cassivellauno,	fines
by common	counsel,	to Cassivellaunus,	the territories

cujus	flumen,	quod	appellatur	Tamĕsis,
of whom	a river,	which	is called	Tamesis (Thames),

divĭdit	à	maritĭmis	civitatĭbus,	circĭter octoginta
divides	from	the maritime	states,	about eighty

millĭa	passŭum	à	mări.	Continentĭa bella
thousands	of paces	from	the sea.	Incessant war

LIBER V.

intercessĕrant	huic	cum	relĭquis	civitatĭbus,
had intervened	*to him*	*with*	*the rest-of*	*the states,*

superiori	tempŏre;	sed	Britanni,	permoti
in the former	*time;*	*but*	*the Britons,*	*alarmed*

nostro	adventu,	præfecĕrant	hunc	toti	bello
by our	*arrival,*	*had appointed*	*him*	*to the whole*	*war*

que imperĭo.
and command.

12. Interĭor pars Britannĭæ incolĭtur ab
The interior part of Britain is inhabited by

iis, quos dicunt prodĭtum memoriâ
those, whom they say (it to have been) delivered by memory

natos in insŭlâ ipsâ: maritĭma pars
having been born in the island itself: the maritime part

ab iis, qui transiĕrant ex
(is inhabited) by those, who had crossed-over out-of

Belgis caussâ prædæ ac belli
the Belgæ by cause (for the sake) of plunder and of war

inferendi; qui omnes fĕre appellantur
to-be-brought-on; who all nearly are called

iis nominĭbus civitatum, ex quĭbus civitatĭbus
by those names of states, out-of which states

orti pervenerunt eŏ, et bello
having sprung they arrived there, and war

illato remanserunt ĭbi, atque cœperunt
being brought-on remained there, and began

colĕre agros. Multitudo homĭnum est
to till the lands. The multitude of men (inhabitants) *is*

infinita, que ædificĭa creberrĭma fĕre
immense, and the buildings most-numerous nearly

consimilĭa Gallĭcis: numĕrus pecŏris
similar to the Gallic: the number of the cattle

magnus. Utuntur aut ære (abl.), aut ferrèis
is) great. They use either brass, or iron

annŭlis examinatis ad certum pondus, pro nummo.
rings regulated to a certain weight, for coin.

Album plumbum nascitur ibi in mediterraneis
White lead (tin) *is produced there in the midland*

regionibus; ferrum in maritimis; sed
countries; iron in the maritime (parts); but

copia ejus est exigua: utuntur importato
the quantity of it is small: they use imported

ære. Est materia cujusque generis, ut in
brass. (There) *is timber of every kind, as in*

Galliâ, præter fagum atque abietem. Putant
Gaul, except the beech and the fir-tree. They think (it)

non fas gustare leporem et gallinam et
not right to taste the hare and the hen and

anserem: tamen alunt hæc caussâ
the goose: however they nourish these by cause (for the

animi que voluptatis. Loca
sake) of mind (diversion) *and of pleasure. The places*

sunt temperatiora quàm in Galliâ, frigoribus
are more-temperate than in Gaul, the colds

remissioribus.
(being) *more-mild.*

13. Insula naturâ triquetra, unum latus
The island (is) *by nature triangular, one side*

cujus est contra Galliam. Alter angulus
of which is opposite Gaul. The other (one) *angle*

hujus lateris, qui est ad Cantium,
of this side, which is at (towards) *Cantium* (Kent),

quò naves ex Galliâ ferè appelluntur,
whither ships from Gaul generally are brought-to-land,

ad orientem solem; inferior spectat
at the rising sun (the East); *the lower* (angle) *looks*

ad meridiem. Hoc latus tenet
(is directed) *to the south. This side holds* (extends)

circiter quingenta millia passuum. Alterum
about five-hundred thousands of paces. The other (side)

vergit ad Hispaniam, atque occidentem solem:
inclines to Spain, and the setting sun:

ex quâ parte est Hibernia, minor dimidio	from (on) which side is Hibernia, less by half
quàm Britannia, ut existimatur; sed transmissus	than Britain, as it is thought; but the passage-across
est pari spatio atque ex Galliâ in	is with equal distance and (as) from Gaul into
Britanniam. In medio hoc cursu est insula,	Britain. In the middle-of this course is an island,
quæ appellatur Mona. Complures minores	which is called Mona (Man). Several less
insulæ præterea existimantur objectæ, de	islands besides are thought (to be) interposed, of
quibus insulis nonnulli scripserunt, noctem esse	which islands some have written, the night to be
triginta continuos dies sub brumâ.	thirty successive days under the winter (in the winter
Nos reperiebamus nihil de eo	season). We did find nothing concerning tha
percunctationibus, nisi videbamus certis mensuris	by inquiries, unless we did see by certain measures
ex aquâ, noctes esse breviores quàm in	of water, the nights to be shorter than on
continente. Longitudo hujus lateris est septin-	he continent. The length of this side is of seven-
gentorum millium passuum, ut opinio	hundred of thousands of paces, as the opinion
illorum fert. Tertium est contra	of them reports. The third (side) is opposite
Septentrionem; cui parti nulla terra est	the North; to which part no land is
objecta, sed angulus ejus lateris spectat	opposed, but the angle of that side looks (is directed)
maximè ad Germaniam Existimatur octingenta	chiefly to Germany. It is thought eight-hundred
millia passuum in longitudinem esse huic.	thousands of paces into length to be to this (side)

R

Ita	omnis	insŭla	est	vicĭes	centena
Thus	*all*	*the island*	*is*	*twenty-times*	*a hundred*

millĭa	passŭum	in	circuĭtu.
thousands	*of paces*	*in*	*compass.*

14.
Ex	omnĭbus	his,	qui	incŏlunt
Out-of	*all*	*these,*	*(those) who*	*inhabit*

Cantĭum,	sunt	longè	humanissĭmi ; omnis
Cantium (Kent),	*are*	*by-far*	*most-civilized ; all*

quæ	regĭo est	maritĭma,	nĕque	diffĕrunt	multùm
which	*tract is*	*maritime,*	*nor*	*do they differ*	*much*

à	Gallĭcâ	consuetudĭne	Plerique	interiores
from	*the Gallic*	*custom.*	*Most-of*	*the interior*

	sĕrunt	non	frumenta (pl.),	sed vivunt
(inhabitants)	*sow*	*not*	*corn,*	*but live*

lacte	et	carne,	que sunt vestiti	pellĭbus.
with (on) milk	*and*	*flesh,*	*and are clad*	*with skins.*

Verò	omnes	Britanni	inficĭunt se	vitro,
But	*all*	*the Britons*	*stain themselves*	*with woad,*

quod	effĭcit	cærulĕum	colorem, atque	hôc
which	*forms*	*a bluish*	*colour, and*	*from this*

sunt	horribiliore	adspectu	in pugnâ :
they are	*with (of) more-frightful*	*look*	*in battle :*

que	sunt	promisso	capillo, atque omni	parte
and	*they are*	*with long*	*hair, and every*	*part*

corpŏris	rasâ,	præter	căput et	superĭus
of the body	*shaved,*	*except*	*the head and*	*upper*

labrum.	Deni que	duodeni	hăbent	uxores
lip.	*Ten and*	*twelve (men)*	*have*	*wives*

communes	inter	se,	et maxĭmè	fratres
common	*among*	*themselves,*	*and chiefly*	*brothers*

cum	fratrĭbus,	et parentes	cum liberis.	Sed si
with	*brothers,*	*and parents*	*with children.*	*But if*

qui sunt	nati	ex his,	habentur
any are	*born*	*out-of these,*	*they are accounted*

libĕri	eorum,	à	quĭbus quæque	virgĭnes
the children	*of those,*	*by*	*whom each*	*(when) virgins*

ductæ-sunt   primùm.
were led (married) *first.*

15. Equĭtes   que   essedarii   hostium
    The cavalry *and* *charioteers* *of the enemies*

conflixerunt   acrĭter   prœlĭo   cum   nostro   equitatu
engaged   *vigorously* *in battle* *with* *our*   *cavalry*

in   itinĕre;   tămen,   ut   nostri   fuĕrint
on *the march;* *however,*   *so-that* *our (men)*   *were*

(perf. subj.)   superiores   omnĭbus   partĭbus,   atque
                superior   *in all*   *parts,*   *and*

compulĕrint (perf. subj.)   ĕos   in   silvas   que
drove   *them* *into* *the woods*   *and*

colles;   sed,   complurĭbus   interfectis,   insecuti
hills;   *but,* *many*   *being killed,*   *having pursued*

            cupidĭùs,   amiserunt   nonnullos
(them)   *more eagerly* (too eagerly), *they lost*   *some*

ex   sŭis.   At   illi,   spatĭo   intermisso,
of   *their-own.* *But* *they,* *an interval* *being intermitted*

             subĭtò   ejecerunt   se   ex
(having elapsed), *suddenly* *threw-out* *themselves* *out-of*

silvis,   nostris   imprudentĭbus   atque
the woods,   *our (men)*   *(being) unaware*   *and*

occupatis   in   munitione   castrorum (pl.);   que
engaged   *in*   *the fortification*   *of the camp;*   *and*

impĕtu   facto   in   ĕos,   qui   collocati-ĕrant
an attack   *being made*   *upon*   *those,*   *who*   *had been placed*

in statione   pro   castris (pl.),   pugnaverunt   acrĭter:
on station   *before* *the camp,*   *they fought*   *vigorously:*

que   duabus   cohortĭbus   missis   subsidĭo   à   Cæsăre,
and   *two*   *cohorts*   *being sent* *for aid*   *by* *Cæsar,*

atque   his   primis   duarum   legionum,   quum   hæ
and   *these* *the first* *of two*   *legions,*   *when* *these*

constitissent (pluperf. subj.),   perexigŭo   spatĭo
had stood-together,   *a very-small* *space*

loci   intermisso   inter   se,   nostris
of ground *being interposed* *between*   *themselves,*   *our (men)*

perterrĭtis	nŏvo	genĕre	pugnæ,	proruperunt
being alarmed	by the new	kind	of battle,	they burst

audacissĭmè	per	medĭos		que	receperunt
most-daringly	through	the midst (of our men)	and	betook

se	inde	incolŭmes.	Eo	dĭe	Quintus
themselves	thence	safe.	In that	day	Quintus

Laberĭus Durus,	tribunus	milĭtum	interficĭtur :	illi
Laberius Durus,	a tribune	of soldiers	is slain :	they

repelluntur,	plurĭbus	cohortĭbus	submissis.
are repulsed,	more	cohorts	being sent-up.

16.
In	hoc	toto	genĕre	pugnæ,	quum
In	this	whole	kind	of battle,	since

dimicaretur (imp. subj.)	sub	ocŭlis	omnĭum	ac
it was fought		under	the eyes	of all	and

pro	castris (pl.),	intellectum-est,	nostros
before	the camp,	it was understood,	our (men)

esse	mĭnùs	aptos	ad	hostem	hujus	genĕris,
to be	less	fit (adapted)	to	an enemy	of this	kind,

propter	gravitatem	armorum,	quòd	possent
on-account-of	the weight	of the arms,	because	they were able

(imp. subj.)	nĕque	insĕqui	cedentes,	nĕque
	neither	to pursue	(them) yielding,	nor

auderent (imp. subj.)	discedĕre	ab	signis ;
did they dare	to depart	from	the standards ;

autem	equĭtes	dimicare	cum	magno	pericŭlo,
but	the cavalry	to contend	with	great	danger,

proptĕrea	quòd	illi	etĭam	cedĕrent (imp. subj.)
because	that	they	also	did yield (retreat)

plerumque	consultò ;	et	quum	removissent (plu-
generally	by-design ;	and	when	they had removed

perf. subj.)	nostros	paullŭlùm	ab	legionĭbus,
	our (men)	a very-little	from	the legions,

desilirent	ex	essĕdis	et	contendĕrent
they would leap-down	from	the chariots	and	would contend

pedĭbus	dispări	prœlĭo.	Autem	ratĭo
with feet (on foot)	in unequal	fight.	But	the method

equestris	prœlii,	et	cedentibus	et
of the cavalry	*fight,*	*(they) both*	*yielding*	*and*
insequentibus,	inferebat	par	atque	idem
pursuing,	*did bring*	*equal*	*and*	*the same*
periculum.	Accedebat	huc,		ut
danger.	*It did approach*	*hither* (added to this),		*that*

prœliarentur (imp. subj.)   nunquam   conferti,   sed
they did fight   *never*   *close-together,*   *but*

rari   que   magnis   intervallis,   que   haberent
few   *and*   *with* (at) *great*   *distances,*   *and*   *did have*

(imp. subj.)   stationes   dispositas;   atque   alii
                 posts   *arranged;*   *and*   *others* (some)

exciperent (imp. subj.)   alios   deinceps,   que   integri
did relieve   *others*   *afterwards,*   *and*   *whole*

et   recentes   succederent (imp. subj.)   defatigatis.
and   *fresh* (men)   *did succeed*   *to the exhausted.*

17.   Postero   die   hostes   constiterunt
         In the following   *day*   *the enemies*   *stood*

procul   à   castris (pl.)   in   collibus;   que   rari
far-off   *from*   *the camp*   *on*   *the hills;*   *and*   *a few*

cœperunt   ostendere   se,   et   lacessere   nostros
began   *to show*   *themselves,*   *and*   *to provoke*   *our*

equites   prœlio   lentius,   quàm   pridie.
cavalry   *to battle*   *more-slowly,*   *than*   *the day-before.*

Sed   meridie,   quum   Cæsar   misisset (pluperf. subj.)
But   *in* (at) *noon,*   *when*   *Cæsar*   *had sent*

tres   legiones   atque   omnem   equitatum   cum   Caio
three   *legions*   *and*   *all*   *the cavalry*   *with*   *Caius*

Trebonio   legato   caussâ
Trebonius   *the lieutenant*   *by cause* (for the purpose)

pabulandi,   advolaverunt   repentè   ad   pabulatores
of foraging,   *they flew*   *suddenly*   *to*   *the foragers*

ex   omnibus   partibus,   sic   uti   absisterent (imp.
from   *all*   *parts,*   *so*   *that*   *they did refrain*

subj.)   non   ab   signis   que   legionibus.
(keep off)   *not*   *from*   *the standards*   *and*   *the legions.*

254 DE BELLO GALLICO. [18

Nostri,	impĕtu	facto	acrĭter	in	ĕos,
Our (men),	an attack	being made	vigorously	upon	them,

repulerunt,	nĕque	fecerunt	finem	insequendi,
repulsed (them),	nor	made they	an end	of pursuing,

quŏad	equĭtes,	confisi	subsidĭo,	quum	viderent
whilst	the cavalry,	relying	to (on) aid,	since	they did see

(imp. subj.) legiones post se, egerunt
the legions behind themselves, drove

hostes præcipĭtes: que magno numĕro eorum
the enemies headlong: and a great number of them

interfecto, nĕque dederunt facultatem sŭi
being killed, neither they gave the power of themselves

colligendi nĕque consistendi, aut desiliendi
to-be-collected, neither of halting, or of leaping-down

ex essĕdis. Auxilĭa, quæ convenĕrant
from the chariots. The auxiliaries, which had assembled

undĭque, discesserunt protĭnus ex
from-every-side, departed immediately from (after)

hâc fŭgâ; nĕque post id tempus hostes
this flight; neither after that time the enemies

unquam contenderunt nobiscum summis
ever contended with us with (their) highest

copĭis
(whole) forces.

18. Cæsar, consilĭo eorum cognĭto, duxit
Cæsar, the design of them being known, led

exercĭtum ad flumen Tamĕsin in
the army to the river Tamesis (Thames) into

fines Cassivellauni: quod flumen pŏtest
the territories of Cassivellaunus: which river is able

transiri pedĭbus omnino uno lŏco,
to be crossed on feet (by fording) altogether (only) in one place,

atque hoc ægrè. Quum venisset (pluperf. subj.)
and in this hardly. When he had come

ĕŏ, animadvertit magnas copĭas hostĭum esse
there, he perceived great forces of the enemies to be

LIBER V.

instructas	ad	altĕram	ripam	flumĭnis.	Autem
arrayed	*at*	*the other*	*bank*	*of the river.*	*But*

ripa	ĕrat	munita	acutis	sudĭbus	præfixis,
the bank	*was*	*fortified*	*with sharp*	*stakes*	*affixed,*

que	sŭdes	ejusdem	genĕris	defixæ	sub
and	*stakes*	*of the same*	*kind*	*fixed-down*	*under*

ăquâ	tegebantur	flumĭne.	Iis	rebus
the water	*were covered*	*by the river.*	*Those*	*things*

cognĭtis	à	captivis	que	perfŭgis,	Cæsar,
being known	*from*	*the prisoners*	*and*	*deserters,*	*Cæsar,*

equitatu	præmisso,	jussit	legiones	subsĕqui
the cavalry	*being sent-before,*	*ordered*	*the legions*	*to follow*

confestim.	Sed	milĭtes	iĕrunt	eâ	celeritate
immediately.	*But*	*the soldiers*	*went*	*with that*	*speed*

atque	impĕtu,	quum	exstarent (imp. subj.)	ex
and	*force,*	*when*	*they did stand-out*	*from*

ăquâ	capĭte	solo,	ut	hostes	possent
the water	*by the head*	*alone,*	*that*	*the enemies*	*were able*

(imp. subj.)	non	sustinere	impĕtum	legionum
	not	*to withstand*	*the attack*	*of the legions*

que	equĭtum,	que	dimittĕrent (imp. subj.)
and	*of the cavalry,*	*and*	*did quit*

ripas	ac	mandarent (imp. subj.)	se	fŭgæ.
the banks	*and*	*did commit*	*themselves*	*to flight.*

19. Cassivellaunus,	omni	spe	contentionis	de-
Cassivellaunus,	*all*	*hope*	*of a contest*	*being*

posĭtâ,	ut	demonstravĭmus	suprà,	amplioribus
laid-aside,	*as*	*we have shown*	*above,*	*(his) larger*

copĭis	dimissis,	circĭter	quatŭor	millĭbus
forces	*being dismissed,*	*about*	*four*	*thousands*

essedariorum	relictis,	servabat	nostra	itinĕra,	que
of charioteers	*being left,*	*did watch*	*our*	*marches,*	*and*

excedebat	paullŭlùm	ex	viâ,	que	occultabat
did depart	*a little*	*out-of*	*the way,*	*and*	*did conceal*

sese	impedĭtis	atque	silvestrĭbus	lŏcis,	atque
himself	*in entangled*	*and*	*woody*	*places,*	*and*

compellebat	pecŏra (pl.)	atque	homĭnes	ex	agris
did drive	*the cattle*	*and*	*men*	*from*	*the lands*

in	silvas	iis	regionĭbus,	quĭbus
into	*the woods*	*from those*	*regions,*	*in which*

cognovĕrat	nos	facturos	ĭter :	et	quum
he had known	*us*	*about-to-make*	*the march :*	*and*	*when*

noster	equitatus	effundĕret	se	liberĭus	in
our	*cavalry*	*did scatter*	*itself*	*more-freely*	*into*

agros	caussâ		vastandi	què
the lands	*by cause* (for the purpose)	*of ravaying*	*and*

prædandi,	emittebat	essedarĭos	ex
of plundering,	*he did send-out*	*the charioteers*	*from*

silvis	omnĭbus	notis	viis	que	semĭtis ; et
the woods	*by all*	*the known*	*ways*	*and*	*paths ; and*

confligebat	cum	iis	cum	magno	perĭculo nostrorum
did engage	*with*	*them*	*with*	*great*	*danger of our*

equĭtum ;	atque	hoc	mĕtu	prohibebat
cavalry ;	*and*	*by this*	*fear*	*did hinder* (them)

vagari	latĭus.	Relinquebatur,	ut	Cæsar
to stray	*more-widely.*	*It was left,*	*that*	*Cæsar*

nĕque	pateretur	discedi	longĭus	ab
neither	*would allow*	(it) *to be departed*	*farther*	*from*

agmĭne	legionum;	et	nocerectur
the troop (main body)	*of the legions ;*	*and*	*it might be injured*

hostĭbus	in	agris	vastandis,	que
to the enemies	*in*	*the lands*	*to-be-ravaged,*	*and*

incendĭis	faciendis,	tantum	quantum	legionarĭi
burnings	*to-be-made,*	*so-much*	*as*	*the legionary*

milĭtes	potĕrant	efficĕre	labore	atque	itinĕre.
soldiers	*were-able*	*to effect*	*by labour*	*and*	*on the march.*

20. Intĕrim	Trinobantes,	propè	firmissĭma
Meantime	*the Trinobantes,*	*nearly*	*the strongest*

civĭtas	earum	regionum,	ex	quâ	Mandubratĭus
state	*of these*	*countries,*	*from*	*which*	*Mandubratius*

adolescens,	secutus	fĭdem
a youth,	*having followed* (embraced)	*the faith* (protection

Cæsăris,	vĕnĕrat	ad	ĕum	in	continentem
of Cæsar,	*had come*	*to*	*him*	*into*	*the continent*

Gallĭam,	(cujus	pater	Imanuentĭus	obtinŭerat
Gaul,	*(whose*	*father*	*Imanuentius*	*had obtained*

regnum		in	ĕâ	civitate,	que
kingdom (royal power)		*in*	*that*	*state,*	*and*

interfectus-ĕrat	à	Cassivellauno ;	ipse	vitavĕrat
had been slain	*by*	*Cassivellaunus;*	*himself*	*had avoided*

mortem	fŭgâ,)	mittunt	legatos	ad	Cæsărem,
death	*by flight,)*	*send*	*ambassadors*	*to*	*Cæsar,*

que	pollicentur		deditūros	sese
and	*promise*		*(to be) about-to-surrender*	*themselves*

ĕi	et	facturos		imperata.
to him	*and*	*about-to-do*		*(the things) commanded.*

Pĕtunt	ut	defendat	Mandubratĭum	ab
They request	*that*	*he may defend*	*Mandubratius*	*from*

injurĭâ	Cassivellauni,	atque	mittat	in
the injury	*of Cassivellaunus,*	*and*	*may send (him)*	*into*

civitatem,	qui	præsit	que	obtinĕat
(their) state,	*who*	*may preside*	*and*	*may obtain*

imperĭum.	Cæsar	impĕrat	his	
the authority.	*Cæsar*	*orders*	*to these (to furnish)*	

quadraginta	obsĭdes	que	frumentum	exercitŭi ;
forty	*hostages*	*and*	*corn*	*to the army ;*

que	mittit	Mandubratĭum	ad	ĕos.	Illi	fecerunt
and	*sends*	*Mandubratius*	*to*	*them.*	*They*	*did (the*

	imperata	celerĭter ;	miserunt	obsides	ad
things) commanded		*quickly ;*	*they sent*	*hostages*	*to*

numĕrum,	que	frumentum.
the number (required),	*and*	*corn.*

21. | Trinobantĭbus | defensis, | atque | prohibĭtis |
|---|---|---|---|
| *The Trinobantes* | *being defended,* | *and* | *being protected* |

ab	omni	injurĭâ	milĭtum,	Cenimagni,
from	*all*	*injury*	*of the soldiers,*	*the Cenimagni,*

Segontiăci,	Ancalites,	Bibrŏci,	Cassi,	legationĭbus
Segontiaci,	*Ancalites,*	*Bibroci,*	*Cassi.*	*embassies*

missis,	dediderunt	sese	Cæsari.	Cognoscit
being sent,	*surrendered*	*themselves*	*to Cæsar.*	*He understands*

ab	his,	oppĭdum	Cassivellauni	abesse
from	*these,*	*the town*	*of Cassivellaunus*	*to-be-distant*

non	longè	ex	ĕo	lŏco,	munitum silvis que
not	*far*	*from*	*that*	*place,*	*fortified by woods and*

paludĭbus,	quò	numĕrus	sătis	magnus
by marshes,	*whither*	*a number*	*sufficiently*	*great*

homĭnum	que	pecŏris	convenĕrit (perf. subj.).
of men	*and*	*of cattle*	*has assembled.*

Autem	Britanni	vŏcant	oppĭdum,	quò
But	*the Britons*	*call*	*(that) a town,*	*where*

consueverunt	convenire,	caussâ
they have been accustomed	*to assemble,*	*by cause* (for the sake)

incursionis	hostĭum	vitandæ,	quum
of an inroad	*of the enemies*	*to be avoided,*	*when*

munîerunt	impeditas	silvas	vallo
they have fortified	*the entangled*	*woods*	*with a rampart*

atque	fossâ.	Eò	proficiscĭtur	cum legionĭbus:
and	*a trench.*	*Thither*	*he sets-out*	*with the legions:*

repĕrit	lŏcum	egregĭè	munitum	naturâ atque
he finds	*the place*	*excellently*	*fortified*	*by nature and*

opĕre;	tămen	contendit	oppugnare	hunc
by work (art);	*however*	*he endeavours*	*to storm*	*this*

ex	duabus	partĭbus.	Hostes morati
from	*two*	*parts.*	*The enemies having delayed*

paullisper,	tulerunt	non	impĕtum	nostrorum
a little-while,	*bore*	*not*	*the attack*	*of our*

milĭtum,	que	ejecerunt	sese	ex	aliâ parte
soldiers,	*and*	*threw-out*	*themselves*	*from*	*another part*

oppĭdi.	Magnus numĕrus	pecŏris	repertus (-est)
of the town.	*A great number*	*of cattle*	*was found*

ĭbi;	que	multi	comprehensi-sunt	atque interfecti
there;	*and*	*many*	*were seized*	*and killed*

in	fŭgâ.
in	*the flight.*

LIBER V.

22. Dum   hæc   geruntur   in   his
   Whilst   these (things are carried-on   in   these

lŏcis,   Cassivellaunus mittit   nuntĭos ad Cantĭum,
places, Cassivellaunus sends   messengers to Cantium

        quod demonstravĭmus suprà esse ad máre,
(Kent), which we have shown above to be at the sea,

quĭbus   regionĭbus   quatŭor reges præĕrant,
to which countries   four   kings   were-over (presided),

Cingetŏrix, Carnilĭus,   Taximagŭlus, Segŏnax; atque
Cingetorix, Carnilius, Taximagulus, Segonax; and

impĕrat   his,   ut   omnĭbus   copĭis
he orders to these, that   all   (their) forces

  coactis,   adoriantur   navalĭa   castra (pl.)
being collected, they may attack the naval   camp

de-improviso, atque   oppugnent.   Quum   hi
unexpectedly, and   may storm (it). When these

venissent (pluperf. subj.) ad   castra (pl.), nostri,
had come   to   the camp,   our (men),

eruptione   factâ,   multis eorum   interfectis, etĭam
a sally   being made, many of them being killed, also

    nobĭli   dŭce Cingetorĭge   capto,   reduxerunt
(their) noble leader Cingetorix being taken, led-back

sŭos   incolŭmes.   Cassivellaunus, hoc   prœlĭo
their (men)   safe.   Cassivellaunus, this   battle

   nuntiato,   tot   detrimentis   acceptis,
being announced, so-many losses   being received,

    finĭbus   vastatis,   etĭam maxĭmè permotus
(his) territories being ravaged, also chiefly alarmed

defectione   civitatum,   mittit   legatos   ad
by the revolt of the states, sends ambassadors   to

Cæsărem   per   Comĭum   Atrebătem   de
Cæsar   by (through)   Comius   the Atrebatian about

deditione.   Quum   Cæsar   statuisset (pluperf. subj.)
a surrender. Since   Cæsar   had resolved

agĕre   hiĕmem   in   continente   propter
to act (spend) the winter on   the continent on-account-of

repentinos	motus	Galliæ;	nĕque	multum
the sudden	*commotions*	*of Gaul;*	*neither*	*much*

æstatis	superesset (imp. subj.);	atque	intel-
of the summer	*did remain;*	*and*	*he did*

ligĕret (imp. subj.),	id	posse	extrăhi	facĭlè,
understand	*that*	*to be-able*	*to be protracted*	*easily,*

impĕrat	obsĭdes;	et	constituit
he commands (him to furnish)	*hostages;*	*and*	*appointed*

quid	vectigalis	Britannĭa	pendĕret
what (portion)	*of tribute*	*Britain*	*should pay*

Romano	popŭlo	in singŭlos	annos.
to the Roman	*people*	*on each*	*years (every year).*

Interdicit	atque	impĕrat	Cassivellauno,
He prohibits	*and*	*commands*	*to Cassivellaunus, (that)*

ne-nocĕat	Mandubratĭo,	neu	Trinobantĭbus.
he may not-injure	*to Mandubratius,*	*nor*	*to the Trinobantes.*

23. Obsidĭbus acceptis, reducit exercĭtum
The hostages being received, he leads-back the army

ad	măre:	invenit	naves refectas.	His
to	*the sea:*	*he finds*	*the ships repaired.*	*These*

deductis,	constituit	reportare
being led-down (launched),	*he resolved*	*to carry-back*

exercĭtum	duobus	commeatĭbus, et	quòd
the army	*by two*	*passages, both*	*because*

habebat	magnum	numĕrum captivorum,	et
he did have	*a great*	*number of prisoners,*	*and*

nonnullæ	naves	deperiĕrant tempestate.	Ac
some	*ships*	*had perished by a tempest.*	*And*

accĭdit	sic, ut	ex tanto	numĕro	navĭum
it happened	*so, that*	*out-of so-great*	*a number*	*of ships*

tot	navigationĭbus, nĕque	ulla navis	omnino,
in so-many	*voyages, neither*	*any ship*	*at-all,*

quæ	portaret (imp. subj.)	milĭtes, desideraretur
which	*did carry*	*the soldiers, was wanting*

(imp. subj.)	hoc	nĕque superiore	anno:
(was lost)	*in this*	*nor in the foregoing*	*year;*

at	ex	iis,	quæ	remitterentur (imp. subj.)
but	*out-of*	*those,*	*which*	*were sent-back*

inanes ad eum ex continente, et militibus
empty to him from the continent, and the soldiers

prioris commeatûs expositis, et quas
of the former passage being landed, and which

Labienus posteă curaverat faciendas, numero
Labienus afterwards had taken-care to-be-made, in number

sexaginta, perpaucæ caperent (imp. subj.) locum,
sixty, very-few did take (reached) the place,

fere omnes reliquæ rejicerentur (imp. subj.).
nearly all the rest were thrown-back.

Quas quum Cæsar exspectâsset (pluperf. subj.)
Which when Cæsar had awaited

aliquandiu frustrà, ne excluderetur
some-time in-vain, lest he might be shut-out

navigatione tempore anni, quòd
from the voyage by the time of the year, because

æquinoctium suberat, necessariò collocavit
the equinox was near, (he) necessarily placed

milites angustiùs. Ac consecutus
the soldiers more-closely. And having attained (obtained)

summam tranquillitatem quum solvisset
the utmost calmness (of weather) when he had loosed

(pluperf. subj.), secundâ vigiliâ initâ,
(had set sail), the second watch being entered,

attigit terram primâ luce, que
he touched (reached) land in the first light, and

perduxit omnes naves incolumes.
conducted all the ships safe.

24. Navibus subductis, que concilio
The ships being drawn-up, and the council

Gallorum Samarobrivæ peractò,
of the Gauls of (at) Samarobriva being completed,

coactus-est collocare exercitum in hibernis
he was compelled to place the army in winter-quarters

alĭter	ac	superiorĭbus	annis,	que	distribuĕre
otherwise	*and* (than)	*in former*	*years,*	*and*	*to distribute*

legiones	in	plures	civitates,	quòd	eo anno
the legions	*into*	*more*	*states,*	*because*	*in that year*

frumentum	provenĕrat		angustĭùs
the corn	*had come-forth* (grown)		*more narrowly* (less

	in	Gallĭâ,	propter siccitates :
abundantly)	*in*	*Gaul,*	*on-account-of the droughts :*

ex	quĭbus	dĕdit	unam	Caĭo	Fabĭo
out-of	*which*	*he gave*	*one* (*legion*)	*to Caius*	*Fabius*

legato	ducendam	in	Morĭnos,	altĕram
the lieutenant	*to-be-led*	*unto*	*the Morini,*	*another*

Quinto	Ciceroni	in	Nervĭos,	tertĭam
to Quintus	*Cicero*	*unto*	*the Nervii,*	*the third*

Lucĭo	Roscĭo	in	Essŭos : jussit	quartam
to Lucius	*Roscius*	*unto*	*the Essui: he ordered*	*the fourth*

hiemare	in	confinĭo	Trevirorum, in	Rhemis
to winter	*on*	*the border*	*of the Treviri, among*	*the Rhemi*

cum	Tito	Labieno :	collocavit tres in	Belgĭo :
with	*Titus*	*Labienus :*	*he placed three in*	*Belgium :*

præfecit	his	Marcum Crassum	quæstorem,
he set-over	*to these*	*Marcus Crassus*	(*as*) *quæstor,*

et	Lucĭum	Munatĭum	Plancum, et	Caĭum
and	*Lucius*	*Munatius*	*Plancus, and*	*Caius*

Trebonĭum	legatos.	Misit	unam	legionem,
Trebonius	(*as*) *lieutenants.*	*He sent*	*one*	*legion,*

quam	conscripsĕrat	proxĭmè	trans Pădum,	et
which	*he had levied*	*very-lately*	*across the Po,*	*and*

quinque	cohortes, in	Eburones,	maxĭma	pars
five	*cohorts, unto*	*the Eburones,*	*the greatest*	*part*

quorum	est	inter Mŏsam et	Rhenum,	qui
of whom	*is*	*between the Meuse and*	*the Rhine,*	*who*

ĕrant	sub	imperĭo	Ambiorĭgis et Cativulci.
were	*under*	*the authority*	*of Ambiorix and of Cativulcus.*

Jussit	legatos	Quintum	Titurĭum	Sabinum
He ordered	*the lieutenants*	*Quintus*	*Titurius*	*Sabinus*

et	Lucium	Aurunculeium	Cottam	præesse	nis
and	*Lucius*	*Aurunculeius*	*Cotta*	*to preside*	*to these*
militibus.	Legionibus	distributis		ad	hunc
soldiers.	*The legions*	*being distributed*		*to* (in)	*this*
modum,	existimavit	sese		posse	mederi
manner,	*he thought*	*himself*		*to be-able*	*to remedy*
facillimè	frumentariæ	inopiæ :		atque	tamen
most-easily	*to the corn*	*scarcity :*		*and*	*however*
hiberna	omnium	harum		legionum	con-
the winter-quarters	*of all*	*of these*		*legions*	*were*
tinebantur	centum	millibus		passuum	(præter
contained	*in a hundred*	*thousands*		*of paces*	(*except*
eam,	quam	dederat		Lucio	Roscio
that (legion),	*which*	*he had given*		*to Lucius*	*Roscius*
ducendam	in	pacatissimam		et	quietissimam
to-be-led	*into*	*the most-appeased*		*and*	*most-tranquil*
partem).	Intereà	ipse	constituit	morari	in
part).	*Meanwhile*	*himself*	*resolved*	*to tarry*	*in*
Galliâ,	quòad	cognovisset	(pluperf. subj.)		legiones
Gaul,	*until*	*he had known*			*the legions*
collocatas,	que	hiberna		munita.	
being settled,	*and*	*the winter-quarters*		*fortified.*	

25. Erat in Carnutibus Tasgetius
There was *in* (among) *the Carnutes* *Tasgetius*

natus summo loco ; cujus majores
born *in the highest* *place* (rank) ; *whose* *ancestors*

obtinuerant regnum in suâ civitate.
had obtained *kingdom* (royal power) *in* *their-own* *state.*

Cæsar restituerat locum majorum huic
Cæsar *had restored* *the situation* *of (his) ancestors* *to him*

pro virtute ejus atque benevolentiâ in
for *the valour* *of him* *and* (*his*) *good-will* *unto*

se, quòd usus-fuerat singulari (abl.) operâ
himself, *because* *he had used* *remarkable* *assistance*

ejus in omnibus bellis. Inimici interfecerunt
of him *in* *all* *the wars.* (*His*) *enemies* *slew*

hunc	pălăm,	regnantem	jam	tertium	annum,	multis
him	*openly,*	*reigning*	*now*	*the third*	*year,*	*many*

etĭam	ex	civitate	auctorĭbus.		Ea
also	*out-of*	*the state*	*(being) authors (of the deed).*		*That*

res	defertur	ad	Cæsărem.	Ille	verĭtus,
matter	*is reported*	*to*	*Cæsar.*	*He*	*having feared,*

ne	civĭtas	deficĕret	impulsu	eorum,
lest	*the state*	*might revolt*	*by the instigation*	*of them,*

quòd	res	pertinebat	ad	plures,	celerĭter
because	*the affair*	*did relate*	*to*	*more (many),*	*quickly*

jŭbet	Lucĭum	Plancum	proficisci	in	Carnutes
orders	*Lucius*	*Plancus*	*to set-out*	*unto*	*the Carnutes*

cum	legione	ex	Belgĭo,	que	hiemare	ĭbi;
with	*a legion*	*out-of*	*Belgium,*	*and*	*to winter*	*there;*

que	mittĕre	hos	comprehensos	ad	se,
and	*to send*	*these*	*seized*	*to*	*himself,*

opĕrâ	quorum	cognovĕrit	Tasgetĭum
by the endeavour	*of whom*	*he may have known*	*Tasgetius*

	interfectum.	Intĕrim	factus-est	certĭor
	(to have been) killed.	*Meantime*	*he was made*	*more-sure*

	ab	omnĭbus	legatis	que
(was informed)	*by*	*all*	*the lieutenants*	*and*

quæstorĭbus,	quĭbus	tradidĕrat	legiones,
quæstors,	*to-whom*	*he had delivered*	*the legions,*

perventum-esse	in	hiberna,	que
to have been arrived (by them)	*into*	*winter-quarters,*	*and*

lŏcum	munitum	hibernis.
the place (to have been)	*fortified*	*for winter-quarters.*

26. | Quindĕcim | diebus | circĭter | quĭbus |
|---|---|---|---|
| *In fifteen* | *days* | *about* | *in (since) which* |

ventum-est	in	hiberna,	initĭum	repentini
it was come	*into*	*winter-quarters,*	*the beginning*	*of a sudden*

tumultûs	ac	defectĭonis	ortum-est	ab	Ambiorĭge
tumult	*and*	*revolt*	*arose*	*from*	*Ambiorix*

et	Catĭvulco:	qui	quum	fuissent (pluperf. subj.)
and	*Cativulcus:*	*who*	*when*	*they had been*

LIBER V.

præstò	Sabino	que	Cottæ	ad	fines	sǔa
near	to Sabinus	and	to Cotta	at	the borders	of their

regni,	que	comportavissent (plup. subj.)	frumentum
kingdom,	and	had carried	corn

in	hiberna,	impulsi	nuntiis
into	winter-quarters,	being instigated	by the messengers

Indutiomări	Treviri,	concitaverunt	sǔos
of Indutiomarus	the Treviran,	roused-up	their-own

(people);	que	lignatorĭbus	oppressis
	and	the wood-cutters	being overwhelmed

subĭtò,	venerunt	magnâ	mănu	oppugnatum
suddenly,	they came	with a great	band	to assault

castra (pl.).	Quum	nostri	cepissent (pluperf.
the camp.	When	our (men)	had taken

subj.)	arma	celerĭter,	que adscendissent (pluperf.
	arms	quickly,	and had ascended

subj.)	vallum,	atque	Hispanis equitĭbus
	the rampart,	and	the Spanish cavalry

emissis	ex	unâ parte,	fuissent (pluperf.
being sent-out	from	one part (side),	had been

subj.)	superiores	equestri prœlĭo,	re
	superior	in the cavalry fight,	the thing

desperatâ,	hostes	reduxerunt sǔos
being despaired-of,	the enemies	led-back their (men)

ab	oppugnatione.	Tum	conclamaverunt sǔo
from	the assault.	Then	they cried-out in their

more,	ŭtì alĭqui	ex nostris	prodirent
manner,	that some	out-of our (people)	might come-forth

ad	colloquĭum;	"sese habere,	quæ
to	a conference;	"themselves to have (things),	which

vellent (imp. subj.)	dicĕre	de communi	re,
they did will	to say	about the common	matter,

quĭbus	sperarent (imp. subj.)	controversĭas	posse
by which	they did hope	the disputes	to be-able

minúi."
to be diminished."

27. Caius Arpinius, Romanus eques, familiaris
    Caius Arpinius, a Roman knight, an acquaintance

Quinti Titurii mittitur ad eos caussâ
of Quintus Titurius is sent to them by cause (for

colloquendi; que Quintus Junius,
the purpose) of conferring; and Quintus Junius,

quidam ex Hispaniâ, qui jam antè
a certain (person) from Spain, who already before

consueverat ventitare ad Ambiorigem,
(this) had been accustomed to come-often to Ambiorix,

missu Cæsaris. Apud quos Ambiorix
by the mission of Cæsar. At (before) whom Ambiorix

locutus-est in hunc modum: "Sese confiteri
spoke unto this (in) manner: "Himself to confess

debere plurimum ei, pro beneficiis Cæsaris
to owe very-much to him, for the kindnesses of Cæsar

in se, quòd operâ ejus
unto himself, because by the assistance of him

liberatus-esset (pluperf. subj.) stipendio, quod
he had been freed from the tribute, which

consuêsset (pluperf. subj.) pendere suis finitimis
he had been accustomed to pay to his neighbours

Atuaticis; que quòd et filius et filius
the Atuatici; and because both (his) son and the son

fratris, quos Atuatici tenuissent (pluperf.
of (his) brother, whom the Atuatici had held

subj.) in servitute et catenis apud se,
in slavery and chains at (with) themselves,

missos numero obsidum, remissi-essent
being sent in the number of the hostages, had been sent-back

(pluperf. subj.) ab Cæsare: neque fecisse id,
by Cæsar: nor to have done that,

quod fecerit (perf. subj.) de oppugnatione
which he has done about the storming

castrorum (pl.), aut judicio aut
of the camp, either from (his-own) judgment or

LIBER V.

sŭâ	voluntate,	sed	coactu	civitatis :	que
his-own	will,	but	by compulsion	of the state.	and

sŭa	imperĭa	esse	ejusmodi,	ut
his-own	authorities (power)	to be	of this-sort,	that

multitudo	haberet (imp. subj.)	non	mĭnus
the multitude	did have	not	less

juris	in	se,	quàm	ipse	in
of jurisdiction	towards	himself,	than	himself	towards

multitudĭnem.	Porrò	hanc	fuisse	caussam
the multitude.	Moreover	this	to have been	the cause

belli	civitati :	quòd	potuĕrit (perf. subj.)
of war	to the state :	because	he was able

non	resistĕre	repentinæ	conjuratione	Gallorum ;
not	to withstand	to the sudden	conspiracy	of the Gauls ;

se	posse	probare	id	facĭlè	ex	sŭâ
himself	to be-able	to prove	that	easily	from	his-own

humilitate ;	quòd	sit	non	adĕò
humbleness (weakness) ;	because	he may be	not	so

imperitus	rerum,	ut	confidat	se
unacquainted	of (with) things,	that	he may trust	himself

posse	superare	Romanum	popŭlum	sŭis
to be-able	to overcome	the Roman	people	with his

copĭis ;	sed	esse	commune	consilĭum
forces ;	but	(the thing) to be	the common	design

Gallĭæ.	Hunc esse dictum	dĭem	omnĭbus
of Gaul.	This to be the said (appointed)	day	for all

hibernis	Cæsăris	oppugnandis,	ne	qua
the winter-quarters	of Cæsar	to-be-assaulted,	lest	any

legĭo	posset	venire	subsidĭo	altĕri	legioni :
legion	might be-able	to come	to aid	to another	legion :

Gallos	non	facĭlè	potuisse	negare
Gauls	not	easily	to have been-able	to deny (their help)

Gallis ;	præsertim	quum	consilĭum	videretur (imp.
to Gauls ;	especially	when	a design	did seem

subj.)	inĭtum	de	communi	libertate
	entered-into	about	(their) common	liberty

recuperandâ. Quĭbus quŏnĭam satisfecĕrit (perf.
to-be-recovered. *To whom* *since* *he has satisfied*

subj.) pro pĭĕtate, se habere
for (as regarded) *duty (to country),* *himself* *to have*

nunc rationem officĭi; monere Cæsărem pro
now *a regard* *of moral-duty;* *to advise* *Cæsar* *for*

beneficĭis, orare Titurĭum pro hospitĭo,
(his) kindnesses, *to beseech* *Titurius* *for* *(his) hospitality,*

ut consŭlat sŭæ saluti ac
that *he may consult* *for his-own* *safety* *and (that)*

milĭtum : magnam mănum Germanorum conductam
of the soldiers: *a great* *band* *of Germans* *being hired*

transîsse Rhenum; hanc affŏre
to have crossed *the Rhine;* *this* *to-be-about-to-be-at-hand*

bidŭo : esse consilĭum ipsorum,
in two-days: *to be* *the counsel* *of themselves* (that it was for

vĕlint-ne ducĕre
Sabinus and Cotta to consider), *whether they will* *to conduct*

milĭtes eductos ex hibernis aut ad
the soldiers *led-out* *from* *winter-quarters* *either* *to*

Ciceronem aut ad Labienum, prĭùs-quàm
Cicero *or* *to* *Labienus,* *before-that* *(their)*

finitĭmi sentĭant; alter quorum
neighbours *may perceive (it);* *the other (one)* *of whom*

absit (pres. subj.) circĭter quinquaginta millĭa
is distant *about* *fifty* *thousands*

passŭum, alter paullò amplĭùs: se polliceri
of paces, *the other* *a little* *more:* *himself* *to promise*

illud et confirmare jurejurando, se daturum
that *and* *to affirm* *by oath,* *himself* *about-to-give*

tutum ĭter per sŭos fines: quod quum
a safe *journey* *through* *his* *territories:* *which* *when*

facĭat, et sese consulĕre civitati, quòd
he may do, *both himself* *to consult* *for the state,* *because*

levetur hibernis, et referre
it may be relieved *from the winter-quarters.* *and* *to return*

LIBER V.

gratĭam Cæsări pro merĭtis ejus." Hâc oratione
favour to Cæsar for the merits of him." This speech

habĭtâ, Ambĭŏrix discedit.
being held (made), Ambiorix departs.

28. Caïus Arpinĭus et Junĭus defĕrunt ad
Caius Arpinius and Junius report to

legatos quæ audiĕrant. Illi
the lieutenants what (things) they had heard. They

perturbati repentinâ re, etsi ĕa
much-disturbed by the sudden affair, although those (things)

dicebantur ab hoste, tămen existimabant
were said by an enemy, however did think (them)

non negligenda: que maxĭmè permovebantur
not to-be-neglected: and especially were much alarmed

hâc re, quòd ĕrat vix credendum
by this affair, because it was hardly to-be-believed

ignobĭlem atque humĭlem civitatem Eburonum
the mean and humble state of the Eburones

ausam (-esse) facĕre bellum suâ sponte
to have dared to make war by its-own accord

Romano popŭlo. Ităque defĕrunt rem
to (on) the Roman people. Therefore they report the matter

ad concilĭum, que magna controversĭa existit
to a council, and a great controversy arises

inter ĕos. Lucĭus Aurunculeĭus que complures
between them. Lucius Aurunculeius and very-many

tribuni milĭtum et centuriones primorum ordĭnum
tribunes of soldiers and centurions of the first ranks

existimabant "nĭhil agendum temĕrè, nĕque
did think "nothing to-be-acted rashly, nor

discedendum ex hibernis injussu
to-be-departed from winter-quarters without-command

Cæsăris." Docebant "quantasvis magnas
of Cæsar." They did teach (show) "howsoever great

copĭas etĭam Germanorum posse sustineri,
forces even of Germans to-be-able to be withstood,

hibernis	munitis."	"Rem
the winter-quarters	*being fortified."*	*" The thing* (expe-

esse	testimonio,	quòd	sustinuěrint
rience) *to be*	*for a testimony,*	*that*	*they have withstood*

(perf. subj.) fortissĭmè primum impĕtum hostĭum,
most-bravely the first attack of the enemies,

multis vulnerĭbus illatis ultrò
many wounds being brought-on (inflicted) *spontaneously.*

Non prĕmi frumentariâ re.
Not to be pressed by corn affair (by want of corn).

Interĕa subsidĭa conventura et ex
Meantime aids (to be) *about-to-assemble both from*

proxĭmis hibernis et à Cæsăre."
the nearest winter-quarters and from Cæsar."

Postremò, quid esse levĭus aut
Lastly, what to be (what could be) *lighter or*

turpĭus, quàm capĕre consilĭum de summis
more-base, than to take counsel about the most-important

rebus, hoste auctore?"
things, an enemy (being) *the adviser?"*

29. Contra ĕa Titurĭus clamitabat,
Against those (reasonings) *Titurius did often cry-out,*

"facturos serò, quum
" about-to-do (that they would do it) *too-late, when*

majores mănus hostĭum, Germanis adjunctis,
greater bands of the enemies, the Germans being united,

convenissent; aut quum alĭquid
should have assembled; or when some (thing)

calamitatis acceptum-esset in proxĭmis
of calamity might have been received in the nearest

hibernis. Occasionem consulendi esse
winter-quarters. The opportunity of consulting to be

brĕvem. Arbitrari Cæsărem
short. To suppose (that he supposed) *Cæsar*

profectum (-esse) in Italĭam: nĕque Carnutes
to have set-out into Italy: neither the Carnutes

LIBER V.

alĭter   fuisse   capturos   consilĭum   Tasgetĭi
otherwise to have been about-to-take   the counsel of Tasgetius

interficiendi ;   nĕque   Ebŭrones   esse   ventŭros
to-be-killed ;   neither   the Eburones to be   about-to-come

ad   castra (pl.)   cum   tantâ   contemptione   nostrî,
to the camp   with   so great contempt   of us,

si ille adesset (imp. subj.).   Non   spectare   hostem
if he   were-near.   Not   to regard   the enemy

auctorem   sed   rem.   Rhenum
(as) an adviser but   the thing (circumstance).   The Rhine

subesse :   mortem   Ariovisti   et   nostras
to be-near : the death   of Ariovistus and   our

superiores   victorĭas,   esse   magno   dolori
former   victories,   to be   for great grief

Germanis :   Gallĭam   ardere   tot
to the Germans : Gaul   to burn (with rage)   so-many

contumelĭis   acceptis,   redactam   sub
insults   being received,   (being) reduced under

imperĭum   Romani   popŭli,   superiore   gloriâ
the authority of the Roman people,   the former   glory

militaris   rĕi   extinctâ."   Postremò,
of (its) military affair being extinguished."   Lastly,

" quis   persuaderet   hoc   sĭbi,   Ambiorĭgem
" who   should persuade this   to himself, Ambiorix

descendisse   ad   consilĭum   ejusmŏdi   sĭne
to have descended to   advice   of this-kind without

certâ   re ?   Sŭam   sententĭam   esse   tutam
a sure thing (purpose)? His   opinion   to be safe

in   utramque   partem :   si   sit   nil
unto   either   part (case): if   there-be   nothing

durĭus,   perventuros (-esse)   ad   proxĭmam
harder (worse), to be about-to-arrive   to   the nearest

legionem   cum   nullo   pericŭlo ;   si   omnis   Gallĭa
legion   with   no   danger ;   if   all   Gaul

consentĭat   cum   Germanis,   unam
may agree (should combine) with the Germans, the one

(only)	salutem safety	esse to be	posĭtam placed	in celeritate. in speed.	Quĭdem Indeed
quem what	exĭtum issue	consilĭum the advice	Cottæ of Cotta	atque and	eorum, of those,
qui who	dissentirent, might dissent (from him),		haberet? might have?	In In	quo which
si if (there be)	non not	præsens present	pericŭlum, danger,	at but	certè surely
fămes famine	esset would be	pertimescenda to-be-dreaded	longinquâ in a long	obsidione." siege."	

30. Hâc   disputatione   habĭtâ   in   utramque
    This   dispute   being held   unto   either

partem,   quum   resisteretur (imp. subj.)   acrĭter
part (side),   when   it was opposed   sharply

à   Cottâ   que   primis   ordinĭbus;   Sabinus   inquit,
by   Cotta   and   the first   ranks;   Sabinus   says,

"Vincĭte,   si   vultis   ĭta,"   et   id   clariore
"Prevail,   if   ye will (it)   so."   and   that   with a louder

voce,   ut   magna   pars   milĭtum   exaudiret:
voice,   that   a great   part   of the soldiers   might hear (him):

"nĕque   sum   is,   inquit,   ex   vobis,   qui
"neither   I am   that (man),   says he,   out-of   you,   who

terrĕar   gravissĭmè   pericŭlo   mortis.
may be affrighted   most-severely   by the danger   of death.

Hi   sapĭent;   et,   si   quid
These (men)   will be-wise (by experience);   and,   if   any

gravĭus   accidĕrit,   reposcent
(thing) more-severe   shall have happened,   they will demand

rationem   abs   te: qui,   si   licĕat
an account   from   thee: who,   if   it be-lawful (be permitted)

per   te,   conjuncti   cum   proxĭmis   hibernis
by   thee,   being united   with   the nearest   winter-quarters

dĭe   perendĭno,   sustinĕant   communem
on the day   after-to-morrow,   may support   a common

casum   cum   relĭquis;   nec   rejecti   et   relegati
chance   with   the rest;   nor   thrown-back   and   banished

longè ab cæteris, intereant aut ferro aut fame."	far from the rest, may perish either by iron (the sword) or by famine."
Consurgitur ex concilio:	It is risen (they rise) from the council:
comprehendunt utrumque et orant;	they lay-hold-of each and beseech;
" ne-deducant rem in summum periculum suâ dissensione et pertinaciâ:	" they may not-bring the thing into the highest danger by their dissension and obstinacy:
rem esse facilem, seu maneant seu proficiscantur, si modò omnes sentiant ac probent unum.	the thing to be easy, whether they may remain or may set-out, if only all may think and may approve one (thing).
Contrà, se perspicere nullam salutem in dissensione."	On-the-other-hand, themselves to perceive no safety in dissension."
Res perducitur disputatione ad mediam noctem.	The thing is protracted by dispute to middle night.

31. Tandem Cotta permotus dat manus: *At-length Cotta being moved gives hands (yields):*

sententia Sabini superat. *the opinion of Sabinus prevails.*

Pronuntiatur ituros primâ luce. *It is declared (them) about-to-go in the first light (day-break).*

Reliqua pars noctis consumitur vigiliis: *The rest (remaining) part of the night is spent in watchings;*

quum quisque miles circumspiceret (imp. subj.) sua, *when each soldier did look-around-for his own (things),*

quid posset portare cum se, *what he might be-able to carry with himself,*

quid cogeretur relinquere ex instrumento hibernorum. *what he might be compelled to leave out-of the furniture of the winter-quarters.*

Omnia excogitantur, *All (things) are devised,*

s

| quare | maneatur | ne | sine |
| wherefore (in order that) | it may be remained | not | without |

| periculo, | et | periculum | augeatur | languore |
| danger, | and | the danger | may be increased | by the languor |

| et | vigiliis | militum. | Proficiscuntur |
| and | by the watchings | of the soldiers. | They set-out |

| primâ | luce | ex | castris (pl.) | sic, | ut | quibus |
| in the first | light | from | the camp | so, | as | to whom |

| esset (imp. subj.) | persuasum | consilium | datum-esse |
| it was | persuaded | advice | to have been given |

| non | ab | hoste, | sed | ab | amicissimo | homine |
| not | by | an enemy, | but | by | a most-friendly | man |

| Ambiorige, | longissimo | agmine | que | magnis |
| Ambiorix, | in a very-long | line | and | with great |

impedimentis.
baggage trains.

32. | At | posteaquàm | hostes | senserunt | de |
| But | after-that | the enemies | perceived | about |

| profectione | eorum | ex | nocturno | fremitu | que |
| the departure | of them | from | the nightly | bustle | and |

| vigiliis, | insidiis | collocatis | bipartitò |
| watchings, | ambuscades | being placed | in two-divisions |

| in | silvis, | opportuno | atque | occulto | loco, |
| in | the woods, | in a convenient | and | secret | place, |

| expectabant | adventum | Romanorum | à |
| they did await | the approach | of the Romans | from (at) |

| circiter | duobus | millibus | passuum : | et | quum |
| about | two | thousands | of paces : | and | when |

| major | pars | agminis | demisisset (pluperf. subj.) |
| the greater | part | of the troop | had sent-down |

| se | in | magnam | convallem, | ostenderunt | sese |
| itself | into | a great | valley, | they showed | themselves |

| subitò | ex | utrâque | parte | ejus | vallis; | que |
| suddenly | from | each | part | of that | valley; | and |

| cœperunt | premere | novissimos | et | prohibere |
| began | to press | the newest (hindmost) | and | to hinder |

primos	adscensu,	atque	committĕre	prœlĭum
the first	*from the ascent,*	*and*	*to engage*	*battle*

lŏco	iniquissĭmo	nostris.
in a place	*most-unfavourable*	*to our (men)*

33.
Tum	demum	Titurĭus	trepidare,
Then	*at-last*	*Titurius*	*(began) to tremble,*

concursare	que	disponĕre	cohortes,	ŭtĭ	qui
to hurry	*and*	*to arrange*	*the cohorts,*	*as*	*(a man) who*

providisset (pluperf. subj.)	nĭhil	antè :	tămen,
had foreseen	*nothing*	*before:*	*however,*

hæc	ɪpsa	timĭdè,	atque	ut
(he did) these (things)	*themselves*	*timidly,*	*and*	*as (-if)*

omnĭa	viderentur (imp. subj.)	deficĕre.	At
all (things)	*did seem*	*to fail (him).*	*But*

Cotta,	qui	cogitâsset (pluperf. subj.)	hæc
Cotta,	*who*	*had thought*	*these (things)*

posse	accidĕre	in	itinĕre,	atque	ob
to be-able	*to happen*	*on*	*the march,*	*and*	*on-account-of*

ĕam	caussam	fuisset (pluperf. subj.)	non	auctor
that	*reason*	*had been*	*not*	*the adviser*

profectionis,	deĕrat	communi	saluti	in
of the departure,	*was wanting*	*to the common*	*safety*	*in*

nullâ	re;	et	præstabat	officĭa	imperatoris
no	*thing;*	*and*	*did perform*	*the duties*	*of a general*

in	militĭbus	appellandis	que	cohortandis;
in	*the soldiers*	*to-be-addressed*	*and*	*to-be-encouraged;*

et	militis	in	pugnâ.	Que	quum	propter
and	*of a soldier*	*in*	*the battle.*	*And*	*when*	*on-account-of*

longitudĭnem	agmĭnis,	possent (imp. subj.)	mĭnùs
the length	*of the troop,*	*they were able*	*less*

facĭlè	obire	omnĭa	per
easily	*to go-through (discharge)*	*all (things)*	*by*

se,	et	providere,	quid	esset	faciendum
themselves,	*and*	*to provide,*	*what*	*might be*	*to-be-done*

quoque	lŏco;	jusserunt	pronuntiari,	ut
in every	*place;*	*they ordered (it)*	*to be announced,*	*that*

s 2

relinquĕrent	impedimenta	atque	consistĕrent
they should leave	*the baggages*	*and*	*should stand-together*

in	orbem.	Quod	consilĭum,	etsi	est	non
into	*a circle.*	*Which*	*plan,*	*although*	*it is*	*not*

reprehendendum	in	casu	ejusmŏdi,	tămen
to-be-blamed	*in*	*a case*	*of this-kind,*	*however*

accĭdit	incommŏdè :	nam	minŭit	spem	nostris
happened	*untowardly :*	*for*	*it diminished*	*hope*	*to our*

militĭbus,	et	effecit	hostes	alacriores
soldiers,	*and*	*rendered*	*the enemies*	*more-alert*

ad-pugnandum ;	quòd	id	videbatur	factum (-esse)
to-fighting ;	*because*	*that*	*did seem*	*to have been done*

non	sĭne	summo	timore	et	desperatione.
not	*without*	*the highest*	*fear*	*and*	*desperation.*

Præterĕa	accĭdit,	quod	ĕrat	necesse	fĭĕri,
Besides	*it happened,*	*what*	*was*	*necessary*	*to be done,*

ut	milĭtes	discedĕrent (imp. subj.)	vulgò
that	*the soldiers*	*did depart*	*in-common*

ab	signis ;	que	quisque	eorum	properaret
from	*the standards ;*	*and*	*every-one*	*of them*	*did hasten*

(imp. subj.)	petĕre	atque	arripĕre	ab	impedimentis,
	to seek	*and*	*to seize*	*from*	*the baggages,*

quæ	habēret	carissĭma ;	et	omnĭa
what (things)	*he might hold*	*most-dear ;*	*and*	*all (places)*

complerentur (imp. subj.)	clamore	ac	fletu.
were filled	*with noise*	*and*	*with weeping.*

34. At	consilĭum	defŭit	non	barbăris.
But	*counsel*	*was-wanting*	*not*	*to the barbarians.*

Nam	dŭces	eorum	jusserunt	pronuntiari
For	*the leaders*	*of them*	*commanded (it)*	*to be announced*

totâ	acĭe,	"ne	quis	discedĕret
in the whole	*line,*	*"that-not*	*any (one)*	*should depart*

ab	lŏco :	quæcunque	Romani
from	*(his) place :*	*whatsoever (things)*	*the Romans*

reliquissent,	esse	prædam	illorum,	atque
might have left,	*to be*	*the plunder*	*of them,*	*and*

reservari	illis:	proinde	existimarent
to be reserved	*for them:*	*wherefore*	*they should think*
omnĭa	posĭta in	victorĭâ."	Nostri ĕrant
all (things)	*placed in*	*victory."*	*Our (men) were*
păres	pugnando et	virtute	et numĕro:
equal	*in fighting both*	*in valour*	*and in number*
tametsi	deserebantur	à	dŭce et
although	*they were deserted*	*by*	*(their) general and by*
fortunâ,	tămen ponebant	omnem spem	salutis
fortune,	*however they did place*	*all hope*	*of safety*
in virtute;	et quotĭes	quæque	cŏhors
in valour;	*and as-often-as*	*every*	*cohort*

procurrĕret (imp. subj.), magnus numĕrus
did-run-forward (did charge), *a great number*

hostĭum cadebat ab ĕâ parte. Quâ
of the enemies did fall from (on) that part. Which

re animadversâ, Ambiŏrix jussit pronuntiari,
thing being observed, Ambiorix ordered (it) to be announced,

ut conjicĭant tela prŏcul neu
that they may cast (their) darts from-a-distance, nor

accedant propĭus; et in quam partem
may-approach nearer; and into what (-ever) part

Romani fecĕrint impĕtum, cedant;
the Romans shall have made an attack, they may give-way;

nĭhil posse noceri ĭis levitate
nothing to be-able to be injured to them by the lightness

armorum et quotidianâ exercitatione:
of (their) arms and by daily exercise:

insequantur recipientes se rursus ad
they may pursue (them) betaking themselves again to

signa.
the standards.

35. Quo præcepto observato diligentissĭmè
Which precept being observed most-carefully

ab ĭis, quum quæpĭam cŏhors excessĕrat ex
by them, when any cohort had gone-out out-of

orbe,	atque	fecĕrat	impĕtum,	hostes
the circle,	*and*	*had made*	*an attack,*	*the enemies*

refugiebant	velocissĭmè;	intĕrim	ĕrat	necesse
did flee-back	*most-swiftly;*	*meantime*	*it was*	*necessary*

nudari	ëâ	parte,	et	tela	recĭpi
to be exposed	*in that*	*part,*	*and*	*darts*	*to be received*

ab	aperto	latĕre.	Rursus,	quum	cœpĕrant
from	*the open*	*flank.*	*Again,*	*when*	*they had begun*

reverti	in	ĕum	lŏcum,	unde	egressi-ĕrant,
to return	*into*	*that*	*place,*	*whence*	*they had gone-out,*

circumveniebantur	et	ab	ïis,	qui	cessĕrant
they were surrounded	*both*	*by*	*those,*	*who*	*had given-way*

et	ab	ïis,	qui	stetĕrant	proxĭmi;	autem	sin
and	*by*	*those,*	*who*	*had stood*	*nearest;*	*but*	*if*

vellent (imp. subj.)	tenere	lŏcum,	nĕque
they did will	*to hold*	*(their) place,*	*neither*

lŏcus	relinquebatur	virtuti,	nĕque
a place (opportunity)	*was left*	*for valour,*	*neither*

conferti	potĕrant	vitare	tela	conjecta	à
crowded	*were they able*	*to avoid*	*the darts*	*hurled*	*by*

tantâ	multitudĭne.	Tămen	conflictati
so-great	*a multitude.*	*However*	*having struggled*

tam-multis	incommŏdis,	multis	vulnerĭbus
with so-many	*disadvantages,*	*many*	*wounds*

acceptis,	resistebant;	et	magnâ	parte
being received,	*they did withstand;*	*and*	*a great*	*part*

diei	consumptâ,	committebant	nĭhil,	quod
of the day	*being spent,*	*they did commit*	*nothing,*	*which*

esset	indignum	ipsis (abl.),	quum
might be	*unworthy*	*themselves,*	*when* (although)

pugnaretur (imp. subj.)	à	primâ	luce	ad	octavam
it was fought	*from*	*the first*	*light*	*to*	*the eighth*

horam.	Tum	utrumque	fĕmur	transjicĭtur
hour (two o'clock).	*Then*	*each*	*thigh*	*is pierced*

tragŭlâ	Tito	Balventĭo,	forti	vĭro,	et
with a dart	*to Titus*	*Balventius,*	*a brave*	*man,*	*and*

magnæ	auctoritatis,	qui	duxĕrat	primum	pilum
of great	*authority,*	*who*	*had led*	*the first*	*javelin*

		superiore	anno.	Quintus
(had been first centurion)		*in the former*	*year.*	Quintus

Lucanĭus	ejusdem	ordĭnis	pugnans	fortissĭmè
Lucanius	*of the same*	*rank*	*fighting*	*most-bravely*

interficĭtur,	dum	subvĕnit	filĭo	circumvento.
is slain,	*whilst*	*he aids*	*to (his) son*	*having been surrounded.*

Lucĭus	Cotta,	legatus	adhortans	omnes
Lucius	*Cotta,*	*the lieutenant*	*encouraging*	*all*

cohortes	que	ordĭnes,	vulneratur	fundâ	in
the cohorts	*and*	*ranks,*	*is wounded*	*with a sling*	*on*

adversum	os.
the opposite	*face.*

36.
Quintus	Titurĭus	permotus	his	rebus,
	Quintus	*Titurius*	*much-alarmed*	*by these things,*

quum	conspexisset	(pluperf. subj.)	Ambiorĭgem
when	*he had beheld*		*Ambiorix*

prŏcul	cohortantem	sŭos,	mittit	sŭum
at-a-distance	*exhorting*	*his (men),*	*sends*	*his*

interprĕtem,	Cnæĭum	Pompeĭum	ad	ĕum,	rogatum,
interpreter,	*Cnæius*	*Pompey*	*to*	*him,*	*to beseech,*

"ut	parcat	sĭbi	que	militĭbus.
"that	*he may spare*	*to himself*	*and*	*to the soldiers.*

Ille	appellatus	respondit,	"licere
He	*being called*	*answered,*	*" to be-lawful* (that he

	collŏqui	secum,	si	vĕlit:
permitted)	*to confer*	*with-himself,*	*if he*	*may-will:*

sperare	posse	impetrari	à	multitudĭne,
to hope	*to be-able*	*to be obtained*	*from*	*the multitude,*

quod	pertinĕat	ad	salutem	milĭtum:	verò
what	*may relate*	*to*	*the safety*	*of the soldiers:*	*but*

nĭhil	nocĭtum-iri	ipsi:	que	se
nothing	*to be about-to-be-hurt*	*to himself:*	*and*	*himself*

interponĕre	sŭam	fĭdem	in	ĕam	rem."
to interpose (to pledge)	*his*	*faith*	*unto*	*that*	*thing."*

Ille	communĭcat		cum	saucĭo	Cottâ;	"si
He	*communicates (this)*		*with*	*the wounded*	*Cotta;*	*"if*

videatur,		ut	excedant		pugnâ,
it may seem (fit),		*that*	*they may retire*		*from the battle,*

et	colloquantur	unà	cum	Ambiorĭge;	se
and	*may confer*	*together*	*with*	*Ambiorix ;*	*himself*

sperare	posse	impetrari	ab	ĕo	de
to hope	*to be-able*	*to be-obtained*	*from*	*him*	*about*

sŭâ	salute	ac		milĭtum."	Cotta	nĕgat
his-own	*safety*	*and*		*(that) of the soldiers."*	*Cotta*	*denies*

se	iturum	ad	armatum	hostem	atque
himself	*about-to-go*	*to*	*an armed*	*enemy*	*and*

persevĕrat	in	ĕo.	(37.)	Sabinus	jŭbet	tribūno
perseveres	*in*	*that.*		*Sabinus*	*orders*	*the tribunes*

milĭtum,	quos	habebat	circum	se	in-præsentĭâ,
of soldiers,	*whom*	*he did have*	*about*	*himself*	*at-present,*

et	centuriones	primorum	ordĭnum,	sĕqui
and	*the centurions*	*of the first*	*ranks,*	*to follow*

se;	et	quum	accessisset (pluperf. subj.)
himself;	*and*	*when*	*he had approached*

propĭùs	Ambiorĭgem,	jussus	abjicĕre
nearer	*Ambiorix,*	*being ordered*	*to throw-away*

arma,	făcit	imperatum,	que	impĕrat
(his) arms,	*he does*	*(the thing) commanded,*	*and*	*commands*

sŭis,	ut	facĭant	ĭdem.	Intĕrim,
to his (men),	*that*	*they may do*	*the same.*	*Mean-time,*

dum	ăgunt	inter	se	de
whilst	*they act (treat)*	*between*	*themselves*	*about*

conditionĭbus,	que	longĭor	sermo	instituĭtur
conditions,	*and*	*a longer*	*speech*	*is framed*

consultò	ab	Ambiorĭge,	circumventus	paullatim
designedly	*by*	*Ambiorix,*	*being surrounded*	*gradually*

interficĭtur.	Tum	verò	conclamant	victorĭam	atque
he is killed.	*Then*	*truly*	*they shout*	*victory*	*and*

tollunt	ululatum	sŭo	more	que	impĕtu
raise	*a howl*	*in their*	*manner,*	*and*	*an attack*

facto	in	nostros,	perturbant	ordines.
being made	*upon*	*our (men),*	*they disorder*	*the ranks.*

Ibi	Lucius	Cotta	pugnans	interficitur,	cum
There	*Lucius*	*Cotta*	*fighting*	*is killed,*	*with*

maximâ	parte	militum:	reliqui	recipiunt
the greatest	*part*	*of the soldiers:*	*the rest*	*betake*

se	in	castra (pl.),	unde	egressi-erant.
themselves	*into*	*the camp,*	*whence*	*they had gone-out.*

Ex	quibus	Lucius	Petrosidius	aquilifer
Out-of	*whom*	*Lucius*	*Petrosidius*	*the eagle-bearer*

(ensign)	projecit	aquilam	intra	vallum,	cum
	cast	*the eagle*	*within*	*the rampart,*	*when*

premeretur (imp. subj.)	magnâ	multitudine
he was pressed	*by a great*	*multitude*

hostium;	ipse	pugnans	fortissimè	pro
of the enemies;	*himself*	*fighting*	*most-bravely.*	*before*

castris (pl.)	occiditur.	Alii	ægrè	sustinent
the camp	*is slain.*	*The others*	*hardly*	*support*

oppugnationem	ad	noctem;	ipsi	omnes
the assault	*to (until)*	*night;*	*themselves*	*all*

ad unum,	salute	desperatâ,	interficiunt
to one (to a man),	*safety*	*being despaired-of,*	*kill*

se	noctu.	Pauci	elapsi	ex	prœlio
themselves	*by night.*	*A few*	*having escaped*	*from*	*the battle*

perveniunt	incertis	itineribus	per	silvas
arrive	*by uncertain*	*routes*	*through*	*the woods*

ad Titum	Labienum	legatum	in	hiberna;
to Titus	*Labienus*	*the lieutenant*	*into*	*winter-quarters;*

atque	faciunt	eum	certiorem	de
and	*make*	*him*	*more-sure (inform him)*	*of*

rebus	gestis.
the things	*carried-on.*

38.
Ambiorix	sublatus	hâc	victoriâ,	statim
Ambiorix	*elated*	*by this*	*victory,*	*immediately*

proficiscitur	cum	equitatu	in	Atuaticos,
sets-out	*with*	*(his) cavalry*	*unto*	*the Atuatici,*

qui	ĕrant	finitĭmi	regno	ejus;	nĕque
who	were	bordering	to the kingdom	of him;	neither

intermittit	dĭem	nĕque	noctem;	que jŭbet
does he intermit	day	nor	night;	and he orders

peditatum	subsĕqui	se.	Re	demonstratâ,
the infantry	to follow	himself.	The affair	being shown,

que	Atuatĭcis	concitatis,	pervĕnit	postĕro
and	the Atuatici	being roused-up,	he arrives	in the following

dĭe	in	Nervĭos,	que	hortatur
day	unto	the Nervii,	and	exhorts (them)

"ne-dimittant	occasionem	sŭi
"they may not-let-slip	the opportunity	of themselves

liberandi	in-perpetŭum,	atque	ulciscendi	Romanos
to-be-freed	for-ever,	and	of avenging	the Romans

pro	ĭis	injurĭis, quas	accepĕrint (perf. subj.):"
for	those	injuries, which	they have received:"

demonstrat	"dŭos	legatos	interfectos-esse,	que
he shows	"two	lieutenants	to have been killed,	and

magnam	partem	exercĭtûs	interîsse:	nĭhil
a great	part	of the army	to have perished:	nothing

negotĭi	esse,	legionem	subĭtò
of business (trouble)	to be,	the legion	suddenly

oppressam,	quæ	hiĕmet (pres. subj.)	cum
being overwhelmed,	which	winter	with

Cicerone,	interfĭci:"	profitetur	"se adjutorem
Cicero,	to be slain:"	he declares	"himself a helper

ad ĕam	rem."
to that	thing."

39. | | | | |
|---|---|---|---|
| Persuadet | Nervĭis | facĭlè | hâc oratione. |
| He persuades | to the Nervii | easily | by this speech. |

Ităque	nuncĭis	dimissis	confestim ad
Therefore	messengers	being dismissed	immediately to

Centrones,	Grudĭos,	Levăcos,	Pleumosĭos,	Gordunos,
the Centrones,	Grudii,	Levaci,	Pleumosii,	Gordŭni,

qui	omnes	sunt	sub	imperĭo. eorum,
who	all	are	under	the authority of them,

LIBER V.

cogunt	mănus	quàm	maxĭmas	possunt;	et
they collect	*bands*	*as*	*greatest*	*they can;*	*and*

advŏlant	de-improviso	ad	hiberna	Ciceronis,
fly	*unexpectedly*	*to*	*the winter-quarters*	*of Cicero,*

famâ	de	morte	Titurĭi	nondum
the report	*about*	*the death*	*of Titurius*	*not-yet*

perlatâ	ad	eum.	Accĭdit	quŏque	huic,
being brought	*to*	*him.*	*It happened*	*also*	*to him,*

quod	fŭit	necesse,	ut	nonnulli	milĭtes,	qui
which	*was*	*necessary,*	*that*	*some*	*soldiers,*	*who*

discessissent	(pluperf. subj.)	in	silvas	caussâ
had departed		*into*	*the woods*	*by cause (for*

	lignationis	que	munitionis
the purpose)	*of wood-cutting*	*and*	*of fortification*

interciperentur	(imp. subj.)	repentino	adventu
were cut-off		*by the sudden*	*arrival*

equĭtum.	His	circumventis,	Eburones,
of (their) cavalry.	*These*	*being surrounded,*	*the Eburones,*

Atuatĭci,	Nervĭi,	atque	socĭi	et	clientes
Atuatici,	*Nervii,*	*and*	*the allies*	*and*	*dependants*

omnĭum	horum,	incipĭunt	oppugnare	legionem
of all	*these,*	*begin*	*to assault*	*the legion*

magnâ	mănu.	Nostri	celerĭter	concurrunt
with a great	*band.*	*Our (men)*	*quickly*	*run-together*

ad	arma;	conscendunt	vallum.	Is	dies
to	*arms;*	*they mount*	*the rampart.*	*That*	*day*

sustentatur	ægrè,	quòd	hostes	ponebant
is supported	*hardly,*	*because*	*the enemies*	*did place*

omnem	spem	in	celeritate,	atque	adepti
all	*hope*	*in*	*expedition,*	*and*	*having obtained*

hanc	victorĭam,	confidebant	se	fŏre
this	*victory,*	*they did trust*	*themselves*	*to be about-to-be*

victores	in-perpetŭum.
conquerors	*for-ever.*

40. | Litĕræ | mittuntur | confestim | ac |
|---|---|---|---|
| ***Letters** (a letter)* | *are sent* | *immediately* | *to* |

DE BELLO GALLICO.

Cæsărem	à Cicerone,	magnis præmiis	propositis,
Cæsar	*by Cicero,*	*great rewards*	*being proposed,*

si pertulissent. Omnĭbus viis
if they might have carried (it). All the ways

obsessis, missi intercipiuntur. Centum
being blocked-up, (those) sent are intercepted. A hundred

et viginti turres excitantur incredibĭli celeritate
and twenty towers are raised with incredible speed

noctu ex ĕâ materĭâ, quam com-
by night out-of that material, which they had

portavĕrant caussâ munitionis.
brought-together by cause (for the purpose) of fortification.

Quæ videbantur deesse opĕri
What (things) did seem to be-wanting to the work

perficiuntur. Hostes, multò majorĭbus copiĭs
are completed. The enemies, by-much greater forces

coactis, oppugnant castra (pl.) postĕro
being collected, assault the camp on the following

die, complent fossam. Resistĭtur à nostris
day, they fill-up the trench. It is withstood by our

eâdem ratione, quâ pridĭe : hoc
(men) in the same manner, in which the day-before: this

ĭdem fit deinceps relĭquis
same (thing) is done afterwards on the rest (remaining)

diebus. Nulla pars nocturni tempŏris intermittĭtur
days. No part of the nightly time is intermitted

ad laborem : facultas quietis dătur non ægris,
to labour : a power of rest is given not to the sick,

non vulneratis. Quæcunque sunt ŏpus
not to the wounded. Whatsoever (things) are necessary

ad oppugnationem · proxĭmi diei, comparantur
to the assault of the next day, are prepared

noctu. Multæ sŭdes præustæ, magnus
by night. Many stakes burnt-at-the-point, a great

numĕrus muralĭum pilorum instituĭtur ; turres
number of mural javelins is prepared; towers

LIBER V.

contabulantur; pinnæ que loricæ attexuntur
are raised ; battlements and parapets are woven

ex cratibus. Cicero ipse, quum
out-of hurdles. Cicero himself, when (although)

esset (imp. subj.) tenuissimâ valetudine, relinquebat
he was in very-delicate health, did leave

ne quidem nocturnum tempus sibi ad
not indeed (even) *the nightly time to himself to*

quietem; ut cogeretur (imp. subj.) parcĕre
rest ; (so) *that he was compelled to spare*

sibi ultrò concursu
to himself spontaneously (in spite of himself) *by the running*

ac vocibus militum.
and voices (of entreaty) *of the soldiers.*

41. Tunc duces que principes Nerviorum,
Then the leaders and chiefs of the Nervii,

qui habebant aliquem aditum sermonis que
who did have some access of speech and

caussam amicitiæ cum Cicerone, dicunt
cause of friendship with Cicero, say

sese velle colloqui. Potestate
themselves to will to confer (with him). *The power* (liberty)

factâ, commemorant eadem, quæ
being made, they narrate the same (things), *which*

Ambiorix egerat cum Titurio: "Omnem
Ambiorix had acted (done) *with Titurius: " All*

Galliam esse in armis: Germanos transîsse
Gaul to be in arms: the Germans to have crossed

Rhenum: hiberna Cæsaris que reliquorum
the Rhine: the winter-quarters of Cæsar and of the rest

oppugnari." Addunt etiam de morte
to be stormed." They add also about the death

Sabini. Ostentant Ambiorigem caussâ
of Sabinus. They display Ambiorix by cause (for the

fidei faciundæ. Dicunt "eos
purpose) *of faith* (credit) *to-be-made. They say " these*

errare,	si	sperent	quidquam	præsidii
to mistake,	if	they may hope	any	of protection

ab	iis,	qui	diffidant (pres. subj.)	suis
from	those,	who	distrust	to their-own

rebus:	tamen	sese	esse	hoc	animo
affairs:	however	themselves	to be	with this	mind

in	Ciceronem	que	Romanum	populum,	ut
unto	Cicero	and	the Roman	people,	that

recusent	nihil,	nisi	hiberna,	atque
they may refuse	nothing,	unless	the winter-quarters,	and

nolint	hanc	consuetudinem	inveterascere:
may be-unwilling	this	custom	to become-old

	licere	illis	discedere
(established):	to be-lawful	for them	to depart

incolumibus	per	se		ex
safe	by	themselves (by their permission)		out-of

hibernis,	et	proficisci	sine	metu	in
the winter-quarters,	and	to set-out	without	fear	into

quascunque	partes	velint."	Cicero	respondit
whatever	parts	they may will."	Cicero	answered

modò	unum	ad	hæc:	"Non	esse
only	one (thing)	to	these:	"Not	to be

consuetudinem	Romani	populi	accipere	ullam
the custom	of the Roman	people	to receive	any

conditionem	ab	armato	hoste:	si	velint
condition	from	an armed	enemy:	if	they may will

discedere	ab	armis,	utantur	se	adjutore,
to depart	from	arms,	they may use	himself	(as) a helper

	que	mittant	legatos	ad	Cæsarem:
(an advocate),	and	may send	ambassadors	to	Cæsar

se	sperare	impetraturos,	quæ
himself	to hope	them (to be) about-to-obtain,	what

petierint,	pro	justitiâ	ejus."
they may have sought,	on-account-of	the justice	of him."

42.

Nervii	repulsi	ab	hâc	spe,
The Nervii	being repulsed	from	this	hope,

cingunt	hiberna	vallo	undĕcim
surround	*the winter-quarters*	*with a rampart*	*of eleven*

pĕdum	et	fossâ	quindĕcim pĕdum.	Cognovĕrant
feet	*and*	*a ditch*	*of fifteen feet.*	*They had known*

	hæc	et	à nostris	consuetudĭne
(learned)	*these (things)*	*also*	*from our (men)*	*by the custom*

superiorum	annorum;	et	nacti	quosdam
of former	*years;*	*and*	*having got*	*some*

captivos	de	exercĭtu,	docebantur	ab his.
prisoners	*of*	*(our) army,*	*they were taught*	*by these.*

Sed	nulla	copĭa	ferramentorum	his,
But	*(there was) no*	*supply*	*of iron-tools*	*to these,*

quæ	esset	idonĕa	ad	hunc	usum.
which	*might be*	*fit*	*to (for)*	*this*	*use.*

Cogebantur	circumcidĕre,	cespĭtem	gladiis,
They were forced	*to cut-round*	*the green-turf*	*with swords,*

exhaurire	terram	manĭbus	que
to draw-out (dig-out)	*the earth*	*with (their) hands*	*and*

	sagŭlis.	Ex	quâ	re	quĭdem,
(carry it) in cloaks.	*From*	*which*	*thing*	*indeed,*

multitudo	homĭnum	potŭit	cognosci.	Nam
the multitude	*of men*	*was-able*	*to be known.*	*For*

mĭnùs	trĭbus	horis	perfecerunt	munitionem
in less	*(than) three*	*hours*	*they finished*	*a fortification*

quindĕcim	millĭum	passŭum	in	circuĭtu.	Que
of fifteen	*thousands*	*of paces*	*in*	*compass.*	*And*

cœperunt	parare	ac	facĕre	tuřres	relĭquis
they began	*to prepare*	*and*	*to make*	*towers*	*on the rest*

	diebus	ad	altitudĭnem	valli;
(remaining)	*days*	*to*	*the height*	*of the rampart;*

falces	que	testudĭnes,	quas	iidem	captivi
scythes	*and*	*mantelets,*	*which*	*the same*	*prisoners*

docuĕrant.
had taught (them).

43.
Septĭmo	dĭe	oppugnationis,	maxĭmo
In the seventh	*day*	*of the siege,*	*a very-great*

vento	coorto,	cœperunt	jacĕre	fundis
wind	*having arisen,*	*they began*	*to throw*	*with slings*

ferventes	glandes	ex	fusĭli	argillâ,	et fervefacta
hot	*balls*	*of*	*fusible*	*clay,*	*and heated*

jacŭla	in	căsas,	quæ	tectæ-ĕrant
darts	*on*	*the cottages*	*which*	*had been covered*

strĕmentis	Gallĭco	more. Hæ	comprehenderunt
with straws	*in the Gallic*	*manner. These*	*caught*

ignem	celerĭter,	et	magnitudĭne	venti,
fire	*quickly,*	*and*	*from the greatness*	*of the wind,*

distulerunt	in	omnem	lŏcum	castrorum (pl.).
carried (it)	*into*	*every*	*place*	*of the camp.*

Hostes	insecuti	maxĭmo	clamore,
The enemies	*having followed*	*with a very-great*	*shout,*

quăsi	victoriâ	partâ	atque	exploratâ
as-if	*the victory*	*being obtained*	*and*	*examined*

jam,	cœperunt agĕre		turres
(assured) already,	*began to act (put in motion)*		*the towers*

que	testudĭnes	et	ascendĕre	vallum scalis.
and	*mantelets*	*and*	*to mount*	*the rampart with ladders*

At	tanta	fŭit	virtus	atque præsentĭa	anĭmi
But	*so-great*	*was*	*the valour*	*and the presence*	*of mind*

milĭtum,	ut,	quum	torrerentur (imp. subj.)
of the soldiers,	*that,*	*when*	*they were scorched*

flammâ	undĭque,	que	premerentur (imp. subj.)
by the flame	*on-every-side,*	*and*	*were pressed*

maxĭmâ	multitudĭne	telorum,	que
with a very-great	*multitude*	*of weapons,*	*and*

intelligĕrent (imp. subj.)	omnĭa	sŭa	impedimenta
did understand	*all*	*their*	*baggages*

atque	omnes	fortunas	conflagrare,	non mŏdò
and	*all*	*(their) fortunes*	*to-be-on-fire,*	*not only*

nemo	decedĕret (imp. subj.)	de	vallo
no-one	*did depart*	*from*	*the rampart*

caussâ		demigrandi,	sed	quisquam ne
by cause (for the sake)		*of going-away,*	*but*	*any-one*

LIBER V.

quĭdem	penè	respicĕret (imp. subj.) ;	ac	tum
indeed (even)	*hardly*	*did look-back ;*	*and*	*then*

omnes	pugnarent (imp. subj.)	acerrĭmè	que
all	*did fight*	*most-vigorously*	*and*

fortissĭmè.	Hic	dĭes	fŭit	longè	gravissĭmus
most-bravely.	*This*	*day*	*was*	*by-far*	*the most-severe*

nostris ;	sed	tămen	habŭit	hunc	eventum,	ut
to our (*men*) ;	*but*	*however*	*it had*	*this*	*issue,*	*that*

ĕo	dĭe	maxĭmus	numĕrus	hostĭum	vulneraretur
on that day	*the greatest*	*number*	*of the enemies*	*was wounded*

(imp. subj.)	atque	interficeretur (imp. sub.) ;	ut
	and	*was killed ;*	(*so*) *that*

constipavĕrant	se	vallo	ipso,
they had crowded	*themselves*	*under*	*the rampart*	*itself,*

que	ultĭmi	dăbant	non	recessum	primis.	Quĭdem
and	*the last*	*did give*	*not*	*a retreat*	*to the first.*	*Indeed*

flammâ	intermissâ	paullŭlùm,	et	turri
the flame	*being interrupted*	*a very-little,*	*and*	*a tower*

adactâ	quodam	lŏco,	et	contingente
being forced-up	*in a certain*	*place,*	*and*	*touching*

vallum,	centuriones	tertĭæ	cohortis
the rampart,	*the centurions*	*of the third*	*cohort*

recesserunt	ex	ĕo	lŏco,	quo	stabant,
retired	*out-of*	*that*	*place,*	*in which*	*they did stand,*

que	removerunt	omnes	sŭos ;	cœperunt
and	*removed*	*all*	*their* (*men*) ;	*they began*

vocāre	hostes	nutu	que	vocĭbus,	"si
to call	*the enemies*	*by nod*	*and*	*by sayings,*	"*if*

vellent	introïre :"	nemo	quorum	ausus-est
they might will	*to enter :"*	*no-one*	*of whom*	*dared*

progrĕdi.	Tum	deturbati (-sunt)	lapidĭbus	conjectis
to advance.	*Then*	*they were beaten-off*	*by stones*	*thrown*

ex	omni	parte,	que	turris	succensa-est.
from	*every*	*part,*	*and*	*the tower*	*was set-on-fire.*

44.

Erant	in	ĕâ	legione	fortissĭmi
There were	*in*	*that*	*legion*	(*two*) *very-brave*

vĭri, centuriones, Titus Pulfĭo et Lucĭus Varenus,	men, centurions, Titus Pulfio and Lucius Varenus,
qui jam appropinquarent (imp. subj.) primis	who now did approach to the first
ordinĭbus. Hi habebant perpetŭas	ranks (of centurions). These did have constant
controversĭas inter se, ŭter	controversies between themselves, whether of-the-two
anteferretur altĕri; que contendebant	should be preferred to the other; and they did contend
summis simultatĭbus de lŏco	with the highest bickerings about place (precedence)
omnĭbus annis. iis Pulfĭo inquit,	in all years. Out-of those Pulfio says,
quum pugnaretur (imp. subj.) acerrĭmè ad	when it was fought most-vigorously at
munitiones, "Quid dubĭtas, Varene?	the fortifications, "Why dost thou hesitate, O Varenus?
aut quem lŏcum tŭæ virtutis probandæ	or what place (opportunity) of thy valour to-be-proved
exspectas? Hic dĭes, hic dĭes judicabit	dost thou wait-for? This day, this day shall decide
de nostris controversĭis." Quum dixisset (pluperf.	about our disputes." When he had said
subj.) hæc, procedit extra munitiones,	these (words), he advances without the fortifications,
et quæ pars hostĭum visa-est confertissĭma,	and what part of the enemies seemed most-dense,
irrumpit in ĕam. Nec Varenus quĭdem	he rushes-in into that. Neither Varenus indeed
tum contĭnet sese vallo; sed verĭtus	then restrains himself on the rampart; but having feared
existimationem omnĭum, subsequĭtur, mediocri	the opinion of all, he follows-closely, a moderate
spatĭo relicto. Pulfĭo mittit pilum in	distance being left. Pulfio sends (his) javelin against

hostes,	atque	transjǐcit	unum	ex	multitudǐne
the enemies,	*and*	*transfixes*	*one*	*out-of*	*the multitude*
procurrentem:	quo	percusso	et		exanimato,
running-forward:	*who*	*being struck*	*and*		*laid-senseless,*
hostes	protĕgunt	hunc		scutis,	et
the enemies	*protect*	*him*		*with (their) shields,*	*and*
universi	conjicǐunt	tela	in	illum,	
all	*hurl*	*(their) darts*	*upon*	*him* (Pulfio),	
nĕque	dant		facultatem		regrediendi.
neither	*do they give (him)*		*a power*		*of returning.*

Scutum transfigǐtur Pulfioni et verŭtum
The shield is transpierced for Pulfio (Pulfio's shield) *and a dart*

defigǐtur	in	baltĕo.	Hic	casus	avertit
is fixed	*in*	*(his) belt.*	*This*	*misfortune*	*turns-away*
vaginam	et	moratur	dextram	mănum	
the scabbard	*and*	*retards*	*the right*	*hand*	*(of him)*
conantis	educĕre	gladǐum,	que		hostes
endeavouring	*to draw-out*	*(his) sword,*	*and*		*the enemies*
circumsistunt		impeditum.	Varenus		inimicus
surround		*(him) entangled.*	*Varenus*		*(his) rival*
succurrit	illi,	et	subvĕnit		laboranti.
succours	*to him,*	*and*	*comes-up*		*(to him) labouring* (in distress).
	Omnis	multitudo	confestim		convertit
	All	*the multitude*	*immediately*		*turns*
se	à	Pulfione	ad	hunc.	Arbitrantur
itself	*from*	*Pulfio*	*to*	*this* (Varenus).	*They thi*
illum	transfixum	verŭto.		Illìc	vĕrò
him (Pulfio)	*run-through*	*with the dart.*		*There*	*truly*
Varenus	occursat	ocǐùs		gladǐo	que
Varenus	*runs-up*	*very-quickly*		*with (his) sword*	*and*
gĕrit	rem	comǐnùs;		atque	uno
carries-on	*the affair*	*hand-to-hand;*		*and*	*one*
interfecto,	propellit	relǐquos	paullùm.		Dum
being killed,	*he repulses*	*the rest*	*a little.*		*Whilst*
instat	cupidiùs	dejectus			concǐdit
he presses-on	*more eagerly,*	*being thrown-down*			*he fell*

in inferiorem locum. Pulfio rursus fert	upon a lower place. Pulfio again brings
subsidium huic circumvento; atque ambo incolumes,	aid to him surrounded; and both safe,
compluribus interfectis, recipiunt sese	several (of the enemy) being killed, betake themselves
cum summâ laude intra munitiones. Sic	with the highest praise within the fortifications. Thus
fortuna versavit utrumque in contentione et	fortune turned each in (their) strife and
certamine, ut alter inimicus esset (imp.	contest, (so) that the other (one) rival was
subj.) auxilio que saluti alteri; neque	for aid and safety to the other; neither
posset (imp. subj.) dijudicari, uter	was it able to be decided, whether-of-the-two
videretur anteferendus utri virtute.	should seem to-be-preferred to which-one in valour.

45. Quantò graviòr atque asperior By how-much more-severe and more-rough

oppugnatio erat indies, et maximè	(desperate) the siege was daily, and chiefly
quòd, magnâ parte militum confectâ	because, a great part of the soldiers being spent
vulneribus, res pervenerat ad paucitatem	with wounds, the thing had come to fewness
defensorum; tantò crebriores literæ que	of defenders; by so-much more-frequent letters and
nuncii mittebantur ad Cæsarem; pars quorum	messengers were sent to Cæsar; part of whom
deprehensa necabatur cum cruciatu in conspectu	being caught was put-to-death with torture in sight
nostrorum militum. Erat unus Nervius intùs,	of our soldiers. There was one Nervian within,
nomine Vertico, natus honesto loco,	by name Vertico, born in honourable place (rank).

qui	profugĕrat	ad	Ciceronem	à	primâ	obsidione,
who	*had fled*	*to*	*Cicero*	*from*	*the first*	*siege,*

que	præstitĕrat	sŭam	fĭdem	êi.	Hic
and	*had exhibited*	*his*	*fidelity*	*to him.*	*This (person)*

persuadet	servo,	spe	libertatis	que	magnis
persuades	*to a slave,*	*by the hope*	*of liberty*	*and*	*by great*

præmĭis,	ut	defĕrat	litĕras (plur.)	ad
rewards,	*that*	*he may carry*	*a letter*	*to*

Cæsărem.	Ille	affert	has	illigatas	in
Cæsar.	*He*	*carries*	*these* (this letter)	*tied-up*	*on*

jacŭlo;	et	Gallus	versatus	inter	Gallos
a javelin;	*and*	*the Gaul*	*being engaged*	*among*	*Gauls*

sĭne	ullâ	suspicĭone,	pervenit	ad	Cæsărem.
without	*any*	*suspicion,*	*arrives*	*to*	*Cæsar.*

Cognoscit	ab	ĕo	de	pericŭlo	Ciceronis
He knows (learns)	*from*	*him*	*of*	*the danger*	*of Cicero*

que	legionis.
and	*of the legion.*

46.
Cæsar,	litĕris (plur.)	acceptis	circĭter
Cæsar,	*the letter*	*being received*	*about*

undecĭmâ	horâ	diei,	mittit	nuncĭum
in the eleventh	*hour*	*of the day,*	*sends*	*a messenger*

statim	ad	Marcum	Crassum	quæstorem	in
immediately	*to*	*Marcus*	*Crassus*	*the quæstor*	*unto*

Bellovăcos,	cujus	hiberna	abĕrant	ab
the Bellovaci,	*whose*	*winter-quarters*	*were-distant*	*from*

ĕo	viginti	quinque	millĭa	passŭum.	Jŭbet
him	*twenty*	*five*	*thousands*	*of paces.*	*He orders*

legionem	proficisci	medĭâ	nocte,	que	venire
the legion	*to set-out*	*in middle*	*night,*	*and*	*to come*

celerĭter	ad	se.	Crassus	exĭit	cum
speedily	*to*	*himself.*	*Crassus*	*came-out*	*with*

nuncĭo.	Mittit	altĕrum	ad	Caïum
the messenger.	*He sends*	*another (messenger)*	*to*	*Caius*

Fabĭum	legatum,	ut	adducat	legionem
Fabius	*the lieutenant,*	*that*	*he may lead*	*(his) legion*

DE BELLO GALLICO.

in	fines	Atrebatium,	quâ	sciebat
into	*the territories*	*of the Atrebates,*	*where*	*he did know*

iter	faciendum	sibi.	Scribit
the march	*to-be-made*	*to (by) himself.*	*He writes*

Labieno,	si	posset	facere	commodo
to Labienus,	*if*	*he might be-able*	*to do (it)*	*with convenience*

Reipublicæ,	veniat	cum	legione	ad
of the State,	*he may come*	*with*	*(his) legion*	*to*

fines	Nerviorum.	Putat	reliquam
the territories	*of the Nervii.*	*He thinks*	*the rest (remaining)*

partem	exercitûs	non	exspectandam,	quòd
part	*of the army*	*not*	*to-be-waited-for,*	*because*

aberat	paullò	longius:	cogit	circiter
it was distant	*a little*	*farther:*	*he collects*	*about*

quadringentos	equites	ex	proximis	hibernis.
four-hundred	*cavalry*	*out-of*	*the nearest*	*winter-quarters.*

47. | Factus-est | certior | de | adventu | Crassi | ab |
|---|---|---|---|---|---|
| *He was made more-sure* | | *of* | *the arrival* | *of Crassus* | *by* |

antecursoribus	circiter	tertiâ	horâ:	progreditur
scouts	*about*	*in the third*	*hour:*	*he advances*

viginti	millia	passuum	eo	die.	Præficit
twenty	*thousands*	*of paces*	*in that*	*day.*	*He sets-over*

Crassum	Samarobrivæ,	que	attribuit	legionem
Crassus	*to Samarobriva,*	*and*	*assigns*	*a legion*

ei;	quòd	relinquebat	ibi	impedimenta
to him;	*because*	*he did leave*	*there*	*the baggages*

exercitûs,	obsides	civitatum,	publicas	literas,
of the army,	*the hostages*	*of the states,*	*the public*	*letters,*

que	omne	frumentum,	quod	devexerat
and	*all*	*the corn,*	*which*	*he had conveyed-down*

eò	caussâ		hiemis
thither	*by cause (for the purpose)*		*of the winter*

tolerandæ.	Fabius,	ut	imperatum-erat,
to-be-supported.	*Fabius,*	*as*	*it had been commanded,*

moratus	non	ita	multùm,
having delayed	*not*	*so*	*much (not very much),*

LIBER V.

occurrit	cum	legione	in	itinĕre.	Labienus,
meets (him)	with	a legion	on	the march.	Labienus,

interĭtu	Sabini,	et	cæde	cohortĭum
the destruction	of Sabinus,	and	the slaughter	of the cohorts

cognĭtâ,	quum	omnes	copĭæ	Trevirorum
being known,	when	all	the forces	of the Treviri

venissent (pluperf. subj.)	ad	ĕum,	verĭtus	ne,
had come	to	him,	having feared	lest,

si	fecisset	profectionem	ex	hibernis
if	he should-have-made	the departure	out-of	winter-quarters

simĭlem	fŭgæ,	ut	posset	non	sustinere
like	to a flight,	that	he might be-able	not	to sustain

impĕtum	hostĭum,	præsertim	quos	sciret
the attack	of the enemies,	especially	whom	he did know

(imp. subj.)	efferri	recenti	victorĭâ,	dimittit
	to be elated	by the late	victory,	despatches

litĕras (plur.)	Cæsări,	cum	quanto	pericŭlo
a letter	to Cæsar,	(to say) with	how-great	danger

esset (imp. subj.)	educturus	legionem	ex
he was	about-to-lead-out	the legion	out-of

hibernis:	perscribit	rem	gestam	in
winter-quarters:	he writes-fully	the affair	carried-on	in

	Eburonĭbus:	dŏcet		omnes
(among)	the Eburones:	he teaches (informs him)		all

copĭas	peditatûs	que	equitatûs	Trevirorum
the forces	of infantry	and	of cavalry	of the Treviri

consedisse		tría	millĭa	passŭum
to have sat-down (encamped)		three	thousands	of paces

longè	ab	sŭis	castris (pl.).
far (distant) from	his	camp.

48.	Cæsar,	consilĭo	ejus	probato,	etsi
Cæsar,	the plan	of him	being approved-of,	although

dejectus	opinione	trĭum
cast-down (disappointed)	in the expectation	of three

legionum,	redĭĕrat	ad	dŭas;	tămen	ponebat
legions,	had returned	to	the two;	however	he did place

unum	auxilium	communis	salutis	in
the one (only)	aid	of the common	safety	in
celeritate.	Venit	magnis	itineribus	in
expedition.	He comes	by great	marches	into
fines	Nerviorum.	Ibi	cognoscit	ex
the territories	of the Nervii.	There	he knows (learns)	from
captivis,	quæ		gerantur (pres. subj.)	
the prisoners,	what (things)		are carried-on	
apud Ciceronem,	que in	quanto	periculo	res
at Cicero,	and in	how-great	danger	the affair
sit (pres. subj.).	Tum	persuadet	cuidam	
is.	Then	he persuades	to a certain (person)	
ex Gallis	equitibus	magnis	præmiis,	uti
out-of the Gallic	horsemen	by great	rewards,	that
deferat	epistolam	ad	Ciceronem.	Mittit hanc
he may carry	a letter	to	Cicero.	He sends this
conscriptam	Græcis	literis;	ne,	epistola
written	in Greek	letters (characters);	lest,	the letter
interceptâ,	nostra	consilia	cognoscantur	ab
being intercepted,	our	plans	may be known	by
hostibus.	Monet,	si	posset	non
the enemies.	He advises (him),	if	he may be-able	not
adire,	ut	objiciat	tragulam	cum
to go-to (Cicero),	that	he may cast	a dart	with
epistolâ deligatâ	ad	amentum	intra	munitiones
the letter tied	to	the thong	within	the fortifications
castrorum (pl.).	Scribit in	literis (plur.),	" se
of the camp.	He writes in	the letter,	" himself
profectum	affore	celeriter	cum
having set-out	to-be-about-to-be-present	speedily	with
legionibus:"	hortatur	" ut	retineat
the legions :"	he encourages (him)	" that	he may retain
pristinam	virtutem."	Gallus	veritus
(his) ancient	valour."	The Gaul	having feared
periculum,	mittit	tragulam,	ut præceptum-erat.
danger,	sends (throws)	the dart,	as it had been ordered.

LIBER V.

Hæc	adhæsit	ad	turrim	casu,	neque
This	*stuck*	*to*	*a tower*	*by chance,*	*nor*

animadversa (-est) bidŭo ab nostris;
was perceived *for two-days* *by* *our (men);*

tertio die conspicitur à quodam milite;
on the third *day* *it is seen* *by* *a certain* *soldier;*

dempta . defertur ad Ciceronem. Ille
being taken-down *it is carried* *to* *Cicero.* *He*

recitat perlectam in conventu
reads-aloud *(it) being read-through* *in* *an assembly*

militum, que afficit omnes maximâ
of the soldiers, *and* *affects* *all* *with the greatest*

lætitiâ. Tum fumi incendiorum videbantur
gladness. *Then* *the smokes* *of the fires* *were seen*

prŏcul: quæ res expulit omnem dubitationem
at-a-distance: *which* *thing* *banished* *all* *doubt*

adventûs legionum.
of the approach *of the legions.*

49 Galli, re cognitâ per exploratores,
The Gauls, *the thing* *being known* *by* *spies,*

relinquunt obsidionem; contendunt ad Cæsărem
leave (raise) *the siege;* *they set-out* *to* *Cæsar*

omnibus copiis: eæ erant circiter sexaginta
with all *(their) forces:* *those* *were* *about* *sixty*

millia armatorum. Cicero, facultate dătâ,
thousands *of armed (men).* *Cicero,* *the power* *being given,*

repetit Gallum ab eodem Verticone, quem
requests *the Gaul* *from* *the same* *Vertico,* *whom*

demonstravimus suprà, qui defěrat literas (plur.)
we have pointed-out *above,* *who* *may carry* *a letter*

ad Cæsărem. Admonet hunc, faciat
to *Cæsar.* *He admonishes* *him,* *(that) he may make*

ĭter cautè que diligenter. Perscribit in
the journey *cautiously* *and* *diligently.* *He writes* *in*

literis (plur.), "Hostes discessisse ab
the letter, *"The enemies* *to have departed* *from*

se,	himself,
que	and
omnem	all
multitudĭnem	the multitude
convertisse	to have turned
ad	to
ĕum."	him."
Quĭbus	Which
litĕris (plur.)	letter
allatis	being brought
Cæsări	to Cæsar
circĭter	about
mediâ	in middle
nocte,	night,
făcit	he makes
sŭos	his (men)
certiores;	more-sure
(informs them);	
que	and
confirmat	strengthens
ĕos	them
anĭmo	in mind
ad-dimicandum.	to-fighting.
Postĕro	In the following
die	day
mŏvet	he moves
castra (pl.)	the camp
primâ	in the first
luce,	light,
et	and
progressus	having advanced
circĭter	about
quatŭor	four
millĭa	thousands
passŭum,	of paces,
conspicatur	he beholds
multitudĭnem	the multitude
hostĭum	of the enemies
trans	beyond
magnam	a great
vallem	valley
et	and
rivum.	rivulet.
Erat	It was
res	a thing
magni	of great
perĭcŭli	danger
dimicare	to contend
cum	with
tantis	so-great
copĭis	forces
iniquo	in an unfavourable
lŏco.	place.
Tămen	However
quonĭam	since
sciebat	he did know
Cicerŏnem	Cicero
liberatum (-fuisse)	to have been delivered
obsidione	from the siege,
que	and
ĕo	therefore
existimabat	did think
remittendum	to-be-relaxed
omnino	altogether
de	of
celeritate,	speed,
consedit,	he sat-down (encamped),
et	and
communit	fortifies
castra (pl.)	the camp
lŏco	in a place
quàm	as
æquissĭmo	most-favourable
pŏtest:	he is able (as favourable as possible):
atque	and
etsi	although
hæc	these
ĕrant	were
exigŭa	small
per	by
se,	themselves,
vix	scarcely
septem	of seven
millĭum	thousands
homĭnum,	of men,
præsertim	especially
cum	with
nullis	no
impedimentis;	baggages:
tămen	yet
contrăhit	he contracts (them)
quàm-maxĭmè	as-much-as

LIBER V.

pŏtest,	ĕo	consilio,	ut	vĕnĭat	in
he is-able,	with that	design,	that	he may come	into

summam	contemptionem	hostĭbus.	Intĕrim
the highest	contempt	to the enemies.	Meantime

speculatorĭbus	dimissis	in	omnes	partes,
scouts	being sent	into	all	parts,

explŏrat	quo	itinĕre	posset	transire
he examines	by what	route	he might be-able	to cross

vallem	commodissĭmè.
the valley	most-conveniently.

50.
Eo	dĭe,	parvŭlis	equestrĭbus	prœlĭis
In that	day,	trifling	cavalry	battles

factis	ad	ăquam,	utrique	contĭnent	sese
being made	at	the water,	each	keep	themselves

sŭo	lŏco.	Galli,	quòd	exspectabant
in their place.		The Gauls (did so),	because	they did await

amplĭores	copĭas,	quæ	convenĕrant	nondum :
more-extensive	forces,	which	had assembled	not-yet :

Cæsar,	si	fortè	posset	elicĕre
Cæsar (did so),	if	perhaps	he might be-able	to entice

hostes	in	sŭum	lŏcum	citra	vallem
the enemies	into	his-own	place	on this-side	the valley

simulatione	timoris,	ut	contendĕret
by a pretence	of fear,	(so) that	he might contend

prœlĭo	pro	castris (pl.) :	si	posset	non
in battle	before	the camp	if	he might be-able	not

efficĕre	id,	ut,	itinerĭbus	exploratis,
to effect	that,	that,	the routes	being examined,

transiret	vallem	que	rivum	cum	minore
he might cross	the valley	and	rivulet	with	less

pericŭlo.	Primâ	luce,	equitatus	hostĭum
danger.	In the first	light,	the cavalry	of the enemies

accedit	ad	castra (pl.),	que	committit	prœlĭum
approaches	to	the camp,	and	engages	battle

cum	nostris	equitĭbus.	Cæsar	consultò	jŭbet
with	our	cavalry.	Cæsar	designedly	orders

equĭtes	cedĕre	que	recipĕre	se	in
the cavalry	*to yield*	*and*	*to betake*	*themselves*	*into*
castra (pl.),		sĭmul	jŭbet		castra (pl.)
the camp,		*at-the-same-time*	*he orders*		*the camp*
munīri	altiore	vallo	ex		omnĭbus
to be fortified	*with a higher*	*rampart*	*from*		*all*
partĭbus,	que	portas	obstrŭi,		atque
parts (sides),	*and*	*the gates*	*to be barricaded,*		*and*
concursari	quàm-maxĭmè		in	iis	rebus
to be hurried	*as-much-as-possible*		*in*	*those*	*things*
administrandis,	et	ăgi	cum		simulatione
to-be-managed,	*and*	*to be acted*	*with*		*a pretence*
timoris.					
of fear.					

51.

Omnĭbus	quĭbus	rebus	hostes	invitati
By all	*which*	*things*	*the enemies*	*being invited*
transducunt		copias,	que constitŭunt	aciem
lead-over		*(their) forces,*	*and station*	*(their) line*
iniquo	lŏco.	Verò	nostris	etĭam
in an unfavourable	*place.*	*But*	*our (men)*	*also*
deductis	de	vallo,	accedunt	propiùs;
being led-down	*from*	*the rampart,*	*they approach*	*nearer ;*
et	conjicĭunt	tela	ex omnĭbus	partĭbus
and	*throw*	*(their) darts*	*from all*	*parts*
intra	munitionem:	que præconĭbus	circummissis,
within	*the fortification:*	*and criers*	*being sent-about,*
jŭbent	pronuntiari;	"Seu	quis	Gallus
they order (it)	*to be declared ;*	*" Whether*	*any*	*Gaul*
seu	Romanus	vĕlit	transire	ad	se
or	*Roman*	*may will*	*to pass-over*	*to*	*themselves*
ante	tertiam	horam,	licere	sĭne	perĭcŭlo:
before	*the third*	*hour,*	*to-be-lawful*	*without*	*danger :*
post	id	tempus,	potestatem	non	fŏre:"
after	*that*	*time,*	*the power*	*not*	*to-be-about-to-be :"*
ac	contempserunt	nostros	sic,	ut,	portis
and	*they despised*	*our (men)*	*so,*	*that,*	*the gates*

LIBER V.

obstructis	in	speciem	singŭlis	ordinĭbus
being barricaded	*into*	*appearance*	*with single*	*rows*

cespĭtum,	quòd	videbantur	non	posse
of turfs,	*because*	*they did seem*	*not*	*to be-able*

introrumpĕre	ĕâ,	alii	incipĕrent (imp. subj.)
to burst-into	*by that (way),*	*others*	*did begin*

scandĕre	vallum	mănu,	alii
to climb	*the rampart*	*by hand (by force),*	*others*

complere	fossas.	Tunc	Cæsar,	eruptione
to fill-up	*the ditches.*	*Then*	*Cæsar,*	*a sally*

factâ	omnĭbus	portis	que	equitatu
being made	*from all*	*the gates*	*and*	*the cavalry*

emisso,	dat	hostes	celerĭter	in
being sent-out,	*gives (puts)*	*the enemies*	*quickly*	*into*

fŭgam;	sic	ut	nemo	omnino	resistĕret (imp. subj.)
flight;	*so*	*that*	*no-one*	*at-all*	*did resist*

caussâ	pugnandi,	que	occidit	magnum
by cause (for the sake)	*of fighting,*	*and*	*he slew*	*a great*

numĕrum	ex	his,	atque	exŭit	omnes
number	*out-of*	*these,*	*and*	*stripped*	*all*

armis.
from (their) arms.

52.
Verĭtus	prosĕqui	longĭùs,	quòd
Having feared	*to pursue (them)*	*farther,*	*because*

silvæ	que	paludes	intercedebant;	nĕque	videbat
woods	*and*	*marshes*	*did intervene;*	*neither*	*did he see*

lŏcum	relinqui	parvŭlo	detrimento	illorum;
the place	*to be left*	*with trifling*	*loss*	*of them;*

omnĭbus	sŭis	copĭis	incolumĭbus,	pervĕnit
all	*his*	*forces*	*(being) safe,*	*he arrives*

eodem	die	ad	Ciceronem.	Admiratur	turres,
in the same	*day*	*to*	*Cicero.*	*He admires*	*the towers,*

testudĭnes,	que	munitiones	hostium,	institutas.
mantelets,	*and*	*fortifications*	*of the enemies,*	*prepared.*

Legione	productâ,	cognoscit	quemque
The legion	*being drawn-out,*	*he knows (observes)*	*every*

DE BELLO GALLICO.

decímum	mílitem	non	relictum-esse	sine
tenth	soldier	not	to have been left	without

vulnĕre.	Ex	omníbus	his	rebus,	judicat,
a wound	Out-of	all	these	things,	he judges,

cum	quanto	perícŭlo,	et	cum	quamâ	virtute,
with	how-great	danger,	and	with	how-great	valour,

res	administratæ-sint (perf. subj.).	Collaudat
affairs	were managed.	He praises

Cicerōnem	pro	merĭto	ejus,	que
Cicero	according-to	the desert	of him,	and

legiōnem:	appellat	sigillatim	centuriones	que
the legion:	he addresses	individually	the centurions	and

tribunos	milítum,	quorum	virtutem	cognŏvĕrat
tribunes	of soldiers,	whose	valour	he had known

fuisse	egregĭam	testimonĭo	Ciceronis.
to have been	excellent	by the testimony	of Cicero.

Cognoscit	certiùs	de	casu	Sabini
He knows (learns)	more-surely	of	the calamity	of Sabinus

et	Cottæ	ex	captivis.	Postĕro	die,
and	of Cotta	from	the prisoners.	On the following	day,

concione	habĭtâ,	proponit	rem
an assembly	being held,	he sets-before (them)	the affair

gestam:	consolatur	et	confirmat	milites:
carried-on:	he consoles	and	encourages	the soldiers:

dŏcet	detrimentum,	quod
he teaches (shows them)	the loss,	which

acceptum-sit (perf. subj.)	culpâ	et	temeritate
has-been-received	by the fault	and	rashness

legati,	ferendum	æquiore	animo
of the lieutenant,	(was) to-be-borne	with more-even	mind

hoc;	quòd	beneficio
from this (on this account);	because	by the kindness

immortalĭum	Deorum,	et	virtute	eorum,
of the immortal	Gods,	and	by the valour	of them,

incommŏdo	expiato,	nĕque	diutĭna
the disadvantage	being atoned-for,	neither	a lasting

LIBER V

lætatio	relinquator (pres. subj.)	hostibus,	neque
rejoicing	*is left*	*to the enemies,*	*nor*
longior	dolor	ipsis.	
longer	*grief*	*to themselves.*	

53. Interim fama de victoriâ Cæsaris
    Meantime the report of the victory of Cæsar

perfertur ad Labienum per Rhemos incredibili
is carried to Labienus by the Rhemi with incredible

celeritate; ut, quum abesset (imp.
expedition; (so) that, .when (though) he was distant

subj.) quinquaginta millia passuum ab
       fifty thousands of paces from

hibernis Ciceronis, que Cæsar pervenisset
the winter-quarters of Cicero, and Cæsar had arrived

(plup. subj.) eò post nonam horam diei,
              thither after the ninth hour of the day,

clamor oriretur (imp. subj.) ante mediam noctem
a shout did arise before middle night

ad portas castrorum (pl.); quo clamore
at the gates of the camp; by which shout

significatio victoriæ que gratulatio fieret
an indication of victory and congratulation was made

(imp. subj.) Labieno ab Rhemis. Hâc famâ
             to Labienus by the Rhemi. This report

perlatâ ad Treviros, Indutiomarus, qui
being carried to the Treviri, Indutiomarus, who

decreverat oppugnare castra (pl.) Labieni
had resolved to assault the camp of Labienus

postero die, profugit noctu que reducit
on the following day, flees by night and leads-back

omnes copias in Treviros. Cæsar remittit
all (his) forces unto the Treviri. Cæsar sends-back

Fabium cum legione in sua hiberna.
Fabius with the legion into their winter-quarters.

Ipse constituit hiemare trinis hibernis
Himself resolved to winter in triple winter-quarters

cum tribus legionibus circum Samarobrivam: et	with three legions about Samarobriva: and
quòd tanti motus Galliæ exstitĕrant	because so-great commotions of Gaul had existed
ipse decrevit manere totam hiĕmem ac	himself determined to remain the whole winter at
exercitum. Nam, illo incommŏdo de morte	the army. For, that disadvantage about the death
Sabini perlato, fērè omnes	of Sabinus being carried-through (them), nearly all
civitates Galliæ consultabant de bello:	the states of Gaul did deliberate about war:
dimittebant nuntios que legationes in omnes	they did dismiss messengers and embassies into all
partes; et explorabant, quid consilii reliqui	parts; and did examine, what of counsel the rest
capĕrent, atque unde initĭum belli	might take, and whence a beginning of war
fiĕret; que habebant nocturna concilia	might be made; and they did hold nightly assemblies
in desertis locis: nĕque ullum tempus fĕrè	in desert places: neither any time nearly
totius hiĕmis intercessit sine sollicitudĭne	of the whole winter intervened without the anxiety
Cæsăris, quin accipĕret (imp. subj.) aliquem	of Cæsar, but-that he did receive some
nuntĭum de conciliis et motu	messenger (message) about the assemblies and disturbance
Gallorum. In his factus-est certĭor	of the Gauls. In (among) these he was made more-sure
ab Lucio Roscio legato, quem	(was informed) by Lucius Roscius the lieutenant, whom
præfecĕrat decĭmæ-tertĭæ legioni, "Magnas	he had placed-over to the thirteenth legion, "Great
copias Gallorum earum civitatum, quæ appellantur	forces of the Gauls of those states, which are called

Armorĭcæ, convenisse caussâ suī
Armoric, to have assembled by cause (for the purpose) *of himself*

oppugnandi; něque abfuisse
to-be-assaulted (of attacking him); *nor to have been-distant*

longĭus octo millĭa passŭum ab sŭis
farther (than) *eight thousands of paces from his*

hibernis; sed, nuntio allato de
winter-quarters; but, a message being brought about

victorĭâ Cæsăris, discessisse, aděò ut
the victory of Cæsar, to have departed, so that (their)

discessus videretur (imp. subj.) simĭlis fŭgæ.
departure did seem like to a flight.

54. At Cæsar, princĭpĭbus cujusque civitatis
But Cæsar, the chiefs of each state

vocatis ad se, tenŭit magnam partem
being called to himself, kept a great part

Gallĭæ in officĭo, aliàs territando,
of Gaul in duty, otherwise (one time) *by alarming,*

quum denuntiaret (imp. subj.), se scire quæ
when he did announce, himself to know what

fĭĕrent (imp. subj.), aliàs
(things) *were done, otherwise* (another time)

cohortando. Tămen Senŏnes, quæ est civĭtas
by encouraging. However the Senones, which is a state

in-primis firma, et magnæ auctoritatis inter
particularly strong, and of great authority among

Gallos, conati (-sunt) interficĕre publĭco consilĭo
the Gauls, attempted to slay by public counsel

Cavarinum, quem Cæsar constituĕrat regem
Cavarinus, whom Cæsar had appointed king

ăpud ĕos, (cujus frater Moritasgus,
at (among) *them,* (whose *brother Moritasgus,*

adventu Cæsăris in Gallĭam, que cujus
at the approach of Cæsar into Gaul, and whose

majores obtinuĕrant regnum;) quum
ancestors had obtained kingdom (royal power);) *when*

ille	præsensisset (pluperf. subj.)	ac	profugisset
he	had previously-understood	and	had escaped,

(pluperf. subj.),	insecuti	usque	ad
	having pursued (him)	until	to

fines,	expulerunt	dŏmo	que
the borders,	they expelled (him)	from home	and

regno;	et	legatis	missis	ad	Cæsărem
the kingdom;	and	ambassadors	being sent	to	Cæsar

caussâ		satisfaciendi,	quum
by cause (for the purpose)		of making-satisfaction,	when

is	jussisset (pluperf. subj.)	omnem	senatum
he	had ordered	all	(their) senate

venire	ad	se,	fuerunt	non	audientes	dicto:
to come	to	himself,	they were	not	hearing	to word

		valŭit	tantum
(obedient to the order):		it availed	so-much (had such an

	ăpud	barbăros	homĭnes,	alĭquos
effect)	at (among)	barbarian	men,	some (any)

princĭpes	belli	inferendi	repertos-esse;
chiefs	of war	to-be-brought-on	to have been found;

que	attŭlit	tantam	commutationem	voluntatum
and	it brought	so-great	a change	of wills

omnĭbus,	ut	fĕrè	nulla	civĭtas	fuĕrit
to all,	that	nearly	no	state	may have been

non	suspecta	nobis,	præter	Ædŭos	et
not	suspected	to (by) us,	except	the Ædui	and

Rhemos,	quos	Cæsar	semper	habŭit	præcipŭo
Rhemi,	whom	Cæsar	always	had	in particular

honore,	altĕros		pro	vetĕrè	ac
honour,	the others (the former)		for	ancient	and

perpetŭâ	fĭde	erga	Romanum	popŭlum;	altĕros
constant	faith	toward	the Roman	people;	the others

	pro	recentĭbus	officĭis	Gallĭci
(the latter)	for	recent	duties	of the Gallic

belli:	que	scĭo	haud,	ne	id	sit
war:	and	I know	not,	whether	that	may be

LIBER V.

mirandum	adeò,	cùm	
to-be-wondered-at	so (much),	when (as well)	from

compluribus	aliis	caussis,	tum	maximè	quòd
many	other	causes,	then (as)	chiefly	because

	qui	præferebantur	omnibus	gentibus
(those)	who	were preferred	to all	nations

virtute	belli,	dolebant	gravissimè,	se
in bravery	of war,	did grieve	most-severely,	themselves

deperdidisse	tantum	opinionis	ejus,
to have lost	so-much	of the opinion (reputation)	of it,

ut	perferrent	imperia	Romani
that	they should endure	the commands	of the Roman

populi.
people.

55. | Verò | Treviri | atque | Indutiomarus |
|---|---|---|---|
| But | the Treviri | and | Indutiomarus |

intermiserunt	nullum	tempus	totius	hiemis,
omitted	no	time	of the whole	winter,

quin	mittěrent	legatos	·trans	Rhenum ;
but-that	they might send	ambassadors	across	the Rhine ;

sollicitarent	civitates ;	pollicerentur	pecunias ;
they might solicit	the states ;	they might-promise	moneys :

dicerent,	magnâ	parte	nostri	exercitûs
they might say,	a great	part	of our	army

interfectâ,	minorem	partem	multò	superesse.
having been slain,	a less	part	by-much	to remain.'

Tamen	neque	potuit	persuaderi	ulli
However	neither	it was-able	to be persuaded	to any

civitati	Germanorum,	ut	transiret	Rhenum ;
state	of the Germans,	that	it should cross	the Rhine ;

quum	dicerent (imp. subj.)	"se	expertos
when	they did say	"themselves	·having tried

bis,	bello	Ariovisti,	et	transitu
twice,	in the war	of Ariovistus,	and	in the crossing

Tenchtherorum,	non	esse	tentaturos	fortunam
of the Tenchtheri,	not	to be	about-to-try	fortune

amplius."   Indutiomărus   lapsus
more."   *Indutiomarus   having slipped* (been disappointed)

hâc   spe,   nihĭlo-mĭnùs   cœpit   cogĕre   copĭas,
in this hope,   nevertheless   began   to collect   forces,

exigĕre   à   finitĭmis,   parare
to demand (them) from   the neighbouring (states),   to procure

ĕquos,   allicĕre   exŭles   que   damnatos   ad
horses,   to entice   exiles   and   condemned (persons)   to

se   magnis   præmĭis   totâ   Galliâ :   ac
himself   by great   rewards   in the whole   Gaul :   and

comparavĕrat   jam   tantam   auctoritatem   sĭbi
he had procured now   so-great   authority   for himself

ŭs   rebus   in   Galliâ,   ut   legationes
by those   things   in   Gaul,   that   embassies

concurrĕrent (imp. subj.)   undĭque   ad   ĕum ;
did run-together   from-every-side   to   him ;

petĕrent (imp. subj.)   gratĭam   atque   amicitĭam
did seek   (his) favour   and   friendship

publĭcè   que   privatim.
publicly   and   privately.

56.   Ubi   intellexit   veniri
     When   he understood (it)   to be come (that they came)

ultrò   ad   se ;   Senŏnes   que   Carnutes
spontaneously   to   himself ;   the Senones   and   Carnutes

instigatos   consciently   facinŏris   ex   altĕrâ
(to be) instigated   by a consciousness   of crime   from   the other

         parte ;   Nervĭos   que   Atuatĭcos   parare
(the one) part ;   the Nervii   and   Atuatici   to prepare

bellum   Romanis   altĕrâ   nĕque   copĭas
war   for the Romans   from the other (side) ;   neither   forces

voluntariorum   defŏre   sĭbi,   si
of volunteers   to be about-to-be-wanting   to himself,   if

cœpisset (plup. subj.)   progrĕdi   ex   sŭis   finĭbus ;
he had begun   to advance   out-of   his-own   borders ;

indicit   armatum   concilĭum.   Hoc,   more
he proclaims   an armed   council.   This,   by the custom

Gallorum,	of the Gauls,
est	is
initium	a commencement
belli;	of war;
quò	whither
omnes	all
puberes	full-grown (persons)
coguntur	are compelled
convenire	to assemble
armati,	armed,
communi	by a common (general)
lege:	law:
et	and
qui	(he) who
ex	out-of
iis	them
venit	comes
novissimus,	newest (last),
affectus	being affected (punished)
omnibus	with all
cruciatibus	tortures
necatur	is put-to-death
in	in
conspectu	sight
multitudinis.	of the multitude.
In	In
eo	that
concilio	council
curat	he takes-care
Cingetorigem,	Cingetorix,
principem	the chief
alterius	of the other
factionis,	party,
suum	his-own
generum,	son-in-law,
judicandum	to-be-judged
hostem	an enemy
(quem	(whom
demonstravimus	we have shown
suprà,	above,
secutum	having followed
fidem	the faith
Cæsaris,	of Cæsar,
non	not
discessisse	to have departed
ab	from
eo),	him),
que	and
publicat	he confiscates
bona	the goods
ejus.	of him.
His	These
rebus	things
confectis,	being finished,
pronunciat	he declares
in	in
concilio	the council
se	himself
accersitum (-esse)	to have been sent-for
à	by
Senonibus	the Senones
et	and
Carnutibus,	Carnutes,
que	and
compluribus	very-many
aliis	other
civitatibus	states
Galliæ:	of Gaul.
facturum (-esse)	to be about-to-make
iter	(his) march
huc	hither
per	through
fines	the territories
Rhemorum,	of the Rhemi,
que	and
populaturum	about-to-ravage
agros	the lands
eorum;	of them;
ac	and
oppugnaturum	about-to-assault
castra (pl.)	the camp
Labieni	of Labienus
priùs-quàm	before-that
faciat	he may do
id:	that:
que	and
præcipit,	he prescribes,
quæ	what
velit	(things) he may will
fieri.	to be done.

57. | Labienus | timebat | nĭhil | de | sŭo
| Labienus | did fear | nothing | about | his-own

perĭcŭlo ac legionis, quum contineret
danger *and* *(that) of the legion,* *when* *he might keep*

sese castris (pl.) munitissĭmis et naturâ
himself *in a camp* *most-fortified* *both* *by the nature*

lŏci, et mănu ; sed cogitabat
of the place, *and* *by hand* (art); *but* *he did think*

ne-dimittĕret quam occasionem rĕi
he should not-omit *any* *opportunity* *of a thing*

gerendæ bĕnè. Ităque oratione Indutiomări,
to-be-carried-on well. *Therefore* *the speech of Indutiomarus,*

quam habuĕrat in concilĭo, cognĭtâ à
which *he had held* *in* *the council,* *being known* *from*

Cingetorĭge atque propinquis ejus, mittit
Cingetorix *and* *the relations* *of him,* *he sends*

nuntĭos ad finitĭmas civitates, que
messengers *to* *the neighbouring* *states,* *and*

convŏcat equĭtes undĭque. Dicit
calls-together *cavalry* *from-every-side.* *He says* (appoints)

certam dĭem conveniendi ĭis. Intĕrim
a certain *day* *of meeting* *for them.* *Meantime*

Indutiomărus vagabatur prŏpè quotidĭe cum
Indutiomarus *did wander* (hover) *almost* *daily* *with*

omni equitatu sub castris (pl.) ejus :
all *(his) cavalry* *under* (near) *the camp* *of him:*

aliàs ut cognoscĕret sĭtum
otherwise (one time) *that* *he might know* (learn) *the situation*

castrorum (pl.); aliàs caussâ
of the camp ; *otherwise* (another time) *by cause* (for

colloquendi aut territandi: omnes
the purpose) *of conferring* *or* *of alarming:* *all*

equĭtes plerumque conjiciebant tela intra
(his) cavalry *generally* *did hurl* *darts* *within*

vallum. Labienus continebant sŭos intra
the rampart. *Labienus* *did keep* *his (men)* *within*

munitiones,	que	augebat	opinionem	timoris
the fortifications,	*and*	*did increase*	*the supposition*	*of fear*

quibuscunque	rebus	poterat.
by whatsoever	*things*	*he was-able.*

58.
Quum	Indutiomarus	accederet (imp. subj.)
When	*Indutiomarus*	*did approach*

indies	ad	castra (pl.)	majore	contemptione,
daily	*to*	*the camp*	*with greater*	*contempt,*

equitibus	omnium	finitimarum	civitatum,	quos
the cavalry	*of all*	*the neighbouring*	*states,*	*which*

curaverat	accersendos,	intromissis	unâ
he had taken-care	*to-be-sent-for,*	*being let-in*	*in one*

nocte,	continuit	omnes	suos	custodiis	intra
night,	*he kept*	*all*	*his (men)*	*in guards*	*within*

castra (pl.)	tantâ	diligentiâ,	ut	ea	res
the camp	*with so-great*	*diligence,*	*that*	*that*	*thing*

posset	enuntiari	nullâ	ratione,	aut	perferri
might be-able	*to be told*	*by no*	*means,*	*or*	*to be carried*

ad	Treviros.	Interim,	ex	quotidianâ
to	*the Treviri.*	*Meantime,*	*according-to*	*daily*

consuetudine,	Indutiomarus	accedit	ad	castra (pl.),
custom,	*Indutiomarus*	*approaches*	*to*	*the camp,*

atque	consumit	magnam	partem	diei	ibi.
and	*wastes*	*a great*	*part*	*of the day*	*there.*

Equites	conjiciunt	tela,	et	evocant	nostros
(His) cavalry	*hurl*	*darts,*	*and*	*call-out*	*our*

	ad	pugnam	magnâ	contumeliâ	verborum.
(men)	*to*	*battle*	*with great*	*insult*	*of words.*

Nullo	responso	dato	à	castris (pl.),	ubi
No	*answer*	*being given*	*from*	*the camp,*	*when*

visum-est,	discedunt	dispersi	ac	dissipati
it seemed (proper),	*they depart*	*dispersed*	*and*	*scattered*

sub		vesperum.	Labienus	subitò
under (a little before)		*evening.*	*Labienus*	*suddenly*

emittit	omnem	equitatum	duabus	portis :
sends-forth	*all*	*the cavalry*	*from two*	*gates ;*

præcipit	atque	interdicit,	hostĭbus	perterrĭtis,
he prescribes	and	forbids,	the enemies	being dismayed,

atque	conjectis	in	fŭgam,	(quod videbat
and	thrown	into	flight,	(which he did see

fŏre,	sicut	accĭdit)	omnes	petĕrent
to be about-to-be,	so-as	it happened)	all	should seek

	Indutiomărum	unum,	neu̇	quis
(attack)	Indutiomarus	one (alone),	nor	any (one)

vulneraret	quemquam,	priŭs	quàm	videret
should wound	any-one,	before	than	he should see

illum	interfectum:	quòd	nolĕbat illum,
him	killed:	because	he was-unwilling him,

nactum	spatĭum	mŏrâ	reliquorum,	effugĕre.
having got	space	by the delay	of the rest,	to escape.

Proponit	magna	præmĭa	iis,	qui
He proposes	great	rewards	to those,	who

occidĕrint:	submittit	cohortes	subsidĭo
should have killed (him):	he sends-up	cohorts	for aid

equitĭbus.	Fortuna	compròbat	consilĭum
to the cavalry.	Fortune	approves (favours)	the plan

homĭnis;	et quum	omnes	petĕrent (imp. subj.)
of the man;	and when	all	did seek

unum,	Indutiomărus	deprehensus	in vădo	ipso
the one,	Indutiomarus	being caught	in the ford	itself

flumĭnis	interficĭtur,	que	căput	ejus
of the river	is slain,	and	the head	of him

refĕrtur	in castra (pl.).	Equĭtes	redeuntes
is carried-back	into the camp.	The cavalry	returning

consectantur	atque	occĭdunt,	quos possunt.
pursue	and	slay (those),	whom they can.

Hâc	re	cognĭtâ,	omnes copĭæ
This	thing	being known,	all the forces

Eburonum	et Nerviorum,	quæ	convenĕrant,
of the Eburones	and of the Nervii,	which	had assembled,

discedunt;	que	paullò post	id factum,	Cæsar
depart;	and	a little after	that being done,	Cæsar

habŭit	Gallĭam	quietiorem.
had	Gaul	more-tranquil.

LIBER SEXTUS
Book Sixth

The sixth book begins with a description of Caesar's rapid and successful campaign against the Senones and Carnutes. The Treviri attack Labienus who conquers them in battle after luring them by a stratagem into an unfavorable place. Caesar builds another bridge across the Rhine. He enters Germany and receives the surrender of the Ubii. He learns that the Suevi have taken refuge in the Bacenis forest. Caesar makes a digression in his narrative and compares the Gauls and Germans in a long descriptive passage. He returns to Gaul, having demolished the farther end of the bridge and fortified the Gallic approach to it. He marches in pursuit of Ambiorix into the Ardennes forest. Meantime the Sugambri cross the Rhine, attack Cicero and return. During this period the Eburones are being plundered and exterminated by a general proclamation as punishment for their treachery of the previous year. Ambiorix is pursued continuously but with a few horsemen succeeds in evading capture. After condemning Acco for the conspiracy of the Senones and Carnutes, Caesar quarters the legions for winter and departs for Italy to hold assemblies.

1. Cæsar de multis causis expectans majorem
Caesar for many reasons expecting (a) greater

motum Galliæ instituit habere delectum,
commotion of Gaul determines to hold a levy

per legatos, M. Silanum, C. Antistium Reginum,
through (his) lieutenants, M. Silanus, C. Antistius Reginus,

T. Sextium. Simul pĕtit ab Cneio
(and) T. Sextius. At the same time he requests from Cneius

Pompeio, proconsŭle, quoniam ipse manēret
Pompey, proconsul, since he (himself) was remaining

ad urbem cum imperio, causā
near the city with (military) command, for the sake of

rei publĭcæ, jubēret quos
the public business, (that) he should order (those) whom

rogavisset (pl. perf. subj.) sacramento consul ex
he had enrolled by oath (as) consul from

Cisalpinā	Galliā	convenire	ad	signa	et
Cisalpine	*Gaul*	*to assemble*	*to*	*the standards*	*and*

proficisci	ad se;	existĭmans		interesse	magni
march	*to him;*	*deeming*	*(it)*	*to be of great importance*	

ad	opinionem	Galliæ	
regarding	*the opinion*	*of Gaul*	*(which they might have)*

etĭam	in	relĭquum	tempus	
also	*for*	*remaining [future]*	*time*	*(that the)*

facultates	Italiæ	videri	tantas	ut	si quid
resources	*of Italy*	*to [should] seem*	*so great*	*that*	*if any*

(neut.)	detrimenti	acceptum esset	in bello,
	(of) detriment [harm]	*should have been received*	*in war,*

id	non modo	posset	sarciri	brĕvi tempŏre,	sed
this	*not only*	*could*	*be repaired*	*in a short time,*	*but*

posset	etĭam	augēri[1]	majoribus	copiis.	Quod
could	*also*	*be supplemented*	*by greater*	*forces.*	*Which*

cum	Pompeius	tribuisset	et	rei publicæ	et
when	*Pompey*	*had granted*	*both*	*for the public interest*	*and*

amicitiæ,	delectu	celeriter	confecto
for (his) friendship,	*a levy*	*quickly*	*having been made*

per	sŭos,	tribus	legionibus	et
through	*his (lieutenants),*	*three*	*legions*	*both*

constitutis	et	adductis	ante	hiemem	ex-
having been raised	*and*	*brought to (him)*	*before*	*the winter*	*had*

actum,	et	numero	earum cohortium,	quas	amisĕrat
passed;	*and*	*the number*	*of these cohorts,*	*which*	*he had lost*

cum	Q. Titurio,	duplicato,	docuit	et
under	*Q. Titurius,*	*having been doubled,*	*he showed*	*both*

celeritate	et	copiis,	quid	disciplīna
by (his) promptness	*and*	*by (his) forces,*	*what*	*the discipline*

atque	opes	Romani	populi	posset.
and	*resources*	*of the Roman*	*people*	*were able (to do).*

2. Indutiomaro	interfecto	ut	docuimus,
Indutiomarus	*having been slain*	*as*	*we have shown,*

imperium	defertur	a Treviris	ad ejus	propinquos.
the government	*is conferred*	*by the Treviri*	*on his*	*relations.*

Illi	non	desistunt	sollicitare	finitimos
They (do)	*not*	*cease*	*to incite (to warfare)*	*the neighboring*

3] LIBER VI. 315

Germanos et pollicēri pecuniam. Cum possent non
Germans and to promise money. When they could not

impetrare ab proximis,[2] tentant ulteriores.[3]
obtain (this) from (those) nearest they try the more remote.

Nonnullis civitatibus inventis, con-
Some states having been found (compliant), they

firmant[4] jurejurando inter se, que
pledge (allegiance) by an oath among themselves, and

cavent obsidibus de pecuniā; adjungunt sibi
give security by hostages for the money; they unite to themselves

Ambiorigem societate et fœdere. Quibus
Ambiorix by alliance and by treaty. Which [These]

rebus cognitis, cum Cæsar vidēret bellum
things having been learned, when Caesar perceived war

parari[5] undique; Nervios, Aduatucos
to be [was] prepared on all sides, (that) the Nervii, the Aduatuci

ac Menapios, omnibus cisrhenanis Germanis
and the Menapii, all the hither-Rhine Germans

adjunctis, esse in armis; Senones non
having been added, were in arms; (that)the Senones (did)not

venire ad imperatum, et communicare
come to (his) command, and (that) they were exchanging

consilia cum Carnutibus que finitimis civitatibus;
counsel with the Carnutes and neighboring states;

Germanos sollicitari a Treviris crebris
(that) the Germans were invited by the Treviri in frequent

legationibus; putavit cogitandum sibi
embassies; he thought to [it must] be considered by himself

maturius de bello.
[*he must consider*] *earlier regarding the war.*

3. Itaque hieme nondum confectā,
Therefore the winter not yet having been completed,

quattuor proximis legionibus coactis,
the four nearest legions having been assembled,

contendit improviso in fines Nerviorum; et
he marched suddenly into the territories of the Nervii; and

prius quam illi aut possent convenire, aut
before (that) they either could assemble, or

profugĕre,	magno	numero	pecoris	atque	hominum
escape	*a great*	*number*	*of cattle*	*and*	*of men*

capto,	atque	ĕā	prædā	concessā
having been captured	*and*	*this*	*booty*	*having been given up*

militibus,	que	agris	vastatis,	coegit
to the soldiers,	*and*	*(their) fields*	*having been laid waste,*	*he forced*

(them)	venire	in	deditionem,	atque	dare
(them)	*to come*	*into*	*a surrender,*	*and*	*to give*

obsides	sibi.	Eo negotio	celeriter
hostages	*to himself.*	*This business [campaign]*	*having been quickly*

confecto,	reduxit	rursus	legiones	in	hiberna.
performed,	*he led back*	*again*	*the legions*	*into*	*winter quarters.*

Concilio	Galliæ	indicto	primo	vere,	ut
A council	*of Gaul*	*having been called*	*in early*	*spring,*	*as*

instituĕrat,	cum	reliqui	præter	Senones,
he had determined,	*since*	*the rest*	*except*	*the Senones,*

Carnutes	que	Treviros	venissent,	arbitratus
the Carnutes	*and*	*Treviri*	*had come,*	*having judged (that)*

hoc	esse	initium	belli	ac	defectionis,
this	*to be [was]*	*the beginning*	*of war*	*and*	*of revolt,*

ut	videretur	postponĕre	omnia,	transfert
although	*he might seem*	*to postpone*	*everything,*	*he transfers*

concilium	in	Lutetiam Parisiorum.	Hi	erant
the council	*to*	*Lutetia of the Parisii (Paris).*	*These*	*were*

confines	Senonibus,	que	memoriā	patrum
neighbors	*to the Senones,*	*and*	*in the memory*	*of the fathers*

conjunxĕrant[6]	civitatem,	sed	existimabantur
had united	*their state (with them),*	*but*	*they were thought*

abfuisse	ab	hoc	concilio.	Hāc	re
to have been absent	*from*	*this*	*council.*	*This*	*thing*

pronuntiatā	pro	suggestu,	proficiscitur
having been proclaimed	*from*	*the tribunal,*	*he marches*

eodem	die	cum	legionibus	in
on the same	*day*	*with*	*the legions*	*into (the country of)*

Senones,	que	pervenit	eo	magnis	itineribus.
the Senones,	*and*	*arrives*	*there*	*by long [forced]*	*marches.*

4. | Ejus | adventu | cognito, | Acco, | qui | fuerat |
|---|---|---|---|---|---|
| *His* | *arrival* | *having been learned,* | *Acco,* | *who* | *had been* |

LIBER VI.

princeps	ejus	concilii	jubet	multitudinem	convenire
the leader	of this	council	orders	the people	to assemble

in	oppida.	Nuntiatur	conantibus,	
into	the towns.	It is announced	to (those) attempting,	(to assemble)

prius quam	id	posset	effici,	Romanos
before	it	could	be accomplished,	(that) the Romans

adesse.	Necessario	desistunt	sententiā,	que
to have [had] come.	Necessarily	they desist	from the design,	and

mittunt	legatos	ad Cæsarem	causā	deprecandi;[7]
send	ambassadors	to Cæsar	for purpose	of interceding;

adeunt	per	Æduos,	in	fide
they approach (him)	through	the Ædui,	under	the protection

quorum	civitas	erat	antiquitus.	Æduis
of whom	(their) state	was	formerly.	The Ædui

petentibus,	Cæsar	libenter	dat	veniam,	que	accipit
petitioning,	Cæsar	readily	gives	pardon,	and	receives

excusationem,	quod	arbitrabatur	æstivum
(their) excuse,	because	he judged	(that) the summer

tempus	esse	instantis	belli	non
time	to be [was] (one)	of [for] impending	war	(and) not

quæstionis.	Centum	obsidibus	imperatis,
of [for] investigation.	A hundred	hostages	having been ordered

tradit	hos	Æduis	custodiendos.	Carnutes
he delivers	these	to the Ædui	to be guarded.	The Carnutes

mittunt	legatos	que	obsides	eodem,
send	ambassadors	and	hostages	to the same place,

usi	Remis	deprecatoribus,	in	clientelā
having made use of the Remi as intercessors,	under the protection

quorum	erant;	ferunt	eadem	responsa.
of whom	they were;	they carry (back)	the same	answers.

Cæsar	peragit	concilium,	que	imperat	equites
Cæsar	holds	the council,	and	orders	horsemen

civitatibus (dat).
(of) the states.

5. Hāc	parte	Galliæ	pacatā,	insistit
This	part	of Gaul	having been pacified,	he applies

	totus	et	mente	et	animo	in bellum
(himself)	altogether	both	in mind	and	soul	to the war

| Trevirorum | et | Ambiorigis. | Jubet | Cavarinum |
| of the Treviri | and | Ambiorix. | He orders | Cavarinus |

| proficisi | secum | cum | equitatu | Senonum, | ne | quis |
| to march | with him | with | the cavalry | of the Senones, | lest | any |

| motus | civitatis | existat | aut | ex | hujus |
| commotion | of the state | may arise | either | from | his |

| iracundiā, | aut | ex | ĕo | odio, | quod | meruĕrat. |
| irascibility, | or | from | that | hatred, | which | he had merited. |

| His | rebus | constitutis, | quod | habebat | pro |
| These | things | having been settled, | because | he regarded (it) | for |

| | explorato | Ambiorigem | non esse certaturum[8] |
| [as] | well known | (that) Ambiorix | would not contend |

| prœlio, | circumspiciebat | animo | ejus | reliqua | consilia. |
| in battle, | he considered | in mind | his | other | plans. |

| Menapii | erant propinqui | finibus | Eburonum, |
| The Menapii | were neighboring | to the frontiers | of the Eburones, |

| muniti | perpetuis | paludibus que silvis; | qui uni | ex |
| protected | by continuous | marshes and woods; | who alone | from |

| Galliā | nunquam | miserant | legatos | ad | Cæsarem |
| Gaul | never | had sent | ambassadors | to | Cæsar |

| de | pace; | sciebat | hospitium | esse |
| concerning | peace; | he knew (that) | hospitality | was [existed] |

| cum | iis | | Ambiorigi (dat.); | item |
| with [between] | them | (and) | Ambiorix; | also |

| cognoverat | venisse | in | amicitiam |
| he had discovered | (that he) to have [had] come | into | friendship |

| Germanis | per | Treviros. | Existimabat |
| to [with] the Germans | through | the Treviri. | He considered (that) |

| hæc | auxilia | detrahenda | illi, | prius quam |
| these | auxiliaries | ought to be detached | from him, | before |

| ipsum | lacessendum | bello; | ne salute | des- |
| (he) himself | ought to be assailed | in war; | lest safety | having been |

| peratā, | aut | abdĕret | se | in | Menapios, |
| despaired of, | either | he might hide | himself | among | the Menapii, |

| aut | cogeretur | congredi | cum | transrhenanis. |
| or | be forced | to unite | with | the over-Rhine (Germans). |

| Hoc | consilio | inito, | mittit | impedimenta |
| This | plan | having been formed | he sends | the baggage |

totius	exercitūs	ad	Labienum	in	Treviros,	que
of the whole	*army*	*to*	*Labienus*	*among*	*the Treviri,*	*and*

jubet	duas	legiones	proficisci	ad	eum.	Ipse
orders	*two*	*legions*	*to proceed*	*to*	*him.*	*(He) himself*

proficiscitur	cum	quinque	expeditis	legionibus	in
marches	*with*	*five*	*light armed*	*legions*	*against*

Menapios.	Illi,	nullā	manu	coactā,
the Menapii.	*They,*	*no*	*force*	*having been assembled,*

freti	præsidio	loci,	confugiunt	in	silvas
relying on the	*protection*	*of the place,*	*retreat*	*into*	*the woods*

que	paludes,	que	conferunt	eodem	sua.
and	*marshes,*	*and*	*convey*	*to the same place*	*their property.*

6. | Cæsar, | copiis | partitis | cum | C. Fabio, |
| --- | --- | --- | --- | --- |
| *Cæsar,* | *the forces* | *having been divided* | *with* | *C. Fabius,* |

legato,	et	M. Crasso,	quæstore,	que	pontibus
the lieutenant,	*and*	*M. Crassus,*	*the quæstor,*	*and*	*bridges*

effectis	celerĭter,	adiit	tripartito;
having been constructed	*hastily,*	*advances*	*in three divisions;*

incendit	ædificia	que	vicos,	potitur	magno
he burns	*the houses*	*and*	*villages*	*(and) gets possession*	*of a great*

numero	pecŏris,	atque	hominum.	Coacti
number	*of cattle,*	*and*	*of men.*	*Having been forced*

quibus	rebus,	Menapii	mittunt	legatos	ad
by which [these] things,	*the Menapii*	*send*	*ambassadors*	*to*

eum,	causā	petendæ[9]	pacis.	Ille,	obsidibus
him,	*for the purpose*	*of seeking*	*peace.*	*He,*	*the hostages*

acceptis,	confirmat	se	habit-
having been received,	*declares*	*(that he) himself*	*about to*

urum	numero	hostium,	si	recepissent
[would] hold (them)	*in the number*	*of enemies*	*if*	*they received*

aut	Ambiorigem,	aut	ejus	legatos	sŭis	finibus.
either	*Ambiorix,*	*or*	*his*	*ambassadors*	*in their*	*territories.*

His	rebus	confirmatis,	relinquit	Commium,
These	*things*	*having been settled*	*he leaves*	*Commius,*

Atrebatem,	cum	equitatu	in	Menapiis	loco
the Atrebatian,	*with*	*the cavalry*	*among*	*the Menapii*	*in place*

custodis;	ipse	proficiscitur	in	Treviros.
of a guard;	*he himself*	*marches*	*against*	*the Treviri.*

7. Dum hæc geruntur a Cæsare, Tre-
While these (things) were being performed by Cæsar, the

viri, magnis copiis peditatūs, que equitatūs coac-
Treviri, great forces of infantry, and of cavalry having been

tis, parabant adoriri Labienum cum unā
assembled, were preparing to attack Labienus with one

legione, quæ hiemaverat in eorum finibus. Que
legion, which had wintered in their territories. And

jam aberant ab eo non longius
already they were distant from him not farther (than)

viā bidui, quum cognoscunt duas
a journey of two days, when they learn (that) two

legiones venisse missū Cæsaris.
legions [to] have arrived by the sending [dispatched] of [by] Cæsar.

Castris positis a quindecim[10] millibus
Their camp having been pitched distant fifteen thousand

passuum constituunt expectare auxilia (pl.)
(of) paces they determine to wait for the aid [auxiliaries]

Germanorum. Labienus, consilio hostium cog-
of the Germans. Labienus, the plan of the enemy having

nito, sperans temeritate eorum
been learned, hoping (that) by the rashness of them

fore aliquam
[by their rashness] to be about to [there would] be some

facultatem dimicandi, præsidio quinque cohortium
opportunity of fighting, a guard of five cohorts

relicto impedimentis, proficiscitur contra hostem
having been left for the baggage, marches against the enemy

cum viginti quinque cohortibus, que magno
with twenty five cohorts, and great [much]

equitatu, et communit castra, spatio mille
cavalry, and fortifies (his) camp, an interval of a thousand

passuum intermisso. Erat, inter Labienum
paces having been left between. There was, between Labienus

atque hostem, flumen difficili transitu, que
and the enemy, a river with a difficult crossing, and

præruptis ripis. Neque ipse habebat in animo
with steep banks. Neither he himself had in mind

LIBER VI.

transire	hoc,	neque	existimabat	hostes
to cross	this,	nor	did he think (that)	the enemy

transituros.	Spes	auxiliorum	augebatur	quotidie.
would cross.	The hope	of auxiliaries	was increased	daily.

Loquitur	palam	in	concilio,	quoniam	Germani
He says	openly	in	council, (that)	since	the Germans

dicuntur	appropinquare	sese	non
are said	to be approaching	(that he) himself (would)	not

devocaturum	in	dubium	suas	que	fortunas
(about to) call	into	doubt [hazard]	his own	and	the fortunes

exercitūs,	et	motorum	castra
of the army,	and	(that he) about to [would] move	the camp

primā luce[11]	postero die.	Hæc	deferuntur
at daybreak	on the next day.	These (words)	are carried

celeriter	ad	hostes,	ut	ex	magno	numero
quickly	to	the enemy,	as	from [of]	the great	number

equitatūs	Gallorum,	natura	cogebat	nonnullos
of cavalry	of the Gauls,	nature	compelled	some

favēre	Gallicis	rebus.	Noctu	Labienus,	tribunis
to favor	the Gallic	affairs.	At night,	Labienus,	the tribunes

militum	que	primis	ordinibus	coac-
of the soldiers	and	the first	orders (of centurions)	having been

tis,	proponit	quid	consilii	sit	sui;
assembled,	sets forth	what	of plan	is	his [what his plan is]

et	quo	facilius	det	hostibus
and	that	the more easily	he may give	to the enemy

suspicionem	timōris,	jubet	castra	movēri
a suspicion	of fear,	he orders	the camp	to be moved

majore	strepitu	et	tumultu,	quam	fert	consuetudo
with greater	noise	and	confusion,	than	is	the custom

Romani	populi.	His	rebus	efficit	profectionem
of the Roman	people.	By these	things	he makes	the departure

similem	fugæ.	Hæc	quoque	in
like	to a flight.	These (things)	also	in [on account of]

tanta	propinquitate	castrorum	deferuntur	ad
so great [such]	nearness	of the camps	are announced	to

hostes	per	exploratores	ante	lucem.
the enemy	through	spies	before	daylight.

8. Vix	novissimum agmen	processerat	extra
Scarcely	*the rear marching-line*	*had proceeded*	*beyond*

munitiones,	cum	Galli	cohortati	inter se[12]
the fortifications,	*when*	*the Gauls*	*having encouraged*	*one another*

ne	dimittĕrent	speratam prædam	ex
(that) they should not	*cast away*	*the hoped for booty*	*from*

manibus;	esse	longum	expectare
(their) hands,	*(that) it would be*	*long [tedious]*	*to wait for*

auxilium	Germanorum, Romanis	perterritis;
the assistance	*of the Germans, the Romans*	*having been terrified;*

neque	suam	dignitatem	pati ut	non
(that) neither	*their*	*dignity*	*suffers that*	*they should not*

audeant	adoriri	tantis	copiis	tam exiguam
dare	*to attack*	*with so great*	*forces*	*so small*

manum,	præsertim	fugientem atque	impeditam;
a band,	*especially*	*fleeing and*	*encumbered;*

	non	dubitant transire
(having encouraged one another thus)	*they do not*	*hesitate to cross*

flumen	et	committĕre prœlium	iniquo	loco.
the river	*and*	*to join battle*	*in an unfavorable*	*place.*

Labienus	suspicatus quæ	fore,
Labienus	*having suspected which [this]*	*to be about to [would] be*

ut	elicĕret	omnes citra flumen,	progredie-
in order that he might lure	*all to this side the river,*	*was march-*

batur	placide usus	eādem simulatione (abl.)	itineris.
ing on	*quietly using*	*the same pretence*	*of a march.*

Tum,	impedimentis	præmissis	paulum, atque
Then,	*the baggage*	*having been sent forward*	*a little, and*

collocatis	quodam tumulo;	"habētis,"	inquit,
having been placed	*on a certain eminence;*	*"you have,"*	*says he,*

"milites,	facultatem	quam petistis;	tenētis
"soldiers,	*the opportunity*	*which you have sought;*	*you hold*

hostem	impedito	atque iniquo	loco;
the enemy	*in an encumbered*	*and unfavorable*	*place;*

præstate	eandem	virtutem	nobis ducibus,	quam
exhibit	*the same*	*courage*	*to us (your) generals,*	*which*

sæpenumero	præstitistis	imperatori; existimate
so often	*you have displayed*	*to your commander; suppose*

eum	adesse,	et	cernĕre	hæc
him	*to be present,*	*and*	*to observe*	*these (deeds as if)*

coram."	Simul	jubet	signa con-
in his presence."	*At the same time*	*he orders*	*the standards to be*

verti	ad	hostem,	que	aciem	dirigi; et
turned	*to*	*the enemy,*	*and*	*the battle-line*	*to be formed, and*

paucis	turmis	dimissis	præsidio	ad
a few	*troops of horsemen*	*having been sent*	*for [as] a guard*	*to*

impedimenta,	disponit	reliquos	equites ad	latera.
the baggage,	*he stations*	*the remaining*	*cavalry on*	*the wings.*

Nostri,	clamore	sublato,	celeriter	jaciunt
Our men,	*a shout*	*having been raised,*	*quickly*	*throw*

pila	in hostes.	Illi, ubi, præter	spem,
(their) weapons	*at the enemy.*	*They, when, contrary*	*to expectation,*

viderunt	quos	credebant	fugĕre ire	ad
they saw	*those whom*	*they believed*	*to be in flight come*	*toward*

se infestis	signis,	non potuerunt	ferre
them with hostile	*standards,*	*were not able*	*to sustain*

impetum nostrorum;	ac	primo	concursu,
the attack of our	*(men); and*	*on the first*	*encounter,*

conjecti	in fugam,	petiverunt	proximas
having been thrown	*into flight,*	*sought*	*the nearest*

silvas;	Labienus consectatus	quos	equitatū,
woods;	*Labienus having followed*	*whom [them]*	*with (his) cavalry,*

magno	numero	interfecto,	compluribus
a great	*number*	*having been slain,*	*(and) very many*

captis,	recēpit civitatem,		paucis
having been captured,	*received the state (in submission),*		*a few*

diebus	post.	Nam Germani,	qui	veniebant
days	*afterwards.*	*For the Germans,*	*who*	*were coming*

auxilio,	fugā	Trevirorum	perceptā,
for [as] aid,	*the flight*	*of the Treviri*	*having been learned,*

contulerunt	sese	domum.	Cum iis	propinqui
betook	*themselves*	*home.*	*With them*	*the relations*

Indutiomari,	qui	fuerant	auctores	defectionis
of Indutiomaris,	*who*	*had been*	*the authors*	*of the revolt*

comitati	eos	excessere	ex	civitate.
having accompanied	*them*	*departed*	*from*	*the state.*

Principatus	atque	imperium	traditum est	Cingetorigi,
The leadership	*and*	*command*	*was assigned*	*to Cingetorix,*

quem	demonstravimus	permansisse	in
whom [who]	*we have shown*	*to have [had] remained*	*in*

officio	ab	initio.
allegiance	*from*	*the beginning.*

9.
Cæsar,	postquam	venit	ex	Menapiis	in
Cæsar,	*after*	*he came*	*from*	*the Menapii*	*into*

Treviros	constituit	de	duabus	causis	transire	Rhenum;
the Treviri	*resolved*	*for*	*two*	*reasons*	*to cross*	*the Rhine;*

altera	quarum	erat,	quod	(Germani)	miserant
the one	*of which*	*was,*	*because*	*(the Germans)*	*had sent*

auxilia	Treviris	contra	se;	altera
auxiliaries	*to the Treviri*	*against*	*himself;*	*the other (that)*

Ambiorix	ne	haberet	receptum	ad	eos.	His
Ambiorix	*might*	*not have*	*a refuge*	*among*	*them.*	*These*

rebus	constitutis,	instituit	facĕre	pontem
things	*having been determined*	*he resolved*	*to make*	*a bridge*

paulum	supra	eum	locum,	quo	antea	trans-
a little	*above*	*this*	*place,*	*at which*	*before*	*he had*

duxerat	exercitum.	Ratione	notā	atque
transported	*the army.*	*The plan*	*having been known*	*and*

institutā,	opus	efficitur,	paucis	diebus,	magno
adopted,	*the work*	*is completed,*	*in a few*	*days,*	*by the great*

studio	militum.	Firmo	præsidio	relicto	ad
zeal	*of the soldiers.*	*A strong*	*guard*	*having been left*	*near*

pontem	in	Treviris,	ne	quis	motus	oriretur
the bridge	*among*	*the Treviri,*	*lest*	*any*	*revolt*	*might arise*

subito	ab	iis,	traducit	reliquas	copias que
suddenly	*from*	*them,*	*he leads across*	*the remaining*	*forces and*

equitatum.	Ubii,	qui	ante	dederant	obsides,
the cavalry.	*The Ubii,*	*who*	*before*	*had given*	*hostages,*

atque	venerant	in	deditionem,	mittunt	ad	eum
and	*had come*	*to*	*a surrender*	*send*	*to*	*him*

causā	purgandi	sui[13]	legatos	qui doceant,
for the purpose	*of clearing*	*themselves*	*ambassadors*	*who may show*

neque	auxilia	missa	in	Treviros	ex
(that) neither	*auxiliaries*	*had been sent*	*to*	*the Treviri*	*from*

suā	civitate,	neque	fidem		læsam ab se;
their	*state,*	*nor*	*faith*	*(had been)*	*violated by them;*

petunt	atque	orant	ut	parcat	sibi, ne
they beg	*and*	*pray*	*that*	*he may spare*	*them, lest*

communi odio Germanorum innocentes pendant
in (his) common hatred of the Germans the innocent pay

pœnas pro nocentibus; si velit amplius obsidum,
the penalties for the guilty; if he desires more [of] hostages,

pollicentur dare. Causā cognitā,
they promise to give (them). The case having been investigated,

Cæsar reperit auxilĭa missa esse ab
Cæsar finds the auxiliaries to have [had] been sent by

Suevis; accepit satisfactionem Ubiorum;
the Suevi; he accepts the explanation of the Ubii; and

perquirit aditus que vias in Suevos.
carefully seeks out the approaches and roads into the Suevi.

10. Interim fit certior[14] ab Ubiis, paucis
In the meanwhile he is informed by the Ubii, a few

diebus pōst, Suevos cogĕre omnes
days after (that) the Suevi to collect [are collecting] all

copĭas in unum locum, atque denuntiare
(their) forces into one place, and to give notice [are

iis nationibus quæ sunt sub eorum imperĭo,
giving notice] to those nations who are under their command.

ut mittant auxilia peditatūs que equitatūs.
that they send auxiliaries of foot [infantry] and of cavalry.

His rebus cognitis providet rem frumentariam,
These things having been learned he provides a corn supply,

deligit idoneum lŏcum castris; imperat
he selects a suitable place for the camp; he commands

Ubiis, ut deducant pecŏra, que conferant
the Ubii that they drive away the cattle, and collect

omnia sua ex agris in oppida; sperans
all their (property) from the fields into the towns; hoping

barbăros atque imperitos homines adductos
(that) the barbarous and ignorant men led

inopiā cibariorum posse deduci ad
by the want of food to be able [might] (to) be brought into

iniquam	conditionem	pugnandi.	Mandat
an unfavorable	*condition*	*of fighting.*	*He orders (the Ubii)*

ut	mittant	crebros	exploratores	in	Suevos,
that	*they send*	*numerous*	*scouts*	*among*	*the Suevi,*

cognoscant	quæque gerantur (pl.)	apud eos.
that they may learn	*whatever is carried on*	*among them.*

Illi	faciunt	imperata,	et,	paucis	diebus	intermissis,
They	*execute*	*the orders*	*and*	*a few*	*days*	*having passed,*

referunt;	omnes	Suevos,	posteaquam	certiores
report;	*(that) all*	*the Suevi*	*after*	*more certain*

nuntii	venerant	de	exercitu
messengers [news]	*had come*	*concerning*	*the army*

Romanorum,	recepisse	sese	penitus	ad
of the Romans	*to have [had] betaken*	*themselves*	*quite*	*to*

extremos	fines	cum omnibus suis	copiis	que
the extreme	*boundaries*	*with all their*	*forces*	*and (those)*

sociorum,	quas	coëgissent.	Esse
of (their) allies,	*which*	*they had collected.*	*To be [There is]*

silvam	ibi	infinitæ	magnitudinis,	quæ
a forest	*there*	*of boundless*	*extent,*	*which*

appellatur	Bacenis;	hanc	pertinēre	longē
is called	*Bacenis;*	*this*	*to extend [extends]*	*far*

introrsus,	et objectam pro	nativo muro,
into the interior	*and is opposed for [as]*	*a natural wall [defence]*

prohibēre	injuriis	que incursionibus	Cheruscos
to check [it checks] from injuries	*and*	*incursions*	*the Cherusci*

a	Suevis,	que	Suevos	a	Cheruscis;	Suevos
from	*the Suevi*	*and*	*the Suevi*	*from*	*the Cherusci;*	*the Suevi*

constituisse	exspectare	adventum	Romanorum,
to have [had] resolved	*to await*	*the arrival*	*of the Romans,*

ad	initium	ejus	silvæ.
at	*the entrance*	*of this*	*forest.*

11. | Quoniam | perventum est | ad hunc locum, |
|---|---|---|
| *Since* | *it has been reached [we have come] to* | *this place,* |

videtur	non esse	alienum	proponere
it seems	*not to be*	*foreign [improper]*	*to present (an account)*

de	moribus	Galliæ	que	Germaniæ,	et
concerning the manners	*of Gaul*	*and*	*of Germany*	*and*

quo	in what (respects)
hæ	these
nationes	nations
differant	may differ
inter	among
sese.[15]	themselves.
In	In
Galliā	Gaul (there)
sunt	are
factiones,	factions,
non solum in omnibus civitatibus atque	not only in all the states and
pagis que partibus, sed etiam pæne in singulis	cantons and parts, but also almost in the individual
domibus; que principes earum factionum sunt	houses; and the chiefs of those factions are (those)
qui existimantur habere, judicio eorum	who are considered to have, in the judgment of them [their
summam auctoritatem; ad arbitrium que	judgment] the highest authority; to the will and
judicium quorum, summa omnium rerum que	judgment of whom, the management of all affairs and
consiliorum redeat. Que id videtur	counsels may return. And this seems (to have been)
institutum (esse) antiquitus causā ejus rei,	instituted anciently for the sake of this thing,
ne quis ex plebe egēret auxilii (gen.)	that no one from [of] the people should lack assistance
contra potentiorem; enim quisque non patitur	against the more powerful; for each one does not suffer
suos opprimi que circumveniri; neque si faciat	his own to be oppressed and overreached; nor if he should do
aliter habeat ullam auctoritatem inter suos.	otherwise would he have any authority among his (people).
Hæc eadem ratio est in summā	This same plan [system] exists in the management [authority]
totius Galliæ. Namque omnes civitates divisæ sunt	of all Gaul. For indeed all the states are divided
in duas partes.	into two parties.

12. Cum Cæsar vēnit in Galliam, Ædui erant
    When Cæsar came into Gaul, the Ædui were

principes alterius factionis, Sequani alterius. Hi,
the chiefs of one faction, the Sequani of the other. These

[The latter]	cum as	valērent they prevailed	minus less	per se, by themselves,
(quod (because	summa the supreme	auctoritas authority	erat was	in Æduis among the Ædui
antiquitus, anciently [of old],	que and	magnæ great		erant eorum were their
clientelæ), tributaries),		adjunxerant they [the Sequani] had united	Germanos the Germans	atque and
Ariovistum Ariovistus	sibi, to themselves,	que and	perduxerant eos ad had brought them over to	
se themselves	magnis jacturis by great sacrifices	que and	pollicitationibus. promises.	Vero Indeed
compluribus very many	secundis successful	prœliis battles	factis, having been fought,	atque and
omni all	nobilitate the nobility	Æduorum of the Ædui		interfectā, having been slain,
	antecesserant they [the Sequani] had surpassed		tantum so much	potentiā, ut in power, that
transducĕrent ad they brought over to	se themselves	magnam partem clientium a great part of the clients		
	ab [tributaries] from	Æduis, the Ædui,	que accipĕrent ab and received from	iis these
filios the sons	principum obsides, of the chiefs as hostages,		et cogĕrent and forced (them)	jurare to swear
publice, publicly,	se (that) they	inituros[16] would enter (into)	nihil nothing	consilii of [no] design
contra against	Sequanos; the Sequani;	et and	possidĕrent they kept	partem a part
finitimi of the neighboring		agri territory	occupatam per seized by	vim, que force, and
obtinērent obtained	principatum the sovereignty	totius of all	Galliæ. Gaul.	Divitiacus Divitiacus
adductus led	quā by which [this]	necessitate, necessity,	profectus having proceeded	Romam to Rome
ad to	senatum the senate	causā for the purpose	petendi of asking	auxilii, aid,
redierat had returned		re infectā. his purpose unaccomplished.		Adventu By the arrival

Cæsaris,	commutatione	rerum	factā,
of Cæsar,	*a change*	*of affairs*	*having been effected,*
obsidibus	redditis	Æduis,	veteribus
the hostages	*having been returned*	*to the Ædui,*	*old*
clientelis	restitutis,	novis	comparatis
tributaries	*having been restored, (and)*	*new*	*having been acquired*
per	Cæsarem,	(quod ii,	qui aggregaverant
through	*Cæsar,*	*(because these,*	*who had united*
se ad	eorum amicitiam,	vidēbant	se
themselves to	*their friendship,*	*saw*	*(that) they*
uti[17]	meliore	conditione atque	æquiore
to use [enjoyed]	*a better*	*condition and*	*more equitable*
imperio)	reliquis	rebus,	eorum gratiā
government)	*(their) other*	*affairs,*	*their authority*
que dignitate		amplificatā,	Sequani
and dignity [influence]		*having been enlarged,*	*the Sequani*
dimisserant	principatum,	Remi	succcesserant
had lost	*the sovereignty, (and) the Remi*		*had succeeded*
in eorum	locum;	quod	intelligebatur
in their	*place;*	*as*	*it was perceived*
quos[18]	adæquare		gratiā apud
whom (that they)	*equaled (the Ædui)*		*in favor with*
Cæsarem, ii,	qui propter	veteres	inimicitias
Cæsar, those,	*who on account of*	*old*	*hostilities*
poterant nullo	modo conjungi	cum	Æduis,
could in no	*manner be united*	*with*	*the Ædui.*
dicabant	se in	clientelam	Remis.
were declaring	*themselves under*	*the protection*	*to [of] the Remi.*
Illi tuebantur	hos diligenter;	et ita	tenēbant
They were protecting	*them carefully;*	*and so*	*they held*
novam et	repente collectam	auctoritatem.	Res
a new and	*suddenly acquired*	*influence.*	*Affairs*
erat tum	eo statu, ut	Ædui	haberentur
were then	*in this state, that*	*the Ædui*	*were held as*
longe principes,		Remi obtinērent	secundum
by far the principal (people),		*while the Remi obtained*	*the second*
locum dignitatis.			
place of dignity [influence].			

DE BELLO GALLICO

13. In omni Gallia sunt duo genera, eorum
    In all Gaul there are two classes, of those

hominum, qui sunt aliquo numero atque honore.
men who are of any account and honor.

Nam plebs habētur pæne loco servorum,
For the common people are held almost in place of slaves,

quæ audet nihil per se, et adhibētur nulli
who dare nothing by themselves, and are admitted to no

concilio. Plerique quum premuntur aut ære alieno,
council. Many when they are oppressed either by debt,

aut magnitudine tributorum, aut injuriā
or by the greatness of the tributes, or by the injury [violence]

potentiorum, dicant sese in servitutem
of the more powerful, declare themselves in servitude

nobilibus; omnia eadem jura sunt in hos, quæ
to the nobles; all the same rights are over these, which

dominis in servos. Sed de his duobus
(are) to masters over slaves. But of these two

generibus, alterum est Druidum, alterum
classes, the one is (that) of the Druids, the other (that)

Equitum. Illi intersunt divinis rebus,
of the knights. They (the Druids) are occupied with sacred things,

procurant publica ac privata sacrificia, inter-
they have charge of public and private sacrifices, (and) inter-

pretantur religiones. Magnus numerus adolescentium
pret religion. A great number of youths

concurrit ad hos causā disciplinæ, que ii,
resort to these for the purpose of training, and they

sunt magno honore apud eos. Nam
(the Druids) are in great honor among them. For

constituunt de fere omnibus controversiis
they decide concerning almost all controversies (both)

publicis que privatis; et si quod facĭnus est
public and private; and if any crime has been

admissum, si cædes facta, si est
committed, if (any) murder has been done if (there) is

controversia de hæreditate, si de finibus, iidem
a dispute about inheritance, if about boundaries the same

LIBER VI.

decernunt que constituunt præmia que pœnas.
decide (it) and determine the recompenses and punishments.

Si quis, aut privatus aut publicus, non
If any (person), either private or public, should not

steterit eorum decreto, interdicunt sacrificiis.
submit to their decree, they ban (him) from the sacrifices.

Hæc est gravissima pœna apud eos. Hi
This is a very serious punishment among them. Those

quibus[19] est ita interdictum, habentur numero
who are thus interdicted, are held in number

impiorum ac sceleratorum; omnes decedunt iis,
of the impious and wicked; all avoid them,

que defugiunt eorum aditum que sermonem; ne
and flee from their approach and conversation; lest

accipiant quid (neut.) incommodi ex
they receive some (of) evil from

contagione; neque jus redditur eis
contact; neither (is) justice administered to them

petentibus neque ullus honos communicatur. Autem
petitioning nor any honor is attributed. But

omnibus his Druidibus unus præest, qui habet
over all these Druids one presides, who has

summam auctoritatem inter eos. Hoc mortuo,
supreme authority among them. This (chief) being dead,

si quis ex reliquis excellit dignitate succedit.
if any one from [of] the others excels in dignity he succeeds.

At si plures sunt pares deligitur suffragio
But if many are equal election is made by the vote

Druidum; etiam nonnunquam contendunt armis
of the Druids; also sometimes they contend with arms

de principatū. Hi considunt in consecrato
for the chieftainship. These (Druids) assemble in a consecrated

loco, certo tempŏre anni in finibus
place, at a certain time of the year in the territories

Carnutum, quæ regĭo habētur media totius Galliæ.
of the Carnutes, which region is held as the center of all Gaul.

Huc undĭque, omnes qui habent controversias,
Here from all sides all who have disputes,

conveniunt, que parent eorum judiciis que decretis.
assemble, and submit to their judgment and decrees.

Disciplina existimatur reperta in Britanniā,
(This) institution [cult] is supposed (to have) originated in Britain,
atque inde (esse) translata in Galliam. Et
and from thence (to have been) transferred into Gaul. And
nunc, qui volunt diligentius cognoscere eam
now, those who wish more perfectly to know this
rem, plerumque proficiscuntur illo causā
thing [sect], often go there for the purpose
discendi.
of learning (it).

14. Druides consueverunt abesse a bello, neque
The Druids are accustomed to be absent from war, nor
pendunt tributa unā cum reliquis; (habent vaca-
do they pay tribute together with the rest; (they have an exemp-
tionem militiæ, que immunitatem omnium
tion from military service and immunity of [in] all
rerum). Excitati tantis præmiis, multi conveniunt in
things). Excited by such advantages, many assemble for
disciplinam, et suā sponte et mittuntur a
instruction, both of their own accord and also are sent by
parentibus que propinquis. Dicuntur ediscere
parents and relations. They are said to learn by heart
magnum numerum versuum ibi. Itaque nonnulli
a great number of verses there. Therefore many
permanent vicenos annos in disciplinā; neque
remain twenty years under instruction; nor
existimant esse fas mandare ea
do they consider (it) to be lawful to commit these (things)
litteris, cum utantur Græcis litteris in fere
to writing, although they use the Greek letters in nearly
reliquis rebus, publicis que privatis rationibus.
(all) other affairs, in public and in private transactions.
Id videtur mihi instituisse de duabus causis;
This seems to me to have been established for two reasons;
quod neque velint disciplinam efferi in
because they neither wish their discipline to be divulged to

volgos,	neque	eos	qui	discunt,	confisos
the common people,	*nor*	*(that) those*	*who*	*learn*	*relying*
litteris,	studēre		memoriæ		minus.
on writing,	*should cultivate (their)*		*memory*		*the less.*

Quod fere accidit plerisque, ut præsidio
Which [This] ordinarily happens to most men, so that by the aid

litterarum remittant diligentiam in perdiscendo,
of writing they relax (their) application in thoroughly learning,

ac memoriam. In primis volunt persuadēre
and (their) memory. In particular they wish to inculcate

hoc; animas non interire, sed post mortem
this; (that) souls [do] not (to) die, but after death

transire ab aliis ad alios[20] atque putant
(to) pass from one (body) to another and they think

hōc maxime excitari ad virtutem,
(that) by this (men) greatly to be [are] roused to courage,

metu mortis neglecto. Præterea disputant,
the fear of death having been disregarded. Moreover they discuss,

et tradunt juventuti multa de sideribus,
and impart to the youths many things concerning the stars,

atque eorum motu, de magnitudine mundi
and their motion, concerning the size of the world

ac terrarum, de naturā rerum, de
and the earth, concerning the nature of things, concerning

vi ac potestate immortalium deorum.
the power and majesty of the immortal gods.

15. Alterum genus est equitum. Hi, cum
The other class is (of) the knights. These, when there

est usus, atque aliquod bellum incidit, (quod ante
is need, and any war occurs, (which before

adventum Cæsaris solēbat accidĕre fere quotannis,
the arrival of Cæsar was wont to happen nearly every year,

uti aut ipsi inferrent injurias, aut
that either they themselves might inflict injuries or

propulsarent illatas) omnes versantur in bello;
might repel (them) inflicted) all are employed in the war;

atque ut quisque eorum est amplissimus
and in proportion as each one of them is very noble

genere que copiis, ita habet plurimos ambactos
by family and resources, so he has very many vassals

que clientes circum se. Noverunt hanc
and clients about himself [him]. They have learned [know] this

gratiam que potentiam unam.
authority and power only.

16. Omnis natio Gallorum est admodum dedita
The whole nation of the Gauls is very much given

religionibus, atque ob eam causam,
to religion [superstitions] and for this reason (those)

qui sunt affecti gravioribus morbis, que qui
who are afflicted with very severe diseases and (those) who

versantur in prœliis que periculis, aut immolant
are engaged in war and dangers, either sacrifice

homines pro victimis, aut vovent se
men for [as] victims, or vow (that they) themselves

immolaturos;[21] que utuntur Druidibus
to be about to [will] sacrifice (them); and they use the Druids

(abl.) administris ad ea sacrificia; quod arbitrantur,
as performers of these sacrifices; because they think

nisi vita hominis reddatur pro vitā
(that) unless the life of a man be rendered for the life

hominis, numen immortalium deorum
of a man, the divine will [divinity] of the immortal gods

non posse aliter placari; que habent sacrificia
can not otherwise be appeased; and they have sacrifices

ejusdem generis instituta publice. Alii habent
of the same kind performed publicly. Others have

simulacra immani magnitudine, membra quorum
images with [of] vast size, the limbs of which

contexta viminibus complent vivis hominibus;
woven with twigs they fill with living men;

quibus succensis homines exanimantur
which [these] having been set on fire the men perish

circumventi flammā. Arbitrantur supplicia
surrounded by flame. They think (that) the sacrifice

eorum, qui sint comprehensi in furto aut in
of those, who have been taken in theft or in

LIBER VI.

latrocinia, aut aliquā noxā esse gratiora
robbery, or some culpable act to be [are] more acceptable

immortalibus diis, sed cum copia ejus
to the immortal gods, but when a supply of this

generis deficit, descendunt etiam ad supplicia
kind is wanting they descend also to the punishment [sacrifice]

innocentium.
of the innocent.

17. Maxime colunt deum Mercurium; sunt
They principally worship the god Mercury; there are

plurima simulacra hujus; ferunt hunc inventorem
many images of him; they regard him (as) the inventor

omnium artium; hunc ducem viarum
of all arts; (they consider) him the guide of their journeys

atque itinerum; arbitrantur hunc habēre maximam
and marches; they believe him to have very great

vim ad quætus pecuniæ que mercaturas (pl.).
power for the acquisition of money and (for) trade.

Post hunc Apollinem et Martem, et
After him (they worship) Apollo and Mars, and

Jovem, et Minervam. De his habent fere
Jupiter, and Minerva. About these they have nearly

eandem opinionem, quam reliquæ gentes;
the same opinion, which (as) other nations; (that)

Appollinem depellĕre[22] morbos, Minervam tradĕre
Apollo drives away diseases, (that) Minerva imparts

initia operum atque artificiorum; Jovem
the principles of crafts and of arts; (that) Jupiter

tenēre imperium cœlestium; Martem regĕre
holds the empire of the celestials; (that) Mars rules

bella. Huic, quum constituerunt dimicare prœlio,
wars. To him when they have resolved to engage in battle,

plerumque devovent, ea quæ ceperint
often they vow, those (things) which they may take

bello; animalia quæ superaverint capta
in war; the animals which may have survived (when) captured

immolant, conferunt reliquas res in
they sacrifice, (and) bring together the remaining things into

unum locum.	In	multis	civitatibus	licet	conspicari
one place.	*In*	*many*	*states*	*there may*	*be seen*

tumulos	exstructos	harum	rerum,	consecratis locis.
piles	*built*	*of these*	*things,*	*in consecrated places.*

Neque	sæpe	accĭdit,	ut	quispiam, religione
Nor	*does it often*	*happen,*	*that*	*any one,* *religion*

neglectā,	audēret	aut occultare	apud se
being disregarded,	*should dare*	*either to conceal*	*at his home*

capta,	aut tollĕre	posita,	que
the things captured,	*or to take away*	*the things deposited,*	*and*

gravissimum	supplicium cum	cruciatu	constitutum est
the most grievous	*punishment with*	*torture*	*has been ordained*

ei	rei.
for this	*thing.*

18.
Omnes	Galli	prædicant	se	prognatos
All	*the Gauls*	*assert*	*(that) they*	*are descended*

ab Dite	patre,	que dicunt	id
from Dis [Pluto]	*as progenitor,*	*and they say (that)*	*this (account)*

prodĭtum[23]	ab	Druidibus.	Ob eam causam
has been handed down	*by*	*the Druids.*	*For this reason*

finiunt	spatia (pl.)	omnis	temporis	non
they determine	*the duration*	*of all*	*time*	*not*

numero	dierum,	sed noctium;	et	observant
by the number	*of days,*	*but of nights;*	*and*	*observe*

natales	dies,	et	initia (pl.)	mensium et
birth	*days,*	*and*	*the commencement*	*of the months and*

annorum,	sic ut dies	subsequatur noctem.	In
of years,	*in such a way that the day*	*may follow the night.*	*In*

reliquis institutis	vitæ differunt	hōc	ab	fere
other usages	*of life they differ*	*in this*	*from*	*nearly all*

reliquis, quod	non patiantur	suos liberos	adire
others,	*that they do not suffer*	*their children*	*to approach*

se	palam,	nisi cum	adoleverint,	ut
them	*publicly,*	*except when*	*they have grown up,*	*so that*

possint	sustinēre	munus	militiæ; que
they may be able	*to bear*	*the duty*	*of military service; and*

ducunt	turpe	filium	in puerili	ætate
they consider (it)	*shameful*	*(for) a son*	*in boyish*	*age*

| assistĕre | in | conspectu | patris, | in | publico. |
| *to attend* | *in* | *the presence* | *of his father,* | *in* | *public.* |

19. | Quantas | pecunias | viri | acceperunt | ab |
| *As much* | *money* | *(as) the husbands* | *have received* | *from* |

| uxoribus, | nomine | dotis, | tantas, | æstimatione |
| *wives,* | *in the name* | *of dower,* | *so much,* | *an estimate* |

| factā, | communicant cum dotibus | ex | suis |
| *having been made,* | *they join with the dower* | *from* | *their own* |

| bonis. | Omnis | hujus | pecuniæ | ratio | conjunctim |
| *goods.* | *Of all* | *this* | *money* | *an account* | *in common.* |

| habetur, | que | fructus | servantur; | uter | eorum |
| *is kept,* | *and* | *the profits* | *are reserved;* | *whichever* | *of them* |

| superārit | vitā. | pars utriusque cum fructibus |
| *shall have survived* | *in life,* | *the share of both with the profits* |

| superiorum | temporum (pl.) | pervĕnit ad eum. | Viri |
| *of the previous* | *time* | *falls to him.* | *Husbands* |

| habent potestatem vitæ | que | nĕcis | in | uxores, |
| *have the power of life* | *and* | *death* | *against [over]* | *the wives,* |

| sicuti | in | libĕros. | Et | cum | pater- |
| *as well as* | *against [over]* | *the children.* | *And* | *when* | *the father* |

| familias | natus | illustriore | loco | decessit, |
| *of a family* | *born* | *in a more illustrious* | *place [rank]* | *has died,* |

| ejus propinqui conveniunt, | et | si | res | vēnit |
| *his relations assemble,* | *and* | *if* | *the event* | *has come* |

| in | suspicionem, | habent | de | morte | quæstionem |
| *into* | *suspicion,* | *they hold* | *about* | *his death* | *an examination* |

| de | uxoribus | in | servilem | modum,[24] | et | si | est |
| *of* | *his wives* | *after* | *the slave* | *manner,* | *and* | *if* | *it is* |

| compertum interficiunt | excruciatas | igni | atque |
| *proved* | *they kill (them)* | *tortured* | *by fire* | *and* |

| omnibus | tormentis. | Funera, | pro | cultu |
| *all* | *torments.* | *The funerals,* | *for* | *the civilization* |

| Gallorum, sunt magnifica | et | sumptuosa, | que | omnia, |
| *of the Gauls, are magnificent* | *and* | *costly,* | *and* | *all things,* |

| quæ | arbitrantur | fuisse | cordi[25] | vivis, | inferunt |
| *which* | *they judge* | *to have been* | *dear* | *to the living,* | *they cast* |

| in | ignem, | etiam | animalia; | ac | paulo | supra | hanc |
| *into* | *the fire,* | *even* | *animals;* | *and* | *a little* | *before* | *this* |

memoriam,	servi	et	clientes,	quos	constabat
memory [time],	*slaves*	*and*	*clients,*	*whom*	*it was understood*

dilectos esse	ab	iis,	cremabantur	unā,
to have [had] been beloved	*by*	*them,*	*were burnt*	*together*

	justis	funeribus confectis.
(with them),	*the proper*	*funeral rites having been performed.*

20. Quæ civitates existimantur administrare
Those states (which) are believed to administer

suam rem publicam (sing.) commodius, habent
their public affairs more advantageously, have

sanctum legibus si quis acceperit
established by law (that) if any one shall have heard

quid a finitimis de re publicā rumore aut
anything from neighbors about the state by rumor or

famā, uti deferat ad magistratum, neve
by report, that he should bring (it) to the magistrate, nor

communicet cum quo alio; quod cognitum est
communicate with any other, because it has been known

sæpe temerarios atque imperitos homines
(that) often rash and inexperienced men

terrēri falsis rumoribus, et impelli
to be [are] terrified by false rumors, and to be [are] impelled

ad facĭnus, et capĕre consilium de summis
to crime, and form a plan about the most important

rebus. Magistratus occultant quæ visa sunt que
things. The magistrates conceal what seem best and

produnt multitudini, quæ judicaverint esse ex usu.
disclose to the people what they have decided to be of use.

Non conceditur loqui de re publicā nisi
It is not allowed to speak concerning a public matter except

per concilium.
through the council.

21. Germani differunt multum ab hāc consue-
The Germans differ much from this way

tudine; nam habent neque Druides, qui præsint
of life; for they have neither Druids, who preside over

divinis rebus; neque student sacrificiis Ducunt
sacred things; nor are they interested in sacrifices. They hold

22] LIBER VI 336

numĕro   deorum   eos solos,   quos   cernunt,
in the number   of the gods, those only   whom   they perceive,

et   quorum   opibus (pl.)   juvantur   aperte,
and   by whose assistance   they are benefitted obviously.

Solem,   et Vulcanum,   et Lunam;   acceperunt
as the Sun, and Vulcan, (fire) and the Moon; they have heard

reliquos ne quidem   famā.   Omnis   vita
(of) the others not even   by report. All   (their) life

consistit   in venationibus (pl.) atque in   studiis
is employed in hunting   and in   the pursuits

militaris   rei (sing);   ab parvulis   student
of military affairs;   from children they accustom themselves

labori   ac   duritiæ.   Qui   permanserunt diutissime
to labor and hardship.   Those who have remained the longest

impuberes, ferunt maximam   laudem   inter suos.
chaste,   obtain the greatest praise among their (people).

Putant   hoc   staturam   ali,
(They) believe (that) by this the stature to be [is] increased,

hoc   vires   ali,   que   nervos
by this the strength to be [is] increased, and   the nerves

confirmari.   Vero   habuisse   notitiam
to be [are] strengthened. Indeed to have had the knowledge

feminæ   intra   vicesimum annum habent in
of a woman within [under] the twentieth year   they hold among

turpissimis   rebus;   cujus   rei   est   nulla
the most shameful things; of this thing there is no

occultatio,   et   quod   perluuntur   promiscue   in
concealment,   both because they bathe   promiscuously in

fluminibus,   et utuntur pellibus, aut parvis tegimentis
the rivers,   and use   skins,   or small coverings

(abl.) renonum, magnā parte corpŏris   nudā.
of deer hides, a great part of the body being naked.

22. Non   student   agri culturæ; que   major
     They are not fond of agriculture; and the greater

pars eorum victūs consistit in   lacte et   caseo
part of their food consists in [of] milk and cheese

et   carne.   Neque   habet quisquam   certum modum
and   meat.   Nor   has   any one   a fixed portion

agri,	aut	proprios	fines;	sed magistratus	ac
of land,	*or*	*his own*	*boundaries;*	*but the magistrates*	*and*

principes,	in singŭlos annos	attribuunt	quantum
chiefs,	*from year to year,*	*assign*	*as much*

agri, et	quo loco	visum est,	gentibus	que
(of) land, and	*in what place*	*it seems best,*	*to the tribes*	*and*

cognationibus	hominum,	qui coierunt	unā,
to the families	*of men,*	*who have united*	*together,*

atque anno	post cogunt	transire alio
and in the year	*after they compel (them)*	*to go somewhere else.*

Adferunt	multas causas	ejus rei (gen.); ne	capti
They offer	*many reasons*	*for this thing;*	*lest captivated*

assiduā	consuetudine	commutent	studium
by continued	*custom*	*they may change*	*(their) zeal*

gerendi	belli	agri culturā; ne	studeant
of [for] waging	*war*	*for agriculture; lest*	*they may be eager*

parare latos	fines, que	potentiores	expellant
to acquire extensive	*estates, and*	*the more powerful*	*may expel*

humiliores	possessionibus;	ne	ædificent
the more humble	*from possessions;*	*lest*	*they may build*

accuratius	ad vitandos frigŏra atque æstus;	ne qua
with too much care	*for avoiding cold and heat;*	*lest any*

cupiditas pecuniæ	oriatur, ex	quā re	factiones
desire of money	*may arise, from*	*which thing*	*factions*

que dissensiones	nascuntur;	ut	contineant
and dissensions	*originate;*	*that*	*they may keep*

plebem	æquitate	animi.	quum quisque
the common people	*in peace*	*of mind,*	*since each one*

videat	suas opes	æquari	cum
may see (that)	*his own means*	*to be [are] equal*	*with*

potentissimis.
the most powerful.

23.
Est	maxima	laus	civitatibus,	habēre
It is	*the greatest*	*honor*	*to the states,*	*to have*

solitudines quam	latissimas[26]	circum	se,
deserts as	*(most) wide (as possible)*	*about*	*themselves,*

finibus	vastatis.	Existimant hoc
their frontiers	*having been laid waste.*	*They consider this*

LIBER VI.

proprium		virtutis,		finitimos	expulsos
a peculiar	*(evidence)*	*of valor,*	*(that)* *their neighbors*	*expelled*

agris		cedĕre,	neque	quemquam
from (their) lands	*(to)*	*abandon (them),*	*and (that) not*	*any*

(sing)	audere	consistĕre	prope	se.
	(to) dare	*(to) settle*	*near*	*them.*

Simul	arbitrantur		se
At the same time	*they think*	*(that)*	*they themselves*

fŏre	tutiores	hōc,	timōre	repentinæ
to be about to [will] be	*more safe*	*by this,*	*the fear*	*of sudden*

incursionis	sublato.	Cum	civitas	aut
invasion	*having been removed.*	*When*	*the state*	*either*

defendit	bellum	illatum,	aut	infert,
repels	*war*	*waged against it,*	*or*	*wages war,*

magistratus	deliguntur,	qui	præsint	ei	bello,
magistrates	*are chosen,*	*who*	*may preside*	*over this*	*war,*

ut	habeant	potestatem	vitæ	que	nĕcis.
so that	*they may have*	*the power*	*of life*	*and*	*death.*

In	pace	est	nullus	communis	magistratus,	sed
In	*peace*	*there is*	*no*	*general*	*magistrate,*	*but*

principes	regionum	atque	pagorum	dicunt
the chiefs	*of the provinces*	*and*	*cantons*	*say [administer]*

jus	inter	suos,	que	minŭunt	controversias.
justice	*among*	*their (people), and*		*settle*	*disputes.*

Habent	nullam	infamiam	latrocinĭa,	quæ	fiunt
They hold	*as no*	*disgrace*	*robberies*	*which are committed*

extra	fines	cujusque	civitatis,	atque	prædicant
beyond the boundaries	*of any*	*state,*	*and*	*they assert*

ea	fieri		causā	exercendæ
these [robberies]	*to be committed*	*for the purpose*	*of exercising*

juventutis	ac	minuendæ	desidiæ.	Atque ubi	quis
the youth	*and*	*of preventing*	*sloth.*	*And when*	*any one*

ex	principibus	dixit	in	concilĭo,	se
from [of]	*the chiefs*	*has said*	*in*	*council*	*[that he] himself*

fŏre	ducem,	ut	qui	velint
to be about to [will] be	*the leader,*	*that*	*those who*	*may wish*

sequi	profiteantur;	ĭi	qui	probant	et
to follow	*may volunteer;*	*those*	*who*	*approve*	*both*

causam et homĭnem consurgunt, que pollicentur	the cause and the man rise up, and promise
suum auxilium, atque collaudantur ab multitudine.	their aid, and are applauded by the multitude.
Qui ex iis, non secuti sunt, ducuntur	Those of them, (who) have not followed, are reckoned
in numero desertorum ac proditorum; que	in the number of deserters and of traitors, and
postea fides abrogatur iis omnium	afterwards credit is taken away from them in all
rerum (gen.). Putant non fas violare	things. They consider it not lawful to injure
hospites; qui venerunt ad eos de quāque	their guests; those who have come to them for any
causā, prohibent ab injuriā, que habent	reason, they defend from harm, and they hold (them)
sanctos; domus omnium patent iis, que	inviolable; the houses of all are open to them, and
victus communicatur.	food is shared (with them).

24. Ac antea fuit tempus, cum Galli — And formerly (there) was a time, when the Gauls

superarent Germanos virtute, et ultro	excelled the Germans in bravery, and of their own accord
inferrent (imp. subj.) bella, ac propter	used to wage war, and on account of
multitudinem hominum que inopiam agri,	the multitude of men and the scarcity of land,
mittĕrent (imp. subj.) colonias trans Rhenum.	used to send colonies across the Rhine.
Itaque Volcæ Tectosages occupārunt ea loca	Therefore the Volcæ Tectosages occupied those places
Germaniæ, quæ sunt fertilissima, atque consederunt	of Germany, which are the most fruitful, and settled
ibi, circum Hercyniam silvam, (quam video	there, about the Hercynian forest, (which I perceive
esse notam Eratostheni et quibusdam	to have been [was] known to Eratosthenes and some other

LIBER VI.

Græcis	famā;	illi	appellant	quam	Orcyniam).
Greeks	*by report;*	*they*	*call*	*which [it]*	*Orcynia).*

Quae	gens	continet	se	iis	sedibus
Which [This]	*nation*	*maintains*	*itself*	*in these*	*settlements*

ad	hoc	tempus,	que	habet	summam	opinionem
to	*this*	*time,*	*and*	*has*	*the highest*	*reputation*

justitiæ	et	bellicæ	laudis;	que	nunc
of [for] justice	*and*	*(of) warlike*	*honor,*	*and*	*now*

permanent	in	eādem	inopia,	egestate,
they remain	*in*	*the same*	*privation [want]*	*poverty [need],*

	patientiā,	quā	Germani;	utuntur
(and)	*resignation*	*in which [as]*	*the Germans;*	*they use*

eodem	victu	et	cultu	corpŏris.	Propinquitas
the same	*food*	*and*	*care*	*of the body.*	*The proximity*

provinciæ	Gallis,	et	notitia	transmarinarum
of (our) province	*to the Gauls,*	*and*	*the knowledge*	*of transmarine*

rerum	largitur (sing.)	multa	ad	copiam
affairs	*provides*	*many (things)*	*for*	*supply [wealth]*

atque	usus.	Paulatim	assuefacti	superari,	que
and	*use.*	*By degrees*	*accustomed*	*to be overcome,*	*and*

victi	multis	prœiis	ipsi	ne	quidem[27]
conquered	*in many*	*battles*	*they*	*do not*	*even*

comparant	se	virtute	cum	illis.
compare	*themselves*	*in valor*	*with*	*them [the Germans].*

25. Latitudo	hujus	Hercyniæ	silvæ,	quæ
The breadth	*of this*	*Hercynian*	*forest,*	*which*

demonstrata est	supra,	patet	iter	novem	dierum
has been mentioned	*above,*	*extends a journey*		*of nine*	*days*

expedito.	Enim	potest non	finiri	aliter,
for an unburdened (man).	*For*	*it can not*	*be bounded*	*otherwise,*

neque	noverunt	mensuras	itinerum.	Oritur
nor	*do they know*	*measures*	*of roads.*	*It begins*

ab	finibus	Helvetiorum,	et	Nemetum,	et
from [at]	*the frontiers*	*of the Helvetii,*	*and*	*of the Nemetes.*	*and*

Rauracorum,	que	pertinet	rectā	regione
of the Rauraci,	*and*	*it extends*	*in a straight*	*direction (along)*

flumĭnis	Danuvi,	ad	fines	Dacorum	et
the river	*Dcnube,*	*to*	*the territories*	*of the Daci*	*and*

Anartium;	hinc	flectit	se	sinistrorsus	diversis
of the Anartes;	*thence*	*it bends*	*itself*	*to the left*	*in different*

regionibus	a	flumĭne,	que	attingit	fines
directions	*from*	*the river,*	*and*	*it touches*	*the boundaries*

multarum	gentium	propter	magnitudinem.	Neque
of many	*nations*	*on account*	*of its great extent.*	*Nor*

est	quisquam	hujus	Germaniæ,	qui	dicat
is (there)	*any one*	*of this (part of)*	*Germany,*	*who*	*may say*

se	aut	adisse	ad
himself (that he)	*either*	*to have gone [has gone]*	*to*

initium	ejus	silvæ,	cum	processerit
the beginning	*of this*	*forest,*	*though*	*he may have proceeded*

iter	sexaginta	dierum,	aut	acceperit	ex	quo
a journey	*of sixty*	*days,*	*or*	*may have heard*	*from*	*what*

loco	oriatur.	Constat	multa	genera
place	*it begins.*	*It is certain (that)*	*many*	*kinds*

ferarum	nasci	in ea,	quæ	sint	non	visa	in
of wild beasts	*are born*	*in it,*	*which*	*are*	*not*	*seen*	*in*

reliquis	locis;	ex	quibus	quæ maxime	differant
other	*places;*	*from*	*which (those) that*	*greatly*	*differ*

ab	ceteris,	et	videantur	prodenda
from	*the rest,*	*and*	*seem*	*worthy to be handed down*

memoriæ,	sunt	hæc.
to memory,	*are*	*these.*

26.

Est	bos	figurā	cervi,	a	mediā
There is	*an ox [animal]*	*in the shape*	*of a stag,*	*from*	*the mid*

fronte	cujus,	inter	aures,	unum	cornu	existit
forehead	*of which,*	*between*	*the ears,*	*a*	*horn*	*grows*

excelsius,	que	măgis	directum	his	cornibus,
higher,	*and*	*more*	*straight (than)*	*those*	*horns,*

quæ	sunt	nota	nobis.	Ab	summo	ejus	rami
which	*are*	*known*	*to us.*	*From*	*the top*	*of this*	*branches*

diffunduntur	late	sicut	palmæ.	Nature
are spread out	*broadly*	*like*	*palm (leaves).*	*The appearance*

feminæ	que	maris	est	eădem,	eădem	forma
of the female	*and*	*male*	*is*	*the same,*	*the same*	*form*

que	magnitudo	cornuum.
and	*size*	*of the horns.*

LIBER VI.

27. Sunt item, quæ appellantur alces.
There are also (animals), which are called elks.

Figura harum, et variĕtas pellium est
The shape of these, and the type of the skins is

consimilis capris, sed magnitudine antecedunt
very like to goats, but in size they surpass

paulo; que sunt mutilæ cornibus, et habent
a little; and they are devoid of horns, and (they) have

crura sine nodis que articulis; neque
legs without articulations and joints; neither

procumbunt causā quietis, neque si afflictæ
do they lie down for the purpose of rest, nor if afflicted

quo casu conciderint, possunt erigĕre
by any accident they have fallen down, can they raise

sese aut sublevare. Arbores sunt his pro
themselves or get up. The trees are to them for [as]

cubilibus; applicant se ad eas, atque
beds; they support themselves against these, and

ita reclinatæ modo paulum capiunt quietem;
so reclined merely a little while take rest;

quum ex vestigiis quarum animadversum est
when from the footsteps of which [these] it has been discovered

a venatoribus quo consueverint recipĕre
by the hunters where they have been accustomed to betake

se, aut subruunt omnes eo
themselves, either they undermine all (the trees) in that

loco a radicibus, aut accidunt arbores tantum ut
place at the roots, or they cut the trees so much that

summa species earum stantium relinquatur.
the total [mere] appearance of them standing may be left.

Huc cum ex consuetudine reclinaverint se,
Here when by custom they have reclined themselves,

affligunt infirmas arbores pondĕre, atque ipsæ
they overturn the weak trees by (their) weight, and they

concidunt una.
fall down together (with them).

28. Est tertium genus eorum, qui
There is a third kind of these (animals), which

appellantur	uri.	Hi	sunt	magnitudine	paulo
are called	*wild oxen.*	*These*	*are*	*in size*	*a little*
infra	elephantos,		specie	et colore	et
below	*the elephants,*		*with the appearance*	*and color*	*and*
figurā	tauri.	Eorum	vis	est magna,	et
form	*of the bull.*	*Their*	*strength*	*is great,*	*and (their)*
velocitas	magna;	parcunt	neque	homĭni neque	feræ
speed	*great;*	*they spare*	*neither*	*man nor*	*beast*
quam	conspexerint;		hos	captos	foveis
that	*they have seen;*		*these*	*captured*	*in pits*
interficiunt	studiose.	Adolescentes	durant	se
they kill	*with much zeal.*	*The youths*	*harden*	*themselves*
hōc	labore,	atque	exercent	hōc	genĕre
by this	*task,*	*and*	*exercise*	*by this*	*kind*
venationis;	et		qui	interfecerunt	plurimos
of hunting,	*and*	*(those)*	*who*	*have killed*	*the most*
ex	his,	ferunt	magnam	laudem,	cornibus
from [of]	*these,*	*obtain*	*great*	*honor,*	*the horns*
relatis		in	publicum	quæ	sint
having been brought		*into*	*public*	*which [that they]*	*may be (as)*
testimonio.	Sed	ne	quidem	parvuli	excepti
evidence.	*But*	*not*	*even*	*the young*	*(when) captured*
possunt		assuescĕre	ad	homĭnes,	et
can		*become accustomed*	*to*	*men,*	*and*
mansuefieri.	Amplitudo	et	figura	et	species
be tamed.	*The size*	*and*	*shape*	*and*	*appearance*
cornuum	differt	multum	a	cornibus	nostrorum
of (their) horns	*differs*	*much*	*from*	*the horns*	*of our*
boum.	Hæc			studiose	conquisita
oxen.	*These (horns)*			*zealously*	*sought*
circumcludunt		ab	labris	argento,	atque
they mount		*from [on]*	*the edges*	*with silver,*	*and*
utuntur		in		amplissimis	epŭlis	pro
use	*(them)*	*in*	*(their)*	*most splendid*	*feasts*	*for*
pocŭlis.					
cups.					

29. | | | | | |
|---|---|---|---|---|
| Cæsar | postquam | compĕrit | per | Ubios |
| *Cæsar* | *after* | *he discovered* | *through* | *the Ubian* |

exploratores,		Suevos	recepisse	sese	in
scouts,	*(that)*	*the Suevi*	*had withdrawn*	*themselves*	*into*

silvas,	longius,	constituit	non	progredi,
the forests,	*further,*	*resolved*	*not*	*to proceed,*

verĭtus	inopiam	frumenti,	(quod,	ut
fearing	*a scarcity*	*of corn,*	*(because,*	*as*

demonstravimus	supra,	omnes	Germani	student
we have shown	*above,*	*all*	*the Germans*	*attend*

minime	agri culturæ);	sed	ne	tollĕret
very little	*to agriculture);*	*but*	*that*	*he might not take away*

omnino	barbăris	metum	sui reditūs atque ut
altogether from the barbarians	*the fear*	*of his return*	*and that*

tardaret	eorum	auxilia,	reducto	exercitu,
he might retard	*their*	*auxiliaries,*	*having led back*	*the army,*

rescindit	ultimam partem pontis,	quæ contingebat
he breaks down	*the farthest part of the bridge*	*which touched*

ripas	Ubiorum,	in	longitudinem	ducentorum
the shores	*of the Ubii,*	*to*	*the length*	*of two hundred*

pedum,	atque	in	extremo	ponte (abl.)
feet,	*and*	*on*	*the extreme [end]*	*(of the) bridge*

constituit	turrim quattuor tabulatorum,	que	ponit
he constructs	*a tower of four stories,*	*and*	*places*

præsidium	duodecim	cohortium	causā	tuendi
a guard	*of twelve*	*cohorts*	*for the purpose*	*of defending*

pontis,	que	firmat	eum	locum	magnis
the bridge,	*and*	*strengthens*	*this*	*place*	*with great*

munitionibus.	Præfecit	ei	loco	que	præsidio,
fortifications.	*He placed over*	*this*	*place*	*and*	*garrison,*

C. Volcatium	Tullum,	adolescentem;	ipse,	cum
C. Volcatius	*Tullus,*	*a young man;*	*he himself,*	*when*

frumenta	incipĕrent	maturescĕre,	profectus	ad
the crops	*began*	*to ripen,*	*having set out*	*to*

bellum	Ambiorigis,	per	Arduennam	
the war	*of [with] Ambiorix,*	*through*	*the Arduennian [Ardennes]*	

silvam,	(quæ	est	maxima	totius	Galliæ,	atque
forest,	*(which*	*is*	*the largest*	*of all*	*Gaul,*	*and*

pertinet	ab	ripis	Rheni	que	finibus
extends	*from*	*the shores*	*of the Rhine*	*and*	*the territories*

Trevirorum ad Nervios, que patet amplius
of the Treviri to the Nervii, and reaches more than

quingentis millibus in longitudmem) præmittit
five hundred miles in length) sends forward

L. Minucium Basilium, cum omni equitatu, si
L. Minucius Basilius, with all the cavalry, (to see) if

possit proficĕre quid celeritate itinĕris,
he may be able to gain anything by quickness of march,

atque opportunitate tempŏris; monet ut
and by the favorableness of the time; he warns that

prohibeat ignes fieri in castris (pl.), ne
he should prohibit fires to be made in the camp, lest

qua significatio fiat procul ejus
any intimation [sign] be made at a distance of his

adventūs; dicit sese subsequi confestim.
coming; he says that he himself to [will] follow speedily.

30. Basilius facit ut imperatum est; itinere
Basilius does as was commanded; the march

confecto celeriter, que contra opinionem
having been performed quickly, and contrary to the expectation

omnium, deprehendit multos inopinantes in agris;
of all, he captures many unaware in the fields;

eorum indicio contendit ad Ambiorigem ipsum,
by their information he marches to Ambiorix himself,

in loco quo dicebatur esse cum paucis
in the place in which he was said to be with a few

equitibus. Fortuna potest multum, cum in
horsemen. Fortune can do much, not only in

omnibus rebus, tum in militari re (sing.).
all (other) things, but also in military affairs.

Nam sicut accidit magno casu, ut incideret
For although it happened by great chance, that he fell

in ipsum incautum atque imparatum, que ejus
on him off his guard and unprepared, and his

adventus videretur ab hominibus prius quam
arrival was seen by the men before

afferretur famā ac nuntiis, sic fuit
it could be announced by report and messengers, yet it was

LIBER VI.

magnæ fortunæ, omni militari instrumento quod
(of) great fortune, all the military equipment that

habēbat circum se erepto, rhedis
he had about him having been seized, his chariots

que equis comprehensis, ipsum
and horses having been captured, (that) he himself

effugĕre mortem. Sed hoc factum est eo quod,
should escape death. But this was effected by the fact that,

ædificio circumdato silvā (ut
the house (having been) surrounded by a wood (as

fere sunt domicilia Gallorum, qui causā
generally are the dwellings of the Gauls, who for the sake

vitandi æstūs, plerumque petunt propinquitates
of avoiding the heat, often seek the vicinity

silvarum ac fluminum), ejus comites que familiares
of woods and rivers), his attendants and friends

sustinuerunt paulisper vim nostrorum equitum
sustained for a little while the force of our calvary

in angusto loco. His pugnantibus (abl.
in a narrow place. (While) these (were) fighting,

abs.), quidam ex suis intulit illum in
a certain one from [of] his (men) placed him on

equum; silvæ texerunt fugientem; sic fortuna
a horse; the woods covered (him) fleeing; thus fortune

valuit multum, et ad subeundum pericŭlum, et
availed much, both for encountering danger, and

ad vitandum.
for avoiding (it).

31. Ne Ambiorix non conduxerit suas copias
Whether Ambiorix did not assemble his forces

judicio, quod existimaverit non dimicandum[28]
on purpose, because he thought (it) not to [must not] be engaged

prœlio; an fuerit exclusus tempore et prohibitus
in battle; or was cut off by time and prevented

repentino adventu equitum, cum
by the sudden arrival of the cavalry, when

credĕret reliquum exercitum subsequi,
he believed (that) the remainder of the army was following

est	dubium,	sed	certe	nuntiis	dimissis
is	*doubtful,*	*but*	*certainly*	*messengers*	*having been sent*

clam	per	agros	jussit
secretly	*through*	*the fields [country]*	*he ordered*

quemque	consulĕre	sibi;	quorum	pars
that each one	*should take care*	*of himself;*	*of whom*	*a part*

profugit	in	Arduennam	silvam,
fled	*into*	*the Arduennan [Ardunes]*	*forest,*

pars	in	continentes	paludes.	Qui
a part	*into*	*the continuous*	*marshes.*	*(Those) who*

fuerunt	proxĭmi	Oceanum,	hi	occultaverunt
were	*nearest*	*the Ocean,*	*these*	*hid*

sese	in	insulis,	quas	æstus
themselves	*in*	*the islands,*	*which*	*the tides*

consuērunt	efficĕre.	Multi	egressi	ex	suis
are accustomed	*to form.*	*Many*	*having emigrated*	*from*	*their*

finibus	crediderunt		se	que	omnia
territories	*confided [consigned]*	*themselves*	*and*	*all*

sua	alienissimis.	Catuvolcus	rex dimidiæ
their (property)	*to entire strangers.*	*Catuvolcus*	*king of the half*

partis	Eburonum	qui	inierat	consilium
part	*of the Eburones*	*who*	*had entered into*	*counsel*

unā	cum	Ambiorĭge,	jam	confectus	ætate,
together	*with*	*Ambiorix,*	*now*	*worn out*	*with age,*

quum	posset	non	ferre	laborem	aut	belli	aut
since	*he could*	*not*	*bear*	*the fatigue*	*either*	*of war*	*or*

fugæ,	detestatus	Ambiorĭgem	omnibus
of flight,	*having cursed*	*Ambiorix*	*with all (kinds of)*

precibus qui		fuisset auctor ejus consilii,
imprecations who [since he] had been the author of this plan [design],

exanimavit	se	taxo,	(cujus est
killed	*himself*	*by yew (leaves),*	*(of which (tree) there is*

magna	copia	in	Galliā	que Germaniā).
a great	*abundance*	*in*	*Gaul*	*and in Germany).*

32. | | | | | | |
|---|---|---|---|---|---|
| Segni | que | Condrusi, | ex | gente | et |
| *The Segni* | *and* | *Condrusi,* | *from [of]* | *the nation* | *and* |

numero	Germanorum,	qui	sunt	inter	Eburones
the number	*of the Germans,*	*who*	*are*	*between*	*the Eburones*

que	Treviros,	miserunt	legatos	ad	Cæsarem
and	*Treviri,*	*sent*	*ambassadors*	*to*	*Cæsar*

oratum	ne	ducĕret		se in	numero
to pray	*that*	*he would not consider*		*them in*	*the number*

hostium,	neve	judicaret		causam	omnium
of enemies,	*nor*	*should he judge (that)*		*the cause*	*of all*

Germanorum,	qui	essent	citra	Rhenum	esse
the Germans,	*who*	*were*	*on this side*	*of the Rhine*	*to be*

	unam;		se cogitāsse	nihil
[was]	*one [the same];*	*(that) they to have [had] thought*		*nothing*

de	bello,	misisse	nulla	auxilia
about	*war,*	*(that) they to have [had] sent*	*no*	*auxiliaries*

Ambiorĭgi.	Cæsar,	re	exploratā
to Ambiorix.	*Cæsar,*	*the thing [matter]*	*having been investigated*

quæstione	captivorum,	imperavit		si qui
by the questioning	*of the prisoners,*	*commanded (that)*		*if any*

Eburones	convenissent	ad	eos	ex fugā	ut
Eburones	*had come*	*to*	*them*	*from flight*	*that*

reducerentur		ad	se. Si	fecissent	ita,
they should be brought back		*to*	*him. If*	*they did*	*so,*

negavit	se		violaturum	eorum
he disavowed (that)	*himself [he]*	*about to [would] harm*		*their*

fines.	Tum	copiis	distributis	in
territories.	*Then*	*(his) forces*	*having been distributed*	*into*

tres	partes,	contulit	impedimenta	omnium	legionum
three	*parts,*	*he removed*	*the baggage*	*of all*	*the legions*

Aduatucam.	Id est	nomen	castelli.	Hoc	est
to Aduatuca.	*This is*	*the name*	*of a fortress.*	*This*	*is*

fere	in	mediis	finibus Eburonum,	ubi
nearly	*in*	*the middle*	*(of the) territories of the Eburones,*	*where*

Titurius	atque	Aurunculeius	consederunt	causā
Titurius	*and*	*Aurunculeius*	*had encamped*	*for the purpose*

hiemandi.	Cæsar	probat	hunc	locum	quum
of wintering.	*Cæsar*	*approves*	*this*	*place*	*not only*

reliquis	rebus,	tum	quod	munitiones
for the other	*things,*	*but also*	*because*	*the fortifications*

superioris	anni	manebant	integræ,	ut
of the preceding	*year*	*were remaining*	*entire,*	*(so) that*

sublevaret	laborem	militum;	reliquit	præsidio
he might lighten	*the labor*	*of the soldiers;*	*he left*	*for [as] a guard*

impedimentis	quattuor-decimam	legionem,	unam
to the baggage	*the fourteenth*	*legion,*	*one*

ex	iis	tribus,	quas	proxime	conscriptas,
of	*those*	*three,*	*which*	*lately*	*(having been) enrolled,*

traduxerat	ex Italiā.	Præfēcit	ei	legioni
he had brought over	*from Italy.*	*He appointed over*	*this*	*legion*

que	castris,	Q. Tullium	Ciceronem,	que	attribuit
and	*the camp,*	*Q. Tullius*	*Cicero,*	*and*	*assigned*

ducentos	equites.
(him) two hundred	*horsemen.*

33. | Exercĭtu | partito, | jubet | T. Labienum |
|---|---|---|---|
| *The army* | *having been divided,* | *he orders* | *T. Labienus* |

proficisi	cum	tribus	legionibus	adversus
to march	*with*	*three*	*legions*	*in the direction of*

Oceanum,	in	eas partes	quæ	attingunt	Menapios.
the Ocean,	*into*	*these parts*	*which*	*touch on*	*the Menapii.*

Mittit	C. Trebonium	cum	pari	numĕro	legionum
He sends	*C. Trebonius*	*with*	*a like*	*number*	*of legions*

ad	depopulandum	eam	regionem,[29]	quæ	adjacet
for	*devastating*	*that*	*district,*	*which*	*borders on*

Aduatucis.	Ipse	cum	tribus	reliquis
the Aduatuci.	*(He) himself*	*with*	*the three*	*remaining (legions)*

constituit	ire	ad	flumen	Scaldim,	quod
resolves	*to go*	*to*	*the river*	*Scaldis [Scheldt],*	*which*

influit	in	Mosam	que	extremas	partes
flows	*into*	*the Mosa [Meuse],*	*and*	*(to) the extreme*	*parts*

Arduennæ,	quo	audiebat
of the Arduennian [Ardennes] (forest),	*whither*	*he heard*

Ambiorĭgem	profectum	cum	paucis	equitibus.
Ambiorix	*to have [had] gone*	*with*	*a few*	*horsemen.*

Discedens	confirmat	sese	reversurum
On departing he promises (that) (he) himself about to [would] return			

septimum	diem	post;	ad	quam	diem	sciebat
(on) the seventh	*day*	*afterwards;*	*on*	*which*	*day*	*he knew*

frumentum	debēri	ei	legioni,	quæ
(that) grain	*to be [was] due*	*to this*	*legion,*	*which*

relinqueoatur	in	præsidio.	Hortatur	Labienum	que
was left	*in*	*garrison.*	*He urges*	*Labienus*	*and*

Trebonium		revertantur	ad	eam	diem, si
Trebonius	*that they should return*		*on*	*this*	*day, if*

possint	facĕre	commodo	rei publicæ,	ut,
they could	*do (it)*	*to the advantage of the republic,*		*that,*

concilio	communicato		rursus, que	rationibus
counsel	*having been communicated*		*mutually, and*	*the plans*

hostium	exploratis,		possint	capĕre
of the enemy	*having been ascertained,*		*they may be able*	*to take*

	aliud	initium	belli.
[adopt]	*another*	*start [beginning]*	*of [in] the war.*

34.
	Erat,	ut	demonstravimus	supra,	nulla certa
	There was,	*as*	*we have shown*	*above,*	*no fixed*

mănus,	non	præsidium,	non	oppidum,	quod
body of men,	*not*	*a garrison,*	*not*	*a town,*	*that*

defendĕret	se	armis,	sed	multitudo	dispersa in
could defend	*itself*	*by arms,*	*but*	*a multitude*	*scattered in*

omnes partes.	Ubi	cuique	aut	abdĭta	vallis, aut
all directions.	*Where*	*to any one*	*either*	*a hidden*	*valley, or*

silvestris	locus,	aut	impedita	palus, offerebat
a woody	*place,*	*or*	*a difficult*	*swamp, offered*

aliquam	spem	præsidii	aut	salutis, consederat.
some	*hope*	*of protection*	*or*	*of safety, he had settled.*

Hæc	loca	erant nota	vicinitatibus,	que	res
These places		*were known*	*to the neighbors,*	*and*	*the thing*

	requirebat	magnam	diligentiam,	non in
[condition]	*required*	*great*	*care,*	*not in*

tuendā	summā (abl.)	exercitūs	(enim nullum
protecting	*the main body*	*of the army*	*(for no*

periculum,	universis,	poterat	accidĕre ab
danger,	*to the whole,*	*could*	*happen from (them)*

perterrĭtis	ac dispersis),	sed in	conservandis singulis
terrified	*and dispersed),*	*but in*	*preserving individual*

militibus; quæ	res	tamen ex parte pertinebat
soldiers; which thing	*[this condition]*	*however in part pertained*

ad	salutem	exercitūs.	Nam	et	cupidĭtas prædæ
to	*the safety*	*of the army.*	*For*	*both*	*the desire of booty*

evocabat multos longius, ac silvæ incertis	
enticed many too far and the woods by their uncertain	
que occultis itineribus prohibebant adire	
and hidden paths prevented (them) to advance [from	
confertos. Si vellet negotium confici	
advancing] close together. If he wished the business to be finished,	
que stirpem sceleratorum homĭnum interfici,	
and a race of infamous men to be exterminated,	
plures mănus dimittendæ, que milites	
a great many bands to [must] be sent out, and the soldiers	
diducendi erant; si vellet continere manipulos	
to [must] be detached; if he desired to keep the companies	
ad signa, ut instituta ratio et consuetudo	
to the ensigns, as the constituted order and custom	
Romani exercitūs postulabat, locus ipse erat	
of the Roman army demanded, the place itself was	
præsidio barbăris; neque dĕerat	
(for) a protection to the barbarians; neither was there wanting	
singulis audacia insidiandi ex occulto, et	
to individuals the daring of ambushing in secret, and	
circumveniendi dispersos. At in difficultatibus	
of surrounding dispersed (soldiers). But in difficulties	
ejusmodi quantum diligentiā poterat provideri	
of this nature as much as by diligence could be provided	
providebatur; ut potius aliquid omitteretur	
was provided so that rather something might be omitted	
in nocendo, esti animi omnium	
in injuring (the enemy), although the minds of all	
ardebant ad ulciscendum, quam nocere-	
were burning to be avenged than that (the enemy) might	
tur cum aliquo detrimento militum.	
be injured with any loss of soldiers.	
Cæsar dimittit nuntios ad finitimas civitates;	
Cæsar sends off messengers to the neighboring states;	
evocat omnes ad se, spe prædæ, ad	
he invites all to himself, by the hope of plunder for	
diripiendos Eburones; ut potius vita Gallorum	
ravaging the Eburones; that rather the life of the Gauls	

LIBER VI.

periclitetur	in	silvis,	quam	legionariorum;
may be hazarded	in	the woods,	than (that)	of the legionary

	simul,	ut	magnā	multitudine
(soldiers);	at the same time,	that	a great	multitude

circumfusā,	stirps	ac	nomen	civitatis
having been sent abroad,	the race	and	name	of the state

tollatur	pro	tali	facinŏre.	Magnus	numĕrus
may be destroyed	for	such	a crime.	A great	number

celeriter convenit undique.
quickly assembled from all places.

35. Hæc gerebantur in omnibus partibus
These (things) were carried on in all parts

Eburonum, que septimus dies appetebat,
of the Eburones, and the seventh day was approaching,

ad	quem	diem	Cæsar	constituerat	reverti	ad
on	which	day	Cæsar	had resolved	to return	to

impedimenta	que	legionem.	Hic	potuit	cognosci,
the baggage	and	the legion.	Here	it might	be learned,

quantum	fortuna	possit	in	bello,	et	quantos
how much	fortune	can do	in	war,	and	how great

casus affĕrat. Hostibus dissipatis
mischances it may bring. The enemy having been dispersed

ac	perterrĭtis,	ut	demonstravimus,	erat	nulla
and	terrified,	as	we have shown,	there was	no

manus,	quæ	afferret	modo	parvam causam
body of men,	which	might create	only [even]	a slight cause

timōris.	Fama	pervenit	trans	Rhenum	ad
of fear.	The report	spread	beyond	the Rhine	to

Germanos,		Eburones	dirĭpi,	atque
the Germans,	(that)	the Eburones	to be [were] pillaged,	and

	omnes	evocari	ultro	ad	prædam.
(that)	all	to be [were] invited	freely	to	the booty

	Sugambri	cogunt	duo	millia	equitum;
[plunder].	The Sugambri	collect	two	thousand	(of) horse;

qui sunt proxĭmi Rheno, a quibus Tenceteros
they are the nearest to the Rhine, by whom [and by them] the Tencteri

atque	Usipetes	receptos	ex		fugā,	
and	Usipetes	were received	in	(their)	flight,	(as)

docuimus	we have shown
supra;	above;
transeuntes	crossing
Rhenum	the Rhine
navibus	in ships
que	and
ratibus	boats
triginta	thirty
millibus	thousand
passuum	paces
infra	below
eum	this
locum	place
ubi	where
pons	the bridge
perfectus erat,	had been made,
que	and
præsidium	the garrison
relictum	left
ab	by
Cæsare,	Cæsar,
adeunt	they enter
primos	the first [nearest]
fines	territories
Eburonum;	of the Eburones;
excipiunt	they surprise
multus	many
dispersos	dispersed
ex	in
fugā;	flight;
potiuntur	they obtain possession of
magno	a great
numĕro	number
pecŏris,	of cattle,
cujus	of which
barbări	the barbarians
sunt	are
cupidissimi.	very covetous.
Invitati	Enticed
prædā	by booty
procedunt	they proceed
longius.	farther.
Non	Neither
palus,	swamp,
non	nor
silvæ,	woods,
morantur	impede
hos	these men
natos	born
in	in
bello	war
que	and
latrocinis.	plundering.
Quærunt	They inquire
ex	of
captivis	the prisoners
in	in
quibus	what
locis	place
Cæsar	Cæsar
sit;	may be;
reperiunt	they find
(that)	(that)
profectum	he has gone
longius,	further,
que	and
cognoscunt	learn
omnem	(that) all
exercĭtum	the army
discessisse.	to have [has] departed.
Atque	Moreover
unus	one
ex	from [of]
captivis	the captives
inquit,	said
"quid	"why
vos	do you
quibus	to whom
jam	now it is allowed
licet	to be
esse	most fortunate
fortunatissimis	follow
sectamini	
hanc	this
miseram	wretched
et	and
tenuem	trifling
prædam?	plunder?
Tribus	In three
horis	hours
potestis	you can
venire	come to
Aduatucam;	Aduatuca;
huc	there
exercitus	the army
Romanorum	of the Romans
contulit	has collected
omnes	all
suas	its
fortunas;	property;
est	there is
tantum	so little
præsidii,	(of a) garrison,
ut	that
ne	not
quidem	even
murus	the wall
possit	can
cingi,	be manned,
neque	nor
audeat	dares
quisquam	any one
agredi	go
extra	beyond
munitiones."	the fortifications."

(Hac)	spe	oblatā,	Germani	relinquunt
(This)	*hope*	*having been offered,*	*the Germans*	*leave*

in	occulto	prædam	quam	nacti erant;
in	*hiding*	*the booty*	*which*	*they had obtained;*

ipsi	contendunt	Aduatucam,	usi	eodem
they	*proceed to*	*Aduatuca,*	*using*	*the same*

duce	cujus	indicio	cognoverant
(person) as guide	*by whose*	*information*	*they had learned*

hæc.
these things.

36. | Cicero, | (qui | per | omnes | superiores | dies, |
| --- | --- | --- | --- | --- | --- |
| *Cicero,* | *(who* | *through* | *all* | *the former* | *days,* |

præceptis	Cæsaris	continuisset	milites	in
according to	*the orders of Cæsar*	*had kept*	*the soldiers*	*in*

castris	summa	diligentiā,	ac	passus est	ne
camp	*with the greatest*	*diligence,*	*and*	*allowed*	*not*

quidem	quemquam	calonem	egredi	extra
even	*any*	*camp follower*	*to go*	*beyond*

munitionem),	septimo die	diffidens	Cæsarem
the fortification),	*on the seventh day*	*distrusting (that)*	*Cæsar*

servaturum	fidem	de	numĕro	dierum,
about to [would] keep	*faith*	*about*	*the number*	*of days,*

quod	audiebat	eum	progressum	longius,
because	*he heard (that)*	*he*	*had proceeded*	*further,*

neque	ulla	fama	de	ejus	redĭtu	afferebatur,
nor	*was any*	*report*	*of*	*his*	*return*	*brought,*

simul	permotus	vocibus	eorum,	qui
at the same time	*moved*	*by the words*	*of those,*	*who*

appellabant	illius	patientiam	pæne	obsessionem	si
were calling	*his*	*endurance*	*nearly*	*a siege*	*if*

quidem	non licēret	egredi	ex	castris;
indeed	*it was not allowed*	*to go out*	*from*	*camp;*

expectans	nullum	casum	hujusmodi	quo
expecting	*no*	*event*	*of such kind*	*by which [that]*

posset	offendi,	in	tribus	milibus,
he could	*be injured,*	*within*	*three*	*miles (of the camp),*

novem	legionibus	oppositis,	que	maximo
nine	*legions*	*having been opposed*	*and*	*a numerous*

equitatu,	hostibus	dispersis	ac	pæne
cavalry,	*the enemy*	*having been dispersed*	*and*	*almost*

deletis,	misit	quinque	cohortes	frumentatum	in
annihilated,	*he sent*	*five*	*cohorts*	*to forage*	*in*

proximas	segĕtes,	inter	quas	et	castra
the neighboring	*corn-fields,*	*between*	*which*	*and*	*the camp*

unus	collis	omnino	intererat.	Complures	ex
one	*hill*	*in all [alone]*	*intervened.*	*Many*	*from*

legionibus	relicti erant	ægri	in	castris;	ex quibus,
the legions	*had been left*	*sick*	*in*	*the camp;*	*of whom,*

qui	hōc	spatio	dierum	convaluerant,
(those) who	*in this*	*period*	*of time*	*had recovered,*

circiter	trecenti	mittuntur	sub	vexillo	unā;
about	*three hundred*	*are sent*	*under*	*a standard*	*together;*

præterea	magna	multitudo	calonum	magna
moreover	*a great*	*multitude*	*of camp followers (and)*	*a great*

vis	jumentorum,	quæ	subsederat	in	castris,
force	*of beasts of burden,*	*that*	*had remained*	*in*	*the camp,*

sequitur,	potestate	factā.
follow (them),	*permission*	*having been given.*

37.
Hoc	ipso	tempŏre	et	casu	Germani
At this	*very*	*time*	*and*	*by chance*	*the German*

equĭtes	interveniunt,	que	protĭnus	eodem	illo
horsemen	*arrive,*	*and*	*immediately*	*with that*	*same*

cursu,	quo	venerant,	conantur	irrumpĕre	in
speed,	*with which*	*they had come,*	*try*	*to break*	*into*

castra	ab	decumanā	portā;	nec	visi sunt,
the camp	*at*	*the decuman*	*gate;*	*nor*	*were they seen,*

(silvis	objectis	ab	eā	parte),	prius
(a wood	*being interposed*	*at [on]*	*this*	*part [side]),*	*until*

quam	appropinquarent	castris;	usque	eo,	ut
they had approached		*the camp;*	*even*	*so,*	*that*

mercatores,	qui	tendĕrent	sub	vallo,
the merchants (sutlers),	*who*	*encamped*	*under*	*the rampart,*

non haberent	facultatem	recipiendi	sui.
had not	*an opportunity*	*of taking*	*themselves away.*

Nostri	inopinantes	pĕrturbantur	novā
Our (men)	*taken unawares*	*are confused*	*with this new*

37] LIBER VI.

re,	ac	cohors	in statione	vix	sustĭnet
condition,	*and*	*the cohort*	*on guard*	*scarcely*	*sustains*
primum	impĕtum;	hostes	circumfunduntur		ex
the first	*attack;*	*the enemy*	*are spread out*		*on*
reliquis	partibus,	si	possent reperire	quem	adĭtum;
the other	*sides, [to see]*	*if*	*they could find*	*some*	*approach;*
nostri	ægre		tuentur	portas;	locus
our	*(men) with difficulty*		*defend*	*the gates;*	*the place*
ipse	per	se	que	munitio	defendit
itself	*through*	*itself*	*and*	*the fortification*	*defends*
reliquos	adĭtus;	totis	castris	trepidatur,	atque
the other	*approaches;*	*in all*	*the camp*	*there is alarm,*	*and*
alius quærit	ex	alio	causam	tumultūs;	neque
one inquires	*of*	*another*	*the cause*	*of the confusion;*	*neither*
provident	quo	signa	ferantur,	neque	in
do they provide	*where*	*the ensigns*	*may be carried,*	*nor*	*into*
quam partem	quisque	conveniat.		Alius	pronuntiat
what part	*each one*	*may assemble.*		*One*	*declares*
	castra	jam	capta,	alius	contendit,
	(that) the camp	*to be [is]*	*already taken,*	*another*	*affirms (that),*
exercitu	atque	imperatore			deleto,
the army	*and*	*the commander*			*having been destroyed,*
victores	barbăros	venisse;		plerique	fingunt
the victorious	*barbarians*	*(to) have come;*		*the greater part*	*form*
novas	religiones	sibi	ex	loco,	que
strange	*superstitions*	*for themselves*	*from*	*the place,*	*and*
ponunt	ante	oculos	calamitatem	Cottæ	et
put	*before (their)*	*eyes*	*the calamity*	*of Cotta*	*and*
Titurii,	qui occiderint	in	eodem	castello.	Omnibus
Titurius,	*who fell*	*in*	*the same*	*fortress.*	*All*
	perterrĭtis	tali	timore,		opinio
(having been) alarmed		*by such*	*fear,*		*the belief*
confirmatur	barbaris,		ut	audierant	ex
it confirmed	*to [among] the barbarians,*		*as*	*they had heard*	*from*
captivo,	nullum	præsidium		esse	intus;
the captive,	*(that) no*	*garrison*		*to be [was]*	*within;*
nituntur	perrumpĕre,		que	ipsi	adhortantur
they endeavor	*to force an entrance,*		*and*	*they*	*exhort*

se,	ne	dimittant	tantam	fortunam	ex
one another,	*lest*	*they may let go*	*so great*	*a prize*	*from*

manibus.
their hands.

38. P. Sextĭus Bacŭlus, qui duxerat primum
P. Sextius Baculus, who had led the first

pilum apud Cæsarem cujus fecimus mentionem
company under Cæsar of whom we have made mention

superioribus prœliis, relictus erat æger in præsidio,
in former battles, had been left sick in the garrison,

ac caruerat cibo jam quintum diem. Hic,
and had been without food now the fifth day. He,

diffisus suæ saluti ac omnium, inermis
mistrusting his safety and (that) of all, unarmed

prodit ex tabernaculo; videt hostes
goes out from the tent; he sees (that) the enemy

imminēre, atque rem esse in
to be [are] pressing on, and that the affair to be [is] in

summo discrimĭne; capit arma a proximis,
the greatest danger; he seizes arms from the nearest,

atque consistit in portā. Centuriones ejus
and places himself in the gate. The centurions of that

cohortis quæ erat in statione sequuntur hunc;
cohort which was on guard follow him;

paulisper sustinent prœlium unā; animus
for a little while they sustain the battle together; his mind

relinquit Sextĭum[30] gravibus vulneribus acceptis;
leaves Sextius severe wounds having been received;

tractus per mănūs (pl.) ægre servatur.
dragged away by hand with difficulty he is saved.

Hoc spatio interposito, reliqui confirmant
This period having been interposed, the others encourage

sese tantum, ut audeant consistĕre
one another so much, that they dare take stand

in mŭnitionibus, qŭe præbeant speciem
on the fortifications, and show the appearance

defensorum.
of defenders.

LIBER VI.

39. Interim frumentatione confectā,
In the meantime the foraging having been completed,

nostri milites exaudiunt clamorem, equites
our soldiers hear the shout, the horsemen

præcurrunt cognoscunt in quanto periculo
hasten on before, and ascertain in what great danger

res sit. Vero hīc est nulla munitio,
the matter is. But here there is no fortification,

quæ recipiat perterritos. Modo conscripti
which may receive (those) affrighted. (Those) lately enrolled

atque imperiti militaris usūs convertunt ora ad
and unskilled in military practice turn faces to

tribunum militum que centuriones; expectant
the tribune of the soldiers and centurions; they await

quid præcipiatur ab his. Nemo est tam
what may be commanded by them. No one is so

fortis, quin perturbetur novitate rei.
brave, but (that) he is disconcerted by the strangeness of the affair

Barbări, conspicati signa procul,
[situation]. The barbarians, having seen the standards at a distance,

desistunt ab oppugnatione; primo credunt
desist from the attack; at first they believe (that,

legiones redisse, quas cognoverant ex
the legions have returned, which they had learned from

captivis discessisse longius; postea, paucitate
the captives had gone further; afterwards, the fewness

despectā, faciunt impetum, ex
having been perceived, they make an attack, from [on]

omnibus partibus.
all parts [sides].

40. Calones procurrunt in proximum tumŭlum
The camp followers run to the nearest high ground

celeriter dejecti hinc, conjiciunt se
(and) having been quickly driven thence, they throw themselves

in signa que manipŭlos; eō măgis
among the standards and companies; so much the more

perterrent timidos milites. Alii censent
they alarm the affrighted soldiers. Some are of the opinion

	cuněo	facto		celeriter
(that)	a wedge	having been formed	they should	quickly

perrumpant,	quoniam	castra	sint	tam	propinqua,
break through,	and as	the camp	is	so	near,

etsi	aliqua	pars	circumventa	ceciderit,
although	some	part	having been surrounded	might fall,

at	confidunt		reliquos	posse
still	they trust	(that)	the remainder	to be able [can]

servari.	Alii	ut	consistant	in
(to) be saved.	Others (advise)	that	they take stand	on

jugo,	atque	omnes	ferant	eundem	casum.
the hill-top,	and	(that) all	undergo	the same	fate.

Veteres	milites,	quos	docuimus
The veteran	soldiers,	whom [who]	we have mentioned

profectos	una	sub	vexillo	non
(to have) marched out	together	under	a standard	do not

probant	hoc. Itaque	cohortati	inter	se,
approve	this. Therefore	having encouraged	one	another,

C. Trebonio,	Romano	equite,	qui	præpositus erat
C. Trebonius,	a Roman	knight,	who	had been placed over

eis,		duce,	perrumpunt per	medios[31]
them,	being their	commander,	they break	through the middle

	hostes	que omnes	ad unum	perveniunt
[central] enemies		and all	to one [a man]	arrive

incolumes	in	castra (acc.).	Calones	que
safe	in	the camp.	The camp followers	and

equites	subsecuti	hos	eodem	impetu,
the horsemen	having followed	these	with the same	dash,

servantur	virtute	militum. At	ii,	qui
are saved	by the bravery	of the soldiers. But	those,	who

constiterant	in	jugo,	etiam nunc	nullo
had taken stand	on	the hill-top,	even now	no

usu	militaris	rei (sing.) percepto,	neque
experience	of military	affairs having been acquired,	neither

potuerunt	permanēre	in	eo	consilio,	quod proba-
were able	to persist	in	this	design,	which they had

verant,	ut	defendĕrent	se	superiore
approved,	that	they should defend	themselves	in the higher

loco,	neque		imitari	eam	vim	que
position,	nor	(were able)	to imitate	that	vigor	and

celeritatem,	quam	viderant	profuisse
speed,	which	they had seen	to have [had] availed

aliis;	sed	conati	recipere	se	in
the others;	but	having attempted	to betake	themselves	into

castra	demiserunt	in	iniquum	locum.
the camp	they descended	into	a disadvantageous	place.

Centuriones,	nonnulli	quorum	transducti	erant
The centurions,	some	of whom	had	been transferred

ex	inferioribus	ordinibus	reliquarum	legionum,
from	the lower	ranks	of the other	legions,

causā	virtutis,	in	superiores	ordines	hujus
by reason of	bravery,	into	the higher	ranks	of this

legionis,	ne	amittĕrent	laudem	militaris
legion,	lest	they might lose	renown	in military

rei (sing.)	partam	ante	conciderunt	pugnantes
affairs	acquired	before,	fell	fighting

fortissime.	Pars	militum,	hostibus
most valiantly.	A part	of (these) soldiers,	the enemy

summotis	virtute	horum,
having been removed	by the bravery	of these [by their bravery],

pervenit	in	castra	incolŭmis,	præter	spem;
arrived	in	the camp	safe,	beyond	expectation;

pars	circumventa	a	barbăris	periit.
a part	surrounded	by	the barbarians	perished.

41. | Germani, | expugnatione | castrorum | des- |
|---|---|---|---|
| The Germans, | the storming | of the camp | having |

peratā,	quod	videbant		nostros
been despaired of,	because	they saw	(that)	our men

jam	constitisse	in	munitionibus	receperunt
had now	taken stand	on	the fortifications	betook

sese	trans	Rhenum,	cum	eā	prædā	quam
themselves	beyond	the Rhine,	with	that	booty	which

deposuerant	in	silvis.	Ac	tantus	fuit
they had deposited	in	the woods.	And	so great	was

terror,	etiam	post	discessum	hostium,	ut
the alarm,	even	after	the departure	of the enemy,	that

eā	on this
nocte,	night,
cum	when
C. Volusenus	C. Volusenus
venisset	had come
ad	to

castra, missus cum equitatu, non
the camp, having been sent with the cavalry, he could not

facĕret fidem Cæsarem adesse cum
make [create] confidence (that) Cæsar was near with

exercĭtu incolŭmi. Timor præoccupaverat animos
the army safe. Fear had preoccupied the souls

omnium sic, ut mente pæne alienatā,
of all so, that with a mind almost unbalanced,

dicĕrent equitatum tantum recepisse se
they were saying, (that) the cavalry only to have [had] returned

ex fugā, omnibus copiis deletis,
from the flight, all the forces having been destroyed,

que contendĕrent Germanos ne fuisse
and they asserted (that) the Germans not to have been

oppugnaturos[32] castra exercĭtu
about to assault [would not have assaulted] the camp (if) the army

incolŭmi; quem timorem Cæsaris adventus
being [was] safe; which fear Cæsar's arrival

sustŭlit.
removed.

42. Ille reversus, non ignarus eventūs
He [Cæsar] having returned, not ignorant of the casualty

belli, questus unum, quod cohortes essent
of war, complained (of) one (thing), that the cohorts had been

emissæ ex statione et præsidio; indicavit
sent from the post and from the garrison; he pointed out

ne quidem minimum locum debuisse
(that) not even the least opportunity ought

relinqui casui; fortunam potuisse
to be left to chance; fortune had been able (to do)

multum in repentino adventu hostium, etiam multō
much by the sudden arrival of the enemy, also much

amplius, quod avertisset barbăros ab
more, because she had turned away the barbarians from

vallo ipso que portis castrorum. Omnium
the rampart itself and the gates of the camp. Of all

quarum	rerum	videbatur	maxime	admirandum,	
which [these]	things	it seemed	most	to be wondered at	

quod	Germani,	qui	transierant	Rhenum	eo
that	the Germans,	who had	crossed	the Rhine	with this

consilio,	ut depopularentur	fines	Ambiorigis,
design,	that they might lay waste	the territories	of Ambiorix,

delati	ad	castra	Romanorum,	obtulerunt
having been led	to	the camp	of the Romans	brought

Ambiorĭgi	optatissimum	beneficium.
to Ambiorix	a most desirable	benefit.

43. Cæsar rursus profectus ad vexandos[33]
  Cæsar again having departed to harass

hostes,	magno	numĕro	coacto	ex
the enemy,	a great	number	having been assembled	from

finitimis	civitatibus	dimittit	in	omnes
the neighboring	states	he sends (them)	into	all

partes.	Omnes	vici	atque omnia	ædificia,
parts.	All	the villages	and all	the buildings,

quæ	quisque	conspexerat,	incendebantur;	præda
which	any one	had noticed	were set on fire;	spoils

agebatur	ex	omnibus	locis;	frumenta	non
were driven off	from	all	places;	the corn	not

solum	consumebantur (pl.)	a	tantā	multitudine
only	was consumed	by	such	a multitude

jumentorum	atque	hominum,	sed etiam	procubuerant
of cattle	and	men,	but also	had fallen down

tempŏre	anni	atque	imbribus;	ut	si	qui
by the time	of year	and	the rains;	so that	if	any

etiam	in	præsentiā	occultāssent	se,	tamen
even	in [for]	the present	had concealed	themselves,	yet

videretur	his	perendum[34]	inopiā	omnium
it would seem (that)	they	must perish	through want	of all

rerum,	exercĭtu	deducto.	Ac	sæpe
things,	the army	having been withdrawn.	And	often

ventum est	in	eum locum,	equitatu	diviso
it came	to	this pass,	the cavalry	having been divided

tanto	in	omnes	partes,	ut	captivi
so much	into [in]	all	directions,	that	the prisoners

| contenderent | | Ambiorigem | | non | modo visum |
| *declared* | *(that)* | *Ambiorix* | | *was not* | *only seen* |

| ab | se | in | fugā, | sed | etiam | | nec abisse |
| *by* | *them* | *in* | *flight,* | *but* | *also* | *(that)* | *he had not gone* |

| plane | ex | conspectu; | ut | spe | consequendi |
| *clearly* | *out* | *of sight;* | *(so) that* | *the hope* | *of overtaking* |

| | illatā, | atque | infinito | labore |
| *(him) having been raised,* | | *and* | *an immense* | *labor* |

| suscepto, | qui | putarent | se |
| *having been undertaken,* | *those who* | *thought* | *(that) they* |

| ituros | summam | gratiam | a | Cæsare, | pæne |
| *would obtain* | *the highest* | *favor* | *from* | *Cæsar,* | *nearly* |

| vincĕrent | naturam | studio, | que semper paulum |
| *conquered* | *nature* | *by (their) efforts,* | *and always but little* |

| videretur | defuisse | ad | summam | felicitatem; |
| *seemed* | *to be wanting* | *to* | *complete* | *success;* |

| atque | ille | eripĕret | se | latēbris | ac | silvis |
| *but* | *he* | *rescued* | *himself* | *by hiding places* | *and* | *woods* |

| aut | saltibus, | et | occultatus | noctu | petĕret | alias |
| *or* | *forests,* | *and* | *concealed* | *by night* | *he sought* | *other* |

| regiones, | que | partes, | non | majore | præsidio |
| *regions,* | *and* | *places,* | *with no* | *greater* | *guard* |

| equitum | quam | quattuor, | quibus | solis | audebat |
| *of horsemen* | *than* | *four,* | *to whom* | *alone* | *he dared* |

| committĕre | suam | vitam. |
| *to entrust* | *his* | *life.* |

44. | Regionibus | vastatis | tali | modo, |
| *The country* | *having been laid waste* | *in such* | *manner,* |

| Cæsar | reducit | exercitum | damno | duarum |
| *Cæsar* | *leads back* | *the army* | *with the loss* | *of two* |

| cohortium | Durocortorum | Rhemorum; | que | concilio |
| *cohorts* | *to Durocortorum* | *of the Rhemi;* | *and* | *a council* |

| | indicto | in | eum | locum | Galliæ, | instituit |
| *having been summoned* | | *into* | *this* | *part* | *of Gaul,* | *he resolved* |

| habēre | quæstionem | de | conjuratione | Senonum |
| *to have* | *an investigation* | *about* | *the conspiracy* | *of the Senones* |

| et | Carnutum; | et | graviore | sententiā | pronun- |
| *and* | *Carnutes;* | *and* | *a very severe* | *sentence* | *having been*

ciatā	de	Accone,	qui	fuerat	princeps
pronounced	*on*	*Acco,*	*who*	*had been*	*the chief*

ejus	consilii,	sumpsit		supplicium,	more
of this	*counsel,*	*he took [inflicted]*		*punishment,*	*after the custom*

majorum.[35]	Nonnulli	verĭti	judicium profugerunt;
of our ancestors.	*Some*	*afraid of*	*a trial* *fled;*

cum	interdixisset	aquā	atque	igni	quibus,
when	*he had interdicted*	*water*	*and*	*fire*	*to them,*

collocavit	in	hibernis	duas legiones	ad	fines
he stationed	*in*	*winter quarters*	*two legions*	*on*	*the frontiers*

Trevirorum,	duas	in	Lingonibus,	reliquas
of the Treviri,	*two*	*among*	*the Lingones,*	*the remaining*

sex	Agendici	in	finibus	Senonum,	que
six	*at Agendicum*	*in*	*the territories*	*of the Senones,*	*and*

frumento		proviso		exercitui,	ut
corn		*having been provided*		*for the army,*	*as*

instituerat	profectus est	in	Italiam	ad	agendos
he had resolved	*he departed*	*for*	*Italy*	*to*	*hold*

conventus.
the assemblies.

LIBER SEPTIMUS
Seventh   Book

The seventh book opens with a statement of the rising of the Gauls upon knowledge of civil disturbances in Rome which might detain Caesar in the city. Caesar at length sets out for his province and unexpectedly crosses the Alps with an army through deep snows. Meantime Vercingetorix, an Arvernian, had been chosen leader of the revolution. Caesar by rapid marches here and there holds the people in check. He captures Velaunodunum, Cenavum, Noviodunum and Avaricum. Labienus goes on an expedition to the north as far as Lutetia, which the Gauls burn, and after defeating the Gauls in battle he rejoins Caesar. In spite of Caesar's efforts the Aedui join the revolt. Caesar obtains cavalry from Germany and with their aid defeats Vercingetorix in several battles. He is forced to raise the siege of Gergovia on account of the increasing activity of the Gallic nations. Caesar concentrates his forces against Vercingetorix and drives him to Alesia. The investment of Alesia and a general uprising of all Gaul now follow. Caesar is attacked by an army of a quarter of a million from without and holds eighty thousand within the city. After having built extensive works and conquering in fierce contests, he defeats the outside forces, repulses the besieged and compels the surrender of the city. Vercingetorix is sent to Rome in chains, and six years later takes part in Caesar's triumph, after which he is executed. The nations make peace with Caesar who quarters his troops in various places in Gaul. He himself winters at Bibracte. On receiving Caesar's letters the senate decrees a thanksgiving of twenty days.

1. Gallia quietā, Cæsar ut constituerat
Gaul being at peace, Cæsar as he had resolved
proficiscitur in Italiam ad agendos conventus;
proceeds to Italy to hold the assemblies;
ubi cognoscit de cæde P. Clodii, que
there he learns of the murder of P. Clodius, and
factus certior de consulto Senatūs,
having been made acquainted with the decree of the Senate,

LIBER VII.

ut omnes juniores Italiæ conjurarent,
that all the young men of Italy should take military oath,

instituit habēre delectum totā provinciā. Eæ
he resolved to hold a levy in all the province. These

res celeriter perferuntur in Transalpinam Galliam.
things quickly are reported into Transalpine Gaul.

Galli ipsi addunt et affingunt rumoribus,
The Gauls themselves add to and enlarge the rumors,

(quod res videbatur poscĕre,) Cæsarem
(as the case seemed to demand,) (that) Cæsar

retinēri urbano motu (sing.), neque posse
was detained by the city commotions, nor could

venire ad exercitum in tantis dissentionibus. Impulsi
come to the army in such dimensions. Incited

hāc occasione, qui jam ante dolērent
by this opportunity, those who even before lamented

se subjectos imperio Romani populi,
(that) they were subjected to the dominion of the Roman people,

incipiunt inire consilia de bello liberius
begin to enter into plans concerning war more freely

atque audacius. Principes Galliæ,
and more daringly. The principal men of Gaul,

conciliis indictis inter se silvestribus
councils having been convoked among themselves in woody

ac remotis locis, queruntur de morte
and remote places, complain concerning the death

Acconis; demonstrant hunc casum posse
of Acco; they represent (that) this fate might

recidĕre ad ipsos; miserantur communem
occur to themselves; they bewail the common

fortunam Galliæ; deposcunt omnibus pollicitationibus
lot of Gaul; they demand with all promises

ac præmiis, qui faciant initium belli,
and rewards, (that) some make a beginning of war,

et vindicent Galliam in libertatem
and defend Gaul into [for] (its) freedom

pericŭlo sui capĭtis.[1] Dicunt in primis
at the peril of their lives. They say especially

rationem	habendam	ejus,	ut
(that) care	*was to [must] be had*	*of [for] this,*	*that*

Cæsar intercludatur ab exercĭtu, priusquam eorum
Cæsar should be cut off from the army, before their

clandestina consilia efferantur. Id esse facile,
secret designs are reported. (That) this was easy,

quod neque legiones, imperatore absente,
because neither the legions, the commander being absent,

audeant egrĕdi ex hibernis, neque possit
dare to come forth from winter quarters, nor can

imperator pervenire ad legiones sine præsidio.
the commander arrive at the legions without a guard.

Postremo præstare interfici in acie,
Finally (that) it was better to be killed in the battle-line,

quam non recuperare vetĕrem gloriam
than not to recover (their) ancient glory

belli que libertatem quam acceperint a
of [in] war and the liberty which they have received from

majoribus.
the forefathers.

2. His rebus agitatis, Carnutes profitentur
These things having been discussed, the Carnutes proclaim

se recusare nullum pericŭlum causā
(that) they to [will] refuse no danger for the sake

commūnis salutis; pollicentur se principes
of the common safety; they promise (that) they the first

ex omnibus facturos bellum; et
from [of] all about to [would] make war; and

quoniam in præsentiā possent non cavēre
since at the present (time) they could not give security

inter se obsidibus, ne res efferatur,
among themselves by hostages, lest the matter be divulged

petunt ut sanciatur jurejurando ac fide,
they request that it be ratified by oath and pledge,

militaribus signis collatis, (quo
the military standards having been stacked together, (by which

more eorum gravissima cærimonia continētur)
usage their most solemn ceremony is guarded [confirmed])

LIBER VII.

ne	initio	belli	facto,
lest	*the commencement*	*of the war*	*having been made,*

deserantur	a	reliquis.	Tunc,	Carnutibus
they should be deserted	*by*	*the others.*	*Then,*	*the Carnutes*

collaudatis,	jurejurando	dato	ab
having been applauded,	*the oath*	*having been given*	*by*

omnibus	qui	aderant,	tempŏre	ejus
all	*who*	*were present,*	*(and) the time*	*of [for] this*

rei	constituto,	disceditur[2]	ab
movement	*having been determined,*	*it is departed[they depart]*	*from*

concilio.
the council.

3. | Ubi | ea | dies | vēnit, | Carnutes, | Cotuato | et |
|---|---|---|---|---|---|---|
| *When* | *this* | *day* | *came,* | *the Carnutes,* | *Cotuatus* | *and* |

Conconnetodumno	ducibus,	desperatis	hominibus,
Conconnetodumnus	*as leaders,*	*desperate*	*men,*

concurrunt	Cenabum,	que	signo
assemble hastily	*at Cenabum [Orleans],*	*and*	*the signal*

dato,	interficiunt	Romanos	cives,
having been given,	*kill*	*the Roman*	*citizens,*

qui	constiterant	ibi	causā	negotiandi,	in
who	*had settled*	*there*	*for the purpose*	*of trading,*	*among*

iis	C. Fufium Citam,	honestum Romanum equitem,
them	*C. Fufius Cita,*	*an honorable Roman knight,*

qui	jussu	Cæsaris,	præerat	frumentariæ	rei;
who	*by order*	*of Cæsar,*	*presided over*	*the grain*	*supply;*

que	diripiunt	eorum	bona.	Fama	celeriter
and	*they plunder*	*their*	*property.*	*The report*	*quickly*

perfertur	ad	omnes	civitates	Galliæ.	Nam	ubi
is spread	*to*	*all*	*the states*	*of Gaul.*	*For*	*when*

major atque	illustrior	res	incidit,	significant
a greater and	*more notable*	*affair*	*occurs,*	*they indicate*

per	agros	que	regiones	clamore;	alii
(it) through	*the lands*	*and*	*territories*	*by a shout;*	*others*

deinceps	excipiunt	hunc,	et	tradunt	proximis,
in succession	*receive*	*this,*	*and*	*transmit (it) to the nearest*

ut	tunc	accidit.	Nam	quæ	gesta essent
as	*then*	*happened.*	*For*	*what (things)*	*had been done*

Cenabi	sole	oriente (abl. abs.),[1]
at Cenabum [Orleans]	*at sun*	*rise,*

audita sunt	ante	primam	vigiliam[4]	confectam,
were heard	*before*	*the first*	*watch*	*was completed.*

in	finibus	Arvernorum,	quod est	spatium
in	*the territories*	*of the Arverni,*	*which is*	*a space*

	circiter	centum et	sexaginta	millium
[distance]	*of about*	*a hundred and*	*sixty*	*thousand*

passuum.
paces.

4. Ibi simili ratione Vircingetorix, Arvernus,
There in like manner Vircingetorix, an Arvernian,

filius Celtilli, adolescens summæ potentiæ,
the son of Celtillus, a young man of the highest power,

(cujus pater obtinuerat principatum totius Galliæ,
(whose father had held the foremost place of all Gaul,

et ob eam causam, quod appetebat regnum
and for this reason, that he was seeking sovereign

 interfectus erat ab civitate), suis clientibus
power had been put to death by the state), his clients

 convocatis, facile incendit eos. Ejus
having been called together, he easily inflamed them. His

consilio cognito concurritur[5] ad arma.
design having been known they rush to arms.

Prohibētur ab Gobannitione suo patruo, que
He is opposed by Gobannitio his uncle, and

reliquis principibus, qui non existimabant
the other chiefs, who did not think (that)

hanc fortunam temptandam; expellitur
this fortune [hazard] ought to be attempted; he is expelled

ex oppido Gergoviā. Tamen non
from the town (of) Gergovia. However he does not

desistit, atque in agris habet delectum
desist, and in the fields [country] holds a levy

egentium ac perditorum. Hāc manu coac-
of needy and desperate (men). This band having

ta, quoscunque ex civitate adit
been collected, whomsoever of the state he approaches

LIBER VII.

perducit	in	suam	sententiam.	Hortatur,	ut
he brings over	*to*	*his*	*opinion.*	*He exhorts,*	*that*
capiant	arma	causā	communis		libertatis;
they take	*arms*	*for the sake*	*of the common*		*liberty;*
que	magnis	copiis	coactis,	expellit	ex
and	*great*	*forces*	*having been collected,*	*he expels*	*from*
civitate	suos	adversarios	a	quibus	ejectus erat
the state	*his*	*adversaries*	*by*	*whom*	*he had been evicted*
paulo	ante.	Appellatur	rex	ab	suis;
a little	*before.*	*He is called*	*king*	*by*	*his (followers);*
dimittit	legationes	quoquoversus;		obtestatur	ut
he sends	*embassies*	*in every direction;*		*he implores*	*that*
maneant	in	fide.	Celeriter	adjungit	sibi
they remain	*in*	*faith.*	*Speedily*	*he attaches*	*to himself*
Senones,	Parisios,	Pictones,	Cadurcos,		Turones,
the Senones,	*the Parisii,*	*the Pictones,*	*the Cadurci,*		*the Turones,*
Aulercos,	Lemovices,	Andos,	que	omnes	reliquos,
the Aulerci,	*the Lemovici,*	*the Andes,*	*and*	*all*	*the rest,*
qui	attingunt	Oceanum.	Imperium		defertur
who	*border on*	*the Ocean.*	*The chief command*		*is conferred*
ad	eum	consensu	omnium.	Quā	potestate
on	*him*	*by the consent*	*of all.*	*Which [This]*	*power*
oblatā,		impĕrat	obsĭdes	omnibus	iis
having been obtained,		*he demands*	*hostages*	*from all*	*these*
civitatibus;	jubet	certum	numĕrum		militum
states;	*he orders*	*a fixed*	*number*		*of soldiers*
celeriter	adduci	ad	se;	constituit	quantum
speedily	*to be brought*	*to*	*him;*	*he decrees*	*what number*
armorum	quæque	civitas	efficiat	domi,	que
of arms	*each*	*state*	*should prepare*	*at home,*	*and*
ante	quod	tempus;	in primis	studet	equitatui.
before	*what*	*time;*	*especially*	*he attends*	*to the cavalry.*
Summæ	diligentiæ	addit	summam		severitatem
To the highest	*diligence*	*he adds*	*the highest*		*severity*
imperii;	magnitudine		supplicii		cogit
of command;	*by the greatness*		*of punishment*		*he forces*
dubitantes.	Nam	majore	delicto	commisso	
the hesitating.	*For*	*a greater*	*crime*	*having been committed*	

necat	igni	atque	omnibus	tormentis;
he puts to death	*by fire*	*and*	*all*	*(kinds of) tortures;*

de	leviore	causā,	auribus	desectis, aut
for	*a slighter*	*cause,*	*the ears*	*having been cut off, or*

singŭlis	oculis (plural)	effosis,	remittit
a single	*eye*	*(having been) put out,*	*he sends (them)*

domum;	ut	sint	documento	reliquis, et
home;	*that*	*they may be*	*(for) an example*	*to the rest, and*

perterreant	alios	magnitudine	pœnæ.
may terrify	*others*	*by the greatness*	*of the punishment.*

5.
Exercĭtu	coacto	celeriter	his
An army	*having been assembled*	*quickly*	*by these*

suppliciis,	mittit	Lucterium	Cadurcum	hominem
punishments,	*he sends*	*Lucterius*	*the Cadurcan*	*a man*

summæ	audaciæ	cum	parte	copiarum	in
of the highest	*daring*	*with*	*a part*	*of the forces*	*to*

Rutenos;	ipse	proficiscitur in	Bituriges.
the Ruteni;	*he himself*	*sets out into*	*the Bituriges.*

Ejus	adventu	Bituriges	mittunt	legatos ad
On his	*arrival*	*the Bituriges*	*send*	*ambassadors to*

Æduos,	(in	quorum	fide	erant,) rogatum
the Ædui,	*(in*	*whose*	*alliance*	*they were,) to ask for*

subsidium,	quo	possint	facilius
aid,	*by which [that]*	*they may be able*	*the more easily*

sustinēre	copias	hostium.	Ædui de consilio
to resist	*the forces*	*of the enemy.*	*The Ædui by the advice*

legatorum,	quos	Cæsar	reliquerat	ad
of the lieutenants,	*whom*	*Cæsar*	*had left*	*at [with]*

exercitum,	mittunt	copias	equitatūs	que peditatūs
the army,	*send*	*forces*	*of cavalry*	*and foot*

Biturigibus;	qui	cum	venissent	ad flumen
to the Bituriges;	*who*	*when*	*they had arrived*	*at the river*

Ligerim,	quod	dividit	Bituriges	ab Æduis,
Loire,	*which*	*divides*	*the Bituriges*	*from the Ædui,*

morati	paucos	dies	ibi,	neque ausi
having delayed	*a few*	*days*	*there,*	*and not having dared*

transire	flumen,	revertunt	domum;	que renuntiant
to cross	*the river,*	*return*	*home;*	*and they report*

LIBER VII.

nostris	legatis	se	veritos	perfidiam
to our	lieutenants	(that) they	having feared	the treachery

Biturigum	revertisse;	quibus[6]	cognoverint
of the Bituriges	to have [had] returned;	to whom	they had ascertained

id	consilii	fuisse,	ut	si	transissent
this	plan	to have [had] been,	that	if	they had crossed

flumen,	ex	una	parte	ipsi,	altera
the river,	on	the one	side	they [the Bituriges],	on the other

Arverni	circumsistĕrent	se.	Ne	fecerint
the Arverni	would surround	them.	Whether	they did

id	de	ea	causa,	quam	pronunciarunt
this	from [for]	that	reason,	which	they alleged

legatis,	an adducti	perfidia,	quod nihil
to the lieutenants,	or were induced	by treachery,	because nothing

constat nobis,	non	videtur	ponendum	esse
is clear to us,	it does not	seem	(that it) ought to be put down	

pro certo.	Biturges	eorum	discessu	statim
for certain.	The Bituriges	on their	retreat	immediately

conjungunt	se	cum	Arvernis.
unite	themselves	with	the Arverni.

6. | His | rebus | nuntiatis | Cæsari, | in | Italiam, |
|---|---|---|---|---|---|
| These | things | having been reported | to Cæsar, | in | Italy, |

cum	jam	ille	intelligĕret	urbanas	res
since	already	he	understood	(that) the city	affairs

pervenisse	in	commodiorem	statum	virtute[i]
had come	into	a more satisfactory	state	by the conduct

Cn. Pompeii,	profectus est	in	Transalpinam	Galliam.
of Cn. Pompey,	he set out	for	Transalpine	Gaul.

Quum	venisset	eo	afficiebatur	magna
When	he had arrived	there	he was troubled	with the great

difficultate,	qua	ratione	posset	pervenire
difficulty,	in [as to] what	manner	he could	reach

ad exercitum.	Nam si	arcessĕret	legiones	in
the army.	For if	he should summon	the legions	into

Provinciam,	intelligebat	dimicaturas
the province,	he understood (that)	they about to [must] fight

prœlio	in	itinĕre,	se	absente;	si	ipse
in battle	on	the march,	he being	absent;	if	he himself

contendĕret	ad	exercĭtum,	videbat,	suam
should hasten	*to*	*the army,*	*he saw (that)*	*his*

salutem	recte	committi	ne	quidem
safety	*properly*	*to [could] be committed*	*not*	*even*

iis,	qui	eo	tempŏre	viderentur
to those,	*who*	*at this*	*time*	*were appearing*

pacti.
(to be) peaceable.

7. Intĕrim Lucterĭus Cadurcus missus
In the mean time   Lucterius   the Cadurcan   having been sent

in Rutenos conciliat eam civitatem Arvernis.
to the Ruteni   gains over   this   state   to the Arveni.

Progressus in Nitiobrĭges et Gabalos, accipit
Having marched into the Nitiobriges and Gabali, he receives

obsĭdes ab utrisque; et magnā manu co-
hostages from both; and a large band having been

actā, contendit facĕre eruptionem in Provinciam
collected, he hastens to make an invasion into the province

versus Narbonem. Quā re nuntiatā,
toward Narbo. Which [This] thing having been reported,

Cæsar existimavit, antevertendum omnibus
Cæsar thought, that (it) to [must] be preferred to all

consiliis, ut proficisceretur Narbonem.
(other) plans, that he should set out to Narbo.

Cum venisset eō, confirmat timentes, constituit
When he had arrived there, he encourages the timid, he places

præsidia in provincialibus Rutenis, Volcis
garrisons among the provincial Ruteni, the Volci

Arecomicis, Tolosatibus, que circum Narbonem, quæ
Arecomici, the Tolosates, and about Narbo, which

loca erant finitima hostibus; jubet partem copiarum
places were near the enemy; he orders a part of the forces

ex Provinciā que supplementum, quod adduxerat
from the province and the recruits, which he had brought

ex Italiā convenire in Helvios qui contingunt
from Italy to assemble among the Helvii who border on

fines Arvernorum.
the territories of the Arverni.

LIBER VII.

8. His rebus comparatis, Lucterio jam
These things having been arranged, Lucterius now

represso et remoto, quod putabat
having been checked and removed, because he thought (it)

periculosum intrare intra præsidia, pro-
dangerous to enter within [among] the garrison, he [Cæsar]

ficiscitur in Helvĭos. Etsi mons Cebenna,
marches into the Helvii. Although mount Cevennes,

qui discludit Arvernos ab Helvĭis impediebat
which separates the Arverni from the Helvii blocked

iter altissimā nive durissimo tempŏre
the road with very deep snow at the severest time [season]

anni, tamen nive sex pedum in altitudinem
of the year, nevertheless the snow six feet in height [depth]

discussā, atqua viis ita patefactis,
having been removed, and the roads thus having been opened,

pervenit ad fines Arvernorum summo
he arrives at the territories of the Arverni by the utmost

labore militum. Quibus oppressis,
labor of his soldiers Who [They] (having been) astounded,

inopinantibus, quod existimabant se
taken unawares, because they thought (that they) themselves

munītos Cebennā ut muro, ac eo
(were) defended by the Cevennes as by a wall, and in this

tempore anni semitæ unquam patuerant
season of the year the paths never had lain open

homini ne singulari quidem, imperat
to a man (not) by himself even, he [Cæsar] commands

equitibus, ut vagentur quam latissime
the cavalry, that they should roam as far as

possint, et inferant quam maximum
they may be able, and should occasion the very greatest

terrorem hostibus. Hæc celeriter perferuntur
fear to the enemy. These (things) are quickly announced

ad Vercingetorigem famā ac nuntiis; quem
to Vercingetorix by report and messengers; whom [him]

omnes Arverni perterrĭti circumsistunt atque
all the Arverni alarmed beset and

obsecrant	ut	consulat	suis	fortunis,	neu
entreat	*that*	*he look out*	*for their*	*property,*	*nor*
patiatur	se	diripi		ab	hostibus,
suffer	*them*	*to be plundered*		*by*	*the enemy*
præsertim	cum	videt	omne	bellum	trans-
especially	*when*	*he sees (that)*	*all*	*the war*	*has been trans-*

latum ad se. Precibus quorum[8] per-
ferred to themselves. By the entreaties of whom [them] having been

motus	ille	movet		castra	ex	Biturigibus
stirred	*he*	*moves*	*(his)*	*camp*	*from*	*the Bituriges*

versus in Arvernos.
towards the Arverni.

9. At Cæsar moratus biduum in iis locis
But Cæsar having delayed two days in these places

quod[9] præceperat opinione, hæc
because he had anticipated in [through] surmise, (that) these

ventura usu de Vercingetorige,
(things) would come in use [to pass] regarding Vercingetorix,

discĕdit	ab	exercĭtu	per	causam	cogendi
departs	*from*	*the army*	*(as) for*	*the cause*	*of raising*

supplementi	que	equitatūs;	præfēcit	Brutum,
recruits	*and*	*cavalry;*	*he placed*	*Brutus,*

adolescentem, iis copiis; monet hunc, ut
a young man, over these forces; he instructs him, that

equites pervagentur quam latissime in
the cavalry should range about as far as possible into

omnes partes, se daturum operam
all directions, (that) he about to [would] take care

ne absit ab castris longius
that he may not be absent from the camp longer (than)

triduo. His rebus constitutis, pervĕnit
three days. These things having been arranged, he arrives

Viennam maximis itineribus quam . potest,
at Vienna [Vienne] by as great marches as he is able,

suis inopinantibus. Ibi nactus recentem
his (men) not expecting (him). There having found the fresh

equitatum, quem præmiserat eō multis
[newly enrolled] cavalry, which he had sent there many

diebus	ante,	itinĕre	intermisso	neque
days	*before,*	*the march*	*having been interrupted*	*neither*

diurno	neque	nocturno, contendit	per	fines
by day	*nor*	*by night, he hastens*	*through*	*the territories*

Æduorum	in	Lingones,	ubi	duæ legiones
of the Ædui	*into*	*the Lingones,*	*where*	*two legions*

hiemabant,	ut	si	etiam	quid	consilii de
were wintering,	*that*	*if*	*also*	*any*	*plan respecting*

suā	salute	iniretur ab Æduis	præcurrĕret,
his	*safety*	*was entered into by the Ædui*	*he might anticipate*

	celeritate.	Cum pervenisset	eō mittit
(it),	*by (his) quickness.*	*When he had arrived there*	*he sends*

ad	reliquas	legiones,	que cogit	omnes in	unum
to	*the other*	*legions,*	*and gathers*	*all into*	*one*

locum,	prius quam	possit	nuntiari
place,	*before*	*it is possible [can]*	*(to) be announced*

Arvernis	de	ejus	adventu.	Hāc re
to the Arverni	*concerning*	*his*	*arrival.*	*This thing*

cognitā,	Vercingetorix	rursus	reducit
having been known,	*Vercingetorix*	*again*	*marches back (his)*

exercĭtum	in	Biturĭges,	atque inde	profectus
army	*to*	*the Bituriges,*	*and thence*	*having set out*

Gorgobinam,	oppidum	Boiorum,	quos
to Gorgobina,	*a town*	*of the Boii,*	*whom (having been)*

victos	Helvetico	prœlio,	Cæsar collocaverat
conquered	*in the Helvetian*	*battle,*	*Cæsar had placed*

ibi,	que attribuerat	Æduis,	instituit oppugnare.
there,	*and had assigned*	*to the Ædui,*	*he resolved to assault (it).*

10. | Hæc | res | afferebat | magnam | difficultatem |
|---|---|---|---|---|
| *This* | *affair* | *was causing* | *great* | *perplexity* |

Cæsari	ad capiendum	consilium;[10]	si	contin-
to Cæsar	*for taking [forming]*	*a plan;*	*if*	*he should*

ēret	legiones in uno loco	reliquam	partem
keep together	*the legions in one place*	*the remaining*	*part*

hiemis,	ne, stipendiariis	Ædui	expugnatis,
of the winter,	*lest, the tributaries*	*of the Ædui*	*having been stormed,*

cuncta	Gallia	deficĕret,	quod videretur
all	*Gaul*	*might revolt,*	*because it would seem (that)*

nullum præsidium		positum esse	in	eo
no	protection	to have been [had been] placed	in	that place

amicis;	sin	educĕret	maturius	ex
for (his) friends;	but	if he should lead	too early	from

hibernis,	ne	laboraret	ab	re frumentariā
winter quarters,	lest	he be troubled	by	the grain supply,

subvectionibus (pl.)	duris.	Visum est	præstare
transportation	(being) difficult.	It seemed	to be better

tamen	perpeti	omnes	difficultates,	quam	tantā
however	to endure	all	difficulties,	than	so great

contumeliā	acceptā,	alienare	voluntates
an insult	having been received,	to alienate	(the) good will

omnium suorum.	Itaque	cohortatus	Æduos
of all	his (allies).	Therefore	having exhorted the Ædui

de	supportando commeatu	præmittit	ad	Boios,
about	transporting provisions	he sends ahead	to	the Boii,

	qui	doceant	de	suo	adventu,	que
(some)	who	may inform (them)	of	his	arrival,	and

hortentur	ut	maneant	in	fide,	atque
may exhort	(them) that	they remain	in	alliance,	and

sustineant	impĕtum	hostium	magno	anĭmo.
resist	the attack	of the enemy	with great	courage [spirit].

Duabus	legionibus,	atque	impedimentis	totius
Two	legions,	and	the baggage	of the entire

exercitūs	relictis	Agendici,	proficiscitur
army	having been left	at Agendicum [Sens],	he marches

ad	Boios.
to	the Boii.

11. | Cum | altĕro | die | venisset | ad | Vellaunodunum |
| --- | --- | --- | --- | --- | --- |
| When | on the next | day | he had come to | | Vellaunodunum |

	oppidum	Senonum,	instituit	oppugnare,
[Beauns]	a town	of the Senones,	he resolved	to attack (it),

ne	relinquĕret	quem	hostem	post	se,
lest	he might leave	any	enemy	behind	him, (and)

quo	uteretur	expeditiore	re frumentariā;	que
that he	might use	more easily	the grain supply;	and

biduo	circumvallavit	id,	terio	die	legatis
in two days	he invested	it.	on the third	day	ambassadors

missis ex oppido de deditione,	having been sent from the town concerning a surrender,
jubet arma proferri, jumenta produci,	he orders the arms to be brought out, the cattle to be produced,
sexcentos obsides dari. Relinquit C. Trebonium,	six hundred hostages to be given. He leaves C. Trebonius,
legatum, qui conficĕret ea, ut ipse	(his) lieutenant, who should execute these things, that he himself
facĕret iter quam primum. Proficiscitur,	might make a march as soon as possible. He sets out,
Cenabum Carnutum, qui, nuntio de	to Cenabum of the Carnutes, who, the information of
oppugnatione Vellaunoduni tum primum	the siege of Vellaunodunum then first [immediately]
allato, causā tuendi Cenabi,	having been brought, for the purpose of defending Cenabum,
comparabant præsidium quod mittĕrent eō, cum	were preparing a garrison which they might send there, since
existimarent eam rem ductum iri	they thought this affair was to be drawn out
longius. Pervenit huc biduo. Castris	longer. He arrived there in three days. The camp
positis ante oppidum, exclusus	having been placed before the town, (being) prevented
tempŏre diei, differt oppugnationem in	by the time of day, he defers the attack to
posterum; imperat militibus quæque	the next (day); he orders to [from] the soldiers whatever
sint usui ad eam rem; et quod pons	may be of use for this affair; and as the bridge
flumĭnis Ligĕris continebat oppidum Cenabum,	of the river Loire joined the town (of) Cenabum,
veritus ne profugĕrent ex oppĭdo noctu,	having feared lest they might flee from the town at night,
jubet duas legiones excubare in armis.	he orders two legions to keep watch under arms.
Cenabenses egressi ex opp do silentio	The people of Cenabum! having departed from the town in silence

paulo ante mediam	a little before mid
noctem cœperunt transire	night began to cross
flumen. Quā	the river. Which [This]
re nuntiatā per	thing having been announced by
exploratores, Cæsar,	the scouts, Cæsar,
portis incensis	the gates having been set afire
intromittit legiones,	sends in the legions,
quas jusserat esse	which he had ordered to be
expeditas, atque potītur oppido (abl.); perpaucis[11]	ready, and seizes the town; very few
ex numĕro hostium desideratis quin	from [of] the number of the enemy having been lacking but that
cuncti caperentur, quod angustiæ (pl.) pontis	the whole should be taken, because the narrowness of the bridge
atque itinerum intercluserant fugam multitudinis.	and of the roads had cut off the flight of the multitude.
Dirĭpit atque incendit oppidum; donat prædam	He pillages and burns the town; he gives the booty
militibus; transducit exercĭtum Ligĕrim, atque	to the soldiers; he leads his army over the Loire, and
pervĕnit in fines Biturigum.	arrives in the territories of the Bituriges.

12. Vercingetorix, ubi cognovit de adventu
Verecingetorix, when he learned of the arrival

Cæsaris, desistit oppugnatio**ne**, atque proficiscitur
of Cæsar, desists from the siege, and marches

obviam Cæsari. Ille instituerat oppugnare
to meet Cæsar. He [Cæsar] had begun to besiege

Noviodunum, oppidum Biturigum, positum
Noviodunum [Saucerre] a town of the Bituriges, situated

ın viā. Ex quo[12] oppido cum legati
on the road. From which town when ambassadors

venissent ad eum oratum ut ignoscĕret sibi,
had come to him to entreat that he would pardon them,

que consulĕret suæ vitæ (sing.), ut conficĕret
and would spare their lives, that he might accomplish

reliquas res celeritate, quā erat consecutus
the remaining affairs with the speed, by which he had won

LIBER VII.

pleraque,	jubet	arma	proferri
the most,	*he orders*	*the arms*	*to be brought forth*

equos	produci,	obsĭdes	dari.	Parte
the horses	*to be produced,*	*(and) hostages*	*to be given.*	*A part*

obsĭdum	jam	traditā,	cum	reli-
of the hostages	*already*	*having been surrendered,*	*while*	*the other*

qua	administrarentur,	centurionibus	et	paucis
things	*were being executed,*	*the centurions*	*and*	*a few*

militum	intromissis,	qui	conquirĕrent
of the soldiers	*having been introduced,*	*who*	*should collect*

arma	que	jumenta,	equitatus	hostium	qui
the arms	*and*	*the horses,*	*the cavalry*	*of the enemy*	*which*

antecesserat agmen Vercingetorigis, est visus procul;
had preceded the army of Vercingetorix, was seen at a distance;

quem[13]	atque	simul	oppidani	conspexerunt,
which	*as*	*soon as*	*the townsmen*	*saw,*

atque	venerunt	in	spem	auxilii,	clamore
and	*came*	*to*	*the hope*	*of aid,*	*a shout*

sublato	cœperunt	capĕre	arma,	claudĕre
having been raised	*they began*	*to take*	*arms,*	*to shut*

portas,	complēre	murum.	Centuriones	in
the gates,	*(and) to fill*	*the walls.*	*The centurions*	*in*

oppĭdo,	cum	intellexissent	ex	significatione
the town,	*when*	*they had understood*	*from*	*the action*

Gallorum	aliquid	novi consilii	iniri	ab
of the Gauls	*(that) some*	*(of) new plan*	*was formed*	*by*

iis,	gladiis	districtis,	occupaverunt
them,	*their swords*	*having been drawn,*	*took possession of*

portas,	que receperunt	omnes	suos	incolŭmes.
the gates,	*and received*	*all*	*their (men)*	*safe.*

13. Cæsar jubet equitatum educi ex castris,
Cæsar orders the cavalry to be led from the camp,

que	committit	equestre	prœlium.	Suis	jam
and	*joins in*	*a cavalry*	*battle.*	*His (men)*	*being now*

laborantibus	submittit	circiter	quadringentos
hard pressed	*he sends*	*about*	*four hundred*

Germanos	equites,	quos	ab	initio	instit-
German	*horsemen.*	*whom*	*from*	*the beginning*	*he had*

uerat	habēre	cum	se.	Galli	potuerunt
determined	*to keep*	*with*	*himself.*	*The Gauls*	*could*

non	sustinēre	eorum	impĕtum, atque	conjecti
not	*sustain*	*their*	*attack, and*	*having been thrown*

in	fugam,	receperunt	se	ad agmen,	multis
into	*flight,*	*betook*	*themselves*	*to the army,*	*many*

amissis.	Quibus	profligatis,	oppidani
having been lost.	*Who [These]*	*having been routed,*	*the townsmen*

rursus	perterrĭti,	perduxerunt	ad Cæsarem	eos
again	*alarmed,*	*led out*	*to Cæsar*	*those*

comprehensos	quorum	operā	existimabant
(having been) arrested	*by whose*	*means*	*they thought*

plebem	concitatam, que	dediderunt	sese
(that) the people	*were incited, and*	*surrendered*	*themselves*

ei.	Quibus rebus	confectis,	Cæsar
to him.	*Which [These] things*	*having been accomplished,*	*Cæsar*

profectus est	ad oppĭdum	Avarĭcum,	quod
marched	*to the town*	*(of) Avaricum [Bourges],*	*which*

erat	maximum	que munitissimum	in	finibus
was	*the largest*	*and best fortified*	*in*	*the territories*

Biturigum,	atque fertillissimā	regione	agri,
of the Biturges,	*and in a most fertile*	*district*	*of country.*

quod	eo oppido	recepto,	confidebat
because	*this town*	*having been taken,*	*he was confident*

se	redacturum	civitatem	Biturigum
(that) he	*about to [would] reduce*	*the state*	*of the Biturges*

in	potestatem.
into (his)	*power.*

14. | Vercingetorix, | tot | | continuis | incommodis |
|---|---|---|---|---|
| *Vercingetorix,* | *so* | *many* | *continual* | *reverses* |

Vellaunoduni,	Cenabi,	Novioduni,	ac-
at Vellaundunum,	*Cenabum, (and)*	*Noviodunum,*	*having been*

ceptis,	convocat suos	ad concilium;	docet
received,	*calls his (followers)*	*to a council;*	*he shows*

bellum	gerendum esse	longe	aliā
(that) the war	*to [must] be carried on*	*with a far*	*different*

ratione,	atque	sit	gestum	antea,	huic rei
plan,	*than*	*it had been*	*carried on*	*before,*	*to this thing*

LIBER VII.

studendum omnibus modis, ut Romani
it must be attended by all means, that the Romans

prohibeantur pabulatione, et commeatu:
should be prohibited from foraging, and from provisions: (that)

id esse facile, quod ipsi abundent equitatu,
this to be [was] easy, because they abound in cavalry,

et quod subleventur tempŏre anni;
and because they are assisted by the season of the year;

pabŭlum posse non secari; hostes
(that) forage could not (to) be cut; (that) the enemy

dispersos necessario petĕre ex ædificiis;
dispersed (must) necessarily (to) seek (it) from the buildings;

omnes hos posse quotidie delēri ab
(that) all these could daily (to) be destroyed by

equitibus. Præterea causā salutis commoda
the horsemen. Moreover for the sake of safety the advantages

familiaris rei (sing.) negligenda;
of private property to [must] be disregarded; (that)

oportēre vicos atque ædificia incen-
to be [it was] necessary (for) the villages and houses to be

di, hoc est, spatio a Boiā quoquoversus,
burnt, that is, in a space from Boia in every direction,

quō videantur posse adire causā
where (the Romans) might seem to be able to go for the purpose

pabulandi. Harum rerum suppetĕre copiam
of foraging. Of these things to be [there is] at hand an abundance

ipsis, quod subleventur opibus eorum
for themselves, because they would be assisted by the means of those

in quorum finibus bellum geratur;
in whose territories war should be waged; (that)

Romanos aut non laturos[14] inopiam,
the Romans either not to be about to [would not] bear privation,

aut progressuros longius a
or (that they) to be about to [would] proceed farther from

castris cum magno pericŭlo; neque inter-
the camp with great danger; nor to be [did it make] any

esse, ne interficiant ipsos ne exuant
difference, whether they kill them or deprive [them] of

386   DE BELLO GALLICO.   [15

         impedimentis, quibus amissis, bellum possit
(their)   baggage,   which having been lost, war   can

non   geri.   Præterea,   oportēre
not   (to) be waged.   Moreover,   (that it) to be [was] necessary

       oppida incendi, quæ sint non tuta ab
(for) the towns to be burnt, which were not safe from

omni pericŭlo munitione et naturā loci;
all   danger by fortification and by the nature of the place;

   neu   sint   suis   receptacula ad
that neither they may be for our (people)   retreats   for

detrectandam militiam neu proposita Romanis
evading   military service nor offered to the Romans

ad tollendam copiam commeatūs que prædam.
for carrying off an abundance of provisions and plunder.

Si hæc videantur gravia aut acerba, debēre (inf.)
If these (things) should seem severe or cruel, they ought

æstimare,   illa   multo gravius
to consider, (that) those things (are) much more severe (that

     liberos   conjuges   abstrahi   in
their) children (and)   wives   to [should] be dragged into

servitutem,   ipsos   interfici; quæ
slavery,   (and they) themselves   (to be) slain;   which

sit   necesse accidĕre victis.
would be certain to befall the conquered.

15. Hāc sententiā   probatā   consensu
This opinion having been approved by the consent

omnium, uno die amplius viginti urbes Biturigum
of all, in one day more than twenty cities of the Bituriges

incenduntur. Hoc idem fit in reliquis civitatibus.
are burned. This same is done in the remaining states.

In omnibus partibus incendia conspiciuntur; quæ
In   all   parts   conflagrations are seen; which

etsi omnes ferebant cum magno dolore, tamen
although all   bore   with great grief,   yet

   proponebant   sibi   hoc   solaci,
they placed before themselves this (as) a consolation,

quod confidebant se, victoriā prope
that   they trusted they, the victory being nearly

LIBER VII.

explorata, celeriter recuperaturos amissa.
assured, quickly about to [would] recover (their) losses.

Deliberatur in communi concilio de Avarico,
It is deliberated in general council about Avaricum,

placeat, incendi
(whether) it is best, (that it) (to) [should] be burnt

an defendi. Bituriges procumbunt
or (to) be defended. The Bituriges fall

ad pedes omnibus Gallis
at the feet (of) all the Gauls, (begging that)

ne cogerentur succendĕre suis
they should not be forced to set fire with their own

manibus pulcherrimam urbem prope totius Galliæ,
hands (to) the most beautiful town nearly of all Gaul,

quæ sit et præsidio et ornamento civitati;
which is both (for) a protection and an ornament to the state;

dicunt se defensuros facile
they say (that) they about to [would] defend (it) easily

naturā loci, quod, circumdata prope
by the nature of the place, because, surrounded almost

ex omnibus partibus flumĭne et palude, habeat
on all sides by the river and by a marsh, it has

unum et perangustum adĭtum. Venia
one [a single] and very narrow entrance. Permission

datur petentibus, Vercingetorige primō dissuadente,
is given to those petitioning. Vercingetorix at first opposing,

post concedente et ipsorum precibus et
afterwards yielding both because of their entreaties and

misericordiā vo!gi. Idonei defensores
because of compassion of [for] the multitude. Suitable defenders

deliguntur oppĭdo.
are selected for the town.

16. Vercingetorix subsequitur Cæsarem minoribus
Vercingetorix follows near Cæsar by lesser

itineribus, et deligit locum castris munitum
marches, and selects a place for the camp defended

paludibus que silvis, longe ab Avarĭco quindecim
by marshes and woods, distant from Avaricum fifteen

millia	passuum.	Ibi	cognoscebat	per	certos
thousand	*paces.*	*There*	*he learned*	*by*	*faithful*

exploratores	in	singŭla	tempŏra (pl.)	diei	quæ
scouts	*at*	*each*	*time [hour]*	*of the day*	*what things*

agerentur (pl.)	ad	Avarĭcum;	et	imperabat
were done	*at*	*Avaricum;*	*and*	*he commanded*

quid	vellet	fieri;	observabat	omnes	nostras
what	*he wished*	*to be done;*	*he watched*	*all*	*our*

pabulationes	que	frumentationes,	que	quum
foragings	*and*	*corn-raids,*	*and*	*when*

necessario	procedĕrent	longius,	adoriebatur
through necessity	*they proceeded*	*rather far,*	*he attacked*

dispersos,	que	afficiebat	magno	incommodo
(them) dispersed	*and*	*inflicted*	*great*	*injury;*

(dat.);	etsi	occurrebatur	ab	nostris
	although (this)	*was obviated*	*by*	*our (men)*

quantum	poterat	providēri	ratione,	ut
as much as	*(it) could*	*(to) be provided against*	*by foresight,*	*that*

irētur (pass. sing.)[15]	incertis	temporibus	que
they should go	*at uncertain*	*times*	*and*

diversis	itineribus.
by different	*routes.*

17.
Castris	positis	ad	eam	partem
The camp	*having been pitched*	*near*	*that*	*part*

oppidi,	quæ	intermissa	ā	flumĭne	et
of the town,	*which*	*having been left*	*by*	*the river*	*and*

palude,	ut	diximus	supra,	habēbat	angustum
marsh,	*as*	*we have said*	*above,*	*had*	*a narrow*

adĭtum,	Cæsar	cœpit	apparare	aggerem,	agĕre
approach,	*Cæsar*	*began*	*to prepare*	*the mound,*	*to move*

vineas,	constituĕre	duas	turres;	nam
the shelters	*(and) to construct*	*two*	*towers;*	*for*

natura	loci	prohibebat	circumvallare.
the nature	*of the place*	*prevented*	*to blockade [investment].*

Non	destitit	adhortari	Boios	atque	Æduos	de
He did not	*cease*	*to exhort*	*the Boii*	*and*	*Ædui*	*about*

frumentariā	re;	altĕri	quorum,	quod	agebant
the corn	*supply;*	*the latter*	*of whom,*	*because*	*they acted*

LIBER VII.

nullo studio,	adjuvabant	non	multum;	altĕri	non
with no zeal,	assisted	not	much;	the others	not

magnis	facultatibus,	quod	civitas	erat	exigua
with [having] great	means,	because	the state	was	small

et	infirma,	consumpserunt	celeriter	quod	habuerunt.
and	weak,	consumed	quickly	what	they had.

Exercĭtu	affecto	summā	difficultate
The army	(having been) afflicted	with the greatest	want

frumentariæ rei,	tenuitate	Boiorum,	indiligentiā
of provisions,	by the poverty	of the Boii,	by the negligence

Æduorum,	incendiis	ædificiorum,	usque
of the Ædui,	(and) by the burning	of the buildings,	even

eo[16]	ut	milites	caruerint	frumento
to this [extent]	that	the soldiers	were without	corn (for)

complures	dies,	et	sustentarent	extremam	famem
many	days,	and	they satisfied	the extreme	hunger

pecŏre	adacto	e	longinquioribus	vicis;
by cattle	driven	from	the more distant	villages;

tamen	nulla	vox	audita est	ab	iis
yet	not	a word	was heard	from	them

indigna	majestate	Romani	popŭli	et
unworthy	the majesty	of the Roman	people	and (their)

superioribus	victoriis.	Quin	etiam	cum	Cæsar
former	victories.	Moreover	also	when	Cæsar

appellaret	singŭlas	legiones	in	opĕre,	et	dicĕret
addressed	the several	legions	at	work	and	said

se	dimissurum	oppugnationem,	si	ferrent
(that) he	would abandon	the siege,	if	they bore

iopiam	acerbius,	universi	petebant	ab
the want	too severely,	all to a man	begged	from [of]

eo	ne	facĕret	id;	se
him	that he would not	do	this; (saying that)	they them-

sic	meruisse	complures	annos
selves in such manner	to have [had] served	very many	years

illo	imperante	ut	accipĕrent	nullam	ignominiam
under his command	that	they admitted	no	dishonor	(and)

nunquam discedĕrent,	re	infectā;
never withdrew,	their purpose (having been)	unaccomplished;

se laturos hoc loco ignominiæ,
they about to[would] regard this (as) an occasion of dishonor,

si relinquissent oppugnationem inceptam; præ-
if they should abandon the siege (once) commenced, to be

stare perferre omnes acerbitates, quam
[it was] preferable to endure all hardships than (that)

non parentarent Romanis civibus, qui
they should not avenge the Roman citizens, who

interissent perfidiā Gallorum Cenabi. Hæc
had perished by the perfidy of the Gauls at Cenabum. These

eadem mandabant centurionibus que
same (words) they entrusted to the centurions and

tribunis, ut per eos deferrentur
tribunes, that through them they might be communicated

ad Cæsarem.
to Cæsar.

18. Cum turres jam appropinquassent muro,
When the towers already had approached the wall,

Cæsar cognovit ex captivis Vercingetorigem,
Cæsar ascertained from the prisoners (that) Vercingetorix,

pabulo consumpto, movisse
the forage having been consumed, to have [had] moved (his)

castra propius Avarĭcum, atque ipsum, cum
camp nearer to Avaricum, and (that) he with

equitatu que expeditis, qui consuēssent
the cavalry and the light armed, who had been trained

proeliari inter equites, causā insidiarum
to fight among the horsemen, for the purpose of ambuscades

profectum eo quo arbitrabatur
to have [had] marched thither, where he thought (that)

nostros venturos pabulatum postĕro
our (men) about to [would] come to forage on the following

die. Quibus rebus cognĭtis profectus
day. Which [These] things having been learned, having set out

silentio mediā nocte, pervēnit ad castra hostium
in silence at mid night, he arrived at the camp of the enemy

mane. Illi, adventu Cæsaris celeriter
early in the morning. They, the arrival of Cæsar speedily

cognito	per	exploratores,	abdiderunt
having been learned	*through*	*scouts,*	*concealed*

carros	que	sua	impedimenta	in	artiores silvas,
the wagons	*and*	*their*	*baggage*	*in*	*the thicker woods,*

	instruxerunt	omnes		copias in edito
(and)	*drew up*	*all*	*(their)*	*forces on an elevated*

atque	aperto	loco.	Quā re	nuntiatā,
and	*open*	*place.*	*Which thing*	*having been announced,*

Cæsar	celeriter	jussit sarcinas	conferri,
Cæsar	*quickly*	*ordered the packs*	*to be collected together,*

arma	expediri.
(and) the arms	*to be made ready.*

19.
Erat	collis	leniter	acclivis	ab infimo.
There was	*a hill*	*gently*	*sloping*	*from below.*

Difficĭlis	atque	impedita	palus	cingebat hunc
A difficult	*and*	*impassable*	*swamp*	*surrounded this*

ex	fere	omnibus	partibus,	non latior
on	*nearly*	*all*	*sides,*	*not wider than*

quinquaginta	pedibus.	Hoc colle,	pontibus
fifty	*feet.*	*On this hill,*	*the bridges*

interruptis,	Galli continebant	se,
having been broken down,	*the Gauls stationed*	*themselves,*

fiduciā	loci;	que distributi	generatim
in confidence	*of the place,*	*and, arranged*	*in tribes*

in	civitates,	obtinebant omnia	vada
according	*to their states,*	*they were holding all*	*the shallows*

ac	saltus	ejus	paludis certis	custodibus; sic
and	*passes*	*of this*	*swamp by trusty*	*guards; thus*

parati	animo,	ut,	si	Romani conarentur
prepared	*in mind,*	*that,*	*if*	*the Romans should attempt*

perrumpĕre	eam paludem,	premĕrent,
to break through	*this swamp,*	*they would crush (them),*

ex	superiore	loco,	hæsitantes, ut
from	*the higher*	*station, while*	*sticking fast; so that*

qui	vidĕrent	propinquitatem	loci,
(any) who	*saw*	*the nearness*	*of the position,*

existimarent	paratos	ad	dimicandum
would think	*(that) they were prepared*	*for*	*fighting*

prope	æquo	Marte;		qui	perspicĕrent
almost	*on equal*	*terms;*	*(but any)*	*who*	*perceived*

iniquitatem	conditionis,	cognoscĕrent
the disadvantage	*of the condition [place],*	*would understand (that)*

sese	ostentare	inani	simulatione.	Cæsar
they	*(to) make show*	*with an empty*	*pretense.*	*Cæsar*

edocet	milites	indignantes,	quod	hostes
shows	*the soldiers*	*(who were) indignant,*	*because*	*the enemy*

possent	ferre	suum	conspectum,	tantulo	spatio
could	*endure*	*their*	*sight,*	*so small*	*a space*

	interjecto,	et		exposcentes	signum
	(having been) interposed,	*and*	*(who were)*	*demanding*	*the signal*

prœlii,	quanto	detrimento,	et	morte
of [for] battle,	*with how great*	*loss,*	*and*	*with the death*

quot	fortium	virorum	sit	necesse
of how many	*brave*	*men*	*it would be*	*necessary*

constare	victoriam;	cum	vidēret	quos	sic
to assure	*the victory;*	*(saying that) since*	*he saw*	*them*	*so*

paratos	animo,	ut	recusarent	nullum	periculum
prepared	*in mind,*	*that*	*they refused*	*no*	*danger*

pro	suā	laude,	se debēre	condemnari	summæ
for	*his*	*glory,*	*he ought*	*to be condemned*	*of the greatest*

iniquitatis,	nisi	habeat	eorum	vitam	cariorem
injustice,	*unless*	*he holds*	*their*	*lives*	*dearer*

	suā	salute.	Consolatus	milites	sic,
than	*his*	*safety.*	*Having consoled*	*the soldiers*	*thus,*

reducit	in	castra	eodem	die;	instituit
he returns	*to*	*the camp*	*on the same*	*day;*	*he undertook*

administrare	reliqua,	quæ	pertinebant	ad
to perform	*the other things,*	*which*	*pertained*	*to*

oppugnationem	oppidi.
the siege	*of the town.*

20.
Vercingetorix,	cum	redisset	ad	suos
Vercingetorix,	*when*	*he had returned*	*to*	*his (men)*

insimulatus	proditionis,	quod	movisset	castra
was accused	*of treason,*	*because*	*he had moved (his)*	*camp*

propius	Romanos;	quod	discessisset	cum	omni
nearer	*to the Romans;*	*because*	*he had departed*	*with*	*all*

equitatu;	quod	relinquisset	tantas	copias	sine
the cavalry;	*because*	*he had left*	*such great*	*forces*	*without*
imperio;	quod	ejus	discessu	Romani	venissent
a command;	*because*	*on his*	*departure*	*the Romans*	*had come*
tantā	opportunitate,		et	celeritate;	omnia
with so great	*timeliness,*		*and*	*celerity;* *(that)*	*all*
hæc	potuisse	non	accidĕre	fortuito,	aut
this	*could*	*not*	*(to) happen*	*accidentally,*	*or*
sine	consilio;	illum	malle[18]		habēre
without	*design;*	*(that) he*	*to prefer*		*[preferred] to have the*
regnum	Galliæ	concessu	Cæsaris, quam ipsorum
sovereignty	*of Gaul*	*with the permission*	*of Cæsar,* *than*	*by their*
beneficio.	Accusatus		tali	modo,	respondit
favor.	*Having been accused*		*in such*	*manner,*	*he replied*
ad hæc		quod	movisset castra,	factum
to these (things) (saying)		*that*	*he had moved the camp*	*was done*
inopiā	pabuli,	ipsis	etiam	hortantibus;	quod
by want	*of forage,*	*they themselves*	*even*	*urging;*	*that*
accessisset		propius	Romanos,		persuasum
he had approached		*nearer*	*the Romans,*		*he was induced*
opportunitate	loci,		qui	ipse	defendĕret
by the advantage	*of the place,*		*which*	*itself*	*would protect*
se	sine	munitione;	vero operam	equitum
itself	*without*	*defence;*	*(that) indeed the service*	*of the horsemen*
debuisse (inf.)	neque	desiderari	in	palustri	loco,
ought	*not*	*to be wanted*	*in*	*a marshy*	*place,*
et	fuisse		utilem	illic,	quo
and	*to have been*		*[was] useful*	*there,*	*where*
profecti sint;		se	consulto		discedentem
they had gone;	*(that)*	*he*	*on purpose*	*(when)*	*departing*
tradidisse	summam	imperii	nulli,	ne
to have [had] conferred	*the chief*	*command*	*on no one,*	*lest*
is	impellĕretur	ad	dimicandum	studio	multi-
he	*might be driven*	*to*	*fighting*	*by the zeal*	*of the*
tudinis;	cui	rei,	vidēret omnes	studēre,
multitude;	*for which*	*thing,*	*he saw* *all*	*to be [were] eager,*
propter	mollitiem[19]	animi,	quod	possent
on account of (their)	*weakness*	*of mind,*	*because*	*they could*

non	diutius	ferre	laborem.	Si	Romani
no	*longer*	*endure*	*labor.*	*If*	*the Romans*

intervenerint	casu		gratiam	habendam
came up	*by chance*	*(that)*	*thanks*	*must be given*

fortunæ; si vocati indicio alicujus,
to fortune; if invited by the information of any one (thanks must

huic;[20] quod et potuerint cognoscĕre eorum
be given) to him; because they could both (to) perceive their

paucitatem ex superiore loco, et despicĕre
small number from the higher ground, and (could) (to) despise

virtutem	qui non	ausi	dimicare turpiter
the courage (of those)	*who not*	*having dared*	*to fight basely*

receperint	se	in	castra. Se	desiderare (inf.)
had betaken	*themselves*	*into*	*camp. He*	*desired*

nullum	imperium	a	Cæsare	per	proditionem,
no	*sovereign power*	*from*	*Cæsar*	*by*	*treason,*

quod	posset	habēre	victoriā,	quæ	esset
because he was able		*(to) have*	*(it) by victory,*	*which*	*was*

jam	explorata	sibi	ac	omnibus	Gallis;	quin
now	*certain*	*to himself and*		*to all*	*the Gauls;*	*but*

etiam	remittĕre	ipsis,	si	videantur	tribuĕre
even	*he to [would] resign*	*to them,*	*if*	*they seemed*	*to confer*

honorem	sibi	magis	quam	accipĕre
honor	*on him*	*rather*	*than*	*to receive*

salutem	ab	se. Inquit,	"ut	intelligatis
safety	*from*	*him. He said,*	*"in order that*	*you may know*

hæc	pronuntiari	sincere	a	me,	audite
these things	*to be [are] announced*	*truly*	*by*	*me,*	*hear*

Romanos	milites."	Producit	servos	quos
the Roman	*soldiers."*	*He brings forward*	*slaves*	*whom*

exceperat	in	pabulatione,	paucis	diebus	ante,
he had captured	*in*	*foraging,*	*a few*	*days*	*before,*

et	excruciaverat	et	fame	que	vinculis.
and	*had tortured*	*both*	*by hunger*	*and*	*chains.*

Hi	edocti	jam	ante, quæ pronunciarent
They	*having been taught*	*already*	*before, what they should declare*

interrogati,	dicunt	se	esse	legionarios,
(when) interrogated,	*say*	*that they*	*were*	*legionary soldiers,*

LIBER VII.

		adductos	fame	et	inopiā
(and)	(having been)	led	by hunger	and	want

	exisse	clam	ex castris		si	possent
to have [had] gone out	secretly	from	camp	(to see)	if they were able

		reperire	quid	frumenti	aut	pecŏris	in
[could]	(to)	find	any	(of) corn	or	cattle	in

agris;		omnem	exercĭtum	premi
the fields;	(that)	all	the army	to be [was] oppressed

simili	inopiā;	nec		vires	cujusquam jam
by a like	want;	nor	(does)	the strength	of any one now

	sufficĕre,	nec		posse	ferre	laborem
(to)	suffice,	nor	to be [are they] able	to bear	the labor

opĕris.	Itaque	imperatorem		statuisse,	si
of the work.	Therefore	the commander	to have [had] resolved,	if

profecissent	nihil	in	oppugnatione	oppidi,
they accomplished	nothing	in	the siege	of the town,

deducĕre	exercĭtum	triduo.	"Hæc beneficia,"
to withdraw (his)	army	in three days.	"These benefits,"

inquit	Vercingetorix,	"habētis	a	me,	quem
said	Vercingetorix,	"you have	from	me,	whom

insimulatis	proditionis,	cujus	operā	vidētis	tantum
you accuse	of treason,	by whose	means	you see	so great

victorem	exercĭtum	pæne	consumptum	fame,
a conquering	army	nearly	destroyed	by hunger,

sine	vestro sanguine;	quem,		turpiter recipien-
without	your blood;	which (army)	disgracefully retreat-

tem se	ex hāc fugā,	provisum est	a me,	ne
ing	from this flight,	it has been provided	by me,	that not

qua	civitas	recipiat	suis	finibus."
any	state	shall receive	in its	territories."

21.
Omnis	multitudo	conclamat	et	concrepat
All	the multitude	shout	and	rattle

armis	suo	more,	quod	consueverunt
with (their) arms	in their	manner,	which	they are accustomed

facĕre	in	eo	cujus	orationem	approbant,
to do	in the case of	him	whose	speech	they approve,

	Vercingetorigem	esse		summum	ducem,	nec
(saying)	Vercingetorix	to be [is]	the greatest	general,	nor

dubitandum	de	ejus	fide,	nec
must it be doubted	*concerning*	*his*	*faithfulness,*	*nor*

posse	bellum	administrari	majore
to be possible [could]	*the war*	*(to) be carried on*	*with greater*

ratione.	Statuunt	ut	decem	millia	hominum
judgment.	*They decree*	*that*	*ten*	*thousand*	*men*

delecta	ex	omnibus	copiis	submittantur	in
selected	*from*	*all*	*the forces*	*should be sent*	*into*

oppidum;	nec	censent	communem	salutem
the town;	*nor*	*do they think*	*the general*	*safety*

committendum	Biturigibus	solis,	quod
ought to be committed	*to the Bituriges*	*alone,*	*because*

intelligebant	summam	victoriæ
they understood	*(that) the completeness*	*of the victory*

constare	pæne	in	eo,	si	retinuissent
would depend	*almost entirely*	*upon*	*this,*	*if*	*they should hold*

oppidum.
the town.

22. | Consilia | cujusque | modi | Gallorum | occurrebant |
|---|---|---|---|---|
| *Plans* | *of every* | *kind* | *of the Gauls* | *opposed* |

singulari	virtuti	nostrorum	militum,	ut	est (sing.)
the uncommon	*bravery*	*of our*	*soldiers,*	*as*	*they are*

genus	summæ	sollertiæ,	atque	aptissimum	ad
a nation	*of the greatest*	*ingenuity,*	*and*	*very apt*	*for [at]*

imitanda	atque	efficienda	omnia,	quæ	traduntur
imitating	*and*	*making*	*all things,*	*which*	*are imparted*

ab	quoque.	Nam	avertebant	laqueis	falces,
by	*every one.*	*For*	*they turned aside*	*with nooses*	*the hooks,*

quos[21]	cum	destinaverant,	reducebant	introrsus
which	*when*	*they had caught,*	*they hauled*	*within*

tormentis,	et	subtrahebant	aggerem	cuniculis,
by engines,	*and*	*they undermined*	*the mound*	*by tunnels,*

eo scientius,	quod	apud	eos	sunt	magnæ
the more skilfully,	*because*	*among*	*them*	*are*	*great*

ferrariæ,	atque	omne	genus	cuniculorum	est	notum
iron mines,	*and*	*all*	*kinds*	*of tunnels*	*are*	*known*

atque	usitatum.	Autem	contabulaverant	totum
and	*employed.*	*Moreover*	*they had fortified*	*the entire*

murum ex omni parte turribus, atque intexerant
wall on every side with towers, and had covered

has coriis; tum crebris diurnis que nocturnis
these with hides; also in (their) frequent daily and nightly

eruptionibus, aut inferebant ignem aggeri,
sallies, either they were setting fire to the mound,

aut adoriebantur milites occupatos in opere; et
or were attacking our soldiers occupied in the work; and

adæquabant altitudinem nostrarum turrium,
they were equaling the height of our towers,

quantum agger quotidianus expresserat has,
as much as the mound daily had raised them,

malis suarum turrium commissis; et
the masts of their towers having been joined [spliced]; and

morabantur apertos cuniculos præustā et
they were retarding (our) open tunnels by burnt and

præcutā materiā, et fervefactā pice, et saxis
very sharp stakes, and by boiling pitch, and by stones

maximi ponderis, que prohibebant
of very great weight, and they were checking (us from)

appropinquare (inf.) mœnibus.
approaching the walls.

23. Autem hæc est fere forma omnibus Gallicis
Now this is generally the form to [of] all the Gallic

muris. Directæ trabes perpetuæ in longitudinem,
walls. Straight beams continuous in length,

binos pedes distantes paribus intervallis inter
two feet distant at equal intervals between

se[22] collocantur in solo. Hæ revinciuntur
one another are placed on the ground. These are made fast

introrsus, et vestiuntur multo aggere.
within, and are covered with much mound-filling.

Autem ea intervalla, quæ diximus
But these intervals, which we have mentioned

effarciuntur in fronte grandibus saxis. Iis
are filled up in front with great stones. These

collocatis et coagmentatis, alius ordo
having been placed and united together, another row

DE BELLO GALLICO.

adjicitur insuper, ut illud idem intervallum
is put above, so that, this same interval

servetur, neque trabes contingant inter
may be observed, nor the beams may touch each

se,[23] sed intermissæ paribus spatiis, singulæ
other, but separated by equal spaces, the several (beams)

contineantur (pl.) arte singulis interjectis saxis;
may be kept in place closely by the several interposed stones;

sic deinceps omne opus contexitur, dum
so successively the whole work is bound together, till

justa altitudo muri expleatur. Cum est
the proper height of the wall is completed. Not only is

hoc opus non deforme in speciem que varietatem
this work not unsightly in appearance and variety

alternis trabibus ac saxis, quæ servant suos
by the alternate beams and stones, which preserve their

ordines rectis lineis, tum habet ad utilitatem,
order in straight lines, but also it has for utility,

et defensionem urbium summam opportunitatem,
and defence of cities great advantage,

quod et lapis defendit ab incendio, et
because both the stone protects from fire, and

ab ariete materia, quæ
from the battering-ram the wood-work, which (having been)

revincta introrsus trabibus plerumque perpetuis
fastened internally by beams mostly continuous (for)

quadragenos pedes, potest neque perrumpi,
forty feet, can neither be broken through,

neque distrahi.
nor rent apart.

24. Oppugnatione impeditā tot iis
The siege having been impeded by so many these

rebus, cum milites tardarentur toto
[such] things, though the soldiers were retarded the whole

tempore luto, frigore, et assiduis imbribus, tamen
time by mud, cold, and continual rains, yet

superaverunt omnia hæc continenti labore,
they overcame all these (things) by their continual labor,

et viginti quinque diebus, extruxerunt aggerem
and in twenty five days, they constructed a mound

trecentos et triginta pedes latum, octoginta
three hundred and thirty feet wide, (and) eighty

pedes altum. Cum is pæne contingĕret
feet high. When this (mound) nearly touched

murum hostium, et Cæsar excubaret ad opus
the wall of the enemy, and Cæsar kept watch at the work

consuetudine, que exhortaretur milites, ne quod
by his custom, and encouraged the soldiers, that not any

tempus omnino intermitteretur ab opere, paulo
time at all should be lost from the work a little

ante tertiam vigiliam, est animadversum
before the third watch, it was observed (that)

aggerem fumare (inf.), quem hostes succenderant
the mound to smoke [was smoking] which the enemy had fired

cuniculo; que eodem tempore clamore sublato
by a mine; and at the same time a shout having been raised

toto muro, eruptio fiebat duabus portis ab
on all the wall, a sally was made from two gates on

utroque latere turrium. Alii eminus jaciebant
each side of the towers. Some from a distance were throwing

faces atque aridam materiem de muro in
torches and dry material from the wall on

aggerem; alii fundebant picem que reliquas res,
the mound; others were pouring pitch and other things,

quibus ignis potest incitari; ut ratio posset
by which the fire might be encouraged; so that a plan could

vix iniri, quo primum occurreretur,[24] aut
scarcely be adopted, where first they should obstruct, or

cui rei auxilium ferretur;
to which affair [predicament] aid should be brought;

tamen quod, instituto Cæsaris, duæ legiones
however as, by the arrangement of Cæsar, two legions

semper excubabant pro castris, que plures partitis
always were watching before the camp, and many at allotted

temporibus erant in opere, celeriter factum est, ut
times were at work, it was quickly managed, that

alli   resisterent   eruptionibus,   alli   redūcĕrent
some   should oppose   the sallies,   others   should draw back

turres   que interscindĕrent aggerem;   vero
the towers and   cut off   the mound;   and indeed

        omnis   multitudo   concurret   ex   castris   ad
(that) a whole   multitude   should run   from the camp   to

restinguendum.
extinguish (the fire).

25. Cum   pugnaretur[25]   in omnibus   locis,
While it was fought [they were] fighting in   all   places,

reliquā   parte   noctis   jam   consumptā,   que
the remaining portion of the night now   having been spent,   and

spes   victoriæ   semper   redintegraretur   hostibus (dat.),
the hope of victory continually   was renewed   in the enemy,

magis   eo   quod   videbant   pluteos   turrium
the more so because they saw the coverings of the towers

deustos,   animadvertebant   apertos   nec
burnt off,   (and)   observed   (that we) unprotected not

facile adire   ad   auxiliandum; que   ipsi
easily to go [approached] for aiding;   and (while) they

recentes   semper   succedĕrent   defessis (dat.),
fresh   all the time were succouring   the wearied,

que   arbitrarentur   omnem   salutem   Galliæ
and (they) were judging (that)   all   the safety of Gaul

    positam[26] in illo vestigio tempŏris,   accidit
(was) placed   in   that   instant   of time, there happened

nobis inspectantibus   quod   visum   dignum
to us observing   (that)   which having seemed (to be) worthy

    memoriā   existimavimus   non prætermittendum.
(of) memory   we have thought   to [must] not be passed over.

Quidam Gallus   ante   portam   oppidi,   qui   e
A certain Gaul before the gate   of the town, who from

regione   turris   projiciebat   in   ignem   glebas
the locality of the tower was thowing into the fire   lumps

sevi   ac   picis   traditas   per   manus (pl.),
of tallow and   pitch   passed along   by   hand,

    trajectus   ab   dextra   latere   scorpione,   que
having been pierced on the right side   by the cross-bow. and

exanimatus	concidit;	unus	ex	proximis
struck lifeless	*fell;*	*one*	*from [of]*	*the nearest*

transgressus	hunc	jacentem	fungebatur	illo
having stepped over	*him*	*lying prostrate*	*performed*	*that*

eodem	munere;	eādem ratione	alteri	exani-
same	*duty;*	*in the same manner*	*the second*	*having been*

mato	ictu	scorpionis,	tertius	successit,
killed	*by a stroke*	*of the cross-bow,*	*a third*	*succeeded,*

et	quartus	tertio;	nec ille	locus	relictus est
and	*a fourth*	*to the third;*	*nor that*	*place*	*was left*

vacuus	a	propugnatoribus,	prius quam	aggere
vacant	*by*	*the defenders,*	*until*	*the mound*

restincto atque hostibus submotis
having been) extinguished and the enemy having been repulsed

omni	parte,	finis factus est	pugnandi.
on every	*side,*	*an end was made*	*of the fighting.*

26. Galli experti omnia, quod nulla res
The Gauls having tried all things, because no thing

successerat, postero die ceperunt consilium profugĕre
had succeeded, on the next day adopted the plan to flee

ex oppido, Vercingetorige hortante et jubente.
from the town, Vercingetorix advising and commanding.

Sperabant, conati id silentio noctis
They were hoping, having attempted it in the silence of the night

sese effecturos non magnā
(that) they about to [would] accomplish (it) with no great

jacturā suorum, propterea quod castra
loss of their (men), because (that) the camp

Vercingetorigis aberant neque longe ab oppido,
of Vercingetorix was distant not far from the town,

et perpetua palus, quæ intercedebat, tardabat[27]
and a continuous marsh, which was intervening, would retard

Romanos ad insequendum. Que jam
the Romans for [in] following. And already

apparabant facĕre hoc noctu, cum matres
they were preparing to do this by night, when the mothers

familias repente procurrerunt in publicum,
of families [matrons] suddenly ran out into public,

que flentes	projectæ		ad	pedes	suorum
and weeping	*having thrown (themselves)*		*at*	*the feet*	*of their*

	petierunt	omnibus precibus,	ne
(husbands)	*they begged*	*with all entreaties,*	*that they would not*

dedĕrent	se	et	communes liberos	hostibus
give up	*themselves*	*and (their)*	*common children*	*to the enemy*

ad	supplicium,	quos	natura, et	infirmitas
for	*punishment,*	*whom*	*nature, and*	*the weakness*

virium (pl).	impediret	ad capiendam	fugam.
of (their) strength	*prevented*	*for [from] taking*	*flight.*

Ubi	viderunt	eos	perstare (inf.)	in
When	*they saw*	*(that) they*	*persisted*	*in (their)*

sententiā,	quod	plerumque	in summo	periculo
design,	*because*	*generally*	*in the greatest*	*danger*

timor	recipit non	misericordiam,	cœperunt	conclamare,
fear	*admits not*	*pity,*	*they began*	*to cry out,*

et	significare	de	fugā	Romanis;
and	*to give warning*	*concerning*	*the flight*	*to the Romans;*

quo	timore	Galli	perterriti,	ne viæ
by which	*fear*	*the Gauls*	*having been alarmed,*	*lest the roads*

præoccuparentur	ab equitatu Romanorum	destiterunt
should be preoccupied	*by the cavalry of the Romans*	*they desisted*

	consilio.
from (their)	*design.*

27. Cæsar,	postero	die	turri	pro-
Cæsar,	*on the next*	*day*	*the tower*	*having been*

motā,	que	operibus	directis,	quæ
moved forward,	*and*	*the works*	*having been arranged,*	*which*

instituerat	facĕre,	magno	imbri	coorto,
he had determined	*to make,*	*a great*	*storm*	*having arisen,*

arbitratus est	hanc	tempestatem	non inutilem	ad
thought	*this*	*time*	*not unsuited*	*for*

capiendum	consilium,	quod	vidēbat	custodias
carrying out	*the plan,*	*because*	*he saw*	*the guards*

in	muro	dispositas	paulo	incautius; que
on	*the wall*	*arranged*	*a little*	*more carelessly; and*

jussit	suos	versari	in	opere langui-
he ordered	*his (men)*	*to be occupied*	*in*	*the work rather et*

dius,	et	ostendit	quid	vellet	fiĕri.
sluggishly,	*and*	*showed*	*what*	*he wished*	*to be done.*

Cohortatus	legiones	expeditas	in	occulto
Having exhorted	*the legions*	*prepared*	*in*	*a concealed place*

intra	vineas,	ut aliquando	percipĕrent	fructum
within	*the sheds,*	*that at length*	*they would receive*	*the fruit*

victoriæ	pro	tantis laboribus,	proposuit	præmia
of victory	*for*	*such great labors,*	*he offered*	*rewards*

iis,	qui	primi	ascendissent	murum,	que dedit
to those,	*who*	*first*	*should scale*	*the wall,*	*and gave*

signum	militibus.	Illi subito	evolaverunt	ex
the signal	*to the soldiers.*	*They suddenly*	*flew out*	*from*

omnibus	partibus,	que celeriter	complērunt	murum.
all	*sides,*	*and quickly*	*filled*	*the wall.*

28.

Hostes	perterriti	novā	re,
The enemy	*having been alarmed*	*by the sudden*	*affair*

	dejecti	muro	que turribus,
[action], (having been)	*driven*	*from the wall*	*and towers,*

constiterunt	cuneatim	foro ac	patentioribus
they drew up	*as a wedge*	*in the square and*	*more open*

locis,	hōc animo,	ut si ex quā	pārte	venire-
places,	*with this idea,*	*that if on any*	*side*	*(any one) should*

tur[28]	contra obviam	depugnarent	acie
come	*against*	*they might fight*	*with a line of battle*

instructā.	Ubi viderunt	neminem	demittĕre
drawn up.	*When they saw (that)*	*no one*	*lowered*

sese	in æquum locum,	sed	undique	circum-
himself	*into the level place,*	*but*	*on every side*	*they were*

fundi	toto	muro,	verĭti	ne omnino
spread around	*on the whole*	*wall,*	*having feared*	*lest altogether*

spes	fugæ	tolleretur,	armis
the hope	*of flight*	*might be taken away,*	*(their) arms*

abjectis	petiverunt	ultimas	partes
having been thrown away	*they sought*	*the farthest*	*parts*

oppidi	continenti	impetu;	que ibi	pars,
of the town	*with a continuous*	*rush;*	*and there*	*a part,*

cum	ipsi	premĕrent	se	angusto exitu
as	*they*	*crowded*	*themselves*	*in the narrow passage*

portarum,	interfecta est	a	militibus.		pars
of the gates,	*was killed*	*by*	*the soldiers*	*(and)*	*a part*
jam	egressa	portis,	ab	equitibus;	nec
already	*having passed*	*the gates,*	*by*	*the horsemen;*	*nor*
fuit	quisquam	qui	studēret	prædæ.	
was there	*any one*	*who*	*was attending*	*to plunder.*	*(Having*
Incitati	sic	et	cæde	Cenabensi,	
been) excited	*so much*	*both*	*by the slaughter*	*at Cenabum,*	
et	labore	opĕris	pepercerunt	non	
and	*by the labor*	*of the work*	*they spared*	*neither (those)*	
confectis	ætate,	non	mulieribus	non	infantibus.
worn out	*with age,*	*nor*	*women*	*nor*	*children.*
Denique	ex	omni	eo	numero,	qui fuit circiter
Finally	*out of*	*all*	*this*	*number,*	*which was about*
quadraginta	millium,	vix	octingenti,	qui	primo
forty	*thousand,*	*scarcely*	*eight hundred,*	*who,*	*the first*
clamore	audito,	ejecerant		se	ex
shout	*having been heard,*	*had thrown*		*themselves*	*from*
oppido,	pervenerunt	incolumes	ad	Vercingetorigem;	
the town,	*came*	*safe*	*to*	*Vercingetorix;*	
quos	ille,	nocte	jam	multā,	excepit
whom	*he,*	*the night (being)*	*now*	*much [late],*	*received*
ex	fugā	silentio, et	veritus	ne qua	seditio
from the flight	*in silence,*	*and*	*having feared*	*lest some*	*sedition*
oreretur	in	castris	ex	eorum	concursu, et
might arise	*in*	*the camp*	*from*	*their*	*gathering, and*
misericordiā		volgi,	suis	familiaribus	que
from the compassion	*of the throng,*	*his*	*friends*	*and*	
principibus	civitatum	dispositis		procul	
the chiefs	*of the states*	*having been located*	*at a distance*		
in	viā,	curavit	disparandos		que
on	*the road,*	*he took care*	*(that) they should be separated*	*and*	
deducendos ad suos,			quæ[29] pars castrorum		
be conducted to their (own people)			*(in) which part of the camp*		
obvenerat	cuique	civitati	ab	initio.	
had fallen to	*each*	*state*	*from*	*the beginning.*	

29. Postero die concilio convocato,
On the following day a council having been called,

consolatus	que	cohortatus est,		ne
he consoled	*and*	*exhorted,*		*they should not be*
admodum	demittĕrent	se animo,	neve	perturbarentur
too much	*cast down*	*in mind,*	*nor*	*troubled*
incommodo:	Romanos		non vicisse	virtute
by (their) loss;	*(that) the Romans*		*had not conquered*	*by bravery*
neque in	acie,	sed	quodam	artificio et
nor in	*a battle-line,*	*but*	*by a certain*	*skill and*
scientiā	oppugnationis,	cujus	rei	ipsi fuerint
by the science	*of siege,*	*of which*	*thing*	*they were*
imperiti;		errare, si	qui expectent	in bello
unskilled;	*(those)*	*err, if*	*they expect*	*in war*
omnes	eventus	rerum	secundos;	nunquam
all	*results*	*of affairs*	*(to be) prosperous;*	*never*
placuisse	sibi	Avarĭcum		defendi,
had it pleased	*him*	*(that) Avaricum*		*to [should] be defended,*
ejus	rei	habēret	ipsos	testes; sed
of which	*thing*	*he had*	*themselves*	*as witnesses; but*
	factum		imprudentiā Biturigum
	to have been (it was) brought about		*by the imprudence of the Bituriges*
et	nimiā	obsequentiā	reliquorom,	uti hoc
and	*by the too great*	*compliance*	*of the rest,*	*that this*
incommodum	acciperetur;	tamen	se	sanaturum
disaster	*was received;*	*however*	*he*	*would remedy*
id	celeriter	majoribus	commodis.	Nam civitates
this	*quickly*	*by greater*	*advantages.*	*For the states*
quæ	dissentirent	ab	reliquis	Gallis, has	suā
which	*dissented*	*from*	*the other*	*Gauls, these*	*by his*
diligentiā adjuncturum, atque effecturum, unum consilium
exertion he would unite, and would make one counsel
totius	Galliæ	cujus	consensui (dat.)	ne orbis
of all	*Gaul*	*whose*	*union*	*not the whole*
terrarum	quidem	possit		obsistĕre;
world	*even*	*would be able [could]*		*(to) oppose;*
que	se	habēre	prope jam	effectum id.
and	*he*	*to have [had]*	*nearly already*	*effected this.*
Interea	esse		æquum	impet-
In the mean time	*to be [it was]*		*iust*	*(that) to [it should]*

rari	ab	iis	causā	communis	salutis,
be obtained	from	them	for the sake	of the general	safety,
ut	instituĕrent		munire	castra,	quo
that	they should decree		to fortify	their camp,	so that
possent		facilius			sustinēre
they would be able [could]		the more easily		(to)	resist
repentinos	impetus	hostium.			
the sudden	attacks	of the enemy.			

30. Hac oratio fuit non ingrata Gallis, quod
This speech was not disagreeable to the Gauls, because

ipse non defecerat animo, tanto incommodo
he himself had not failed in courage, so great a loss

accepto, neque abdiderat se in occultum,
having been received, neither had he hidden himself in secret,

neque fugerat conspectum multitudinis; que
nor fled the sight of the multitude; and

existimabatur providēre et præsentire plus
he was thought to foresee and to forecast more

animo quod, re integrā, cen-
in mind because, the matter (being) not begun, he had

suerat primo Avaricum incendendum,
decided first (that) Avaricum to [should] be burnt,

post deserendum Itaque ut adversæ
afterwards (that) it to [should] be deserted. And so as adverse

res minuunt auctoritatem reliquorum imperatorum;
affairs diminish the authority of other commanders;

sic ex contrario dignitas hujus incommodo
so on the contrary the authority of this one a loss

accepto, augebatur in dies;
having been sustained, was increased (from day) to day;

simul veniebant in spem, ejus
at the same time they were coming into the hope, because of his

affirmatione, de adjungendis reliquis civitatibus; que
assertion, of uniting the other states; and

primum Galli eo tempore instituerunt munire
first the Gauls at this time undertook to fortify

castra; et sic homines insueti laboris
their camp; and so men unaccustomed to labor

LIBER VII.

confirmati sunt	animo,	ut	existimarent	omnia
were encouraged	*in mind,*	*that*	*they should think*	*(that) all*

quæ	imperarentur	patienda	sibi.
(things) which	*were commanded*	*must be endured*	*by them.*

31.
Nec Vercingetorix	laborabat	minus animo
Nor Vercingetorix	*was exerting himself*	*less in mind*

quam	pollicitus est,	ut	adjungĕret	reliquas
than	*he had promised,*	*that*	*he might attach*	*the other*

civitates,	atque	alliciebat	eorum	principes	donis
states,	*and*	*he was enticing*	*their*	*chiefs*	*by presents*

que	pollicitationibus.	Deligebat	idoneos	homines
and	*promises.*	*He selected*	*suitable*	*men*

huic	rei,	aut	subdolā	oratione	aut	amicitiā
for this	*affair,*	*either*	*by the wily*	*speech*	*or*	*friendship*

quorum	quisque	posset	facillime	capi.
of whom	*each*	*(chief) might*	*most easily*	*be gained.*

Qui	refugerant	Avarico	expugnato,
Those who	*had escaped*	*Avaricum*	*having been stormed,*

curat	armandos	que	vestiendos.	Simul
he takes care	*should be armed*	*and*	*clothed.*	*At the same time*

ut	diminutæ	copiæ	redintegrarentur,	imperat
that	*his diminished*	*forces*	*might be renewed,*	*he orders*

certum	numerum	militum	civitatibus,	quem,	et
a certain	*number*	*of soldiers*	*from the states,*	*whom,*	*and*

ante	quam	diem,	velit	adduci	in	castra;
before	*what*	*day,*	*he wishes*	*to be brought*	*into*	*the camp;*

que	jubet	omnes	sagittarios,	quorum	erat
and	*he orders*	*all*	*the archers,*	*of whom*	*there was*

permagnus	numerus	in	Galliā,	conquiri,	et	mitti
a very great	*number*	*in*	*Gaul,*	*to be sought,*	*and*	*sent*

ad	se.	His	rebus,	id	quod	deperierat
to	*him.*	*By these*	*means,*	*that*	*which*	*he had lost*

Avarici	celeriter.	expletur.	Interim
at Avaricum	*speedily,*	*is replaced.*	*in the mean time*

Teutomatus,	filius	Olloviconis,	rex	Nitiobrigum,
Teutomatus,	*the son*	*of Ollovicon,*	*king*	*of the Nitiobriges,*

cujus	pater	appellatus erat	amicus	ab	nostro	Senatu,
whose	*father*	*had been called*	*friend*	*by*	*our*	*Senate,*

pervēnit ad eum, cum magno numero suorum equitum,
came   to him, with a great number of his cavalry,

et   quos   conduxerat   ex   Aquitaniā.
and (those) that he had hired from Aquitania.

32. Cæsar   commoratus   complures   dies   Avarĭci,
Cæsar   having delayed   several   days at Avaricum,

que   nactus   ibi   summam   copiam   frumenti   et
and having obtained there the greatest supply of corn and

reliqui   commeatus,   refecit   exercitum   ex   labore
of other   provisions,   refreshed   his army   from   labor

atque   inopiā.   Hieme   jam   prope   confectā,
and   want.   The winter   now   nearly having been ended,

cum   tempore   ipso   anni   vocaretur   ad
when   by the season   itself   of the year   he was invited   to

gerendum   bellum,   et   constituisset   proficisci
carrying on   war,   and   he had determined   to march

ad   hostem,   sive   elicĕre   eum   ex   paludibus
against   the enemy,   either   to entice   him   from   the marshes

que   silvis,   sive   posset   premĕre   obsidione,
and   woods,   or   that he might   crush   by a siege,

principes   Æduorum veniunt   ad   cum   legati
chiefs   of the Ædui   come   to   him   as ambassadors

oratum   ut   maxime   necessario   tempore
to entreat   that   in an especially   necessary [critical]   time

subveniat   civitati;   rem   esse   in
he should assist the state; (saying that) their affairs to be [are] in

summo   periculo;   quod   cum   singuli   magistratus   cre-
extreme   danger;   that   whereas   single   magistrates   were

ari   antiquitus,   atque   consuēssent   obtinēre
appointed   of old,   and   had been accustomed   to possess

regiam   potestatem   annum,   duo gerant magistratum,
a kingly   power   for one year,   two   hold   the magistracy,

et   uterque   eorum   dicat   se creatum esse
and   each   of them   asserts (that)   he was appointed

legibus.   Horum   alterum   esse   Convictrolitavem
by the laws.   Of these   the one   was   Convictrolitavis

florentem   et   illustrem adolescentem, alterum Cotum
a distinguished and illustrous   young man,   the other   Cotus

natum	antiquissimā	familiā,	atque ipsum	hominem
sprung	*from a most ancient*	*family,*	*and himself*	*a man*

summæ	potentiæ,	et magnæ cognationis,	cujus
of the highest	*power,*	*and of great connections,*	*whose*

frater	Valetiacus	gesserit	eundem	magistratum
brother	*Valetiacus*	*had held*	*the same*	*magistracy*

proximo	anno;	omnem	civitatem	esse in	armis;
the last	*year;*	*the whole*	*state*	*was in*	*arms;*

senatum	divisum,	populum	divisum,	suas
the senate	*was divided,*	*the people*	*divided,*	*their*

clientelas[30]	cujusque	eorum:	quod si	controversia
partisans	*of each*	*of them;*	*but if*	*the dispute*

alatur	diutius,	fore uti	pars	civitatis
is formented	*longer,*	*it would happen that*	*a part*	*of the state*

confligat	cum	parte;	id	ne accidat
would collide	*with*	*a part;*	*(that) this*	*should not happen*

positum	in ejus	diligentiā atque	auctoritate.
was placed [rested]	*in his*	*exertion and*	*authority.*

33. | | | | |
|---|---|---|---|
| Cæsar, | etsi | existimabat | detrimentosum |
| *Cæsar,* | *although* | *he thought it* | *injurious* |

discedĕre	a	bello atque	hoste,	tamen non
to depart	*from*	*the war and*	*the enemy,*	*yet not*

ignorans	quanta	incommoda	consuēssent	oriri
being ignorant	*how great*	*wrongs*	*were wont*	*to arise*

ex	dissensionibus,	ne	tanta	civitas et tam
from	*dissensions,*	*lest*	*so great*	*a state and (one) so*

conjuncta	Romano	populo,	quam	ipse semper
connected	*with the Roman*	*people,*	*which*	*he always*

aluisset,	que ornāsset	omnibus	rebus,	descendĕret
had cherished,	*and honored*	*in all*	*things,*	*should resort*

ad	vim	atque ad arma, atque	ea	pars	quæ
to	*violence*	*and to arms, and (lest)*	*that*	*part*	*which*

confidĕret	minus	sibi	accersĕret	auxilia a
trusted	*least*	*in him*	*should call for*	*assistance from*

Vercingetorige,	existimavit	huic rei	præ-
Vercingetorix,	*thought (that)*	*this action*	*ought*

vertendum;	et quod	legibus	Æduorum,
to be anticipated;	*and because*	*by the laws*	*of the Ædui,*

iis	qui	obtinērent	summum	magistratum
to those	*who*	*possessed*	*the chief*	*magistracy*

non licēret	excedĕre	ex	finibus,	ne
it was not allowed	*to depart*	*from (their) territories,*		*lest*

videretur	deminuisse	quid	de	eorum
he should seem	*to have curtailed*	*any thing*	*respecting*	*their*

jure	aut legibus,	ipse	statuit	proficisci	in
authority	*or laws,*	*he himself*	*resolved*	*to set out*	*to*

Æduos,	que	evocavit	omnem senatum,	et
the Ædui,	*and*	*summoned*	*all the senate,*	*and (those)*

intra	quos	controversia	esset,	ad	se
among	*whom*	*the controversy*	*might be,*	*to (meet)*	*him*

Decetiam.	Cum	prope	omnis	civitas
at Decetia [Decize].	*When*	*nearly*	*the whole*	*state*

convenisset	eo,	que	doceretur	fratrem
had assembled	*there,*	*and*	*he was informed*	*(that) a brother*

renunciatum	a fratre,	paucis	clam vocatis,
had been proclaimed by a brother, a few having been secretly called,			

alio	loco,	alio	tempore,	atque
in another	*place,*	*(and) at another*	*time,*	*than*

oportuerit;	cum	leges	non	solum	vetarent
was proper;	*since*	*the laws*	*not*	*only*	*forbade*

duos	ex	unā familiā,	utroque	vivo,	creari
two	*of*	*one family,*	*both*	*being alive,*	*to be chosen*

magistratus,	sed	etiam	prohibērent	esse	in
magistrates,	*but*	*also*	*forbade (them)*	*to be*	*in*

senatu;	coegit	Cotum	deponĕre	magistratum;
the senate;	*he compelled*	*Cotus*	*to resign*	*the magistracy*

jussit	Convictolitavem,	qui creatus esset	per
he ordered	*Convictolitavis,*	*who had been chosen*	*through*

sacerdotes	more	civitatis,	magistratibus
the priests	*after the custom*	*of the state,*	*the magistracy*

intermissis,	obtinēre	potestatem.
having lapsed,	*to hold*	*the power [office].*

34. | Hōc | decreto | interposito, | cohortatus |
|---|---|---|---|
| *This* | *decree* | *having been delivered,* | *he exhorted* |

Æduos	ut	obliviscerentur	controversiarum
the Ædui	*that*	*they should forget*	*(their) controversies*

LIBER VII.

ac	dissensionum,	atque	omnibus	rebus	omis-
and	dissensions,	and	all	things	having been

sis,	servirent	huic bello,	que	exspectarent
laid aside,	they should attend to	this war,	and	might expect

ea	præmia,	quæ	meruissent,	ab	se,	Galliā
those	rewards,	which	they should merit,	from	him,	Gaul

devictā,	que	mittĕrent	omnem
having been conquered,	and (that)	they should send	all

equitatum,	et	decem	millia	peditum	celeriter
the cavalry,	and	ten	thousand	footmen	speedily

sibi,	quæ	disponĕret	in	præsidiis	causā
to him.	whom	he might place	in	garrisons	for the sake

rei frumentariæ;	divisit	exercitum	in	duas
of the grain supply;	he divided (his)	army	into	two

partes;	dedit	quattuor legiones	Labieno	ducendas
parts;	he gave	four legions	to Labienus	to be led

in	Senones	que	Parisios;	ipse	duxit	sex	in
into	the Senones	and	Parisii;	he himself	led	six	into

Arvernos	ad	oppidum	Gergoviam	secundum	flumen
the Arverni	to	the town (of)	Gergovia	down	the river

Elaver:	attribuit	partem	equitatūs	illi,
Allier:	he gave	a part	of the cavalry	to him (Labienus)

reliquit	partem	sibi.	Quā	re	cognitā,
he left	a part	for himself.	Which	thing	having been learned

Vercingetorix,	omnibus	pontibus	ejus	fluminis
Vercingetorix,	all	the bridges	of this	river

interruptis,	cœpit	facĕre	iter	ab
having been demolished,	began	to make	his march	on

alterā	parte	fluminis.
the other	side	of the river.

35.

Cum	uterque	exercitus	esset	in	conspectu
Since	each	army	was	in	view

utrique	que	poneret	castra	fere	e
to (of) the other	and	was pitching	a camp	almost	over

regione	castris,	exploratoribus	dispositis,
against	a camp,	scouts	having been stationed,

necubi	Romani	transducĕrent	copias,
(so) that in no place	the Romans	could lead across	the forces,

ponte	effecto;		res	erat
a bridge	*having been built;*		*(this) thing*	*[condition] was*

Cæsari	in	magnis	difficultatibus,	ne	imped-
to [placed] Cæsar	*in*	*great*	*difficulties,*	*lest*	*he should*

iretur	flumine,	majorem	partem	æstatis,
be hindered	*by the river,*	*for the greater*	*part*	*of the summer,*

quod	Elaver	fere	soleat	non	transiri
because	*the Allier*	*generally*	*is wont*	*not*	*to be crossed*

vado	ante	autumnum.	Itaque	ne	id
by fording	*before*	*autumn.*	*Therefore*	*lest*	*this*

accidĕret,	castris positis	silvestri	loco
might happen,	*the camp having been pitched*	*in a woody*	*place*

e regione	unius	eorum	pontium,	quos	Vercin-
opposite	*one*	*of these*	*bridges,*	*which*	*Vercin-*

getorix	curaverat	rescindendos,	postero	die
getorix	*had provided*	*should be destroyed,*	*on the next*	*day*

restitit	in	occulto,	cum duabus	legionibus,
he remained	*in*	*a concealed place,*	*with two*	*legions;*

misit,	ut	consueverat	reliquas	copias
he sent,	*as*	*he had been accustomed*	*the remaining*	*forces*

cum	omnibus	impedimentis,	quibusque	quartis
with	*all*	*the baggage,*	*each*	*fourth*

cohortibus	demptis,	uti	numerus	legionum
cohort	*having been removed,*	*so that*	*the number*	*of the legions*

videretur	constare.	Iis	jussis	progredi
should seem	*to agree.*	*These having been ordered*	*to advance*

quam	longissime	possent,	cum	jam	ex
as	*far*	*(as) they could,*	*when*	*at last*	*from*

tempore	diei	capĕret	conjecturam	per-
the time	*of day*	*he could make*	*the conjecture*	*(that) they*

ventum	in	castra,	cœpit	reficĕre	pontem
had arrived	*to [in]*	*camp,*	*he began*	*to rebuild*	*the bridge*

iisdem	sublicis	inferior	pars	quarum	remanebat
on the same	*piles*	*the lower*	*part*	*of which*	*was remaining*

integra.	Opere	celeriter	effecto,	que
entire.	*The work*	*quickly*	*having been completed*	*and*

legionibus	transductis,	et	idoneo	loco
the legions	*having been led over,*	*and*	*a suitable*	*place*

castris	delecto,	revocavit	reliquas	copias.
for a camp	*having been selected,*	*he recalled*	*the remaining*	*forces.*
Vercingetorix,	re		cognitā,	ne
Vercingetorix,	*the thing [event]*		*having been learned,*	*lest*
cogeretur	dimicare	contra	suam	voluntatem,
he might be forced	*to fight*	*against*	*his*	*will,*
antecessit		magnis	itineribus.	
preceded (him)		*by great [forced]*	*marches.*	

36. Cæsar pervēnit Gergoviam, ex eo loco,
Cæsar *reached* *Gergovia,* *from this place,*

quintis	castris	que	levi	equestri	prœlio
on the fifth	*encampment*	*and*	*a slight*	*cavalry*	*battle*
facto	eo	die,	situ		urbis
having been fought	*on this*	*day,*	*the situation*		*of the town*
perspecto,		quæ		posita	in
having been reconnoitered,		*which*	*(having been)*	*placed*	*on*
altissimo	monte,	habebat	omnes		aditus
a very high	*mountain,*	*had*	*all*		*the approaches*
difficiles,	desperavit	de	expugnatione;		constituit
difficult,	*he despaired*	*of*	*an assault;*		*he determined*
non	agendum[31]		de		obsessione
(that) not	*to be [it must not be] acted*		*respecting*		*the siege*
prius	quam	expedisset	rem frumentariam.		At
before	*(that)*	*he had secured*	*a grain supply.*		*But*

Vercingetorix castris positis prope oppidum,
Vercingetorix *(his) camp* *having been placed near* *the town,*

in	monte,	collocaverat	copias	singularum
on	*the mountain,*	*had stationed*	*the forces*	*of each*
civitatum	separatim,	circum	se,	mediocribus
state	*separately,*	*around*	*himself,*	*at moderate*
intervallis,	atque	omnibus	collibus	ejus jugi
intervals,	*and*	*all*	*the hills*	*of this range*
occupatis	qua	poterat		despici,
having been occupied	*where*	*it was possible*		*to be viewed,*
præbebat	horribilem speciem;	que		jubebat
he was presenting	*a formidable appearance;*	*and*		*he was ordering*
principes	earum	civitatum,	quos	delegerat
the chiefs	*of these*	*states*	*whom*	*he had selected*

sibi	ad	capiendum	consilium,	convenire	ad
for himself	*for*	*taking*	*counsel,*	*to come*	*to*
se	quotidie	primā	luce	seu	quid
him	*daily*	*at first*	*light [early dawn],*	*whether*	*anything*
videretur		communicandum,	seu	quid	minis-
might seem best		*to be discussed,*	*or*	*anything*	*(to) be*
trandum;	neque	intermittebat	fere	ullum	diem,
performed;	*nor*	*did he omit*	*scarcely*	*any*	*day;*
quin	periclitaretur	quid	animi	ac	virtutis
but that	*he might try*	*what*	*(of) spirit*	*and*	*(of) courage*
esset	in	quoque	suorum	equestri	prœlio,
might be	*in*	*each*	*of his men*	*by cavalry*	*engagements,*
sagittariis		interjectis.		Erat	collis e
the archers		*having been intermixed.*		*There was*	*a hill*
regione	oppidi	sub	ipsis	radicibus	montis
opposite	*the town*	*at*	*the very*	*roots [foot]*	*of the mountain*
egregie	munitus,	atque	circumcisus	ex	omni parte
excellently	*fortified,*	*and*	*precipitous*	*on*	*every side*
(quem	si	nostri	tenērent,	videbantur	
(which	*if*	*our men*	*could hold,*	*they would seem*	*(able)*
prohibituri	hostes	et[32]	ex	magnā	parte
to prevent	*the enemy*	*both*	*in*	*great*	*part (from)*
aquæ (gen.),	et	liberā	pabulatione);	sed	is
water,	*and*	*from free*	*foraging);*	*but*	*this*
locus	tenebatur	ab	iis	præsidio	non nimis
place	*was held*	*by*	*them*	*with a garrison*	*not very*
firmo;	tamen,	Cæsar	egressus	ex	castris
strong;	*however,*	*Cæsar*	*having marched out*	*from*	*the camp*
silento	noctis,	prius	quam subsidium	posset	
in the silence	*of the night,*	*before*	*(that) aid*	*could*	
venire	ex	oppido,	præsidio	dejecto,	
come	*from*	*the town,*	*the garrison*	*having been dislodged,*	
potitus	loco,	collocavit	duas legiones,	ibi,	
having seized	*the place,*	*he stationed*	*two legions*	*there,*	
que perduxit	duplicem	fossam		duodenūm	pedum
and led	*a double*	*trench*	*(of)*	*twelve*	*feet*
a	majoribus	castris	ad	minora,	ut
(wide) from	*the greater*	*camp*	*to*	*the lesser.*	*(so) that*

etiam	singuli	possent	commeare	tuto	ab
even	*single (soldiers)*	*could*	*pass*	*safely*	*from [on]*

repentino	incursu	hostium.
the sudden	*attack*	*of the enemy.*

37.
Dum	hæc	geruntur	ad	Gergoviam,
While	*these things*	*were happening*	*at*	*Gergovia,*

Convictolitais.	Æduus,	cui	demonstravimus
Convictolitais.	*the Æduan,*	*to whom*	*we have shown*

magistratum	abjudicatum	a Cæsare	sollicitatus
the magistracy	*was adjudged*	*by Cæsar*	*having been solicited*

pecuniā	ab	Arvernis	colloquitur	cum quibusdam
with money	*by*	*the Arverni*	*confers*	*with certain*

adolescentibus	quorum	Litavicus erat	princeps, atque
young men	*of whom*	*Litavicus was*	*the chief, and*

ejus fratres,	adolescentes	nati	amplissimā familiā.
his brothers,	*young men*	*born*	*of most illustrious family.*

Communicat	præmium cum iis,	que hortatur	eos
He shares	*the money with them,*	*and exhorts*	*them*

ut	meminerint	se liberos, et	natos
that	*they should remember*	*(that) they (were) free, and*	*born*

imperio;	esse unam civitatem Æduorum quæ
for empire;	*(saying that) it is alone the state of the Ædui which*

distineat	certissimam	victoriam Galliæ;	reliquas
retards	*the most certain*	*victory of the Gauls;*	*the rest*

contineri	ejus auctoritate, quā	transductā,
are restrained	*by its authority*	*which having been brought over*

	non	fore locum	Romanis
[and if it were won over],	*there would not be*	*a place for the Romans*

consistendi in	Galliā;	se esse affectum	nonnullo
to stand on in	*Gaul;*	*(that) he was treated*	*by a considerable*

beneficio	Cæsaris,	tamen	sic ut	obtinuerit
benefit	*of Cæsar,*	*however*	*(only) so that*	*he obtained*

justissimam	causam	apud	eum; sed	tribuĕre (inf.)
a most just	*cause*	*through*	*him; but*	*(he) owes*

plus	communi	libertati.	Enim cur	Ædui
more to (their)	*common*	*liberty.*	*For why*	*should the Ædui*

veniant	ad	Cæsarem	disceptatorem	de	suo jure
come	*to*	*Cæsar*	*as arbiter*	*about*	*their rights*

et	de	legibus	potius	quam	Romani	ad
and	about	their laws	rather	than	the Romans	to

Æduos?	Adolescentibus	deductis
the Ædui?	The young men	having been brought over

celeriter,	et	oratione	magistratūs,	et	præmio,
speedily,	both	by the speech	of the magistrate,	and	the bribe,

cum	profiterentur,	se	vel	fore	principes
when	they promised,	that they	indeed	would be	leaders

ejus	consilii,	ratio	perficiendi	quærebatur,
of this	enterprise,	a plan	of executing (it)	was inquired into,

quod	confidebant	civitatem	non	posse
because	they were confident (that)	the state	could	not be

adduci	temere	ad	suscipiendum	bellum.
induced	rashly	to	undertaking	the war.

Placuit	ut	Litavicus	præficeretur	illis
it was resolved	that	Litavicus	should be appointed over	those

decem	millibus	quæ	mitterentur	Cæsari	ad	bellum,
ten	thousand	that	were to be sent	to Cæsar	for	the war,

atque	curaret	ducenda	ea,	que	ejus
and	should have charge	of conducting	them,	and (that)	his

fratres	præcurrerent	ad	Cæsarem.	Constituunt
brothers	should go before (him)	to	Cæsar.	They determine

quā ratione	placeat	reliqua	agi.
in what manner it may be well (that)	the rest to be [should be]	performed.

38. Litavicus,	exercitu	accepto,	cum
Litavicus,	the army	having been received,	when

abesset	circiter	triginta	millia	passuum	ab
he was distant	about	thirty	thousand	paces	from

Gergovia,	subito	convocatis	militibus,
Gergovia,	having suddenly	called together	the soldiers,

lacrumans	inquit,	"Quo	milites	proficiscimur?
weeping	he said,	"Whither	O soldiers	are we going?

omnis	noster	equitatus,	omnis	nobilitas	interiit.
all	our	Knighthood	all	the nobility	has perished.

Eporedorix	et	Viridomarus	principes	civitatis
Eporedorix	and	Viridomarus	chiefs	of the state

insimulati	proditionis	interfecti sunt	ab
having been accused	of treason	have been killed	by

38]

Romanis causā indictā. Cognoscite
the Romans the case not having been called. [without a trial] Know

hæc ab iis, qui fugerunt ex ipsā cæde. Nam
this from these, who have fled from the very massacre. For

ego fratribus atque omnibus meis propinquis
I (my) brothers and all my relations

interfectis prohibeor dolore pronunciare quæ
having been killed am prevented by grief from announcing what

gesta sunt." Ii producuntur, quos ille edocuerat
has been done." Those are produced, whom he had taught

quæ vellet dici, atque eadem, quæ Litavicus
what he wished to be said, and the same, which Litavicus

pronunciaverat, exponunt multitudini: omnes
had announced, they explain to the multitude: (that) all

equites Æduorum interfectos, quod dicerentur
the knights of the Ædui were slain, because they were said

collocuti cum Arvernis; ipsos occultasse se
to have conspired with the Arverni; they had hid themselves

inter multitudinem militum, atque profugisse ex
among the multitude of soldiers, and had fled from

mediā cæde. Ædui conclamant, et
the midst (of the) massacre. The Ædui exclaim, and

obsecrant Litavicum ut consulat sibi,
entreat Litavicus that he should deliberate for themselves,

"Quasi vero," inquit ille, "res sit
"As if indeed," said he, "the thing were (a matter)

consilii, ac non sit necesse nobis contendĕre
of [for] a plan, and it were not necessary for us to hasten

Gergoviam et conjungĕre nosmet cum Arvernis?
to Gergovia and to unite ourselves with the Arverni?

An dubitamus, quin, nefario facinŏre
Or can we doubt, but that, so nefarious a crime

admisso, Romani jam concurrant ad
having been committed, the Romans now gather for

interficiendos nos? Proinde si est quid animi
slaying us? Therefore if there is any spirit

in nobis persequamur eorum mortem, qui
in us let us follow [avenge] their death, who

interierunt	indignissime,	atque	interficiamus	hos
have perished	*most ignobly,*	*and*	*let us slay*	*these*
latrones."	Ostendit	Romanos	cives,	qui erant
robbers."	*He shows*	*the Roman*	*citizens,*	*who were*

unā fiduciā ejus præsidii. Continuo diripit
with them in the confidence of his protection. He forthwith seizes

magnum numerum frumenti que commeatus;
a great quantity of corn and provisions;

interficit ipsos crudeliter excruciatos;
he kills them (the Romans) having cruelly tortured (them);

dimittit nuntios totā civitate Æduorum; permovet
he sends messengers in all the state of the Ædui; he excites

(them) eodem mendacio de cæde
(them) with the same falsehood about the massacre

equitum et principum; hortatur ut simili
of knights and chiefs; he exhorts (them) that in like

ratione, atque ipse fecerit, persequantur suas
manner, as he had done, they should avenge their

injurias.
injuries.

39. Eporedorix adolescens natus summo loco,
Eporedorix a young man born in the highest rank,

et summæ potentiæ domi, et unā Viridomarus,
and of the highest power at home, and also Viridomarus,

pari ætate et gratiā, sed dispari genĕre,
of equal age and influence, but of unequal lineage

quem Cæsar perduxerat ad summam dignitatem
whom Cæsar had elevated to the highest dignity

ex humili loco, traditum sibi
from humble station, he having been recommended to him

ab Divitiaco, convenerant in numero equitum,
by Divitiacus, had come in the number of the horsemen,

evocati nominatim ab eo. Erat
(having been) called by name by him (Cæsar). There was

contentio his inter se de
a contest (between) these (two) among thrmselves concerning

principatu; et in illā controversiā magistratuum
rank, and in that dispute of the magistrates

alter pugnaverat pro Convictolitavi alter pro	the one had contended for Convictrolitais the other for
Coto summis opibus. Ex iis Eporedorix,	Cotus with (their) greatest resources. Of these Eporedorix,
consilio Litavici cognito defert rem	the designs of Litavicus having been learned reports the matter
ad Cæsarem fere mediā nocte; orat	to Cæsar about mid night; he begs (that)
ne patiatur civitatem pravis consiliis	he would not suffer the state by the wicked counsels
adolescentium deficĕre ab amicitiā Romani	of young men to fall from the friendship of the Roman
populi, quod provideat futurum, si tot millia	people, which he foresaw would happen, if so many thousands
hominum conjunxerint se cum hostibus,	of men should have united themselve with the enemy,
quorum salutem neque propinqui	whose safety neither (their) relations (could)
negligĕre neque posset civitas æstimare levi	neglect nor could the state consider (it) of slight
momento.	importance.

40. Cæsar affectus magnā sollicitudine
    Cæsar, (having been) affected with great anxiety

hōc nuntio, quod semper præcipue	by this intelligence, because he had always particularly
indulserat civitati Æduorum, nullā dubitatione	favored the state of the Ædui, no delay
interpositā, educit ex castris quattuor	having been interposed, leads forth from the camp four
expeditas legiones, que omnem equitatum. Nec	light-armed legions, and all the cavalry. Nor
fuit spatium tali tempŏre ad contrahenda	was there an interval at such a time for contracting
castra, quod res videbatur posita	the camp, because the matter seemed placed [depending]
in celeritate. Relinquit C. Fabium legatum	on speed [dispatch]. He leaves C. Fabius (his) lieutenant

cum	quabus	legionibus	præsidio	castris;
with	*two*	*legions*	*for [as] a garrison*	*to the camp;*

quum	jussisset	fratres	Litavici	comprehendi,
when	*he had ordered*	*the brothers*	*of Litavicus*	*to be arrested,*

reperit	profugisse	paulo ante	ad	hostes.
he finds	*(that) they have fled*	*a little before*	*to*	*the enemy.*

Adhortatus	milites,	ne permoveantur
Having encouraged (his)	*soldiers,*	*(that) they should not be troubled*

labōre	itinĕris	necessario tempŏre,	omnibus
by the labor	*of the march*	*at (so) necessary a time,*	*all*

	cupidissimis,	progressus	viginti	quinque
(being)	*most eager,*	*having proceeded*	*twenty*	*five*

millia	passuum,	conspicatus	agmen	Æduorum,
thousand	*paces [miles],*	*having seen*	*the army*	*of the Ædui*

equitatu	immisso,		moratur atque
the cavalry	*having been sent against (them),*		*he retards and*

impedit	eorum	iter;	que	interdicit	omnibus,
impedes	*their*	*march;*	*and*	*he forbids*	*all,*

ne interficiant	quemquam.	Jubet	Eporedorigem
that they should kill	*any one.*	*He orders*	*Eporedorix*

et Viridomarum,	quos	ille	existimabant	interfectos,
and Viridomarus,	*whom*	*they*	*were thinking*	*had been killed,*

versari	inter	equites,	que	appellare	suos
to mingle	*among*	*the horsemen,*	*and*	*to address*	*their*

	Iis	cognitis,	et	fraude
(countrymen).	*These*	*having been recognized,*	*and*	*the fraud*

Litavici	perspectā,	Ædui	incipiunt
of Litavicus	*having been perceived,*	*the Ædui*	*begin*

tendĕre	manus	et	significare	deditionem,	et
to extend	*(their) hands*	*and*	*to signify*	*submission,*	*and*

	projectis	armis	deprecari	mortem.
having thrown away	*(their) arms*	*to beg off*	*death.*

Litavicus	profugit	Gergoviam,	cum	suis	clientibus,
Litavicus	*flees*	*to Gergovia,*	*with*	*his*	*clients,*

quibus	est	nefas,	more	Gallorum,	deserĕre
with whom	*it is*	*a crime,*	*by the custom*	*of the Gauls,*	*to desert*

	patronos,	etiam	in	extremā	fortunā.
(their)	*patrons,*	*even*	*in*	*extreme [bad]*	*fortune.*

LIBER VII.

41. Cæsar, nuntiis missis ad civitatem
Cæsar, messengers having been sent to the state

Æduorum, qui docěrent conservatos suo
of the Ædui, who should show (that those) had been saved by his

beneficio, quos potuisset interficěre jure belli,
favor, whom he could have killed by the right of war,

que tribus horis noctis datis exercitui
and three hours of the night having been given to the army

ad quietem, movit castra ad Gergoviam.
for rest, he moved the camp toward Gergovia.

Fere medio itiněre equites, missi a Fabio,
About the middle (of the) march horsemen sent by Fabius,

exponunt in quanto periculo res fuerit;
reveal in how great danger the affair has been;

demonstrant castra oppugnata summis
they explain (that) the camp was attacked by very great

copiis, quum integri crebro succederent
forces, as fresh (men) frequently succeeded

defessis, que defatigarent nostros assiduo
the tired, and exhausted our (men) by the continual

laborě, quibus (dat.)[33] propter magnitudinem
labor, by whom on account of the size

castrorum perpetuo permanendum esset
of the camp it must continually be remained [stationed]

vallo, iisdem, multos vulneratos
on the rampart (by) the same, (that) many were wounded

multitudine sagittarum, atque omnis geněris
by the multitude of arrows, and of every kind

telorum; ad sustinenda hæc tormenta
of weapons; for resisting these the hurling engines

fuisse magno usui; Fabium eorum dicessu,
were (of) great use; (that) Fabius on their departure,

duabus portis relictis obstruěre
two gates having been left (open) was blocking up

ceteras, que adděre pluteos vallo, et se
the rest, and adding breastworks to the wall, and (that) he

parare ad similem casum in posterum diem.
was preparing for a like fate on the next day.

Iis	rebus	cognitis,	Cæsar	pervēnit	in
These	*things*	*having been learned,*	*Cæsar*	*arrived*	*at*

castra	ante	ortum	solis	summo	studio
the camp	*before*	*the rising*	*of the sun*	*by the highest*	*exertion*

militum.
of the soldiers.

42. Dum hæc gerunter ad Gergoviam,
While these things are going on at Gergovia,

Ædui, primis nuntiis a Litavico accep-
the Ædui, the first messages from Litavicus having been

tis, relinquunt sibi nullum spatium ad
received, leave to themselves no time for

cognoscendum. Avaritia impellit alios iracundia
verifying (it). Avarice impels some passion

et temeritas alios, quæ est maxime innata
and rashness others, which (last) is especially natural

illi genĕri hominum, ut habeant levem
to that kind of men, (so that) they hold a slight

auditionem pro re compertā. Deripiunt bona
hearsay for a thing assured. They plunder the goods

Romanorum civium, faciunt cædes, abstra-
of Roman citizens, they commit murder, they drag (them)

hunt in servitutem. Convictolitavis adjuvat
away into slavery. Convictolitavis advances

proclinatam rem, que impellit plebem ad
the ruined condition, and drives the people to

furorem, ut facinŏre admisso
madness, that an enormity having been committed,

pudeat reverti ad sanitatem.
it may shame (them) to return to soundness of mind.

Educunt ex oppido Cobillono M. Aristium
They drag out from the town (of) Cobillonus M. Aristius

tribunum militum facientem iter ad
a tribune of the soldiers making (his) way to (his)

legionem, fide datā;
legion (although), a pledge (of safety) having been [had been] given;

cogunt eos facĕre idem, qui constiterant ibi
they force those to do the same, who had sojourned there

causā	negotiandi.	Continuo adorti	hos
for the purpose	of trading.	Having continually attacked	these

in	itinĕre,	exuunt	omnibus
on	(their) journey,	they strip (them)	of all (their)

impedimentis;	obsident	repugnantes	diem	que
baggage;	they besiege (those)	opposing	day	and

noctem,	multis	utrimque	interfectis,	concitant
night,	many	on both sides	having been slain	they summon

majorem	multitudinem	ad	arma.
a greater	multitude	to	arms.

43.
Interim	nuntiis	allatis,	omnes
Meantime	news	having been brought,	(that) all

eorum	milites	tenēri	in	potestate	Cæsaris,
of their	soldiers	to be [were] held	in	the power	of Cæsar,

concurrunt	ad	Aristium,	demonstrant	nihil
they gather	to	Aristium,	they show	(that) nothing

factum	publico	consilio;	decernunt	quæstionem
(was) done	by public	design;	they decree	an investigation

de	bonis	direptis;	publicant	bona
concerning	the goods	plundered;	they confiscate	the goods

Litavici	que	fratrum;	mittunt	legatos	ad
of Litavicus	and	(his) brothers;	they send	ambassadors	to

Cæsarem	gratiā	purgandi	sui.	Hæc,
Cæsar	for the sake of	clearing	themselves.	These things,

faciunt	gratiā	recuperandorum	suorum;
they do	for the sake	of recovering	their (soldiers);

sed	contaminati	facinŏre	et	capti	compendio
but	implicated	in the crime	and	allured	by the gain

ex	direptis	bonis,	quod	ea	res	pertinebat
from	the plundered	goods,	because	this	matter	related

ad	multos,	et	exterriti	timōre	pœnæ,
to	many,	and	having been alarmed	by the fear	of punishment,

incipiunt	clam	inire	consilia	de	bello
they begin	secretly	to entertain	plans	concerning	war

que	solicitant	legationibus	reliquas	civitates,
and	incite	with embassies	the remaining	states.

Quæ[34]	tametsi Cæsar intellegebat,	tamen quam
Which [these] things	although Cæsar knew,	yet as

mitissime potuit appellat legatos,
mildly as he was able he addresses the ambassadors, (saying that)

nihil se judicare gravius de civitate
in no wise does he judge more severely concerning the state

propter inscientiam que levitatem volgi,
on account of the ignorance and fickleness of the common people,

neque deminuĕre de suā benevolentiā in Æduos.
nor doe he abate from his good will toward the Ædui.

Ipse expectans majorem motum Galliæ,
He himself apprehending a greater commotion of Gaul,

ne circumsisteretur ab omnibus civitatibus,
lest he should be surrounded by all the states,

inibat consilia, quemadmodum discedĕret a
was devising plans, as to what manner he might depart from

Gergoviā ac rursus contraheret omnem
Gergovia and again might draw together all (his)

exercitum, ne profectio nata a timore
army, lest a departure arising from fear

defectionis, videretur similis fugæ.
of a revolt, might seem like (to) a flight.

44. Facultas gerendæ rei bene visa est
An opportunity of executing the affair well seemed

accidĕre cogitanti hæc. Nam cum
to occur (to him) meditating these (things). For when

venisset in minora castra causā perspiciendi
he had come to the smaller camp for the purpose of inspecting

operis, animadvertit collem, qui tenebatur
the work, he observed (that) the hill, which was held

ab hostibus nudatum hominibus, qui superioribus
by the enemy was bared of men, which on former

diebus vix poterat cerni præ multitudine.
days scarcely could be discerned for the multitude.

Admiratus, quærit causam ex perfugis, quorum
Surprised, he inquires the cause of the deserters, of whom

magnus numerus quotidie confluebat ad eum.
a great number daily were pouring in to him.

Constabat inter omnes, quod Cæsar ipse
It was agreed by all, which [as] Cæsar himself

cognoverat	jam	per	exploratores,		dorsum
had known	*already*	*through*	*(his) scouts,*		*(that) the back*

	ejus	jugi	esse prope æquum,	sed	silvestre
[summit]	*of this*	*hill*	*was nearly level,*	*but*	*woody*

et	angustum,	quā	esset	aditus ad	alteram
and	*narrow,*	*where*	*was*	*a passage to*	*the other*

partem	oppidi;	illos	timēre	vehementer
part	*of the town;*	*(that) they*	*feared*	*exceedingly*

huic	loco;	nec jam	sentire	aliter,	uno
for this	*place;*	*nor now*	*did they feel*	*otherwise,*	*one*

colle	occupato	ab Romanis,	quin	si
hill	*having been occupied*	*by the Romans,*	*(but) that*	*if*

amisissent	alterum,	viderentur	pæne
they should lose	*the other,*	*they would appear*	*nearly*

circumvallati	atque interclusi	omni exitu et	pabulatione;
surrounded	*and cut off*	*from all egress and*	*foraging;*

omnes	evocatos	a Vercingetorige ad muniendum
(that) all	*had been called out by*	*Vercingetorix for fortifying*

hunc locum.
this place.

45. Hāc re cognitā, Cæsar mittit
This thing having been learned, Cæsar sends

complures	turmas	equitum	eo	de	mediā
several	*troops*	*of horsemen*	*thither*	*at*	*mid-*

nocte;	imperat iis,	ut	pervagentur
night;	*he commands them,*	*that*	*they should range about*

in omnibus locis paulo tumultuosius. Primā
in all places somewhat more tumultuously [noisily]. At the first

luce	jubet	magnum	numerum
light [early dawn]	*he orders*	*a great*	*quantity*

impedimentorum	produci	ex castris,	que
of baggage	*to be brought forth*	*from the camp,*	*and*

mulorum,	que	stramenta	detrahi iis,	que
of mules,	*and*	*the pack-saddles*	*to be taken from them,*	*and*

muliones	cum	cassidibus	circumvehi collibus
the mule'eers	*with*	*helmets*	*to ride round the hills*

	specie	ac simulatione	equitum. His
in the appearance		*and manner*	*of horsemen. To these*

addit paucos equites, qui vagarentur latius	he adds a few horsemen, who might range more widely
causā ostentationis. Jubet omnes	for the purpose of display. He orders (them) all
petĕre easdem regiones longo circuitu. Hæc	to seek the same places by a long circuit. These
videbantur procul ex oppido, ut erat	things were seen at a distance from the town, as there was
despectus a Gergoviā in castra; neque, tanto	a view from Gergovia into the camp; nor, at such
spatio, poterat explorari quid certi	a distance, could it be made out what of [to a] certainty
esset. Mittit unam legionem eodem jugo, et	it might be. He sends one legion on the same hill, and
constituit progressam paulum, inferiore	he stations (it) advanced a little, in a lower
loco, que occultat silvis. Suspicio	place, and hides (it) in the woods. The suspicion (of)
Gallis augetur, atque omnes copiæ munitionum	the Gauls is increased, and all the forces of the fortifications
transducuntur illo. Cæsar conspicatus	are brought over thither. Cæsar having perceived (that)
castra hostium vacua, insignibus suorum	the camp of the enemy was deserted, the insignia of his
tectis, que militaribus signis	(men) having been covered, and the military ensigns
occultatis, traducit milites raros ex	having been concealed, transfers (his) soldiers in squads from
majoribus castris in minora, ne animad-	the larger camp into the smaller, lest they should
verterentur ex oppido; que ostendit	be observed from the town; and he shows [explains]
legatis, quos præfecerat singulis legionibus,	to the lieutenants whom he had appointed over each legion,
quid velit fieri; in primis monet, ut	what he wishes to be done; especially he admonishes that
contineant milites, ne progrediantur	they should restrain the soldiers, lest they should proceed

longius,	studio	pugnandi	aut	spe	prædæ.
too far,	*by the desire*	*of fighting*	*or*	*by the hope*	*of plunder.*

Proponit	quid		incommodi	iniquitas
He explains	*what*	*(of)*	*disadvantage*	*the unfavorableness*

loci	habeat		hoc	posse	vitari
of the place	*may have,*	*(that)*	*this*	*can*	*be avoided*

celerite	unā,		rem	occasionis,	non
by quickness [speed]	*alone,*	*(that it is)*	*a matter of opportunity,*		*not*

prœli.	His	rebus	expositis,	dat	signum,
of battle.	*These*	*things*	*having been stated,*	*he gives*	*the signal,*

et	mittit	Æduos,	eodem tempŏre,	ab	dextrā
and	*sends*	*the Ædui,*	*at the same time,*	*from*	*the right*

parte	alio	adscensu.
side *[flank]*	*by another*	*ascent.*

46.
Murus	oppidi	aberat	mille	et	du-
The wall	*of the town*	*was distant*	*a thousand*	*and*	*two*

centos [MCC]	passus	ab planitie,	atque	initio
hundred	*paces*	*from the plain,*	*and from*	*the beginning*

adscensūs,	recta	regione,	si	nullus	anfractus
of the ascent,	*in a straight*	*direction,*	*if*	*no*	*bend*

intercederet.	Quidquid	accesserat	huic
should intervene.	*Whatever*	*had been added*	*to this*

circuitūs	ad	molliendum	clivum,	id	augebat
(of) circuit	*for*	*easing*	*the slope [ascent],*	*this*	*increased*

spatium	itineris.	Galli	præduxerant	murum
the length	*of the route.*	*The Gauls*	*had extended*	*a wall*

sex	pedum	ex	grandibus	saxis,	fere	a
six	*feet*	*(high) of*	*great*	*stones,*	*nearly*	*in*

medio	colle	in	longitudine		ut
the middle (of)	*the hill*	*on*	*the length*	*[lengthwise],*	*as*

natura	montis	ferebat,	qui	tardaret
the nature	*of the mountain*	*allowed,*	*which*	*might retard*

impetum	nostrorum;	atque	omni	inferiore	spatio
the attack	*of our men;*	*and*	*all*	*the lower*	*space*

relicto	vacuo,	compleverant	superiorem partem
having been left	*vacant,*	*they had filled*	*the higher part*

collis	usque	ad	murum	oppidi	castris
of the hill	*even*	*to*	*the wall*	*of the town*	*with camps*

densissimis. Milites, signo dato,
very close. The soldiers, the signal having been given

celeriter perveniunt ad munitionem, que
quickly arrive at (this) fortification, and

transgressi eam, potiuntur trinis
having passed over it, take possession (of) three (separate)

castris. Ac tanta fuit celeritas in capiendis
camps. And so great was the speed in capturing

castris, ut Teutomatus, rex Nitiobrigum,
the camps, that Teutomatus, king of the Nitiobriges,

oppressus subito in tabernaculo, ut
having been surprised suddenly in (his) tent, when

conquieverat meridie, vix eripĕret se
he had gone to rest at noon, scarcely saved himself

ex manibus prædantium militum, superiore
from the hands of the plundering soldiers, with the upper

parte corpŏris nuda, equo
part of (his) body naked, (and his) horse

vulnerato.
wounded.

47. Cæsar consecutus id quod proposuerat
Cæsar having attained that which he had proposed

animo, jussit cani receptui, que
in mind, ordered (the bugle) to be sounded for retreat, and

constituit signa decimæ legionis, quā erat
set up the standards of the tenth legion, by which he was

tum comitatus. At milites reliquarum legionum,
then accompanied. But the soldiers of the other legions,

non exaudito sono tubæ, quod
not having heard the sound of the trumpet, because

vallis satis magna intercedebat, tamen
a valley sufficiently [quite] large was intervening, nevertheless

retinebantur a tribunis militum que
were kept back by the tribunes of the soldiers and

legatis, ut præceptum erat a Cæsare.
by the lieutenants, as (it) had been commanded by Cæsar.

Sed elati spe celeris victoriæ et fuga
But elated by the hope of a speedy victory and by the flight

LIBER VII.

hostium,	que	secundis	prœliis	superiorum
of the enemy,	*and*	*the favorable*	*battles*	*of former*

temporum existimabant nihil adeo arduum
times   they thought (that)   nothing (was)   so   difficult

sibi, quod possent non consequi virtute;
for them,   which   they could   not   accomplish   by valor;

neque fecerunt finem sequendi, prius
nor   did they   make   an end   of following,   before

quam appropinquārunt muro que portis oppidi.
(that)   they had approached   the wall   and   the gates   of the town.

Vero tum clamore orto ex omnibus partibus
But   then   a shout   having arisen   from   all   parts

urbis, qui aberant longius perterriti
of the town,   those who   were distant   farther   frightened

repentino tumultu, quum existimarent hostes
by the sudden   tumult,   as   they thought   the enemy

esse intra portas, jecerunt sese ex
to be [were]   within   the gates,   threw   themselves   from

oppido. Matres familiās jactabant
the town.   The mothers   of families [matrons]   threw

vestem que argentum de muro, et
(their) clothes   and   silver   from   the wall,   and

prominentes nudo pectŏre, passis manibus
bending forward with naked   breast,   with outstretched hands,

obtestabantur Romanos, ut parcĕrent sibi; neu
they implored   the Romans,   that   they should spare   them;   nor

sicut fecissent Avarici, abstinērent ne
as   they had done   at Avaricum,   abstain from [spare]   not

quidem mulieribus atque infantibus. Nonnullæ
even   the women   and   children.   Some

demissæ de muris per manus,
having let themselves down   from   the wall   by   their hands,

tradebant sese militibus. L. Fabius
surrendered   themselves   to the soldiers.   L. Fabius

centurio octavæ legionis, quem, constabat
a centurion   of the eighth   legion,   whom [who],   it appeared

dixisse eo die inter suos, se
to have [had] said   this   day   among   his (men, that)   he

excitari	Avaricensibus	præmiis,	neque	commissurum,
was excited	by the Avarican	rewards,	nor	would he allow,

ut	quisquam	adscendĕret	murum	prius,
that	any one	should mount	the wall	before (himself),

nactus	tres	suos	manipulares	atque
having taken	three	(of) his	company	and

sublevatus	ab	iis	adscendit	murum;
having been raised up	by	them	mounted	the wall;

ipse	rursus	exceptans	singulos	extulit	eos	in
he	in turn	taking up	one at a time	drew	them	onto

murum.
the wall.

48. Interim ii, qui convenerant ad alteram
In the meantime those, who had assembled at the other

partem oppidi, ut demonstravimus supra causā
part of the town, as we have shown above for the purpose

munitionis, primo clamōre exaudito, inde
of fortifying, the first shout having been heard, afterward

etiam incitati crebris nuntiis, oppidum
also incited by frequent reports, (that) the town

tenēri ab Romanis, præmissis equitibus,
was held by the Romans, having sent forward the horsemen,

contenderunt eo magno concursu. Ut quisque
they hastened there in a great throng. As each

eorum primus vēnerat consistebat sub muro,
of them first came he halted under the wall,

que augebat numerum suorum pugnantium.
and increased the number of their (men) fighting.

Cum magna multitudo quorum convenisset,
When a great multitude of these had assembled,

matres familiās quæ paulo ante
the mothers of families [matrons] who a little before

tendebant manus de muro Romanis,
were stretching out hands from the wall to the Romans,

cœperunt obtestari suos et Gallico more
began to beseech their (people) and in the Gallic manner

ostentare passum capillum, que proferre
to show dishevelled hair, and to bring forth

liberos	in	conspectum.	Contentio	erat	æqua
the children	into	view.	The contest	was	equal

Romanis	nec	loco nec	numero (sing.);	simul
for the Romans	neither	in place nor	in numbers;	at the same time

defatigati	et	cursu	et	spatio	pugnæ
fatigued	both	by running	and	by the duration	of the fight,

non facile sustinebant	recentes	atque	integros.
they did not easily withstand	(those) fresh	and	vigorous.

49.
Cæsar	cum	videret	pugnari
Cæsar	when	he saw	to be fought [the fighting was]

iniquo	loco,	que	copias	hostium
in a disadvantageous	place,	and	the forces	of the enemy

augeri,	præmetuens	suis	mittit	ad
to be [were] increased,	being anxious	for his (men)	he sends	to

T. Sextium	legatum,	quem reliquerat	præsidio
T. Sextius	(his) lieutenant,	whom he had left	for [as] a guard

minoribus	castris,	ut	celeriter educeret
to the smaller	camp,	that	he should quickly lead forth

cohortes	ex	castris,	et	constitueret	sub
the cohorts	from	the camp,	and	should station	(them) at

infimo	colle	ab dextro	latere	hostium;
the lowest (part of)	the hill	on the right	wing	of the enemy;

ut si	vidisset	nostros	depulsos	loco,
that if	he should see	our (men)	repulsed	from the place,

terreret	hostes	quo	insequerentur	minus
he might alarm	the enemy	so that	they would follow	less

libere.	Ipse	progressus	paulum	ex	eo
freely.	He himself	having proceeded	a little	from	this

loco	cum	legione,	ubi	constiterat,	expectabat
place	with	the legion,	where	he had halted,	was awaiting

eventum	pugnæ.
the issue	of the battle.

50.
Cum	pugnaretur	accerime	comminus,
While	it was fought	most violently	hand to hand,

hostes	confiderent	loco	et	numero,
the enemy	trusted	in the place	and (their)	number,

nostri	virtute;	Ædui sunt	subito	visi,	ab
our men	in (their) courage;	the Ædui were	suddenly	seen,	by

nostris aperto latěre, quos Cæsar miserat	our (men) on the exposed flank, whom Cæsar had sent
ab dextrā parte alio ascensu, causā	from the right side [flank] by another ascent, for the purpose
distinendæ manus.³⁶ Hi vehementer perterruerunt	of cutting off the force. They very much alarmed
nostros similitudine armorum; ac tametsi	our men by the similarity of (their) arms, and although
animadvertebantur dextris humeris exsertis	they were observed with the right shoulder uncovered,
quod consueverat esse insigne pacatorum,	which was accustomed to be the sign of the peaceful,
tamen milites existimabant id ipsum	yet the soldiers thought (that) this same
factum ab hostibus causā fallendi sui.	(was) done by the enemy for the sake of deceiving them.
Eodem tempore centurio, L. Fabius, que	At the same time the centurion, L. Fabius, and
qui adscenderant murum unā,	(those) who had ascended the wall together (with him),
circumventi atque interfecti, præcipitabantur	having been surrounded and slain, were thrown
de muro. M. Petronius, centurio ejusdem	from the wall. M. Petronius, a centurion of the same
legionis, quum conatus esset exscindere portas,	legion, when he had attempted to cut down the gates,
oppressus a multitudine, ac desperans	overpowered by the multitude, and despairing of safety
sibi, vulneribus jam acceptis, inquit	for himself, wounds already having been received, said
suis manipularibus qui secuti erant illum.	to his comrades who had followed him.
"Quoniam possum non servare me unā vobiscum,	"Since I can not save myself together with you,
quidem certe prospiciam vestræ saluti, quos,	indeed certainly I will provide for your safety, whom,
adductos cupiditate gloriæ deduxi in	led by the desire of glory, I have brought into

periculum;	vos,	facultate	datā
danger;	*you,*	*an opportunity*	*having been given,*

		consulite	vobis."
[when an opportunity occurs]		*consult*	*for yourselves."*

Simul	irrupit	in medios	hostes,
At the same time	*he threw himself*	*into the midst (of the)*	*enemy,*

que	duobus	interfectis,	submovit reliquos paulum
and	*two*	*having been killed,*	*he drove back the rest a little*

a	portā.	Suis	conantibus	auxiliari	inquit,
from	*the gate.*	*To his (men)*	*endeavoring*	*to assist*	*he said,*

"Frustra	conamini	subvenire	meæ	vitæ	quem	sanguis
"In vain	*you try*	*to save*	*my*	*life*	*whom*	*blood*

que	vires	jam	deficiunt,	proinde	abite	hinc,
and	*strength*	*now*	*fail,*	*therefore*	*go*	*from here,*

dum	est	facultas,	que recipite	vos	ad
while	*there is*	*the chance,*	*and get [betake]*	*yourselves*	*to*

legionem."	Pugnans	ita	concidit	post	paulum,
the legion."	*Fighting*	*thus*	*he fell*	*after*	*a little,*

ac	fuit	saluti[37]	suis.
and	*was*	*(for) a safety*	*to his (men).*

51. Cum	nostri		premerentur	undique,
As	*our*	*(men)*	*were pressed*	*on every side,*

quadraginta	sex	centurionibus	amissis,
forty	*six*	*centurions*	*having been lost,*

dejecti sunt	loco.	Sed	decima	legio,
they were driven	*from the place.*	*But*	*the tenth*	*legion,*

quæ	constiterat	pro	subsidio	paulo	æquiore
which	*had taken stand*	*for*	*a reserve*	*on a little*	*more level*

loco	tardavit	Gallos	insequentes	intolerantius
place	*checked*	*the Gauls*	*following*	*too eagerly.*

Cohortes	decimæ tertiæ legionis,	rursus	exceperunt
The cohorts	*of the thirteenth legion,*	*in turn*	*supported*

hanc,[38]	quæ	eductæ	ex minoribus castris,
this,	*which [for they]*	*having been led*	*from the smaller camp,*

cum	T. Sextio,	legato,	ceperant	superiorem
with	*T. Sextius,*	*the lieutenant,*	*had occupied*	*the higher*

locum.	Ubi legiones	primum	attigerunt	planitiem
ground.	*When the legions*	*first*	*reached*	*the plain*

constiterunt,	they halted,
signis	the standards
infestis	having been turned
contra	against
hostes.	the enemy.
Vercingetorix	Vercingetorix
reduxit	led back
suos	his (men)
ab	from
radicibus	the foot
collis	of the hill
intra	within
munitiones.	the fortifications.
Eo	On this
die	day
paulo	a little
minus	less (than)
septingenti	seven hundred
milites	soldiers
desiderati sunt.	were missing.

52. Postero die, Cæsar, contione advocata,
On the next day, Cæsar, an assembly having been called,

reprehendit	censured
temeritatem	the rashness
que	and
cupiditatem	avarice
militum,	of the soldiers,
quod	because
ipsi	they
judicavissent	had judged
sibi,	for themselves,
quō	where
viderētur	it seemed
(that they)	ought to go
procedendum,	
aut	or
quid	what
agendum,	ought to be done,
neque,	neither,
signo	the signal
recipiendi	for halting
dato,	having been given,
constitissent,	did they halt,
neque	nor
potuissent	could they
retineri	be restrained
a	by
tribunis	the tribunes
militum	of the soldiers
que	and
legatis.	by the lieutenants.
Exposuit	He showed
quid	what
iniquitas	the disadvantage
loci	of position
posset,	would be able (to effect),
quid	what
ipse	(he) himself
sensisset	had perceived
ad	at
Avarĭcum,	Avaricum,
cum,	when,
hostibus	the enemy
deprehensis,	having been surprised
sine	without
duce	a leader
et	and
sine	without
equitatu,	cavalry,
demisisset	he had given up
exploratam	a certain
victoriam,	victory,
ne	lest
accipĕret	he might receive
modo	even
parvum	a small
detrimentum	injury
in	in
contentione,	the contest,
propter	on account of
iniquitatem	the disadvantage
loci.	of the place.
Quantopere	As much as
admīraretur	he admired
eorum	their
magnitudinem	greatness
animi,	of spirit,

LIBRE VII.

quos non munitiones castrorum, non altitudo
whom neither the fortifications of the camp, nor the height

montis, non murus oppidi potuisset
of the mountain, nor the wall of the town could

tardare, reprehendĕre tantopere licentiam que
retard, he censured so greatly (their) lawlessness and

arrogantiam, quod existimarent se sentire
presumption, because they were thinking (that) they understood

plus quam imperatorem de victoriā atque
more than (their) commander about victory and

exitu rerum; se desiderare in milite nec
the issue of affairs; (saying that) he desired in a soldier no

minus modestiam et continentiam, quam virtutem
less moderation and submission, than valor

atque magnitudinem animi.
and greatness of spirit.

53. Hāc contione habitā, et ad extremum
This council having been held, and to the highest degree

militibus confirmatis oratione, ne
the soldiers having been encouraged by (his) speech, that (they)

permoverentur animo ob hanc causam, neu
should not be disturbed in mind on account of this affair, nor

tribuĕrent id virtuti hostium, quod
should they attribute this to the valor of the enemy, which

iniquitas loci attulisset; cogitans
the disadvantage of position had brought on (them); thinking

eadem de profectione, quæ senserat
the same concerning a departure, which [as] he had felt

ante, eduxit legiones ex castris, que
before, he led forth the legions from the camp, and

constituit aciem idoneo loco. Cum
drew up the battle line in a favorable place. When

Vercingetorix nihilo magis descendĕret in æquum
Vercingetorix no more would descend into level

locum, levi equestri prœlio facto,
ground, a slight cavalry engagement having occurred,

atque eo secundo, reduxit exercitum
and this (being) favorable, he led back (his) army

in castra.	into the camp.
Cum fecisset hoc idem postero die,	When he had done this same thing the next day,
existimans satis factum ad minuendam Gallicam ostentationem,	believing (that) enough was done for lessening the Gallic arrogance,
que confirmandos animos militum,	and for encouraging the minds of (his) soldiers,
movit castra in Æduos.	he moved (his) camp into the Ædui.
Hostibus ne cuidem tum insecutis,	The enemy not even then having followed,
tertio die refecit pontem ad flumen Elaver,	on the third day he repaired the bridge over the river Allier,
atque traduxit exercitum.	and led over (his) army.

54. Ibi appellatus a Viridomaro atque Eporedorige Æduis, discit Litavicum, cum omni equitatu profectum ad sollicitandos Æduos; et esse opus ipsos antecedĕre ad confirmandam civitatem. Etsi Cæsar jam multis rebus habebat perfidiam Æduorum perspectam atque existimabat discessu horum defectionem civitatis admaturari; tamen censuit eos non retinendos, ne videretur aut inferre injuriam, aut dare aliquam suspicionem timoris. His discedentibus, breviter exposuit sua merita in Æduos, quos

There, having been waited on by Viridomarus and Eporedorix the Æduans, he learns (that) Litavicus, with all the cavalry had set out for instigating the Ædui; and (that) it was necessary (that) they should go before for restraining the state. Although Cæsar already in many things had the unfaithfulness of the Ædui clearly understood and he believed (that) by the departure of these the defection of the state to [would] be hastened; however he was of the opinion that they should not be detained, lest he might appear either to impose a wrong, or to give some suspicion of fear. To them departing, he briefly set forth his services to the Ædui, whom

LIBER VII.

accepisset		et	quam	humiles,	compulsos	in
he had taken in charge		*and*	*how*	*humbled*,	*driven*	*into*

oppida,	multatos	agris,	omnibus		copiis
their towns,	*deprived*	*of their lands,*	*all*		*(their) means*

ereptis,	stipendio	imposito,	
having been taken away,	*a tribute*	*having been imposed,*	*(and)*

obsidibus	extortis	cum	summā	contumeliā,
hostages	*having been exacted*	*with*	*the greatest*	*insult,*

in	quam	fortunam,	que	in	quam	amplitudinem
to	*what*	*fortune,*	*and*	*to*	*what*	*greatness*

deduxisset,	ut	non solum	redissent	in
he had raised (them),	*so that*	*they had not only*	*returned*	*to (their)*

pristinum	statum,	sed	viderentur	antecessisse
former	*state,*	*but*	*seemed*	*to have surpassed*

dignitatem	et	gratiam	omnium	temporum.	His
the dignity	*and*	*influence*	*of all*	*times.*	*This*

mandatis	datis,	dimisit	eos	ab
charge	*having been given,*	*he dismissed*	*them*	*from*

se.
his presence.

55.
Novidunum		erat	oppidum	Æduorum
Novidunum	*[Nevers]*	*was*	*a town*	*of the Ædui*

positum	opportuno	loco	ad	ripas	Ligĕris.
situated	*in an advantageous*	*place*	*on*	*the banks*	*of the Loire.*

Cæsar	contulerat	huc	omnes	obsides	Galliæ,
Cæsar	*had brought*	*hither*	*all*	*the hostages*	*of Gaul,*

frumentum,	publicam	pecuniam,	magnam	partem
the corn,	*the public*	*money,*	*a great*	*part*

suorum	impedimentorum,	atque		exercitūs.
of his	*baggage,*	*and*		*(that) of the army.*

Miserat	huc	magnum	numerum	equorum
He had sent	*hither*	*a great*	*number*	*of horses*

coëmptorum	in	Italiā	atque	Hispaniā,	causā
bought	*in*	*Italy*	*and*	*Spain,*	*for the purpose*

hujus	belli.	Cum	Eporedorix	que	Viridomarus
of this	*war.*	*When*	*Eporedorix*	*and*	*Viridomarus*

venissent	eo,	et	cognovissent	de	statu
had arrived	*there,*	*and*	*had learned*	*about*	*the condition*

[attitude] civitatis;	[attitude] of the state;
Litavicum receptum ab	(that) Litavicus was received by
Æduis Bibracte,	the Ædui in Bibracte,
quod est oppidum maximæ	which is a town of the greatest
auctoritatis apud eos;	importance among them;
Convictolitavem	(that) Convictolitavis
magistratum que magnam partem senatūs	the magistrate and a great part of the senate
convēnisse ad eum;	had gone to him;
legatos publice	ambassadors were openly
missos ad Vercingetorigem de conciliandā pace	sent to Vercingetorix concerning procuring peace
et amicitiā; existimaverunt tantum commodum	and alliance; they thought so great an advantage
non prætermittendum. Itaque custodibus Novioduni	must not (to) be neglected. Therefore the guards of Noviodunum
que qui convenerant eo causā	and those who had assembled there for the sake
negotiandi, aut itinĕris, interfectis, partiti sunt	of trading, or travel, having been killed, they divided
pecuniam atque equos inter se; curaverunt	the money and the horses among themselves; they took care
obsides civitatum deducendos Bibracte	(that) the hostages of the states should be conducted to Bibracte
ad magistratum; oppidum, quod judicabant	to the magistrate; the town, because they thought (it)
posse non teneri ab se, incenderunt, ne	could not be held by them, they burned, lest
esset cui usui Romanis. Avexerunt	it might be (of) some use to the Romans. They carried away
subito navibus quod potuerunt frumenti; corru-	suddenly in ships what they could of corn; they
perunt reliquum flumine atque incendio; ipsi	destroyed the rest in the river and by fire; they
cœperunt cogĕre copias ex finitimis regionibus,	began to collect forces from the neighboring districts,
disponĕre præsidia que custodias ad ripas	~ place garrisons and guards along the banks

Ligeris,	que	ostentare	equitatum	omnibus	locis
of the Loire,	and	to display	cavalry	in all	places

causā	injiciendi	timōris,	si	aut	possent
for the purpose	of exciting	alarm,	if	either	they could

excludĕre	Romanos	re frumentariā,	aut	expellĕre
cut off	the Romans	(from) a corn supply,	or could expel	(them)

adductos	inopiā,	ex	Provinciā;	
driven	by want	from	the province;	(it)

adjuvabat	eos	multum	ad	quam	spem,	quod
assisted	them	much	to	such	hope,	because

Liger	creverat	ex	nivibus,	ut	videretur
the Loire	had swollen	from	snows,	so that	it seemed

omnino	posse	non	transiri	vado.
altogether (that)	it could	not	be crossed	by a ford.

56.
Quibus rebus	cognitis,	Cæsar	censuit
Which things	having been learned,	Cæsar	was of the opinion

	sibi	maturandum,[39]	si	esset	periclitandum
(that)	he	must hasten,	if	he must	take the risk

in	perficiendis	pontibus,	ut	dimicaret	prius
in	building	the bridges,	so that	he might fight	before

quam	majores copiæ	coactæ essent	eo.	Nam	ut,
(that)	greater forces	had been collected	there.	For	that,

	consilio	commutato,	convertĕret	iter
(his)	plan	having been changed,	he might alter	(his) route

in	Provinciam,	existimabat	id	ne	tum
into	the Province,	he thought	(that) this	not	then

quidem	necessario	faciendum;	cum	infamia
even	of necessity	must be done;	not only	the disgrace

atque	indignitas	rei,	et	oppositus mons
and	humiliation	of the thing,	and	the opposed mount

Cebenna,	que	difficultas	viarum	impediebat (sing.),
Cevennes,	and	the difficulty	of the roads	prevented,

tum	maxime	quod	cupiebat	vehementer
but also	especially	because	he desired	very much

adjungi	Labiēno,	atque	iis	legionibus quas
to be united	with Labienus,	and	those	legions which

miserat	unā.	Itaque	admodum magnis
he had sent	together (with him).	Therefore	very long

| itineribus | diurnis | atque | nocturnis | confectis, |
| marches | by day | and | by night | having been made, |

| pervenit | ad | Ligěrim, | contra | opinionem | omnium; |
| he arrived | at | the Loire, | contrary | to the expectation | of all; |

| que | vado | invento | per | equites, | opportuno |
| and | a ford | having been found | by | the horsemen | suitable |

| pro | necessitate | rei, | ut | brachia | modo, | atque |
| for | the urgency | of the case, | that | the arms | only | and |

| humeri | possent | esse | liberi | ab | aquā | ad |
| the shoulders | might | be | free | from | the water | for |

| sustinenda | arma, | equitatu | disposito |
| supporting (their) equipments, | the cavalry | having been stationed |

| | qui | refringěret | vim | fluminis, | atque |
| (that) | they | might break | the force | of the river, | and |

| hostibus | | perturbatis | primo adspectu, |
| the enemy | (having been) | thrown into disorder | at first sight, |

| traduxit | exercitum | incolumen | que | nactus |
| he led over | the army | safe | and | having found |

| frumentum | in | agris, | et | copiam | pecŏris, |
| corn | in | the fields, | and | abundance | of cattle, |

| exercitu | repleto | iis | rebus, | instituit |
| the army | having been supplied | with those | things, | he determines |

| facěre | iter | in | Senones. |
| to make | (his) march | into | the Senones. |

57. | Dum | hæc | geruntur | apud Cæsarem, |
| While | these things | are happening | under Cæsar, |

| Labienus, | eo | supplemento, | quod nuper venerat |
| Labienus, | that | contingent [addition], | which had lately come |

| ex | Italiā | relicto | Agendici, | ut |
| from | Italy | having been left | at Agendicum [Sens], | that |

| esset | | præsidio | impedimentis, | proficiscitur |
| it might be | (for) | a guard | to the baggage, | marches |

| cum | quattuor | legionibus | Lutetiam. | Id | est |
| with | four | legions | to Lutetia [Paris]. | This | is |

| oppidum | Parisiorum | positum | in | insulā | fluminis |
| a town | of the Parisii | situated | on | an island | of the river |

| Sequanæ. | Cujus | adventu | cognito | ab |
| Seine. | Whose | arrival | having been learned | by |

LIBER VII. 441

hostibus, magnae copiae convenerunt ex finitimis
the enemy,   great   forces   assembled   from   the neighboring

civitatibus. Summa imperii traditur Camulogeno
states.   The supreme command is given to Camulogenus

Aulerco; qui prope confectus aetate,
the Aulercan; who (though) nearly worn out with age,

tamen evocatus est ad eum honorem propter
yet   was called   to this   honor on account of (his)

singularem scientiam militaris rei. Is, quum
singular   knowledge of military affairs. He, when

animadvertisset esse perpetuam paludem
he had observed (that there) was a continuous marsh

quae influĕret in Sequanam, atque magnopere
which opened into the Seine, and   greatly

impediret omnem illum locum, consedit hic, que
obstructed all that place, encamped there, and

instituit prohibēre nostros transitu.
resolved to prohibit our (soldiers) from passing.

58. Labienus primo conabatur agĕre vineas,
Labienus at first endeavored to work the sheds.

explere paludem cratibus atque aggere, atque
to fill up the marsh with hurdles and a mound, and

munire iter. Postquam animadvertit id
to open a road. After he observed (that) this

confieri difficilius, egressus
would be accomplished with great difficulty, having marched out

e castris silentio tertiā vigiliā, pervēnit
from (his) camp in silence at the third watch, he arrived

Metiosedum,[40] eodem itinĕre, quo
at Metiosedum [Melun] by the same road, by which

venerat. Id est oppidum Senonum positum
he had come. This is a town of the Senones situated

in insulā Sequanae, ut paulo ante diximus
on an island of the Seine, as a little before we have said

Lutetiam. Circiter quinquaginta navibus depre-
(was) Lutetia. About fifty ships having been

hensis, que conjunctis celerite, atque
seized, and (having been) joined together quickly, and

militibus	impositis	eo,	et	oppidanis
soldiers	having been placed	thereon,	and	the people of the town

magna	pars	quorum	erat	evocata	ad
a great	part	of whom	had	been called away	to

bellum,		perterritis	novitate	rei,
the war,	(having been)	alarmed	by the novelty	of the thing,

potitur	oppido	sine	contentione.	Ponte
he seizes	the town	without	a contest.	The bridge

refecto,	quem	hostes	resciderant
having been rebuilt,	which	the enemy	had destroyed

superioribus	diebus,	traducit	exercitum,	et
on the preceding	days,	he leads over (his)	army,	and

cœpit	facĕre	iter	secundo	flumine	ad	Lutetiam.
begins	to make (his)	way	down	the river	to	Lutetia.

Hostes,	re	cognitā	ab	iis	qui
The enemy,	the matter	having been learned	from	those	who

profugerant	a	Metiosedo,	jubent	Lutetiam
had fled	from	Metiosedum,	order	Lutetia

incendi	que	pontes	ejus	oppidi	rescindi;
to be burned	and	the bridges	of this	town	to be destroyed,

ipsi	profecti	palude,	considunt	in
they themselves	having left	the marsh,	place themselves	on

ripis	Sequanæ	e	regione	Lutetiæ	contra
the banks	of the Seine	over	against	Lutetia	opposite

castra	Labieni.
the camp	of Labienus.

59.

Jam	Cæsar	audiebatur	discessisse	a
Already	Cæsar	was heard	to have departed	from

Gergoviā;	jam	rumores	afferebantur	de	defectione
Gergovia;	already	reports	were brought	of	the revolt

Æduorum,	et	secundo	motu	Galliæ,	que
of the Ædui,	and	of the successful	rising	of Gaul,	and

Galli	in	colloquis	confirmabant	Cæsarem
the Gauls	in	their conversations	were asserting (that)	Cæsar

interclusum	itinere	et	Ligĕre,	
cut off	from (his) route	and	from the Loire	(and)

coactum	inopiā	frumenti,	contendisse	in
forced	by the want	of corn,	had marched	into

Provinciam.	Autem	Bellovaci,	defectione	Æduorum
the province.	But	the Bellovaci,	the defection	of the Ædui

cognitā,	qui	ante	erant	per	se
having been learned	who	before	were	of	themselves

infideles,	cœperunt	cogĕre	manus,	atque	aperte
unfaithful,	began	to collect	forces,	and	openly

parare	bellum.	Tum	Labienus,	tantā
to prepare (for)	war.	Then	Labienus,	in so great

commutatione	rerum	intelligebat	longe	aliud
a change	of affairs	thought	(that) a far	different

consilium	capiendum	sibi,	atque	senserat
plan	to [must] be taken	by him,	than	he had considered

antea.	Neque	jam	cogitabat,	ut	acquirĕret
before.	Nor	now	was he thinking,	that	he should acquire

aliquid,	que	lacessĕret	hostes	prœlio,	sed	ut
anything	and	should attack	the enemy	in battle,	but	that

reducĕret	exercitum	incolumen	Agendicum.
he should lead back (his)	army	safe	to Agendicum.

Namque	ex	alterā	parte	Bellovaci,	civitas	quæ
For	on	the one	side	the Bellovaci,	a state	which

habet	maximam	opinionem	virtutis	in	Galliā,
has	the greatest	reputation	of [for] bravery	in	Gaul,

instabant;	alteram	Camulogenus	tenebat
were pressing;	the other (side)	Camulogenus	was holding

parato	atque	instructo	exercitu;	tum
with an organized	and	equipped	army;	also

maximum	flumen	distinebat	legiones
a very large	river	separated	the legions (having been)

interclusas	a	præsidio	atque	impedimentis.
cut off	from	the garrison	and	baggage.

Tantis	difficultatibus	subito	objectis,
Such great	difficulties	suddenly	having been presented,

videbat	auxilium	petendum	ab	virtute[41]
he saw (that)	aid	to [must] be sought	from	strength

animi.
of mind.

60.
Itaque	sub	vesperum,	concilio	con-
Therefore	towards	evening,	a council	having been

vocato,	cohortatus,		ut	diligenter	que
called,	he exhorted (his soldiers),		that	diligently	and

industrie	administrarent	ea	quæ
industriously	they should execute [perform]	those (things)	which

imperāsset;	naves,	quas	deduxerat	a
he had commanded;	the ships,	which	he had brought	from

Metiosedo,	attribuit	singulas	Romanis equitibus;	et
Metiosedum,	he assigns	singly	to Roman knights;	and

jubet,	primā	vigiliā	confectā,
orders (them),	the first	watch	having been completed,

progredi	quattuor millia	passuum	secundo	flumine,
to proceed	four thousand	paces	down	the river,

silentio,	que	ibi	expectare	se. Relinquit
in silence,	and	there	to await	himself. He leaves

quinque	cohortes,	quas	existimabat	esse minime
five	cohorts,	which	he considered	to be least

firmas	ad dimicandum,	præsidio	castris;
sturdy	for fighting,	for [as] a guard	to the camp;

imperat	reliquas	quinque	ejusdem	legionis
he commands	the remaining	five	of the same	legion

proficisci	de mediā	nocte	cum omnibus	impedimentis
to proceed	at mid	night	with all	(their) baggage

adverso	flumine	magno tumultu.	Etiam
up	the river	with a great din.	Also

conquirit	lintres; has	mittit in	eandem	partem,
he collects	boats; these	he sends in	the same	direction,

incitatas magno sonitu	remorum.	Ipse,	paulo
driven by a great sound [noise]	of oars.	He himself,	a little

post,	egressus	silentio cum	tribus legionibus,
after,	having marched out	in silence with	three legions,

petit	eum	locum,	quo jusserat	naves
seeks	that	place,	where he had ordered	the ships

appelli.
to be brought.

61.

Cum	esset ventum[42]	eo,	exploratores
When	it was come [he came]	there,	the scouts

hostium,	ut	dispositi erant	omni	parte
of the enemy,	as	they were stationed	in every	part

| 61] | | | **LIBER VII.** | | 445 |

fluminis,	inopinantes,	quod	magna	tempestas
of the river,	*off their guard,*	*because*	*a great*	*storm*

subito coorta erat,	opprimuntur	ab	nostris;
had suddenly arisen,	*were overpowered*	*by*	*our (men);*

exercitus	que	equitatus	celeriter transmittitur,
the infantry	*and*	*cavalry*	*are speedily transported,*

Romanis equitibus administrantibus,	quos
the Roman knights superintending,	*whom he (Labienus)*

præficĕret	ei	negotio.	Fere	uno
had appointed for	*this*	*task.*	*Nearly*	*at one [the same]*

tempŏre	sub	lucem	nuntiatur	hostibus,
time	*about*	*daylight*	*it is announced*	*to the enemy,*

tumultuari	in	castris	Romanorum	præter
(that) there was confusion	*in*	*the camp*	*of the Romans*	*exceeding*

consuetudinem,	et	magnum	agmen	ire
(their) custom,	*and (that)*	*a great*	*force*	*was going*

adverso	flumine,	que	sonitum	remorum
up	*the river,*	*and*	*(that) the sound [noise]*	*of oars*

exaudiri	in	eādem	parte,	et	paulo
was heard	*in*	*the same*	*direction,*	*and*	*(that) a little*

infra	milites	transportari	navibus.	Quibus	rebus
below	*soldiers*	*were transported*	*in ships.*	*Which*	*things*

auditis,	quod	existimabant	legiones
having been heard,	*because*	*they thought*	*(that) the legions*

transire	tribus	locis, atque	omnes perturbatos
were crossing	*in three*	*places, and*	*(that) all alarmed*

defectione	Æduorum	parare	fugam,
by the defection	*of the Ædui*	*were preparing*	*for flight,*

quoque distribuĕrunt	suas	copias	in	tres	partes.
they also divided	*their*	*forces*	*into*	*three*	*parts.*

Nam,	præsidio	relicto	a regione	castrorum,
For,	*a guard*	*having been left*	*opposite*	*the camp,*

et	parvā	manu	missā	versus	Metiosedum,
and	*a small*	*force*	*having been sent*	*toward*	*Metiosedum,*

quæ	progrederetur	tantum	quantum	naves	pro-
which	*should advance*	*only*	*as far as*	*the ships*	*had*

cessisent,	duxerunt	reliquas	copias	contra	Labienum.
proceeded,	*they led*	*the remaining*	*forces*	*against*	*Labienus.*

62. Prima luce et omnes nostri
At first light [daylight] both all our (soldiers)

transportati erant, et acies hostium cernebatur.
had been transported, and the army of the enemy was discerned

Labienus cohortatus milites ut tenerent
[seen]. Labienus exhorted the soldiers that they should hold

memoriam suae pristinae virtutis, et tot
the memory (of) their former valor, and (of) so many

secundissimorum proeliorum, atque existimarent
very successful battles, and that they should think

Caesarem ipsum, cujus ductu saepenum-
(that) Caesar himself, under whose leadership they had so

ero superassent hostes adesse; dat signum
often conquered the enemy, was present; he gives the signal

proeli. Primo concursu, ab dextro cornu, ubi
of battle. On the first encounter, on the right wing, where

septima legio constiterat, hostes pelluntur,
the seventh legion stood, the enemy are repulsed,

atque conjiciuntur in fugam; ab sinistro,
and are thrown into flight; on the left (wing),

quem locum duodecima legio tenebat, quum
which place the twelfth legion was holding, when

primi ordines hostium concidissent transfixi
the first ranks of the enemy had fallen transfixed

pilis, reliqui tamen resistebant acerrime, nec
by javelins, the rest yet were resisting most actively, nor

quisquam dabat suspicionem fugae. Dux
was any one giving suspicion of flight. The general

ipse hostium Camulogenus aderat suis,
himself of the enemy Camulogenus was present with his

atque cohortabatur eos. At exitu
(men), and was encouraging them. But the issue

victoriae etiam nunc incerto, quum
of the victory even now (being) uncertain, when

nuntiatum esset tribunis septimae legionis,
it was announced to the tribunes of the seventh legion,

quae gererentur in sinistro cornu, ostenderunt
what was transpiring on the left wing, they displayed

LIBER VII.

legionem post tergum hostium, que intulerunt	the legion behind [on] the rear of the enemy, and advanced
signa. Ne eo tempōre quidem quisquam cessit	the standards. Not at this time even did any one leave
loco, sed omnes circumventi sunt que	the place, but all were surrounded and
interfecti; Camulogenus tulit eandem	slain; Camulogenus bore [met] the same
fortunam. At ii qui relicti erant præsidio	fortune [fate]. But those who were left for a garrison
contra castra Labieni, quum audissent	over against the camp of Labienus, when they had heard
prœlium commissum, ierunt subsidio	(that) the battle (had) commenced, went for [as] an aid
suis, que ceperunt collem, neque	to their [people], and took [occupied] the hill, nor
potuerunt sustinēre impetum nostrorum militum	could they endure the attack of our soldiers
victorum; sic permixti cum suis fugientibus,	(when) conquerors; so mingled with their own (men) retreating,
quos silvæ que montes non texerunt	those whom the woods and the mountains did not conceal
interfecti sunt ab equitatu. Hoc negotio con-	were killed by the cavalry. This affair having
fecto, Labienus revertitur Agedincum, ubi	been completed, Labienus returns to Agedincum, where
impedimenta totius exercitūs relicta erant; inde	the baggage of all the army had been left; thence
pervenit ad Cæsarem cum omnibus copius.	he came to Cæsar with all (his) forces.

63. Defectione Æduorum cognitā, bellum
The revolt of the Ædui having been known, the war

augetur; legationes circummittuntur in omnes
is increased; embassies are sent about in all

partes; nituntur ad sollicitandas civitates quantum
directions; they strive to solicit the states as much as

valent gratiā, auctoritate, pecuniā.
they may avail by favor, by authority, (or) by money

Nacti	obsides,	quos	Caesar	deposuerat
Having obtained	the hostages,	whom	Caesar	had deposited

apud	eos,	territant	dubitantes	supplicio
with	them,	they frighten	the hesitating	by the punishment

horum.	Ædui	petunt	a	Vercingetorige	ut
of these.	The Ædui	request	of	Vercingetorix	that

veniat	ad	se,	que	communicet	rationes
he come	to	them,	and	communicate	the plans

gerendi	belli.	Re	impetratā,
of carrying on	the war.	This request having been obtained,

contendunt,	ut	summa	imperii	tradatur
they maintain,	that	the chief	command	should be assigned

ipsis	et,	re	deductā	in	controversiam,
to them	and,	the thing having been brought	into	dispute,

concilium	totius	Galliæ	indicitur	Bibracte.
a council	of all	Gaul	is convoked	at Bibracte.

Frequentes	undique	conveniunt	eodum;	res
Great numbers	from everywhere	assemble	there;	the matter

permittitur	suffragiis	multitudinis;	omnes	ad	unum
is consigned	to the votes	of the multitude;	all	to	one

	probant	Vercingetorigem		imperatorem.
[a man]	approve of	Vercingetorix	(as)	commander.

Remi,	Lingones,		Treviri,	abfuerunt	ab
The Remi,	Lingones,	(and)	Treviri,	were absent	from

hōc	concilio;	illi	quod	sequebantur
this	council;	those [two first]	because	they were following

	amicitiam	Romanorum;	Treviri	quod
[observing]	the friendship	of the Romans;	the Treviri	because

longius	aberant,	et	premebantur ab Germanis;
they were far	distant,	and	were hard pressed by the Germans;

quæ	fuit	causa	quare	abessent	toto
which	was	the reason	why	they were absent in	the whole

bello,	et	mittĕrent	auxilia	neutris.	Ædui
war,	and	sent	auxiliaries	to neither.	The Ædui

ferunt	magno	dolōre	se	dejectos
bear	with great	resentment	(that) they	were deprived

principatu;	queruntur	commutationem	fortunæ,
of the leadership;	they lament	the change	of fortune,

LIBER VII.

et	requirunt	Cæsaris	indulgentiam	in	se;
and	*they miss*	*Cæsar's*	*indulgence*	*toward*	*themselves,*

neque	tamen,	bello	suscepto,	audent
nor	*however,*	*the war*	*having been undertaken,*	*do they dare*

separare	suum	consilium	ab	reliquis.
to separate	*their*	*plan [course]*	*from*	*the rest.*

Eporedorix	et	Viridomarus	adolescentes	summæ
Eporedorix	*and*	*Viridomarus*	*young men*	*of the highest*

spei (sing.)	inviti	parent	Vercingetorigi.
expectations	*unwillingly*	*obey*	*Vercingetorix.*

64. Ille	imperat	obsides	reliquis
He [Vercingetorix]	*demands*	*hostages*	*from the other*

civitatibus.	Denique	constituit	diem	ei	rei;
states.	*Finally*	*he appoints*	*a day*	*for this*	*matter;*

huc	jubet	omnes	equites,	numero
here	*he orders*	*all*	*the horsemen,*	*to the number*

quindecim	millia,	convenire	celeriter.	Dicit
of fifteen	*thousand,*	*to assemble*	*quickly.*	*He says*

se	fore	contentum	peditatu	quem
(that) he	*would be*	*content*	*with the infantry*	*which*

habuerit	ante;	neque	tentaturum	fortunam,	neque
he had	*before;*	*nor*	*would he tempt*	*fortune,*	*nor*

dimicaturum	acie;[43]	sed,	quoniam	abundet
would he fight	*in the battle-line;*	*but,*	*since*	*he abounds*

equitatu,	esse	perfacile	factu	prohibēre
in cavalry,	*it would be*	*very easy*	*in fact*	*to check*

Romanos	frumentationibus	que	pabulationibus;	modo
the Romans	*from corn*	*and*	*forage;*	*provided*

ipsi	æquo	animo	corrumpant	sua
they themselves	*with a calm*	*mind*	*destroy*	*their own*

frumenta,	que	incendant	ædificia;	qua
corn,	*and*	*burn*	*(their) houses;*	*by which*

jacturā	familaris	rei	videant	se
loss	*of private*	*property*	*they may see*	*(that) they would*

consequi	perpetuum	imperium	que	libertatem.	His
obtain	*perpetual*	*empire*	*and*	*freedom.*	*These*

rebus	constitutis,	imperat	Æduis	que
things	*having been arranged,*	*he demands*	*from the Ædui*	*and*

Segusianis,	qui	sunt	finitimi	Provinciæ,	decem
the Segusiani,	*who*	*are*	*nearest*	*to the Province,*	*ten*

millia	peditum;	huc	addit	octingentos
thousand	*(of) infantry;*	*to this*	*he adds*	*eight hundred*

equites;	his	præficit	fratrem	Eporedorigis,
horsemen;	*over these*	*he appoints*	*the brother*	*of Eporidorix,*

que	jubet	inferre	bellum	Allobrogibus.
and	*orders (him)*	*to wage*	*war*	*with the Allobroges.*

Ex	alterā	parte	mittit	Gabalos	que proximos
On	*the other*	*side*	*he sends*	*the Gabali*	*and the nearest*

pagos	Arvernorum	in	Helvios;	item Rutenos,
cantons	*of the Arverni*	*against*	*the Helvii;*	*likewise the Ruteni,*

que	Cadurcos	ad depopulandos	fines	Volcarum
and	*the Cadurci*	*to lay waste*	*the territories*	*of the Volcæ*

Arecomicorum.	Nihilominus	sollicitat	Allobroges
Arecomici.	*Nevertheless*	*he solicits*	*the Allobroges*

clandestinis	nuntiis	que	legationibus,	quorum mentes
by secret	*messages*	*and*	*embassies,*	*whose minds*

sperabat	nondum	resedisse	a
he was hoping	*not yet*	*to have [had] recovered*	*from*

superiore	bello.	Horum principibus	pollicetur pecunias,
the former	*war.*	*To their leaders*	*he promises money,*

autem	civitati	imperium totius	Provinciæ.
but	*to the state*	*the empire of all*	*the Province.*

65.
Ad	omnes hos	casus	præsidia
Against	*all these contingencies*	*[crises]*	*the protection*

viginti	et	duarum cohortium	provisa erant,	quæ
of twenty	*and*	*two cohorts*	*had been provided,*	*which*

coacta	ex	Provinciā ipsā	ab L. Cæsare,
having been collected	*from*	*the province itself*	*by L. Cæsar,*

legato,	opponebantur	ad	omnes partes.
(his) lieutenant.	*were opposing*	*at [on]*	*all sides.*

Helvii,	suā	sponte congressi	prœlio cum
The Helvii,	*of their own*	*accord having engaged*	*in battle with*

finitimis,	pelluntur,	et	C. Valerio Donotauro,
their neighbors,	*are defeated,*	*and*	*C. Valerius Donaturus,*

filio	Caburi,	principe civitatis,	que compluribus
the son	*of Caburus,*	*a chief of the state,*	*and many*

aliis	interfectis,	compelluntur	intra	oppida
others	having been killed,	they are driven	into	the towns

que	muros.	Allobroges	crebris	præsidiis
and	fortifications.	The Allobroges	frequent	guards

dispositis	ad	Rhodanum,	tuentur	suos
having been placed	at [along]	the Rhone,	defend	their

fines	cum	magnā	curā	et	diligentiā.	Cæsar,
frontiers	with	great	care	and	diligence.	Cæsar,

quod	intelligebat		hostes	esse
because	he perceived	(that)	the enemy	to be [were]

superiores	equitatu,	et	omnibus	itineribus
superior	in cavalry,	and,	all	the roads

interclusis,	poterat sublevari nullā	re
having been shut up,	he could be assisted in no	thing [respect]

ex	Provinciā	atque	Italiā,	mittit	trans	Rhenum
from the	Province	and	Italy,	sends	across	the Rhine

in	Germaniam	ad eas	civitates,	quas	pacaverat
into	Germany	to these	states,	which	he had conquered

superioribus	annis,	que	arcessit	equites	ab	his,
in former	years,	and	demanded	cavalry	from	them,

et	pedites	levis	armaturæ,	qui	consueverant
and	infantry	of light	armor,	that	were accustomed

prœliari	inter	eos.	Eorum	adventu,	quod
to battle	among	them.	On their	coming,	because

utebantur	minus	idoneis	equis,	sumit	equos
they used	less	suitable	horses,	he takes	horses

a	tribunis	militum,	que	reliquis
from	the tribunes	of the soldiers,	and from the other

Romanis	equitibus,	atque	evocatis,	que	distribuit
Roman	knights,	and	veterans,	and	distributes

Germanis.
to the Germans.

66. Interea	dum	hæc	geruntur,	copiæ
Mean time	while	these things	are transpiring,	the forces

ex	Arvernis,	que	equites,	qui	imperati erant
from	the Arverni,	and	the cavalry,	that	had been demanded

toti	Galliæ,	conveniunt.	Magno	numero	horum
to [from] all	Gaul,	assemble.	A great	number	of these

452 DE BELLO GALLICO. [66

coacto,	cum	Caesar	facĕret	iter in
having been collected,	when	Caesar	made	(his) way into

Sequanos,	per	extremos	fines	Lingonum,
the Sequani,	through	the extreme	borders	of the Lingones,

quo	posset	facilius	ferre	subsidium	Provinciae,
so that	he could	more easily	bring	aid	to the Province,

Vercingetorix	consedit,	trinis	castris,	circiter	decem
Vercingetorix	halted,	in three	camps,	about	ten

millia	passuum	ab	Romanis; que	praefectis
thousand	(of) paces	from	the Romans; and	the commanders

equitum	convocatis	ad concilium,	demonstrat
of the cavalry	having been called	to a council,	he shows (that)

tempus	victoriae	venisse;	Romanos	fugĕre in
the time	of victory	had come;	the Romans	were fleeing into

Provinciam,	que	excedĕre	Galliā;	id esse	satis
the Province,	and	were leaving	Gaul;	(that) this was	enough

sibi	ad	obtinendam	praesentem	libertatem;
for them	for	obtaining	present [immediate]	freedom;

profici	parum	ad	pacem	atque	otium
(but it)	profited	little	for	the peace	and	repose

reliqui	tempŏris;	enim	majoribus	copiis
of the remaining	time;	for	greater	forces

coactis	reversuros	neque	facturos
having been collected	they would return	nor	would they make

finem	bellandi;	proinde	adoriantur	
an end	of warring;	therefore	let them attack	(them)

impeditos	agmine.	Si	pedites	ferant	auxilium
encumbered	on the march.	If	the infantry	should bring	assistance

suis,	atque	morentur	eo,	iter posse
to their (men),	and	delay	for this,	(that) the march could

non	confici;	sin,	id	quod	magis
not be performed;	but if,	that	which [as]	the rather	[the more]

confidat	futurum,	impedimentis	relictis,
he expects	would be,	the baggage	having been abandoned,

consulant	suae	saluti,	iri	spoliatum
they consult	their	safety,	they would be	deprived

et	usu	necessariarum	rerum,	et	dignitate.
both	of the use	of necessary	things,	and	of their honor.

LIBER VII.

Nam	de	equitibus	hostium,	ne	ipsos
For	*concerning*	*the cavalry*	*of the enemy,*	*not*	*they*

quidem	debēre	dubitare,	quin	nemo	eorum
even	*ought*	*to doubt,*	*(but)* *that*	*no one*	*of them*

audeat	modo	progredi	extra	agmen.
would dare	*even*	*to advance*	*beyond*	*the marching-line.*

Quo	faciant	id	majore	animo,	se habiturum
That	*they may do*	*this*	*with greater*	*spirit,*	*he would hold*

omnes	copias	pro	castris,	et	futurum
all (his)	*forces*	*before*	*the camp,*	*and*	*would be*

terrōri	hostibus.	Equites	conclamant
(for) a terror	*to the enemy.*	*The cavalry*	*shout (that)*

oportēre	confirmari	sanctissimo	jurejurando,
it was proper	*to confirm (this)*	*by a most sacred*	*oath,*

ne recipiatur	tecto,	habeat aditum
that he should not be received	*under a roof,*	*(nor) have access*

ne	ad	liberos	ne	ad	parentes,	ne	ad	uxorem,
either	*to*	*children*	*or*	*to*	*parents,*	*or*	*to*	*wife,*

qui	non	bis	perequitāsset	per	agmen
who	*had not*	*twice*	*ridden*	*through*	*the army*

hostium.
of the enemy.

67. Re	probatā,	atque	omnibus
The thing	*having been approved,*	*and*	*all*

adactis	ad	jusjurandum,	postero	die
having been bound	*to*	*an oath,*	*on the next*	*day*

equitatu	distributo	in	tres	partes,	duæ
the cavalry	*having been divided*	*into*	*three*	*parts,*	*two*

ostendunt	se	a	duobus	lateribus;	una	cœpit
show	*themselves*	*on*	*the two*	*flanks;*	*one*	*began*

impedire	iter	a	primo	agmĭne.	Quā
to impede	*the march*	*on*	*the first*	*line [the front].*	*Which*

re	nuntiatā,	Cæsar	quoque jubet suum
thing	*having been announced,*	*Cæsar*	*also orders his*

equitatum	divisum	tripartito	ire	contra	hostem.
cavalry	*divided*	*into three parts*	*to go*	*against*	*the enemy.*

Pugnatur (pass. sing.)	unā	in	omnibus	partibus.
They fight	*together*	*on*	*all*	*sides.*

Agmen consistit. Impedimenta recipiuntur	*The marching-column halts. The baggage is received*
inter legiones. Si in quā parte nostri	*among the legions. If in any part our (men)*
videbantur laborare, aut premi gravius, eo	*seemed to labor, or be pressed too severely, there*
Cæsar jubebat signa inferri, que	*Cæsar ordered the standards to be borne, and*
aciem converti; quæ res et tardabat	*the battle-line to be turned; which thing both retarded*
hostes ad insequendum, et confirmabat	*the enemy for [from] following, and encouraged*
nostros spe auxili. Tandem Germani	*our (men) with the hope of aid. At length the Germans*
ab dextro latĕre, nacti summum jugum	*on the right wing, having gained the top of the hill*
depellunt hostes loco; persequuntur	*force the enemy from the place; they pursue*
fugientes usque ad flumen, ubi Vercingetorix	*(them) fleeing even to the river, where Vercingetorix*
consederat cum pedestribus copiis, que interficiunt	*had halted with the foot forces, and they kill*
complures. Quā re animadversā, reliqui	*very many. Which thing having been observed, the rest*
verĭti, ne circumvenirentur, mandant se	*afraid, lest they might be surrounded, consign themselves*
fugæ. Cædes fit omnibus locis. Tres	*to flight. Slaughter is made in all parts. Three*
nobilissimi Ædui capti perducuntur ad Cæsarem;	*most noble Æduans captured are led back to Cæsar;*
Cotus præfectus equitum, qui habuerat	*Cotus the commander of the cavalry, who had held*
controversiam cum Convictolitave proximis comitiis;	*the contest with Convictolitav's in the late elections;*
et Cavarillus, qui, post defectionem Litavici	*and Cavarillus, who, after the revolt of Litavicus*
præfuerat pedestribus copiis, et Eporedorix,	*had commanded the foot forces, and Eporedorix,*

loco *the place*	admodum *very high,* edito,	ut *so that*	videretur *it seemed*	non posse ex- *it could not (to)*
pugnari *by captured*	nisi *unless*	obsidione. *by a blockade.*	Duo *Two*	flumina ex *rivers on*
duabus *two*	partibus *sides*	subluebant *washed*	radices *the foot*	cujus collis. *of this hill.*
Ante *Before*	oppidum *the town*	planities *a plain*	patebat *extended*	circiter trium *about three*
millia *thousand*	passuum *paces*	in *[miles] in*	longitudinem. *length*	Ex omnibus *On all*
reliquis *the remaining*	partibus, *sides,*	colles, *hills,*	mediocri *a moderate*	saptio *distance*
(having been)	interjecto *interposed*	pari *with equal*	fastigio *elevation*	*[degree]*
altitudinis *of height*	cingebant *encircled*	oppidum. *the town.*	Sub *Under*	muro, *the wall,*
pars *the part*	collis, *of the hill,*	quæ *which*	spectabat *looked*	ad orientem, *to the east,*
omnem *all*	hunc *this*	locum *place*	copiæ *the forces* Gallorum *of the Gauls*	compleverant, *had filled,*
que *and*	præduxerant *had led [thrown] around*		fossam, *a ditch,*	et maceriam *and a cement wall*
sex *six*	pedum *feet*	in *in*	altitudinem. *height.*	Circuitus ejus *The circuit of this*
munitionis, *fortification,*	quæ *which*	instituebatur *was undertaken*	ab *by*	Romanis *the Romans*
tenebat *extended*	undecim *eleven*	millia *thousand*	passuum. *paces [miles].*	Castra *The camp*
posita erant *was placed*	opportunis *in favorable*	locis; *positions;*	que *and*	ibi viginti *there twenty*
tria *three*	castella *fortresses*	facta, *were made,*	in quibus *in which*	interdiu stationes *by day guards*
disponebantur, *were placed,*	ne *lest*	qua *any*	irruptio *sally* fieret *might be made*	subito. *suddenly.*
Hæc *These*	eadem *same*	tenebantur *were held [occupied]*	noctu *at night*	excubitoribus, *by pickets,*
ac *and*	firmis *strong*	præsidiis. *posts.*		

70] LIBER VII. 457

70. Opĕre instituto,   equestre   prœlium
    The work having been undertaken,   *a cavalry*   *battle*

fit   in   eā   planitie,   quam,   demonstravimus
took place *on* *this* *plain,* *which,* *we have shown*

supra,   patēre   tria   millia   passuum   in   longitudinem,
above, *extends* *three* *thousand* *paces* *in*   *length,*

intermissam   collibus.   Contenditur
limited   *by the hills.*   *It is contended* [*They contend*]

summā   vi   ab   utrisque.   Cæsar
with the highest [*utmost*] *vigor* *by* [*on*] *both sides.*   *Cæsar*

submittit   Germanos   nostris   laborantibus,   que
sends   *the Germans*   *to our men*   *hard pressed,* *and*

constituit   legiones   pro   castris,   ne   qua   irruptio
draws up   *the legions* *before* *the camp,* *lest* *any* *sally*

subito   fiat   peditatu   hostium.   Præsidio
suddenly should be made by the infantry of the enemy. The protection

legionum   addito,   animus   augetur   nostris;
of the legions having been added, courage is increased in our men;

hostes   conjecti   in   fugam,   ipsi   impediunt
the enemy *thrown*   *into*   *flight,* *they*   *impede*

se   multitudine;   atque   coartantur   angustioribus
themselves *by their mass;* *and* *are crowded* *in the narrower*

portis   relictis.   Germani   sequuntur
gates   *left*   (*open*). *The Germans* *follow*   (*them*)

acrius   usque ad   munitiones;   magna   cædes
more vigorously   *even*   *to*   *the fortifications;* *a great slaughter*

fit;   nonnulli,   equis relictis,   conantur
is made; *some,*   *the horses having been abandoned,* *endeavor*

transire   fossam,   et   transcendĕre   maceriam.
to cross over *the ditch,* *and*   *climb*   *the cement wall.*

Cæsar   jubet   legiones,   quas   constituerat
Cæsar   *orders*   *the legions,* *which*   *he had drawn up*

pro vallo   promoveri   paulum.   Galli,
before the rampart   *to be moved forward* *a little.*   *The Gauls*

qui   erant   intra   munitiones,   non   minus
who   *were*   *within*   *the fortifications,* *no*   *less*

perturbantur;   existimantes   veniri
were terrified;   *thinking*   (*our men*) *were coming*

confestim	ad	se,	conclamant	ad	arma.	Nonnulli
quickly		*against them,*	*they call*	*to*	*arms.*	*Some*

perterriti	irrumpunt	in	oppidum.	Vercingetorix
panic stricken	*burst*	*into*	*the town.*	*Vercingetorix*

jubet	portas	claudi,	ne	castra	nudentur.
orders	*the gates*	*to be closed,*	*lest*	*the camp*	*should be left bare.*

Multis	interfectis,		compluribus	equis
Many having been slain,		*(and)*	*very many*	*horses*

captis,	Germani	recipiunt sese.
having been captured,	*the Germans*	*retreat.*

71.	Vercingetorix	capit	consilium	dimittere	a
	Vercingetorix	*adopts*	*the plan*	*to send away*	*from*

se	omnem	equitatum	noctu,	priusquam	munitiones
him	*all*	*the cavalry*	*by night,*	*before*	*the fortifications*

perficiantur	ab Romanis.	Mandat	discedentibus,
should be finished	*by the Romans.*	*He commands them departing,*	

ut,	quisque eorum	adeat	suam	civitatem,	que
that,	*each one of them*	*should go to*	*his own*	*state,*	*and*

	cogant	ad	bellum	omnes,	qui	per
(that)	*they should assemble*	*for*	*the war*	*all,*	*who*	*by*

ætatem	possint	ferre	arma.	Proponit	sua
their age	*would be able*	*to bear*	*arms.*	*He states*	*his*

merita	in	illos, que obtestatur,	ut	habeant
services	*toward*	*them, and implores,*	*that they should have*	

rationem	suæ	salutis,	neu	dedant	se	hostibus
a regard	*for his*	*safety,*	*nor*	*deliver*	*him*	*to the enemy*

in	cruciatum,	meritum	optime	de
for	*torture,*	*having merited*	*so well*	*concerning*

communi libertate;	qui[45]	si	fuerint	indiligentiores,
the common liberty;	*who*	*if they should be*	*somewhat remiss,*	

demonstrat		octoginta	millia	delecta hominum
he shows	*(that)*	*eighty*	*thousand*	*chosen men*

interitura	cum	se;	ratione	inita,
would perish	*with*	*him;*	*a calculation*	*having been entered [made],*

se habere	frumentum	exigue	triginta	dierum,	sed
he had	*corn*	*scarcely*	*of [for] thirty*	*days,*	*but*

posse	tolerare	etiam	paulo	longius	parcendo.
he could	*endure*	*even*	*a little*	*longer*	*by sparing.*

His	mandatis	datis,	dimittit equitatum
These	orders	having been given,	he dismisses the cavalry

silentio,	secundā	vigiliā,	quā	nostrum	opus
in silence,	in the second	watch,	when	our	work

intermissum erat;	jubet	omne frumentum	ferri	ad
had ceased;	he orders	all	the corn	to be brought to

se;	constituit	poenam	capitis[46]	iis,
himself;	he ordains the punishment of the head	[of death]	to those,

qui	non	paruerint;	distribuit	pecus,	cujus
who	should not	obey;	he distributes	the cattle,	of which

magna	copia	compulsa erat	ab	Mandubiis,
a great	abundance	had been driven (there)	by the	Mandubii,

viritim;	instituit	frumentum	metiri
man by man; he regulates	(that) the corn	to [should]	be measured

parce	et	paulatim;	recipit	omnes	copias,
sparingly	and	by little;	he receives	all	the forces,

quas	collocaverat	pro	oppido,	in	oppidum.
which	he had placed	before	the town,	into	the town.

His	rationibus	parat	expectare	auxilia	Galliæ,
In this	manner	he prepares	to await	the aid	of Gaul,

et	administrare	bellum.
and	to carry on	the war.

72. Quibus	rebus	cognitis	ex	perfugis
Which	things	having been learned	from	deserters

et	captivis,	Cæsar	instituit	hæc	genĕra (pl.)
and	prisoners,	Cæsar	adopts	this	kind

munitionis.	Duxit	fossam	viginti	pedum
of fortification.	He constructed	a ditch	(of) twenty	feet

latam	directis	lateribus,	ut	ejus	solum
broad	with perpendicular	sides,	so that	its	bottom

pateret	tantundem quantum	summa	labra distabant.
might open just as muc	as	the upper	edges were apart.

Reduxit	omnes	reliquas munitiones	quadringentis
He drew back	all	the other fortifications	(by) four hundred

pedibus	ab	eā	fossā;	id	hōc	consilio
feet	from	this	ditch;	this	with this	design

(quoniam	tantum	spatium	necessario esset	complexus,
(since	so great	a space	necessarily was	embraced

totum	opus	nec	facile	cingeretur
(that) the whole	work	not	easily	could be surrounded

coronā militum);	ne aut	multitudo	hostium
by a circle of soldiers);	*lest either*	*a mass*	*of the enemy*

advolaret	ad	munitiones	de	improviso noctu,
should sally out	*to*	*the works*	*of*	*a sudden by night,*

aut interdiu	possent	conjicĕre tela	in
or by day	*they might be able*	*to throw weapons*	*against*

nostros destinatos	opĕri.	Hōc spatio	inter-
our men assigned	*to the work.*	*This space having been*	

misso, perduxit duas	fossas quindecim	pedes	latas,
left, he formed two	*trenches fifteen*	*feet*	*wide,*

eādem altitudine;	interiorem	quarum	
with the same depth;	*the inner one*	*of which*	*(being)*

campestribus ac demissis locis,	complevit	aquā
in level and low ground,	*he filled*	*with water*

derivatā	ex	flumine.	Post eas	extruxit
led	*from*	*the river.*	*Behind these*	*he constructed*

aggerem	et	vallum duodecim pedum.	Huic
a mound	*and*	*rampart of twelve feet.*	*To this*

adjecit	loricam	que pinnas, grandibus	cervis
he added	*a parapet*	*and battlements, with great*	*stag-horns*

eminentibus	ad	commissuras (pl.) pluteorum (pl.)
projecting	*at*	*the junction of the parapet*

atque	aggĕris,	qui tardarent	adscensum
and	*the mound,*	*which might hinder*	*the ascent*

hostium;	et circumdedit	turres toto opere,	quæ
of the enemy;	*and he put around*	*towers on all the work,*	*which*

distarent	inter	se[47] octoginta	pedes.
were distant	*from each other*	*eighty*	*feet.*

73. Erat	necesse	eodem	tempŏre et
It was	*necessary*	*at the same*	*time both*

materiari,	et	frumentari,	et	tantas
to bring wood,	*and*	*to get corn,*	*and (that)*	*so great*

munitiones	fieri,	nostris copiis	dim-
fortifications	*to [should] be made,*	*our forces*	*having been*

inutis,	quæ	progrediebantur	longuis ab
diminished,	*that*	*were proceeding*	*rather far from*

castris;	et	Galli	nonnunquam	conabantur
the camp;	*and*	*the Gauls*	*sometimes*	*endeavored*

tentare	nostra	opĕra,	atque	facĕre	eruptionem
to attack	*our*	*works,*	*and*	*to make*	*a sally*

ex	oppido	summā	vi	pluribus	portis.
from	*the town*	*with the utmost*	*vigor*	*by several*	*gates.*

Quare	Caesar	putavit	ad	haec	rursus		
Therefore	*Caesar*	*thought*	*to*	*these*	*again*	*(to)*	*[there must]*

addendum	opera,	quō	munitiones	possent
be added	*works,*	*so that*	*the fortifications*	*might*

defendi   minore   numero   militum.   Itaque truncis
be defended   with a less   number   of men [soldiers]. Therefore trunks

arborum,	aut	ramis	admodum	firmis	abscissis,
of trees,	*or*	*branches*	*somewhat*	*stout*	*having been cut down,*

atque	cacuminibus	horum	delibratis	atque
and	*the tops*	*of these*	*having been peeled*	*and*

preacutis;	perpetuae	fossae	quinos	pedes	altae
sharpened;	*continuous*	*ditches*	*five*	*feet*	*deep*

ducebantur.	Huc	illi	stipites	demissi,	et
were cut.	*Here*	*these*	*stakes*	*having been put down,*	*and*

revincti	ab	infimo		possent ne	revelli,
fastened	*at*	*the bottom*	*(so that)*	*they could not*	*be pulled up,*

eminebant	ab	ramis.	Quini	ordines
were projecting	*by*	*their branches.*	*Every five*	*rows*

erant	conjuncti,	atque	implicati	inter se,
were	*united,*	*and*	*intertwined*	*one with another,*

quō	ipsi	qui[48]	intraverant,	induebant	se
where	*those*	*who*	*had entered,*	*impaled*	*themselves*

acutissimis	vallis;	appellabant	hos	cippos.
on very sharp	*stakes;*	*they called*	*these*	*cippi [boundary*

	Ante	hos	obliquis	ordinibus,		
posts].	*Before*	*these*	*in oblique*	*rows,*	*and*	*(having been)*

dispositis	in	quincuncem,	scrobes,	in	altitudinem
arranged	*in*	*quincunx,*	*pits,*	*to*	*the depth*

trium	pedum	fodiebantur	paulatim	angustiore
of three	*feet*	*were dug*	*with a little*	*narrower*

fastigio	ad	summum.	Huc	teretes	stipites	crassitudine
surface	*at*	*the top.*	*Here*	*round*	*stakes*	*of the thickness*

feminis,	ab	summo	præcuti	et	præusti,
of the thigh,	at	the top	very sharp	and	burnt,

demittebantur;	ita	ut	non	amplius	quattuor
were set in;	so	that	not	more	(than) by four

digitis	eminērent	ex	terrā.	Simul
inches	they might project	from	the ground.	At the same time

causā	confirmandi	et	stabiliendi,	singuli[49]
for the purpose	of strengthening	and	steadying,	each

pedes (pl.)	ab	infimo	solo	terrā
foot	from	the lowest	ground	with earth

exculcabantur;	reliqua	pars	scrobis	integebatur
was trodden down;	the remaining	part	of the pit	was covered

viminibus	ac	virgultis	ad	occultandas	insidias.
with osiers	and	twigs	for	concealing	the traps.

Octoni	ordines	hujus	genĕris	ducti,	distabant
Eight	rows	of this	kind	were set,	they were distant

ternos	pedes	inter	se.	Id,	ex	similitudine
three	feet	from each other.		This,	from	the likeness

floris,	appellabant	lilium.	Ante	hæc	taleæ,
to the flower,	they called	a lily.	Before	these,	stakes,

pedem	longæ,	ferreis	hamis	infixis,	totæ
a foot	long,	with iron	hooks	fixed in,	all [wholly]

infodiebantur	in	terram;	que,	mediocribus
were sunk	into	the ground;	and,	moderate

spatiis		intermissis,	disserebantur	omnibus
spaces	(having been)	interposed,	were planted	in all

locis,	quos	nominabant	stimulos.
places,	which	they called	spurs.

74. | | | | |
|---|---|---|---|
| His | rebus | perfectis, | secutus |
| These | things | having been completed, | having followed |

regiones	æquissimas	quam	potuit,	pro
localities	(as) [most] level	as	was possible,	considering

naturā	loci	complexus	quattuordecim millia
the nature	of the place	(and) having enclosed	fourteen thousand

passuum,	perfēcit	pares	munitiones	ejusdem
paces,	he completed	like	fortifications	of the same

generis,	diversas	ab	his,	contra	exteriorem
kind.	opposite	from	these,	against	an external

LIBER VII.

hostem;	ut	præsidia	munitionum	possent
enemy;	*that*	*the guards*	*of the fortifications*	*could*

circumfundi	ne	quidem	magna[50]	multitudine,	(si
be surrounded	*not*	*even*	*by a great*	*multitude,*	*(if*

accidat	ita).	Ac	he	cogerentur
it should happen	*so).*	*And*	*that they*	*might not be forced*

egredi	ex	castris	cum	periculo,	jubet	omnes
to go	*from*	*the camp*	*with*	*danger,*	*he orders*	*all*

habēre	pabulum	convectum	que	frumentum
to have	*forage*	*collected*	*and*	*corn*

triginta	dierum.
for thirty	*days.*

75.

Dum	hæc		geruntur	ad	Alesiam,
While	*these*	*(things)*	*are transpiring*	*at*	*Alesia,*

Galli,	concilio	principum	indicto,
the Gauls,	*a council*	*of the chiefs*	*having been convoked*

statuunt,		non	omnes	convocandos	qui
ordain,	*(that)*	*not*	*all*	*should be called out*	*who*

possent	ferre	arma	(ut	Vercingetorix	censuit),
could	*bear*	*arms*	*(as*	*Vercingetorix*	*decided);*

sed		certum	numerum	imperandum	cuique
but	*(that)*	*a certain*	*number*	*should be ordered*	*for each*

civitati;	ne,	tantā		confusā	multitudine
state;	*lest,*	*in so great*	*(and)*	*mixed*	*a multitude*

possent	nec	moderari,	nec	discernĕre	suos
they could	*neither*	*govern,*	*nor*	*distinguish*	*their (men)*

nec	habēre	rationem	frumentandi.	Imperant
nor	*have*	*the means*	*of provisioning.*	*They demand*

triginta	quinque	millia	Æduis	atque
thirty	*five*	*thousand*	*from the Ædui*	*and*

eorum	clientibus,	Segusianis,	Ambivaretis,	Aulercis,
their	*clients,*	*the Segusiani,*	*the Ambivareti,*	*the Aulerci,*

Brannovicibus,	(Blannoviis);	parem	numerum
the Brannovices,	*(Blannovii);*	*a like*	*number*

Arvernis,	adjunctis	Eleutetis,	Cadurcis,
from the Arverni,	*united*	*with the Eleuteti,*	*the Cadurci,*

Gabalis,		Vellaviis,	qui	consueverunt
the Gabali.	*(and)*	*the Vellavii,*	*who*	*have been accustomed*

esse sub	imperio	Arvernorum;	Senonibus,
to be under	the command	of the Arverni;	from the Senones,

Sequanis,	Biturigibus,	Santonibus,	Rutenis,
the Sequani,	the Bituriges,	the Santones,	the Ruteni,

Carnutibus,	duodena millia;	Bellovacis,	decim;
the Carnutes,	twelve thousand;	the Bellovaci,	ten;

totidem Lemovicibus;	octona Pictonibus,	et
the same from the Lemovice;	eight from the Pictones,	and

Turonis,	et	Parisiis,	et Helvetiis;	sena
the Turoni,	and	the Parisii,	and the Helvetii,	six

Audibus,	Ambianis,	Mediomatricis,	Petrocoriis,
from the Audes,	the Ambiani,	the Mediomatrici,	the Petrocorii,

Nerviis,	Morinis,	Nitiobrigibus;	quina milia
the Nervii,	the Morini,	the Nitiobriges,	five thousand

Aulercis Cenomanis;	totidem	Atrebatibus;
from the Aulercis Cenomani;	the same number	from the Atrebates

quatuor	Veliocassis;	(Lexoviis et)	Aulercis
four	from the Veliocassi;	(the Lexovii and)	the Aulerci

Eburovicibus terna;	Rauracis	et	Boiis bina.
Eburovices three;	from the Rauraci	and	Boii two.

Decim	universis	civitatibus,	quæ attingunt
Ten from	all	the states,	which border on

Oceanum,	quæque eorum	consuetudine	appellantur
the Ocean,	and that by their	custom	are called

Armoricæ,	in quo	numero sunt	Coriosolites,
Armoricæ,	in which	number are	the Coriosolites,

Redones,	Ambibarii,	Caletes,	Osismi,	Veneti,
the Redones,	the Ambibarii,	the Caletes,	the Osismi,	the Veneti,

Lexovii,	Venelli.	Ex his	Bellovaci	non
Lexovii,	Venelli.	Of these	the Bellovaci	did not

contulerunt	suum	numerum;	quod	dixerunt
contribute	their	number;	because	they said (that)

se gesturos	bellum cum	Romanis	suo
they would carry on	war with	the Romans	by their own

nomine	atque	arbitrio,	neque obtemperaturos
name	and	will,	nor would they obey

imperio	cujusquam.	Rogati	a Commio,
the command	of any one.	Requested	by Commius,

tamen,	pro	ejus	hospitio,	miserunt
however,	on account of	his	tie of hospitality,	they sent

duo millia.
two thousand

76. Caesar, ita ut antea demonstravimus, usus erat
    Caesar, just as before we have shown, had used

fideli	atque	utili	operā	hujus	Commii,
the faithful	and	helpful	services	of this	Commius,

superioribus	annis	in	Britanniā,	pro	quibus meritis
in former	years	in	Britain,	for	which deserts

jusserat	ejus	civitatem	esse	immunem,
he had ordered	his	state	to be	exempt (from tribute),

reddiderat	jura	que	leges;	atque	attribuerat
had restored	the rights	and	laws;	and	had conferred

ipsi   Morinos. Tamen tanta fuit consensio
on himself [him] the Morini. Yet so great was the unanimity

universae	Galliae	vindicandae	libertatis,	et
of the whole	of Gaul	of [for] establishing	liberty,	and

recuperandae		pristinae	laudis	belli,	ut
of [for] recovering	(their)	ancient	renown	in war,	that

moverentur	neque	beneficiis,	neque	memoriā
they could be moved	neither	by benefits,	nor	by the memory

amicitiae,	que	omnes	incumběrent	in	id
of friendship,	and	all	were devoting themselves	to	this

bellum	et	animo	et	opibus;	octo
war	with both	mind [thought]	and	means,	eight

millibus	equitum,	et	circiter	ducentis	et
thousand	cavalry,	and	about	two hundred	and

quadraginta	millibus	peditum	coactis.
forty	thousand	infantry	having been collected.

Haec	recensebantur	in	finibus	Aeduorum;	que
These	were received	in	the country	of the Aedui;	and

numerus	inibatur;	praefecti	constituebantur;
the number	was secured;	commanders	were appointed;

summa   imperii   traditur   Commio   Atrebati,
the supreme command is conferred on Commius the Atrebatian,

Viridomaro	et	Eporedorigi	Aeduis,	
Viridomarus	and	Eporedorix	the Aeduans,	(and

DE BELLO GALLICO.

Vercassivellauno Arverno, consobrino Vercinge-
Vercassivellaunus *the Arvernian,* *cousin-german* *to Vercinge-*

torigis. Iis delecti ex civitatibus
torix. *To them* *(those)* *selected* *from* *the states*

attribuntur, quorum consilio bellum administraretur.
are assigned, *by those* *counsel* *the war* *should be conducted.*

Omnes proficiscuntur ad Alesiam alacres et pleni
All *set out* *to* *Alesia* *eager* *and* *full*

fiduciae. Nec erat quisquam omnium, qui,
of confidence. *Nor* *was there* *any one* *of all,* *who,*

arbitraretur adspectum modo tantae
supposed *that* *the sight* *even* *of so great*

multitudinis posse sustineri, praesertim ancipiti
a multitude *could* *be endured,* *especially* *in a two-fold*

proelio; quum pugnaretur[52] eruptione ex
battle; *when* *it would be [they] fought* *by [in] a sally* *from*

oppido, et foris tantae copiae equitatus que
the town, *and* *outside* *so great* *forces* *of cavalry* *and*

peditatus cernerentur.
infantry *should be discerned.*

77. At ii qui obsidebantur Alesiae, die
But *those* *who* *were besieged* *in Alesia,* *the day*

praeterita, qua expectaverant auxilia suorum,
having passed, *on which* *they had expected* *the aid* *of their (allies),*

omni frumento consumpto, inscii quid
all *the corn* *having been consumed,* *ignorant* *what*

gereretur in Æduis, concilio coacto,
was going on *among* *the Ædui,* *a council having been assembled*

consultabant de exitu suarum fortunarum.
they were deliberating *about* *the issue* *of their* *fortunes.*

Ac variis sententiis dictis, quarum pars
And *various* *opinions* *having been expressed,* *of which* *a part*

censebant deditionem, pars eruptionem dum
recommended *a surrender,* *a part* *a sally* *while*

vires (pl.) suppetĕrent. Oratio Critognati
(their) strength *was sufficient.* *The speech* *of Critognatus*

videtur non praetereunda, propter ejus
it seems *ought not to be passed over,* *on account of* *its*

singularem	singular
ac	and
nefariam	infamous
crudelitatem.	cruelty.
Hic,	He,
natus	born

singularem ac nefariam crudelitatem. Hic, natus
singular and infamous cruelty. He, born

summo loco in Arvernis, et habitus
of the highest rank among the Arverni, and possessed

magnæ auctoritatis, inquit: "dicturus sum nihil
of great influence, said: "I am about to say nothing

de sententiā eorum, qui appellant
concerning the opinion of those, who call

turpissimam servitutem nomĭne deditionis;
the basest slavery by the name of surrender;

censeo hos neque habendos loco
I am of the opinion (that) these neither ought to be held in the place

civium, neque adhibendos ad
[role] of citizens, nor ought they to be admitted to

concilium. Res est mihi cum iis, qui
the counsel. The business is for me with those, who

probant eruptionem; in consilio quorum consensu
sanction a sally; in the advice of whom with the consent

vestrum omnium memoria pristinæ virtutis
of you all the memory of the old-time valor

videtur residēre. Ista est mollities animi non
seems to abide. This is a weakness of mind not

virtus, non posse ferre inopiam paulisper.
courage, not to be able to endure privation for a little time.

Qui ultro offerant se morti facilius
(Those) who willingly offer themselves to death more easily

reperiuntur, quam qui patienter ferant dolōrem.
are found, than (those) who patiently endure distress.

Atque ego probarem hanc sententiam (tantum
And I would approve this opinion (so much

apud me dignitas potest), si vidērem
with me honor is able [avails]), if I could see (that)

nullam jacturam fieri præterquam nostræ
no loss would be made except of our

vitæ (sing.). Sed in capiendo consilio,
lives. But in taking [forming] a plan

respiciamus omnem Galliam, quam concitavimus
let us regard all Gaul, which we have aroused

ad nostrum	auxilium.	Octoginta	millibus	hominum
to our	assistance.	Eighty	thousand	men

interfectis,	uno	loco,	quid	animi	existimatis
having been slain,	in one	place,	what	(of) spirit	do you think

fore	nostris	propinquis	que	consanguineis,	si
(this) would be	to our	relatives	and	kinsmen,	if

cogentur	decertare	prœlio	pæne	in
they should be forced	to engage	in battle	almost	over (our)

cadaveribus	ipsis?	Nolite	spoliare	hos	vestro
dead bodies	themselves?	Do not	deprive	those	of your

auxilio,	qui	causā	vestræ	salutis	neglexerint
aid,	who	for the sake	of your	safety	have disregarded

suum	periculum,	nec	vestrā	stultitiā	ac
their own	peril,	nor	by your	folly	and

temeritate,	aut	imbecillitate	animi	prosternĕre
recklessness,	or	imbecility	of mind	prostrate

omnem	Galliam,	ac	addicĕre	perpetuæ	servituti.
all	Gaul,	and	consign (it)	to perpetual	slavery.

An	quod	non venerint	ad	diem
Why	because	they may not have come	at [on]	the day

dubitatis	de	eorum	fide	que	constantiā?	Quid
do you doubt	of	their	fidelity	and	constancy?	What

ergo?	Putatis	Romanos	exercēri	quotidie
then?	Do you suppose (that)	the Romans	are training	daily

in	illis	ulterioribus	munitionibus	ne	causā
in	those	outer	fortifications	only	for the sake

animi?[53]	Si	potestis	non	confirmari	nun-
of the mind?	If	you can	not	be strengthened	by the

tiis	illorum,	omni	aditu	præsepto,
messages	of those,	all	approach	having been prevented

utimini	iis	testibus	eorum	adventum
use	these (as)	witnesses	(that) their	arrival

appropinquare,	exterriti	timōre	cujus	rei
draws near, (the fact that)	alarmed	by the fear	of this	thing

versantur	diem	que	noctem	in	opĕre.	Quid
they are busied	day	and	night	in	the work.	What

ergo	est	mei	consilii?	Facĕre	quod	nostri
therefore	is	my	advice?	To do	what	our

majores	fecerunt	nequaquam	pari	bello	Cimbrorum
forefathers	did	in the by no means	equal	war	of the Cimbri

que	Teutonum,	qui	compulsi	in	oppida, ac
and	Teutones,	who	driven	into	towns, and

subacti	simili	inopiā,	toleraverunt vitam	corporibus
forced	by a like	want,	supported life	by the bodies

eorum,	qui	ætate	videbantur inutiles	ad bellum,
of those,	who	by age	seemed useless	for war,

neque	tradiderunt	se	hostibus. Si
nor	did they surrender	themselves	to the enemy. If

haberemus	non	exemplum	cujus	rei,	tamen
we had	not	the example	of this	thing,	yet

judicarem	pulcherrimum	causā	libertatis
I should judge it	most glorious	for the sake	of liberty

institui,	et	prodi	posteris. Nam
to be established,	and	be handed down	to posterity. For

quid	fuit	simile	illi	bello?[54] Gallia
what	was there	like	that	war? Gaul (having been)

depopulatā,	que magnā	calamitate	illatā,
depopulated,	and a great	disaster	(having been) inflicted,

Cimbri	aliquando	excesserunt nostris	finibus,	atque
the Cimbri	at length	departed from our	territories,	and

petierunt	alias	terras;	reliquerunt nobis	jura,
sought	other	lands;	they left us	the rights,

leges,	agros	libertatem.	Vero Romani
the laws,	the lands (and)	liberty.	But the Romans

quid	aliud	petunt,	aut quid volunt,	nisi
what	else	do they seek,	or what do they wish,	except

adducti	invidiā,	considĕre	in	agris que
induced	by greed,	to settle	in	the fields and

civitatibus	horum, quos	cognoverunt	famā
states	of these (those) whom	they have learned	by report

	nobiles que	potentes	bello,	atque his
(are)	noble and	powerful	in war,	and on these

injungĕre	æternam	servitutem?	Enim neque unquam
to impose	perpetual	slavery?	For never

gesserunt	bella	aliā	conditione. Quod
have they waged	wars	on any other	terms. For

si	ignoratis	ea	quæ	geruntur	in
if	*you know not*	*those things*	*which*	*are being done*	*in*

longinquis	nationibus,	respicite	finitimam	Galliam,
distant	*nations,*	*look ye [you] at*	*neighboring*	*Gaul,*

quæ	redacta	in	provinciam,		jure	et	legibus
which	*reduced*	*to*	*a province,*	*(its)*	*rights*	*and*	*laws*

	commutatis,		subjecta	securi-
(having been)	*subverted*	*(having been)*	*subjected to the*	*(lic-*

bus	premitur	perpetuā	servitute!"
tors')	*axes,*	*is oppressed*	*by perpetual*	*slavery!"*

78. | Sententiis | | dictis, | constituunt, | ut |
|---|---|---|---|---|
| *The opinions* | *having been delivered,* | *they resolve,* | *that* |

qui	valetudine,	aut	ætate	sunt	inutiles	bello
(those)	*who*	*by sickness,*	*or*	*age*	*are*	*uselsss*	*for war*

excedant	oppido,	atque	omnia	experiantur,
should leave	*the town,*	*and*	*all things*	*should be tried,*

prius	quam	descendant	ad	sententiam
before	*(that)*	*they descend*	*to*	*the recommendation*

Critognati;	tamen	utendum	illo consilio, si res
of Critognatus;	*however*	*(that they must) use*	*his advice, if the case*

cogat,	atque	auxilia	morentur,	potius	quam
compels,	*and*	*aid*	*be delayed,*	*rather*	*than (that)*

conditionem	deditionis	aut	pacis	subeundam.
a condition	*of surrender*	*or*	*of peace*	*should be endured.*

Mandubii,	qui	receperant	eos	oppido	coguntur
The Mandubii,	*who*	*had received*	*them*	*in the town*	*are forced*

exire	cum	liberis	atque	uxoribus.	Hi
to depart	*with*	*the children*	*and*	*wives.*	*These*

quum	accessissent	ad	munitones	Romanorum,
when	*they had approached*	*to*	*the fortifications*	*of the Romans,*

flentes	orabant	omnibus	precibus,	ut	recep-
weeping	*prayed*	*with all*	*entreaties,*	*that*	*having been*

tos	in	servitutem,	juvarent	cibo.
received	*into*	*slavery,*	*they would relieve (them)*	*with food.*

Hos	Cæsar,	custodiis	dispositis	in	vallo,
These	*Cæsar,*	*sentinels*	*having been posted*	*on*	*the rampart,*

prohibebat	recipi.
prevented to be [from being] received.

LIBER VII.

79. | Interea | Commius, | et | reliqui | duces, |
| --- | --- | --- | --- | --- |
| *In the meantime* | *Commius,* | *and* | *the other* | *leaders,* |

quibus	summa	imperii	permissa erant,	perveniunt
to whom	*the supreme*	*command*	*had been assigned,*	*arrive*

ad	Alesiam	cum	omnibus	copiis,	et	exteriore
at	*Alesia*	*with*	*all*	*the forces,*	*and*	*an outer*

colle	occupato,	considunt	non	longius
hill	*having been occupied,*	*they encamp*	*not*	*farther (than)*

mille	passibus	a	nostris	munitionibus.	Postero
a thousand	*paces*	*from*	*our*	*fortifications.*	*The next*

die,	equitatu	educto	ex	castris,
day,	*the cavalry*	*having been led forth*	*from (their)*	*camp,*

complent	omnem	eam	planitiem,	quam	demonstravimus
they fill	*all*	*this*	*plain,*	*which*	*we have shown*

patēre	tria	millia	passuum	in	longitudinem;
to extend [extends]	*three*	*thousand*	*paces*	*in*	*length;*

que	constituunt	pedestres	copias	paulum	ab	eo
and	*they station*	*the foot*	*soldiers*	*a little*	*from*	*this*

loco,	abditas	in	superioribus	locis (pl.).	Erat
place,	*removed*	*on*	*higher*	*ground.*	*There was*

despectus	ex	oppido	Alesiā	in	campum.
a view	*from*	*the town*	*(of) Alesia*	*over*	*the plain.*

His	auxiliis	visis,	concurritur,
These	*auxiliaries*	*having been seen,*	*there is running together*

gratulatio	fit (sing.)	inter	eos,	atque	animi
congratulations	*are made*	*among*	*them,*	*and*	*the souls*

omnium	excitantur	ad	lætitiam.	Itaque,	copiis
of all	*are excited*	*to*	*joy.*	*Therefore, (their)*	*forces*

productis	ante	oppidum,	considunt	et
having been drawn out	*before*	*the town,*	*they take stand*	*and*

integunt	proximam	fossam	cratibus,	atque	explent
cover	*the nearest*	*ditch*	*with hurdles,*	*and*	*fill (it)*

aggĕre,	que	comparant	se	ad	eruptionem,
with dirt,	*and*	*prepare*	*themselves*	*for*	*a sally,*

atque	omnes	casus.
and	*all*	*chances.*

80. Cæsar,	omni	exercitu	disposito	ad
Cæsar,	*all*	*the army*	*having been stationed*	*at*

472 DE BELLO GALLICO. [80

utramque	partem	munitionum,	ut	si	usus
both	sides	of the fortifications,	(so) that	if	the need

veniat,	quisque	noverit	et	teneat	suum	locum,
should come	each	might know	and	keep	his own	place.

jubet	equitatum	educi	ex	castris,	et
orders	the cavalry	to be led	from	the camp,	and

committi	prœlium.	Erat	despectus	ex	omnibus
to join	battle.	There was	a view	from	all

castris,	quæ	undique	tenebant	summum
the camp,	which	everywhere	occupied	the highest

jugum,	atque	animi	omnium	militum	intenti
ridge,	and	the minds	of all	the soldiers	intent

pugnæ	exspectabant	eventum.	Galli
on battle	were anticipating	the issue.	The Gauls

interjecerant	inter	equites	raros	sagittarios,
had placed	among	the horsemen	scattered	archers,

que	expeditos	levis	armaturæ,[55]	qui	succurrĕrent
and	ready soldiers	lightly	armed,	who	might succor

auxilio	suis	cedentibus	et	sustinērent
by (their) aid	their (men)	retreating	and	hold

impetum	nostrorum	equitum.	Complures
the charge	of our	cavalry.	Many (of our men)

vulnerati	de improviso	ab	his	excedebant
wounded	unexpectedly	by	these	withdrew

prœlio.	Cum	Galli	confidĕrent	suos
from the battle.	When	the Gauls	believed	(that) their

	esse	superiores	pugnā,	et	vidērent
(men)	were	superior	in the fight,	and	saw

nostros		premi	multitudine;	ex	om-
our	(men)	(to be) hard pressed	by the throng,	from	[on]

nibus	partibus,	et	ii	qui	continebantur
all	parts [sides],	both	those	who	were retained

munitionibus,	et	ii	qui	convenerant	ad
within the fortifications,	and	those	who	had come	for

auxilium,	confirmabant	animos	suorum	clamore
aid,	strengthened	the spirits	of their men	by a shout

et	ululatu.	Quod	res	gerebatur	in conspectu
and	yell.	As	the action	was carried on	in the sight

omnium,	neque	factum	recte	aut
of all,	neither	(a thing) done	rightly [nobly]	or

turpiter	poterat	celari,	et	cupiditas	laudis,
shamefully	could	be concealed,	both	the desire	of praise,

et	timor	ignominiae	excitabat (sing.)	utrosque	ad
and	the fear	of disgrace	were inciting	both sides	to

virtutem.	Quum	pugnaretur	a	meridie
valor.	When	it was [they] fought	from	noon

prope ad	occasum	solis	dubiā	victoriā,
nearly to	the setting	of the sun	with a doubtful	victory,

Germani	in	unā	parte	confertis	turmis	fecerunt
the Germans	on	one	side	in compact	troops	made

impetum	in	hostes,	que	propulerunt	eos.
an attack	on	the enemy,	and	routed	them.

Quibus			conjectis	in	fugam,
Whom	[These]	(having been)	thrown	into	flight,

sagittarii	circumventi sunt	que	interfecti.	Item
the archers	were surrounded	and	slain.	Also

ex	reliquis	partibus	nostri	insecuti	
in	other	quarters	our men	followed	(those)

cedentes	usque	ad	castra,		dederunt
retreating	even	to	the camp,	(and)	gave

non	facultatem	colligendi	sui.	At
no	opportunity	of [for] collecting	their (men).	But

ii,	qui	processerant	ab	Alesiā,	victoriā
those,	who	had come	from	Alesia,	the victory

prope	desperatā,	receperunt	se
nearly	(having been) despaired of	betook	themselves

maesti,	in	oppidum.
sorrowful,	into	the town.

81.	Uno	die	intermisso,	atque	hōc	spatio
One	day	having intervened,	and	in this	period

magno	numero	cratium,	scalarum,	harpagonum
a great	number	of hurdles,	ladders,	pole-hooks

effecto,	Galli,	mediā nocte,	silentio,
having been made,	the Gauls,	at mid night	(and) in silence,

egressi	ex		castris	accedunt	ad
having marched	from	(their)	camp	approach	to

campestres	munitiones.	Subito	clamōre
the field [outside]	fortifications.	A sudden	shout

sublato,	qua	significatione,	qui
having been raised,	by which	signal, (those)	who

obsidebantur	in	oppido,	possent	cognoscĕre	de
were besieged	in	the town,	might	know	of

suo	adventu,	projicĕre	crates	deturbare
their	arrival, (and)	throw out	the hurdles,	force

nostros	de	vallo	fundis,	sagittis	lapidibus,
our men	from	the rampart	by slings,	arrows (and)	stones,

que	administrare	reliqua	quæ	pertinent	ad
and	(to) perform	the other things	which	belong	to

oppugnationem.	Eodem	tempŏre,	clamōre
an assault.	At the same	time,	the shout

exaudito,	Vercingetorix	dat	signum	suis
having been heard,	Vercingetorix	gives	the signal	to his men

tubā,	atque	educit		ex	oppido.
by the trumpet,	and	leads	(them forth)	from	the town.

Nostri,	ut	superioribus	diebus,	suus	locus
Our men,	as	on the previous	days,	his	place

attributus erat	cuique, accedunt ad	munitiones;
had been assigned	to each one, proceed	to the fortifications;

perterrent	Gallos	fundis	libralibus[57]	que
they alarm	the Gauls	by slings	(of) pound-weight	and

sudibus,	quas	disposuerant	in	opĕre,	ac
stakes,	which	they had placed	in	the works,	and

glandibus.	Prospectu	adempto tenebris,
by lead bullets.	The view (having been)	cut off by darkness,

multa	vulnĕra	accipiuntur	utrimque,	complura
many	wounds	are received	on both sides,	numerous

tela	conjiciuntur	tormentis.	At	M. Antonius,[58]
weapons	are thrown	by the engines.	But	M. Antonius,

et C. Trebonius,	legati,	quibus	eae	partes
and C. Trebonius,	the lieutenants,	to whom	these	parts

obvenerant	ad	defendendum,	ex	qua
had fallen	for	defending,	on	what [whatever]

parte	intellexerunt	nostros	premi,
side	they understood (that)	our men	were hard pressed,

82]   LIBER VII.   473

submittebant	iis	auxilio	deductos	ex
they sent	*to them*	*for [as] aid*	*(those) drawn [led]*	*out from*

ulterioribus	castellis.
the more remote	*fortresses.*

82. | Dum | Galli | aberant | longius | ab |
|---|---|---|---|---|
| *While* | *the Gauls* | *were distant* | *rather far* | *from* |

munitione,	proficiebant,	plus	multitudine
the fortifications,	*they made progress,*	*more*	*by the multitude*

	telorum;	posteaquam	successerunt	proprius,
[*mass*]	*of weapons;*	*after*	*they approached*	*nearer,*

aut	ipsi	inopinantes	induebant	se	stimulis,
either	*they*	*unawares*	*impaled*	*themselves*	*on the spurs,*

aut	delapsi	in	scrobes	transfodiebantur,	aut
or	*having fallen*	*into*	*the pits*	*were transfixed,*	*or*

interibant	trajecti	murialibus	pilis	ex
perished	*pierced*	*by the wall*	*javelins (thrown)*	*from*

vallo	et	turribus.	Multis	vulneribus accep-
the rampart	*and*	*towers.*	*Many*	*wounds having*

tis	undique,	nulla	munitione	perrupta,
been received	*on all sides,*	*no*	*fortification*	*having been forced,*

cum	lux	appeteret,	veriti	ne
when	*(day) light*	*was approaching,*	*having feared*	*lest*

circumvenirentur	ab	aperto	latere,	eruptione
they might be surrounded	*on*	*the exposed*	*flank,*	*by a sally*

ex	superioribus castris,	receperunt se	ad suos.
from	*the higher camp,*	*they retreated*	*to their (people).*

At	interiores,	dum	proferunt	ea
But	*those within (the town),*	*while*	*they bring out*	*these things*

quæ	præparata erant	a	Vercingetorige	ad
which	*had been prepared*	*by*	*Vercingetorix*	*for*

eruptionem,	explent priores	fossas;	morati
the sally,	*fill up the first*	*ditches;*	*having been delayed*

diutius	in	administrandis	iis	rebus,	cogno-
rather long	*in*	*performing*	*these*	*things,*	*they*

verunt	suos	discessisse	prius	quam
learned	*(that) their men*	*had withdrawn*	*before*	*(that)*

appropinquarent		munitionibus.	Ita,	re
they had approached	*(to)*	*the fortifications.*	*Thus,*	*the thing*

	infectā,	reverterunt	in
[design]	having been unaccomplished,	they returned	into

oppidum.
the town.

83. Galli bis repulsi cum magno
The Gauls twice having been repulsed with great

detrimento, consulunt quid agant. Adhibent
loss, consult what they should do. They admit

peritos locorum (pl.). Cognoscunt ab
(those) acquainted with the locality. They learn from

his situs superiorum castrorum que
these the position of the higher camp and

munitiones. Erat collis a septentrionibus,
the fortifications. There was a hill on the north,

quem[59] nostri non potuerant circumplecti opĕre,
which our men had not been able to enclose in the works,

propter magnitudinem circuitus; pæne
on account of the greatness of the circuit; almost

necessario fecerant castra iniquo et
necessarily they had pitched (their) camp in an unfavorable and

leniter declivi loco. C. Antistius Reginus, et
gently descending place. C. Antistius Reginus, and

C. Caninius Rubilus, legati, obtinebant hæc
C. Caninius Rubilus, the lieutenants, were holding this

cum duabus legionibus. Regionibus cognitis
with two legions. The country having been explored

per exploratores, duces hostium deligunt
by scouts, the leaders of the enemy select

sexaginta millia ex omni numero earum
sixty thousand from all the number of those

civitatum, quæ habeant maximam opinionem
states, which have the greatest reputation

virtutis; occulte constituunt inter se, quid,
of [for] bravery; secretly they arrange among themselves, what,

que quo pacto placeat agi.
and in what manner it is pleasing [is best] to be done.

Definiunt tempus adeundi quum videatur
They determine the time of advancing when it may seem

esse	meridies.	Præficiunt	iis	copiis
to be	noon.	They place over	these	forces

Vercassivellaunum	Arvernum,	unum	ex	
Vercassivellaunus	the Arvernian,	one	from	[of,

quattuor	ducibus,	propinquum	Vercingetorigis.	Ille
the four	leaders,	a kinsman	of Vercingetorix.	He

egressus	ex	castris	primā vigiliā	itinĕre
having departed	from	the camp	at the first watch	the march

confecto	prope	sub	lucem,	occultavit
having been completed	nearly	about	(day) light,	concealed

se	post	montem,	que	jussit	milites
himself	behind	the mountain,	and	ordered	the soldiers

reficĕre	sese	ex	nocturno labore. Cum
to refresh	themselves	from [after]	(their) nocturnal labor. When

jam	meridies	videretur	appropinquare,	contendit
now	noon	was seen	to draw near,	he marched

ad	ea	castra,	quæ	demonstravimus	supra,	que
to	that	camp.	which	we have mentioned	above	and

eodem	tempŏre	equitatus	cœperunt	accedĕre
at the same	time	the cavalry	commenced	to approach

ad	campestres	munitiones,	et	reliquæ
to	the field [outer]	fortifications,	and	the remaining

copiæ	ostendĕre	sese	pro	castris.
forces	to show	themselves	before	the camp.

84. | Vercingetorix | conspicatus | suos, | ex |
|---|---|---|---|
| Vercingetorix | having beheld | his (allies), | from |

arce	Alesiæ,	egreditur ex	oppido,	profert
the citadel	of Alesia,	marches from	the town,	brings forth

e	castris	longurios,	musculos,	falces,	que
from	the camp	long poles,	moveable sheds,	wall hooks,	and

reliqua,	quæ	paraverat	causā	eruptionis.
other things,	which he had prepared for the purpose of the sally.

Pugnatur[60]	uno tempŏre, omnibus locis, atque
It is fought [Fighting occurs] at one time,	in all places, and

omnia	tentantur.	Quæ pars visa	esse minime
all things	are attempted.	What part is seen	to be least

firma,	huc	concurritur.	Manus	Romanorum
strong,	hither	(they) run together.	The force	of the Romans

distinetur	tantis	munitionibus	nec	facile
is extended	in so great	fortifications	and not	easily

occurrit	pluribus	locis.	Clamor, qui	exstitit
meets (the attack)	in many	places.	The din, that	arose

post	tergum	pugnantibus,	valuit	multum ad
in	the rear	to [of] the combatants,	served	much for

terrendos	nostros,	quod	vident	suum
alarming	our men,	because	they see (that)	their

periculum	consistĕre	in virtute	alienā.	Enim
peril	depends	on the bravery (of)	others.	For

plerumque	omnia	quæ	absunt	perturbant
generally	all things	which	are absent	alarm

mentes	hominum	vehementius.
the minds	of men	more violently.

85.
Cæsar	nactus	idoneum	locum,	cognoscit
Cæsar,	having chosen	a suitable	place,	learns

quid	geratur in	quāque parte,	submittit	(aid)
what	is done in	every part,	sends	

	laborantibus.	Occurrit ad	animum utrisque.
(to those)	hard pressed.	It occurs to	the mind to each,

	illud esse	unum	tempus, quo	conveniat
(that)	that is	the one	time, in which	it is fitting

maxime	contendi.[61]	Galli,	nisi
to the greatest degree	to be fought [to fight].	The Gauls,	unless

perfregerint	munitiones,	desperant	de	omni
they break through	the fortifications,	despair	of	all

salute.	Romani, si	obtinuerint	rem
safety.	The Romans, if	they should gain	the affair [action]

expectant	finem	omnium	laborum.	Maxime
expect	an end	of all (their)	labors.	Especially

laboratur	ad superiores munitiones, quō
it is struggled [there is a struggle]	at the higher fortifications, where

demonstravimus	Vercassivellaunum	missum.
we have shown (that)	Vercassivellaunus	(had been) sent.

Exiguum	fastigium	loci	ad declivitatem,
The small	elevation	of the place	with the slope,

habet	magnum	momentum.	Alii	conjiciunt tela,
has	great	importance.	Some	throw weapons

alii	testudine	factā,	subeunt,	integri
cthers	a testudo	having been made	advance,	fresh men

succedunt	defatigatis	in vicem.	Agger	conjectus
relicce	the wearied	by turns.	The earth	thrown

ab	universis	in	munitionem,	et	dat
by	all	against	the fortifications,	both	gives

ı dscensum	Gallis,	et	contegit	quæ
an ascent	to the Gauls,	and	covers	what

Romani	occultaverant	in	terrā.	Nec	arma,
the Romans	had concealed	in	the ground.	Neither	arms,

)m	nec	vires	suppetunt	nostris.
ow	nor	strength	suffice	for our men.

86. | His | rebus | cognitis, | Cæsar | mittit |
|---|---|---|---|---|
| These | things | having been learned, | Cæsar | sends |

Labienum	cum	sex	cohortibus	subsidio
Labienus	with	six	cohorts	for [as]	aid

	laborantibus.	Imperat,	si	possit non
(to these)	struggling.	He commands	(him),	if he could not

sustinēre,	cohortibus	deductis,	pugnet
withstand,	the cohorts	having been drawn [led] out,	he should fight

eruptione;	non	faciat	id,	nisi	necessario.
in a sally;	(but) not	do	this,	unless	necessary.

Ipse	adit	reliquos;	cohortatur	ne
He	goes	to the rest;	he exhorts (them) that they should not

succumbant	labor;	docet	fructum	omnium
succumb	to the work;	he shows (that)	the fruit	of all

	superiorum	dimicationum	consistĕre	in	eo
(their)	former	battles	depended	on	this

die	atque	horā.	Interiores		campestribus
day	and	hour.	Those within [The besieged]		the level

locis	desperatis,	propter	magnitudinem
places	having been despaired of,	on account of	the size

munitionum,	tentant	loca	præcrupta	ex
of the fortifications,	attempt	the places	steep	in

adscensu;	huc	conferunt	ea	quæ	para-
ascent;	here	they bring	those	things which	they had

verant,	deturbant	propugnantes	ex	turribus
prepared,	they drive back	the defenders	from	the towers

multitudine telorum; explent fossas aggĕre
by the multitude of weapons; they fill up the trenches with earth

et cratibus expediunt aditus; rescindunt
and fascines they prepare an approach, they tear down

vallum ac loricam falcibus.
the rampart and parapet with hooks.

87. Caesar primo mittit Brutum, adolescentem,
Caesar at first sends Brutus, a young man,

cum sex cohortibus, post Fabium legatum cum
with six cohorts, afterwards Fabius (his) lieutenant with

septem aliis. Postremo ipse, quum pugnaretur[62]
seven others. At length he himself, when it was fought

vehementius, adducit integros subsidio.
more desperately, leads up fresh (men) for aid.

Proelio restituto, ac hostibus repul-
The battle having been renewed, and the enemy having been

sis, contendit eō quō miserat Labienum;
repulsed, he marches thither where he had sent Labienus;

educit quattuor cohortes ex proximo castello;
he draws out four cohorts from the nearest fortress;

jubet partem equitum sequi se, partem
he orders a part of the cavalry to follow himself, a part

circumire exteriores munitiones, et adoriri
to go around the outer fortifications, and to attack

hostes ab tergo. Labienus, postquam
the enemy from [in] the rear. Labienus, after (that)

neque aggeres neque fossae poterant sustinēre
neither the mounds nor the trenches could resist

vim hostium, una de quadraginta cohortibus
the force of the enemy, thirty-nine cohorts

coactis, quas deductas ex proximis
having been assembled, which drawn from the nearest

praesidiis, sors obtulit, facit certiorem Caesarem,
posts, chance offered, informs Caesar,

per nuntios quid existimet faciendum, Caesar
by messengers what he thinks must be done. Caesar

accelerat ut intersit proelio.
hastens that he may be present at the battle.

88] LIBER VII. 481

88. Ejus	adventu	cognito	ex	colōre
His	arrival	having been known	from	the color

vestitūs,	(quō	insigni	consueverat	uti
of (his) robe,	(which	(as) an insignia	he was accustomed	to use

in	prœliis),	que	turmis	equitum	et	cohortibus
in	battle),	both	the troops	of cavalry	and	cohorts

visis,	quas	jusserat	sequi	se,	ut	de
having been seen,	which	he had ordered	to follow	him,	as	from

superioribus	locis	hæc	declivia	et	devexa
the higher	places	these	sloping	and	inclined (places)

cernebantur,	hostes	committunt	prœlium.	Clamōre
were visible,	the enemy	join	battle.	A shout

sublato	utrimque,	clamōr	rursus excipit
having been raised	on both sides,	a shout	again follows

ex	vallo	atque	omnibus	munitionibus.
from	the rampart	and	all	the fortifications.

Nostri	pilis	omissis,	gerunt
Our	(men) the javelins	having been laid aside,	carry on

rem	gladiis (pl.).	Equitatus	repente cernitur
the action	with the sword.	The cavalry	suddenly is seen

post	tergum;	aliæ	cohortes	appropinquant;
in	the rear (of the Gauls);	other	cohorts	advance;

hostes	vertunt	terga;	equites	occurrunt
the enemy	turn (their)	backs;	the cavalry	meet

	fugientibus;	magna	cædes	fit.	Sedulius
(those)	fleeing;	a great	slaughter	is made.	Sedulius

dux	et	princeps	Lemovicum	occiditur;
general	and	chief	of the Lemovices	is slain;

Vercassivellaunus	Arvernus	comprehenditur	vivus
Vercassivellaunus	the Arvernian	is taken	alive

in	fugā;	septuaginta	quattuor	militaria	signa
in	flight;	seventy	four	military	standards

referuntur	ad	Cæsarem;	pauci	ex	tanto
are brought	to	Cæsar;	few	from [of]	so great

numero	recipiunt se	incolumes	in castra.	Conspicati
a number	return	safe	into the camp.	Having beheld

ex	oppido	cædem	et	fugam	suorum,
from	the town	the slaughter	and	flight	of their (people)

salute	desperatā,	reducunt	copias
safety	having been despaired of,	they lead back (their)	forces

a	munitionibus.	Hāc	re	auditā,
from	the fortifications.	This	news	having been heard,

fuga	protinus	fit,	ex	castris	Gallorum;
a flight	immediately	is made,	from	the camp	of the Gauls;

quod	nisi	milites	fuissent defessi
as to [regarding] which [this]	unless	the soldiers	had been fatigued

crebris	subsidiis	ac	labōre	totius
by the frequent	reinforcements	and	by the labor	of the whole

diei, omnes	copiæ	hostium	potuissent delēri.
day, all	the forces	of the enemy	might have been destroyed

De	mediā	nocte,	equitatus	missus	consequitur
About	mid	night,	the cavalry	having been sent	overtakes

novissimum	agmen.	Magnus	numerus	capitur,
the rear	line.	A great	number	are taken

atque	interficitur;	reliqui	discedunt	ex	fugā
and	killed;	the rest	escape	from	the flight [rout

in	civitates.
into	their states.

89.

Postero	die,	concilio	convocato,
On the next	day,	a council	having been called

Vercingetorix	demonstrat		se	suscepisse
Vercingetorix	shows	(that)	he	had undertaken

bellum	non	causā	suarum	necessitatum (pl.),	sed
the war	not	for the sake	of his own	necessity,	but

communis	libertatis,	et	quoniam	sit
of (their) common	liberty,	and	because	it must

cedendum	fortunæ,	offerre	se	illis
be yielded	to fortune,	(that he) offered	himself	to them

ad	utramque	rem,	seu	velint
for	either	thing [alternative],	whether	they wish

satisfacĕre	Romanis	suā	morte,	seu	tradĕre
to satisfy	the Romans	by his	death,	or	to surrender

	vivum.	Legati	mittuntur	ad	Cæsarem
(him)	alive.	Ambassadors	are sent	to	Cæsar

de	his	rebus.	Jubet		arma
concerning	these	things.	He orders	(their)	arms

tradi,	principes	produci.	Ipse
to be surrendered,	(and their) chiefs	to be led forth.	He

consedit	in	munitione	pro	castris;	eo
seated himself	at	the fortification	before	the camp;	there

principes	producuntur.	Vercingetorix	deditur;
the chiefs	are led forth.	Vercingetorix	is surrendered

arma	projiciuntur.	Æduis	atque	Arvernis
the arms	are thrown down.	The Ædui	and	Arverni

reservatis,	si	per	eos	posset	recuperare
having been reserved,	if	through	them	he could	gain over

	civitates,	ex	reliquis	captivis	distribuit
(their)	states,	from	the remaining	captives	he distributed

singula	capita	toti	exercitui	nomine
one	each	to the whole	army	under the name

prædæ.
of booty.

90. | His | rebus | confectis, | proficiscitur |
|---|---|---|---|
| These | things | having been accomplished, | he marches |

in	Æduos;	recipit	civitatem.	Legati
into	the Ædui;	he receives	the state.	Ambassadors

missi	eo	ab	Arvernis	pollicentur
sent	thither	from	the Arverni	promise

	se	facturos,	quæ	imperaret.	Imperat
(that)	they	would do,	what	he might command.	He orders

magnum	numerum	obsidum.	Mittit	legiones	in
a great	number	of hostages.	He sends	the legions	into

hiberna.	Reddit	circiter	viginti	millia
winter-quarters.	He restores	about	twenty	thousand

	captivorum	Æduis	que	Arvernis.	Jubet
(of)	prisoners	to the Ædui	and	Arverni.	He orders

T. Labienum	proficisci	in	Sequanos	cum
T. Labienus	to march	into	the Sequani	with

duabus	legionibus	et	equitatu.	Huic	attribuit
two	legions	and	the cavalry.	To him	he assigns

M. Sempronium	Rutilum.	Collocat	C. Fabium
M. Sempronius	Rutilus.	He places	C. Fabius

et	L. Minucium	Basilum	in	Remis	cum
and	L. Minucius	Basilus	among	the Remi	with

duabus	legionibus,	ne		accipiant	quam
two	*legions,*	*that they may not*		*receive*	*any*
calamitatem	a	finitimis	Bellovacis.		Mittit
injury	*from*	*the neighboring*	*Bellovaci.*		*He sends*

C. Antistium   Reginum   in   Ambivaretos,
C. Antistius   *Reginus*   *among*   *the Ambivareti,*

T. Sextium   in   Bituriges,   C. Caninum   Rebilum
T. Sextius *among* *the Bituriges,* *C. Caninus* *Rebilus*

in   Rutenos,   cum   legionibus   singulis;   collocat
among *the Ruteni,* *with* *a legion* *each;* *he stations*

Q. Tullium   Ciceronem,   et   P. Sulpicium   Caboloni
Q. Tullius *Cicero,*   *and* *P. Sulpicius* *at Cabilo*

et   Matiscone   ad   Ararim   in   Æduis
and   *Matisco*   *on [near]* *the (river) Saone* *among* *the Ædui*

causa   frumentariæ rei;   ipse   constituit
for the purpose *of the corn supply;* *he himself* *determines*

hiemare   Bibracte.   His   rebus   cognitis
to winter *at Bibracte.* *These* *things* *having been learned*

Romæ   litteris   Cæsaris,   supplicatio   viginti
at Rome   *by a letter* *of Cæsar,*   *a thanksgiving* *of twenty*

dierum   indicitur.
days   *is decreed.*